PACIFIC NORTHWEST
◇ CAMPING ◇

You'll never get stuck on the road again! Find the perfect
campground in PACIFIC NORTHWEST CAMPING from the
more than 1,400 campground descriptions with over 40,000
different sites!

FIRST EDITION NAMED REGIONAL BEST SELLER
by the Portland Oregonian and Seattle Times!

NOW IN A NEW EASY-TO-USE 2ND EDITION!
Completely updated and expanded
More information
Lakes, rivers, parks and forests highlighted
Extensive index

A THANK YOU FROM FOGHORN PRESS

Thanks to all of you who in the past year have written in with your comments on **PACIFIC NORTHWEST CAMPING!** It's great to have a link to other campers (besides ourselves). Here's a sampling: Says Richard White of Seattle Washington, **PACIFIC NORTHWEST CAMPING** is a "nicely organized and informative reference guide." Bill Barzler of Beaverton, Oregon writes it's "a very thorough book." Says Randy Hubbard of Longview, Washington, " It's a good guide for the camper new to the area." We appreciate your comments.

Special thanks to those of you who suggested areas for improvement. Because of you, this new second edition of **PACIFIC NORTHWEST CAMPING** is even better than before. First, we've added more information and expanded and updated the book. We now report which sites allow pets and whether facilities are wheelchair accessible. And we've made the book easier to use. Each site now includes a location reference in its title and each zone has a chapter page showing all the highlights.

But our major achievement has been to enlarge the index to cross reference campsites. For example, let's say you are looking for a free site with boat launching facilities. You want to bring your pet and not venture further than 100 miles from your house. Using the index, you can now find specific sites to meet this description. Armed with this book, you have the key ingredient for a perfect camping trip.

We are constantly monitoring campgrounds for changes in fees and facilities. Each campground is contacted regularly to verify fees and information. But, in spite of our efforts to give you the latest information, fees are subject to change throughout the year. Many of those updates appear in our outdoor newsletter, which is yours for the asking. Please write us with your suggestions or comments. Include your address, and for your efforts, we'll send you the newsletter free. Our mailing address is Foghorn Press, P.O. Box 77845, San Francisco, CA 94107.

Vicki Morgan
Publisher

2ND EDITION

PACIFIC NORTHWEST ◆ CAMPING ◆

The Complete Guide to Recreation Areas in Washington and Oregon

Tom Stienstra

Julie Lancelle

Foghorn Press
San Francisco

Editor	SARA SHOPKOW
Senior Research Editor	JULIE LANCELLE
Book Design	LUKE THRASHER
Proofreader	LAURA WILEY
Cover photo	GARY E. HOLSCHER

Library of Congress Cataloging-in-Publication Data

Stienstra, Tom.
    Pacific Northwest camping: the complete guide to recreation areas in Washington and Oregon / Tom Stienstra & Julie Lancelle -- 2nd ed.
       p. cm.
     ISBN 0-935701-24-9
     1. Camp sites, facilities, etc.--Washington (State)--Directories. 2. Camp sites, facilities, etc.--Oregon--Directories. 3. Washington (State)--Description and travel--1981- --Guide-books. I. Lancelle, Julie.
    II. Title.
    GV191.42.W2S75 1990
    647.94797--dc20   89-77865
                 CIP

·CONTENTS·

· JOINING THE FIVE · PERCENT CLUB

Going on a camping trip can be like trying to put hiking boots on an octopus. You've tried it too, eh? Instead of the relaxing, exciting sojourn it was intended, a camping trip can turn into a scenario called You Against The World. You want something easy? Try fighting an earthquake.

But it doesn't have to be that way and that's what this book is all about. If you give it a chance, this book can put the mystery, excitement and fun back into your camping vacations—and remove the fear of snarls, confusion and occasional temper explosions of volcanic proportions that keep people at home, locked away from where the action is.

Mystery? There are hundreds of hidden, rarely used campgrounds listed and mapped in this book that you have never dreamed of. Excitement? With many of them comes the sizzle with the steak, the hike to a great lookout, the big fish at the end of the line. Fun? The how-to section of the book can take the futility out of your trips so you can put the fun back in. Add it up, put it in your cash register and you can turn camping into the satisfying adventure it is meant to be, whether for just an overnight quicky or for a month-long fortune hunt.

It has been documented that 95 percent of the vacationers use only five percent of the available recreation areas. With this book, you can leave the herd to wander and be free, and join the inner circle, the five percenters who know the great, hidden areas used by so few people. To join the Five Percent Club, you should take a hard look at the maps for the areas you wish to visit, and in turn, the numbered listings for the campgrounds that follow. As you study the camps, you will start to feel a sense of excitement building, a sense that you are about to unlock a door—and catch a glimpse of a world that is rarely viewed. When you feel that excitement, act on it, parlay the energy into a great trip, so you can spend your time making memories, rather than remembering old ones.

The campground maps and guide lists can serve two ways: **1.** If you're on the road, it's late in the day and you are stuck for a spot for the night, you can likely find one nearby, or **2.** for planning in advance, you can custom tailor a vacation to fit exactly into your plans, rather than heading off, and hoping—maybe praying—it turns out all right.

For the latter, you may wish to obtain additional maps, particularly if you are venturing into areas governed by the U.S Forest Service or Bureau of Land Management. Both are federal agencies and have low-cost maps available that detail all hiking trails, lakes, streams and backcountry camps reached via logging roads. How to obtain these and other maps is described in Chapter 7. The backcountry camps are often in primitive and rugged settings, but provide the sense of isolation that many need on a trip. In addition, they can provide good jump-off points for backpacking trips, if that is your calling. These camps are also often free, and we have included hundreds of them in this book.

At the other end of the spectrum are the developed parks for motor homes, parks that offer a home away from home with everything from full hookups to a grocery store to a laundromat. These spots are just as important as the remote camps with no facilities. Instead of isolation, RV parks provide a place to shower, get outfitted for food and clean clothes, and for the motor home cruisers, spots to stay in high style while touring the area. They tend to cost from $10 to $20 per night and an advance deposit may be necessary in summer months.

Somewhere between the two—the remote, unimproved camps and the lavish motor home parks—are hundreds and hundreds of campgrounds that provide a compromise—beautiful settings, some facilities, and a small overnight fee. Piped water, vault toilets, and picnic tables tend to come with the territory, along with a fee of $4 to $12. Because they offer a bit of both worlds, this is where demand is highest. Reservations are usually advised, and at state parks, particularly during the summer season, you can expect company. This does not mean you need to abandon them in hope of a less confined environment. For one, most state parks have set up quotas so you don't feel like you've been squeezed in with a shoehorn, and for two, the same parks often provide off-season or weekday prospects when there can be virtually no use.

Prior to your trip, you will want to get organized, and that's where you will want to start putting socks on that giant octopus. The key to organization for any task is breaking it down to its key components, then solving each element independently of the others. Remember the octopus. Grab a moving leg, jam a boot on, and make sure it's on tight before reaching for another leg. Do one thing at a time, in order, and all will get done quick and right.

As a result, we have isolated the different elements of camping, and you should do the same when planning for your trip. There are separate sections on each of the primary ingredients for a successful trip: **1.** Food and cooking gear; **2.** Clothes and weather protection; **3.** Foot, leg care, and how to choose the right boots and socks; **4.** Sleeping gear and how to get your rest; **5.** Combatting bugs and some common-sense first-aid; **6.** Recreation gear and catching fish; **7.** How to obtain good maps and put them in use.

Each section has a list at the end of its respective chapter. This way you can become completely organized for your trip in just one week—spending just a little time each evening, working a different section each night. In itself, getting organized is an unnatural act for many; by splitting it up, you take the pressure out and put the fun back in.

As a full-time outdoor writer, the question I get asked more than any other is, "Where are you going this week?" All of the answers are in this book.

·FOOD & COOKING· GEAR

It was a warm, crystal clear day, the kind of day when if you had ever wanted to go sky diving, you would go sky diving. That was exactly the case for my old pal Foonsky, who had never before tried the sport. But a funny thing happened after he jumped out of the plane and pulled on the rip cord for the first time: The parachute didn't open.

In total free fall, Foonsky watched the earth below getting closer and closer. Not one to panic, he calmly pulled the rip cord on the emergency parachute. But nothing happened then either. No parachute, no nothing.

The ground was getting closer and closer, and as he tried to search out for a soft place to land, Foonsky detected a small object shooting up toward him, getting larger as it approached. It looked like a camper.

Foonsky figured this could be his last chance, so as they passed in mid-flight, he shouted, "Hey, do you know anything about parachutes?"

The other fellow just shouted back as he headed off into space, "Do you know anything about lighting camping stoves?"

Well, Foonsky got lucky and his parachute opened. But as for the other fellow, well, he's probably in orbit like a NASA weather satellite. If you've ever had a mishap lighting a camping stove, you know exactly what I'm talking about.

When it comes to camping, all things are not created equal. Nothing is more important than lighting your stove easily and having it reach full heat without feeling like you're playing with a short fuse to a miniature bomb. If your stove does not work right, your trip can turn into a disaster, regardless of how well you have planned the other elements. In addition, a bad stove will add an underlying feel of futility to your day, especially if you have carefully detailed your cooking gear and food for the trip. You will constantly have the inner suspicion that your darn stove is going to foul up on you again.

CAMPING STOVES

If you are buying a camping stove, remember this one critical rule: Do not leave the store with a new stove unless you have been shown exactly how to use it.

Know what you are getting. Many stores that specialize in outdoor recreation equipment now provide experienced campers/employees who will demonstrate the use of every stove they sell, and while they're at it, describe the respective strengths and weaknesses.

A second rule to remember is never buy a stove that uses kerosene for fuel. Kerosene is smelly and messy, provides low heat, needs priming, and in America, is virtually obsolete as a camp fuel. As a test experience, I tried using a kerosene stove once. I could scarcely boil a pot of water. In addition, some kerosene leaked out when the stove was packed, and it ruined everything it touched. The smell of kerosene never did go away. Kerosene remains popular in Europe only because the campers haven't heard much of white gas yet, and when they do, they will demand it.

That leaves white gas or butane as the best fuels, and either can be right for you, depending on your special preferences.

White gas is the most popular, because it can be purchased at most outdoor recreation stores, at many supermarkets, and is inexpensive and effective. It burns hot, has virtually no smell, and evaporates quickly if it should spill. If you get caught in wet, miserable weather and can't get a fire going, you can use it as an emergency fire starter though its use as such should be sparing and never on an open flame.

White gas is a popular fuel both for car campers who use the large, two-burner stoves equipped with a fuel tank and a pump, or for hikers who use one of the lightweight backpacking stoves. On the latter, lighting can require priming with a gel called priming paste, which some people dislike. Another problem with white gas is that it can be extremely explosive.

As an example, I once almost burned my beard completely off in a mini-explosion while lighting one of the larger stoves styled for car camping. I was in the middle of cooking dinner when the flame suddenly shut down. Sure enough, the fuel tank was empty, and after refilling it, I pumped the tank 50 or 60 times to regain pressure. When I lit a match, the sucker ignited from three feet away. The concussion from the explosion was like a stick of dynamite going off, and immediately, the smell of burning beard was in the air. In the quick flash of an erred moment, my once thick, dark beard had been reduced to a mass of little, yellow burned curly-queues.

My error? After filling the tank, I forgot to shut the fuel cock off while pumping up the pressure in the tank. As a result, as I pumped the tank, the stove burners were slowly producing the gas/air mixture, filling the air space above the stove. The strike of a match even from a few feet away and ka-boom!

That problem can be solved by using stoves that use bottled butane fuel. On the plus side, butane requires no pouring, pumping, or priming, and stoves that use butane are the easiest to light of all camping stoves. Just turn a knob and light, that's it. On the minus side, because it comes in bottles, you never know precisely how much fuel you have left, and when a bottle is empty, you have a potential piece of litter. Never litter. Ever.

The other problem with butane as a fuel is that it just plain does not work well in cold weather, or when there is little fuel left in the cartridge. Since you cannot predict mountain weather in spring or fall, and most certainly will eventually use most of the fuel in the cartridge, butane can thus make a frustrating choice. With most butane cartridges, if there is any chance of the temperature falling below freezing, you must sleep with it to keep it warm; otherwise, forget using it come morning.

Personally, I prefer using a small, lightweight stove that uses white gas so I can closely gauge fuel consumption. My pal Foonsky uses one with a butane bottle because it lights so easily. We have contests to see who can boil a pot of water faster and the difference is usually negligible. Thus, other factors are important when choosing a stove.

Of the other elements, ease of cleaning the burner is the most important. If you camp much, especially with the smaller stoves, the burner holes will eventually become clogged. Some stoves have a built-in cleaning needle; a quick twist of a knob and you're in business. On the other hand, others require disassembling and a protracted session using special cleaning tools. If a stove is difficult to clean, you will tend to put off doing it, and your stove will sputter and pant while you get humiliated watching the cold pot of water sitting atop it.

Thus, before making a purchase, require the salesman to show you how to clean the burner head. Except in the case of the large, multi-burner family camping stoves, which rarely require cleaning, this test can do more to determine the long-term value of a stove than any other factor.

BUILDING FIRES

One summer expedition took me to the Canadian wilderness in British Columbia for a 75-mile canoe trip on the Bowron Lake Circuit, a chain of 13 lakes, six rivers, and seven portages. It is one of the true great canoe trips in the world, a loop trip that ends just a few hundred feet distant from the start. But at the first camp at Kibbee Lake, my camp stove developed a fuel leak at the base of the burner and the nuclear-like blast that followed just about turned Canada into a giant crater.

As a result, the final 70 miles of the trip had to be completed without a stove, cooking on open fires each night. The problem was compounded by the weather. It rained eight of the ten days. Rain? In Canada, raindrops the size of silver dollars fall so hard they actually bounce on the lake surface. We had to stop paddling a few times in order to empty the rain water out of the canoe. At the end of the day, we'd make camp, and then came the test. Either make a fire or go to bed cold and hungry.

With an axe, at least we had a chance for success. As soaked as all the downed wood was, I was able to make my own fire-starting tinder from the chips of splitting logs; no matter how hard it rains, the inside of a log is always dry.

In miserable weather, matches don't stay lit long enough to get the tinder started. Instead, we used either a candle or the little, wax-like, fire-starter cubes that stay lit for several minutes. From that, we could get the tinder going. Then we added small, slender strips of wood that had been axed from the interior of the logs. When the flame reached a foot high, we added the logs, with the dry interior of them facing in. By the time the inside of the logs had caught fire, the outside would be drying from the heat. It wasn't long and a royal blaze was brightening the rainy night.

That's a worst possible case scenario and perhaps you will never face anything like it. Nevertheless, being able to build a good fire and cook on it can be one of the more satisfying elements of a camping trip. At times, just looking into the flames can provide a special satisfaction at the end of a good day.

However, never expect to build a fire for every meal, or in some cases, even to build one at all. Many state and federal campgrounds have been picked clean of downed wood, or forest fire danger will force rangers to prohibit fires altogether during the fire season. In either case, you either use your camp stove or go hungry.

But when you can build a fire, and the resources are available to do so, it will add depth and a personal touch to your camping trip. Of the campgrounds listed in the directory of this book, the sites that allow for fires will likely already have fire rings available. In primitive areas where you can make your own, you should dig a ring eight inches deep, line the edges with rock, and clear all the needles and twigs in a five-foot radius. The next day, when the fire is dead, you can discard the rocks, fill over the black charcoal with dirt, then scatter pine needles and twigs over it. Nobody will even know you camped there. That's the best way I know to keep a secret spot a real secret.

When you start to build a campfire, the first thing you will notice is that no matter how good your intentions, your fellow campers will not be able to resist moving the wood around. Watch. You'll just be getting ready to add a key piece of wood at just the right spot, and your companion will stick his mitts in, quietly believing he has a better idea, shift the fire around, and undermine your best thought-out plans.

So I make a rule on camping trips. One person makes the fire and everybody else stands clear, or is involved with other camp tasks, like gathering wood, getting water, putting up tents, or planning dinner. Once the fire is going strong, then it's fair game; anyone adds logs at their discretion. But in the early, delicate stages of the campfire, it's best to leave it to one person.

Before a match is first struck, a complete pile of firewood should be gathered alongside. Then start small, with the tiniest twigs you can find, and slowly add in larger twigs as you go, criss-crossing them like a miniature tepee. Eventually, you will get to the big chunks that will produce high heat. The key is to get one piece of wood burning into another, which then burns to another, setting off what I call the chain-of-flame. Conversely, single pieces of wood, set apart from each other, will not burn.

On a dry, summer evening at a campsite where plenty of wood is available, about the only way you can blow the deal is to get impatient and try to add the big pieces too quickly. Do that and you'll just get smoke, not flames, and it won't be long before every one of your fellow campers is poking at your fire. It will drive you crazy, but they just can't help it.

COOKING GEAR

I like traveling light, and I've found all one needs is a cooking pot, small frying pan, metal pot grabber, fork, knife, cup, and matches for a cook kit. In fact, I keep it all in one small bag, which fits into my pack. If I'm camping out of my four-wheel drive rig, the little bag of cooking gear is easy to keep track of. Simple, not complicated, is the key to keeping a camping trip on the right track.

You can get more elaborate by purchasing complete cook kits with plates, a coffee pot, large pots, and other cookware, but what really counts is having one single pot you're happy with. It needs to be just the right size, not too big or small, and be stable enough so it won't tip over, even if it is at a slight angle on a fire, full of water at a full boil. Mine is just six inches wide and 4.5 inches deep, holds better than a quart of water, and has served well for several hundred camp dinners.

The rest of your cook kit is easy to complete. The frying pan should be small, light-gauge aluminum, teflon-coated, with a fold-in handle so it's no hassle to store. A pot grabber is a great addition, that is, a little aluminum gadget that will clamp to the edge of pots and allow you to lift them and pour water with total control and without burning your fingers. A fork, knife, and cup are at your discretion. For cleanup, take a small bottle filled with dish cleaner and a plastic scrubber, and you're in business.

A Sierra Cup, which is a wide aluminum cup with a wire handle, is ideal because you can eat out of them as well as use them for drinking. This means no plates to clean after dinner, so cleanup is quick and easy. In addition, if you go for a hike, you can clip them to your belt with the wire handle.

If you want a more formal setup, complete with plates, glasses, silverware, and the like, you can end up spending more time preparing and cleaning up from meals than you do enjoying the country you are exploring. In addition, the more equipment you bring, the more loose ends you will have to deal with and loose ends can cause plenty of frustration. If you have a choice, choose simple.

And remember what Thoreau said: "A man is rich in proportion to what he can do without."

FOOD AND COOKING TRICKS

On a trip to the Bob Marshall Wilderness in western Montana, I woke up one morning, yawned, and said, "What've we got for breakfast?"

The silence was ominous. "Well," finally came the response, "we don't have any food left."

"What!?"

"Well, I figured we'd catch trout for meals every other night."

On the return trip, we ended up eating wild berries, buds, and yes, even tried roots (not too tasty). When we finally landed the next day at a Kalispell pizza parlor, we nearly ate the wooden tables.

Running out of food on a camping trip can do more to turn reasonable people into violent grumps than any other event. There's no excuse for it, not when a system for figuring meals can be outlined with precision and little effort. You should not go out and buy a bunch of food, throw it in your rig, and head off for yonder. That leaves too much to chance. And if you've ever been in the woods and real hungry, you'll know to take a little effort to make sure a day or two of starvation will not reoccur. A three-step process offers a solution:

1. Make a general meal-by-meal plan and make sure your companions like what is on it. Never expect to catch fish for any meals.

2. Tell your companions to buy any specialty items (like a special brand of coffee) on their own and not to expect you to take care of everything.

3. Put all the food on your living room floor and literally figure every day of your trip meal-by-meal, bagging the food in plastic bags as you go. You will know exact food quotas and will not go hungry.

Fish for meals? There's a guaranteed rule for that: If you expect to catch fish for meals, you will most certainly get skunked. If you don't expect to catch fish for meals, you will probably catch so many they'll be coming out of your ears. I've seen it a hundred times.

One of the best camp dinner meals you can make is a self-designed soup/stew mix. After bringing a pot of water to a full boil, add in ramen or pasta, then cut up a potato, carrot, onion, and garlic clove and let it simmer then add in a soup mix or two. Because vegetables can take ten minutes to cook, it is often a good idea to add in the soup mix well after the vegetables. Read the directions on the soup mix to determine cooking time. Make sure you stir it up, otherwise your concoction may fall victim to "The Clumps." That done, pull a surprise bottle of wine out of your pack and we're talking about a gourmet dinner in the outback.

If you are car camping and have a big ice chest, you can bring virtually anything to eat and drink. If you want to go on the trail, well, then the rules of the game change.

There will be no steaks, beer, or french fries waiting in your pack when you reach the top of the mountain. But that doesn't mean you don't get to eat well. Some of the biggest advances in the outdoor industry have come in freeze-dried dinners now available for campers. Some of them are almost good enough to serve in restaurants. Sweet-and-sour pork over rice, tostadas, burgundy chicken . . . it sure beats the poopy goop we used to eat, like the old, soupy chili mac dinners that tasted bad and looked so unlike "food" that consumption was near impossible, even for my dog.

To provide an idea of how to plan a menu, consider what my companions and I ate while hiking 250 miles on California's John Muir Trail:

Breakfast: Instant soup, oatmeal (never get plain), one beef jerky stick, coffee or hot chocolate.

Lunch: One beef stick, two jerky sticks, one Granola bar, dried fruit, half cup of pistachio nuts, Tang, small bag of M&Ms.

Dinner: Instant soup, freeze-dried dinner, milk bar, rainbow trout.

What was that last item? Rainbow trout? Right! Lest you plan on it, you can catch them every night.

COOKING GEAR LIST

Matches bagged in different zip-lock bags
Fire-starter cubes or candle
Camp stove
Camp fuel
Pot, pan, cup
Pot grabber
Knife, fork
Dish soap and scrubber
Salt, pepper, spices
Itemized food
Plastic spade

OPTIONAL

Axe or hatchet
Wood or charcoal for barbecue
Ice chest
Spatula
Grill
Tin foil
Whisk broom and dust pan
Tablecloth
Clothespins

·CLOTHING & WEATHER· PROTECTION

W hat started as an innocent pursuit of a perfect campground had evolved into one heck of a predicament for Foonsky and me.

We had parked at the end of a logging road and then bushwhacked our way down a canyon to a pristine trout stream. And on my first cast, a little flip into the plunge pool of a waterfall, I caught a 16-inch rainbow trout, a real beauty that jumped three times. Magic stuff.

Then just across stream, we saw it. The Perfect Camping Spot. On a sandbar on the edge of the forest, there lay a flat, high and dry spot above the river. Nearby was plenty of downed wood collected by past winter storms that we could use for firewood. And, of course, this beautiful trout stream was bubbling along just 40 yards from the site.

But nothing is perfect, right? To reach it, we had to wade across the river, though it didn't appear too difficult a task. The cold water tingled a bit, and the river came up surprisingly high, just above the belt. But it would be worth it to camp at The Perfect Spot.

Once across the river, we put on some dry clothes, set up camp, explored the woods, and fished the stream, catching several nice trout for dinner. But late that afternoon, it started raining. What? Rain in the summertime? Nature makes its own rules. By next morning it was still raining, pouring like a Yosemite waterfall from a solid gray sky.

That's when we noticed The Perfect Spot wasn't so perfect. The rain had raised the river level too high for us to wade back across. We were marooned, wet, and hungry.

"Now we're in a heck of a predicament," said Foonsky, the water streaming off him.

Getting cold and wet on a camping trip with no way to get warm is not only unnecessary and uncomfortable, but it can be a fast ticket to hypothermia, the number one killer of campers in the woods. By definition, hypothermia is a condition where body temperature is lowered to the point where it causes illness. It is particularly dangerous because the afflicted are usually unaware it is setting in. The first sign is a sense of apathy, then a state of confusion, which can lead eventually to collapse (or what appears to be sleep), then death.

You must always have a way to get warm and dry in short order, regardless of any condition you may face. If you have no way of getting dry, then to prevent hypothermia you must take emergency steps. Those steps are detailed in the chapter on first-aid.

But you should never reach that point. For starters, always have different sets of clothes tucked away, so no matter how cold and wet you might get, you always have something dry. On hiking trips, I always carry a second set of clothes, sealed to stay dry, in a plastic garbage bag. I keep a third set waiting back at the truck.

If you are car camping, the vehicle can cause an illusionary sense of security. But with an extra set of dry clothes stashed safely away, there is no illusion. The security is real. And remember, no matter how hot the weather is when you start on your trip, always be prepared for the worst. Foonsky and I learned the hard way.

So both of us were soaking wet on that sandbar, and with no other choice, we tried holing up in the tent for the night. A sleeping bag with Quallofil, or another polyester fiber fill, can retain warmth too, even when wet, because the fill is hollow and retains its loft. So as miserable as it was, we made it through the night.

The rain finally stopped the next day, and the river dropped a bit, but it was still rolling big and angry. Using a stick as a wading staff, Foonsky crossed about 80 percent of the stream before he was dumped, but he made a jump for it and managed to scramble to the river bank. He waved for me to follow. "No problem," I thought.

It took me some 20 minutes to reach nearly the same spot where Foonsky had been dumped. The heavy river current was above my belt and pushing hard. Then, in the flash of an instant, my wading staff slipped on a rock. I teetered in the river current, and was knocked over like a bowling pin. I became completely submerged. I went tumbling down the river, heading right toward the waterfall. While underwater, I looked up at the river surface and can remember how close it appeared, yet how out of control I was. Right then, this giant hand appeared, and I grabbed it. It was Foonsky. If it wasn't for that hand, I would have sailed right over the nearby waterfall.

My momentum drew Foonsky right into the river, and we scrambled in the current, but I suddenly sensed the river bottom under my knees. On all fours, the two of us clambered ashore. We were safe.

"Thanks ol' buddy," I said.

"Man, we're wet," he responded. "Let's get to the rig and get some dry clothes on.

DRESSING IN LAYERS

After falling in the river, Foonsky and I looked like a couple of cold swamp rats. When we eventually reached the truck, and finally started getting into warm clothes, a strange phenomenon hit both of us Now that we were warming up, we started shivering and shaking like an old engine trying to start. It's the body's built-in heater. Shivering is how the body tries to warm itself, producing as much heat as if you were jogging.

To retain that heat, you should dress in "layers." The interior layer, what you wear closest to your skin, and the exterior layer, what you wear to repel the weather, are the most important.

In the good ol' days, campers wore long underwear made out of wool, which was scratchy, heavy, and sometimes sweaty. Well, times have changed. You can now wear long underwear made of Polypropylene, a synthetic material that is warm, light, and wicks dampness away from your skin. It's ideal to wear in a sleeping bag on cold nights, during cool evenings after the sun goes down, or for winter snow sports. Poly shirts come in three weights: light, medium, and heavy. The medium weight is ideal for campers. The light weight clings too much to your body. We call it Indian Underwear, because it keeps creeping up on you. And the heavy weight is too warm and bulky. For most folks the medium is just right.

The next layer of clothes should be a light cotton shirt or a long-sleeve cotton/wool shirt, or both, depending on coolness of the day. For pants, many just wear blue jeans when camping, but blue jeans can be hot, tight, and once wet, they tend to stay that way. Putting on wet blue jeans on a cold morning is a torturous way to start the day. I can tell you that from experience since I have suffered that fate a number of times. A better choice are pants made from a cotton/canvas mix, which are available at outdoor shops. They are light, have a lot of give, and dry quickly. If the weather is quite warm, shorts that have some room to them can be the best choice.

VESTS, PARKAS

In cold weather, you should take the layer system one step further with a warm vest and a parka jacket. Vests are especially useful because they provide warmth without the bulkiness of a parka.

The warmest vests and parkas are either filled with down, Quallofil, or are made with a cotton/wool mix. Each has its respective merits and problems. Downfill provides the most warmth for the amount of weight, but becomes useless when wet, taking on a close resemblance to a wet dish rag. Quallofil keeps much of its heat-retaining qualities even when wet, but is expensive. Vests made of cotton/wool mixes are the most attractive and also are quite warm, but can be as heavy as a ship's anchor when wet.

Sometimes the answer is combining the two. One of my best camping companions wears a good-looking, cotton-wool vest, and a parka filled with Quallofil. The vest never gets wet, so weight is less of a factor.

RAIN GEAR

One of the most miserable nights I ever spent in my life was on a camping trip where I didn't bring my rain gear or a tent. Hey, it was early August, the temperature had been in the 90s for weeks, and if anybody told me it was going to rain, I would have asked them to consult a brain doctor.

But rain it did. And as I got more and more wet, I kept saying to myself, "Hey, it's summer, it's not supposed to rain." Then I remembered one of the Ten Commandments of camping: Forget your rain gear and you can guarantee it will rain.

To stay dry, you need some form of water repellent shell. It can be as simple as a $5 poncho made out of plastic or as elaborate as a Gore-Tex rain jacket and pants that cost $300 a set. What counts is not how much you spend, but how dry you stay.

Some can do just fine with a cheap poncho, and note that ponchos can serve other uses in addition to a rain coat. Ponchos can be used as a ground tarp, a rain cover for supplies or a backpack, or in a pinch, can be roped up to trees to provide a quick storm ceiling if you don't have a tent. The problem with ponchos is that in a hard rain, you just don't stay dry. First your legs get wet, then they get soaked. Then your arms follow the same pattern. If you're wearing cotton, you'll find that once part of the garment gets wet, the water will spread until, alas, you are dripping wet, poncho and all. Before long you start to feel like a walking refrigerator.

One high-cost option is buying a Gore-Tex rain jacket and pants. Gore-Tex is actually not a fabric, as is commonly believed, but a laminated film that coats a breathable fabric. The result is a lightweight, water repellent, breathable jacket and pants. They are perfect for campers, but they cost a fortune.

Some hiking buddies of mine have complained that the older Gore-Tex rain gear loses some water repellent qualities over time. However, manufacturers insist that this is the result of water seeping through seams, not leaks in the jacket. At each seam, tiny needles will have pierced through the fabric, and as tiny as the holes are, water will find a way through. An application of Seam Lock, especially at major seams around the shoulders of a jacket, can usually end the problem.

If you don't want to spend the big bucks for Gore-Tex rain gear, but want more rain protection than a poncho affords, a coated nylon jacket is the middle road that many choose. They are inexpensive, have the highest water repellent qualities of any rain gear, and are warm, providing a good outer shell for your layers of clothing. But they are not without fault. These jackets don't breathe at all, and if you zip it up tight, you can sweat like an Eskimo.

My brother, Rambob, gave me a $20 nylon jacket prior to an expedition we took climbing northern California's Mt. Shasta, one of America's most impressive peaks at 14,162 feet. I wore that $20 special all the way to the top and with no complaints; it's warm and 100 percent waterproof. At $20, it seems like a treasure, especially compared to the $180 Gore-Tex jackets. And its value increases every time it rains.

OTHER GEAR, AND A FEW TIPS

What are the three items most commonly forgotten on a camping trip?

"A cook, a dishwasher, and a fish cleaner," says my pal, the Z-Man.

C'mon now, Z-man, the real answers? A hat, sunglasses, and chapstick. A hot day is unforgiving without them.

A hat is crucial, especially when you are visiting high elevations. Without one you are constantly exposed to everything nature can give you. The sun will dehydrate you, sap your energy, sunburn your head, and in worst cases, cause sunstroke. Start with a comfortable hat. Then finish with sunglasses, chapstick, and sunscreen for additional protection. That will help protect you from extreme heat.

To guard against extreme cold, it's a good idea to keep a pair of thin ski gloves stashed away with your emergency clothes, along with a wool ski cap. The gloves should be thick enough to keep your fingers from stiffening up, but pliable enough to allow full movement, so you don't have to take them off to complete simple tasks, like lighting a stove. An option to gloves are glovelets, which look like gloves with no fingers. In any case, just because the weather turns cold doesn't mean that your hands have to.

And if you fall into a river like Foonsky and I did, well, I hope you have a set of dry clothes waiting back at your rig. Oh, and a hand reaching out to you.

CAMPING CLOTHES LIST

Polypropylene underwear
Cotton shirt
Long sleeve cotton/wool shirt
Cotton/canvas pants
Vest
Parka
Rain jacket, pants, or poncho
Hat
Sunglasses
Chapstick
Sunscreen

OPTIONAL

Seam Lock
Shorts
Swimming suit
Gloves
Ski cap

✦HIKING & FOOT✦ CARE

We had set up a nice, little camp in the woods, and my buddy, Foonsky, sitting against a big Douglas fir, was strapping on his hiking boots.

"New boots," he said with a grin. "But they seem pretty stiff."

We decided to hoof it on down the trail for a few hours, exploring the mountain wildlands that are said to hide Bigfoot and other strange creatures. These woods are quiet and secret, and after just a short while on the trail, a sense of peace and calm seemed to settle in. The forest provides the chance to be cleansed with clean air and the smell of trees, freeing you from all troubles.

But it wasn't long and the look of trouble was on Foonsky's face. And no, it wasn't from seeing Bigfoot.

"Got a hot spot on a toe," he said.

Immediately we stopped. He pulled off his right boot, then socks, and inspected the left side of his big toe. Sure enough, a blister had bubbled up, filled with fluid, but not popped. From his medical kit, Foonsky cut a small piece of moleskin to fit over the blister, then taped it to hold it in place. A few minutes later, we were back on the trail.

A half hour later, there was still no sign of Bigfoot. But Foonsky stopped again and pulled off his other boot. "Another hot spot." Another small blister had started on the little toe of his left foot, over which he taped a Band-Aid to keep it from further chafing against the inside of his new boot.

In just a few days, ol' Foonsky a big, strong guy who goes 6-foot-5, 200-plus pounds was walking around like a sore-hoofed hoss that had been loaded with a month of supplies and then ridden over sharp rocks. Well, it wasn't the distance that had done Foonsky in, it was those blisters. He had them on eight of his ten toes and was going through Band-Aids, moleskin, and tape like he was a walking emergency ward. If he used any more tape, he was going to look like a mummy from an Egyptian tomb.

If you've ever been in a similar predicament, then you know the frustration of wanting to have a good time, wanting to hike and explore the area at which you have set up a secluded camp, only to be turned gimp-legged by several blisters. No one is immune, not big, strong guys nor small, innocent-looking women. All are created equal before the blister god. You can be forced to bow to it unless you get your act together.

That means wearing the right style boots for what you have in mind and then protecting your feet with a careful selection of socks. And then, if you are still so unfortunate as to get a blister or two, it means knowing how to treat them fast so they don't turn your walk into a sore-footed endurance test.

What causes blisters? In almost all cases, it is the simple rubbing of your foot against the rugged interior of your boot. That act can be worsened by several factors:

1. A very stiff boot, that is, one in which your foot moves inside the boot as you walk, instead of the boot flexing as if it was another layer of skin.

2. Thin, holey, or dirty socks. This is the fastest route to blister death. Thin socks will allow your feet to move inside of your boots, holey socks will allow your skin to chafe directly again the boot's interior, and dirty socks will wrinkle and fold, also rubbing against your feet instead of cushioning them.

3. Soft feet. By itself, soft feet will not cause blisters, but in combination with a stiff boot or thin socks, can cause terrible problems. The best way to toughen up your feet is to go barefoot. In fact, some of the biggest, toughest-looking guys you'll ever see from Hell's Angels to pro football players have feet that are as soft as a baby's butt. Why? Because they never go barefoot and don't hike much.

SELECTING THE RIGHT BOOTS

One summer I hiked 400 miles, including 250 miles in three weeks, along the crest of California's Sierra Nevada, and another 150 miles over several months in an earlier general training program. In that span, I got just one blister, suffered on the fourth day of the 250-miler. I treated it immediately, and suffered no more. One key is wearing the right boot, and for me, that means a boot that acts as a thick layer of skin that is flexible and pliable to my foot. I want my feet to fit snugly in them, with no interior movement.

There are three kinds of boots: mountaineering boots, hiking boots, and walking shoes. Either select the right one for you or pay the consequences.

The stiffest of the lot is the mountaineering boot. These boots are often identified by mid-range tops, laces that extend almost as far as the toe area, and ankle areas that are as stiff as a board. The lack of "give" in them is what enamors them to mountaineers. The stiffness is preferred when rock climbing, walking off-trail on craggy surfaces, or hiking down the edge of stream beds where walking across small rocks can cause you to turn your ankle. Because these boots don't give on rugged, craggy terrain, it reduces ankle injuries and provides better traction.

The backlash of stiff boots is that if careful selection of socks is not made and your foot starts slipping around in them, you will get a set of blisters that would raise even Foonsky's eyebrows. But if you just want to go for a walk, or a good tromp with a backpack, then hiking shoes or backpacking boots are better designed for those respective uses.

Walking shoes are the lightest of all footwear, designed for day walks or short backpacking trips. Some of the newer models are like rugged tennis shoes, designed with a canvas top for lightness and a lug sole for traction. These are perfect for people who like to walk but rarely carry a backpack. Because they are flexible, they are easy to break in, and with fresh socks, rarely cause blister problems. And because they are light, general hiking fatigue is greatly reduced.

On the negative side, because they have shallow lug soles, traction can be far from good on slippery surfaces. In addition, canvas walking shoes provide less than ideal ankle support, which can be a problem in rocky areas, such as along a stream where you might want to go trout fishing. Turn your ankle and your trip can be ruined.

My preference is for a premium hiking boot, the perfect medium between the stiff mountaineering boots and the soft canvas walking shoes. The deep lug bottom provides traction, high ankle coverage provides support, yet the soft, waterproof leather body gives each foot a snug fit—add it up and that means no blisters. On the negative side, they can be quite hot, weigh a ton, and, if they get wet, take days to dry.

There are a zillion styles, brands, and price ranges of boots to choose from. If you wander about, looking at them equally, you will get as confused as a kid in a toy store. Instead go into the store with your mind clear with what you want, then find it, and buy it. If you want the best, expect to spend $60 to $80 for hiking shoes, from $100 to $140 and sometimes more for hiking or mountaineering boots. This is one area you don't want to scrimp on, so try not to yelp about the high cost. Instead, walk out of the store believing you deserve the best, and that's exactly what you just paid for.

If you plan on using the advice of a shoe salesman for your purchase, first look at what kind of boots he is wearing. If he isn't even wearing boots, then any advice he might attempt to tender may not be worth a plug nickel. Most people I know who own quality boots, including salesmen, will wear them almost daily if their job allows, since boots are the best footwear available. However, even these well-meaning folks can offer skeptical advice. Every hiker I've ever met will tell you he wears the world's greatest boot.

Instead, enter the store with a precise use and style in mind. Rather than fish for suggestions, tell the salesman exactly what you want, try two or three different brands of the same style, and always try on the matching pair of boots simultaneously so you know exactly how they'll feel. If possible, walk up and down stairs with them. Are they too stiff? Are your feet snug yet comfortable, or do they slip? Do they have that "right" kind of feel when you walk?

If you get the right answers to those questions, then you're on your way to blister-free, pleasure-filled days of walking.

SOCKS

The poor gent was scratching his feet like ants were crawling over them. I looked closer. Huge yellow calluses had covered the bottom of his feet, and at the ball and heel, the calluses were about a quarter of an inch thick, cracking, and sore.

"I don't understand it," he said. "I'm on my feet a lot, so I bought a real good pair of hiking boots. But look what they've done to my feet. My feet itch so much I'm going crazy."

People can spend so much energy selecting the right kind of boot, that they can virtually overlook wearing the right kind of socks. One goes with the other.

Your socks should be thick enough to provide a cushion for your foot, as well as a good, snug fit. Without good socks, you might try to get the boot laces too tight and that's like putting a tourniquet on your feet. You should have plenty of clean socks on hand, or plan on washing what you have on your trip. As socks are worn, they become compressed, dirty, and damp. Any one of those factors can cause problems.

My camping companions believe I go overboard when it comes to socks, that I bring too many, wear too many. But it works, so that's where the complaints stop. So how many do I wear? Well, would you believe three socks on each foot? It may sound like overkill, but each has its purpose, and like I said, it works.

The interior sock is thin, lightweight, and made out of Polypropylene or silk synthetic materials that actually transport moisture away from your skin. With a poly-interior sock, your foot stays dry when it sweats. Without a poly sock, your foot can get damp, mix with dirt, which in turn can cause a "hot spot" to start on your foot. Eventually you get blisters, lots of them.

The second sock is for comfort, and can be cotton, but a thin wool-based composite is ideal. Some made of the latter can wick moisture away from the skin, much like the qualities of Polypropylene. If wool itches your feet, a thick cotton sock can be suitable, though cotton collects moisture and compacts more quickly than other socks. If you're on a short hike though, cotton will do just fine.

The exterior sock should be made of high quality, thick wool at least 80 percent wool. It will cushion your feet, provide that "just right" snug fit in your boot, and in cold weather, give you some additional warmth and insulation. It is critical to keep the wool sock clean. If you wear a dirty wool sock over and over again, it will compact and lose its cushion, start wrinkling while you hike, and with that chain of events, your feet will catch on fire from the blisters that start popping up.

A FEW TIPS

If you are like most folks, that is, the bottom of your feet are rarely exposed and quite soft, you can take additional steps in their care. The best tip is keeping a fresh foot pad in your boot made of sponge rubber. Another cure for soft feet is to get out and walk or jog on a regular basis prior to your camping trip.

If you plan to use a foot pad and wear three socks, you will need to use these items when sizing boots. It is an unforgiving error to wear thin cotton socks when buying boots, then later trying to squeeze all this stuff, plus your feet, into your boots. There just won't be enough room.

The key to treating blisters is fast work at the first sign of a hot spot. But before you remove your socks, first check to see if the sock has a wrinkle in it, a likely cause to the problem. If so, either change socks or get them pulled tight, removing the tiny folds, after taking care of the blister. Cut a piece of moleskin to cover the offending toe, securing the moleskin with white medical tape. If moleskin is not available, small Band-Aids can do the job, but have to be replaced daily, and sometimes with even more frequency. At night, clean your feet and sleep without socks.

Two other items that can help your walking is an Ace bandage and a pair of gaiters.

For sprained ankles and twisted knees, an Ace bandage can be like an insurance policy to get you back on the trail and out of trouble. Over the years, I have had serious ankle problems and have relied on a good wrap with a four-inch bandage to get me home. The newer bandages come with the clips permanently attached, so you don't have to worry about losing them.

Gaiters are leggings made of plastic, nylon or Gore-Tex which fit from just below your knees, over your calves, and attach under your boots. They are of particular help when walking in damp areas, or places where rain is common. As your legs brush against ferns or low-lying plants, gaiters will deflect the moisture. Without them, your pants will be soaking wet in short order.

Should your boots become wet, a good tip is to never try to force dry them. Some well-meaning folks will try to speed dry them at the edge of a campfire or actually put the boots in an oven. While this may dry the boots, it can also loosen the glue that holds them together, ultimately weakening your shoe until one day they fall apart in a heap.

A better bet is to treat the leather so the boots become water repellent. Silicone-based liquids are the easiest to use and least greasy of the treatments available.

A final tip is to have another pair of lightweight shoes or moccasins that you can wear around camp, and in the process, give your feet the rest they deserved.

HIKING AND FOOT CARE LIST

Quality hiking boots
Backup lightweight shoes
Polypropylene socks
Thick cotton socks
80 percent wool socks
Strong boot laces
Inner sole or foot cushion
Ace bandage
Moleskin and medical tape
Band-Aids
Gaiters
Water repellent boot treatment

· SLEEPING ·
GEAR

One mountain night in the pines on an eve long ago, my dad, brother, and I had rolled out our sleeping bags and were bedded down for the night. After the pre-trip excitement, a long drive, an evening of trout fishing, and a barbecue, we were like three tired doggies who had played too much.

But as I looked up at the stars, I was suddenly wide awake. The kid was still wired. A half hour later? No change—wide awake.

And as little kids can do, I had to wake up ol' dad to tell him about it. "Hey, Dad, I can't sleep."

"This is what you do," he said. "Watch the sky for a shooting star and tell yourself that you cannot go to sleep until you see at least one. As you wait and watch, you will start getting tired, and it will be difficult to keep your eyes open. But tell yourself you must keep watching. Then you'll start to really feel tired. When you finally see a shooting star, you'll go to sleep so fast you won't know what hit you."

Well, I tried it that night and I don't even remember seeing a shooting star, I went to sleep so fast.

It's a good trick, and along with having a good sleeping bag, ground insulation, maybe a tent—or a few tricks for bedding down in a pickup truck or motor home—you can get a good sleep on every camping trip.

Some 20 years later after that camping episode with my dad and brother, we made a trip to the Planetarium at the Academy of Sciences in San Francisco to see a show on Halley's Comet. The lights dimmed, and the ceiling turned into a night sky, filled with stars and a setting moon. A scientist began explaining phenomenons of the heavens.

After a few minutes, I began to feel drowsy. Just then, a shooting star zipped across the Planetarium ceiling. I went into a deep sleep so fast it was like I was in a coma. I didn't wake up until the show was over, the lights were turned back on, and the people were leaving.

Drowsy, I turned to see if ol' Dad had liked the show. Oh yeah? He not only had gone to sleep too, but apparently had no intention of waking up, no matter what. Just like a camping trip.

SLEEPING BAGS

What could be worse than trying to sleep in a cold, wet sleeping bag on a rainy night without a tent in the mountains?

Answer: Trying to sleep in a cold, wet sleeping bag on a rainy night without a tent in the mountains—when your sleeping bag is filled with down.

Water will turn a down-filled sleeping bag into a mushy heap. Many campers do not like a high-tech approach, but the state-of-the-art polyfiber sleeping bags can keep you warm even when wet. That factor, along with temperature rating and weight, are key factors when selecting a sleeping bag.

A sleeping bag is a shell filled with a heat-retaining insulation. By itself, it is not warm. Your body provides the heat, and the sleeping bag's ability to retain that heat is what makes it warm or cold.

The old-styled canvas bags are heavy, bulky, cold, and, when wet, useless. With other options available, their use is limited. Anybody who sleeps outdoors or backpacks should choose otherwise. Instead, buy and use a sleeping bag filled with down or one of the quality poly-fills. Down is light, warm, and aesthetically pleasing to those who don't think camping and technology mix. If you like down bags, be sure to keep it double wrapped in plastic garbage bags on your trips in order to keep it dry. Once wet, you'll spend your nights howling at the moon.

The polyfiber-filled bags are not necessarily better that those filled with down, but can be. The one key advantage is that even when wet, some poly-fills can retain up to 80 to 85 percent of your body heat. This allows you to sleep and get valuable rest even in miserable conditions. And my camping experience is that no matter how lucky you may be, there comes a time when you will get caught in an unexpected, violent storm and everything you've got will get wet, including your sleeping bag. That's when the value of a poly-fill bag becomes priceless. You either have one and can sleep—or you don't have one and suffer. It is that simple. Of the synthetic fills, Quallofil made by Dupont is the leader of the industry.

But as mentioned, just because a sleeping bag uses a high-tech poly-fill doesn't necessarily make it a better bag. There are other factors.

The most important are a bag's temperature rating and weight. The temperature rating of a sleeping bag refers to how cold it can get before you start actually feeling cold. Many campers make the mistake of thinking, "I only camp in the summer, so a bag rated at a 30 or 40 degrees should be fine." Later, they find out it isn't so fine, and all it takes is one cold night to convince them of that. When selecting the right temperature rating, visualize the coldest weather you might ever confront, and then get a bag rated for even colder weather.

For instance, if you are a summer camper, you may rarely experience a night in the low 30s or high 20s. A sleeping bag rated at 20 degrees would thus be appropriate, keeping you snug, warm, and asleep. For most campers, I advise bags rated at zero or ten degrees.

If you buy a poly-filled sleeping bag, never leave it squished in your stuff sack between camping trips. Instead keep it on a hanger in a closet or use it as a blanket. One thing that can reduce a polyfilled bag's heat-retaining qualities is if you lose the loft out of the tiny hollow fibers that make up the fill. You can avoid this with proper storage.

The weight of a sleeping bag can also be a key factor, especially for backpackers. When you have to carry your gear on your back, every ounce becomes important. To keep your weight to a minimum, sleeping bags that weigh just three pounds are available, though expensive. But if you hike much, it's worth the price. For an overnighter, you can get away with a four or 4.5-pound bag without much stress. However, bags weighing five pounds and up should be left back at the car.

I have two sleeping bags: A seven-pounder that feels like I'm in a giant sponge, and a little three-pounder. The heavy duty model is for pickup truck camping in cold weather and doubles as a blanket at home. The lightweight bag is for hikes. Between the two, I'm set.

INSULATION PADS

Even with the warmest sleeping bag in the world, if you just lay it down on the ground and try to sleep, you will likely get as cold as a winter cucumber. That is because the cold ground will suck the warmth right out of your body. The solution is to have a layer of insulation between you and the ground. For this, you can use a thin Insulite pad, a light-weight Therm-a-Rest inflatable pad, or an air mattress. Here is a capsule summary of them:

Insulite pads: They are light, inexpensive, roll up quick for transport, and can double as a seat pad at your camp. The negative side is that in one night, they will compress, making you feel like you are sleeping on granite.

Therm-a-Rest pads: They are a real luxury, because they do everything an Insulite pad does, but also provide a cushion. The negative side to them is that they are expensive by comparison, and if they get a hole in them, they become worthless unless you have a patch kit.

Air mattress: Okay for car campers, but their bulk, weight and the amount of effort necessary to blow them up makes them a nuisance.

A FEW TRICKS

When surveying a camp area, the most important consideration should be to select a good spot to sleep. Everything else is secondary. Ideally, you want a flat spot that is wind sheltered on ground soft enough to drive stakes into. Yeah, and I want to win the lottery too.

Sometimes that ground will have a slight slope to it. In that case, always sleep with your head on the uphill side. If you sleep parallel to the slope, every time you roll over in your sleep, you can find yourself rolling down the hill. If you sleep with your head on the downhill side, you can get a headache that feels like an axe is embedded in your brain.

When you have found a good spot, clear it of all branches, twigs, and rocks, of course. A good tip is to then dig a slight indentation in the ground where your hip will fit. Since your body is not flat, but has curves and edges, it will not feel comfortable on flat ground. Some people even get severely bruised on the sides of their hips when sleeping on flat, hard ground. For that reason alone, they learn to hate camping. Instead, bring a spade, dig a little depression in the ground for your hip, and sleep well.

After the ground is prepared, throw a ground cloth over the spot, which will keep much of the morning dew off you. In some areas, particularly where fog is a problem, morning dew can be quite heavy and get the outside of your sleeping bag quite wet. In that case, you either need a tent or some kind of roof, like that of a poncho or tarp, with its ends tied to trees.

TENTS AND WEATHER PROTECTION

All it takes is to get caught in the rain once without a tent and you will never go anywhere without one again. A tent provides protection from rain, wind, and mosquito attacks. In exchange, you can lose a starry night's view, though some tents now even provide moon roofs.

A tent can be as complex as a four-season, tubular-jointed dome with rain fly, or nothing more complicated than two ponchos snapped together and roped up to a tree. They can be as cheap as a $10 tube tent, which is nothing more than a hollow piece of plastic, to as expensive as a $500 five-person deluxe expedition dome model. They vary greatly in size, price, and put-up time. If you plan on getting a good one, then plan on doing plenty of shopping and asking lots of questions. The key ones are: Will it keep me dry? How hard is it to put up? Is it roomy enough? How much does it weigh?

With a little bit of homework, you can get the right answers to these questions.

Will it keep me dry? On many one and two-person tents, the rain fly does not extend far enough to keep water off the bottom sidewalls of the tent. In a driving rain, water can also drip from the rain fly and to the bottom sidewalls of the tent. Eventually the water can leak through to the inside, particularly through the seams where the tent has been sewed together. Water can sneak through the tiny needle holes.

You must be able to stake out your rain fly so it completely covers all of the tent. If you are tent shopping and this does not appear possible, then don't buy the tent. To prevent potential leaks, use a seam water proofer like Seam Lock, a glue-like substance, to close potential leak areas on tent seams. On the large umbrella tents, keep a patch kit handy and dig a canal around your tent to channel rain water.

Another way to keep water out of your tent is to store all wet garments outside the tent, under a poncho. Moisture from wet clothes stashed in the tent will condense on the interior tent walls. If you bring enough wet clothes in the tent, by the next morning you can feel like you're camping in a duck blind.

How hard is it to put up? If a tent is difficult to erect in full sunlight, you can just about forget it at night. Some tents can go up in just a few minutes, without you requiring help from another camper. This might be the kind of tent you want.

The way to compare put-up time of tents when shopping is to count the number of connecting points from the tent poles to the tent, and also the number of stakes required. The fewer, the better. Think simple. My tent has seven connecting points and, minus the rain fly, requires no stakes. It goes up in a few minutes. If you need a lot of stakes, it is a sure tipoff to a long put-up time. Try it at night or in the rain, and you'll be ready to cash your chips and go for broke.

Another factor is the tent poles themselves. Some small tents have poles that are broken into small sections that are connected by Bungy cords. It takes only an instant to convert it to a complete pole.

Some outdoor shops have tents on display on their showroom floor. Before buying the tent, have the salesman take the tent down and put it back up. If it takes him more than five minutes, or he says he "doesn't have time," then keep looking.

Is it roomy enough? Don't judge the size of a tent on floor space alone. Some tents small on floor space can give the illusion of roominess with a high ceiling. You can be quite comfortable in them and snug.

But remember that a one-person or two-person tent is just that. A two-person tent has room for two people plus gear. That's it. Don't buy a tent expecting it to hold more than it is intended to.

How much does it weigh? If you're a hiker, this becomes the preeminent question. If it's much more than six or seven pounds, forget it. A 12-pound tent is bad enough, but get it wet and its like carrying a piano on your back. On the other hand, weight is scarcely a factor if you camp only where you can take your car. My dad, for instance, used to have this giant canvas umbrella tent that folded down to this neat little pack that weighed about 500 pounds.

AN OPTION

If you like going solo and choose not to own a tent at all, a bivy bag (from the word "bivouac") can provide the weather protection you require. A bivy bag is a water repellent shell in which your sleeping bag fits. They are light and tough, and for some, are a perfect option to a heavy tent. On the down side, however, there is a strange sensation when you try to ride out a rainy night in one. You can hear the rain hitting you, sometimes even feel the pounding of the drops through the bivy bag. It can be unsettling to try and sleep under such a circumstance..

PICKUP TRUCK CAMPERS

If you own a pickup truck with a camper shell, you can turn it into a self-contained campground with a little work. This can be an ideal way to go: it's fast, portable, and you are guaranteed a dry environment.

But that does not necessarily mean it is a warm environment. In fact, without insulation from the metal truck bed, it can be like trying to sleep on an iceberg. That is because the metal truck bed will get as cold as the air temperature, which is often much colder than the ground temperature. Without insulation, it can be much colder in your camper shell than it would be on the open ground.

When I camp in my rig, I use a large piece of foam for a mattress and insulation. The foam measures four inches thick, is 48 inches wide and 76 inches long. It makes for a bed as comfortable as anything one might ask for. In fact, during the winter, if I don't go camping for a few weeks because of writing obligations, I sometimes will throw the foam on the living room floor, lay down the old sleeping bag, light a fire, and camp right in my living room. It's in my blood, I tell you.

If you camp in cold areas in your pick-up truck camper shell, a Coleman catalytic heater can keep you toasty. When using a catalytic heater, it is a good idea to keep ventilation windows partially open to keep the air fresh. Don't worry about how cold it is—the heater will take the snap out of it.

MOTOR HOMES

The problems motor home owners encounter come from two primary sources: Lack of privacy and light intrusion.

The lack of privacy stems from the natural restrictions of where a "land yacht" can go. Without careful use of the guide portion of this book, motor home owners can find themselves in parking lot settings, jammed in with plenty of neighbors. Because motor homes often have large picture windows, you lose your privacy, causing some late nights, and come daybreak, light intrusion forces an early wake-up. The result is you get short on your sleep.

The answer is to always carry inserts to fit over the inside of your windows. This closes off the outside and retains your privacy. And if you don't want to wake up with the sun coming daybreak, you don't have to. It will still be dark.

GOOD NIGHT'S SLEEP LIST

Sleeping bag
Insulite pad or Therm-a-rest
Tent
Ground tarp

OPTIONAL

Air pillows
Mosquito netting
Foam pad for truck bed
Windshield light screen for motor home
Catalytic heater

◆FIRST AID & PROTECTION◆
AGAINST INSECTS

A mountain night could not have been more perfect, I thought as I lay in my sleeping bag.

The sky looked like a mass of jewels and the air tasted sweet and smelled of pines. A shooting star fireballed across the sky, and I remember thinking, "It just doesn't get any better."

Just then, as I was drifting into sleep, this mysterious buzz appeared from nowhere and deposited itself inside my left ear. Suddenly awake, I whacked my ear with the palm of my hand about hard enough to cause a minor concussion. The buzz disappeared. I pulled out my flashlight and shined it on my palm, and there, lit in the blackness of night, lay the squished intruder. A mosquito, dead amid a stain of blood.

Satisfied, I turned off the light, closed my eyes, and thought of the fishing trip planned for the next day. Then I heard them. It was a squadron of mosquitos, flying landing patterns around my head. I tried to grab them with an open hand, but they dodged the assault and flew off. Just 30 seconds later another landed back in my left ear. I promptly dispatched the invader with a rip of the palm.

Now I was completely awake, so I got out of my sleeping bag to retrieve some mosquito repellent. But while en route, several of the buggers swarmed and nailed me in the back and arms. Later, after application of the repellent and again snug in my sleeping bag, the mosquitos would buzz a few inches from my ear. After getting a whiff of the poison, they would fly off. It was like sleeping in a sawmill.

The next day, drowsy from little sleep, I set out to fish. I'd walked but 15 minutes when I brushed against a bush and felt this stinging sensation on the inside of my arm, just above the wrist. I looked down: A tick had got his clamps into me. I ripped it out before he could embed his head into my skin.

After catching a few fish, I sat down against a tree to eat lunch, and just watch the water go by. My dog, Rebel, sat down next to me and stared at the beef jerky I was munching as if it was a T-bone steak. I finished eating, gave him a small piece, patted him on the head, and said, "Good dog." Right then, I noticed an itch on my arm where a mosquito had drilled me. I unconsciously scratched it. Two days later, in that exact spot, some nasty red splotches started popping up. Poison oak. By petting my dog and then scratching my arm, I had transferred the oil residue of the poison oak leaves from Rebel's fur to my arm.

On returning back home, Foonsky asked me about the trip.

"Great," I said. "Mosquitos, ticks, poison oak. Can hardly wait to go back."

"Sorry I missed it," he said sarcastically.

"On the next trip," I said, "We'll declare war on those buggers."

MOSQUITOS, NO-SEE-UMS, GNATS, AND HORSEFLIES

On a trip to Canada, Foonsky and I were fishing a small lake from the shore when suddenly a black horde of mosquitos could be seen moving across the lake toward us. It was like when the French Army looked across the Rhine and saw the Wehrmacht coming. There was a literal buzz in the air. We fought them off for a few minutes, then made a fast retreat to the truck and jumped in, content the buggers had been fooled. But somehow, still unknown to us, the mosquitos started gaining entry to the truck. In 10 minutes, we squished 15 of them while they attempted to plant their oil derricks in our skin. Just outside the truck, the black horde waited for us to make a tactical error, like rolling down a window. It finally took a miracle hailstorm to wipe out the attack.

When it comes to mosquitos, no-see-ums, gnats, and horseflies, there are times when there is nothing you can do. However, in most situations you can muster a defense to repel the attack.

The first key with mosquitos is to wear clothing too heavy for them to drill through. Expose a minimum of skin, wear a hat, and, around your neck, tie a bandanna, one that has preferably been sprayed with repellent. If you try to get by with just a cotton T-shirt, you will be declared a federal mosquito sanctuary.

So first your skin must be well covered, exposing only your hands and face. Second, you should have your companion spray your clothes with repellent. Third, you should dab liquid repellent directly on your skin.

Taking Vitamin B1 and eating garlic are reputed to act as natural insect repellents, but I've met a lot of mosquitos that are not convinced. A better bet is to take the mystery out of the task and examine the contents of the repellent in question. The key is the percentage of the ingredient called "non-diethyl-metatoluamide." That is the poison, and the percentage of it in the container must be listed and will indicate that brand's effectiveness. Inert ingredients are just excess fluids used to fill the bottles.

At night, the easiest way to get a good sleep without mosquitos buzzing in your ear is to sleep in a bug-proof tent. If the nights are warm and you want to see the stars, new tent models are available that have a skylight covered with mosquito netting. If you don't like tents on summer evenings, mosquito netting rigged with an air space at your head can solve the problem. Otherwise prepare to get bit, even with the use of mosquito repellent.

If your problems are with no-see-ums or biting horseflies, then you need a slightly different approach.

No-see-ums are a tiny, black insect that can look like nothing more than a sliver of dirt on your skin. Then you notice something stinging—and when you rub the area, you scratch up a little no-see-um. The results are similar to mosquito bites, making your skin itch, splotch, and, when you get them bad, puffy. In addition to using the techniques described to repel mosquitos, you should go one step further.

The problem is, no-see-ums are tricky little devils. Somehow they can actually get under your socks and around your ankles where they will bite to their heart's content all night long while you sleep, itch, sleep, and itch some more. The best solution is to apply a liquid repellent to your ankles, then wear clean socks.

Horseflies are another story. They are rarely a problem, but when they get their dander up, they can cause problems you'll never forget.

One such episode occurred when Foonsky and I were paddling a canoe along the shoreline of a large lake. This giant horsefly, about the size of a fingertip, started dive bombing the canoe. After 20 minutes, it landed on his thigh. Foonsky immediately slammed it with an open hand—then let out a blood-curdling "yeeeee-ow" that practically sent ripples across the lake. When Foonsky whacked it, the horsefly had turned around and bit him in the hand, leaving a huge, red welt.

In the next 10 minutes, that big fly strafed the canoe on more dive-bomb runs. I finally got ready with my canoe paddle, as if it was a baseball bat, swung, and nailed that horsefly like I'd hit a home run. It landed about 15 feet from the boat, still alive and buzzing in the water. While I was trying to figure what it would take to kill this bugger, a large rainbow trout surfaced and snatched it out of the water finally avenging the assault.

If you have horsefly or yellow jacket problems, you'd best just leave the area. One, two or a few can be dealt with. More than that and your fun camping trip will be about as fun as being roped to a tree and stung by an electric shock rod.

On most trips, you will spend time doing everything possible to keep from getting bit by mosquitos or no-see-ums. When that fails, you must know what to do next—and fast, if you are among those ill-fated campers who get big, red lumps from a bite inflicted from even a microscopic-sized mosquito.

A fluid called "After Bite," or a dab of ammonia, should be applied immediately to the bite. To start the healing process, apply a first-aid gel, not liquid, such as Campho-Phenique.

TICKS

Ticks are a nasty, little vermin that will wait in ambush, jump on unsuspecting prey, and eventually crawl to a prime location before trying to fill his body with his victim's blood.

I call them the Dracula Bug, but by any name they can be a terrible camp pest. Ticks rest on grass and low plants and attach themselves to those who brush against the vegetation (dogs are particularly vulnerable). Typically, they are no more than 18 inches above ground, and if you stay on the trails, you can usually avoid them.

There are two common species of ticks. The common coastal tick is larger, brownish in color, and prefers to crawl around prior to putting the clamps on you. The latter habit can give you the creeps, but when you feel it crawling, you can just pick it off and dispatch it. Their preferred destination is usually the back of your neck, just where the hairline starts. The other species, a wood tick, is small, black, and when he puts the clamps in, it's immediately painful. When a wood tick gets into a dog for a few days, it can cause a large, red welt. In either case, ticks should be removed as soon as possible.

If you have hiked in areas infested with them, it is advisable to shower as soon as possible, discarding and washing your clothes immediately. If you just leave your clothes in a heap, a tick can crawl from your clothes and thus invade your home. They like warmth, and, one way or another, they can end up in your bed. Waking up in the middle of the night with a tick crawling across you chest can really give you the creeps.

Once a tick has the clampers on you, you must decide how long it has been there. If it has been a short time, the most painless, and effective method is to just take a pair of sharp tweezers and grasp the little devil, making certain to isolate the mouth area, then pull him out.

If the tick has been in longer, you may wish a doctor to extract it. Some people will burn it with a cigarette, or poison it with lighter fluid, but this is not advisable. In any case, you must take care to remove all of it, especially its claw-like mouth.

The wound, however small, should then be cleansed and dressed. This is done by applying liquid peroxide, which cleans and sterilizes the wound and then coating a dressing with a first-aid gel such as First-Aid Cream, Campho-Pehnique, or Neosporin ointment.

Lyme disease, which is transmitted by the bite of the deer tick, is rare in California, but common enough to warrant some attention. To prevent tick bites, tuck your pant legs into your hiking socks and always wear a shirt, making sure it is tucked into your pants. Then spray tick repellent, called Permamone, on your pants.

The first symptom of Lyme disease is the bite area will develop a bright-red, splotchy rash. Other early symptoms sometimes include headache, nausaea, fever and/or a stiff neck. If this happens or if you have any doubts, you should see your doctor immediately. If you do get Lyme disease, don't panic. Doctors say it is easily treated in the early stages with simple antibiotics. If you are nervous about the possibility of getting Lyme disease, put the tick in a plastic bag as soon as it is removed and take it to your doctor for analysis.

POISON OAK

After a nice afternoon hike, about a five-miler, I was concerned about possible exposure to poison oak, so I immediately showered and put on clean clothes. Then I settled into a chair with my favorite foamy, body-building elixir to watch the end of a baseball game. The game went 18 innings and meanwhile, my dog, tired from the hike, had gone to sleep on my bare ankles.

A few days later I had a case of poison oak. My feet looked like they had been on fire and put out with an ice pick. The lesson? Don't always trust your dog, give him a bath as well, and beware of extra-inning ball games.

You can get poison oak only from direct contact with the oil residue from the leaves. It can be passed in a variety of fashions, as direct as skin to leaf contact or as indirect as leaf to dog, dog to sofa, sofa to skin. Once you have it, there is little you can do but itch yourself to death. Applying Caladryl lotion or its equivalent can help because it contains antihistamines, which attack and dry the itch.

A tip that may sound crazy but seems to work is advised by my pal Furniss. You should expose the afflicted area to the hottest water you can stand, then suddenly immerse it in cold water. The hot water opens the skin pores and gets the "itch" out, and the cold water then quickly seals the pores.

In any case, you're a lot better off if you don't get poison oak to begin with. Remember the old Boy Scout saying: "Leaves of three, let them be." Also remember that poison oak can disguise itself. In the spring it is green, then gradually turns reddish in the summer. By fall, it becomes a bloody, ugly-looking red. In the winter, it loses its leaves altogether and appears to be nothing more than barren, brown sticks of small plant. However, at any time and in any form, skin contact can cause quick infection.

Some people are more easily afflicted than others, but if you are one of the lucky few, don't cheer too loudly. While some people can be exposed to the oil residue of poison oak with little or no effect, the body's resistance can gradually be worn down with repeated exposures. At one time, I could practically play in the stuff and the only symptom would be a few little bumps on the inside of my wrist. Now, some 15 years later, times have changed. My resistance has broken down. If I merely rub against poison oak now, in a few days the exposed area can look like it has been used for a track meet.

So regardless if you consider yourself vulnerable or not, you should take heed to reduce exposure. That can be done by staying on trails when you hike and making sure your dog does the same. Remember, the worst stands of poison oak are usually brush-infested areas just off the trail. Protect yourself also by dressing so your skin is completely covered, wearing long-sleeve shirts, long pants, and boots. If you suspect you've been exposed, immediately wash your clothes, then wash yourself with aloe vera, rinsing with a cool shower.

And don't forget to give your dog a bath as well.

SUNBURN

The most common injury suffered on camping trips is sunburn, yet some people wear it as a badge of honor, believing that it somehow enhances their virility. Well it doesn't. Neither do suntans. And too much sun can lead to serious burns or sunstroke.

It is easy enough to avoid. Use a high-level sunscreen on your skin, chapstick on your lips, and wear sunglasses and a hat. If any area gets burned, apply First-Aid Cream, which will sooth, and provide moisture for the parched, burned skin.

The best advice from Doctor Bogney is not to even get a suntan. Those that do are involved in a practice that can be eventually ruinous to their skins.

A WORD ABOUT GIARDIA

You have just hiked in to your secret backwoods fishing or hunting spot, thirsty and a bit tired, but you smile as you consider the prospects. Everything seems perfect: You have a campsite along a stream that tumbles into a nearby lake, there's not a stranger in sight, and you have nothing to do for a week but fish or hunt with your pals.

You toss down your gear, grab your cup and dip it into the stream, and take a long drink of that ice cold mountain water. It seems crystal pure and sweeter than anything you've ever tasted. It's later that you find out that it can be just like drinking a cup of poison.

By drinking what appears to be pure mountain water without treating it, you can ingest a microscopic protozoan called *Giardia lamblia*. The pain of the abdominal cramps can make you feel like your stomach and intestinal tract are in a knot, ready to explode. With that comes long-term diarrhea that is worse than even a bear could imagine.

Doctors call the disease giardiasis, or Giardia for short, but it is difficult to even diagnose. One friend of mine who contracted Giardia was first told she might have stomach cancer before the proper diagnosis was eventually made.

Drinking directly from a stream or lake does not mean you will get Giardia, but you are taking a giant chance. Yet there is no reason to take such a risk, potentially ruining your trip and enduring weeks of misery.

A lot of fishermen and hunters are taking that risk. I made a personal survey of backpackers in the Yosemite National Park Wilderness last year, and found roughly only one in 20 were equipped with some kind of water purification system. The result, according to the federal Public Health Service, is that about four percent suffer giardiasis. Across the country, the rates range from one percent to 20 percent, depending on the geographic location and age of the person studied, according to the Parasitic Diseases Division of the Center for Infectious Diseases.

But if you get Giardia, you are not going to care about the statistics. "When I got Giardia, I just about wanted to die," said Henry McCarthy, a California camper. "For about ten days, it was the most terrible thing I have ever experienced. And through the whole thing, I kept thinking, 'I shouldn't have drunk that water,' but it seemed all right at the time."

That is the mistake most campers make. The stream might be running free, gurgling over boulders in the high country, tumbling into deep, oxygenated pools. It looks pure. Then the next day, the problems suddenly start. Drinking untreated water from mountain streams is a lot like Russian roulette. Sooner or later, the gun goes off.

If you camp, fish, and hunt in primitive settings, there are some clear-cut answers to use at your discretion. I hike about 200 miles per year, and in the process have tested them all. Here are my findings.

Katadyn Water Filter: This is the best system for screening out Giardia, as well as other microscopic bacteria more commonly found in stream and lake water that can also cause stomach problems.

This filter works by placing the nozzle in the water, then pumping the water directly from a spout at the top of the pump into a canteen. The pumping can be fairly rigorous, especially as the filter becomes plugged. On the average, it takes a few minutes to fill a canteen.

The best advantages are that the device has a highly advanced screening system (a ceramic element), and it can be cleaned repeatedly with a small brush.

The drawbacks are that the filter is expensive at $170, it can easily break when dropped because its body is made of porcelain, and if you pack very light, its weight (about two pounds) may be a factor. But those are good trade-offs when you can drink ice cold stream water without risk.

First-Need Water Purifier: This is the most cost-effective water purification system for a variety of reasons.

At $35, the unit is far less expensive than the Katadyn, yet provides much better protection than anything cheaper. They are small and lightweight, so they don't add much to the weight of your pack. And if you use some care to pump water from sediment-free sources, they easily last a week, the length of most outdoorsmen's trips.

These devices consist of a plastic pump and a hose that connects to a separate filter canister. They pump faster and with less effort than the Katadyn, but one of the reasons for that is because the filter is not as fine-screened.

The big drawback is that if you pump water from a mucky lake, the filter can clog in a few days. Therein lies the weakness. Once plugged up, it is useless and you have to replace it ($25) or take your chances.

One trick to extend the filter life is to fill your cook pot with water, let the sediment settle, then pump from there. It is also advisable to always have a spare filter canister as an insurance policy.

Boiling Water: Except for water filtration, this is the only treatment that you can use with complete confidence. According to the federal Center of Disease Control, it takes a few minutes at a rolling boil to be certain to kill *Giardia lamblia*. At high elevations, the advice is to boil for three to five minutes. A side benefit is that you'll also kill other dangerous bacteria that also live undetected in natural waters.

But to be honest, boiling water is a thorn for most people on backcountry fishing and hunting trips. For one thing, if you boil water on an open fire, what should taste like crystal-pure mountain water tastes instead like a mouthful of warm ashes. If you don't have a campfire, it wastes stove fuel. And if you are thirsty *now,* forget it. The water takes hours to cool.

The one time boiling always makes sense, however, is when you are preparing dinner. The ash taste will disappear in whatever freeze-dried dinner, soup, or hot drink you have planned.

Water purification pills are the preference for most anglers and hunters—and it can get them in trouble. The pills come cheap at just $3 to $8 per bottle, which can figure to just a few cents per canteen. In addition, they kill most of the bacteria, regardless of whether you use iodine crystals or potable aqua iodine tablets.

They just don't always kill *Giardia lamblia*, and that is the one critter worth worrying about on your trip. That makes water treatment pills unreliable and dangerous.

Another key element is the time factor. Depending on the water's temperature, organic content, and pH level, these pills can take a long time to do the job—a minimum wait of 20 minutes is prescribed. Most guys don't like waiting that long, especially when hot and thirsty after a long hike, "and what the heck, the water looks fine."

And then there is the taste. On one trip, my water filter clogged and we had to use the iodine pills instead. It doesn't take long to get tired of the iodine-tinged taste of the water. Mountain water should be one of the great-tasting beverages of the world, but the iodine kills that.

No treatment: This is your last resort and, using extreme care, can be executed with success. One of my best hiking buddies is a hydrologist for the Forest Service, Michael Furniss, and on wilderness fishing trips he has showed me the difference between "safe" and "dangerous" water sources.

At one time, just finding water running over a rock used to be a guarantee of its purity. No longer. The safe water sources are almost always small creeks or springs located in high, craggy mountain areas. The key is making sure no one has been upstream from where you drink.

He mentioned that another problem you can have if you bypass water treatment is that even in settings free of Giardia, you can still ingest other bacteria that can cause stomach problems.

The only sure way to beat the problem is to pump filter or boil the water before drinking, eating, or brushing your teeth. And the best way to prevent its spread is to be certain to bury your waste products at least eight inches deep and at least 100 feet away from natural waters.

HYPOTHERMIA

No matter how well planned your trip might be, a sudden change in weather can turn it into a puzzle for which there are few answers. Bad weather or an accident can result in a dangerous chain of events.

Such a chain of episodes occurred for my brother, Rambob, and myself on a fishing trip one fall day just below the snow line. The weather had suddenly turned very cold and ice was forming along the shore of the lake. Suddenly, the canoe was placed in terrible imbalance and just that quick, it flipped. The little life vest seat cushions were useless, and using the canoe as a paddle board, we tried to kick our way back to shore where my dad was going crazy at the thought of his two sons drowning before his eyes.

It took 17 minutes in that 38-degree water, but we finally made it to the shore. When they pulled me out of the water, my legs were dead, not strong enough to even hold up my weight. In fact, I didn't feel so much cold as tired, and I just wanted to lay down and go to sleep.

I closed my eyes, and my brother-in-law, Lloyd Angal, slapped me in the face several times, then got me on my feet and pushed and pulled me about.

In the celebration over making it to shore, only Lloyd had realized that hypothermia was setting in—where the temperature of the body is lowered to the point that it causes poor reasoning, apathy, and collapse. It can look like the endangered is just tired and needs to sleep, but that sleep can be the next step to a coma.

Ultimately, my brother and I shared what little dry clothing remained. We then began hiking around to get muscle movement, creating internal warmth. Shivering is another way the body creates warmth for itself. We ate whatever munchies were available because the body produces heat by digestion. But most important, we got our heads as dry as possible. More body heat is lost through wet hair than any other single factor.

A few hours later, we were in a pizza parlor replaying the incident, talking about how only a life vest can do the job of a life vest. We decided never again to rely on those little floatation seat cushions that disappear when the boat flips.

Almost by instinct we had done everything right to prevent hypothermia: Don't go to sleep, start a physical activity, induce shivering, put dry clothes on, dry your head, and eat something. That's how you fight hypothermia. In a dangerous setting, whether you fall in a lake, a stream, or get caught unprepared in a storm, that's how you can stay alive.

After being in that ice-bordered lake for almost 20 minutes, and then finally pulling ourselves to the shoreline, a strange, eerie phenomena occurred. My canoe was flipped right-side up, and lost were almost all of its contents: tackle box, floatation cushions, and cooler. But remaining was one paddle and one fishing rod, the trout rod my grandfather had given me for my 12th birthday.

Lloyd gave me a smile. "This means that you are meant to paddle and fish again," he said with a laugh.

FIRST AID KIT LIST

Band-Aids
Sterile gauze pads
Roller gauze
Athletic tape
Moleskin
Thermometer
Aspirin
Ace bandage

SECONDARY KIT LIST

Mosquito repellent
After Bite or ammonia
Campho-Phenique gel
First Aid cream
Sunscreen
Neosporin ointment
Caladryl
Biodegradable soap
Towelettes

OPTIONAL

Water purification system
Coins for emergency phone call
Extra set of matches
Tweezers
Mirror for signaling

♦ FISHING & RECREATIONAL ♦
EQUIPMENT

Feet tired and hot, stomachs hungry, we stopped our hike for lunch beside a beautiful little river pool that was catching the flows from a long but gentle waterfall. My brother, Rambob, passed me a piece of jerky. I took my boots off, then slowly dunked my feet into the cool, foaming water.

I was gazing at a towering peak across a canyon, when suddenly— Wham! There was sudden jolt at the heel of my right foot. I pulled my foot out of the water and incredibly, a trout had bitten it.

My brother looked at me like I had antlers growing out of my head. "Wow!" he exclaimed, "that trout almost caught himself an outdoors writer!"

It's true that in remote areas trout sometimes bite on almost anything, even feet. In California's High Sierra, I have caught limits of trout using nothing but a bare hook. The only problem is the fish will often hit the splitshot sinker instead of the hook. Of course, fishing isn't usually that easy. But it gives you an idea of what is possible.

America's wildlands are home for a remarkable abundance of fish and wildlife. Deer browse with little fear of man, bear keep an eye out for your food, and little critters like squirrels and chipmunks are daily companions. Add in the fishing and you've got yourself a camping trip.

Your camping trips will evolve into premium outdoor experiences if you can parlay in a few good fishing trips, avoid bear problems, and occasionally add a little offbeat fun with some camp games.

TROUT AND BASS

He creeps up on the stream as quiet as an old Indian, keeping his shadow off the water. With his little spinning rod, he'll zip his lure within an inch or two of its desired mark, probing along rocks, the edges of riffles, pocket water; wherever he can find a change in river habitat. It's my brother, Rambob, trout fishing, and he's a master at it.

In most cases, he'll catch a trout on his first or second cast. After that it's time to move up river, giving no spot much more than five minutes due. Stick and move, stick and move, stalking the stream like a bobcat zeroing in on a unsuspecting rabbit. He might keep a few trout for dinner, but mostly he releases what he catches. Rambob doesn't necessarily fish for food. It's the feeling that comes with it.

Fishing can give you a sense of exhilaration, like taking a hot shower after being coated with dust. On your walk back to camp, the steps come easy. You suddenly understand what John Muir meant when he talked of developing a oneness with nature, because you have it. That's what fishing can help provide.

You don't need a million dollars worth of fancy gear to catch fish. What you need is the right outlook, and that can be learned. That goes regardless if you are fishing for trout or bass, the two most popular fisheries in America. Your fishing tackle selection should be as simple and as clutter-free as possible.

At home, I've got every piece of fishing tackle you might imagine, more than 30 rods and many tackle boxes, racks, and cabinets filled with all kinds of stuff. I've got one lure that looks like a chipmunk and another that resembles a miniature can of beer with hooks. If I hear of something new, I want to try it, and usually do. It's a result of my lifelong fascination with the sport.

But if you just want to catch fish, there's an easier way to go. And when I go fishing, I take that path. I don't try to bring everything. It would be impossible. Instead, I bring a relatively small amount of gear. At home I will scan my tackle boxes for equipment and lures, make my selections, and bring just the essentials. Rod, reel, and tackle will fit into a side pocket of my backpack or a small carrying bag.

So what kind of rod should be used on an outdoor trip? For most camper-anglers, I suggest the use of a light, multi-piece spinning rod that will break down to a small size. One of the best deals on the fishing market is the six-piece Daiwa 6.5-foot pack rod, No. 6752. It retails for as low as $30 yet is made of a graphite/glass composite that gives it a quality of a much more expensive model. And it comes in a hard plastic carrying tube for protection. Other major rod manufacturers, such as Fenwick, Sabre, and Contender, offer similar premium rods. It's tough to miss with any of them.

The use of graphite-glass composites in fishing rods has made them lighter and more sensitive, yet stronger. The only downside to graphite as a rod material is that it can be brittle. If you rap your rod against something, it can crack or cause a weak spot. That weak spot can eventually snap when under even light pressure, like setting a hook or casting. Of course, a bit of care will prevent that from ever occurring.

If you haven't bought a fishing reel in some time, you will be surprised at the quality and price of micro spinning reels on the market. The reels come tiny and strong, with rear-control drag systems. Sigma, Shimano, Cardinal, Abu, and others all make premium reels. They also come expensive, usually $50 to $75. They're worth it. With your purchase, you've just bought a reel that will last for years and years.

The one downside to spinning reels is that after long term use, the bail spring will weaken. The result is that after casting and beginning to reel, the bail will sometimes not flip over and allow the reel to retrieve the line. You then have to do it by hand. This can be incredibly frustrating, particularly when stream fishing, where instant line pickup is essential. The solution is to have a new bail spring installed every few years. This is a cheap, quick operation for a tackle expert.

You might own a giant tackle box filled with lures, but on your fishing trip you are better off to fit just the essentials into a small container. One of the best ways to do that is to use the Plano Micro-Magnum 3414, a tiny two-sided tackle box for trout fishermen that fits into a shirt pocket. In mine, I can fit 20 lures in one side of the box and 20 flies, splitshot and snap swivels in the other. For bass lures, which are larger, you need a slightly larger box, but the same principle applies.

There are more fishing lures on the market than you can imagine, but a few special ones can do the job. I make sure these are in my box on every trip. For trout I carry: Small black Panther Martin spinner with yellow spots, small gold Kastmaster, yellow Roostertail, gold Z-Ray with red spots, Super Duper, and Mepps Lightning spinner.

You can take it a step further using insider's wisdom. My old pal Ed the Dunk showed me his trick of taking a tiny Dardevle spoon, then spray painting it flat black and dabbing five tiny red dots on it. It's a real killer, particularly in tiny streams where the trout are spooky.

The best trout catcher I've ever used on rivers is a small metal lure called a Met-L Fly. On days when nothing else works, it can be like going to a shooting gallery. The problem is that the lure is near impossible to find. Rambob and I consider the few we have remaining so valuable that if the lure is snagged on a rock, a cold swim is deemed mandatory for its retrieval. These lures are as elusive to find in tackle shops as trout can be to catch without one.

For bass, you can also fit all you need into a small plastic tackle box. I have fished with many bass pros and all of them actually use just a few lures: a white spinner bait, a small jig called a Git's It, a surface plug called a Zara Spook, and plastic worms. At times, like when the bass move into shoreline areas during the spring, shad minnow imitations such as made by Rebel or Rapala can be dynamite. For instance, my favorite is the one-inch blue-silver Rapala. Every spring, as the lakes begin to warm and the fish snap out of their winter doldrums, I like to float and paddle around small lakes in my small raft. I'll cast that little Rapala along the shoreline and catch and release hundreds of bass, bluegill, and sunfish. The fish are usually sitting close to the shoreline, awaiting my offering.

A FEW TRICKS

There's an old angler's joke about how you need to "think like a fish." But if you're the one getting zilched, you may not think it's so funny.

The irony is that it is your mental approach, what you see and what you miss, that often determines your fishing luck. Some people will spend a lot of money on tackle, lures, and fishing clothes, and that done, just saunter up to a stream or lake, cast out and wonder why they are not catching fish. The answer is their mental outlook. They are not attuning themselves to their surroundings.

You must live on nature's level, not your own. Try this and you will start to feel things you never believed even existed. Soon you will see things that will allow you to catch fish. You can get a head start by reading about fishing, but to get your degree in fishing, you must attend the University of Nature.

On every fishing trip, regardless what you fish for, try to follow three hard-and-fast rules:

1. Always approach the fishing spot so you will be undetected.

2. Present your lure, fly or bait in a manner so it appears completely natural, as if no line was attached.

3. Stick and move, hitting one spot, working it the best you can, then move to the next.

Here's a more detailed explanation.

1. Approach: No one can just walk up to a stream or lake, cast out, and start catching fish as if someone had waved a magic wand. Instead, give the fish credit for being smart. After all, they live there.

Your approach must be completely undetected by the fish. Fish can sense your presence through sight and sound, though this is misinterpreted by most people. By sight, this rarely means the fish actually see you, but more likely, they will see your shadow on the water, or the movement of your arm or rod while casting. By sound, it doesn't mean they hear you talking, but that they will detect the vibrations of your footsteps along the shore, kicking a rock, or the unnatural plunking sound of a heavy cast hitting the water. Any of these elements can spook them off the bite. In order to fish undetected, you must walk softly, keep your shadow off the water, and keep your casting motion low. All of these keys become easier at sunrise or sunset, when shadows are on the water. At mid-day, a high sun causes high level of light penetration in the water, which can make the fish skittish to any foreign presence.

Like hunting, you must stalk the spots. When my brother Rambob sneaks up on a fishing spot, he looks like a burglar sneaking through an unlocked window.

2. Presentation: Your lure, fly, or bait must appear in the water as if no line was attached, so it appears as natural as possible. My pal Mo Furniss has skin-dived in rivers to watch what the fish see when somebody is fishing.

"You wouldn't believe it," he said. "When the lure hits the water, every trout within 40 feet, like 15, 20 trout, will do a little zig-zag. They all see the lure and are aware something is going on. Meanwhile, on-shore the guy casting doesn't get a bite and thinks there aren't any fish in the river."

If your offering is aimed at fooling a fish into striking, it must appear as part of its natural habitat, as if it is an insect just hatched or a small fish looking for a spot to hide. That's where you come in.

After you have snuck up on a fishing spot, you should zip your cast upstream, then start your retrieve as soon as it hits the water. If you let the lure sink to the bottom, then start the retrieve, you have no chance. A minnow, for instance, does not sink to the bottom then start swimming. On rivers, the retrieve should be more of a drift, as if the "minnow" was in trouble and the current was sweeping it downstream.

When fishing on trout streams, always hike and cast up river, then retrieve as the offering drifts downstream in the current. This is effective because trout will sit almost motionless, pointed upstream, finning against the current. This way they can see anything coming their direction, and if a potential food morsel arrives, all they need to do is move over a few inches, open their mouths, and they've got an easy lunch. Thus you must cast upstream.

Conversely, if you cast downstream, your retrieve will bring the lure from behind the fish, where he cannot see it approaching. And I've never seen a trout that had eyes in its tail. In addition, when retrieving a downstream lure, the river current will tend to sweep your lure inshore to the rocks.

3. Finding spots: A lot of fishermen don't catch fish and a lot of hikers never see any wildlife. The key is where they are looking.

The rule of the wild is that fish and wildlife will congregate wherever there is a distinct change in the habitat. This is where you should begin your search. To find deer, for instance, forget probing a thick forest, but look for when it breaks into a meadow, or a clear-cut has splayed a stand of trees. That's where the deer will be. Look for the change.

In a river, it can be where a riffle pours into a small pool, a rapid that plunges into a deep hole and flattens, a big boulder in the middle of a long riffle, a shoreline point, a rock pile, a submerged tree. Look for the changes. Conversely, long straight stretches of shoreline will not hold fish—the habitat is lousy.

On rivers, the most productive areas are often where short riffles tumble into small oxygenated pools. After sneaking up from the downstream side and staying low, you should zip your cast so the lure plops gently in the white water just above the pool. Starting your retrieve instantly, the lure will drift downstream and plunk into the pool. Bang! That's where the trout will hit. Take a few more casts, then head upstream to the next spot.

With a careful approach and lure presentation, and by fishing in the right spots, you have the ticket to many exciting days on the water.

OF BEARS AND FOOD

The first time you come nose-to-nose with a bear, it can make your skin quiver.

Even mild-mannered black bears, the most common bear in America (and the one you see in the West) can send shock waves through your body. They range from 250 to 400 pounds and have large claws and teeth that are made to scare campers. When they bound, the muscles on their shoulders seem to roll like ocean breakers.

Bears in camping areas are accustomed to sharing the mountains with hikers and campers. They have become specialists in the food-raiding business. As a result, you must be able to make a bear-proof food hang, or be able to scare the fellow off. Many campgrounds provide bear and raccoon-proof food lockers. You can also stash your food in your vehicle, but that puts a limit on your trip.

If you are in a particularly remote area, there will be no food lockers available. Your car will not be there either. The answer is making a bear-proof food hang—suspending all of your food wrapped in a plastic garbage bag from a rope in mid-air, ten feet from the trunk of a tree and 20 feet off the ground. (Counter-balancing two bags with a rope thrown over a tree limb is very effective, but an extensive search must often be made to find an appropriate limb.)

This is accomplished by tying a rock to a rope, then throwing it over a high but sturdy tree limb. Next, tie your food bag to the rope, and hoist it up in the air. When you are satisfied with the position of the food bag, tie off the end of the rope to another tree. Nothing else will do, especially for hikers in bear-troubled areas such as national parks where hunting is not allowed. For instance, one day in Yosemite near Tuolumne Meadows, I met five consecutive teams of hikers head- ing the other direction who had all lost food to bears.

I've been there. On one trip, Foonsky and Rambob had left to fish, and I was stoking up an evening campfire when I felt the eyes of an intruder on my back. I turned around and this big bear was heading straight for our camp. In the next half hour, I scared the bear off twice, but then he got a whiff of something sweet in my brother's pack.

In most situations you can spook a black bear by banging on a pot and shouting like a lunatic. But some bears are on to the old banging-the-pot trick. If so, and he gets a whiff of your Tang, banging on a pot and shouting can be like trying to stop a tank with a roadblock.

In this case, the bear rolled into camp like a semi truck, grabbed my brother's pack, ripped it open and plucked out the Tang and the Swiss Miss. The bear, a 350-pounder, then sat astride a nearby log and lapped at the goodies like a thirsty dog finding water.

I took two steps toward the pack and that bear jumped off the log and galloped across the camp right at me. Scientists say a man can't outrun a bear, but they've never seen how fast I can go up a granite block with a bear on my tail. Once a bear gets his mitts on your gear, he considers it his.

Shortly thereafter, Foonsky returned while I was still perched on top of the rock, and demanded to know how I could let a bear get our Tang. But it took all three of us, Foonsky, Rambob, and myself, all charging at once and shouting like madmen to clear the bear out of the camp and send him off over the ridge. It was a lesson to never let food sit unattended again—a lesson learned the hard way.

THE GRIZZLY

When it comes to grizzlies, well, my friends, you need what we call an "attitude adjustment." Or that big ol' bear may just decide to adjust your attitude for you and make your stay at the park a short one.

Grizzlies are nothing like black bears. They are bigger, stronger, have little fear, and take what they want. Some people believe there are many different species of this critter, like Alaskan brown, silvertop, cinnamon, kodiak, but the truth is they are all grizzlies. Any difference in appearance has to do with diet, habitat, and life habits, not speciation. But by any name, they all come big. Although you won't find grizzlies in Oregon and most of Washington (the North Cascades excepted), it is good to know what to do in case you ever do run into one.

The first thing you must do to prepare is determine if there are grizzlies in the area where you are camping. That can usually be done easily enough by asking rangers in the area. If you are heading into Yellowstone or Glacier National Park, or the Bob Marshall Wilderness of Montana, well, you don't have to ask. They're out there, and they're the biggest and potentially most dangerous critters you could run into.

One general way to figure the size of a bear is from his footprint. Take the width of the footprint in inches, add one to it -- and you'll have an estimated length of the bear in feet. For instance, a nine-inch footprint equals a 10-foot bear. Any bear that big is a grizzly, my friends. In fact, most grizzly footprints average about nine to ten inches across, and black bears (though they may be brown in color) tend to have footprints only 4.5 to six inches across.

If you are hiking in a wilderness area that may have grizzlies, then it becomes a necessity to wear bells on your pack. That way, the bear will hear you coming and likely get out of your way. Keep talking, singing, or maybe even debate the country's foreign policy, but whatever, do not fall into a silent hiking vigil. And if a breeze is blowing in your face, you must make even more noise (now a good excuse to rant and rave about the government's domestic affairs). Noise is important, because your smell will not be carried in the direction you are hiking. As a result, the bear will not smell you coming.

If a bear can hear you and smell you, they will tend to get out of the way and let you pass without your knowing they were even close by. The exception is, if you are carrying fish, lots of sweets in your pack, or are wearing heavy, sweet deodorants or makeup. All three are bear attractants.

Most encounters with grizzlies occur when hikers fall into a silent march in the wilderness with the wind in their faces—and they walk around a corner and right into a big, unsuspecting grizzly. If you do this, and see a big hump just behind its neck, well, gulp, don't think twice, it's a grizzly.

And then what should you do? Get up a tree, that's what. Grizzlies are so big that their claws cannot support their immense weight, and thus they cannot climb trees. And although their young can climb, they rarely want to get their mitts on you.

If you do get grabbed, every instinct in your body will tell you to fight back. Don't believe it. This is a time to listen to logic; not the heart. Play dead. Go limp. Let the bear throw you around a little, because after awhile you become unexciting play material, and the bear will get bored. My grandmother was grabbed by a grizzly in Glacier National Park and after a few tosses and hugs, was finally left alone to escape.

Some say it's a good idea to tuck your head under his chin, and therefore, the bear will be unable to bite your head. I'll take a pass on that one. If you are taking action, any action, it's a signal that you are a force to be reckoned with, and he'll likely respond with more aggression. And bears don't lose many wrestling matches.

What grizzlies really like to do, believe it or not, is to pile a lot of sticks and leaves on you. Just let them, and keep perfectly still. Don't fight them; don't run. And when you have a 100-percent chance (not 98 or 99) to dash up a nearby tree, that's when you let fly. Once safely in a tree, then you can hurl down insults, and let your aggression out. Remember, logic.

In a wilderness camp, there are special precautions you should take. Always hang your food at least 100 yards down wind of your camp. and get it high; 30 feet is reasonable. In addition, circle your camp with rope, and hang the bells from your pack onto it. Thus, if a bear walks into your camp, he'll run into your rope; the bells will ring, and everybody will have a chance to get up a tree before ol' griz figures out what's going on. Often, the unexpected ringing of bells is enough to send him off in search of a quieter environment.

You see, more often than not, grizzlies tend to clear the way for campers and hikers. So, be smart, and don't act like bear bait, and always have a plan if you are confronted by one.

My pal Foonsky had such a plan during a wilderness expedition in Montana's northern Rockies. On our second day of hiking, we started seeing scratch marks on the trees, like 13 to 14 feet off the ground.

"Mr. Griz made those," Foonsky said. "With spring here, the grizzlies are coming out of hibernation and using the trees like a cat uses a scratch board to stretch the muscles."

The next day, I noticed Foonsky had a pair of track shoes tied to the back of his pack. I just laughed.

"You're not going to outrun a griz," I said. "In fact, there's hardly any animals out here in the wilderness that man can outrun."

Foonsky just smiled.

"I don't have to outrun a griz," he said. "I just have to outrun you!"

FUN AND GAMES

You can bring an added dimension to your camping trip with a few recreational tools.

One such tool is an inexpensive star chart. They allow you to identify stars, constellations, and planets on clear mountain nights. Another good addition is a pocket-size handbook on tree identification. Both of these can provide a unique perspective to your trip, and make you feel more a participant of the wild, rather than an observer.

If you want more excitement, and maybe a little competition with your companions, a good game using twigs or rocks is called "3-5-7." You set up the game by laying out three rows of twigs, with three twigs in one row, five in another, seven in the other. Alternating turns with one competitor, you are allowed to remove all or as few as one twig from a row, but from only one row per turn. You alternate turns removing twigs, and whoever is left picking up the last twig is the loser.

Some folks bring a deck of cards and a tiny cribbage board, or will set up a poker game. Of the latter, I've been in a few doozies on backpacking trips. Money is meaningless in the woods, but something like penny candy has a high value. Betting a pack of M&Ms and a beef stick in a poker game in the outback is like laying down a million dollars in Las Vegas.

In a game of seven-card stud, I caught a straight on the last card of the deal, but Foonsky was showing three sevens and bluffing full house. When I bet five M&Ms with nuts and two Skittles, Rambob folded. "Too much for me." But Foonsky matched my bet, and then with painful slowness, raised me a grape stick.

All was quiet. It was the highest bet ever made. I felt nervous, my heart started pounding, and again I looked hard at my cards. The decision came tough: I folded. The potential lose of a grape stick, even with a great hand like I had, was just too much to gamble.

But I still had my grape stick.

FISHING & RECREATIONAL GEAR LIST
Fishing rod
Fishing reel with fresh line
Small tackle box with lures, splitshot, and snap swivels
Pliers
Knife

OPTIONAL
Knapsack for each person
Stargazing chart
Tree identification handbook
Deck of cards
Backpacking cribbage board

·Maps & How To· USE THEM

Now you're ready to join the Five Percent Club, that is, the five percent of campers who know the secret spots where they can camp, fish and hike and have the time of their lives doing it.

To aid in that pursuit, there are a number of contacts, map sources and reservation systems available for your use. These include contacts for national forests, state parks, national parks, the Bureau of Land Management and motor home parks. The state and federal agencies listed can provide detailed maps at low cost and any additional information you might require.

NATIONAL FORESTS

The Forest Service provides many secluded camps and permits camping anywhere except where it is specifically prohibited. If you ever want to clear the cobwebs and get away from it all, this is the way to go.

Many Forest Service campgrounds are quite remote and have no developed water. You don't need to check-in, you don't need reservations and there is no fee. At many Forest Service campgrounds that provide piped water, the camp fee is often only a few dollars, with payment made on the honor system. Because most of these camps are in mountain areas, they are subject to closure for snow or mud during the winter.

Dogs are permitted in National Forests at no extra charge and with no hassle. They must be on leashes in the campgrounds. Conversely, in state and national parks, dogs are not allowed on trails.

Maps for National Forests are among the best you can get. They detail all backcountry streams, lakes, hiking trails and logging roads for access. They cost $2 and can be obtained by writing to USDA-Forest Service, Outdoor Recreation Information Office, 1018 First Avenue, Seattle, WA 98104.

I've found the Forest Service personnel to be the most helpful of the government agencies when obtaining camping or hiking trail information. Unless you are buying a map, it is advisable to phone, not write, to get the best service. For specific information on a National Forest, write or phone the following addresses and phone numbers.

Washington

Gilford Pinchot National Forest: write to 6926 East 4th Plain Boulevard, Vancouver, WA 98668-8944 or phone (206)696-7500.

Olympic National Forest: write to P.O. Box 2288, Olympia, WA 98507 or phone (206)753-9534.

Mount Baker-Snoqualmie National Forest: write to Holyoke Building, 1022 First Avenue, Seattle, WA 98104 or phone (206)442-0170.

Colville National Forest: write to 695 South Main Street, Colville, WA 99144 or phone (509)684-3711.

Wenatchee National Forest: write to P.O. Box 811, Wenatchee, WA 98807 or phone (509)622-4335.

Okanogan National Forest: write to P.O. Box 950, Okanogan, WA 98840 or phone (509)422-2704.

Oregon

Deschutes National Forest: write to 1645 Highway 20 East, Bend, OR 97701 or phone (503)388-2715.

Fremont National Forest: write to 524 North G Street, Lakeview, OR 97630 or phone (503)947-2151.

Malheur National Forest: write to 139 NE Dayton Street, John Day, OR 97845 or phone (503)575-1731.

Mount Hood National Forest: write to 2955 NW Division Street, Gresham, OR 97030 or phone (503)666-0700.

Ochoco National Forest: write to P.O. Box 490, Prineville, OR 97754 or phone (503)447-6247.

Rogue River National Forest: write to 333 West 8th Street, Medford, OR 97501 or phone (503)776-3600.

Siskiyou National Forest: write to P.O. Box 440, Grants Pass, OR 97526 or phone (503)479-5301.

Siuslaw National Forest: write to P.O. Box 1148, Corvallis, OR 97339 or phone (503)750-7000.

Umatilla National Forest: write to 2517 SW Hailey Avenue, Pendleton, OR 97801 or phone (503)276-3811.

Umpqua National Forest: write to 2900 NW Stewert Parkway, Roseburg, OR 97470 or phone (503)672-6601.

Wallowa-Witman National Forest: write to P.O. Box 907, Baker, OR 97814 or phone (503)523-6391.

Willamette National Forest: write to P.O. Box 10607, Eugene, OR 97440 or phone (503)465-6521.

Winema National Forest: write to 2819 Dahlia Street, Klamath Falls, OR 97601 or phone (503)883-6714.

STATE PARKS

The Washington and Oregon State Parks systems provide many popular camping spots. Reservations are often a necessity during the summer months. The camps include drive-in, numbered sites, tent spaces, picnic tables, with showers and bathrooms provided nearby. Although some parks are well-known, there are still some little-known gems in the State

Parks systems where campers can get seclusion, even in the summer months.

In Washington, there are nine parks that offer a reservation service. Reservations are accepted from the second Monday in January until 14 days before Labor Day. You can request camping dates within the current calendar year only. There is a $4 non-refundable fee for each reservation made at each park. The $4 payment and the standard campsite fee for the first night must accompany your reservation request.

For more information, the Washington State Parks system provides a toll-free number, operational between May 1 and Labor Day, at (800)562-0990. The rest of the year, call (206)753-2027 for information.

Washington

Belfair State Park: write to NE 410 Beck Road, Belfair, WA 98528 or phone (206)478-4625.

Birch Bay State Park: write to 5105 Helwig Road, Blaine, WA 98230 or phone (206)371-2800.

Fort Canby State Park: write to P.O.Box 488, Ilwaco, WA 98624 or phone (206)642-3078.

Fort Flagler State Park: write to Norland, WA 98358 or phone (206)385-1259.

Lake Chelan State Park: write to Route 1, Box 90, Chelan, WA 98816 or phone (509)687-3710.

Moran Sate Park: write to Star Route, Box 22, Eastwood, WA 98245 or phone (206)376-2326.

Pearrygin Lake State Park: write to P.O.Box 300, Winthrop, WA 98862 or phone (509)996-2370.

Steamboat Rock State Park: write to P.O.Box 352, Electric City, WA 99123 or phone (509)633-1304.

Twin Harbors-Grayland Beach: write c/o Twin Harbors State Park, Westport, WA 98595 (206)268-9717.

Oregon

State Parks and Recreation Division: write to 3554 SE 82nd Avenue, Salem, OR 97310 or phone (503)378-6305.

State Parks, Portland Office: write to 3554 South 82nd Avenue, Portland, OR 97266 or phone (503)238-7488.

State Parks, Tillamook Office: write to 3600 East Third Street, Tillamook, OR 97141 or phone (503)842-5501.

State Parks, Coos Bay Office: write to 365 North Forest Street, Coos Bay, OR 97420 or phone (503)269-9410.

State Parks, Bend Office: write to 63055 North Highway 97, Bend, OR 97701 or phone (503)388-6211.

State Parks, LaGrande Office: write to 211 Adams Avenue, LaGrande, OR 97850 or phone (503)963-6444.

NATIONAL PARKS

The National Parks in Washington and Oregon are natural wonders, ranging from the spectacular Mount Rainer National Park to the lava-strewn Mount St. Helens National Monument to the often fog-bound Olympic National Park.

For information on each of the national parks in Washington and Oregon, you should contact the parks directly at the following numbers or addresses.

Washington

Olympic National Park: write to 600 East Park Avenue, Port Angeles, WA 98362 or phone (206)452-4501.

Mount St. Helens National Volcanic Monument: write to Route 1, Box 369, Amboy, WA 98601 or phone (206)247-5473.

Mount Rainier National Park: write to Tahoma Woods, Star Route, Ashford, WA 98304 or phone 1(206)569-2211.

North Cascades National Park: write to Ross Lake and Lake Chelan National Recreation Areas, 800 State Street, Sedro Wooley, WA 98284 or phone (206)856-5700.

Coulee Dam National Recreation Area: write to P.O.Box 37, Coulee Dam, WA 99116 or phone (509)663-9441.

Oregon

Crater Lake National Park: write to P.O.Box 7, Crater Lake, OR 97604 or phone (503)594-2211.

Fort Clatsop National Memorial: write to Route 3, Box 604-FC, Astoria, OR 97103 or phone (503)861-2471.

John Day Fossil Beds National Monument: write to 420 West Main Street, St. John Day, OR 97845 or phone (503)575-0721.

Oregon Caves National Monument: write to 19000 Caves Highway, Cave Junction, OR 97523 or phone (503)592-2100.

DEPARTMENT OF NATURAL RESOURCES

The Department of Natural Resources manages about five million acres of public land in Washington. All of it is managed under the concept of "multiple use," designed to provide the greatest recreational opportunities while still protecting the natural resources of the area.

The campgrounds in these areas are among the most primitive, remote and least known of the camps listed in this book. The cost is usually free and you are asked to remove all litter and trash from the area, leaving only your footprints behind.

In addition to maps of the area it manages, the Department of Natural Resources also has U.S. Geological Survey maps and U.S. Army Corps of Engineer maps. For information, write or phone:

Department of Natural Resources, Photo and Map Sales, AW-11, 1065 South Capitol Way, Olympia, WA 98504. Phone (206)753-5338.

BUREAU OF LAND MANAGEMENT

Oregon State Office: write to 825 NE Multnomah Street, Portland, OR 97232 or phone (503)231-6274.

Hines District: write to HC74-12533 Highway 20 West,Hines, OR 97738 or phone (503)575-5241.

Coos Bay District: write to 1300 Airport Lane, North Bend, OR 97459 or phone (503)756-0100.

Eugene District: write to 1255 Pearl Street, Eugene, OR 97440 or phone (503)683-6600.

Lakeview District: write to 1000 South 9th Street, Lakeview, OR 97630 or phone (503)947-2177.

Medford District: write to 3040 Biddle Road, Medford, OR 97504 or phone (503)776-4174.

CAMPING GEAR CHECK LIST

1. COOKING GEAR

- ☐ Matches bagged in different zip lock bags
- ☐ Fire-starter cubes or candle
- ☐ Camp stove
- ☐ Camp fuel
- ☐ Pot, pan, cup
- ☐ Pot grabber
- ☐ Knife, fork
- ☐ Dish soap and scrubber
- ☐ Salt, pepper, spices
- ☐ Itemized food
- ☐ Plastic spade

OPTIONAL

- ☐ Axe or hatchet
- ☐ Wood or charcoal for barbecue
- ☐ Ice chest
- ☐ Spatula
- ☐ Grill
- ☐ Tin foil
- ☐ Dust pan
- ☐ Tablecloth
- ☐ Whisk broom
- ☐ Clothespins

2. CAMPING CLOTHES

- ☐ Polypropylene underwear
- ☐ Cotton shirt
- ☐ Long sleeve cotton/wool shirt
- ☐ Cotton/canvas pants
- ☐ Vest
- ☐ Parka
- ☐ Rain jacket, pants, or poncho
- ☐ Hat
- ☐ Sunglasses
- ☐ Chapstick

OPTIONAL

- ☐ Seam lock
- ☐ Shorts
- ☐ Swimming suit
- ☐ Gloves
- ☐ Ski cap

3. HIKING AND FOOT CARE LIST

- ☐ Quality hiking boots
- ☐ Backup lightweight shoes
- ☐ Polypropylene socks
- ☐ Thick cotton socks
- ☐ 80 percent wool socks
- ☐ Strong boot laces
- ☐ Innersole or foot cushion
- ☐ Moleskin and medical tape

- ☐ Gaiters
- ☐ Water repellent boot treatment

4. GOOD NIGHT'S SLEEP LIST

- ☐ Sleeping bag
- ☐ Insulite pad or Therm-a-rest
- ☐ Ground tarp
- ☐ Tent

OPTIONAL

- ☐ Air pillow
- ☐ Mosquito netting
- ☐ Foam pad for truck bed
- ☐ Windshield light screen for RV
- ☐ Catalytic heater

5. FIRST-AID KIT

- ☐ Band-Aids
- ☐ Sterile gauze pads
- ☐ Roller gauze
- ☐ Athletic tape
- ☐ Moleskin
- ☐ Thermometer
- ☐ Aspirin
- ☐ Ace bandage
- ☐ Mosquito repellent
- ☐ After Bite or ammonia
- ☐ Campho-Phenique gel
- ☐ First-Aid cream
- ☐ Sunscreen
- ☐ Neosporin Ointment
- ☐ Caladryl
- ☐ Biodegradable soap
- ☐ Towelette

OPTIONAL

- ☐ Water purification system
- ☐ Coins for emergency phoning
- ☐ Extra set of matches
- ☐ Tweezers
- ☐ Mirror for signaling

6. FISHING/RECREATIONAL GEAR

- ☐ Fishing rod
- ☐ Fishing reel with fresh line
- ☐ Small tackle box with lures, splitshot, and snap swivels
- ☐ Pliers
- ☐ Knife

OPTIONAL

- ☐ Stargazing chart
- ☐ Tree identification hand book
- ☐ Deck of cards
- ☐ Backpacking cribbage board
- ☐ Knapsack for each person

7. MISCELLANEOUS

- ☐ Maps
- ☐ Flashlight
- ☐ Nylon rope for food hang
- ☐ Handkerchief
- ☐ Camera and film
- ☐ Plastic garbage bags
- ☐ Toilet paper
- ☐ Compass
- ☐ Watch

OPTIONAL

- ☐ Binoculars
- ☐ Notebook and pen
- ☐ Towel

GUIDE TO THE
WASHINGTON
CAMPING AREAS

OLYMPIC PENINSULA
♦

SOME HIGHLIGHTS

94 CAMPGROUNDS

Olympic National Forest

Sequim Bay

Strait of Juan De Fuca

Bert Cole State Park

Clallam Bay

Neah Bay

Quinault Lake

Wonder Mountain Wilderness

Hood Canal

Hamma Hamma River

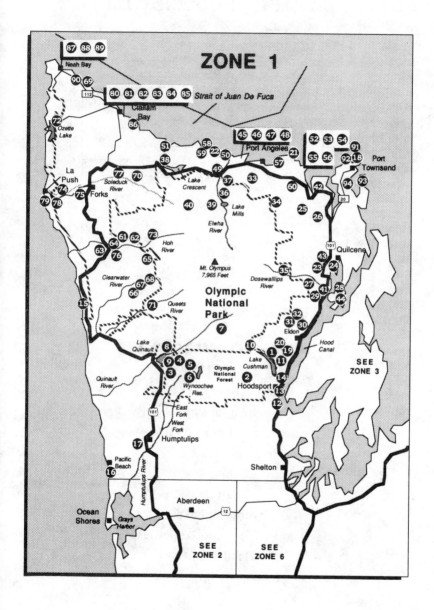

BIG CREEK
Site **1**   near Lake Cushman
OLYMPIC NATIONAL FOREST

Campsites, facilities: There are 23 sites for tents or motor homes up to 30 feet long. Picnic tables are provided. Pump water, vault toilets, firewood and wheelchair facilities are available. A store and a cafe are nearby. Leashed pets are permitted. A boat dock and ramp are located at nearby Lake Cushman.

Reservations, fee: No reservations necessary; $4 fee per night. Open from May through mid-November.

Who to contact: Phone the Hood Canal Ranger Station at (206)877-5254 or write to P.O. Box 68, Hoodsport, WA 94548.

Location: From Hoodsport, drive eight miles northwest on Highway 44 to the "T" intersection and you're there.

Trip note: This camp is a good alternative to Sites 10 and 11, which are set right along Lake Cushman and get heavier use. The camp is set 700 feet elevation and covers 30 acres.

BROWN CREEK
Site **2**   on Brown Creek
OLYMPIC NATIONAL FOREST

Campsites, facilities: There are seven tent sites and 12 sites for trailers or motor homes up to 21 feet long. Picnic tables are provided. Well water, vault toilets and firewood are available. Pets are permitted.

Reservations, fee: No reservations necessary; $4 fee per night. Open year-round.

Who to contact: Phone the Hood Canal Ranger Station at (206)877-5254 or write to Hood Canal Ranger Station, P.O. Box 68, Hoodsport, WA 94548.

Location: Drive north out of Shelton on US 101 for 22 miles, then turn left at the Skokomish Valley on County Road 23 and drive for about 14 miles on County Road 23 and Forest Service roads. A Forest Service map is essential.

Trip note: This camp is virtually unknown to outsiders. It is accessible to two-wheel drive vehicles, but the road connects to a network of primitive, backcountry Forest Service roads. The camp is small, just six acres, but is within the vast Olympic National Forest. Obtain a Forest Service map to expand your trip.

WILLABY
Site **3**   on Quinault Lake
OLYMPIC NATIONAL FOREST

Campsites, facilities: There are seven tent sites and 15 sites for trailers or motor homes up to 21 feet long. Picnic tables are provided. Piped water, flush toilets, electricity in the bathrooms and firewood are available. Leashed pets are permitted. Boat docks, boat launching facilitieslaunching facilities and rentals are available at nearby Quinault Lake.

Reservations, fee: No reservations necessary; $6 fee per night. Open early May to November.

Who to contact: Phone the Quinault Ranger Station at (206)288-2525 or write to Quinault Ranger Station, Route 1, Box 9, Quinault, WA 98575.

Location: Drive on US 101 to Quinault turn-off (County Road 5), then drive 1.5 miles to where the camp is located along the shore of Quinault Lake.

Trip note: This seven-acre camp is set on the shore of Quinault Lake at 200 feet elevation. The Quinault Rain Forest Nature Trail and the Quinault Loop

National Recreation Trail are nearby. Quinault Lake covers about six square miles.

Site **4**

FALLS CREEK
on Quinault Lake
OLYMPIC NATIONAL FOREST

Campsites, facilities: There are ten tent sites and 21 sites for trailers or motor homes up to 16 feet long. Picnic tables are provided. Piped water, flush toilets, electricity in the bathrooms and firewood are available. Pets on leashes are permitted. Boat docks, launching facilities and rentals are available at nearby Quinault Lake. Wheelchair facilities are available.

Reservations, fee: No reservations necessary; $6 fee per night. Open mid-May to early October.

Who to contact: Phone the Quinault Ranger Station, Olympic National Forest at (206)288-2525 or write to Quinault Ranger Station, Route 1, Box 9, Quinault, WA 98575.

Location: Drive on US 101 to Quinault turn-off (County Road 5). Drive three miles to where camp is located on the shore of Quinault Lake.

Trip note: This three-acre camp is set at 200 feet elevation, on the shore of Quinault Lake where Falls Creek empties into it. The Quinault Rain Forest Nature Trail and Quinault Loop National Recreation Trail are nearby. This is a rustic setting on the edge of Olympic National Park.

Site **5**

CAMPBELL TREE GROVE
on Humptulips River
OLYMPIC NATIONAL FOREST

Campsites, facilities: There are eight tent sites and three sites for trailers or motor homes up to 21 feet long. Picnic tables are provided. Vault toilets, well water and firewood are available. Leashed pets are permitted.

Reservations, fee: No reservations necessary, no fee. Open from mid-May to December.

Who to contact: Phone the Quinault Ranger Station, Olympic National Forest at (206)288-2525 or write to Quinault Ranger Station, Route 1, Box 9, Quinault, WA 98575.

Location: This is located on the edge of the Colonel Bob Wilderness. To reach it you drive 26 miles northeast of Humptulips on Forest Service roads. A Forest Service map is essential.

Trip note: This 14-acre camp is set at about 1,100 feet elevation. Trails leading into the Colonel Bob Wilderness are nearby; see a Forest Service map for locations. The West Fork of the Humptulips River runs near the camp. It's a prime base camp for wilderness expedition.

Site **6**

COHO
on Wynoochee Lake
OLYMPIC NATIONAL FOREST

Campsites, facilities: There are ten tent sites and 46 sites for trailers or motor homes up to 34 feet long. Walk-in tent sites are also available. Picnic tables are provided. Flush toilets, piped water and wheelchair facilities are available. Leashed pets are permitted. Boat docks and boat launching facilitieslaunching facilities are available at Wynoochee Lake.

Reservations, fee: No reservations necessary; $6 fee per night. Open late May to early September.

Who to contact: Phone the Hood Canal Ranger Station at (206)877-5254 or write to Hood Canal Ranger Station, at P.O. Box 520, Shelton, WA 98548.

Location: From Montesano, drive 12 miles north on County Road 58, then continue north for another 22 miles on Forest Service roads to where camp is located on the west shore of Wynoochee Lake. A Forest Service map would be helpful.

Trip note: This eight-acre camp is set on the shore of Wynoochee Lake at 900 feet elevation. Points of interest include a working forest nature trail, Wynoochee Dam Viewpoint, and a ten-mile national recreation trail that goes around the lake. This is one of the most idyllic drive-to settings you could hope to find.

GRAVES CREEK
Site **7**
near Quinault River
OLYMPIC NATIONAL PARK

Campsites, facilities: There are 30 sites for tents or motor homes up to 21 feet long. Picnic tables, fire grills, drinking water and rest rooms are available. Leashed pets are permitted.

Reservations, fee: No reservations necessary; no fee. Open all year with limited winter facilities.

Who to contact: Phone the Olympic National Park at (206)452-4501 or write to 600 East Park, Port Angeles, WA 98362.

Location: Drive 15 miles northeast of Quinault on an all-weather Forest Service road. The campground and Graves Creek Ranger Station are located at road's end.

Trip note: This camp is set at 540 feet elevation and set a short distance from a trailhead leading into many areas in the backcountry of Olympic National Park. See an Olympic Forest Service National Park Map for details. The upper Quinault River is nearby, but there are lakes in the area.

JULY CREEK
Site **8**
on Quinault Lake, walk-in only
OLYMPIC NATIONAL PARK

Campsites, facilities: There are 29 walk-in tent sites. Picnic tables and fire grills are provided. Toilets and drinking water are available. Pets are permitted on leash in camp.

Reservations, fee: No reservations necessary; no fee. Open all year.

Who to contact: Phone the Olympic National Park at (206)452-4501 or write to 600 East Park, Port Angeles, WA 98362.

Location: Drive two miles north of the town of Amanda Park on US 101, then turn right and drive for two miles along north shore of Quinault Lake to the camp where July Creek empties into Quinault Lake.

Trip note: This primitive alternative is on the north shore of Quinault Lake. Full supplies are available on the southern shoreline of the lake, which has a marina.

GATTON CREEK
Site **9**
on Quinault Lake
OLYMPIC NATIONAL FOREST

Campsites, facilities: There are five walk-in tent sites and three day-use picnic sites. An additional ten overflow sites are available in the paved parking area for motor homes up to 21 feet long. Picnic tables are provided, vault toilets and firewood are available. Leashed pets are permitted.

Reservations, fee: No reservations necessary; $3 fee per night. No charge for picnicking. Open May to October.

Who to contact: Phone the Quinault Ranger Station at (206)288-2525 or write to Quinault Ranger Station, Route 1, Box 9, Quinault, WA 98575.

Location: Drive on US 101 to the Quinault turn-off (County Road 5), then drive 3.5 miles to where the camp is located along the shore of Quinault Lake.

Trip note: This five-acre camp is set on the shore of Quinault Lake at 200 feet elevation where Gatton Creek empties into it. The Quinault Rain Forest Nature Trail and the Quinault Loop National Recreation Trail are nearby. Quinault Lake covers about six square miles.

Site 10   STAIRCASE
near Wonder Mountain Wilderness
OLYMPIC NATIONAL PARK

Campsites, facilities: There are 59 sites for tents or motor homes up to 21 feet long. Picnic tables and fire grills are provided. Rest rooms, drinking water and wheelchair facilities are available. Leashed pets are permitted in camp.

Reservations, fee: No reservations necessary; $5 fee per night. Open all year.

Who to contact: Phone the Olympic National Park at (206)452-4501 or write to 600 East Park, Port Angeles, WA 98362.

Location: From town of Hoodsport, drive 19 miles northwest via Staircase and Skokomish River Roads. The camp is located on the Staircase Rapids of the North Fork of the Skokomish River, about one mile from where it empties into Lake Cushman.

Trip note: This is a take-your-pick spot. Lake Cushman is located just south, the Skokomish River runs adjacent and the Wonder Mountain Wilderness is set to the northeast. A major trailhead at the camp leads to many areas in the backcountry of Olympic National Park. See an Olympic National Park and a Forest Map for details. In the summer there are ranger programs and a nature trail is nearby.

Site 11   LAKE CUSHMAN STATE PARK
on Lake Cushman

Campsites, facilities: There are 51 tent sites and 30 sites with full hookups for trailers or motor homes up to 60 feet long. Picnic tables and fire grills are provided. Sanitary disposal services, drinking water, rest rooms, showers and wheelchair facilities are available. A store, restaurant and ice are available within one mile. Firewood is available for an extra fee. Leashed pets are permitted. Boat docks and launching facilities are available at nearby Lake Cushman.

Reservations, fee: No reservations necessary; $7-9.50 fee per night. Open year-round.

Who to contact: Phone the Lake Cushman State Park at (206)877-5491 or write to P.O. Box 128, Hoodsport, WA 98548.

Location: Drive seven miles west of Hoodsport on Staircase Road.

Trip note: This 603-acre camp is set at on the shore of Lake Cushman and has beach access and good trout fishing. Lake Cushman is a ten-mile long lake that is surrounded by the Olympic Mountains. Nearby recreation options include an 18-hole golf course and marked hiking trails.

Site 12   POTLACH STATE PARK
on Hood Canal

Campsites, facilities: There are 17 tent sites and 18 drive-through sites with full hookups for trailers or motor homes up to 60 feet long. Picnic tables, fire grills and drinking water are provided. Sanitary disposal services and rest rooms with showers are available. Firewood is available for an extra fee. Leashed pets are permitted. Boat docks are available at nearby Hood Canal.

Reservations, fee: No reservations necessary; $7-9.50 fee per night. Open all year.

Who to contact: Phone Potlach State Park at (206)877-5361 or write to P.O. Box D, Hoodsport, WA 98548.

Location: Drive 12 miles north of Shelton on US 101 to the park, located along the shoreline of Hood Canal.

Trip note: This is a good camp for vacationers towing boats because the drive-through sites provide plenty of space. This 57-acre park is set along Hood Canal which offers opportunities for fishing, clamming, crabbing and scuba diving. Nearby recreation options include marked hiking trails.

Site **13**   **GLEN AYR RV PARK**
on Hood Canal

Campsites, facilities: There are 57 drive-through sites for trailers or motor homes of any length. Electricity, piped water, sewer hookups and picnic tables are provided. Bottled gas, toilets, showers, a recreation hall and laundry are available. A store, a cafe and ice are within one mile. Pets are permitted.

Reservations, fee: Reservations accepted; $14 fee per night; MasterCard and Visa accepted. Open all year.

Who to contact: Phone the park at (206)877-9522 or write to P.O. Box 432, Hoodsport, WA 98548.

Location: Drive one mile north of Hoodsport on US 101.

Trip note: This fully-developed, nine-acre park is located at sea level on Hood Canal, where there are opportunities to fish and scuba dive. Nearby recreation options include an 18-hole golf course.

Site **14**   **REST A WHILE**
on Hood Canal

Campsites, facilities: There are 15 tent sites and 92 drive-through sites for trailers or motor homes of any length. Electricity, piped water, sewer hookups and picnic tables are provided. Bottled gas, toilets, firewood, a recreation hall, a store, laundry, ice are available. A cafe is less than a mile from the park. Showers are available for an extra fee. Pets and motorbikes are permitted. Boat docks and launching facilities are available at nearby Hood Canal.

Reservations, fee: Reservations accepted; $13 fee per night. Open all year.

Who to contact: Phone the park at (206)877-9474 or write to N 27001 Highway 101, Hoodsport, WA 98548.

Location: Drive three miles north of Hoodsport on US 101.

Trip note: This seven-acre park, located at sea level, is on Hood Canal. There are numerous opportunities to fish and scuba dive. It's an alternative to Sites 12 and 13.

Site **15**   **KALALOCH**
near the Pacific Ocean
OLYMPIC NATIONAL PARK

Campsites, facilities: There are 177 sites for tents or motor homes up to 21 feet long. Picnic tables and fire grills are provided. Rest rooms, drinking water, wheelchair facilities and trailer sanitary station are available. A store and restaurant are within one mile. Pets on leashes are permitted in the campground.

Reservations, fee: No reservations necessary; $5 fee per night. Open all year.

Who to contact: Phone the Olympic National Park at (206)452-4501 or write to 600 East Park, Port Angeles, WA 98362.

Location: Drive 25 miles south of Forks on US 101.

Trip note: This camp is located on the beach, and like other camps set on the coast of the Olympic Peninsula, gets heavy rain in winter and spring. It's often foggy in summer. It is set along the coastal National Wildlife Refuge. A naturalist program is offered in summer months.

Site 16   PACIFIC BEACH STATE PARK
on the Pacific Ocean

Campsites, facilities: There are 118 tent sites and 20 sites for trailers or motor homes up to 45 feet long. Picnic tables are provided, and sanitary disposal station and toilets are available. Electricity, piped water and showers are available for an extra fee. Leashed pets are permitted.

Reservations, fee: No reservations necessary; $7 fee per night. Open all year.

Who to contact: Phone the state park at (206)289-3553 or write to Route 4, Box 2900, Hoquiam, WA 98550.

Location: This camp is in the town of Pacific Beach on Highway 109.

Trip note: This nine-acre, in-town campground is on the beach, but it tends to get crowded since there are no other coastal camps in the immediate vicinity.

Site 17   RIVERVIEW RV PARK AND CAMPGROUND
on Humptulips River

Campsites, facilities: There are eight tent sites and 12 drive-through sites for trailers or motor homes of any length. Picnic tables are provided. Sanitary services, toilets and firewood are available. A store, a cafe and ice are within one mile. Electricity, piped water, sewer hookups and showers are available for an extra fee. Pets and motorbikes are permitted. Boat launching facilities are available at the nearby Humptulips River.

Reservations, fee: No reservations necessary; $5.50-9.25 fee per night. Open all year.

Who to contact: Phone the park at (206)987-2216 or write to P.O. Box 97, Humptulips, WA 98552.

Location: In Humptulips, drive one-quarter mile west on Beach Cutoff Road.

Trip note: This five-acre camp is set at about 1,000 feet elevation along the Humptulips River. It's a good layover if you're cruising US 101.

Site 18   FORT WORDEN
near Puget Sound

Campsites, facilities: There are 50 sites for trailers or motor homes up to 50 feet long. Picnic tables and fire grills are provided. Toilets, a cafe, laundromat, a store, a playground and conference facilities are available. Electricity, piped water, sewer hookups, showers and firewood are available for an extra fee. Leashed pets are permitted. Boat docks, buoys, floats and launching facilities are nearby. Wheelchair accessible facilities are available.

Reservations, fee: Reservations required; $7 fee per night. Open all year.

Who to contact: Phone the park at (206)385-4730 or write to Box 574, Port Townsend, WA 98368.

Location: This park is set on the northeastern tip of the Olympic Peninsula, at the northern end of Port Townsend. From US 101, turn north on Highway 20 and drive about ten miles to Port Townsend.

Trip note: The highlights here are the great lookouts over the Strait of Juan De Fuca as it feeds into Puget Sound. This 339-acre park is at historic Fort Worden and includes buildings from the turn of the century. Nearby recreation options include marked hiking trails, marked bike trails and tennis courts.

Site **19**
MELBOURNE
on Melbourne Lake
BERT COLE STATE FOREST

Campsites, facilities: There are five campsites for tents or small trailers. Picnic tables, fire grills and tent pads are provided. Pit toilets are available. There is **no piped water,** so bring your own. Firearms are prohibited. Leashed pets are permitted.

Reservations, fee: No reservations necessary; no fee. Open all year.

Who to contact: Phone the Department of Natural Resources at (800)527-3305 or write to Department of Natural Resources AW-11, 1065 South Capitol Way, Olympia, WA 98504.

Location: Drive 11 miles north from Hoodsport on US 101, then turn left on Jorsted Creek Road (Forest Service Road 24) and drive 5.5 miles. Turn left and travel on a gravel road for 1.7 miles, then bear left and drive three quarters of a mile to the camp which is on Melbourne Lake.

Trip note: This primitive camp is on Melbourne Lake at about 1,000 feet elevation in a little-known, rustic setting. If you want quiet, and don't mind a lack of facilities, this is a good drive-to option.

Site **20**
LILLIWAUP CREEK
BERT COLE STATE FOREST

Campsites, facilities: There are 13 campsites for tents or small trailers. Picnic tables, fire grills and tent pads are provided. Pit toilets and piped water are available. Leashed pets are permitted.

Reservations, fee: No reservations necessary; no fee. Open all year.

Who to contact: Phone the Department of Natural Resources at (800)527-3305 or write to Department of Natural Resources AW-11, 1065 South Capitol, Olympia, WA 98504.

Location: Drive 11 miles north of Hoodsport on US 101, then turn left on Jorsted Creek Road (Forest Service Road 24) and drive 6.5 miles to the camp. It is on the right of Lilliwaup Creek.

Trip note: An alternative to Site 19, this is also a primitive, quiet setting, but this has piped water provided. Lilliwaup Creek makes for a nice backdrop.

Site **21**
DUNGENESS RECREATION AREA
near Strait of Juan de Fuca

Campsites, facilities: There are 65 tent sites and 65 drive-through sites for trailers or motor homes of any length. Picnic tables are provided. Sanitary services, toilets and a playground are available. Showers and firewood are available for an extra fee. Pets are permitted.

Reservations, fee: No reservations necessary; $6 fee per night. Open February to October with limited winter facilities.

Who to contact: Phone the park at (206)683-5847 or write to 223 East 4th, Port Angeles, WA 98362.

Location: From Sequim, drive five miles west on US 101, then turn right on Kitchen Road and drive four miles to the park.

Trip note: This park overlooks the Strait of Juan De Fuca, and is set along the Dungeness National Wildlife Refuge. Nearby recreation options include marked hiking trails. The toll ferry at Port Angeles can take you to Victoria.

Site 22   SALT CREEK RECREATION AREA
near Strait of Juan De Fuca

Campsites, facilities: There are 65 tent sites and 65 sites for trailers or motor homes of any length. Picnic tables are provided. Sanitary services, toilets, showers, a playground are available. Firewood is available for an extra fee. Pets are permitted.

Reservations, fee: No reservations necessary; $6 fee per night. Open all year.

Who to contact: Phone the park at (206)928-3441 or write to 223 East 4th, Port Angeles, WA 98362.

Location: From Port Angeles, drive ten miles west on Highway 112, then turn right on Camp Hayden Road and drive three miles to the park.

Trip note: This 192-acre camp overlooks the Strait of Juan De Fuca. Nearby recreation options include marked hiking trails. It's a good layover spot if you're planning to take the ferry out of Port Angeles to Victoria.

Site 23   FALLS VIEW
on Big Quilcene River
OLYMPIC NATIONAL FOREST

Campsites, facilities: There are 16 tent sites and 14 sites for trailers or motor homes up to 27 feet long. Picnic tables are provided. Piped water, flush toilets are available. Leashed pets are permitted. Wheelchair facilities are available.

Reservations, fee: Reservations accepted but not required; $5 fee per night. Open May to mid-September.

Who to contact: Phone the Quilcene Ranger Station, Olympic National Forest at (206)765-3368 or write to Quilcene Ranger Station, Box 280, Quilcene, WA 98376.

Location: From Quilcene, drive four miles southwest on US 101. The camp is located on a terrace above the Big Quilcene River.

Trip note: In spite of the rustic setting, this spot on the edge of the Olympic National Forest has most facilities available.

Site 24   RAINBOW
near Quilcene
OLYMPIC NATIONAL FOREST

Campsites, facilities: There are nine tent sites. Picnic tables and fire grills are provided. Vault toilets, piped drinking water are available. A store, a cafe, laundromat and ice are within five miles. Leashed pets are permitted.

Reservations, fee: Reservations accepted but not required for single sites; $3 fee per night. The entire campground can be reserved for groups (up to 50 people); $30 fee per night; reservations required through MISTIX at (800)283-CAMP. Open year-round.

Who to contact: Phone the Quilcene Ranger Station, Olympic National Forest at (206)765-3368 or write to Quilcene Ranger Station, Box 280, Quilcene, WA 98376.

Location: Drive five miles southwest of Quilcene on US 101.

Trip note: This is a rugged, primitive setting on edge of Olympic National Forest, with backcountry access provided on Forest Service roads. It's advisable to obtain Forest Service map.

Site 25   DUNGENESS FORKS
on Dungeness and Gray Wolf Rivers
OLYMPIC NATIONAL FOREST

Campsites, facilities: There are ten tent sites. Picnic tables are provided. Well water, vault toilets are available. Leashed pets are permitted.

Reservations, fee: No reservations necessary; $4 fee per night. Open late May to early September.

Who to contact: Phone the Quilcene Ranger Station, Olympic National Forest at (206)765-3368 or write to Quilcene Ranger Station, Box 280, Quilcene, WA 98376.

Location: From Sequim, drive four miles southeast on US 101, then turn right and drive eight miles on county and Forest Service roads to get to the camp. A Forest Service map is essential.

Trip note: This pretty spot is set at the confluence of Dungeness and Gray Wolf Rivers. If you want quiet, you'll find it here.

Site 26   EAST CROSSING
OLYMPIC NATIONAL FOREST

Campsites, facilities: There are ten sites for tents, trailers or motor homes up to 16 feet long. Picnic tables are provided. Well water and vault toilets are available. Leashed pets are permitted.

Reservations, fee: No reservations necessary; $4 fee per night. Open late May to early September.

Who to contact: Phone the Quilcene Ranger Station, Olympic National Forest at (206)765-3368 or write to Quilcene Ranger Station, Box 280, Quilcene, WA 98376.

Location: From Sequim, drive four miles southeast on US 101, then turn right and drive 11 miles on county and Forest Service roads to get to the camp. A Forest Service map is essential.

Trip note: A nearby option to Site 25, this seven-acre camp is set at about 1,200 feet elevation. It offers some improvements, but it is still for individuals seeking an out-of-the-way spot.

Site 27   ELKHORN
on Dosewallips River
OLYMPIC NATIONAL FOREST

Campsites, facilities: There are 16 tent sites and four sites for trailers or motor homes up to 21 feet long. Picnic tables are provided. Well water, vault toilets are available. Leashed pets are permitted.

Reservations, fee: No reservations necessary; $4 fee per night. Open mid-May to September.

Who to contact: Phone the Quilcene Ranger Station, Olympic National Forest at (206)765-3368 or write to Quilcene Ranger Station, Box 280, Quilcene, WA 98376.

Location: From Brinnon, drive one mile north on US 101 then turn left and drive ten miles west on County Road 10 and Forest Service Road 2610 (same road). The camp is on the left.

Trip note: This eight-acre camp is set on the Dosewallips River at 600 feet elevation. Site 35 is a more primitive option.

Site 28
SEAL ROCK
on Dabob Bay
OLYMPIC NATIONAL FOREST

Campsites, facilities: There are 42 sites for tents, trailers or motor homes up to 31 feet long. Picnic tables are provided. Piped water, flush toilets and wheelchair facilities are available. Leashed pets are permitted. Boat docks and launching facilities are nearby on the Hood Canal and in Dabob Bay.

Reservations, fee: Reservations accepted but not required; $8 fee per night. Open mid-April to November.

Who to contact: Phone the Olympic National Forest at (206)877-5254 or write to Hood Canal Ranger Station, P.O. Box 68, Hoodsport, WA 98376.

Location: From Brinnon, drive two miles north on US 101. The camp is on the shore at Seal Rock.

Trip note: This 30-acre camp is set along the shore near the mouth of Dabob Bay. The modern, developed setting provides a good spot for boat owners.

Site 29
COLLINS
on Duckabush River
OLYMPIC NATIONAL FOREST

Campsites, facilities: There are six tent sites and ten sites for trailers or motor homes up to 21 feet long. Picnic tables are provided. Well water, vault toilets and firewood are available. Leashed pets are permitted.

Reservations, fee: No reservations necessary; $4 fee per night. Open mid-May to mid-November.

Who to contact: Phone the Hood Canal Ranger Station, Olympic National Forest at (206)877-5254 or write to Hood Canal Ranger Station, P.O. Box 68, Hoodsport, WA 98548.

Location: From Brinnon, drive two miles south on US 101, then turn right and drive five miles west on Forest Service Road 2515. The camp is on the left.

Trip note: Tourists cruising US 101 don't have a clue about this spot, yet it's not far from the highway. This four-acre camp is set on the Duckabush River at 200 feet elevation.

Site 30
HAMMA HAMMA
on Hamma Hamma River
OLYMPIC NATIONAL FOREST

Campsites, facilities: There are three tent sites and 12 sites for trailers or motor homes up to 21 feet long. Picnic tables are provided. Well water, vault toilets and firewood are available. Leashed pets are permitted. Some facilities are wheelchair accessible.

Reservations, fee: No reservations necessary; $4 fee per night. Open March to mid-November.

Who to contact: Phone the Hood Canal Ranger Station, Olympic National Forest at (206)877-5254 or write to Hood Canal Ranger Station, P.O. Box 68, Hoodsport, WA 98548.

Location: From Eldon, drive two miles north on US 101, then turn left and drive 6.5 miles west to the camp on Forest Service Road 25.

Trip note: Good holdover for vacationers cruising US 101. This camp is set on the

Hamma Hamma River at about 600 feet elevation.

Site **31**
LENA CREEK
on Hamma Hamma River
OLYMPIC NATIONAL FOREST

Campsites, facilities: There are 13 sites for tents, trailers or motor homes up to 21 feet long. Picnic tables are provided. Well water, vault toilets and firewood are available. Leashed pets are permitted. The camp is wheelchair accessible.

Reservations, fee: No reservations necessary; $4 fee per night. Open mid-May to September.

Who to contact: Phone the Hood Canal Ranger District, Olympic National Forest at (206)877-5254 or write to Hood Canal Ranger Station, P.O. Box 68, Hoodsport, WA 98548.

Location: From Eldon, drive two miles north on US 101, then turn left and drive nine miles on Forest Service Road 25 to the camp.

Trip note: This seven-acre camp is set where Lena Creek empties into the Hamma Hamma River. A trail from the camp leads two miles to Lena Lake and four miles to Upper Lena Lake. A map of the Olympic National Forest details the trail and road system. The camp is rustic with some improvements.

Site **32**
LENA LAKE
near Hamma Hamma River, walk-in only
OLYMPIC NATIONAL FOREST

Campsites, facilities: There are 29 rustic campsites at this hike-in campground. Pit toilets are available, but there is **no piped water.** Leashed pets are permitted.

Reservations, fee: No reservations necessary; no fee. Open late May to early September.

Who to contact: Phone the Hood Canal Ranger Station, the Olympic National Forest at (206)877-5254 or write to Hood Canal Ranger Station, Box 68, Hoodsport, WA 98548.

Location: From Eldon, drive two miles north on US 101, then head west for nine miles on Forest Service Road 25 to Lena Creek. Hike two miles to Lena Lake, campsites are scattered around the lake.

Trip note: You can't beat the price--free. This 135-acre camp is set on Lena Lake. Popular in the summer. Two-mile hike from Lena Creek to the campground is suitable for entire family.

Site **33**
HEART O' THE HILLS
OLYMPIC NATIONAL PARK

Campsites, facilities: There are 105 sites for tents, trailers or motor homes to 21 feet long. Picnic tables are provided. Rest rooms, and drinking water are available. Leashed pets are permitted. Wheelchair facilities are available.

Reservations, fee: No reservations necessary; $5 fee per night. Open all year.

Who to contact: Phone the Olympic National Park at (206)452-4501 or write to 600 East Park, Port Angeles, CA 98362.

Location: From Port Angeles, drive five miles south on Hurricane Ridge Road. The camp is on the left.

Trip note: Set on the northern edge of Olympic National Park. You can drive deeper into the interior of the park on Hurricane Ridge Road and take one of numerous hiking trails. This camp is set at 1,800 feet elevation. Evening ranger programs are available in the summer.

Site **34**   **DEER PARK**
                        near Blue Mountain
                      OLYMPIC NATIONAL PARK

Campsites, facilities: There are 18 tent sites. Picnic tables and fire grills are
    provided. Rest rooms and drinking water are available. Leashed pets are
    permitted.
Reservations, fee: No reservations necessary; no fee. Open mid-June to late
    September with limited winter facilities.
Who to contact: Phone the Olympic National Park at (206)452-4501 or write to 600
    East Park, Port Angeles, CA 98362.
Location: From Port Angeles, drive six miles east on US 101, then turn right and
    drive 18 miles south on Deer Park Road.
Trip note: This camp is set in the Olympic Peninsula's high country at 5,400 feet
    elevation, just below 6,000-foot Blue Mountain. There are numerous trails in
    area, including a major trailhead into the backcountry of Olympic National
    Park and the Buckhorn Wilderness.

Site **35**   **DOSEWALLIPS**
                        on Dosewallips River
                      OLYMPIC NATIONAL PARK

Campsites, facilities: There are 32 tent sites. Picnic tables and fire grills are
    provided. Rest rooms, drinking water and wheelchair facilities are available.
    Leashed pets are permitted.
Reservations, fee: No reservations necessary; no fee. Open from June to late
    September.
Who to contact: Phone the Olympic National Park at (206)452-4501 or write to 600
    East Park, Port Angeles, WA 98362.
Location: From Quilcene, drive 13 miles south on US 101, then turn right and drive
    15 miles west along Dosewallips River.
Trip note: This offers a more remote option to Sites 27 and 29. This camp is set on
    the Dosewallips River at 1,600 feet elevation. It provices a major trailhead into
    the backcountry of Olympic National Park. The trail follows Dosewallips River
    over Anderson Pass then along Quinault River and ultimately reaches Quinault
    Lake. A naturalist program is available in the summer.

Site **36**   **ALTAIRE**
                        on Elwha River
                      OLYMPIC NATIONAL PARK

Campsites, facilities: There are 30 sites for tents, trailers or motor homes up to 18
    feet long. Picnic tables and fire grills are provided. Rest rooms and drinking
    water are available. Leashed pets are permitted.
Reservations, fee: No reservations necessary; $5 fee per night. Open June to late
    September.
Who to contact: Phone the Olympic National Park at (206)452-4501 or write to 600
    East Park, Port Angeles, WA 98362.
Location: From Port Angeles, drive nine miles west on US 101, then turn left and
    drive four miles south along Elwha River.
Trip note: This camp is set on the Elwha River about a mile from Lake Mills. It's
    a nice layover spot for a one-nighter before taking ferry boat at Port Angeles
    to Victoria.

Site 37
ELWHA
on Elwha River
OLYMPIC NATIONAL PARK

Campsites, facilities: There are 41 sites for tents, trailers or motor homes up to 21 feet long. Picnic tables and fire grills are provided. Rest rooms and drinking water are available. Leashed pets are permitted.

Reservations, fee: No reservations necessary; $5 fee per night. Open all year.

Who to contact: Phone the Olympic National Park at (206)452-4501 or write to 600 East Park, Port Angeles, WA 98362.

Location: From Port Angeles, drive nine miles west on US 101, then turn right and drive three miles south along Elwha River.

Trip note: This camp is set along the Elwha River and gets regular use. Some trails are available. The evening ranger programs are very popular here in the summer.

Site 38
FAIRHOLM
on Crescent Lake
OLYMPIC NATIONAL PARK

Campsites, facilities: There are 87 sites for tents, trailers or motor homes up to 21 feet long. Picnic tables and fire grills are provided. Sanitary disposal station, rest rooms, drinking water and wheelchair facilities are available. A store and a cafe are within one mile. Pets are permitted. Boat launching facilities are nearby on Lake Crescent.

Reservations, fee: No reservations necessary; $5 fee per night. Open all year.

Who to contact: Phone the Olympic National Park at (206)452-4501 or write to 600 East Park, Port Angeles, WA 98362.

Location: From Port Angeles, drive 26 miles west on US 101, then turn right and drive one mile to the camp on North Shore Road.

Trip note: This camp is set on the shore of Lake Crescent. This pretty lake is situated within boundaries of Olympic National Forest. It is a mile off US 101 and gets heavy use during tourist months. A naturalist program is available in summer months.

Site 39
BOULDER CREEK
near Olympic Hot Springs, walk-in only
OLYMPIC NATIONAL PARK

Campsites, facilities: There are 50 primitive tent sites at this hike-in campground. Picnic tables and fire grills are provided. **No piped water** is available, so bring your own. Pit toilets are available. Leashed pets are permitted.

Reservations, fee: No reservations necessary; no fee. Open mid-June to late September with limited winter facilities.

Who to contact: Phone the Olympic National Park at (206)452-4501 or write to 600 East Park, Port Angeles, WA 98362.

Location: From Port Angeles, drive nine miles west on US 101, then 12 miles southwest along Elwha River. Backpack 2.5 miles to the campground.

Trip note: This is a primitive option in national park setting, set at 2,000 feet elevation, with some walking necessary. It is on Boulder Creek, near the Olympic Hot Springs. The trail here leads into the backcountry and eventually to Boulder Lake.

Site **40**
SOLEDUCK
on Soleduck River
OLYMPIC NATIONAL PARK

Campsites, facilities: There are 80 sites for tents or motor homes up to 21 feet long. Picnic tables and fire grills are provided. Sanitary disposal station, rest rooms, drinking water and wheelchair facilities are available. A store and a cafe are within one mile. Pets are permitted.

Reservations, fee: No reservations necessary; $5 fee per night. Open May to late October with limited winter facilities.

Who to contact: Phone the Olympic National Park at (206)452-4501 or write to 600 East Park, Port Angeles, WA 98362.

Location: From Port Angeles, drive 27 miles west on US 101, then fork left at Soleduck turn-off and drive 12 miles to the camp.

Trip note: This site is a nice hideaway, with Sol Duc Hot Springs a highlight. The problem is that it's becoming quite popular. The camp fills up quickly on weekends, and a fee is charged to use the hot springs, which are now fully developed. The camp is set at 2,000 feet elevation along Soleduck River. A naturalist program is available in summer months.

Site **41**
DOSEWALLIPS STATE PARK
on Dosewallips Creek

Campsites, facilities: There are 87 tent sites and 40 sites for trailers or motor homes up to 60 feet long. Picnic tables and fire grills are provided. Rest rooms and drinking water are available. A recreation hall, a store, a cafe and laundry are within one mile. Electricity, piped water, sewer hookups, and showers are available for an extra fee. Leashed pets are permitted. Facilities are wheelchair accessible.

Reservations, fee: No reservations necessary; $7-9.50 fee per night. Open all year.

Who to contact: Phone the Dosewallips State Park at (206)796-4415 or write to Drawer K, Brinnon, WA 98320.

Location: From Brinnon, drive one mile south on US 101. Park is located on shore of the Hood Canal.

Trip note: This 425-acre park is set at the mouth of Dosewallips Creek, which gets a fair run of steelhead in winter months. In Hood Canal, rockfish and salmon fishing is popular. Beachcombers might consider clamming, but check with Department of Health prior to harvesting any shellfish, due to seasonal and local conditions.

Site **42**
SEQUIM BAY
on Sequim Bay

Campsites, facilities: There are 60 sites for tents or self-contained motor homes and 26 sites with full hookups for trailers or motor homes up to 30 feet long. Picnic tables and fire grills are provided. Sanitary disposal station, toilets, drinking water, showers and a playground are available. Leashed pets are permitted. Boat docks, launching facilities and moorage camping are nearby on Sequim Bay. Facilities are wheelchair accessible.

Reservations, fee: No reservations necessary; $6 fee per night. Open all year.

Who to contact: Phone the Sequim Bay State Park at (206)683-4235 or write to 1872 Highway 101 East, Sequim, WA 98382.

Location: From Sequim, drive four miles southeast on US 101 to the park entrance.

Trip note: This 90-acre camp is on Sequim Bay. Nearby recreation options include marked hiking trails and tennis courts. Because of its unique location, it gets far less rain than other areas on the Olympic Peninsula.

Site 43   TRANQUILCENE TRAILER PARK
near Quilcene Bay

Campsites, facilities: There are 12 sites for tents or motor homes of any length. Electricity, piped water, sewer hookups and picnic tables are provided. Firewood is available. Bottled gas, sanitary services, a store, a cafe, laundry and ice are within one mile. Pets and motorbikes are permitted. Boat launching facilities are nearby on Quilcene Bay.

Reservations, fee: Reservations accepted; $7.50 fee per night. Open all year.

Who to contact: Phone the park at (206)765-3409 or write to P.O. Box 188, Quilcene, WA 98376.

Location: From Quilcene, drive one-half mile south on US 101.

Trip note: Set at about 1,000 feet elevation, this five-acre camp is near the shore of Quilcene Bay in a wooded setting. Nearby recreation options include marked hiking trails and a full-service marina. It's a developed, private camp.

Site 44   COVE PARK CAMPGROUND
near Dabob Bay

Campsites, facilities: There are 35 sites for trailers or motor homes up to 30 feet long. Electricity, piped water, sewer hookups and picnic tables are provided. Bottled gas, sanitary services, toilets, a store, laundry and ice are available. Showers are available for an extra fee. Pets are permitted. Boat docks and launching facilities are nearby on the Hood Canal.

Reservations, fee: Reservations accepted; $9.50 fee per night. Open all year.

Who to contact: Phone the park at (206)796-4723 or write to 28453 Highway 101, Brinnon, WA 98320.

Location: From Brinnon, drive three miles north on US 101.

Trip note: This five-acre, private camp is in a rural setting, yet it is fully developed. It is near the shore of Dabob Bay at sea level.

Site 45   ELMER'S TRAVEL TRAILER PARK
near the Pacific Ocean

Campsites, facilities: There are five tent sites and 12 sites for trailers or motor homes up to 31 feet long in this adult only campground. Electricity, piped water and sewer hookups are provided. Sanitary services, toilets and laundry are available. Bottled gas, a store, a cafe and ice are within one mile. Showers are available for an extra fee. Pets are permitted.

Reservations, fee: No reservations necessary; $10 fee per night. Open all year.

Who to contact: Write to Elmer's Travel Trailer Park, 2430 Highway 101, Port Angeles, CA 98362 or call (206)457-4392.

Location: From Port Angeles, drive two miles east on US 101.

Trip note: Located at about 1,000 feet elevation, this ten-acre camp is near the ocean, yet in an urban setting. Nearby recreation options include an 18-hole golf course, marked hiking trails and a full-service marina.

Site 46   AL'S RV TRAILER PARK
near Port Angeles

Campsites, facilities: There are 31 sites for trailers or motor homes up to 33 feet long in this adult-only campground. Electricity, piped water and sewer hookups are provided. Bottled gas, toilets, showers and laundry are available. A store, a cafe and ice are within one mile. Boat docks and launching facilities are nearby.

Reservations, fee: No reservations necessary; $13 plus tax per night. Open all year.

Who to contact: Phone the park at (206)457-9844 or write to 522 North Lees Creek Road, Port Angeles, WA 98362.

Location: From Port Angeles, drive two miles east on US 101, then turn left on Lees Creek Road and drive one-half mile to park.

Trip note: This is a good choice for motor home owners. It is set in the country at about 1,000 feet elevation, yet not far from the Strait of Juan De Fuca. Nearby recreation options include an 18-hole golf course and a full-service marina.

Site 47   CITY CENTER TRAILER PARK
in Port Angeles

Campsites, facilities: There are 36 sites for trailers or motor homes of any length. Electricity, piped water and sewer hookups are provided. Bottled gas, sanitary services, toilets and laundry are available. A store, a cafe and ice are within one mile. Showers are available for an extra fee. Pets are permitted. Boat docks, launching facilities and rentals are nearby.

Reservations, fee: Reservations accepted; $14 fee per night. Open all year.

Who to contact: Phone the park at (206)457-7092 or write to 127 South Lincoln, Port Angeles, WA 98362.

Location: In Port Angeles, drive on US 101 to the corner of Lincoln and 2nd.

Trip note: Private camp. This three acre RV park is in the woods next to a river. Nearby recreation options include an 18-hole golf course, marked biking trails, a full-service marina and tennis courts.

Site 48   WELCOME INN TRAILER AND RV PARK
near Port Angeles

Campsites, facilities: There are 15 tent sites and 130 drive-through sites for trailers or motor homes of any length. Electricity, piped water, sewer hookups, dump stations and picnic tables are provided. Bottled gas, sanitary services, toilets and laundry are available. A store, a cafe and ice are within one mile. Showers are available for an extra fee. Pets and motorbikes are permitted. Boat docks and launching facilities are nearby.

Reservations, fee: Reservations accepted; $14 fee per night. Open all year.

Who to contact: Phone the park at (206)457-1553 or write to 112 Highway 101 West, Port Angeles, WA 98362.

Location: From Port Angeles, drive 1.5 miles west on US 101 to the park.

Trip note: A privately-developed campground for motor homes and tent campers. An eight-acre camp set in the woods. Nearby recreation options include an 18-hole golf course, marked hiking trails, a full-service marina and tennis courts.

Site 49   ELWHA RESORT AND CAMPGROUND
on Elwha River

Campsites, facilities: There are nine tent sites and four sites for trailers or motor homes up to 32 feet long. Electricity, piped water, sewer hookups and picnic tables are provided. Bottled gas, toilets, a store, a cafe, ice, a playground are available. Sanitary services and laundry are located within one mile. Showers and firewood are available for an extra fee. Pets and motorbikes are permitted. Boat docks, launching facilities and cabin rentals are nearby at the Elwha River.

Reservations, fee: Reservations accepted; $6 fee per night; MasterCard and Visa accepted. Open all year.

Who to contact: Phone the park at (206)457-7011 or write to 464 Highway 101 West, Port Angeles, WA 98362.

Location: From Port Angeles, drive nine miles west on US 101.

Trip note: This small, private campground, set at sea level next to the Elwha River, offers more seclusion than nearby Sites 45-48. Nearby recreation options include marked hiking trails and Lake Adwell.

Site 50   LYRE RIVER PARK
near Lyre River

Campsites, facilities: There are 15 tent sites and 60 drive-through sites for trailers or motor homes of any length. Electricity, piped water, sewer hookups and picnic tables are provided. Bottled gas, sanitary services, toilets, a store, laundry and ice are available. Showers and firewood are available for an extra fee. Pets and motorbikes are permitted.

Reservations, fee: Reservations accepted; $10.50 fee per night. Open all year.

Who to contact: Phone the park at (206)928-3436 or write to 5960 Lyre River Road, Port Angeles, WA 98362.

Location: From Port Angeles, drive five miles west on US 101, then get on Highway 112 and drive 15 miles west. Turn right on Lyre River Road and drive one-half mile to the park.

Trip note: This 80-acre camp is in a wooded area tucked between the Strait of Juan De Fuca and the Lyre River. Marked hiking trails are accessible in the immediate area.

Site 51   SILVER KING RESORT
in Strait of Juan De Fuca

Campsites, facilities: There are ten tent sites and 165 sites for trailers or motor homes of any length. Electricity, piped water and picnic tables are provided. Bottled gas, sanitary services, toilets, firewood, a store, laundry and ice are available. Showers are available for an extra fee. Pets and motorbikes are permitted. Boat docks and launching facilities are located at nearby the Pillar Point Recreation Area.

Reservations, fee: Reservations required; $9.50 fee per night. Open all year.

Who to contact: Phone the park at (206)963-2800 or write to Star Route 2, Box 10A, Clallam Bay, WA 98326.

Location: From Port Angeles, drive five miles west on US 101, then get on Highway 120 and drive west for 30 miles. At Jim Creek, turn right and drive one-half mile to the park.

Trip note: A good summer camp for salmon fishermen, with mooching the most popular technique for big salmon in Strait of Juan De Fuca. The camp is developed and privately run.

Site 52   SUNSHINE MOBILE AND RV PARK
near Sequim

Campsites, facilities: There are 12 tent sites and 35 drive-through sites for trailers or motor homes of any length. Electricity, piped water, sewer hookups and picnic tables are provided. Toilets, showers, a recreation hall, laundry and ice are available. Sanitary services, a store and a cafe are located within one mile. Pets and motorbikes are permitted.

Reservations, fee: Reservations accepted; $12.50 fee per night. Open all year.

Who to contact: Phone the park at (206)683-4769 or write to 1875 Highway 101 West, Sequim, WA 98382.

Location: From Sequim, drive four miles west on US 101 to park.

Trip note: This six-acre, private camp is set at about 1,000 feet elevation in a wooded area outside of Sequim. Nearby recreation options include an 18-hole golf course and a full-service marina at Sequim Bay.

Site **53**   **SEQUIM WEST RV PARK**
near Dungeness River

Campsites, facilities: There are 28 drive-through sites for trailers or motor homes of any length. Electricity, piped water, sewer hookups and picnic tables are provided. Toilets, showers, laundry and ice are available. Bottled gas, sanitary services, a store, a cafe are located within one mile. Pets are permitted.

Reservations, fee: Reservations accepted; $14.50 fee per night; American Express, MasterCard, Visa, Discover and Diner's Club accepted. Open all year.

Who to contact: Phone the park at (206)683-4144 or write to 740 West Washington, Sequim, WA 98382.

Location: The park is in Sequim on the west end of US 101.

Trip note: This two-acre camp is near the Dungeness River within ten miles of Dungeness Spit State Park. Nearby recreation options include an 18-hole golf course and a full-service marina at Sequim Bay.

Site **54**   **SOUTH SEQUIM BAY RV PARK**
on Sequim Bay

Campsites, facilities: There are ten tent sites and 20 drive-through sites for trailers or motor homes of any length. Picnic tables are provided. Bottled gas, sanitary services, toilets, showers and a playground are available. Electricity, piped water, sewer hookups are available for an extra fee. Pets and motorbikes are permitted. Boat rentals are at nearby Sequim Bay.

Reservations, fee: Reservations accepted; $11-13 fee per night. Open year-round.

Who to contact: Phone the park at (206)683-7194 or write to Box 152, Old Bly Highway, Sequim, WA 98382.

Location: From Sequim, drive five miles southeast on US 101 to park.

Trip note: This six-acre park set along Sequim Bay is especially good when salmon are running. Nearby recreation options include an 18-hole golf course, marked bike trails and tennis courts.

Site **55**   **SEQUIM BAY MARINA**
on Sequim Bay

Campsites, facilities: There are 43 pull-through sites for trailers or motor homes of any length. Electricity, piped water and sewer hookups are provided. Sanitary services, toilets, a store and laundry are available. Showers are available for an extra fee. Pets are permitted if on leashes. Boat docks and launching facilities are nearby.

Reservations, fee: No reservations necessary; $12 fee per night. Open all year.

Who to contact: Phone the park at (206)683-4050 or write to 630 West Sequim Bay, Sequim, WA 98382.

Location: From Sequim, drive one mile east on US 101, then turn left on West

Sequim Bay Road and drive three miles to marina.

Trip note: This is the headquarters on Sequim Bay for salmon fishermen. Nearby recreation options include an 18-hole golf course.

Site **56**   **RAINBOW'S END**
on Sequim Bay

Campsites, facilities: There are 15 tent sites and 37 sites for trailers or motor homes of any length. Electricity, piped water, sewer hookups, cable TV hookups and picnic tables are provided. Sanitary services, toilets, showers and laundry are available. Bottled gas, a store, a cafe and ice are located within one mile. Firewood is available for an extra fee. Pets (if on leashes or otherwise controlled) and motorbikes are permitted.

Reservations, fee: Reservations accepted; $11-17 fee per night. Open year-round.

Who to contact: Phone the park at (206)683-3863 or write to 1464 Highway 101 West, Sequim, WA 98382.

Location: From Sequim, drive two miles west on US 101 to the park.

Trip note: Of the group of five camps on Sequim Bay (your other options are Sites 52, 53, 54 and 55), this is one of the nicest. Nearby recreation options include an 18-hole golf course, marked bike trails, a full-service marina and tennis courts.

Site **57** **DIAMOND POINT RV PARK AND CAMPGROUND**
near Sequim

Campsites, facilities: There are 13 tent sites and 31 pull-through sites for trailers or motor homes of any length. Electricity, piped water, sewer hookups and picnic tables are provided. Bottled gas, sanitary services, toilets, firewood, a recreation hall, laundry and ice are available. A store and a cafe are located within one mile. Showers are available for an extra fee. Pets and motorbikes are permitted. Boat launching facilities are at nearby Sequim Bay.

Reservations, fee: Reservations accepted; $13 fee per night. Open all year.

Who to contact: Phone the park at (206)683-2284 or write to 137 Industrial Parkway, Sequim, WA 98382.

Location: From Sequim, drive ten miles east on US 101, then turn left on Diamond Point Road and drive 3.5 miles to the camp.

Trip note: Privately-developed and operated, this camp provides a good layover before heading to Victoria by ferry.

Site **58**   **WHISKEY CREEK BEACH**
on Strait of Juan De Fuca

Campsites, facilities: There are 40 tent sites and 11 sites for trailers or motor homes of any length. Piped water, sewer hookups and picnic tables are provided. Sanitary services and laundry are available. Pets are permitted. Boat launching facilities are nearby.

Reservations, fee: Reservations accepted; $5-8 fee per night. Open May to late September.

Who to contact: Phone the park at (206)928-3489 or write to Joyce, WA 98343.

Location: From Port Angeles, travel five miles west on US 101, 13 miles west on Highway 112, then turn north on Schmitt Road.

Trip note: Set on the beach along Strait of Juan De Fuca, this campground covers 400 acres, with Agate Beach nearby.

Site 59
LOG CABIN RESORT
on Lake Crescent

Campsites, facilities: There are ten tent sites and 40 sites for trailers or motor homes of any length. Electricity, piped water, sewer hookups and picnic tables are provided. Sanitary services, toilets, a store, a cafe, laundry, ice, a playground are available. Showers and firewood are available for an extra fee. Pets are permitted. Boat docks, launching facilities and rentals are located at Lake Crescent.

Reservations, fee: Reservations accepted; $10 fee per night; MasterCard and Visa accepted. Open April to November.

Who to contact: Phone the park at (206)928-3325 or write to 6540 East Beach, Port Angeles, WA 98362.

Location: From Port Angeles, drive 16 miles west on US 101, then turn right on East Beach Road and drive three miles to the camp.

Trip note: This pretty spot lies along the shore of Lake Crescent and is a good spot for boaters. A marked hiking trail traces lake's shoreline.

Site 60
KOA PORT ANGELES-SEQUIM
near Port Angeles

Campsites, facilities: There are 15 tent sites and 73 drive-through sites for trailers or motor homes of any length. Picnic tables are provided. Bottled gas, sanitary services, toilets, showers, a store, laundry, ice, a playground, a recreation room and a swimming pool are available. A cafe is located within two miles. Electricity, piped water, sewer hookups and firewood are available for an extra fee. Pets and motorbikes are permitted.

Reservations, fee: Reservations accepted; $14.50 fee per night; MasterCard and Visa accepted. Open May to late October.

Who to contact: Phone the park at (206)457-5916 or write to 2065 Highway 101 East, Port Angeles, WA 98362.

Location: From Port Angeles, drive six miles east on US 101 then turn right on O'Brien Road and go one block to the campground.

Trip note: This private, developed camp covers 41 acres and is in a country setting. An 18-hole golf course, marked hiking trails and tennis courts are options.

Site 61
WILLOUGHBY CREEK
BERT COLE STATE FOREST

Campsites, facilities: There are three campsites for tents or small trailers. Picnic tables, fire grills and tent pads are provided. Pit toilets are available. There is **no piped water,** so bring your own. Pets on leashes are permitted.

Reservations, fee: No reservations necessary; no fee. Open all year.

Who to contact: Phone the Department of Natural Resources at (800)527-3305 or write to Department of Natural Resources AW-11, 1065 South Capitol Way, Olympia, WA 98504.

Location: Drive 14 miles south of Forks on US 101 and turn east on Hoh Rain Forest Road. Drive 3.5 miles to the camp. The camp is on the right.

Trip note: This is a little-known, tiny and rustic camp set along Willoughby Creek and the Hoh River. The area gets heavy rainfall.

Site **62**
MINNIE PETERSON
on Hoh River

Campsites, facilities: There are six campsites for tents or small trailers. Picnic tables, fire grills and tent pads are provided. Pit toilets and piped water are available. Firearms are prohibited. Pets on leashes are permitted.

Reservations, fee: No reservations necessary; no fee. Open all year.

Who to contact: Phone the Department of Natural Resources at (800)527-3305 or write to Department of Natural Resources AW-11, 1065 South Capitol Way, Olympia, WA 98504.

Location: Drive 14 miles south of Forks on US 101 and turn east on Hoh Rain Forest Road. Drive 4.5 miles to the camp on the left.

Trip note: This is a primitive camp, set on the Hoh River on the edge of the Hoh Rain Forest. Bring your rain gear. Not many folks know about this spot.

Site **63**
COTTONWOOD
on Hoh River

Campsites, facilities: There are six campsites for tents or small trailers. Picnic tables, fire grills and tent pads are provided. Pit toilets, piped water and a boat launch are available. Pets on leashes are permitted.

Reservations, fee: No reservations necessary; no fee. Open all year.

Who to contact: Phone the Department of Natural Resources at (800)527-3305 or write to Department of Natural Resources AW-11, 1065 South Capitol Way, Olympia, WA 98504.

Location: Drive 15 miles south of Forks on US 101, and then go west on Oil City road for 2.3 miles. Turn left on a gravel road (H 4060) and drive one mile to the camp.

Trip note: An option to Sites 61-64, this primitive, little-used site is also set along Hoh River.

Site **64**
HOH OXBOW
on Hoh River

Campsites, facilities: There are five campsites for tents or small trailers. Picnic tables, fire grills and tent pads are provided. Pit toilets and a hand boat launch are available. Firearms are prohibited. **No piped water** is available so bring your own. Pets on leashes are permitted.

Reservations, fee: No reservations necessary; no fee. Open all year.

Who to contact: Phone the Department of Natural Resources at (800)527-3305 or write to Department of Natural Resources AW-11, 1065 South Capitol Way, Olympia, WA 98504.

Location: Drive 14 miles south of Forks on US 101 and camp east of highway next to the river.

Trip note: This is the most populated of the five camps on the Hoh River. Primitive and close to the highway and the price is right.

Site **65**
SOUTH FORK HOH
BERT COLE STATE FOREST

Campsites, facilities: There are three campsites for tents or small trailers. Picnic tables, fire grills and tent pads are provided. Pit toilets are available. There is **no piped water,** so bring your own. Pets on leashes are permitted.

Reservations, fee: No reservations necessary; no fee. Open all year.

Who to contact: Phone the Department of Natural Resources at (800)527-3305 or write to Department of Natural Resources AW-11, 1065 South Capitol Way, Olympia, WA 98504.

Location: Drive 15 miles south of Forks, then go east on Hoh Mainline Road for 6.5 miles. Turn left on H1000 Road and drive 7.5 miles to the camp on the right. A Forest Service map is essential.

Trip note: This one is way out there. It's a rarely used camp set along the South Fork of Hoh River. Not many folks know about it.

Site 66   COPPER MINE BOTTOM
on Clearwater River

Campsites, facilities: There are nine campsites for tents or small trailers. Picnic tables, fire grills and tent pads are provided. Pit toilets and a hand boat launch are available. There is **no piped water** available. Pets on leashes are permitted.

Reservations, fee: No reservations necessary; no fee. Open all year.

Who to contact: Phone the Department of Natural Resources at (800)527-3305 or write to Department of Natural Resources AW-11, 1065 South Capitol Way, Olympia, WA 98504.

Location: On US 101 begin at milepost 147, go north on Hoh Clearwater Mainline Rd for 12.5 miles, then right on C1010 (gravel one-lane road) for 1.5 miles. The camp is on the left.

Trip note: Few tourists ever visit this primitive, hidden campground with river dory launching facilities. It's set on Clearwater River, a tributary to the Queets River, which runs to the ocean.

Site 67   UPPER CLEARWATER
on Clearwater River

Campsites, facilities: There are six campsites for tents or small trailers. Picnic tables, fire grills and tent pads are provided. Pit toilets, piped water and a hand boat launch are available. Pets on leashes are permitted.

Reservations, fee: No reservations necessary; no fee. Open all year.

Who to contact: Phone the Department of Natural Resources at (800)527-3305 or write to Department of Natural Resources AW-11, 1065 South Capitol Way, Olympia, WA 98504.

Location: From US 101 milepost 147, go north on Hoh Clearwater Mainline Rd. for 13 miles, then turn right on C3000 (gravel one-lane road) and drive 3.3 miles. The camp entrance is on the right.

Trip note: This is one of the three primitive camps set along the Clearwater River. It has river dory launching facilities.

Site 68   YAHOO LAKE
BERT COLE STATE FOREST

Campsites, facilities: There are six tent sites and a group shelter at this primitive hike-in camp. Pit toilets, a group shelter and a boat dock are available. There is **no piped water,** so bring your own. Pets on leashes are permitted.

Reservations, fee: No reservations necessary; no fee. Open all year.

Who to contact: Phone the Department of Natural Resources at (800)527-3305 or write to Department of Natural Resources AW-11, 1065 South Capitol Way, Olympia, WA 98504.

Location: Follow directions to Upper Clearwater (Site 67) and continue on C 3000 (gravel road) for three-quarters of a mile. Turn right on C 3100 (gravel two-lane road), keep left and continue on C 3100 another three-quarters of a mile to the trailhead. Hike in.

Trip note: This camp is set at about 2,000 feet elevation on the edge of tiny Yahoo Lake. It's an idyllic setting that few people take advantage of.

Site 69
PILLAR POINT RECREATION AREA
near the Strait of Juan De Fuca

Campsites, facilities: There are 20 tent sites and 18 sites for trailers or motor homes up to 24 feet long. Sewer hookups and picnic tables are provided. Toilets are available. A store is located within one mile. Firewood can be purchased. There is **no piped water,** so bring your own. Pets and motorbikes are permitted. Boat launching facilities are nearby.

Reservations, fee: No reservations necessary; $6 fee per night. Open mid-May to mid-September.

Who to contact: Phone the park at (206)928-3201 or write to Star Route 2, Box 8, Clallam Bay, WA 98326.

Location: From Clallam Bay drive 14 miles east on Highway 112, then one-half mile north on Pillar Point Road to the campground.

Trip note: This camp is set in the northwestern end of the Olympic Peninsula, near the mouth of the Strait of Juan De Fuca. Fishermen will launch here and try to intercept migrating salmon. It is an option to Sites 87-90.

Site 70
KLAHOWYA
on Soleduck River
OLYMPIC NATIONAL FOREST

Campsites, facilities: There are 25 tent sites and 30 sites for trailers or motor homes up to 21 feet long. Picnic tables are provided. Piped water, vault and flush toilets, and firewood are available. Leashed pets are permitted. Wheelchair facilities are available. Boat ramp is nearby.

Reservations, fee: Reservations accepted but not required; $5 fee per night. Open May to mid-October with full service. Limited service in the off-season.

Who to contact: Phone the Soleduck Ranger Station, Olympic National Forest at (206)374-6522 or write to Soleduck Ranger Station, Star Route 1, Box 185, Forks, WA 98331.

Location: From Forks, drive 20 miles northeast on US 101.

Trip note: This is a good choice if you don't want to venture far from US 101, yet want to retain the feel of Olympic National Forest. The camp is 32 acres and set along the headwaters of the Soleduck River.

Site 71
QUEETS
on Queets River

Campsites, facilities: There are 20 primitive tent sites. Picnic tables and fire grills are provided. Toilets are available, but there is **no piped water.** Pets are permitted. Rest rooms are wheelchair accessible.

Reservations, fee: No reservations necessary; no fee. Open year-round.

Who to contact: Phone the Olympic National Park at (206)452-4501 or write to 600 East Park, Port Angeles, WA 98362.

Location: From Queets, drive five miles east on US 101, then 14 miles northeast on unpaved road along Queets River. The campground is at the end of the road.

Trip note: This is a gem of a find if you don't mind bringing your own water or purifying river water. The camp is little-known, primitive and set on the shore of the Queets River. A trailhead is available for hikes into the interior of Olympic National Park.

Site 72 ERICKSON'S BAY
on Lake Ozette, walk-in or boat-in only

Campsites, facilities: There are 15 primitive tent sites at this boat-in or hike-in camp. Picnic tables, fire grills and pit toilets are provided. **No piped water** is available. Pets are permitted.

Reservations, fee: No reservations necessary; no fee. Open all year.

Who to contact: Phone the Olympic National Park at (206)452-4501 or write to 600 East Park, Port Angeles, WA 98362.

Location: From Ozette, drive one-half mile south to Lake Ozette (Boat or backpack access only).

Trip note: Very few people visit this site, set on the shore of Ozette Lake and just a few miles from the Pacific Ocean. This is a boaters' delight. Access is limited to boaters and backpackers.

Site 73 HOH RAIN FOREST
OLYMPIC NATIONAL PARK

Campsites, facilities: There are 89 sites for tents or motor homes up to 21 feet long. Picnic tables and fire grills are provided. Sanitary disposal station, rest rooms and drinking water are available. Pets are permitted. Facilities are wheelchair accessible.

Reservations, fee: No reservations necessary; $5 fee per night. Open all year.

Who to contact: Phone the Olympic National Park at (206)452-4501 or write to 600 East Park, Port Angeles, WA 98362.

Location: From Forks, drive 14 miles south on US 101, then 19 miles east along the Hoh River until you arrive at the campground.

Trip note: This camp is at the trailhead leading into the interior of Olympic National Park. It provides an option to Sites 61-64, which are set downriver on the Hoh. In the summer there are evening naturalist programs.

Site 74 MORA
near the Pacific Ocean
OLYMPIC NATIONAL PARK

Campsites, facilities: There are 94 sites for tents or motor homes up to 21 feet long. Picnic tables, fire grills are provided. Drinking water, sanitary disposal station, and rest rooms are available. Pets are permitted. Wheelchair facilities are available.

Reservations, fee: No reservations necessary; $5 fee per night. Open all year.

Who to contact: Phone the Olympic National Park at (206)452-4501 or write to 600 East Park, Port Angeles, WA 98362.

Location: From Forks, drive two miles north on US 101 then west 12 miles on La Push Highway to the campground.

Trip note: This is a good out-of-the-way choice set near Pacific Ocean and the coastal National Wildlife Refuge. Soleduck River feeds into the ocean near here. In summer months, a naturalist program is available.

Site 75 BOGACHIEL STATE PARK
on Bogachiel River

Campsites, facilities: There are 41 sites for tents or small motor homes up to 35 feet long. Picnic tables, fire grills are provided. Sanitary disposal station, rest rooms and drinking water are available. A store and ice are located within one mile. Showers and firewood are available for an extra fee. Leashed pets are permitted.

Reservations, fee: No reservations necessary; $7 fee per night. Open all year.

Who to contact: Phone the state park at (206)374-6356 or write to HC 80 Box 500, Forks, WA 98331.

Location: From Forks, drive six miles south on US 101 to the park.

Trip note: This is a good base camp for salmon or steelhead fishing trips. This 119-acre park is set on the Bogachiel River. There are marked hiking trails in the area. A problem that sometimes occurs is noise during the day from the logging mill located directly across the river from the campground and noise at night from logging trucks on the nearby highway.

Site 76   HOH RIVER RESORT

Campsites, facilities: There are eight tent sites and 27 drive-through sites for trailers or motor homes of any length. Electricity, piped water, sewer hookups and picnic tables are provided. Toilets, a store, laundry and ice are available. Showers and firewood are available for an extra fee. Pets and motorbikes are permitted.

Reservations, fee: No reservations necessary; $7.50-12 fee per night. Open all year.

Who to contact: Phone the park at (206)374-5566 or write to Star HC 80-750, Forks, WA 98331.

Location: From Forks, drive 15 miles south on US 101.

Trip note: This is a nice camp along US 101. Marked hiking trails are in the area.

Site 77   BEAR CREEK MOTEL AND RV PARK
                     on Bear Creek

Campsites, facilities: There are eight tent sites and 15 drive-through sites for trailers or motor homes of any length. Electricity, piped water, sewer hookups and picnic tables are provided. Bottled gas, sanitary services, toilets, showers and firewood are available. A cafe is located within one mile. Pets are permitted. Boat launching facilities are nearby.

Reservations, fee: No reservations necessary; $10 fee per night; American Express, MasterCard and Visa accepted. Open all year.

Who to contact: Phone the park at (206)327-3660 or write to Box 213, Beaver, WA 98305.

Location: From Forks, drive 15 miles north on US 101, watch for milepost 206. The camp is nearby.

Trip note: This quiet, little spot is set where Bear Creek empties into the Soleduck River. It's private and developed.

Site 78   THREE RIVERS RESORT
                     on Soleduck River

Campsites, facilities: There are ten sites for tents, trailers or motor homes of any length. Picnic tables are provided. Bottled gas, toilets, a store, a cafe, laundry and ice are available. Electricity, piped water, sewer hookups, showers and firewood can be purchased for an extra fee. Pets are permitted.

Reservations, fee: Reservations accepted; $8 fee per night; MasterCard, Visa and Chevron accepted. Open all year.

Who to contact: Phone the park at (206)374-5300 or write to HC 79, Box 280, Forks,

WA 98331.

Location: From Forks, drive nine miles west on La Push Road.

Trip note: This small, private camp is set on the Soleduck River. The coastal National Wildlife Refuge and Pacific Ocean are a short drive to the west.

Site **79**   **SHORELINE RESORT AND TRAILER PARK**
on the Pacific Ocean

Campsites, facilities: There are 62 drive-through sites for trailers or motor homes of any length. Electricity, piped water and sewer hookups are provided. Bottled gas, sanitary services, toilets, a store, laundry are available. A cafe and ice are located within one mile. Showers are available for an extra fee. Pets are permitted. Boat docks and launching facilities are nearby.

Reservations, fee: No reservations necessary; $10-11 fee per night; MasterCard and Visa accepted. Open all year.

Who to contact: Phone the park at (206)374-6488 or write to Box 26, La Push, WA 98350.

Location: From Forks, drive 14 miles west on US 101. Turn onto La Push Road and drive 17 miles to the campground.

Trip note: This private , developed park is set along the Pacific Ocean and the coastal National Wildlife Refuge.

Site **80**   **COHO RESORT AND TRAILER PARK**
near Sekiu

Campsites, facilities: There are 25 tent sites and 100 sites for trailers or motor homes of any length. Electricity, piped water, sewer hookups and cable TV are provided. Sanitary services, toilets, a cafe, laundry and ice are available. Bottled gas and a store are located within one mile. Showers are available for an extra fee. Pets and motorbikes are permitted. Boat docks, launching facilities and rentals are available.

Reservations, fee: No reservations necessary; $6-11 fee per night. Open March to October.

Who to contact: Phone the park at (206)963-2333 or write to HCR 61, Box 15, Sekiu, WA 98381.

Location: From Sekiu, drive one mile east on Highway 112 to park.

Trip note: This is one of the seven camps in immediate area besides Sites 81-86. A full-service marina nearby provides boating access.

Site **81**   **SURFSIDE RESORT**
in Sekiu

Campsites, facilities: There are 20 tent sites and 24 drive-through sites for trailers or motor homes of any length. Electricity, piped water, sewer hookups and picnic tables are provided. Sanitary services, toilets and showers are available. Bottled gas, a store, a cafe, laundry and ice are located within one mile. Firewood is available for an extra fee. Pets and motorbikes are permitted. Boat docks, launching facilities and rentals are nearby.

Reservations, fee: Reservations accepted; $9 fee per night. Open May to September.

Who to contact: Phone the park at (206)963-2723 or write to P.O. Box 151, Sekiu, WA 98381.

Location: In Sekiu on the east edge of town.

Trip note: Nearby recreation options include marked hiking trails, marked bike trails and a full-service marina.

Site **82**
CURLEY'S RESORT
on Clallam Bay

Campsites, facilities: There are 12 sites for trailers or motor homes up to 22 feet
  long. Electricity, piped water and sewer hookups are provided. Toilets, showers
  and ice, and cable TV are available. Bottled gas, sanitary services, a store, a
  cafe and laundry are located within one block. Pets and motorbikes are
  permitted. Boat docks, launching facilities and rentals are nearby.
Reservations, fee: Reservations accepted; $11 fee per night; MasterCard and Visa
  accepted. Open April to late October.
Who to contact: Phone the park at (206)963-2281 or write to Box 265, Sekiu, WA
  98381.
Location: In Sekiu.
Trip note: A small RV park set on the edge of Clallam Bay.

Site **83**
OLSON'S RESORT
in Sekiu

Campsites, facilities: There are 30 tent sites and 100 sites for trailers or motor homes
  of any length. Electricity, piped water, sewer hookups and picnic tables are
  provided. Toilets, showers, a store, a cafe and ice are available. Sanitary services
  and laundry are located within one mile. Pets and motorbikes are permitted. Boat
  docks, launching facilities and rentals are nearby.
Reservations, fee: No reservations necessary; $8-11 fee per night; MasterCard and
  Visa accepted. Open February to mid-October.
Who to contact: Phone the park at (206)963-2311 or write to Box 216, Sekiu, WA
  98381.
Location: In Sekiu, off Highway 112, at the north end of Front Street.
Trip note: This large, private camp is developed with full-services. A marina nearby
  is salmon fishing headquarters.

Site **84**
VAN RIPERS' RESORT HOTEL
AND CAMPGROUND
on Clallam Bay

Campsites, facilities: There are 60 drive-through sites for trailers or motor homes
  of any length. Electricity, piped water and picnic tables are provided. Sanitary
  services, toilets, showers and ice are available. Bottled gas, a store, a cafe and
  laundry are located within one mile. Sewer hookups and firewood are available
  for an extra fee. Pets and motorbikes are permitted. Boat docks, launching
  facilities and rentals are nearby.
Reservations, fee: No reservations necessary; $8.50 fee per night; MasterCard and
  Visa accepted. Open April to late September.
Who to contact: Phone the park at (206)963-2334 or write to Box 246, Sekiu, WA
  98381.
Location: In Sekiu, off Highway 112, north on Front Street.
Trip note: This is for motor homes and trailers only. It's urban camping along
  Clallam Bay!

Site **85**
RICE'S RESORT
in Sekiu

Campsites, facilities: There are 41 tent sites and 16 sites for trailers or motor homes
  up to 30 feet long. Electricity, piped water, sewer hookups and picnic tables

are provided. Sanitary services, toilets, showers, firewood, ice and a playground are available. Bottled gas, a store, a cafe and laundry are located within one mile. Pets and motorbikes are permitted. Boat docks, launching facilities and rentals are nearby.

Reservations, fee: Reservations accepted; $8 fee per night. Open all year with limited winter facilities.

Who to contact: Phone the park at (206)963-2300 or write to Box 218, Sekiu, WA 98381.

Location: In Sekiu, off Highway 112, one-half mile north and one-eighth mile west on Rice Street.

Trip note: Of the seven campgrounds in the immediate area around Clallam Bay, this one is set up more for tent campers than the others.

Site 86   SAM'S TRAILER AND RV PARK
on Clallam Bay

Campsites, facilities: There are ten tent sites and 20 drive-through sites for trailers or motor homes of any length. Electricity, piped water, sewer hookups and picnic tables are provided. Sanitary services, toilets, showers and laundry are available. Bottled gas, a store, a cafe and ice are located within one mile. Pets and motorbikes are permitted. Boat docks, launching facilities and rentals are nearby.

Reservations, fee: Reservations accepted; $7 fee per night. Open all year.

Who to contact: Phone the park at (206)963-2402 or write to Box 45, Clallam Bay, WA 98326.

Location: In the town of Clallam Bay on Highway 112.

Trip note: This is an option to Sites 80-84 on Clallam Bay.

Site 87   THUNDERBIRD RV PARK
in Neah Bay

Campsites, facilities: There are 45 pull-through sites for trailers or motor homes of any length. Electricity, piped water and sewer hookups are provided. Bottled gas, toilets, laundry and ice are available. Sanitary services, a store, a cafe are located within one mile. Showers are available for an extra fee. Pets and motorbikes are permitted. Boat docks, launching facilities and rentals are nearby.

Reservations, fee: Reservations accepted; $8-13 fee per night; MasterCard and Visa accepted. Open April to late September.

Who to contact: Phone the park at (206)645-2450 or write to Box 218, Neah Bay, WA 98357.

Location: In the town of Neah Bay on Highway 112.

Trip note: This three-acre RV park has safety valve option of five tent sites. It's an okay base of operations for anglers when salmon migrate through the area. There is a full-service marina nearby.

Site 88   TYEE MOTEL AND RV PARK
in Neah Bay

Campsites, facilities: There are 40 pull-through sites for trailers or motor homes of any length. Electricity, piped water and sewer hookups are provided. Bottled gas, sanitary services, toilets, laundry and ice are available. A store and a cafe are located within one mile. Showers are available for an extra fee. Pets and motorbikes are permitted. Boat docks, launching facilities and rentals are nearby.

Reservations, fee: Reservations accepted; $8-13 fee per night; MasterCard and Visa accepted. Open all year.

Who to contact: Phone the park at (206)645-2223 or write to Box 193, Neah Bay, WA 98357.

Location: In Neah Bay on Highway 112.

Trip note: For motor homes and trailers only, this private, developed campground is located near the northwestern tip of Olympic Peninsula.

Site 89
WESTWIND RESORT
in Neah Bay

Campsites, facilities: There are 28 sites for tents, trailers or motor homes up to 30 feet long. Electricity, piped water, sewer hookups and picnic tables are provided. Toilets, showers, laundry and ice are available. Bottled gas, a store, a cafe are located within one block. Pets are permitted if on leashes. Boat docks, launching facilities and rentals are nearby.

Reservations, fee: Reservations accepted; $8.50 fee per night; MasterCard and Visa accepted. Open May to October.

Who to contact: Phone the park at (206)645-2751 or write to Box 918, Neah Bay, WA 98357.

Location: In the town of Neah Bay on Highway 112.

Trip note: This is one of the better choices in immediate area for tent campers.

Site 90
NEAH BAY RESORT
near Cape Flattery

Campsites, facilities: There are ten tent sites and 38 sites for trailers or motor homes of any length. Electricity, piped water, sewer hookups and picnic tables are provided. Bottled gas, sanitary services, toilets, showers, a store, a cafe and ice are available. Pets are permitted. Boat docks, launching facilities and rentals are nearby.

Reservations, fee: Reservations accepted; $12 fee per night. Open May to mid-September.

Who to contact: Phone the park at (206)645-2288 or write to Box 97, Neah Bay, WA 98357.

Location: From the town of Neah Bay, drive five miles east on Highway 112 to resort.

Trip note: This private camp is a good alternative to Sites 87-89, all on the tip of Olympic Peninsula. It's set near Makah Indian Reservation and Cape Flattery.

Site 91
POINT HUDSON CAMPGROUND
in Port Townsend

Campsites, facilities: There are 20 drive-through sites for trailers or motor homes of any length. Picnic tables and full hookups are provided. Flush toilets, a store, a cafe, laundromat, and ice are available. Showers are available for an extra fee. A boat dock and launching ramp is nearby.

Reservations, fee: Reservations accepted; $11 fee per night. Open all year.

Who to contact: Phone (206)385-2828 or write to the campground in Port Townsend, WA 98368.

Location: In Port Townsend, from the junction of Highway 20 and Water Street, drive to the Port Hudson Boat Basin.

Trip note: Nearby recreation options include an 18-hole golf course, a full-service

marina, Old Fort Townsend State Park, Fort Flagler State Park and Fort Worden
State Park.

Site 92
SEA BREEZE CENTER
MOTORHOME AND RV PARK
in Port Townsend

Campsites, facilities: There are 32 sites for self-contained motor homes or trailers
of any size. Full hookups are provided. A store, laundromat, boat dock, launch
ramp and ice are available. A sanitary dump station, bottled gas and a cafe are
nearby.

Reservations, fee: Reservations accepted; $8.50 fee per night; Visa and MasterCard
accepted. Open all year.

Who to contact: phone the park at (206)692-4648.

Location: Drive to the west edge of Port Townsend on Highway 20 and you'll see
the park.

Trip note: Nearby recreation options include an 18-hole golf course, horseback
riding rentals, tennis courts, Old Fort Townsend State Park, Fort Flagler State
Park and Fort Worden State Park.

Site 93
FORT FLAGLER STATE PARK
near Port Townsend

Campsites, facilities: There are 116 sites for tents or motor homes up to 50 feet
long. Picnic tables, fire grills are provided. Flush toilets, a sanitary dump
station, a store, a cafe, boat buoys and floats, and a boat launch are available.
Facilities are wheelchair accessible. Showers are available for an extra fee.
Leashed pets are permitted.

Reservations, fee: Reservations accepted only by mail; $6 fee per night.

Who to contact: Phone (206)385-1259 or write to Nordland, WA 98358.

Location: Drive to Marrowstone Island just south of Port Townsend. The state park
is eight miles northeast of Hadlock.

Trip note: The campgrounds are right on the beach. It's a good place for fisherman
with year-round rockfish and salmon fishing. Crabbing and clamming are good
in season. Tours are available for Fort Flagler, which was built in 1898.

Site 94
OLD FORT TOWNSEND STATE PARK
near Quilcene

Campsites, facilities: There are 40 sites for tents or motor homes up to 40 feet long.
Picnic tables, fire grills are provided. Flush toilets, a playground and boat buoys
are available. Firewood and showers are available for an extra fee. Leashed
pets are permitted.

Reservations, fee: No reservations; $7 fee per night. Open all year with limited
winter facilities.

Who to contact: Phone (206)385-3595 or write to Route 1, Port Townsend, WA
98368.

Location: From Quilcene, drive 12 miles north on US 101, then go north on Highway
20 for seven miles to the park.

Trip note: This fort was built in 1859, one of the oldest remaining in the state. The
campground has access to a good clamming beach, and there are stables nearby.

SOUTHWEST COAST

◆

SOME HIGHLIGHTS
---

55 CAMPGROUNDS

Leadbetter Point

Westport Light State Park

Westhaven State Park

Grayland Beach State Park

Willapa Bay

Fort Canby State Park

Fort Columbia State Park

Columbia River

Grays Harbor

Westport Harbor

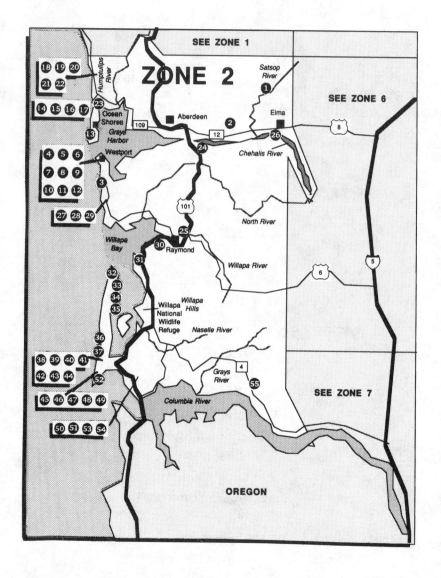

SCHAFER STATE PARK
Site **1**   on Satsop River

Campsites, facilities: There are 47 tent sites and six sites with water and electric hookups for trailers or motor homes up to 40 feet long. Picnic tables and fire grills are provided. Sanitary disposal station, toilets and a playground are available. Water, showers and firewood are an additional charge. Some facilities are wheelchair accessible. Leashed pets are permitted.

Reservations, fee: No reservations necessary; $7-9 fee per night. Open all year with limited winter facilities.

Who to contact: Phone (206)482-3852 or write to Route 1, Box 87, Elma, WA 98541.

Location: Drive four miles east of Montesano on Highway 12, then head north for eight miles on East Satsop Road to the Park.

Trip note: This heavily-wooded, rural camp covers 119 acres and is on the East Fork of the Satsop River. There are good canoe and kayaking spots, some with Class II and Class III rapids, along the Middle and West Forks of the Satsop River. At one time this park was the Schafer Company Park and was used by the employees and their families.

LAKE SYLVIA
Site **2**   on Lake Sylvia

Campsites, facilities: There are 35 tent sites which also can accommodate vehicles or motor homes up to 30 feet long. Picnic tables, fire grills are provided. Piped water, sanitary disposal station, toilets, a store, fishing supplies, a car-top boat launch, boat rentals and a playground are available. Showers and firewood are available for an extra fee. Laundry and ice are located within one mile. Some facilities are wheelchair accessible. Leashed pets are permitted.

Reservations, fee: No reservations necessary; $6 fee per night. Open all year.

Who to contact: Phone (206)249-3621 or write to Box 701, Montesano, WA 98563.

Location: From Montesano, drive north one mile to the park.

Trip note: This camp is on the shore of Lake Sylvia and covers 234 acres. There are numerous marked hiking trails. Additional options include trout fishing and swimming. If this camp is full, nearby options are Sites 1, 24 and 26.

TWIN HARBORS STATE PARK
Site **3**   on the Pacific Ocean

Campsites, facilities: There are 272 tent sites and 49 sites for trailers or motor homes up to 35 feet long. Picnic tables, fire grills are provided. Piped water, sanitary disposal station, toilets and a playground are available. A store, a cafe and ice are available within one mile. Electricity, sewer hookups, showers and firewood are available for an extra fee. Some facilities are wheelchair accessible. Leashed pets are permitted.

Reservations, fee: Reservations accepted; $7-9.50 fee per night. Open all year.

Who to contact: Phone (206)753-4055 or write to Twin Harbors State Park, Westport, WA 98595.

Location: The park is three miles south of Westport on Highway 105.

Trip note: This park covers 1,881 acres, and has beach access and marked hiking trails, including the Shifting Sands Nature Trail. Nearby in Westport there are fishing boats to charter. This is one of the largest campgrounds on the coast.

Site 4
WESTPORT WATERFRONT RV PARK
in Westport

Campsites, facilities: There are 30 sites with full hookups for trailers or motor homes of any length. Sanitary services, toilets and ice and showers are available. Boat docks, launching facilities and rentals are located at the park. Bottled gas, a store and laundry are within one mile.

Reservations, fee: Reservations not accepted; $11 fee per night. Open May to late October.

Who to contact: Phone the park at (206)268-0137 or write to 609 Revetment, Westport, WA 98595.

Location: In Westport, take Revetment Drive to boat basin to the park at 609 Revetment.

Trip note: This motor home park and marina covers two acres. Westport Light and Westhaven State Parks are both nearby and offer day-use facilities on the beach. It also offers good salmon fishing in summer months along the local coast.

Site 5
LIGHTHOUSE RV RESORT
near Grays Harbor

Campsites, facilities: There are 15 tent sites and 43 drive-through sites for trailers or motor homes of any length. Electricity, piped water, sewer hookups and picnic tables are provided. Toilets, showers and laundry are available. Bottled gas, sanitary services, a store, a cafe and ice are within one mile. Pets are permitted. Boat docks and launching facilities are available nearby.

Reservations, fee: Reservations accepted; $8-11 fee per night. Open all year.

Who to contact: Phone (206)268-0001 or write to P.O. Box 1237, Westport, WA 98595.

Location: In Westport, drive three blocks east on Tacoma Avenue from Highway 109 and you're there.

Trip note: This private park covers three acres and is near Grays Harbor and Westport Light State Park, a day-use park popular for surfing, scuba diving and rock collecting. There is a full-service marina within five miles of the campground at Grays Harbor.

Site 6
ISLANDER RV PARK
on Grays Harbor

Campsites, facilities: There are 60 sites with full hookups for trailers or motor homes of any length. Toilets, showers, a cafe, laundry, ice, a swimming pool, boat docks, are available. Bottled gas, sanitary services and a store are located within one mile. Pets and motorbikes are permitted.

Reservations, fee: Reservations accepted; $10.50-12.50 fee per night; American Express, MasterCard, Visa and Diners Club accepted. Open all year.

Who to contact: Phone (206)268-9166 or write to P.O. Box 488, Westport, WA 98595.

Location: In Westport, drive to boat basin on Neddie Rose Drive.

Trip note: This park covers three acres and is on Grays Harbor, not far from Westport Light and Westhaven State Parks, which offer ocean-front, day-use facilities. Additional facilities found within five miles of the campground include a full-service marina.

Site 7   G & M CHARTER TRAILER PARK
near Westport Harbor

Campsites, facilities: There are 30 drive-through sites with full hookups for trailers or motor homes of any length. Picnic tables are provided. Sanitary services, toilets, boat docks, rentals and ice are available. Showers are available for an extra fee. Bottled gas, a store, a cafe and laundry are available within one mile. Pets and motorbikes are permitted.

Reservations, fee: Reservations accepted; $11 fee per night. Open year-round.

Who to contact: Phone the park at (206)268-0265 or write to P.O. Box 342, Westport, WA 98595.

Location: In Westport, drive to Point Chehalis on Neddie Rose Drive. Park is at the Westport Docks.

Trip note: This park covers one acre and is near Westport Harbor. Westport Light and Westhaven State Parks are nearby and offer day-use facilities along the ocean.

Site 8   COHO TRAILER PARK
near Westport Harbor

Campsites, facilities: There are 80 sites with full hookups for trailers or motor homes of any length. Picnic tables are provided. Sanitary services, cable TV, toilets, showers, laundry and ice are available. Bottled gas, a store and a cafe are within one mile. Pets are permitted. Boat docks, launching facilities and rentals also are located one block from this park. Good Sam Membership discount.

Reservations, fee: Reservations accepted; $11-12.50 fee per night. Open all year.

Who to contact: Phone (206)268-0111 or write to 2501 Nyhus, Westport, WA 98595.

Location: In Westport, from Highway 105 drive north on Nyhus Street to the Westport Docks.

Trip note: This park covers two acres and is one of ten camp options in the immediate area. Both Westhaven and Westport Light State Parks are nearby. They are popular places for rock hounds, scuba divers and surf fishermen. Additional facilities found within five miles of the campground include a full-service marina.

Site 9   HAMMOND TRAILER PARK
in Westport

Campsites, facilities: There are eight tent sites and 25 sites with full hookups for trailers or motor homes of any length. Picnic tables are provided. Sanitary services, toilets, showers, firewood and laundry are available. Bottled gas, a store, a cafe and ice are within one mile. Pets are permitted. Boat docks, launching facilities and boat rentals are nearby.

Reservations, fee: Reservations accepted; $7 fee per night. Open all year.

Who to contact: Phone (206)268-9645 or write to P.O. Box 1648, Westport, WA 98595.

Location: In Westport, drive one-quarter mile south on Montesano Street to 1845 Roberts Road.

Trip note: This park covers five acres. Additional facilities found within five miles of the campground include a full-service marina.

Site 10
HOLAND CENTER
in Westport

Campsites, facilities: There are 80 drive-through sites with full hookups for trailers or motor homes of any length. Picnic tables are provided. Toilets and showers are available. Bottled gas, a store, a cafe, laundry and ice are located within one mile. Pets are permitted. Boat docks and launching facilities are nearby.

Reservations, fee: Reservations accepted; $9 fee per night. Open all year.

Who to contact: Phone (206)268-9582 or write to P.O. Box 468, Westport, WA 98595.

Location: In Westport, this park is at the corner of Highway 105 and Wilson Street.

Trip note: This camp covers 18 acres. Additional facilities found within five miles of the campground include a full-service marina.

Site 11
TOTEM RV AND TRAILER PARK
in Westport

Campsites, facilities: There are ten tent sites and 77 drive-through sites for trailers or motor homes of any length. Electricity, piped water, sewer hookups and picnic tables are provided. Sanitary services, toilets, showers, a store, laundry and ice are available. Bottled gas and a cafe are located within one mile. Pets and motorbikes are permitted. Boat docks, launching facilities and rentals are nearby.

Reservations, fee: Reservations accepted; $9 fee per night. Open March to October.

Who to contact: Phone (206)268-0025 or write to P.O. Box 1166, Westport, WA 98595.

Location: In Westport, from the junction of Highway 105 and Montesano Street, drive 1.5 miles north on Highway 105, then two blocks northeast to Nyhus (1st Avenue).

Trip note: This park covers two acres and is near Westhaven State Park which offers day-use facilities. Additional facilities found within five miles of the campground include marked bike trails, a full-service marina and tennis courts.

Site 12
PACIFIC MOTEL AND TRAILER PARK
near Twin Harbors

Campsites, facilities: There are 40 tent sites and 80 drive-through sites for trailers or motor homes of any length. Electricity, piped water and sewer hookups are provided. Sanitary services, toilets, a recreation hall and a swimming pool are available, and showers are available for an extra fee. Bottled gas, a store, a cafe, laundry and ice are located within one mile. Pets and motorbikes are permitted. Boat docks and launching facilities are nearby.

Reservations, fee: Reservations accepted; $10 fee per night; MasterCard and Visa accepted. Open all year.

Who to contact: Phone (206)268-9325 or write to 330 W. Forrest, Westport, WA 98595.

Location: The motel and trailer park are in Westport. To get there, drive two miles north of Twin Harbors State Park on Highway 105.

Trip note: This park covers five acres and is near Twin Harbors and Westport Light State Parks, both of which have beach access. Additional facilities found within five miles of the campground include a full-service marina.

Site 13

MARINA VIEW RV PARK TENT
on Point Brown

Campsites, facilities: There are 50 tent sites and 93 drive-through sites for trailers or motor homes of any length. Electricity, piped water, sewer hookups and picnic tables are provided. Sanitary services, toilets, showers, a store, a cafe and ice are available. Pets and motorbikes are permitted. Boat docks, launching facilities and rentals are nearby.

Reservations, fee: Reservations accepted; $9 fee per night; American Express, MasterCard and Visa accepted. Open all year.

Who to contact: Phone (206)289-3391 or write to P.O. Box 1291, Ocean Shores, WA 98569.

Location: From Ocean Shores, drive five miles south on Point Brown Avenue and you're there.

Trip note: This camp covers 13 acres and is on Point Brown. Additional facilities found within five miles of the campground include an 18-hole golf course, marked hiking trails, marked bike trails and a riding stable.

Site 14

STURGEON TRAILER HARBOR
in Ocean City

Campsites, facilities: There are 66 sites (32 drive-through) for trailers or motor homes of any length. Electricity, piped water, sewer hookups and picnic tables are provided. Toilets, showers and a recreation hall are available. Bottled gas, a store, a cafe and ice are located within one mile. Pets are permitted.

Reservations, fee: Reservations accepted; $12 fee per night. Open all year.

Who to contact: Phone (206)289-2101 or write to P.O. Box 536, Ocean City, WA 98569.

Location: This trailer park is on Highway 109 in Ocean City at the southern end of town.

Trip note: This park covers five acres and offers beach access. Additional facilities found within five miles of the campground include an 18-hole golf course, marked hiking trails, a full-service marina and a riding stable.

Site 15

LOOKOUT RV PARK
in Ocean City

Campsites, facilities: There are 23 sites for trailers or motor homes of any length. Electricity, piped water, sewer hookups, cable TV hookups and picnic tables are provided. Sanitary services, toilets, showers and a recreation hall are available. Bottled gas, a store, a cafe and ice are located within one mile. Pets are permitted.

Reservations, fee: Reservations accepted; $10 fee per night. Open all year.

Who to contact: Phone (206)289-2220 or write to Route 4, Box 570, Ocean City, WA 98569.

Location: Follow the signs in Ocean City to the Lookout RV Park.

Trip note: This park covers one acre and has beach access. It's one of 11 campgrounds on six miles of coastline.

Site 16

BLUE PACIFIC MOTEL AND TRAILER PARK
near Ocean City

Campsites, facilities: There are 19 sites for trailers or motor homes up to 30 feet long. Electricity, piped water, sewer hookups and picnic tables are provided.

Toilets, showers and a a playground are available. Bottled gas, a store, a cafe and ice are located within one mile. Pets are permitted if on leashes.

Reservations, fee: Reservations accepted; $13 fee per night; MasterCard and Visa accepted. Open all year, but with limited winter facilities.

Who to contact: Phone (206)289-2262 or write to Route 4, Box 615, Ocean City, WA 98569.

Location: Drive north from Ocean City on Highway 109 for one-half mile to this park.

Trip note: This park covers two acres and has beach access. An 18-hole golf course is available nearby.

Site **17**   ROD'S BEACH RESORT
near Copalis Beach

Campsites, facilities: There are 85 drive-through sites for trailers or motor homes of any length. Electricity, piped water, sewer hookups and picnic tables are provided. Sanitary services, toilets, showers, a recreation hall, a store, a cafe, ice and a playground are available. Bottled gas is located within one mile. A swimming pool is available for an extra fee. Pets are permitted.

Reservations, fee: Reservations accepted; $12 fee per night; MasterCard and Visa accepted. Open February to late November.

Who to contact: Phone the park at (206)289-2222 or write to Rod's Beach Resort, Copalis Beach, WA 98535.

Location: Drive south from Copalis Beach on Highway 109 for 1.5 miles to this park.

Trip note: This park covers ten acres and has beach access, plus nice sunsets.

Site **18**   TIDELANDS ON THE BEACH
near Copalis Beach

Campsites, facilities: There are 100 tent sites and 60 drive-through sites for trailers or motor homes of any length. Electricity, piped water, sewer hookups and picnic tables are provided. Sanitary services, toilets, firewood and a playground are available. Bottled gas, a store, a cafe and ice are located within one mile. Showers are available for an extra fee. Pets are permitted.

Reservations, fee: Reservations accepted; $12 fee per night. Open all year.

Who to contact: Phone (206)289-8963 or write to P.O. Box 36, Copalis Beach, WA 98535.

Location: Drive south from Copalis Beach on Highway 109 for one mile.

Trip note: This wooded park covers 47 acres and has beach access. It's a more remote option than Sites 14-17.

Site **19**   SURF AND SAND RV PARK
in Copalis Beach

Campsites, facilities: There are 45 drive-through sites for trailers or motor homes of any length. Electricity, piped water, sewer hookups, cable TV hookups and picnic tables are provided. Sanitary services, toilets, showers, a cafe and ice are available. Bottled gas and a store are located within one mile. Pets are permitted.

Reservations, fee: Reservations accepted; $13 fee per night; MasterCard and Visa accepted. Open all year.

Who to contact: Phone (206)289-2707 or write to P.O. Box 87, Copalis Beach, WA 98535.

Location: In Copalis Beach, take the Copalis Beach Access Road off Highway 109 and drive one-quarter mile to the park.

Trip note: This park covers five acres and has beach access. It's a decent layover for motor home vacation.

Site 20   DRIFTWOOD ACRES OCEAN CAMPGROUND
near Copalis Beach

Campsites, facilities: There are 50 tent sites and 50 sites for trailers or motor homes of any length. Piped water, sewer hookups and picnic tables are provided. Electricity, showers, sanitary services, toilets and firewood are available. Bottled gas, a store, a cafe and ice are located within one mile. Pets are permitted if on leashes.

Reservations, fee: Reservations accepted; Call ahead for fees, as they vary. Open April to late October.

Who to contact: Phone (206)289-3484 or write to P.O. Box 216, Copalis Beach, WA 98535.

Location: Drive one-quarter mile south of Copalis Beach on Highway 109 to park.

Trip note: This wooded campground covers 150 acres and has beach access and marked hiking trails. Additional facilities found within five miles of the campground include an 18-hole golf course and a riding stable.

Site 21   SHADES BY THE SEA
in Copalis Beach

Campsites, facilities: There are eight tent sites and 35 sites for trailers or motor homes of any length. Electricity, piped water, sewer hookups and picnic tables are provided. Sanitary services, toilets and firewood are available, and showers are available for an extra fee. Bottled gas, a store, a cafe and ice are located within one mile. Pets and motorbikes are permitted.

Reservations, fee: Reservations accepted; $11-12 fee per night; MasterCard and Visa accepted. Open February through November.

Who to contact: Phone (206)289-3358 or write to P.O. Box 67, Copalis Beach, WA 98535.

Location: This park is in Copalis Beach at the north end of town on Highway 109.

Trip note: The park covers 20 acres and offers beach and river access. An 18-hole golf course is a short drive distant.

Site 22   RIVERSIDE TRAILER COURT
near Copalis Beach

Campsites, facilities: There are 15 tent sites and 53 drive-through sites for trailers or motor homes of any length. Electricity, piped water, sewer hookups and picnic tables are provided. Bottled gas, sanitary services, toilets, showers, firewood and a recreation hall are available. A store, a cafe and ice are located within one mile. Pets and motorbikes are permitted.

Reservations, fee: Reservations accepted; $8-11 fee per night; MasterCard and Visa accepted. Open all year.

Who to contact: Phone (206)289-2111 or write to P.O. Box 307, Copalis Beach, WA 98535.

Location: From Copalis Beach, drive across the river to the park.

Trip note: This park covers three acres and has beach and river access.

Site 23   OCEAN CITY STATE PARK

Campsites, facilities: There are 149 tent sites and 29 sites with full hookups for trailers or motor homes up to 55 feet long. Picnic tables are provided, and sanitary services and toilets are available. Showers and firewood (in the summer) are available for an extra fee. Some facilities are wheelchair accessible. Pets are permitted.

Reservations, fee: No reservations necessary; $6 fee per night. Open all year.

Who to contact: Phone the state park at (206)289-3553 or write to Route 4, Box 2900, Hoquiam, WA 98550.

Location: Drive 20 miles west from Aberdeen on Highway 109, then turn left on Highway 105 and drive three miles to park.

Trip note: This is one of the choice spots in the area for tent campers. The camp is on the ocean and covers 131 acres. It is near many interesting shops and restaurants in town, and a short drive from an 18-hole golf course.

Site 24   ARTIC RV PARK
near North River

Campsites, facilities: There are 12 tent sites and ten sites for trailers or motor homes of any length. Electricity, piped water and sewer hookups are provided. Sanitary services and a cafe are available. Firewood can be purchased for an extra fee. Pets and motorbikes are permitted.

Reservations, fee: Reservations accepted; $7 fee per night. Open all year.

Who to contact: Phone (206)532-9811 or write to HCR 77, Box 64, Cosmopolis, WA 98537.

Location: Drive seven miles south of Aberdeen on US 101.

Trip note: This wooded park covers four acres and provides access to the North River. It offers a more remote setting than Sites 3-23 on Grays Harbor. An 18-hole golf course is a short drive distant.

Site 25   TIMBERLAND RV PARK
near Willapa River

Campsites, facilities: There are six tent sites and 24 drive-through sites for trailers or motor homes of any length. Electricity, piped water, sewer hookups, cable TV hookups and picnic tables are provided. Toilets and showers are available. Bottled gas, sanitary services, a store, a cafe, laundry and ice are located within one mile. Pets and motorbikes are permitted. Boat docks are nearby where the Willapa River empties into Willapa Bay.

Reservations, fee: Reservations accepted; $7-10 fee per night. Open mid-March to November.

Who to contact: Phone (206)942-3325 or write to 850 Crescent, Raymond, WA 98577.

Location: To get to this park, drive on US 101 to Raymond, then turn west on Highway 105 and drive six blocks. Turn left on Crescent for two blocks and you're there.

Trip note: This park covers three acres and has access to the Willapa River, a popular river during salmon or steelhead runs. Additional facilities found within five miles of the campground include an 18-hole golf course and tennis courts.

Site **26**

RL'S RV PARK
on Chehalis River

Campsites, facilities: There are 20 tent sites and 100 drive-through sites for trailers or motor homes of any length. Electricity, piped water and sewer hookups are provided. Bottled gas, sanitary services, toilets, showers and laundry are available. A store and a cafe are located within one mile. Pets and motorbikes are permitted. Boat docks, launching facilities and rentals are nearby on the Chehalis River.

Reservations, fee: Reservations accepted; $10 fee per night. Open all year.

Who to contact: Phone (206)482-5623 or write to P.O. Box K2, Elma, WA 98541.

Location: From Elma, drive one-half mile south on US 12 to the park.

Trip note: This rural park covers eight acres and sits along the Chehalis River. Additional facilities found within five miles of the campground include an 18-hole golf course, a riding stable and tennis courts.

Site **27**

OCEAN GATE RESORT
in Grayland

Campsites, facilities: There are 20 tent sites and 24 drive-through sites for trailers or motor homes of any length. Electricity, piped water, sewer hookups and picnic tables are provided. Toilets, showers, laundry and a playground are available, and firewood is available for an extra fee. Bottled gas, a store, a cafe and ice are found within one mile. Pets and motorbikes are permitted.

Reservations, fee: Reservations accepted; $9 fee per night. Open all year.

Who to contact: Phone (206)267-1956 or write to P.O. Box 67, Grayland, WA 98547.

Location: Drive to Grayland on Highway 105. The park is located in town.

Trip note: This is a privately-run park that provides an option to Site 29, the publicly run Grayland Beach State Park. This park covers seven acres and has beach access.

Site **28**

WESTERN SHORES TRAILER PARK
in Grayland

Campsites, facilities: There are ten tent sites and 25 drive-through sites for trailers or motor homes of any length. Electricity, piped water, sewer hookups and picnic tables are provided. Bottled gas, toilets, a recreation hall, ice and a playground are available, and showers are available for an extra fee. Sanitary services, firewood, a store and a cafe are located within one mile. Pets and motorbikes are permitted.

Reservations, fee: Reservations accepted; $7 fee per night; MasterCard and Visa accepted. Open all year.

Who to contact: Phone (800)562-0189 or write to Star Route 1, Box 79, Grayland, WA 98547.

Location: Drive to Grayland on Highway 105. The camp is located in town.

Trip note: A small, private park designed for families. This is a good option to Site 38, since kids are welcome.

Site **29**

GRAYLAND BEACH STATE PARK
on the Pacific Ocean

Campsites, facilities: There are 60 campsites with full hookups for trailers or motor homes up to 40 feet long. Picnic tables, fire grills are provided, toilets are available and showers are available for an extra fee. Some facilities are wheelchair accessible.

Reservations, fee: Reservations accepted; $10.50 fee per night. Open all year.

Who to contact: Write Grayland State Park, Westport, WA 98595.

Location: Drive to Grayland on Highway 105. The park is just south of town.

Trip note: This ocean-front park covers 317 acres and has a self-guided interpretive trail. It's one of the best parks in the immediate area and quite popular with out-of-towners, especially in the summer season.

Site **30**   **GYPSY RV PARK**
                          on Willapa River

Campsites, facilities: There are two tent sites and 12 drive-through sites for trailers or motor homes of any length. Electricity, piped water and sewer hookups are provided. Toilets, showers, a recreation hall and laundry are available. Bottled gas, a store, a cafe and ice can be found within one mile. Pets and motorbikes are permitted. Boat docks and launching facilities are nearby where the Willapa River empties into Willapa Bay.

Reservations, fee: Reservations accepted; $8 fee per night. Open all year.

Who to contact: Phone (206)875-5165 or write to P.O. Box 191, South Bend, WA 98586.

Location: Drive to South Bend on US 101, then go south on Central. The camp is located in town.

Trip note: This wooded park covers two acres and is on the Willapa River. Additional facilities found within five miles of the campground include an 18-hole golf course.

Site **31**   **KOA HAPPY TRAILS**
                          on Willapa Bay

Campsites, facilities: There are ten tent sites and 32 drive-through sites for trailers or motor homes of any length. Piped water and picnic tables are provided. Bottled gas, sanitary services, toilets, showers, a recreation hall, a store, laundry and ice are available. Electricity, sewer hookups and firewood can be purchased for an extra fee. There is a cafe nearby. Pets and motorbikes are permitted. Boat docks and launching facilities are about three miles from camp on Willapa Bay.

Reservations, fee: Reservations accepted; $11 fee per night; MasterCard and Visa accepted. Open March to December.

Who to contact: Phone (206)875-6344 or write to P.O. Box 315, Bay Center, WA 98527.

Location: Take the Bay Center exit off US 101 and drive one mile south to campground.

Trip note: This camp covers 11 acres and is on the shore of Willapa Bay. A trail from the campground leads to the beach.

Site **32**   **EVERGREEN COURT**
                          near Leadbetter Point State Park

Campsites, facilities: There are 16 tent sites and 18 sites for trailers or motor homes of any length. Electricity, piped water, sewer hookups, cable TV hookups and picnic tables are provided. Sanitary services, toilets, showers, firewood and a a playground are available. A store, a cafe and laundry can be found within one mile. Pets and motorbikes are permitted.

Reservations, fee: Reservations accepted; $6-9 fee per night; MasterCard and Visa accepted. Open all year.

Who to contact: Phone the park at (206)665-6351 or write to P.O. Box 488, Ocean Park, WA 98640.

Location: Drive seven miles south of Long Beach on Highway 103 to get to the park.

Trip note: This wooded campground covers five acres and has beach access. Nearby is Leadbetter Point State Park, a day-use park and natural area that adjoins a wildlife refuge. The trails at Leadbetter Point State Park lead through the dunes and woods and provide opportunities for seeing both marine birds and waterfowl, especially in the spring and fall. There is also a boat launch there. Additional facilities found within five miles of the campground include an 18-hole golf course and marked bike trails.

Site **33**   **OCEAN AIRE**
                         near Willapa Bay

Campsites, facilities: There are 40 drive-through sites for trailers or motor homes of any length. Electricity, piped water, sewer hookups and picnic tables are provided. Bottled gas, sanitary services, toilets, showers, laundry and ice are available. A store and a cafe can be found within one mile. Pets are permitted. Boat rentals are nearby on Willapa Bay.

Reservations, fee: Reservations accepted; $8 fee per night. Open all year.

Who to contact: Phone (206)665-4027 or write to P.O. Box 155, Ocean Park, WA 98640.

Location: Drive 12 miles north of Long Beach on Highway 103, then turn east on 259th Street, drive two blocks and you're there.

Trip note: This camp covers two acres and has access to the shoreline of Willapa Bay. Additional facilities found within five miles of the campground include tennis courts. About eight miles north of this campground is Leadbetter Point State Park which is open for day use and provides footpaths for walking through the state-designated natural area and wildlife refuge.

Site **34**   **OCEAN PARK RESORT**
                         on Willapa Bay

Campsites, facilities: There are six tent sites and 100 drive-through sites for trailers or motor homes of any length. Electricity, piped water, sewer hookups and picnic tables are provided. Bottled gas, toilets, a recreation hall, laundry, ice, a playground and a swimming pool are available. Showers are available for an extra fee. Firewood, a store and a cafe can be found within one mile. Pets and motorbikes are permitted. Boat docks and launching facilities are nearby on Willapa Bay.

Reservations, fee: Reservations accepted; $12.50 fee per night; MasterCard, Discover and Visa accepted. Open all year.

Who to contact: Phone the park at (206)665-4585 or write to P.O. Box 339, Ocean Park, WA 98640.

Location: Drive nine miles north of Long Beach on Highway 103. This resort is in Ocean Park.

Trip note: This wooded campground covers ten acres and has access to the shoreline of Willapa Bay. It's primarily for motor homes.

Site 35   WESTGATE MOTOR AND TRAILER COURT
near Long Beach

Campsites, facilities: There are 34 drive-through sites for trailers or motor homes of any length. Electricity, piped water and sewer hookups are provided. Bottled gas, toilets, showers, a recreation hall and ice are available. A store, a cafe and laundry can be found within one mile. Pets are permitted. Boat docks and launching facilities are nearby on Willapa Bay.

Reservations, fee: Reservations accepted; $10 fee per night; MasterCard and Visa accepted. Open all year.

Who to contact: Phone the park at (206)665-4211 or write to Route 1, Box 394, Ocean Park, WA 98640.

Location: Drive seven miles north of Long Beach on Highway 103. The park sits along the highway; you'll see it.

Trip note: This camp covers four acres and has beach access. Additional facilities found within five miles of the campground include an 18-hole golf course.

Site 36   PEGG'S OCEANSIDE TRAILER PARK
near Long Beach

Campsites, facilities: There are six tent sites and 30 sites for trailers or motor homes of any length. Electricity, piped water, sewer hookups and picnic tables are provided. Sanitary services, toilets, a recreation hall and ice are available. Showers are available for an extra fee. Bottled gas, a store, a cafe and laundry can be found within one mile. Pets and motorbikes are permitted.

Reservations, fee: Reservations accepted; $7 fee per night. Open mid-April to mid-September.

Who to contact: Phone (206)642-2451 or write to Route 1, Box 460, Long Beach, WA 98631.

Location: Drive four miles north of Long Beach on Highway 103 and you're there.

Trip note: This wooded campground covers three acres and has beach access. Additional facilities found within five miles of the campground include an 18-hole golf course.

Site 37   ANDERSEN'S TRAILER COURT AND MOTEL
near Long Beach

Campsites, facilities: There are 15 tent sites and 56 sites for trailers or motor homes of any length. Electricity, piped water, sewer hookups and picnic tables are provided. Sanitary services, toilets, showers, a recreation hall, laundry, ice and a playground are available. Bottled gas, a store and a cafe can be found within one mile. Pets are permitted.

Reservations, fee: Reservations accepted; $9-12 fee per night. Open year-round.

Who to contact: Phone (206)642-2231 or write to Route 1, Box 480, Long Beach, WA 98631.

Location: Drive 3.5 miles north of Long Beach on Highway 103 and you're there.

Trip note: This camp covers five acres and has beach access. Additional facilities found within five miles of the campground include an 18-hole golf course, a riding stable and tennis courts.

Site 38   CRANBERRY ADULT PARK
near Long Beach

Campsites, facilities: There are 24 drive-through sites for trailers or motor homes

of any length in this adult-only campground. Electricity, piped water, sewer hookups and picnic tables are provided. Sanitary services, toilets, showers and ice are available. Bottled gas, a store, a cafe and laundry can be found within one mile. Pets are permitted.

Reservations, fee: Reservations accepted; $9 fee per night. Open all year.

Who to contact: Phone (206)642-2027 or write to Route 1, Box 522B, Long Beach, WA 98631.

Location: Drive two miles north of Long Beach on Highway 103 and you're there.

Trip note: This park covers two acres, and has beach access. Additional facilities found within five miles of the campground include an 18-hole golf course, marked bike trails and a riding stable.

Site **39**   **PACIFIC PARK TRAILER PARK**
near Long Beach

Campsites, facilities: There are 53 sites for trailers or motor homes of any length. Electricity, piped water, sewer hookups and picnic tables are provided. Toilets, laundry and ice are available, and showers are available for an extra fee. Bottled gas, a store and a cafe can be found within one mile. Pets are permitted.

Reservations, fee: Reservations accepted; $7 fee per night. Open all year.

Who to contact: Phone (206)642-3253 or write to Route 1, Box 543, Long Beach, WA 98631.

Location: Drive two miles north of Long Beach on Highway 103 and you're there.

Trip note: This park covers two acres, and has beach access. Additional facilities found within five miles of the campground include an 18-hole golf course, marked bike trails and a riding stable.

Site **40**   **SAND-LO MOTEL AND RV PARK**
near Long Beach

Campsites, facilities: There are six sites for trailers or motor homes of any length. Electricity, piped water, cable TV hookups and sewer hookups are provided. Sanitary services, toilets, showers and laundry are available. Bottled gas, a store, a cafe and ice are available within one mile. Pets and motorbikes are permitted.

Reservations, fee: Reservations accepted; $9.50 fee per night; MasterCard and Visa accepted. Open all year.

Who to contact: Phone (206)642-2600 or write to P.O. Box 736, Long Beach, WA 98631.

Location: Drive one mile north of Long Beach on Highway 103 and you're there.

Trip note: This park covers three acres and has beach access. Additional facilities found within five miles of the campground include an 18-hole golf course, a full-service marina and a riding stable.

Site **41**   **DRIFTWOOD RV TRAV-L PARK**
near Long Beach

Campsites, facilities: There are 50 drive-through sites for trailers or motor homes of any length. Electricity, piped water, sewer hookups and picnic tables are provided. Toilets, showers, a recreation hall and ice are available. Bottled gas, a store, a cafe and laundry can be found within one mile. Pets are permitted.

Reservations, fee: Reservations accepted; $9 fee per night. Open March to November.

Who to contact: Phone (206)642-2711 or write to P.O. Box 296, Long Beach, WA

98631.

Location: Drive three-quarters of a mile north of Long Beach on Highway 103 and you're there.

Trip note: This park covers two acres and has beach access. Additional facilities found within five miles of the campground include an 18-hole golf course and a full-service marina.

Site 42   ANTHONY'S HOME COURT MOTEL PARK
in Long Beach

Campsites, facilities: There are 20 sites for trailers or motor homes. Electricity, piped water, sewer hookups and picnic tables are provided. Toilets, laundry, ice and a playground are available, and showers are available for an extra fee. Bottled gas, sanitary services, a store and a cafe are located within one mile. Pets are permitted.

Reservations, fee: Reservations accepted; $11 fee per night; MasterCard and Visa accepted. Open all year.

Who to contact: Phone (206)642-2802 or write to Route 1, Box 610, Long Beach, WA 98631.

Location: Drive one-half mile north of the downtown light in the town of Long Beach on Highway 103 and you're there.

Trip note: This park covers two acres and has beach access. Additional facilities found within five miles of the campground include an 18-hole golf course, marked bike trails and a riding stable.

Site 43   OCEANIC RV PARK
in Long Beach

Campsites, facilities: There are 20 drive-through sites for trailers or motor homes of any length. Electricity, piped water and sewer hookups are provided. Toilets and showers are available. Bottled gas, sanitary services, a store, a cafe, laundry and ice are located within one mile. Pets are permitted. Boat docks, launching facilities and rentals are nearby.

Reservations, fee: Reservations accepted; $11 fee per night; MasterCard and Visa accepted. Open all year.

Who to contact: Phone (206)642-3836 or write to Route 1, P.O. Box 169E, Long Beach, WA 98631.

Location: This park is in Long Beach at the south junction of Pacific Highway and 5th Avenue.

Trip note: This camp covers two acres and has beach access. Additional facilities found within five miles of the campground include an 18-hole golf course, marked bike trails and a full-service marina.

Site 44   WHITMAN'S RV PARK
in Long Beach

Campsites, facilities: There are ten tent sites and 29 drive-through sites for trailers or motor homes of any length. Electricity, piped water, sewer hookups and picnic tables are provided. Sanitary services, toilets, laundry and ice are available, and showers are obtained for an extra fee. Bottled gas, a store and a cafe can be found within one mile. Pets and motorbikes are permitted. Boat docks, launching facilities and rentals are nearby.

Reservations, fee: Reservations accepted; $8 fee per night. Open all year.

Who to contact: Phone (206)642-2174 or write to Route 1, Box 614, Long Beach,

WA 98631.

Location: This park is in Long Beach on Highway 103 at the north end of town.

Trip note: This park covers two acres and has beach access. Additional facilities found within five miles of the campground include an 18-hole golf course, marked bike trails, a full-service marina and a riding stable.

Site 45   SOUWESTER LODGE AND TRAILER PARK
in Long Beach

Campsites, facilities: There are ten tent sites and 60 drive-through sites for trailers or motor homes of any length. Electricity, piped water and sewer hookups are provided. Toilets, showers and laundry are available. Bottled gas, sanitary services, a store, a cafe and ice are located within one mile. Pets and motorbikes are permitted. Boat launching facilities are nearby.

Reservations, fee: Reservations accepted; $11-12 fee per night. Open all year.

Who to contact: Phone the park at (206)642-2542 or write to P.O. Box 102, Seaview, WA 98644.

Location: From the junction of US 101 and Highway 103 in Seaview, drive one block south on US 101, then one block west on 38th Place and you're there.

Trip note: One of the few sites in immediate area that provides spots for tent camping. It covers three acres and has beach access. Additional facilities found within five miles of the campground include an 18-hole golf course, a full-service marina and a riding stable.

Site 46   WILDWOOD RV PARK AND CAMPGROUND
near Fort Canby State Park

Campsites, facilities: There are 20 tent sites and 30 sites for trailers or motor homes of any length. Electricity, piped water, sewer hookups and picnic tables are provided. Sanitary services and toilets are available, and showers can be obtained for an extra fee. Bottled gas, firewood, a store, a cafe, laundry and ice are located within one mile. Pets and motorbikes are permitted.

Reservations, fee: Reservations accepted; $11 fee per night. Open mid-May to mid-September.

Who to contact: Phone the park at (206)642-2131 or write to Route 1, Box 76, Long Beach, WA 98631.

Location: From the junction of US 101 and Highway 103 in Seaview, drive one-half mile east on US 101, three-quarters of a mile north on Sand Ridge Road and you're there.

Trip note: This wooded park, for citizens of age 50 and over, covers five acres and has beach access. Additional facilities found within five miles of the campground include an 18-hole golf course, a full-service marina and tennis courts. See Site 47 for attractions at nearby Fort Canby State Park.

Site 47   THE BEACON-CHARTERS RV PARK
near Fort Canby State Park

Campsites, facilities: There are 39 drive-through sites for trailers or motor homes of any length. Electricity, piped water and sewer hookups are provided. Toilets and ice are available. Showers can be obtained for an extra fee. Bottled gas, a store, a cafe and laundry are located within one mile. Pets are permitted. Boat docks and launching facilities are nearby.

Reservations, fee: Reservations accepted; $9 fee per night. Open late May to mid-September.

Who to contact: Phone (206)642-2138 or write to P.O. Box 74, Ilwaco, WA 98624.

Location: Drive to Ilwaco. The park is on the corner of Howerton and Elizabeth.

Trip note: This park covers two acres and has beach and riverside access. Fort Canby State Park is nearby. It offers an interpretive center on maritime and military history, and numerous hiking trails. Additional facilities found within five miles of the campground include an 18-hole golf course.

Site 48   COVE RV AND TRAILER PARK
near Fort Canby State Park

Campsites, facilities: There are 25 sites for trailers or motor homes of any length. Electricity, piped water, sewer hookups and picnic tables are provided. Sanitary services, toilets and laundry are available. Showers can be obtained for an extra fee. Bottled gas, a store, a cafe and ice are located within one mile. Pets are permitted. Boat docks, launching facilities and rentals are nearby.

Reservations, fee: Reservations accepted; $12 fee per night. Open all year.

Who to contact: Phone (206)642-3689 or write to P.O. Box 38, Ilwaco, WA 98624.

Location: Drive to Ilwaco. Turn south on 2nd Street and drive four blocks to the park.

Trip note: This park covers five acres and has beach access. Additional facilities found within five miles of the campground include a maritime museum and hiking trails at nearby Fort Canby State Park, a full-service marina and a riding stable.

Site 49   KOA ILWACO
near Fort Canby State Park

Campsites, facilities: There are 50 tent sites and 120 drive-through sites for trailers or motor homes of any length. Picnic tables are provided. Bottled gas, sanitary services, toilets, showers, firewood, a recreation hall, a store, laundry, ice and a playground are available. Electricity, piped water and sewer hookups can be obtained for an extra fee. Pets are permitted.

Reservations, fee: Reservations accepted; $11 fee per night; MasterCard and Visa accepted. Open April to November.

Who to contact: Phone the park at (206)642-3292 or write to P.O. Box 549, Ilwaco, WA 98624.

Location: This campground is in Ilwaco at the junction of US 101 South and US 101 Alternate.

Trip note: This campground covers 17 acres and has ocean and river access. Additional facilities found within five miles of the campground include a maritime museum and hiking trails at nearby Fort Canby State Park, and an 18-hole golf course.

Site 50   MAUCH'S SUNDOWN RV PARK
near Fort Columbia State Park

Campsites, facilities: There are ten tent sites and 50 sites (some drive-through) for trailers or motor homes of any length. Electricity, piped water, sewer hookups and picnic tables are provided. Sanitary services, toilets, firewood, laundry and ice are available. Showers can be obtained for an extra fee. Bottled gas, a store and a cafe are located within one mile. Pets and motorbikes are permitted. Boat docks and launching facilities are nearby on the Columbia River.

Reservations, fee: Reservations accepted; $9 fee per night. Open all year.

Who to contact: Phone (206)777-8713 or write to P.O. Box 129, Chinook, WA

98614.

Location: This park is in Chinook near the Astoria Bridge, one-half mile west of town on US 101.

Trip note: Mauch's covers four acres and has riverside access. It is near Fort Columbia State Park which has a newly renovated interpretive center featuring the history of coastal artillery.

Site 51   RIVER'S END CAMPGROUND TENT
near Fort Columbia State Park

Campsites, facilities: There are 40 tent sites and 60 drive-through sites for trailers or motor homes of any length. Electricity, piped water, sewer hookups, cable TV, dump station and picnic tables are provided. Sanitary services, toilets, a recreation hall, laundry, ice and a playground are available. Showers and firewood can be obtained for an extra fee. Bottled gas, a store and a cafe are located within one mile. Pets and motorbikes are permitted. Boat docks, launching facilities and rentals are nearby on the Columbia River.

Reservations, fee: Reservations accepted; $8-10 fee per night. Open April to late October.

Who to contact: Phone (206)777-8317 or write to P.O. Box 66, Chinook, WA 98614.

Location: The campground is in Chinook at the north end of town on US 101.

Trip note: This wooded campground covers five acres and has riverside access. Additional facilities found within five miles of the campground include marked bike trails and a full-service marina. Also nearby is Fort Columbia State Park which has an interpretive center featuring the history of coastal artillery.

Site 52   FORT CANBY
on the Pacific Ocean

Campsites, facilities: There are 190 sites for tents, trailers or motor homes up to 45 feet long, 60 with full hookups. Picnic tables and fire grills are provided. Sanitary disposal station and toilets are available. Showers can be obtained for an extra fee. A store and restaurant are located within one mile. Pets are permitted. Boat launching facilities are nearby.

Reservations, fee: Reservations accepted; $7-$10.50 fee per night. Open all year.

Who to contact: Phone the state park at (206)642-3078 or write to P.O. Box 488, Ilwaco, WA 98624.

Location: From Ilwaco, drive two miles southwest on US 101 to the park.

Trip note: This is the choice spot of the area for tent campers. This park covers 1,881 acres and provides hiking trails and opportunities for surf, jetty and ocean fishing by boat. There is an interpretive center that highlights Lewis and Clark, maritime and military history.

Site 53   OLSENS
in Chinook

Campsites, facilities: There are 40 tent sites and 60 drive-through sites for trailers or motor homes. Electricity and piped water are provided. Sanitary services, toilets, a store and ice are available. Showers can be obtained for an extra fee. Bottled gas, a cafe and laundry are located within one mile. Pets are permitted. Boat docks, launching facilities and rentals are nearby on the Columbia River.

Reservations, fee: No reservations necessary; $8 fee per night. Open May to late October.

Who to contact: Phone (206)777-8475 or write to P.O. Box 44, Chinook, WA 98614.

Location: This park is in Chinook on US 101.

Trip note: This camp covers seven acres and has river access. Additional facilities found within five miles of the campground include a full-service marina.

Site 54
CHINOOK COUNTY PARK
on Columbia River

Campsites, facilities: There are 100 tent sites and 100 drive-through sites, some with water and electrical hookups, for trailers or motor homes of any length. Picnic tables and fire pits are provided. Piped water, toilets showers and a playground are available. Bottled gas, a store, a cafe and ice are located within one mile. Pets are permitted. Boat docks and launching facilities are nearby on the Columbia River.

Reservations, fee: Reservations accepted; $3-9 fee per night. Open May to mid-October.

Who to contact: Phone (206)777-8442 or write to P.O. Box 261, Chinook, WA 98614.

Location: The park is just east of Chinook on US 101.

Trip note: This campground covers 19 acres and has access to a small beach on the Columbia River. It is near Fort Columbia State Park.

Site 55
SKAMOKAWA VISTA PARK
near Columbia River

Campsites, facilities: There are four tent sites and 15 sites for trailers or motor homes of any length. Electricity and picnic tables are provided, but **no piped water** is available. Sanitary services, toilets, showers, firewood and a playground are available. Bottled gas, a store, a cafe and ice are located within one mile. Pets and motorbikes are permitted. Boat docks and launching facilities are nearby.

Reservations, fee: Reservations accepted; $7 fee per night. Open all year.

Who to contact: Phone the park at (206)795-8605 or write to 13 School Road, Skamokawa, WA 98647.

Location: In Skamokawa on Highway 4, turn one-quarter mile west on County School Road.

Trip note: This camp covers 30 acres and has access to the Columbia River. Additional facilities found within five miles of the campground include a full-service marina and tennis courts.

PUGET SOUND

♦

SOME HIGHLIGHTS

56 CAMPGROUNDS

Orcas Island

San Juan Island

Puget Sound

Hood Canal

Tahuya State Forest

Mount Constitution

Whidbey Island

San Juan National Historic Park

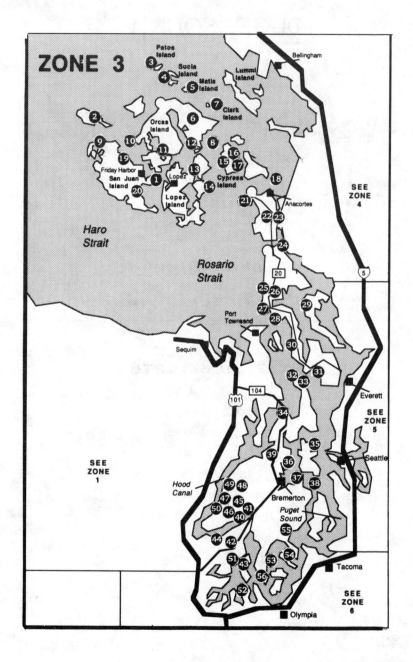

Site **1**   **TURN ISLAND STATE PARK**
near Friday Harbor, boat-in only

Campsites, facilities: There are ten primitive campsites. Picnic tables are provided and pit toilets are available. There is **no piped water.** Boat buoys are available for overnight moorage.

Reservations, fee: No reservations necessary; $3 fee per night. Open all year.

Who to contact: Phone (206)376-2326 or write to 6158 Lighthouse Road, Friday Harbor, WA 98250.

Location: This little island is just east of Friday Harbor and San Juan Island and is accessible only by boat.

Trip note: This is one of about 30 campgrounds we detail in Zone 3 that can be reached only by boat. Quiet, primitive and beautiful, this spot offers good hiking trails and year around rockfishing. No cars allowed, unless they float.

Site **2**   **STUART ISLAND MARINE STATE PARK**
near San Juan Island, boat-in only

Campsites, facilities: There are 19 primitive campsites. Picnic tables are provided and pit toilets are available. There is **no piped water.** Boat buoys and floats are available for overnight moorage.

Reservations, fee: No reservations necessary; $4-6 fee per night. Open May 1 through Labor Day.

Who to contact: Phone (206)378-2044 or write to 6158 Lighthouse Road, Friday Harbor, WA 98250.

Location: Stuart Island is located northwest of San Juan Island and is accessible only by boat.

Trip note: This is really stalking the unknown. It's a remote little island on the edge of Canadian waters that covers 153 acres and has good harbors for mooring. There is good fishing at nearby Reed and Provost Harbors.

Site **3**   **PATOS ISLAND STATE PARK**
near Sucia Island, boat-in only

Campsites, facilities: There are four primitive campsites. Pit toilets are available, but there is **no piped water.** Boat buoys are available for overnight moorage.

Reservations, fee: No reservations necessary; $3 fee per night. Open all year.

Who to contact: Phone (206)378-2044 or write to 6158 Lighthouse Road, Friday Harbor, WA 98250.

Location: Patos Island is four miles northwest of Sucia Island and is accessible only by boat.

Trip note: If you are going to get stranded on an island, this is not a bad choice, providing you like your companion. There are good hiking trails and excellent salmon and bottom fishing opportunities here.

Site **4**   **SUCIA ISLAND MARINE STATE PARK**
near Orcas Island, boat-in only

Campsites, facilities: There are 51 primitive campsites. Picnic tables are provided and vault toilets are available. There is **no piped water.** Boat buoys and floats are available for overnight moorage.

Reservations, fee: No reservations necessary; $4-6 fee per night. Open May 1 through Labor Day.

Who to contact: Phone (206)376-2044 or write to Star Route, Box 28, Eastsound,

WA 98245.

Location: Sucia Island is 2.5 miles north of Orcas Island and is accessible only by boat.

Trip note: A classic spot, with rocky outcrops for lookout points and good beach and fishing areas. This island covers 562 acres, and provides opportunities for hiking, clamming, crabbing, canoeing and scuba diving.

Site 5   MATIA ISLAND STATE PARK
near Orcas Island, boat-in only

Campsites, facilities: There are six primitive campsites. Pit toilets are available. There is **no piped water.** There is a boat dock, and buoys and floats are available for overnight moorage.

Reservations, fee: No reservations necessary; $4-6 fee per night. Open May 1 through Labor Day.

Who to contact: Phone (206)378-2044 or write to 6158 Lighthouse Road, Friday Harbor, WA 98250.

Location: Matia Island is 2.5 miles northeast of Orcas Island and is accessible only by boat.

Trip note: The campsites are located just a short walk from the docking facilities. Many of the other island campgrounds don't have docks. Good fishing and beachcombing are among the highlights.

Site 6   MORAN STATE PARK
on Orcas Island

Campsites, facilities: There are 135 campsites for tents or motor homes up to 45 feet long, but there are no hookups. Picnic tables and fire grills are provided. Flush toilets, showers and firewood are available. Some facilities are wheelchair accessible. Leashed pets are permitted. Boat docks, fishing supplies, launching facilities and boat rentals are located at the concession stand in the park.

Reservations, fee: Reservations accepted; $7.50 fee per night. Open all year.

Who to contact: Phone (206)378-2044 or write to 6158 Lighthouse Road, Friday Harbor, WA 98250.

Location: This park is on Orcas Island and is accessible by ferry from the town of Anacortes, which is five miles west of Burlington.

Trip note: This is a big park, 4,604 acres, that offers hiking trails and lake fishing. If you drive to the top of Mount Constitution, you will have a view of Vancouver, Mount Baker and the San Juan Islands. No motor homes are allowed on this winding road. Nearby recreation options include an 18-hole golf course.

Site 7   CLARK ISLAND STATE PARK
near Orcas Island, boat-in only

Campsites, facilities: There are eight primitive campsites. Pit toilets are available, but there is **no piped water.** Boat buoys are available for overnight moorage. Please pack out your garbage.

Reservations, fee: No reservations necessary; $3 fee per night. Open all year.

Who to contact: Phone (206)378-2044 or write to 6158 Lighthouse Road, Friday Harbor, WA 98250.

Location: These campsites are on Clark Island northeast of Orcas Island and are accessible only by boat.

Trip note: This island state park offers beautiful beaches with opportunities for scuba diving. There are excellent views of the other islands.

Site 8   DOE ISLAND STATE PARK
near Orcas Island, boat-in only

Campsites, facilities: There are five primitive campsites. Pit toilets are available, but there is **no piped water.** Boat floats are available for moorage.

Reservations, fee: No reservations necessary; $3 fee per night. Open all year.

Who to contact: Phone (206)378-2044 or write to 6158 Lighthouse Road, Friday Harbor, WA 98250.

Location: This small, secluded island is southeast of Orcas Island and accessible only by boat.

Trip note: This island has a rocky shoreline, which makes for an ideal fish habitat. Scuba diving and fishing are exceptional.

Site 9   POSEY ISLAND STATE PARK
near Roche Harbor, boat-in only

Campsites, facilities: There is one primitive campsite. **No piped water** is available.

Reservations, fee: No reservations necessary; $3 fee per night. Open all year.

Who to contact: Phone (206)378-2044 or write to 6158 Lighthouse Road, Friday Harbor, WA 98250.

Location: This little island is at the north end of Roche Harbor and is accesible only by small boat.

Trip note: If you want a beautiful little spot all to yourself, this is it, the smallest campground in Washington. It is difficult to get here, however. The best way is by kayak or canoe, a short paddle from San Juan Island.

Site 10   JONES ISLAND MARINE STATE PARK
near Orcas Island, boat-in only

Campsites, facilities: There are 21 primitive campsites. Picnic tables are provided and pit toilets are available. There is **no piped water.** Boat buoys and floats are available for overnight moorage.

Reservations, fee: No reservations necessary; $4-6 fee per night. Open May through Labor Day.

Who to contact: Phone (206)378-2044 or write to 6158 Lighthouse Road, Friday Harbor, WA 98250.

Location: This island is one mile off the southwest tip of Orcas Island and is accessible only by boat.

Trip note: This little island is another hidden spot that gets little use. The campground is near the beach, so you don't have to carry your gear very far. The area provides good fishing and scuba diving.

Site 11   BLIND ISLAND STATE PARK
near Shaw Island, boat-in only

Campsites, facilities: There are four primitive campsites. Pit toilets are available, but there is no **no piped water.** Boat buoys are available for overnight moorage.

Reservations, fee: No reservations necessary; $3 fee per night. Open all year.

Who to contact: Phone (206)378-2044 or write to 6158 Lighthouse Road, Friday Harbor, WA 98250.

Location: This island is north of Shaw Island and is accessible only by boat.

Trip note: This island has few trees and is known for its rocky shoreline. It is dangerous and ill-advised to try beaching cruiser-style boats. Bring a life raft to paddle ashore.

Site 12   OBSTRUCTION PASS MULTIPLE USE AREA
on Orcas Island, hike-in only

Campsites, facilities: There are nine primitive campsites. Picnic tables are provided and vault toilets are available. There is **no piped water.** Boat buoys are available for overnight moorage.

Reservations, fee: No reservations; no fee. Open all year.

Who to contact: Phone (800)527-3305 or write to Department of Natural Resources, 1065 South Capitol Way, Olympia, WA 98504.

Location: On Orcas Island, start at the town of Olga and go east on Doe Bay Road for one-half mile, then turn right on Obstruction Pass Road and go two-thirds of a mile. Keep right for one-third mile, then go straight for one mile to the parking area. Hike one-half mile to the campground.

Trip note: It takes a ferry boat ride, a tricky drive and then a short walk to reach this campground, but that helps set it apart from others—you'll find a unique, primitive spot set in a forested area near the shore of Orcas Island with good hiking.

Site 13   SPENCER SPIT STATE PARK
on Lopez Island

Campsites, facilities: There are 30 campsites here for tents or self-contained motor homes up to 28 feet long. Picnic tables and fire grills are provided. A sanitary disposal station and toilets are available. Boat docks are nearby. Leashed pets are permitted.

Reservations, fee: No reservations necessary; $6 fee per night. Open all year.

Who to contact: Phone (206)468-2251 or write to Route 2, Box 3600, Lopez, WA 98261.

Location: From Anacortes, take the ferry to the eastern shore of Lopez Island.

Trip note: One of the few island campgrounds accessible to cars via a ferry boat ride. A long sliver of sand extends far into the water and provides good access to prime clamming areas.

Site 14   JAMES ISLAND STATE PARK
near Decatur Island, boat-in only

Campsites, facilities: There are 13 primitive campsites that are accessible only by boat. Pit toilets are available, but there is **no piped water.** Boat floats and buoys are available for moorage off the east side of the island. A moorage dock on the west side of the island is open from May through Labor Day.

Reservations, fee: No reservations necessary; $4-$6 fee per night from May 1 through Labor Day. Open all year.

Who to contact: Phone (206)468-2251 or write to Route 2, Box 3600, Lopez, WA 98261.

Location: This island is east of Decatur Island on Rosario Strait and is only accessible by boat.

Trip note: This small, hidden island provides good opportunities for hiking, fishing and scuba diving. It's quiet and primitive.

Site 15 STRAWBERRY ISLAND MULTIPLE USE AREA
near Blakeley Island, boat-in only

Campsites, facilities: There are three primitive campsites. Picnic tables are provided and vault toilets are available. There is **no piped water.**

Reservations, fee: No reservations necessary; no fee. Open all year.

Who to contact: Phone (800)527-3305 or write to Department of Natural Resources, 1065 South Capitol Way, Olympia, WA 98504.

Location: This island is off the west coast of Blakeley Island and is accessible only by small boat.

Trip note: This campground is not used much because of strong currents and submerged rock make boat landing difficult. Boaters should anchor, then make shore using a raft or kayak.

Site 16 PELICAN BEACH MULTIPLE USE AREA
on Cypress Island, boat-in only

Campsites, facilities: There are four primitive campsites. Picnic tables and vault toilets are available. There is **no piped water** available. Buoys are available for overnight moorage.

Reservations, fee: No reservations necessary; no fee. Open all year.

Who to contact: Phone (800)527-3305 or write to Department of Natural Resources, 1065 South Capitol Way, Olympia, WA 98504.

Location: This camp is set on the east shore of Cypress Island and is accessible only by boat.

Trip note: This forested island campground offers a group shelter, beach access and hiking trails. The 1.2-mile trail to Eagle Cliff is a must.

Site 17 CYPRESS HEAD MULTIPLE USE AREA
on Cypress Island, boat-in only

Campsites, facilities: There are five primitive campsites. Picnic tables and vault toilets are available. There is **no piped water.** Boat buoys are available for overnight moorage. The float is for off-loading only.

Reservations, fee: No reservations necessary; no fee. Open all year.

Who to contact: Phone (800)527-3305 or write to Department of Natural Resources, 1065 South Capitol Way, Olympia, WA 98504.

Location: This camp is set on the east shore of Cypress Island and is accessible only by boat.

Trip note: This is an option to Site 16. The dock makes off-loading equipment a lot easier than most island campgrounds.

Site 18 SADDLEBAG ISLAND STATE PARK
near Guemes Island, boat-in only

Campsites, facilities: There are five primitive campsites. Pit toilets are available, but there is **no piped water.**

Reservations, fee: No reservations necessary; $3 fee per night. Open all year.

Who to contact: Phone (206)378-2044 or write to 6158 Lighthouse Road, Friday Harbor, WA 98250.

Location: This little island is north of Anacortes and east of Guemes Island. It is accessible only by boat.

Trip note: This is a good cruise from Anacortes. The island is quiet and primitive. There's a nice beach nearby for beachcombing and good crabbing in the bay.

Site **19**   **LAKEDALE CAMPGROUND**
              on San Juan Island

Campsites, facilities: There are 84 tent sites and 12 drive-through sites for trailers or motor homes up to 34 feet long. Electricity, piped water and picnic tables are provided. Toilets, a store and ice are available. Showers and firewood are available for an extra fee. Pets and motorbikes are permitted. Boat docks and boat rentals are nearby.

Reservations, fee: Reservations accepted; $13-15 fee per night; MasterCard and Visa accepted. Open April to late September.

Who to contact: Phone (206)378-2350 or write to 2627 Roche Harbor, Friday Harbor, WA 98250.

Location: Take the ferry from Anacortes to Friday Harbor on San Juan Island, then drive 4.5 miles north on Roche Harbor Road to the campground.

Trip note: This is a real nice spot for visitors who want the solitude of an island camp, yet all the amenities of a privately-run campground.

Site **20**   **GRIFFIN BAY MULTIPLE USE AREA**
              on San Juan Island, boat-in only

Campsites, facilities: There is one primitive campsite and three picnic sites. Piped water and picnic tables are provided, and pit toilets are available. Boat buoys are available for overnight moorage.

Reservations, fee: No reservations necessary; no fee. Open all year.

Who to contact: Phone (800)527-3305 (in Washington only) or (206)753-2400. Or write to Department of Natural Resources, 1065 South Capitol Way, Olympia, WA 98504.

Location: Griffin Bay is on San Juan Island south of Friday Harbor and is accessible only by boat.

Trip note: Hardly anybody knows about this spot, yet San Juan Island is one of the prettiest islands in the area. The camp is within a few miles of the San Juan National Historic Park, a day-use area. This camp has been recently rebuilt and reopened.

Site **21**   **SKYLINE RV PARK**
              near Anacortes

Campsites, facilities: There are 35 sites for trailers or motor homes of any length in this adult-only campground. Electricity, piped water and sewer hookups are provided. Sanitary services, toilets, showers and a laundromat are available. Bottled gas, a store, a cafe and ice are located within one mile. Pets are permitted. Boat docks, launching facilities and boat rentals are nearby.

Reservations, fee: No reservations necessary; $13 fee per night. Open all year.

Who to contact: Phone (206)293-4277 or write to 5809 Sands Way, Anacortes, WA 98221.

Location: This park is located just outside of Anacortes. To get there drive 4.2 miles west on Highway 20 (12th Street), then go one-half mile west on Sunset, and one-quarter mile south on Skyline Way.

Trip note: This is one of several options to Sites 22-24, which are located in the vicinity. Nearby recreation options include a full-service marina and tennis courts.

Site 22
FERN HILL CAMPGROUND
near Anacortes

Campsites, facilities: There are 35 tent sites and 77 drive-through sites for trailers or motor homes of any length. Electricity, piped water, sewer hookups and picnic tables are provided. Bottled gas, sanitary services, toilets, a recreation hall, a laundromat, ice and a playground are available. A store and a cafe are located within one mile. Showers and firewood can be obtained for an extra fee. Pets and motorbikes are permitted.

Reservations, fee: Reservations accepted; $10-15 fee per night; MasterCard and Visa accepted. Open all year.

Who to contact: Phone (206)293-5355 or write to 527 Miller Road, Anacortes, WA 98221.

Location: From Anacortes, drive west on Highway 20 to Deception Pass junction, then go three-quarters of a mile south to Miller Road, and west to 527 Miller Road.

Trip note: Nearby recreation options include an 18-hole golf course, a full-service marina and tennis courts.

Site 23
ANACORTES RV PARK
in Anacortes

Campsites, facilities: There are six tent sites and 40 sites for trailers or motor homes of any length. Electricity, piped water, sewer hookups and picnic tables are provided. Bottled gas, sanitary services, toilets, showers, a recreation hall, a laundromat and a playground are available. A store and a cafe are located within one mile. Firewood can be purchased. Pets and motorbikes are permitted.

Reservations, fee: Reservations accepted; $15 fee per night. Open all year.

Who to contact: Phone (206)293-3700 or write to 1255 Highway 20, Anacortes, WA 98221.

Location: From Mount Vernon or the junction of Interstate 5 and Highway 20, drive 18 miles west to Whidbey Island junction. The campground is one block south at 1255 Highway 20.

Trip note: This wooded park covers six acres and is set along the shoreline. Nearby recreation options include an 18-hole golf course, a full-service marina and tennis courts.

Site 24
HOPE ISLAND STATE PARK
in Skagit Bay, boat-in only

Campsites, facilities: There are five primitive campsites. **No piped water** is available.

Reservations, fee: No reservations necessary; $3 fee per night.

Who to contact: Phone (206)676-2417 or write to 5175 NSH 20, Oak Harbor, WA 98277.

Location: This little island is in Skagit Bay, two miles north of the entrance to Swinomish Bay. It is accessible only by boat.

Trip note: This site is a primitive alternative to the nearby and more developed Sites 21-23. The only catch is you must have a boat to reach it.

Site 25
WESTERN VILLAGE MOBILE ESTATES
in Oak Harbor

Campsites, facilities: There are 12 sites for trailers or motor homes of any length in this adult only campground. Electricity, piped water and sewer hookups are provided. Toilets, a recreation hall and a laundromat are available. Bottled gas, sanitary services, a store, a cafe and ice are located within one mile. Boat launching facilities are at nearby Oak Harbor.

Reservations, fee: No reservations necessary; $9 fee per night. Open all year.

Who to contact: Phone (206)675-1210 or write to 6451 60th Street NW, Oak Harbor, WA 98277.

Location: Take Highway 20 to the town of Oak Harbor. Turn northwest at 60th Street and drive one block to the park.

Trip note: This is a privately-developed RV park located in town. It provides beach access. Nearby recreation options include an 18-hole golf course, marked bike trails, a full-service marina and tennis courts.

Site 26   OAK HARBOR CITY BEACH PARK
in Oak Harbor

Campsites, facilities: There are 55 sites for trailers or motor homes of any length. Electricity, piped water and picnic tables are provided. Sanitary services, toilets and a playground are available. Bottled gas, a store, a cafe, a laundromat and ice are located within one mile. Showers can be obtained for an extra fee. Pets are permitted. Boat launching facilities are at nearby Oak Harbor.

Reservations, fee: No reservations necessary; $7 fee per night. Open mid-April to late October.

Who to contact: Phone (206)679-5551 or write to 3075-300 Avenue West, Oak Harbor, WA 98277.

Location: Take Highway 20 to the town of Oak Harbor. Turn south on Pioneer Way and drive one block to the park.

Trip note: This developed park offers no tent camping but has beach access. Nearby recreation options include an 18-hole golf course, a full-service marina and tennis courts.

Site 27   FORT EBEY STATE PARK
near Oak Harbor

Campsites, facilities: There are 50 campsites for tents or self-contained motor homes up to 50 feet long. Picnic tables and fire grills are provided. Sanitary disposal service, toilets and showers are available. Leashed pets are permitted.

Reservations, fee: No reservations necessary; $6 fee per night. Open mid-April to late September.

Who to contact: Phone (206)678-4636 or write to 395 North Fort Ebey Road, Coupeville, WA 98239.

Location: To get to the park, drive eight miles south of Oak Harbor on Highway 20.

Trip note: This park covers 228 acres and has access to a beach that is rocky and good for hiking. It is the site of an historic World War II bunker. There is also a freshwater lake.

Site 28   FORT CASEY STATE PARK
near Coupeville

Campsites, facilities: There are 35 campsites for tents or self-contained motor homes up to 40 feet long. Picnic tables and fire grills are provided and toilets are available. Showers and firewood can be obtained for an extra fee. Some facilities are wheelchair accessible. Pets are permitted. Boat launching facilities are located in the park.

Reservations, fee: No reservations necessary; $7 fee per night. Open all year.

Who to contact: Phone (206)678-4519 or write to 1280 Fort Casey, Coupeville, WA 98239.

Location: To get to the park drive three miles south of Coupeville on Highway 20.

Trip note: A good spot to set up a base camp for a fishing trip. There is good rockfishing year around, and good salmon and steelhead fishing in season. This park covers 137 acres and is the site of an historic U.S Defense Post.

Site 29   CAMANO ISLAND STATE PARK
near Stanwood

Campsites, facilities: There are 87 campsites for tents or self-enclosed motor homes up to 30 feet long, and two primitive campsites. Picnic tables and fire grills are provided. Sanitary disposal service, toilets and a playground are available. Showers and firewood can be obtained for an extra fee. Leashed pets are permitted. Boat launching facilities are located in the park.

Reservations, fee: No reservations necessary; $7 fee per night. Open all year.

Who to contact: Phone (206)387-3031 or write to 2269 South Park Road, Stanwood, WA 98292.

Location: Take Highway 532 off Interstate 5 at Stanwood and drive eight miles southwest to the park.

Trip note: The campsites are quiet and private in this wooded park. Good inshore rockfishing is available year-round and salmon fishing is also good in season. Clamming is excellent during low tides in winter and spring. There is a five mile self-guided nature trail.

Site 30   SOUTH WHIDBEY STATE PARK
on Whidbey Island

Campsites, facilities: There are 54 campsites for tents or self-contained motor homes up to 45 feet long, and six primitive campsites. Picnic tables and fire grills are provided. Sanitary disposal services and toilets are available. Showers and firewood can be obtained for an extra fee. Some facilities are wheelchair accessible. Pets are permitted.

Reservations, fee: No reservations necessary; $7 fee per night. Open all year.

Who to contact: Phone (206)321-4559 or write to 4128 Smugglers Cove Road, Freeland, WA 98429.

Location: This park is located on the west side of Whidbey Island. To get there drive 4.5 miles southwest of Highway 525.

Trip note: This wooded park covers 85 acres and provides opportunities for hiking, scuba diving, picnicking, beachcombing and clam digging along a sandy beach. There are spectacular views of Puget Sound and the Olympic Mountains.

Site 31   MUTINY BAY RESORT
on Whidbey Island

Campsites, facilities: There are 30 sites for trailers or motor homes up to 28 feet long. No tent sites. Electricity, piped water, sewer hookups and picnic tables are provided. Toilets, showers and ice are available. Bottled gas, a store, a cafe and a laundromat are within one mile. Boat docks and launching facilities are nearby.

Reservations, fee: Reservations accepted; $15-20 fee per night; MasterCard and Visa accepted. Open all year.

Who to contact: Phone (206)321-4500 or write to P.O. Box 249, Freeland, WA

98429.

Location: This park is located on the southwest side of Whidbey Island. To get there drive ten miles northwest of Clinton on Highway 525, then go one mile west on Fish Road to the resort.

Trip note: This privately-operated park provides an option to the nearby South Whidbey State Park.

Site 32   POINT NO POINT BEACH RESORT
in Hansville

Campsites, facilities: There are four tent sites and 38 drive-through sites for trailers or motor homes up to 32 feet long. Electricity, piped water, sewer hookups and picnic tables are provided. Bottled gas, toilets, showers, a cafe, a laundromat and ice are available. A store is located within one mile. Boat docks and boat rentals are nearby.

Reservations, fee: Reservations accepted; $8-13 fee per night. Open mid-May to mid-October.

Who to contact: Phone (206)638-2233 or write to 8708 NE Point No Point Road, Hansville, WA 98340.

Location: You can get to Hansville via Highway 16 or Highway 104, then go one-half mile east of Hansville on Point No Point Road.

Trip note: This is a summer resort with beach access.

Site 33   FORBES LANDING
on Bremerton Island

Campsites, facilities: There are 40 tent sites and 22 drive-through sites for trailers or motor homes of any length. Electricity, piped water, sewer hookups and picnic tables are provided. Bottled gas, sanitary services, toilets, showers, a store and ice are available. Pets are permitted. Boat docks, launching facilities and boat rentals are nearby.

Reservations, fee: Reservations accepted; $10 fee per night. Open all year.

Who to contact: Phone (206)638-2257 or write to P.O. Box 113, Hansville, WA 98340.

Location: This park is at the northern tip of Bremerton Island. You can get to Hansville via Highway 16 or Highway 104. The park is located in town.

Trip note: This campground provides an option to Site 32 for tent campers. Nearby recreation options include an 18-hole golf course and a full-service marina.

Site 34   KITSAP MEMORIAL STATE PARK
on Hood Canal

Campsites, facilities: There are 43 sites for tents or motor homes to 30 feet long. Picnic tables and fire grills are provided. Sanitary disposal service, toilets and a playground are available. Showers and firewood can be obtained for an extra fee. Leashed pets are permitted. Boat buoys are available. Some facilities are wheelchair accessible.

Reservations, fee: No reservations necessary; $7 fee per night. Open all year.

Who to contact: Phone (206)779-3205 or write to 202 NE Park Street, Poulsbo, WA 98370.

Location: Drive on Highway 3 to Poulsbo, and then go north past the Hood Canal Ferry Terminal to the park.

Trip note: This is a nice spot for tent campers along the Hood Canal. Nearby recreation options include an 18-hole golf course.

Site **35**   FAY-BAINBRIDGE STATE PARK
on Bainbridge Island

Campsites, facilities: There are 26 sites for trailers or motor homes up to 30 feet
long. Picnic tables and fire grills are provided. Sanitary disposal service, toilets
and a playground are available. A store and a cafe are located within one mile.
Piped water, showers and firewood can be obtained for an extra fee. Some
facilities are wheelchair accessible. Pets are permitted. Boat docks and
launching facilities are nearby.

Reservations, fee: No reservations necessary; $7.50 fee per night. Open all year.

Who to contact: Phone (206)842-3931 or write to 15546 Sunrise, Bainbridge Island,
WA 98110.

Location: Drive to Bainbridge Island via Highway 305. The park is located at the
southern tip of the island.

Trip note: Set on the edge of Puget Sound, this site provides beautiful night vistas
of Seattle.

Site **36**   ILLAHEE STATE PARK
near Bremerton

Campsites, facilities: There are 25 sites for tents for motor homes up to 30 feet long.
Picnic tables and fire grills are provided, and sanitary disposal service, toilets
and a a playground are available. Showers and firewood can be obtained for
an extra fee. A laundromat and ice are located within one mile. Some facilities
are wheelchair accessible. Leashed pets are permitted. Boat docks and
launching facilities are nearby.

Reservations, fee: No reservations necessary; $7 fee per night. Open all year.

Who to contact: Phone (206)478-6460 or write to 3540 Bahia Vista, Bremerton,
WA 98310.

Location: Drive three miles northeast of Bremerton on Highway 303, then take the
east turnoff to the park.

Trip note: This nice spot is just three miles from civilization in Bremerton, yet
unknown to out-of-towners touring the area.

Site **37**   MANCHESTER STATE PARK
in Puget Sound

Campsites, facilities: There are 50 sites for tents or motor homes up to 42 feet long
and three primitive tent sites. Picnic tables and fire grills are provided. Piped
water, sanitary disposal station and toilets are available. Showers and firewood
can be obtained for an extra fee. Some facilities are wheelchair accessible.
Leashed pets are permitted.

Reservations, fee: No reservations necessary; $7 fee per night. Open all year with
limited winter facilities.

Who to contact: Phone (206)871-4065 or write to P.O. Box 36, Manchester, WA
98353.

Location: Coming from Olympic Peninsula in the northwest, take Highway 3 to
Highway 16, then take the Highway 160-Port Orchard exit. Stay on Highway
160 and signs will direct you to the park. Coming from the Seattle area and
Interstate 5, take the Highway 16 exit to Bremerton, then take the Sedgwick
exit off Highway 16. Follow the signs that direct you to the park.

Trip note: Set on the edge of Point Orchard, this campground has good lookouts
across Puget Sound. There's good hiking in the park.

Site 38   BLAKE ISLAND STATE PARK (BOAT-IN)
near Seattle, boat-in only

Campsites, facilities: There are 30 tent sites. Picnic tables and fire grills are provided. Piped water, sanitary disposal station, toilets, showers, firewood and a unique restaurant (see the trip note) are available. Some facilities are wheelchair accessible. Leashed pets are permitted. Boat buoys and floats are available.

Reservations,fee: No reservations necessary; $6 fee per night. Open all year.

Who to contact: Phone (206)947-0905 or write to P.O. Box 287, Manchester, WA 98353.

Location: This little island is three miles west of Seattle and is accessible only by boat.

Trip note: Set right in the middle of the massive Seattle metropolitan area on a small island, this camp offers a combination of primitive settings and developed facilities. Tillicum Village offers unique northwest Indian dining.

Site 39   GREEN MOUNTAIN CAMP
TAHUYA STATE FOREST

Campsites, facilities: There are nine campsites for tents or small trailers. Picnic tables, fire grills and tent pads are provided. Pit toilets, piped water and facilities for horses are available.

Reservations, fee: No reservations necessary; no fee. Open all year.

Who to contact: Phone (800)527-3305 or write to Department of Natural Resources, 1065 South Capitol Way, Olympia, WA 98504.

Location: Start on Highway 3 south of Silverdale and go west on Newberry Hill Road for three miles, then turn left on Seabeck Highway and drive for two miles. Turn right on Holly Road and go four miles, then turn left on Tahuya Lake Road and drive one mile. Turn left again on Green Mountain Road (gravel) and drive 2.5 miles to the junction, then turn left and drive one mile to the campground.

Trip note: A prime spot, primitive yet with piped water provided, this campground is operated by the Department of Natural Resources and is located in Tahuya State Forest. There are facilities for horses here and trails for hiking and horseback riding.

Site 40   SNOOZE JUNCTION TRAILER PARK
near Belfair

Campsites, facilities: There are 38 drive-through sites for trailers or motor homes of any length. Electricity, piped water, sewer hookups and picnic tables are provided. Bottled gas, sanitary services, toilets, showers and a recreation hall are available. A store, a cafe, a laundromat and ice are located within one mile. Pets and motorbikes are permitted. Boat docks and launching facilities are nearby.

Reservations, fee: Reservations accepted; $11 fee per night. Open all year.

Who to contact: Phone (206)275-2381 or write to P.O. Box 880, Belfair, WA 98528.

Location: Drive to Belfair (eight miles southwest of Bremerton on Highway 3). From the junction of Highways 3 and 300, go one block northwest, then turn southwest and drive three miles and turn south on Gladwin Beach Road.

Trip note: This is a good holdover spot for motor home campers preparing to head north. Recreation options include an 18-hole golf course and marked bike trails.

Site 41
BELFAIR STATE PARK
on Hood Canal

Campsites, facilities: There are 147 tent sites and 47 sites for trailers or motor homes up to 36 feet long. Picnic tables and fire grills are provided. Sanitary disposal station, toilets and a playground are available. A store and a restaurant are located within one mile. Electricity, piped water, sewer hookups, showers and firewood can be obtained for an extra fee. Leashed pets are permitted.

Reservations, fee: Reservations accepted; $7.50-10.50 fee per night. Open all year.

Who to contact: Phone (206)478-4625 or write to NE 410 Beck Road, Belfair, WA 98528.

Location: Drive to Belfair (eight miles southwest of Bremerton on Highway 3) on Bremerton Island, and go west three miles on Highway 300. Then turn north on access road to the park.

Trip note: Tent campers will consider this a good alternative to Site 40. Set along edge of the Hood Canal.

Site 42
TWANOH STATE PARK
near Union

Campsites, facilities: There are 39 sites for trailers or motor homes up to 35 feet long. Picnic tables and fire grills are provided. Toilets, a store and a playground are available. Electricity, piped water, sewer hookups, showers and firewood can be obtained for an extra fee. Some facilities are wheelchair accessible. Leashed pets are permitted.

Reservations, fee: No reservations necessary; $7.50-9.50 fee per night. Open all year with limited winter facilities.

Who to contact: Phone (206)275-2222 or write to P.O. Box 2520, Belfair, WA 98528.

Location: Drive five miles east of the town of Union on Highway 106 to get to the park.

Trip note: If you are cruising US 101, this camp is only a short drive east off Highway 106. It is often bypassed by visitors touring Washington. It's a nice spot with option of visiting Mason Lake to the south or Hood Canal to the north.

Site 43
JARELLS'S COVE MARINA
near Shelton

Campsites, facilities: There are four tent sites and 16 drive-through sites for trailers or motor homes up to 27 feet long. Piped water and picnic tables are provided, and bottled gas, toilets, a store, a laundromat and ice are available. Electricity, showers and firewood are obtained for an extra fee. Pets are permitted. Boat docks and boat rentals are available.

Reservations, fee: Reservations accepted; $10-12 fee per night; MasterCard and Visa accepted. Open all year.

Who to contact: Phone (206)426-8823 or write to East 220 Wilson Road, Shelton, WA 98584.

Location: From the town of Shelton, drive eight miles north on Highway 3, then drive four miles east on Spencer Lake Road. Cross Hartstone Bridge and continue north on Island Drive, then turn west on Haskell Hill Road and drive one mile to the marina.

Trip note: Marina and boat rentals are the big bonus. The drive-through sites are ideal for pickup campers towing boats on trailers.

Site 44   ROBIN HOOD TRAILER VILLAGE
near Hood Canal

Campsites, facilities: There are ten tent sites and 16 sites for trailers or motor homes of any length. Electricity, piped water, sewer hookups and picnic tables are provided. Toilets, showers, a cafe and a laundromat are available. Bottled gas, sanitary services, a store and ice are available within one mile. Pets and motorbikes are permitted. Boat docks and launching facilities are nearby.

Reservations, fee: Reservations accepted; $10 fee per night; MasterCard and Visa accepted. Open all year.

Who to contact: Phone (206)898-2163 or write to East 6780 Highway 106, Union, WA 98592.

Location: Drive eight miles southwest of Bremerton to Belfair, then continue southwest on Highway 106 for 13 miles to East 6780 Highway 106.

Trip note: This wooded park, an option to Sites 45 and 46, has access to the Hood Canal. Nearby recreation options include an 18-hole golf course and a full-service marina.

Site 45   TOONERVILLE MULTIPLE USE AREA
TAHUYA STATE FOREST

Campsites, facilities: There are four campsites for tents or small trailers. Picnic tables, fire grills and tent pads are provided. Pit toilets are available, but there is **no piped water.** Motorbikes are permitted. Pets on leashes are permitted.

Reservations, fee: No reservations necessary; no fee. Open all year.

Who to contact: Phone (800)527-3305 or write to Department of Natural Resources, 1065 South Capitol Way, Olympia, WA 98504.

Location: Drive eight miles southwest of Bremerton on Highway 3 to the town of Belfair. From Belfair, take Highway 300 for one-third mile, then bear left and continue for another 3.3 miles. Turn right on Belfair-Tahuya Road and go one-half mile, then turn right on Elfendahl Pass Road for 2.5 miles (past the Tahuya four-wheel drive trailhead). Go straight through the intersection with Goat Ranch Road and drive 3.3 miles to the camp, which is on the left.

Trip note: Primitive and rustic, this wooded campground is managed by the Department of Natural Resources and has trails for use by hikers, horses and motorbikes.

Site 46   HOWELL LAKE
TAHUYA STATE FOREST

Campsites, facilities: There are six campsites for tents or small trailers. Picnic tables, fire grills and tent pads are provided. Pit toilets and piped water are available. A boat launch for small craft is located at Howell Lake. Motorbikes are permitted. Pets on leashes are also allowed.

Reservations, fee: No reservations necessary; no fee. Open all year.

Who to contact: Phone (800)527-3305 or write to Department of Natural Resources, 1065 South Capitol Way, Olympia, WA 98504.

Location: Drive eight miles southwest of Bremerton on Highway 3 to the town of Belfair. From Belfair, take Highway 300 for one-third mile and then follow it left for another 3.3 miles. Turn right on Belfair-Tahuya Road and go 4.5 miles.

Trip note: This pretty spot doesn't get a lot of use. The campground is managed by the Department of Natural Resources and set along Lake Howell. There are trails for use by hikers, horses, or motorbikes.

Site 47   TAHUYA RIVER HORSE CAMP
on Tahuya River
TAHUYA STATE FOREST

Campsites, facilities: There are nine primitive campsites for tents or small trailers. Picnic tables, fire grills and tent pads are provided. Pit toilets, piped water and equestrian facilities are available. Motorbikes are permitted. Pets on leashes are also permitted.

Reservations, fee: No reservations; no fee. Open all year.

Who to contact: Phone (800)527-3305 or write to Department of Natural Resources, 1065 South Capitol Way, Olympia, WA 98504.

Location: Drive eight miles southwest of Bremerton on Highway 3 to the town of Belfair. From Belfair, take Highway 300 for one-third mile and follow it left for 3.3 miles, then turn right on Belfair-Tahuya Road and go 1.7 miles. Turn right on Spillman Road for two miles, then turn left and drive three-quarters of a mile to the campground.

Trip note: This camp is set along the Tahuya River and is a good base camp for trips into the Tahuya State Forest. The trails can be used by hikers, horses or motorbikes.

Site 48   CAMP SPILLMAN MULTIPLE USE AREA
on Tahuya River
TAHUYA STATE FOREST

Campsites, facilities: There are six primitive campsites for tents or small trailers. Picnic tables, fire grills and tent pads are provided. Pit toilets and piped water are available. Motorbikes are permitted. Pets on leashes are also permitted.

Reservations, fee: No reservations necessary; no fee. Open all year.

Who to contact: Phone (800)527-3305 or write to Department of Natural Resources, 1065 South Capitol Way, Olympia, WA 98504.

Location: Drive eight miles southwest of Bremerton on Highway 3 to the town of Belfair. From Belfair, drive one-third mile on Highway 300, continue to follow it left for 3.3 miles, turn right on Belfair-Tahuya Road and go one-half mile, then turn right on Elfendahl Pass Road and drive 2.5 miles. At Twin Lakes Road turn left and drive two-thirds of a mile to the camp.

Trip note: This is one of four campgrounds (Sites 46-49) set in the immediate vicinity of the Tahuya State Forest. This one sits along the Tahuya River.

Site 49   TWIN LAKES MULTIPLE USE AREA
TAHUYA STATE FOREST

Campsites, facilities: There are six primitive campsites for tents or small trailers. Picnic tables, fire grills and tent pads are provided. Pit toilets are available, but there is **no piped water.** A hand launch for small boats is available at the lake. Pets on leashes are permitted.

Reservations, fee: No reservations necessary; no fee. Open all year.

Who to contact: Phone (800)527-3305 or write to Department of Natural Resources, 1065 South Capitol Way, Olympia, WA 98504.

Location: From Camp Spillman (see Site 48), continue west on Twin Lakes Road for one mile, then turn right and drive one-half mile to the camp.

Trip note: Little known, free and quiet, this wooded campground is in Tahuya State Forest and is managed by the Department of Natural Resources.

Site **50**
ALDRICH LAKE MULTIPLE USE AREA
on Lake Aldrich
TAHUYA STATE FOREST

Campsites, facilities: There are four primitive campsites for tents or small trailers. Picnic tables, fire grills and tent pads are provided. Pit toilets and piped water are available. A hand launch for small boats is located at the lake. Pets on leashes are permitted.

Reservations, fee: No reservations necessary; no fee. Open all year.

Who to contact: Phone (800)527-3305 or write to Department of Natural Resources, 1065 South Capitol Way, Olympia, WA 98504.

Location: From the town of Tahuya, drive north on Belfair-Tahuya Road for four miles, turn left on Dewatto Road and drive two miles, turn left again on Robbins Lake Road and drive one-half mile. Then turn right and drive two-thirds of a mile, turn right again and drive 200 yards to the campsites.

Trip note: This campground is on Aldrich Lake and is managed by the Department of Natural Resources. Robbins Lake is nearby and has day-use facilities and a hand launch for small boats. To reach Robbins Lake, follow the directions above--except that after turning left on Robbins Lake Road and driving one-half mile, you make another left and drive one mile to the lake.

Site **51**
JARRELL COVE STATE PARK
on Hartstene Island

Campsites, facilities: There are 20 sites for tents or motor homes up to 30 feet long. Picnic tables and fire grills are provided. Flush toilets are available. Showers can be obtained for an extra fee. Some facilities are wheelchair accessible. Leashed pets are permitted. Boat docks are available for overnight moorage for a fee.

Reservations, fee: No reservations necessary; $7 fee per night. Open all year.

Who to contact: Phone (206)426-9226 or write to East 391 Wingert Road, Shelton, WA 98584.

Location: From the town of Shelton, drive east on Highway 3 to Hartstene Island. The park is at the northwest end of the island.

Trip note: This wooded park is rarely crowded and offers a protected cove for boating and docking facilities. A private marina is nearby.

Site **52**
SQUAXIN ISLAND STATE PARK
on Squaxin Island, boat-in only

Campsites, facilities: There are 31 primitive campsites. Picnic tables are provided and pit toilets are available. There is **no piped water.** Leashed pets are permitted. Boat docks can be obtained for overnight moorage.

Reservations, fee: No reservations necessary; $4-6 fee per night. Open all year.

Who to contact: Phone (206)426-9226 or write to East 391 Wingert Road, Shelton, WA 98584.

Location: This camp is on Squaxin Island, which is north of the city of Olympia and accessible only by boat.

Trip note: Very few people know about this spot. It's a secluded island, yet not far from Olympia. This island covers 31 acres and has trails for hiking.

Site 53   PENROSE POINT STATE PARK
on Puget Sound

Campsites, facilities: There are 83 campsites for tents or self-contained motor homes up to 35 feet long. Picnic tables and fire grills are provided. A sanitary disposal station and toilets are available. Showers and firewood can be obtained for an extra fee. Some facilities are wheelchair accessible. Pets are permitted. Boat docks are nearby, available for overnight moorage for a fee.

Reservations, fee: No reservations necessary; $7 fee per night. Open all year.

Who to contact: Phone (206)884-2514 or write to 321-158th KPS, Lakebay, WA 98439.

Location: From Tacoma, drive ten miles north on Highway 16, then take Highway 302 and drive 17 miles to the park.

Trip note: This park overlooks Lake Bay in the Puget Sound near Tacoma. Because of the circle-like driving route it takes to get here, a lot of people bypass it.

Site 54   KOPACHUEK STATE PARK
on Puget Sound

Campsites, facilities: There are 41 campsites for tents or self-contained motor homes up to 35 feet long. Picnic tables and fire grills are provided. A sanitary disposal station and toilets are available. Showers and firewood can be obtained for an extra fee. Some facilities are wheelchair accessible. Leashed pets are permitted. Boat buoys are nearby.

Reservations, fee: No reservations necessary; $7 fee per night. Open all year.

Who to contact: Phone (206)265-3606 or write to 11101 56th Street NW, Gig Harbor, WA 98335.

Location: From Tacoma, drive seven miles north on Highway 16, then take turn-off west and drive five miles to park.

Trip note: This park overlooks Lake Bay in the Puget Sound, near Tacoma. It's a nice, developed park with full facilities for tent campers.

Site 55   KOA TACOMA-GIG HARBOR
near Tacoma

Campsites, facilities: There are 40 tent sites and 100 drive-through sites for trailers or motor homes of any length. Electricity, piped water, sewer hookups and picnic tables are provided. Bottled gas, sanitary services, toilets, showers, a recreation hall, a store, a cafe, a laundromat, ice, a playground and a swimming pool are available. Firewood can be obtained for an extra fee. Pets and motorbikes are permitted.

Reservations, fee: Reservations accepted; $16 fee per night; MasterCard and Visa accepted. Open all year.

Who to contact: Phone (206)858-8138 or write to 9515 Burnham, Gig Harbor, WA 98335.

Location: Take the Highway 16 exit off Interstate 5 in Tacoma and drive 12 miles northwest on Highway 16. There will be signs showing the way to the KOA.

Trip note: Nearby recreation options include an 18-hole golf course, a full-service marina and tennis courts.

Site 56   R.F. KENNEDY MULTIPLE USE AREA
on Puget Sound

Campsites, facilities: There are eight campsites for tents or small trailers. Picnic tables, fire grills and tent pads are provided. Pit toilets, piped water, boat launching facilities and a floating dock are available. Pets on leashes are permitted.

Reservations, fee: No reservations necessary; no fee. Open all year.

Who to contact: Phone (800)527-3305 or write to Department of Natural Resources, 1065 South Capitol Way, Olympia, WA 98504.

Location: Drive ten miles northwest of Tacoma via Highway 16, then go west for about 15 miles on Highway 302 to the town of Home. Start at the bridge in Home and follow Longbranch Road south for 1.3 miles, turn right on Whiteman Road and drive 2.3 miles, then turn right on Bay Road and drive one mile to the campsite.

Trip note: This beautiful yet free camp is set along the shore of the peninsula. Piped water makes it a sure winner.

NORTH CASCADES

♦

SOME HIGHLIGHTS

42 CAMPGROUNDS

Birch Bay

Mountain Baker-Snoqualmie National Forest

North Cascades National Park

Ross Lake National Recreation Area

Nooksack River

Baker Lake

Skagit River

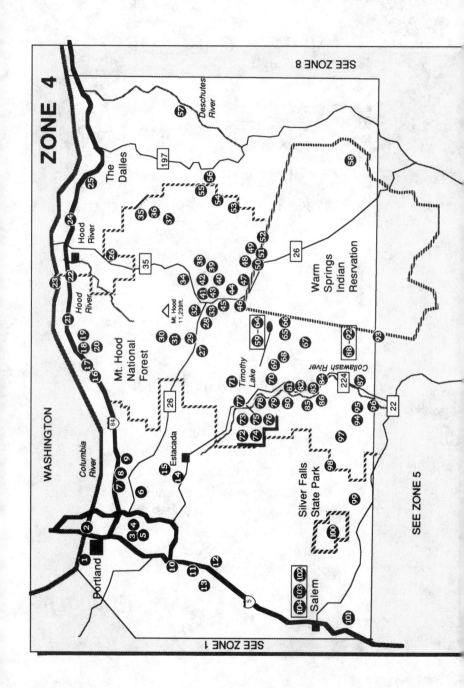

WHALEN'S RV PARK
Site **1**   on Point Roberts

Campsites, facilities: There are 100 tent sites and 65 sites for trailers or motor homes of any length. Electricity, piped water and picnic tables are provided. Flush toilets, bottled gas, sanitary services, firewood and showers are available. A store, a cafe, a laundromat and ice are located within one mile. Pets are permitted. Boat docks, launching facilities and rentals are nearby.

Reservations, fee: Reservations accepted; $11-13 fee per night. Open May to late October.

Who to contact: Phone (206)945-2874 or write to Box 985, Point Roberts, WA 98281.

Location: This campground is located on Point Roberts. To get there, go north on Highway 99N to the Lander exit, west on Highway 10 to Highway 17, south on Highway 17 to 56th Street, south on 56th Street to Roosevelt Way, then turn east and drive to the campground.

Trip note: This great spot, a mix of mountains and water, is very special to the few people who know about it. Nearby recreational options include an 18-hole golf course, a full-service marina and tennis courts.

BIRCH BAY STATE PARK
Site **2**   on Birch Bay

Campsites, facilities: There are 147 sites for tents and self-contained motor homes, some have electricity and water hookups. Picnic tables and fire grills are provided. Flush toilets, showers, firewood and sanitary disposal station are available. A store, restaurant, a laundromat and ice are located within one mile. Some facilities are wheelchair accessible. Leashed pets are permitted.

Reservations, fee: Reservations accepted; $7.50-10.50 fee per night. Open all year.

Who to contact: Phone (206)371-2800 or write to 5105 Helwig Road, Blaine, WA 98230.

Location: From Blaine, drive eight miles south on a paved road to the park. This is the easiest route. Other routes on county roads from Custer and Pleasant Valley are available.

Trip note: This park covers 193 acres and includes a mile-long beach. More than 300 different species of birds, many of which are migrating on the Pacific Flyway, can be seen here. An 18-hole golf course is available nearby.

BAYWOOD PARK
Site **3**   on Birch Bay

Campsites, facilities: There are 50 tent sites for trailers or motor homes of any length. Electricity, piped water and sewer hookups are provided. Flush toilets, sanitary services, showers, a recreation hall, a laundromat and a playground are available. Bottled gas, a store, a cafe and ice are located within one mile. Pets are permitted. Boat launching facilities are nearby.

Reservations, fee: Reservations accepted; $12 fee per night. Open all year.

Who to contact: Phone (206)371-7211 or write to 4672 Birch Bay-Lynden Road, Blaine, WA 98230.

Location: Take exit 270 off Interstate 5 south of Blaine, then drive three miles west on Birch Bay-Lynden Road to park.

Trip note: This camp provides opportunities for clamming and saltwater fishing. Nearby recreational options include an 18-hole golf course, a full-service marina and a riding stable.

BIRCH BAY TRAILER PARK

Site **4**

on Birch Bay

Campsites, facilities: There are 320 drive-through sites for trailers or motor homes of any length. Electricity, piped water, sewer hookups and picnic tables are provided. Flush toilets, bottled gas, sanitary services, showers, a recreation hall, satellite TV and a laundromat are available. A store, a cafe and ice are located within one mile. Pets and motorbikes are permitted. Boat launching facilities are nearby.

Reservations, fee: Reservations accepted; $17 fee per night; MasterCard and Visa accepted. Open all year.

Who to contact: Phone (206)371-7922 or write to 8080 Harbor View, Blaine, WA 98230.

Location: Take exit 270 off Interstate 5 south of Blaine and drive four miles west on Birch Bay-Lynden Road, then 300 feet south on Harbor View to the park.

Trip note: This private campground provides good ocean access on Birch Bay. Nearby recreational options include a full-service marina and tennis courts.

BORDER LINE RV PARK

Site **5**

on Birch Bay

Campsites, facilities: There are ten tent sites and 48 drive-through sites for trailers or motor homes of any length. Electricity, piped water, sewer hookups and picnic tables are provided. Flush toilets, bottled gas, sanitary services, showers, a cafe and ice are available. A store and a laundromat are located within one mile. Pets and motorbikes are permitted. Boat docks and launching facilities are nearby.

Reservations, fee: Reservations accepted; $17 fee per night; MasterCard and Visa accepted. Open April to October.

Who to contact: Phone (206)332-6909 or write to 1690 Peace Portal, Blaine, WA 98230.

Location: Take exit 274 off Interstate 5 south of Blaine, then drive 200 yards west on Peace Portal Way.

Trip note: This small, private camp is one of six in the immediate area. Nearby recreational options include an 18-hole golf course, marked bike trails and a full-service marina.

PLAZA PARK

Site **6**

on Birch Bay

Campsites, facilities: There are 100 tent sites and 49 drive-through sites for trailers or motor homes of any length. Electricity, piped water, sewer hookups and picnic tables are provided. Flush toilets, bottled gas, sanitary services, showers, firewood and a laundromat are available. A store, a cafe and ice are located within one mile. Pets and motorbikes are permitted.

Reservations, fee: Reservations accepted; $11 fee per night. Open all year.

Who to contact: Phone (206)371-7822 or write to 4414 Birch Bay, Blaine, WA 98230.

Location: Take exit 270 off Interstate 5 and drive two miles west on Lynden-Birch Bay Road to 4414 Birch Bay.

Trip note: This is an option to Sites 3-5 and 7, which are also located in vicinity.

RICHMOND RESORT
Site **7**
in Blaine

Campsites, facilities: There are 50 sites for trailers or motor homes up to 33 feet long. Electricity, piped water, sewer hookups and picnic tables are provided. Flush toilets, showers and a laundromat are available. Bottled gas, sanitary services, a store, a cafe and ice are located within one mile. Boat launching facilities are nearby.

Reservations, fee: Reservations accepted; $14 fee per night. Open April to early October.

Who to contact: Phone (206)371-2262 or write to 8086 Birch Bay, Blaine, WA 98230.

Location: Take exit 270 off Interstate 5 and drive two miles west on Lynden-Birch Bay Road. Go south one block on Harbor View, then northwest on Birch Bay Road to 4414 Birch Bay Road.

Trip note: This campground provides an option to Sites 3-6.

SUMAS RV PARK
Site **8**
in Sumas

Campsites, facilities: There are six tent sites and 35 drive-through sites for trailers or motor homes of any length. Electricity, piped water and picnic tables are provided. Flush toilets, sanitary services, showers, firewood and a ballpark are available. Bottled gas, a store, a cafe, a laundromat and ice are located within one mile. Pets and motorbikes are permitted.

Reservations, fee: Reservations accepted; $10-12 fee per night. Open all year.

Who to contact: Phone (206)988-8875 or write to 9600 Easterbrook, Sumas, WA 98295.

Location: The park is located in Sumas which is 25 miles northeast of Bellingham. To get there, drive to the junction of Highways 9 and 547, then go one-quarter mile south on Cherry Street. The campground is in the center of town.

Trip note: Set on edge of the United States-Canada border, this campground is a holdover spot to spend American dollars before heading into British Columbia. Nearby recreational options include an 18-hole golf course and tennis courts.

KOA LYNDEN
Site **9**

Campsites, facilities: There are 80 tent sites and 100 sites (20 drive-through) for trailers or motor homes of any length. Electricity, piped water, sewer hookups and picnic tables are provided. Flush toilets, bottled gas, sanitary services, showers, firewood, a recreation hall, store, a cafe, a laundromat, ice, a playground and a swimming pool are available. Pets are permitted. Boat rentals nearby.

Reservations, fee: Reservations accepted; $14-19 fee per night; MasterCard and Visa accepted. Open year-round

Who to contact: Phone (206)354-4772 or write to 8717 Line Road, Lynden, WA 98264.

Location: From Bellingham, drive 14 miles north on Highway 539, then go east for three miles on Highway 546.

Trip note: This campground is a holdover spot for vacationers heading north to Canada via Highways 539 and 546. Nearby recreational options include 18-hole golf course and tennis courts. It is set in a rural area with many small farms.

Site **10**
WINDMILL INN
near Nooksack River

Campsites, facilities: There are eight sites for trailers or motor homes of any length. Electricity, piped water, sewer hookups and picnic tables are provided. Flush toilets, showers, bottled gas, a store, a cafe, a laundromat and ice are available within one mile. Pets and motorbikes are permitted. Boat launching facilities are nearby.

Reservations, fee: Reservations accepted; $10 fee per night; MasterCard and Visa accepted. Open all year.

Who to contact: Phone (206)354-3424 or write to 8022 Guide Meridian Road, Lynden, WA 98264.

Location: From Bellingham, drive ten miles north on Highway 539.

Trip note: This nice little spot is set near the Nooksack River and Wiser Lake.

Site **11**
FERNDALE EVERGREEN MOBILE PARK
in Ferndale

Campsites, facilities: There are 16 sites for trailers or motor homes of any length in this adults-only campground. Electricity, piped water and sewer hookups are provided. Flush toilets, showers, bottled gas, a laundromat and a playground are available. A store and ice are located within one mile. Pets are permitted.

Reservations, fee: Reservations accepted; $10 fee per night. Open all year.

Who to contact: Phone (206)384-1241 or write to 6800 Enterprise, Ferndale, WA 98248.

Location: This park is located in Ferndale. To get there, take exit 266 off Interstate 5 and drive one-half mile east on Grandview, then one block south to the campground.

Trip note: An option to Sites 9 and 10, this campground provides more direct access from Interstate 5. A golf course and riding stable provide nearby options.

Site **12**
CANYON CREEK
near Canadian border
MOUNT BAKER-SNOQUALMIE NATIONAL FOREST

Campsites, facilities: There are eight primitive sites for tents or trailers up to 16 feet long. Picnic tables and fire grills are provided. Firewood and vault toilets are available. **No piped water** or toilets are available. Pets are permitted.

Reservations, fee: No reservations necessary; no fee. Call ahead for availability; usually open mid-May to mid-September.

Who to contact: Phone the Mount Baker-Snoqualmie National Forest at (206)856-5700 or (206)599-2714 or write to the Forest Service in Glacier, WA 98244.

Location: From Glacier, drive two miles northeast on Highway 542, then go north on Forest Service Road 31 for seven miles to the campground. A Forest Service map is essential.

Trip note: This campground and access road was washed out by storms and will take awhile to rebuild. It most likely will be out of commission for all of 1990. Call first. The campground is set on Canyon Creek about three miles from the Canadian border. When it's up, it's a secluded, little-known spot.

Site **13**
HANNEGAN
on Ruth Creek
MOUNT BAKER-SNOQUALMIE NATIONAL FOREST

Campsites, facilities: This is a primitive camping area with no designated campsites and no facilities (**no piped water**) provided. Pets are permitted.

Reservations, fee: No reservations necessary; no fee. Open mid-May to mid-September.

Who to contact: Phone the Mount Baker-Snoqualmie National Forest at (206)856-5700 or (206)599-2714 or write to the Forest Service in Glacier, WA 98244.

Location: From Glacier, drive 12.5 miles east on Highway 542, then turn east on Forest Service Road 32 and drive four miles to the campground. A Forest Service map is essential.

Trip note: This rustic spot is set on Ruth Creek on the border of the Mount Baker Wilderness and is at the trailhead that leads into the Mount Baker Wilderness across Hannegan Pass.

Site **14**
SILVER FIR
on the North Fork of Nooksack River
MOUNT BAKER-SNOQUALMIE NATIONAL FOREST

Campsites, facilities: There are 31 sites for tents, trailers or motor homes up to 31 feet long. Picnic tables are provided. Piped water, vault toilets, firewood, a community kitchen and group picnic area are available. Leashed pets are permitted.

Reservations, fee: No reservations necessary; $6 fee for the first night and $3 for each following night. Open May to October.

Who to contact: Phone the Mount Baker-Snoqualmie National Forest at (206)856-5700 or (206)599-2714 or write to the Forest Service in Glacier, WA 98244.

Location: From Glacier, drive 12.5 miles east on Highway 542 to the campground.

Trip note: This campground is set on the North Fork of the Nooksack River, just a short distance from the North Fork Nooksack Research Natural Area. You are strongly advised to obtain a Forest Service map in order take maximum advantage of the recreational opportunities in the area.

Site **15**
EXCELSIOR GROUP CAMP
near Nooksack River
MOUNT BAKER-SNOQUALMIE NATIONAL FOREST

Campsites, facilities: There are 13 tent sites. Picnic tables and fire grills are provided, but there is **no piped water.** Firewood is available. Pets are permitted.

Reservations, fee: Reservations required for all groups.

Who to contact: Phone the Mount Baker-Snoqualmie National Forest at (206)856-5700 or (206)599-2714 or write to the Forest Service in Glacier, WA 98244.

Location: From Glacier, drive 6.5 miles east on Highway 542 to the campground.

Trip note: This campground is set near the Nooksack River less than a mile from Nooksack Falls and 1.5 miles from the site of the Excelsior Mine. Remember to bring your own water.

DOUGLAS FIR

Site **16**

on Nooksack River

MOUNT BAKER-SNOQUALMIE NATIONAL FOREST

Campsites, facilities: There are 36 sites for tents, trailers or motor homes up to 31
feet long. Picnic tables and fire grills are provided. Piped water, vault toilets
and firewood are available. A store, a cafe, a laundromat and ice are located
within five miles. Pets are permitted.

Reservations, fee: No reservations necessary; $7 fee per night. Call ahead for
availability; usually open mid-May to mid-September.

Who to contact: Phone the Mount Baker-Snoqualmie National Forest at
(206)856-5700 or (206)599-2714 or write to the Forest Service at Glacier, WA
98244.

Location: From Glacier, drive two miles northeast on Highway 542 to the
campground.

Trip note: This camp may have residue storm damage, but is up again for the summer
of 1990. Set along the Nooksack River, it's an option to Sites 14-17.

LARRABEE STATE PARK

Site **17**

on Samish Bay

Campsites, facilities: There are 74 tent sites and 26 sites for trailers or motor homes
with full hookups. Picnic tables and fire grills are provided. Flush toilets,
sanitary disposal station, piped water, sewer hookups, showers and firewood
are available. Leashed pets are permitted. Boat launching facilities are available
nearby.

Reservations, fee: No reservations necessary; $7.50-9.50 fee per night. Open all
year.

Who to contact: Phone (206)676-2093 or write to 245 Chuckanut, Bellingham, WA
98225.

Location: From Bellingham, drive seven miles south on Chuckanut Drive (Highway
11) to the park.

Trip note: This 1,885-acre state park is on Samish Bay in Puget Sound. It offers
tide pools and eight miles of hiking trails, including two that go to small lakes.

BAY VIEW STATE PARK

Site **18**

on Padilla Bay

Campsites, facilities: There are 90 sites for tents or self-contained motor homes,
with full hookups available. Picnic tables are provided. Flush toilets, a
playground, a swimming pool, piped water, sewer hookups and showers are
available. A store and a laundromat are located within one mile. Leashed pets
are permitted.

Reservations, fee: No reservations necessary; $7.50-10.50 fee per night. Open all
year.

Who to contact: Phone (206)757-0227 or write to 1093 Bay View-Edison Road,
Brighton, WA 98233.

Location: From Burlington, drive five miles west on Highway 20, then turn north
and drive two miles to the park.

Trip note: This is a good family campground with a large play area for kids. It's set
on Padilla Bay.

Site **19**

RIVERBEND PARK
on Skagit River

Campsites, facilities: There are 25 tent sites and 95 drive-through sites for trailers or motor homes of any length. Electricity, piped water, sewer hookups and picnic tables are provided. Flush toilets, sanitary services, showers, a laundromat and a playground are available. Bottled gas, a store, a cafe, ice and a swimming pool are located within one mile. Pets are permitted.

Reservations, fee: Reservations accepted; $13 fee per night; MasterCard and Visa accepted. Open all year.

Who to contact: Phone (206)428-4044 or write to 305 Stewart, Mount Vernon, WA 98273.

Location: In Mount Vernon, take the College Way exit off Interstate 5 and drive one block west to Freeway Drive, then turn north and go one-half mile to the park.

Trip note: Access to the Skagit River here is a high point. Nearby recreational options include an 18-hole golf course, marked bike trails and tennis courts.

Site **20**

MOUNTAIN VIEW MOBILE HOME PARK
on Skagit River

Campsites, facilities: There are 14 sites for trailers or motor homes of any length in this adults-only campground. Electricity, piped water and sewer hookups are provided. Flush toilets, sanitary services and a laundromat are available. Bottled gas, a store, a cafe, showers and ice are located within one mile. Pets are permitted. Boat launching facilities are nearby.

Reservations, fee: No reservations necessary; $10 fee per night. Open all year.

Who to contact: Phone (206)424-3775 or write to 1685 Highway 99, Mount Vernon, WA 98273.

Location: In Mount Vernon, take exit 225 off Interstate 5 and drive one-quarter mile west, then turn north and drive one-quarter mile to 1685 Highway 99.

Trip note: This camp is an alternative to Site 19, both on Skagit River, not far off Interstate 5.

Site **21**

POTLATCH RV RESORT
near Skagit Bay

Campsites, facilities: There are 68 sites for trailers or motor homes of any length. Electricity, piped water, sewer hookups and picnic tables are provided. Flush toilets, showers, bottled gas, a club house, a cafe, a laundromat, ice, a large indoor swimming pool, spas, and cable TV are available. A store is located within one mile. Pets and motorbikes are permitted. Boat docks, launching facilities and rentals are nearby on Skagit Bay.

Reservations, fee: Reservations accepted; $14-18.50 fee per night; MasterCard and Visa accepted. Open all year.

Who to contact: Phone (206)466-4468 or write to P.O. Box 344, LaConner, WA 98257.

Location: This resort is near LaConner. From the junction of Interstate 5 and Highway 20, take exit 230. Drive west on Highway 20, then go south on LaConner-Whitney Road, then north on 3rd Street.

Trip note: This park has access to the shore of Skagit Bay. Nearby recreation options include an 18-hole golf course, marked bike trails and a full-service marina.

Site **22**
HORSESHOE COVE
on Baker Lake
MOUNT BAKER-SNOQUALMIE NATIONAL FOREST

Campsites, facilities: There are 34 sites for tents, trailers or motor homes up to 21 feet long. Picnic tables are provided. Piped water, flush toilets, sanitary disposal station and firewood are available. Leashed pets are permitted. Boat launching facilities are located nearby on Baker Lake.

Reservations, fee: No reservations necessary; $7 fee per night. Open May to October.

Who to contact: Phone the Mount Baker-Snoqualmie National Forest at (206)856-5700 or write to Mount Baker Ranger District, 2105 Highway 20, Sedro Woolley, WA 98284.

Location: From Concrete, drive 9.5 miles north on County Road 25, then 2.5 miles north on Forest Service Road 11. Take Forest Service Road 1118 east for two miles to the campground. A Forest Service map is essential.

Trip note: This campground is set on the shore of 5,000-acre Baker Lake, a good fishing lake for rainbow trout, kokanee salmon, cutthroat trout, Dolly Varden trout and whitefish.

Site **23**
BOULDER CREEK
near Baker Lake
MOUNT BAKER-SNOQUALMIE NATIONAL FOREST

Campsites, facilities: There are ten sites for tents or trailers up to 15 feet long. Picnic tables and fire grills are provided. Firewood and pit toilets are available, but there is **no piped water.** A store, a cafe and ice are located within five miles. Pets are permitted. Boat docks and launching facilities are nearby on Baker Lake.

Reservations, fee: No reservations necessary; no fee. Call ahead for availability; usually open mid-May to mid-September.

Who to contact: Phone the Mount Baker-Snoqualmie National Forest at (206)856-5700 or write to Mount Baker Ranger District, 2105 Highway 20, Sedro Woolley, WA 98284.

Location: From Concrete, drive 9.5 miles north on County Road 25, then head north for 5.5 miles on Forest Service Road 11. Campground is on the right.

Trip note: The campground is an alternative to Site 22, set on Boulder Creek about one mile from the shore of Baker Lake. A boat launch is located at Panorama Point. In season, wild berries are available in the area.

Site **24**
MAPLE GROVE
on Baker Lake, walk-in or boat-in only
MOUNT BAKER-SNOQUALMIE NATIONAL FOREST

Campsites, facilities: There are five primitive tent sites which are only accessible by boat or on foot. Picnic tables are provided. Firewood is available, but there is **no piped water.** Pets are permitted. Boat launching facilities are located nearby on Baker Lake.

Reservations, fee: No reservations necessary; no fee. Open mid-May to mid-September.

Who to contact: Phone the Mount Baker-Snoqualmie National Forest at (206)856-5700 or write to Mount Baker Ranger District, 2105 Highway 20, Sedro Woolley, WA 98284.

Location: From Concrete, drive 9.5 miles north on County Road 25, then turn north on Forest Service Road 11 and drive 2.5 miles. Turn east on Forest Service Road 1118 and go two miles, then park your car, launch your boat and go one mile northeast across Lake Baker to the campground. A Forest Service map is essential.

Trip note: You want a quiet spot on the edge of a lake? Okay, here it is. This rustic campground is on the shore of Baker Lake and is hike-in or boat-in only.

Site **25**
PANORAMA POINT
on Baker Lake
MOUNT BAKER-SNOQUALMIE NATIONAL FOREST

Campsites, facilities: There are 16 sites for tents, trailers or motor homes up to 21 feet long. Picnic tables are provided. Piped water, flush toilets and firewood are available. A store, a cafe and ice are located within one mile. Pets are permitted. Boat docks, launching facilities and rentals are nearby on Baker Lake.

Reservations, fee: No reservations necessary; $5 fee per night. Open May to October.

Who to contact: Phone the Mount Baker-Snoqualmie National Forest at (206)856-5700 or write to Mount Baker Ranger District, 2105 Highway 20, Sedro Woolley, WA 98284.

Location: From Concrete, drive 9.5 miles north on County Road 25, then drive 6.5 miles north on Forest Service Road 11 to the campground.

Trip note: This well-maintained campground is on the shore of Baker Lake. The reservoir is one of the better fishing lakes in the area.

Site **26**
PARK CREEK
near Baker Lake
MOUNT BAKER-SNOQUALMIE NATIONAL FOREST

Campsites, facilities: There are 12 sites for tents or trailers up to 15 feet long. Picnic tables are provided. Firewood and pit toilets are available, but there is **no piped water.** A store and a cafe are located within one mile. Pets are permitted. Boat docks, launching facilities and rentals are nearby on Lake Baker.

Reservations, fee: No reservations necessary; no fee. Open mid-May to mid-September.

Who to contact: Phone the Mount Baker-Snoqualmie National Forest at (206)856-5700 or write to Mount Baker Ranger District, 2105 Highway 20, Sedro Woolley, WA 98284.

Location: From Concrete, drive 9.5 miles north on County Road 25, then 7.5 miles north on Forest Service Road 11. Take Forest Service Road 1144 about 200 yards northwest and you're there. A Forest Service map is essential.

Trip note: This campground is set on Park Creek a short distance from the north shore of Baker Lake.

Site **27**
KOA GRADY CREEK
near Baker Lake

Campsites, facilities: There are 30 tent sites and 40 drive-through sites for trailers or motor homes of any length. Picnic tables are provided. Flush toilets, sanitary services, showers, a recreation hall, a store, a laundromat, ice, a playground, electricity, piped water, sewer hookups, firewood and a swimming pool are available. Bottled gas and a cafe are located within one mile. Pets and motorbikes are permitted.

Reservations, fee: Reservations accepted; $10 fee per night; MasterCard and Visa accepted. Open mid-April to late October.

Who to contact: Phone (206)826-3554 or write to 736 Russell, Concrete, WA 98237.

Location: From Concrete, drive six miles west on Highway 20, then turn north on Russell Road and go one-quarter mile to the campground.

Trip note: This wooded campground is a good base for trips to Skagit River and Baker Lake. There are numerous hiking trails nearby.

Site **28**
CREEKSIDE RV PARK
near Skagit River

Campsites, facilities: There are 25 sites for tents, trailers or motor homes of any length. Electricity, piped water, sewer hookups and picnic tables are provided. Flush toilets, sanitary services, a store, a laundromat, ice, a playground and showers are available. A store and a cafe are located within one mile. Pets and motorbikes are permitted.

Reservations, fee: Reservations accepted; $10 fee per night. Open all year.

Who to contact: Phone (206)826-3566 or write to 761 Baker Lake Road, Concrete, WA 98237.

Location: From north of Mount Vernon and south of Bellingham on Interstate 5, take exit 232 (Cooke Road). Turn left at the junction of Highway 20 and Cooke Road and follow it for 17 miles. Turn left on Baker Lake Road and drive one-half mile to the camp.

Trip note: This wooded campground is centrally located to nearby recreational opportunities at Baker Lake and the Skagit River.

Site **29**
HUTCHISON CREEK
near South Fork in Nooksack River

Campsites, facilities: There are 11 sites for tents or small trailers. Picnic tables, fire grills and tent pads are provided. Vault toilets and firewood are available, but there is **no piped water.** A store is located within one mile. Leashed pets are permitted.

Reservations, fee: No reservations necessary; no fee. Open all year.

Who to contact: Phone the Department of Natural Resources at (800)527-3305 or write to Department of Natural Resources AW-11, 1065 South Capitol Way, Olympia, WA 98504.

Location: Start on Highway 9 at Acme, just north of the Nooksack River Bridge, go east for 2.5 miles on Mosquito Lake Road, then turn right on a gravel road, continue one-half mile to the campground.

Trip note: This campground is set in the forest along Hutchinson Creek near the South Fork of the Nooksack River. Managed by the Department of Natural Resources, it's rustic, beautiful, primitive and unknown to out-of-towners.

Site **30**
HOWARD MILLER STEELHEAD
on Skagit River

Campsites, facilities: There are 40 tent sites and 20 sites for trailers or motor homes of any length. Electricity, piped water and picnic tables are provided. Flush toilets, sanitary services, showers and a playground are available. Bottled gas, a store, a cafe and ice are located within one mile. Pets and motorbikes are permitted. Boat launching facilities are nearby on Skagit River.

Reservations, fee: No reservations necessary; $8 fee per night. Open all year.

Who to contact: Phone (206)853-8808 or write to P.O. Box 97, Rockport, WA 98283.

Location: This city park is located in Rockport. Drive to the junction of Highway 20 and Rockport-Darrington Road, then turn south and drive to the camp.

Trip note: This city park has access to the Skagit River, which has been designated a wild and scenic river. There is good steelhead fishing in season.

Site **31**
ROCKPORT STATE PARK
near Skagit River

Campsites, facilities: There are 11 tent sites and 50 sites for trailers or motor homes. Picnic tables and fire grills are provided. Flush toilets, sanitary disposal station, electricity, piped water, sewer hookups, showers and firewood are available. Facilities are wheelchair accessible. A store, restaurant, and ice are located within one mile. Leashed pets are permitted.

Reservations, fee: No reservations necessary; $7.50-10.50 fee per night. Open April to late October.

Who to contact: Phone (206)853-8461 or write to Route 1, Box 296, Concrete, WA 98237.

Location: Rockport is 40 miles east of Mount Vernon. This state park is located one mile west of Rockport on Highway 20.

Trip note: This state park covers 457 acres and offers five miles of hiking trails, some of which are wheelchair accessible. The campground is set among old-growth Douglas firs, and is near the Skagit River, a good steelhead stream.

Site **32**
WILDERNESS VILLAGE AND RV PARK
near Skagit River

Campsites, facilities: There are 20 tent sites and 32 drive-through sites for trailers or motor homes of any length. Electricity, piped water, sewer hookups and picnic tables are provided. Flush toilets, sanitary services, showers, a recreation hall and a laundromat are available. A cafe and ice are located within one mile. Pets are permitted.

Reservations, fee: Reservations accepted; $6-12 fee per night. Open all year.

Who to contact: Phone (206)873-2571 or write to 5550 Highway 20, Rockport, WA 98283.

Location: From Rockport, drive five miles east on Highway 20. The park is past mile post 102.

Trip note: This park is near the Skagit River. Rockport State Park and hiking trails are nearby.

Site **33**
ALPINE RV PARK AND CAMPGROUND
near Skagit River

Campsites, facilities: There are 15 tent sites and 30 drive-through sites for trailers or motor homes of any length. Electricity, piped water, sewer hookups and picnic tables are provided. Flush toilets, firewood, a laundromat, showers and a playground are available. Bottled gas, a store, a cafe and ice are located within one mile. Pets and motorbikes are permitted.

Reservations, fee: Reservations accepted; $8 fee per night; MasterCard and Visa accepted. Open all year.

Who to contact: Phone (206)873-4142 or write to P.O. Box 148, Marblemount, WA 98267.

Location: Drive east of Rockport on Highway 20 to Marblemount, then go 1.5 miles past town and you'll see the campground.

Trip note: This campground has access to the Skagit River. A trail from the nearby National Park Service Ranger Station ascends to Helen Buttes.

Site **34**
CASCADE ISLANDS
on Cascade River

Campsites, facilities: There are 15 sites for tents or small motor homes. Picnic tables, fire grills and tent pads are provided. Vault toilets, piped water and firewood are available. A store, a cafe and ice are located within one mile. Leashed pets are permitted.

Reservations, fee: No reservations necessary; no fee. Open all year.

Who to contact: Phone the Department of Natural Resources at (800)527-3305 or write to Department of Natural Resources AW-11, 1065 South Capitol Way, Olympia, WA 98504.

Location: Start on Highway 20 in Marblemount. Go east for two-thirds of a mile on Old Cascade Road, then turn right on Rockport Cascade Road, go 200 yards and turn left on South Cascade Road. Drive 1.2 miles to the campground.

Trip note: This Department of Natural Resources campground is set on the shore of the Cascade River about two miles upstream from its confluence with the Skagit River. The price is right and so is the streamside setting.

Site **35**
MARBLE CREEK
on Marble Creek
MOUNT BAKER-SNOQUALMIE NATIONAL FOREST

Campsites, facilities: There are 24 sites for tents, trailers or motor homes up to 31 feet long. Picnic tables and fire grills are provided. Pit toilets and firewood are available, but there is **no piped water.** Pets are permitted.

Reservations, fee: No reservations necessary; no fee. Open mid-May to mid-September.

Who to contact: Phone the Mount Baker-Snoqualmie National Forest at (206)856-5700 or write to Mount Baker Ranger District, 2105 Highway 20, Sedro Woolley, WA 98284.

Location: From Marblemount, drive east for eight miles on County Road 3528, then turn south on Forest Service Road 1530 and drive one mile to the campground. A Forest Service map is essential.

Trip note: This rustic campground is set on Marble Creek. Continuing on Forest Service Road 1530 will take you up to Bush Lake. A trailhead to Hidden Lake just inside the boundary of North Cascades National Park can be found about five miles from camp at the end of Forest Service Road 1540. See a Forest Service map for details.

Site **36**
MINERAL PARK
on Cascade River
MOUNT BAKER-SNOQUALMIE NATIONAL FOREST

Campsites, facilities: There are four undesignated, dispersed primitive sites for trailers up to 15 feet long. Firewood is available, but there is **no piped water.** Pets are permitted.

Reservations, fee: No reservation necessary; no fee. Call ahead for availability; usually open mid-May to mid-September.

Who to contact: Phone the Mount Baker-Snoqualmie National Forest at (206)856-5700 or write to Mount Baker Ranger District, 2105 Highway 20, Sedro Woolley, WA 98284.

Location: From Marblemount, drive east on County Road 3528 for 15 miles and you'll find the campground.

Trip note: Here's another classic unknown camping area that can provide a jump-off for many adventures. This rustic site is set on the Cascade River and is near numerous trails leading into Glacier Peak Wilderness. This camp was closed because of storm damage and has since reopened. It wouldn't hurt to call ahead.

Site 37 WILLIAM C. DEARINGER
on Sauk River

Campsites, facilities: There are 12 sites for tents or small trailers. Picnic tables, fire grills and tent pads are provided. Vault toilets and firewood are available, but there is **no piped water.** Leashed pets are permitted.

Reservations, fee: No reservations necessary; no fee. Open all year.

Who to contact: Phone the Department of Natural Resources at (800)527-3305 or write to Department of Natural Resources AW-11, 1065 South Capitol Way, Olympia, WA 98504.

Location: Start on Highway 530 and drive one-third mile north of Darrington, then go east on Mountain Loop Road for one-half mile. Continue straight for five miles, then turn left and drive two-thirds of a mile on East Sauk Prairie Road. Stay right on Road SWD 5000 and go 2.6 miles, then bear right for one mile. Turn left on Road SWD 5400 and drive about 400 yards to the campground.

Trip note: This wooded campground is on the Sauk River and is managed by the Department of Natural Resources. It may be a little difficult to get there, but that's why you'll probably be the only one there.

Site 38 COLONIAL CREEK CAMPGROUND
on Diablo Lake
ROSS LAKE NATIONAL RECREATION AREA

Campsites, facilities: There are 164 campsites for tents or motor homes up to 22 feet long. Picnic tables and fireplaces are provided. Flush toilets, piped water, a sanitary dump station and a boat ramp are available. Some facilities are wheelchair accessible. Leashed pets are permitted.

Reservations, fee: No reservations; $5 fee per night. Open from mid-April to mid-October.

Who to contact: Phone the Skagit District of the North Cascades National Park at (206)873-4590 or write to them in Marblemount, WA 98267.

Location: Drive 25 miles east of Marblemount on Highway 20 and you'll see the campground entrance.

Trip note: This campground is located at 1,200 feet elevation along the shore of Diablo Lake in the Ross Lake National Recreation Area. The lake is about five, six miles long and offers numerous hiking and fishing possibilities. A naturalist program is available in summer months.

Site 39 NEWHALEM CREEK CAMPGROUND
on Skagit River
NORTH CASCADES NATIONAL PARK

Campsites, facilities: There are 129 campsites for tents or motor homes. Picnic tables and fireplaces are provided. Flush toilets, piped water and a sanitary dump station are available. Some facilities are wheelchair accessible. Leashed pets are permitted.

Reservations, fee: No reservations; $5 fee per night. Open from mid-June to Labor Day.

Who to contact: Phone the Skagit District of the North Cascades National Park at

(206)873-4590 or write to them in Marblemount, WA 98267.

Location: Drive 15 miles northeast of Marblemount on Highway 20 and you'll see the entrance to the campground.

Trip note: One of the newer camps set in the Ross Lake Recreation Area, this spot is set along the Skagit River below Newhalem. There are good hiking possibilities in the immediate area.

Site **40**   **GOODELL CREEK CAMPGROUND**
on Goodell Creek and Skagit River
ROSS LAKE NATIONAL RECREATION AREA

Campsites, facilities: There are 22 campsites for tents or motor homes up to 22 feet long. Picnic tables and fireplaces are provided. Pit toilets, piped water, a sanitary dump station and group sites are available.

Reservations, fee: No reservations; $3 fee per night.

Who to contact: Phone the Skagit District of the North Cascades National Park at (206)873-4590 or write to them in Marblemount, WA 98267.

Location: Drive 14 miles east of Marblemount on Highway 20 to this side of Newhalem and you'll see the campground entrance.

Trip note: This campground is an alternative to the nearby and larger Site 39. This one is set where Goodell Creek pours into the Skagit River in the Ross Lake National Recreation Area. It's a popular place for raft trips down river.

Site **41**   **HOZOMEEN**
on Ross Lake
ROSS LAKE NATIONAL RECREATION AREA

Campsites, facilities: There are 122 campsites for tents or motor homes up to 22 feet long. Picnic tables and fireplaces are provided. Pit toilets, piped water, a sanitary dump station and a boat launch on Ross Lake are available.

Reservations, fee: No reservations; no fee. Open from mid-May to late November.

Who to contact: Phone the Skagit District of the North Cascades National Park at (206)873-4590 or write to them in Marblemount, WA 98267.

Location: Drive 40 miles south of Hope (British Columbia) on Silver Skagit Road and you'll find the campground at the north end of Ross Lake. Much of it is a rough dirt road.

Trip note: This camp is set just inside the border at the United States-Canada line on the north shore of Ross Lake. Note that access is best from the north, leaving from Hope. It takes an effort to get here. To some, it is worth it.

Site **42**   **GORGE LAKE**
on Gorge Lake
ROSS LAKE NATIONAL RECREATION AREA

Campsites, facilities: There are six sites for tents or motor homes of any length. Picnic tables and fire grills are provided. Vault toilets, a boat launch are available. **No piped water** is available. Leashed pets are permitted.

Reservations, fee: No reservations; no fee. Open from mid-April to mid-October.

Who to contact: Phone the Skagit District of the North Cascades National Park at (206)873-4590 or write to them in Marblemount, WA 98267.

Location: Drive 21 miles east of Marblemount. Turn left (north) on the road to Diablo and drive less than one mile to the campground entrance.

Trip note: This small campground is set along the shore of Gorge Lake. There is a series of dams nearby along the Skagit River.

MOUNT BAKER

♦

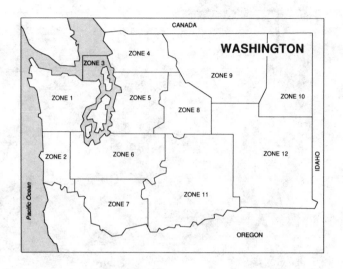

SOME HIGHLIGHTS

45 CAMPGROUNDS

Mount Baker

Lake Goodwin

Mount Baker-Snoqualmie National Forest

Stillaquamish River

Seattle

Snoqualmie River

Lake Sammamish State Park

Alpine Lakes Wilderness

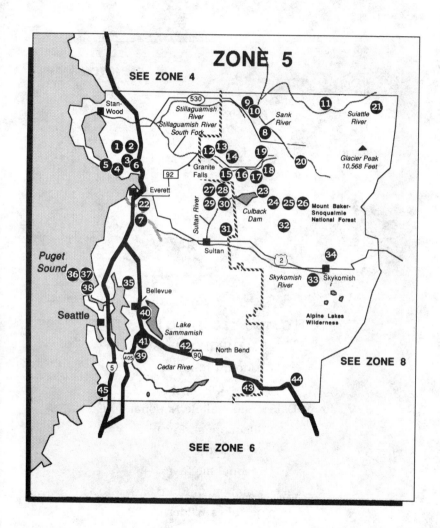

ZONE 5

SEE ZONE 4

530
Stillaguamish
River
Stillaguamish River
South Fork

Stan-
Wood

Sank
River

Suiattle
River

Glacier Peak
10,568 Feet

92

Granite
Falls

Everett

Sultan River

Culback
Dam

Mount Baker-
Snoqualmie
National Forest

Sultan

2

Skykomish
River

Skykomish

Puget
Sound

Alpine Lakes
Wilderness

Bellevue

Seattle

Lake
Sammamish

North Bend

90

SEE ZONE 8

405

Cedar River

5

0

SEE ZONE 6

Site 1
WENBERG STATE PARK
on Lake Goodwin

Campsites, facilities: There are 65 sites for tents or self-contained motor homes, some with water and electrical hookups. Picnic tables are provided and a sanitary disposal station, flush toilets, piped water, a store, a cafe and a playground are available. Showers are available for an extra fee. Leashed pets are permitted. Boat launching facilities and rentals are located on Lake Goodwin.

Reservations, fee: No reservations necessary; $7.50-10.50 fee per night. Open all year.

Who to contact: Phone (206)652-7417 or write to 15430 East Lake Goodwin Road, Stanwood, WA 98292.

Location: Drive 13 miles north of Everett on Interstate 5 to exit 206 (Smokey Point), then head west for five miles to the park.

Trip note: This state park is set along the shore of Lake Goodwin, where the trout fishing can be great. Power boats are allowed and there is a concession stand that provides food and fishing supplies. Lifeguards are on duty in the summer. There is a large day-use area and hiking trails nearby.

Site 2
LAKE GOODWIN RESORT
on Lake Goodwin

Campsites, facilities: There are 20 tent sites and 85 drive-through sites for trailers or motor homes of any length. Electricity, piped water, sewer hookups and picnic tables are provided. Flush toilets, bottled gas, sanitary services, a recreation hall, a store, a cafe, a laundromat, ice, a playground, showers and firewood are available. Boat docks, launching facilities and rentals are nearby on Lake Goodwin.

Reservations, fee: Reservations accepted; $16 fee per night; American Express, MasterCard and Visa accepted. Open all year.

Who to contact: Phone (206)652-8169 or write to 4726 176th NW, Stanwood, WA 98292.

Location: From Everett, drive 13 miles north on Interstate 5 to exit 206 (Smokey Point), then drive west for five miles and you'll see the park.

Trip note: This private campground is set on Lake Goodwin, a lake known for good trout fishing. Motorboats are permitted on the lake and there is an 18-hole golf course nearby.

Site 3
CEDAR GROVE RESORT
on Lake Goodwin

Campsites, facilities: There are ten tent sites and 44 sites for trailers or motor homes. Electricity, piped water, sewer hookups and picnic tables are provided. Flush toilets, showers, a playground and firewood are available. Bottled gas, sanitary services, a store, a cafe, a laundromat and ice are located within one mile. Boat docks, launching facilities and rentals are nearby on Lake Goodwin.

Reservations, fee: Reservations accepted; $12 fee per night. Open all year.

Who to contact: Phone (206)652-7083 or write to 16529 52nd Avenue NW, Stanwood, WA 98292.

Location: From Everett, drive 13 miles north on Interstate 5, then take exit 206 (Smokey Point) and drive five miles west to 52nd Avenue NW, then turn south and go one-half mile to park.

Trip note: This wooded resort is set on the shore of Lake Goodwin near Wenberg State Park. Trout fishing and swimming are the highlights. Nearby recreation options include an 18-hole golf course.

Site 4   JIM MARION'S LAKE MARTHA RESORT
near Lake Goodwin

Campsites, facilities: There are seven tent sites and 24 drive-through sites for trailers or motor homes of any length. Electricity, piped water, sewer hookups and picnic tables are provided. Flush toilets, sanitary services, showers and a laundromat are available. A store and ice are located within one mile. Boat docks and launching facilities are nearby on Lake Martha.

Reservations, fee: Reservations accepted; $12 fee per night. Open all year.

Who to contact: Phone (206)652-8412 or write to 8105 Lakewood Road, Stanwood, WA 98292.

Location: From Everett, drive 13 miles north on Interstate 5 to exit 206 (Smokey Point), then go seven miles west and bear left at fork in the road. Lake Martha is one-half mile away.

Trip note: Camping here is an option to the nearby and slightly larger Lake Goodwin. It's a good summer spot for fishing and swimming. Nearby recreation options include an 18-hole golf course.

Site 5   KAYAK POINT COUNTY PARK
on Puget Sound

Campsites, facilities: There are nine tent sites and 23 drive-through sites for trailers or motor homes up to 25 feet long. Piped water and picnic tables are provided. Flush toilets, firewood and a playground are available. Pets are permitted. Boat docks and launching facilities are nearby on Puget Sound.

Reservations, fee: No reservations necessary; $7 fee per night. Open May to late September.

Who to contact: Phone (206)339-1208 or write to P.O. Box 310, Monroe, WA 98272.

Location: From Everett, drive north on Interstate 5, then take exit 199 (Tulalip) at Marysville. The road winds for 14 miles through the Tulalip Indian Reservation, then you'll see the park entrance on your left.

Trip note: This large, wooded county park is set on the shore of Puget Sound. Nearby recreation options include an 18-hole golf course.

Site 6   SMOKEY POINT RV PARK
near Lake Goodwin

Campsites, facilities: There are 115 sites (50 drive-through) for trailers or motor homes of any length. Piped water and picnic tables are provided. Flush toilets, sanitary services, showers, a recreation hall, a laundromat, a playground, electricity and sewer hookups are available. Bottled gas, firewood, a store, a cafe and ice are located within one mile. Pets are permitted.

Reservations, fee: Reservations accepted; $13.50-18 fee per night; MasterCard and Visa accepted. Open all year.

Who to contact: Phone (206)652-7300 or write to 2910 172nd Street, Arlington, WA 98223.

Location: From Everett, drive 13 miles north on Interstate 5 to exit 206 (Smokey Point). Go west for one-tenth mile on 172nd Street and you'll see the park on the south side.

Trip note: This is an ideal stopover for motor home cruisers heading up Interstate 5 and looking for a place to spend the night. It is located just off the freeway and is only five miles from the state park and resorts on Lake Goodwin. Nearby recreation options include marked bike trails.

Site **7**   ### SILVER SHORES RV PARK
on Silver Lake

Campsites, facilities: There are ten tent sites and 83 sites for trailers or motor homes. Electricity, piped water and picnic tables are provided. Flush toilets, sanitary services, showers and a laundromat are available. Firewood, a store, a cafe and ice are located within one mile.

Reservations, fee: Reservations accepted; $11-18 fee per night. Open all year.

Who to contact: Phone (206)337-8741 or write to 11621 West Silver Lake Road, Everett, WA 98208.

Location: From Everett, take exit 186 off Interstate 5, and head east. You will see signs showing you the way to the park.

Trip note: This is a good option to Site 6 for travelers heading up Interstate 5. This wooded park is set along the shores of Silver Lake, a quiet lake with an eight-mph speed limit, good trout fishing and swimming opportunities. It is centrally located, close to shopping and Seattle. There are tennis courts nearby.

Site **8**   ### CLEAR CREEK
on Clear Creek and Sauk River
MOUNT BAKER-SNOQUALMIE NATIONAL FOREST

Campsites, facilities: There are ten sites for tents, trailers or motor homes up to 21 feet long. Picnic tables and fire grills are provided. Vault toilets and firewood are available. There is **no piped water.** A store, a cafe, a laundromat and ice are located within two miles. Pets are permitted.

Reservations, fee: No reservations necessary; no fee. Open late May to early September.

Who to contact: Phone the Mount Baker-Snoqualmie National Forest at (206)436-1155 or write to Darrington Ranger District, 1405 Emmens Street, Darrington, WA 98241.

Location: From Darrington, drive 2.5 miles south on Highway 20, and you'll see the campground entrance.

Trip note: This nice, secluded spot does not get heavy use. This campground is set at the confluence of Clear Creek and the Sauk River, a designated wild and scenic river. A trail from camp leads about one mile up to Frog Lake.

Site **9**   ### SQUIRE CREEK COUNTY PARK
on Squire Creek

Campsites, facilities: There are 30 drive-through sites for trailers or motor homes up to 25 feet long. Piped water, sewer hookups and picnic tables are provided. Flush toilets, sanitary services and firewood are available. Pets are permitted. A store is located nearby in Darrington.

Reservations, fee: No reservations necessary; $5 fee per night. Open mid-May to mid-September.

Who to contact: Phone (206)339-1208 or write to P.O. Box 310, Monroe, WA 98272.

Location: From Darrington, drive three miles west on Highway 530 and you'll see the park.

Trip note: This wooded park is set along Squire Creek about three miles from the boundaries of the Boulder River Wilderness. A low-cost motor home park set near the outback.

Site 10   CASCADE KAMLOOP TROUT PARK
in Darrington

Campsites, facilities: There are eight tent sites and 24 sites for trailers or motor homes of any length. Electricity, piped water, sewer hookups and picnic tables are provided. Flush toilets, sanitary services, showers, firewood and a recreation hall are available. Bottled gas, a store, a cafe, a laundromat and ice are located within one mile. Motorbikes are permitted.

Reservations, fee: Reservations accepted; $5-9 fee per night; American Express, MasterCard and Visa accepted. Open all year.

Who to contact: Phone (206)436-1003 or write to P.O. Box 353, Darrington, WA 98241.

Location: This campground is in Darrington. Take exit 208 off Interstate 5, then drive 31 miles east on Highway 530 and follow the camping and fishing signs to the campground.

Trip note: This campground offers a little bit of both worlds—a rustic quietness with all facilities available. A bonus is a nearby trout pond, which is stocked in season. No boats are allowed. Nearby recreation options include marked hiking trails and tennis courts.

Site 11   BUCK CREEK
near Suiattle River
MOUNT BAKER-SNOQUALMIE NATIONAL FOREST

Campsites, facilities: There are 25 tent sites and one site for a trailer or motor home up to 21 feet long. Picnic tables are provided. Pit and vault toilets, and firewood are available, but **no piped water** is available. Pets are permitted.

Reservations, fee: No reservations necessary; $3 fee per night. Open late May to early September.

Who to contact: Phone the Mount Baker-Snoqualmie National Forest at (206)436-1155 or write to Darrington Ranger District, 1405 Emmens Street, Darrington, WA 98241.

Location: From Darrington, drive 7.5 miles north on Highway 530, then turn southeast on Forest Service Road 26 and drive 15.2 miles to the campground. A Forest Service map is essential.

Trip note: This primitive campground is set along Buck Creek near its confluence with the Suiattle River in the Glacier Peak Wilderness. It's quiet and remote.

Site 12   TURLO
on the South Fork of Stillaguamish River
MOUNT BAKER-SNOQUALMIE NATIONAL FOREST

Campsites, facilities: There are 19 sites for tents or motor homes up to 31 feet long. Picnic tables are provided. Pit or vault toilets, piped water and firewood are available. A store, a cafe and ice are located one mile away in Robe. Pets are permitted.

Reservations, fee: No reservations necessary; $6 fee per night. Open mid-May to late September.

Who to contact: Phone the Mount Baker-Snoqualmie National Forest at (206)436-1155 or write to Darrington Ranger Station, 1405 Emmens Street,

Darrington, WA 98241.

Location: From the town of Granite Falls, go 10.6 miles east on Highway 92 and you'll see the campground entrance.

Trip note: This campground is set along the South Fork of the Stillaguamish River, the most westerly of six Sites, 12-18, located on this stretch of Highway 92. A Forest Service Public Information Center is nearby.

Site 13
VERLOT
on the South Fork of Stillaguamish River
MOUNT BAKER-SNOQUALMIE NATIONAL FOREST

Campsites, facilities: There are 26 sites for tents, trailers or motor homes up to 31 feet long. Picnic tables are provided. Flush toilets, firewood and piped water are available. A store, a cafe and ice are located within one mile. Pets are permitted.

Reservations, fee: No reservations necessary; $6 fee per night. Open mid-May to late September.

Who to contact: Phone the Mount Baker-Snoqualmie National Forest at (206)436-1155 or write to Darrington Ranger District, 1405 Emmens Street, Darrington, WA 98241.

Location: From the town of Granite Falls, go 11 miles east on Highway 92 and you'll see the campground entrance.

Trip note: This campground is set along the South Fork of the Stillaguamish River, a short distance from the Lake Twenty-Two Research Natural Area and the Maid of the Woods Trail. A Forest Service map details back roads and hiking trails.

Site 14
GOLD BASIN
on the South Fork of Stillaguamish River
MOUNT BAKER-SNOQUALMIE NATIONAL FOREST

Campsites, facilities: There are 93 tent sites and 83 sites for trailers or motor homes up to 31 feet long. Picnic tables are provided. Vault toilets, piped water and firewood are available. A store, a cafe and ice are located nearby. Some facilities are wheelchair accessible. Pets are permitted.

Reservations, fee: No reservations necessary $6 fee per night. Open mid-May to early September.

Who to contact: Phone the Mount Baker-Snoqualmie National Forest at (206)436-1155 or write to Darrington Ranger District, 1405 Emmens Street, Darrington, WA 98241.

Location: From the town of Granite Falls, go 13.5 miles east on Highway 92 and you'll see the campground entrance.

Trip note: One of the larger parks in the vicinity. With all facilities available this site is preferable for most motor home campers. Set along the South Fork of the Stillaguamish River.

Site 15
ESSWINE
MOUNT BAKER-SNOQUALMIE NATIONAL FOREST

Campsites, facilities: There are six tent sites and one site for trailers or motor homes of any length. Picnic tables are provided. Pit or vault toilets and firewood are available, but there is **no piped water**. A store, a cafe and ice are located within one mile. Pets are permitted.

Reservations, fee: No reservations necessary; $3 fee per night. Open mid-May to early September.

Who to contact: Phone the Mount Baker-Snoqualmie National Forest at (206)436-1155 or write to Darrington Ranger District, 1405 Emmens Street, Darrington, WA 98241.

Location: From the town of Granite Falls, go 16 miles east on Highway 92 and you'll see the campground entrance.

Trip note: Only three miles from Site 14, but a very small, quiet and secluded camp. The lack of piped water is the only drawback.

Site 16   BOARDMAN CREEK
on the South Fork of Stillaguamish River
MOUNT BAKER-SNOQUALMIE NATIONAL FOREST

Campsites, facilities: This a specially-designated group campground. Picnic tables are provided. Pit or vault toilets and firewood are available, but there is no piped water. Pets are permitted.

Reservations, fee: Reservations necessary; $25 fee per night. Open mid-May to early September.

Who to contact: Phone the Mount Baker-Snoqualmie National Forest at (206)436-1155 or write to Darrington Ranger District, 1405 Emmens Street, Darrington, WA 98241.

Location: From the town of Granite Falls, go 16.5 miles east on Highway 92 and you'll see the campground entrance.

Trip note: Nearby Forest Service Roads will take you to several backcountry lakes, including Boardman Lake, Lake Evan, Clear Lake and Ashland Lakes. Get a Forest Service map, set up your camp and go for it.

Site 17   RED BRIDGE
on the South Fork of Stillaguamish River
MOUNT BAKER-SNOQUALMIE NATIONAL FOREST

Campsites, facilities: There are 16 tent sites and 14 sites for trailers or motor homes up to 31 feet long. Picnic tables are provided. Pit or vault toilets are available, but there is **no piped water.** Pets are permitted.

Reservations, fee: No reservations necessary; no fee. Open late May to early September.

Who to contact: Phone the Mount Baker-Snoqualmie National Forest at (206)436-1155 or write to Darrington Ranger District, 1405 Emmens Street, Darrington, WA 98241.

Location: From the town ofGranite Falls, go 18 miles east on Highway 92 and you'll see the campground entrance.

Trip note: This is another classic spot, one of several in vicinity. This campground is set on the South Fork of the Stillaguamish River near Mahardy Creek. A trailhead two miles east of camp leads to Granite Pass in the Boulder River Wilderness. It makes a good base camp for backpacking expedition.

Site 18   TULALIP MILLSITE GROUP CAMP
on the South Fork of Stillaguamish River
MOUNT BAKER-SNOQUALMIE NATIONAL FOREST

Campsites, facilities: This is a specially-designated group camp and will accommodate up to 80 people. Picnic tables and fire grills are provided. Vault toilets are available, but **no piped water** is available. Pets are permitted.

Reservations, fee: Reservations required; $30 fee. Open mid-May to late September.

Who to contact: Phone the Mount Baker-Snoqualmie National Forest at (206)436-1155 or write to Mount Baker-Snoqualmie National Forest, Granite, WA 98252.

Location: From the town of Granite Falls, go 18.5 miles east on Highway 92 and you'll see the campground entrance.

Trip note: Like Sites 12-19, this campground is set along the South Fork of the Stillaguamish River. A trailhead about one mile east of camp leads north into the Boulder River Wilderness. There are numerous creeks and streams that criss-cross this area.

Site **19**   **COAL CREEK BAR**
on the South Fork of Stillaguamish River
MOUNT BAKER-SNOQUALMIE NATIONAL FOREST

Campsites, facilities: There are four sites for tents. Picnic tables and fire grills are provided. Pit or vault toilets and firewood are available. There is **no piped water.** Pets are permitted. The entire camp can be reserved by a group.

Reservations, fee: No reservations necessary; $15 to reserve entire campground. Open mid-May to late September.

Who to contact: Phone the Mount Baker-Snoqualmie National Forest at (206)436-1155 or write to Mount Baker-Snoqualmie National Forest, Granite, WA 98252.

Location: From the town of Granite Falls, go 23.5 miles east on Highway 92 and you'll see the campground entrance.

Trip note: This campground is set along the South Fork of the Stillaguamish River near Coal Creek. Nearby Forest Service roads lead to Coal Lake and a trailhead that leads to other backcountry lakes. A Forest Service map will unlock this beautiful country for you.

Site **20**   **BEDAL**
on Sauk River
MOUNT BAKER-SNOQUALMIE NATIONAL FOREST

Campsites, facilities: There are 19 sites for tents, trailers or motor homes up to 21 feet long. Picnic tables are provided. Pit or vault toilets are available, but there is **no piped water.** A Forest Service district office is nearby.

Reservations, fee: No reservations necessary; no fee. Open June to early September.

Who to contact: Phone the Mount Baker-Snoqualmie National Forest at (206)436-1155 or write to Darrington Ranger District, 1405 Emmens Street, Darrington, WA 98241.

Location: From the town of Granite Falls, go 30 miles east on Highway 92, then head northeast for 6.5 miles on Forest Service Road 20. A Forest Service map is essential.

Trip note: This campground is set at the confluence of the North and South Forks of the Sauk River. North Fork Falls is about a mile up the North Fork of the Sauk from camp and worth the trip.

Site **21**   **SULPHER CREEK**
on Suiattle River
MOUNT BAKER-SNOQUALMIE NATIONAL FOREST

Campsites, facilities: There are 28 sites for tents, trailers or motor homes up to 15 feet long. Picnic tables and fire grills are provided. Pit or vault toilets and firewood are available. There is **no piped water.** Leashed pets are permitted.

Reservations, fee: No reservations necessary; no fee. Open June to early September.

Who to contact: Phone the Mount Baker-Snoqualmie National Forest at (206)436-1155 or write to Darrington Ranger District, 1405 Emmens Street, Darrington, WA 98252.

Location: From Darrington, drive 7.5 miles north on Highway 530, then go 22.5 miles southeast on Forest Service Road 26. Forest Service map is advisable.

Trip note: This campground is set along the Suiattle River near the border of Glacier Peak Wilderness. It is a good base camp for a wilderness expedition. A horse ramp and a trailhead leading deep into the backcountry can be found about a mile south of the campground. The trail hooks up with the Pacific Crest Trail.

Site 22   FLOWING LAKE COUNTY PARK
near Snohomish

Campsites, facilities: There are eight tent sites and 29 drive-through sites for trailers or motor homes up to 25 feet long. Electricity, piped water, sewer hookups and picnic tables are provided. Flush toilets, sanitary services, firewood and a playground are available. Pets are permitted. Boat docks and launching facilities are nearby.

Reservations, fee: No reservations necessary; $7 fee per night. Open mid-May to mid-September.

Who to contact: Phone (206)339-1208 or write to P.O. Box 310, Monroe, WA 98272.

Location: Drive eight miles northeast of Snohomish.

Trip note: This campground has a little something for everyone. The recreational possibilities include swimming, power boating, waterskiing and good fishing at the lake.

Site 23   CUTTHROAT LAKES
on Bald Mountain, hike-in only

Campsites, facilities: There are ten tent sites at this primitive, hike-in campground. Picnic tables, fire grills and tent pads are provided. Pit toilets are available, but there is **no piped water.** Leashed pets are permitted.

Reservations, fee: No reservations necessary; no fee. Open all year.

Who to contact: Phone the Department of Natural Resources at (800)527-3305 or write to Department of Natural Resources AW-11, 1065 South Capitol Way, Olympia, WA 98504.

Location: Start on US 2, one-half mile east of Sultan, go north on Sultan Basin Road for 14 miles, then keep left on Road SLS 4200 for two miles. Continue straight on Road P 5800 for one mile, then turn right on Road P 5000 and go 7.5 miles. Continue on Road SLS 6000 for 1.6 miles, then turn left on SLS6100 Road and go 1.5 miles to the East Bald Mountain Trailhead. From East Bald Mountain Trailhead, hike three miles to the campsite.

Trip note: To reach this spot requires following difficult directions, but it is worth the effort because of the beautiful lakeside camps and the good trout fishing and hiking.

Site 24   LITTLE GREIDER LAKE
on Little Greider Lake, hike-in only

Campsites, facilities: There are nine tent sites at this primitive hike-in campground. Picnic tables, fire grills and tent pads are provided. Pit toilets and firewood are available. There is **no piped water.** Leashed pets are permitted.

Reservations, fee: No reservations necessary; no fee. Open all year.

Who to contact: Phone the Department of Natural Resources at (800)527-3305 or write to Department of Natural Resources AW-11, 1065 South Capitol Way, Olympia, WA 98504.

Location: Start on US 2, one-half mile east of Sultan and go north on Sultan Basin Road for 13.5 miles, then go straight on the middle road (Road SLS 4000) for about 8.5 miles to the Greider Lake Trailhead. From Greider Lake Trailhead, hike 2.5 miles to campsite.

Trip note: This is prime country for hiking, backpacking and trout fishing. The primitive, wooded campground is on Little Greider Lake. A detailed map of the area from Department of Natural Resources is essential before taking off for the backcountry.

Site 25   BIG GREIDER LAKE
on Big Greider Lake, hike-in only

Campsites, facilities: There are five tent sites at this primitive hike-in campground. Picnic tables, fire grills and tent pads are provided. Pit toilets and firewood are available, but there is **no piped water.** Leashed pets are permitted.

Reservations, fee: No reservations necessary; no fee. Open all year.

Who to contact: Phone the Department of Natural Resources at (800)527-3305 or write to Department of Natural Resources AW-11, 1065 South Capitol Way, Olympia, WA 98504.

Location: Start on US 2, one-half mile east of Sultan and go north on Sultan Basin Road for 13.6 miles. Take the middle road (Road SLS 4000) for about 8.5 miles to the Greider Lake Trailhead. From Greider Lake Trailhead, hike three miles to campsite.

Trip note: This primitive campground is on Big Greider Lake. A good alternative to Site 24, which is on adjacent Little Greider Lake.

Site 26   BOULDER LAKE
on Boulder Lake, hike-in only

Campsites, facilities: There are nine campsites for tents at this primitive hike-in campground. Picnic tables, fire grills and tent pads are provided. Pit toilets and firewood are available. There is **no piped water.** Leashed pets are permitted.

Reservations, fee: No reservations necessary; no fee. Open all year.

Who to contact: Phone the Department of Natural Resources at (800)527-3305 or write to Department of Natural Resources AW-11, 1065 South Capitol Way, Olympia, WA 98504.

Location: Start on US 2, one-half mile east of Sultan and go north on Sultan Basin Road for 13.5 miles. Then go straight on the middle road (Road SLS 4000) for about 8.5 miles to the Greider Lake Trailhead. Stay right on Road SLS 7000 and drive one mile to the Boulder Lake Trailhead. From the Boulder Lake Trailhead hike 3.5 miles to campsite.

Trip note: This primitive hike-in campground is on Boulder Lake. One of three hike-in camps, Sites 24-26, spotlighted in immediate area.

Site 27   BEAVER PLANT LAKE
on Beaver Plant Lake, hike-in only

Campsites, facilities: There are six tent sites at this primitive, hike-in campground. Picnic tables, fire grills and tent pads are provided. Pit toilets and firewood are available. There is **no piped water.** Leashed pets are permitted.

Reservations, fee: No reservations necessary; no fee. Open all year.

Who to contact: Phone the Department of Natural Resources at (800)527-3305 or write to Department of Natural Resources AW-11, 1065 South Capitol Way, Olympia, WA 98504.

Location: Start at the east end of the town of Granite Falls on Highway 92 and go north on Mountain Loop Highway for 15 miles. Turn north on Forest Service Road 4020 and drive 2.5 miles. Turn right on Forest Service Road 4021 and drive two miles to the Ashland Lakes Trailhead. From Ashland Lakes Trailhead, hike one mile to campsite.

Trip note: This campground is on Beaver Plant Lake, one of four campgrounds (Sites 27-30) highlighted in area. A map from Department of Natural Resources details trails and backcountry.

Site **28**   **UPPER ASHLAND LAKE**
near Upper Ashland Lake, hike-in only

Campsites, facilities: There are six tent sites at this primitive, hike-in campground. Picnic tables, fire grills and tent pads are provided. Pit toilets and firewood are available, but there is **no piped water.** Leashed pets are permitted.

Reservations, fee: No reservations necessary; no fee. Open all year.

Who to contact: Phone the Department of Natural Resources at (800)527-3305 or write to Department of Natural Resources AW-11, 1065 South Capitol Way, Olympia, WA 98504.

Location: Start at the east end of the town of Granite Falls on Highway 92, go north on Mountain Loop Highway for 15 miles. Turn north on Forest Service Road 4020 and drive 2.5 miles. Turn right on Forest Service Road 4021 and drive two miles to the Ashland Lakes Trailhead. From Ashland Lakes Trailhead hike 1.5 miles to campsite.

Trip note: The lake is just a short hike away and well worth the effort. A detailed map of the area is essential.

Site **29**   **LOWER ASHLAND LAKE**
on Lower Ashland Lake, hike-in only

Campsites, facilities: There are six tent sites at this primitive, hike-in campground. Picnic tables, fire grills and tent pads are provided. Pit toilets and firewood are available. There is **no piped water.** Leashed pets are permitted.

Reservations, fee: No reservations necessary; no fee. Open all year.

Who to contact: Phone the Department of Natural Resources at (800)527-3305 or write to Department of Natural Resources AW-11, 1065 South Capitol Way, Olympia, WA 98504.

Location: Start at the east end of the town of Granite Falls on Highway 92. Go north on Mountain Loop Highway for 15 miles. Turn north on Forest Service Road 4020 and drive 2.5 miles. Turn right on Forest Service Road 4021 and drive two miles to the Ashland Lakes Trailhead, then hike two miles to campsite.

Trip note: This campground is on Lower Ashland Lake, set adjacent to Site 28.

Site **30**   **TWIN FALLS LAKE**
on Twin Falls Lake, hike-in only

Campsites, facilities: There are five tent sites at this primitive hike-in campground. Picnic tables are provided. Pit or vault toilets and firewood are available. There is **no piped water.** Leashed pets are permitted.

Reservations, fee: No reservations necessary; no fee. Open all year.

Who to contact: Phone the Department of Natural Resources at (800)527-3305 or write to Department of Natural Resources AW-11, 1065 South Capitol Way, Olympia, WA 98504.

Location: Start at the east end of the town of Granite Falls on Highway 92. Go north on Mountain Loop Highway for 15 miles. Turn north on Forest Service Road 4020 and drive 2.5 miles. Turn right on Forest Service Road 4021 and drive two miles to the Ashland Lakes Trailhead. From Ashland Lakes Trailhead hike 3.5 miles to campsite.

Trip note: There is good hiking, backpacking and trout fishing at this site for people willing to grunt a little. It's such a beautiful and secluded area, yet it's not a long drive from Seattle.

Site 31
WALLACE FALLS STATE PARK
near Goldbar

Campsites, facilities: There are six tent sites. Picnic tables and fire grills are provided. Flush toilets and piped water are available. Leashed pets are permitted. Some facilities are wheelchair accessible.

Reservations, fee: No reservations necessary; $7 fee per night. Open all year.

Who to contact: Phone (206)793-0420 or write to P.O. Box 106, Goldbar, WA 98251.

Location: Drive 38 miles north and east of Bellevue via Interstate 405, Highway 522 and US 2. The park is two miles northeast of Goldbar.

Trip note: This beautiful, tiny spot is nestled in the forest near the scenic Wallace Falls. Seattle is loaded with people, but very few of them know of this jewel.

Site 32
TROUBLESOME CREEK A & B
on the North Fork of Skykomish River
MOUNT BAKER-SNOQUALMIE NATIONAL FOREST

Campsites, facilities: There are 22 sites for tents, trailers or motor homes up to 21 feet long. Picnic tables are provided. Pit or vault toilets and firewood are available. Leashed pets are permitted.

Reservations, fee: No reservations; no fee. Open mid-May to mid-September.

Who to contact: Phone the Mount Baker-Snoqualmie National Forest at (206)677-2414 or write to Skykomish Ranger District, Box 305, Skykomish, WA 98288.

Location: From the junction of US 2 and Highway 522, head east for 20 miles until you get to the town of Index. From there, drive 12 miles northeast on Galena Road to the campground.

Trip note: Here's another one I bet you never heard of. This campground is set along the North Fork of the Skykomish River. There is a nature trail adjacent to camp, and a mineral springs about three miles to the east along the county road.

Site 33
MILLER RIVER
near Alpine Lakes Wilderness
MOUNT BAKER-SNOQUALMIE NATIONAL FOREST

Campsites, facilities: This is a group camp with 20 sites for tents, trailers or motor homes up to 21 feet long. Picnic tables and fire grills are provided. Vault toilets, piped water, group barbecue are available. A store, a cafe, a laundromat and ice are available within one mile. Leashed pets are permitted.

Reservations, fee: Reservations required; $50 fee. Open mid-May to October.

Who to contact: Phone the Mount Baker-Snoqualmie National Forest at

(206)677-2414 or write to Skykomish Ranger District, Box 305, Skykomish, WA 98288.

Location: From Skykomish, drive 2.5 miles west on US 2, then go south on Old Cascade Highway for one mile. Turn on Forest Service Road 6410 and go two miles south.

Trip note: This campground is set along the Miller River a short distance from the boundary of the Alpine Lakes Wilderness. It is prime mountain territory. If you continue another four miles on Forest Service Road 6412 you will get to a trailhead leading to Lake Dorothy and many other backcountry lakes. A Forest Service map is essential.

Site **34**   **BECKLER RIVER**
on Beckler River
MOUNT BAKER-SNOQUALMIE NATIONAL FOREST

Campsites, facilities: There are seven tent sites and 20 sites for tents, trailers or motor homes up to 21 feet long. Picnic tables are provided. Vault toilets, piped water and firewood are available. A store, a cafe, a laundromat and ice are located within one mile. Pets are permitted.

Reservations, fee: No reservations necessary; $8 fee per night. Open mid-May to mid-September.

Who to contact: Phone the Mount Baker-Snoqualmie National Forest at (206)677-2414 or write to Skykomish Ranger District, Box 305, Skykomish, WA 98288.

Location: From Skykomish, go one mile east on US 2, then two miles north on Forest Service Road 65.

Trip note: This spot is on the Beckler River and is a good option to Site 33. Located just 60 miles from Seattle, yet little known.

Site **35**   **BOTHELL CANYON MOTORHOME AND RV PARK**
in Bothell

Campsites, facilities: There are 26 sites for trailers or motor homes of any length. Electricity, piped water and sewer hookups are provided. Flush toilets, piped water and a laundromat are available. Showers are available for an extra fee. Bottled gas, sanitary services, a store, a cafe and ice are located within one mile. Pets are permitted.

Reservations, fee: Reservations accepted; $15 fee per night. Open all year.

Who to contact: Phone (206)481-3005 or write to 22625 31st Avenue SE, Bothell, WA 98021.

Location: Drive eight miles north of Bellevue on Interstate 405 to Bothell. In Bothell, take exit 26 off Interstate 405 and drive south to 228th Street, then turn east and drive 1.2 miles to 22625 31st Avenue SE.

Trip note: This wooded park is near Seattle and is for motor homes and trailers only. Nearby recreation options include an 18-hole golf course, hiking trails, marked bike trails and a riding stable.

Site **36**   **TRAILER HAVEN**
in Seattle

Campsites, facilities: There are 15 sites for trailers or motor homes of any length in this adult only campground. Electricity, piped water and sewer hookups are provided. Flush toilets, bottled gas, showers and a laundromat are available. A store, a cafe and ice are located within one mile.

Reservations, fee: No reservations necessary. Call ahead for fees. Open all year.

Who to contact: Phone (206)362-4211 or write to 11724 Aurora Avenue North, Seattle, WA 98133.

Location: From Interstate 5 in Seattle, take exit 173 and go west to North Gateway and then to Highway 99. When you get to Aurora, turn north and go to 11724 Aurora Avenue North.

Trip note: Nearby recreation options include an 18-hole golf course, hiking trails, a full-service marina and tennis courts.

Site 37   HOLIDAY PARK RESORT
in Seattle

Campsites, facilities: There are 22 sites for trailers or motor homes up to 32 feet long. Electricity, piped water, sewer hookups and picnic tables are provided. Flush toilets, showers, a cafe and a laundromat are available. Bottled gas, sanitary services, a store and ice are located within one mile.

Reservations, fee: Reservations accepted; $15 fee per night. Open all year.

Who to contact: Phone (206)542-2760 or write to 19250 Aurora Avenue North, Seattle, WA 98133.

Location: From Interstate 5 in Seattle, take the 175th Avenue exit and go west to Aurora Avenue. Turn north and head to 19250 Aurora Avenue North.

Trip note: An alternative to Site 36, this campground is situated nearby. Recreation options include an 18-hole golf course, marked bike trails and tennis courts.

Site 38   ORCHARD TRAILER PARK
in Seattle

Campsites, facilities: There are ten sites for trailers or motor homes of any length. Electricity, piped water and sewer hookups are provided. Flush toilets, showers and a laundromat are available. Bottled gas, a store, a cafe and ice are located within one mile. Pets are permitted.

Reservations, fee: No reservations necessary; $15 fee per night. Open all year.

Who to contact: Phone (206)243-1210 or write to 4011 South 146th Street, Seattle, WA 98168.

Location: From Interstate 5 in Seattle, take exit 154 (Burien) and go one mile west to Highway 99. Drive north for three-quarters of a mile to South 146th Street, turn east (right) and drive to trailer park.

Trip note: This is the smallest and most intimate of the motor home parks in the Seattle area. Nearby recreation options include an 18-hole golf course.

Site 39   LAKE SHORE MANOR
in Seattle

Campsites, facilities: There are 25 sites for trailers or motor homes of any length. Electricity, piped water and sewer hookups are provided. Flush toilets, showers, a recreation hall and a laundromat are available. A store, a cafe and ice are located within one mile. Pets are permitted.

Reservations, fee: No reservations necessary; $11 fee per night. Open all year.

Who to contact: Phone (206)772-0299 or write to 11448 Rainier South, Seattle, WA 98178.

Location: From the junction of Interstate 5 and Interstate 405 in Seattle, take the Renton exit and drive three miles north to Rainier Avenue and 11448 Rainier South.

Trip note: Nearby recreation options include an 18-hole golf course, hiking trails, marked bike trails and a full-service marina.

Site 40
VASA PARK RESORT
on Lake Sammamish

Campsites, facilities: There are 16 tent sites and five sites for trailers or motor homes of any length. Piped water, sewer hookups and picnic tables are provided. Flush toilets, sanitary services, a playground, electricity and showers are available. Bottled gas, firewood, a store, a cafe and a laundromat are located within one mile. Pets and motorbikes are permitted. Boat launching facilities are nearby on Lake Sammamish.

Reservations, fee: Reservations accepted; $10 fee per night. Open mid-May to October.

Who to contact: Phone (206)746-3260 or write to 3560 West Lake Sammamish, Bellevue, WA 98008.

Location: From Interstate 90 in Bellevue, take exit 13 and drive one mile north. The campground is on the west side of Lake Sammamish.

Trip note: This is the most rustic of the parks in the immediate Seattle area, The resort is on Lake Sammamish. The state park is at the south end of the lake. Nearby recreation options include an 18-hole golf course, hiking trails, marked bike trails and a riding stable.

Site 41
TRAILER INNS RV PARK AND RECREATION CENTER
near Lake Sammamish State Park

Campsites, facilities: There are 115 drive-through sites for trailers or motor homes of any length. Electricity, piped water, sewer hookups and picnic tables are provided. Flush toilets, bottled gas, showers, a recreation hall, a swimming pool, a laundromat, ice and a playground are available. Sanitary services, a store and a cafe are available within one mile. Pets and motorbikes are permitted.

Reservations, fee: Reservations accepted; $18-20 fee per night; MasterCard and Visa accepted. Open all year.

Who to contact: Phone (206)747-9181 or write to 15531 Interstate 90, Bellevue, WA 98006.

Location: From the junction of Interstate 405 and Interstate 90 in Bellevue, go east on Interstate 90 for two miles to exit 11A, then go south on the frontage road to the park.

Trip note: A nice spot for motor home travelers, with nearby Lake Sammamish State Park a highlight. Nearby recreation options include an 18-hole golf course, hiking trails, marked bike trails and tennis courts.

Site 42
SNOQUALMIE RIVER CAMPGROUND
on Snoqualmie River

Campsites, facilities: There are 100 tent sites and 80 drive-through sites for trailers or motor homes of any length. Piped water and picnic tables are provided. Flush toilets, sanitary services, showers and a playground are available. Electricity and firewood can be obtained for an extra fee. Bottled gas, a store, a cafe, a laundromat and ice are located within one mile. Pets and motorbikes are permitted. Boat launching facilities are nearby.

Reservations, fee: Reservations accepted; $8.50-10 fee per night; Open April to late

October and some off-season weekends.

Who to contact: Phone (206)222-5545 or write to P.O. Box 16, Fall City, WA 98024.

Location: Go 14 miles east of Bellevue on Interstate 90 until you get to exit 22 (Preston-Fall City). Go five miles north on Highway 203 and follow the signs to the campground.

Trip note: If you're in the Seattle area and stuck for a place for the night, this is a prime choice. This wooded campground is set along the Snoqualmie River. Nearby recreation options include an 18-hole golf course, hiking trails and marked bike trails.

Site **43**
TINKHAM
on Snoqualmie River
MOUNT BAKER-SNOQUALMIE NATIONAL FOREST

Campsites, facilities: There are 13 tent sites and 34 sites for trailers or motor homes up to 21 feet long. Picnic tables are provided. Pit or vault toilets, firewood and piped water are available. Some facilities are wheelchair accessible. Pets are permitted.

Reservations, fee: No reservations necessary; $6 fee per night. Open mid-May to mid-September.

Who to contact: Phone the Mount Baker-Snoqualmie National Forest at (206)888-1421 or write to North Bend Ranger District, 42404 SE North Bend Way, North Bend, WA 98045.

Location: Drive 31 miles southeast of Bellevue on Interstate 90 (ten miles southeast of North Bend), then go 1.5 miles southeast on Forest Service Road 55 to campground. A Forest Service map is advisable.

Trip note: This campground is set along the Snoqualmie River, and is a good layover for the night for travelers heading west to Seattle. Nearby backcountry roads are detailed on a Forest Service map.

Site **44**
COMMONWEALTH
on Snoqualmie River
MOUNT BAKER-SNOQUALMIE NATIONAL FOREST

Campsites, facilities: There are six tent sites. Picnic tables are provided. Pit or vault toilets, and firewood are available. There is **no piped water.** A cafe is located within one mile. Pets are permitted.

Reservations, fee: No reservations necessary; no fee. Open June to mid-September.

Who to contact: Phone the Mount Baker-Snoqualmie National Forest at (206)888-1421 or write to North Bend Ranger District, 42404 SE North Bend Way, North Bend, WA 98045.

Location: Drive 43 miles southeast of Bellevue on Interstate 90 (22 miles southeast of North Bend), then go 200 yards north on Forest Service Road 58 and you'll see the campground. A Forest Service map is essential.

Trip note: This campground is set along the Snoqualmie River near the Snoqualmie Summit Ski Area. There are several trails nearby that lead into the Alpine Lakes Wilderness backcountry. Massive Keechulus Lake is about three miles south from camp, across Highway 90.

Site **45**
SALTWATER STATE PARK
near Seattle

Campsites, facilities: There are 52 sites for tents, self-contained motor homes up to 50 feet long. Picnic tables and fire grills are provided. Flush toilets, a sanitary disposal station, showers, a playground and firewood are available. A store, a restaurant and ice are located within one mile. Some facilities are wheelchair accessible. Leashed pets are permitted. Boat buoys are nearby on Puget Sound.

Reservations, fee: No reservations necessary; $7 fee per night. Open all year.

Who to contact: Phone (206)764-4128 or write to 25205 8th Place South, Kent, WA 98031.

Location: Drive eight miles south of Seattle on Interstate 5 to Des Moines, then go two miles south on Highway 509 to the park.

Trip note: This is a nice state park for tent or motor home campers, set on the edge of Seattle and beautiful Puget Sound. Beaches offer clamming and picnic facilities. There are also foot trails that lead through Kent Smith Canyon.

MOUNT RAINIER

♦

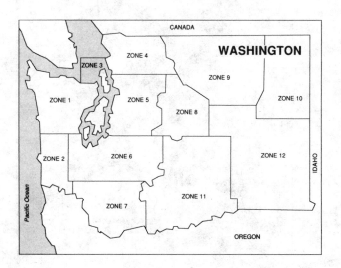

SOME HIGHLIGHTS

102 CAMPGROUNDS

Mount Rainier

Mount Rainier National Park

Gifford Pinchot National Forest

Mount Baker-Snoqualmie National Forest

Wenatchee National Forest

American River

Nisqually National Wildlife Refuge

Yakima River

William O. Douglas Wilderness

Mayfield Lake

Tieton River

Capitol Forest

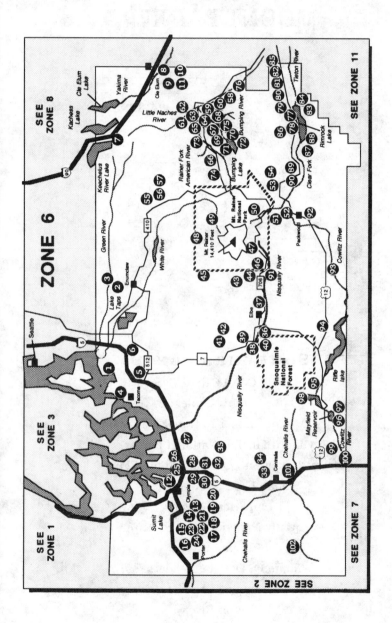

DASH POINT STATE PARK
Site **1**
near Tacoma

Campsites, facilities: There are 108 sites for tents, trailers or motor homes up to 35 feet long. Water and electrical hookups are available. Picnic tables are provided. Flush toilets, sanitary disposal station, a playground, electricity, piped water, showers and firewood are available. Leashed pets are permitted.

Reservations, fee: No reservations necessary; $7.50-10.50 fee per night. Open all year.

Who to contact: Phone (206)593-2206 or write to 5700 West Dash Point Road, Federal Way, WA 98003.

Location: From Tacoma, drive five miles northeast on Highway 509.

Trip note: This urban state park has beach access. Nearby recreation options include an 18-hole golf course and marked hiking trails. Tacoma offers a variety of activities and attractions, including the Tacoma Art Museum with a children's gallery, the Washington State Historical Society Museum, the Seymour Botanical Conservatory at Wrights Park, Point Defiance Park, Zoo and Aquarium, the Western Washington Forest Industries Museum and the Fort Lewis Military Museum. The Old Town area along the waterfront has been renovated and there are two public fishing piers there.

KANASKAT-PALMER RECREATION AREA
Site **2**
on Green River

Campsites, facilities: There are 31 tent sites and 19 drive-through sites for trailers or motor homes up to 35 feet long. Electricity and picnic tables are provided. Flush toilets, showers and sanitary services are available. Some facilities are wheelchair accessible. Pets and motorbikes are permitted. Boat rentals are available on the Green River.

Reservations, fee: No reservations necessary; $6 fee per night. Open all year with limited facilities in the winter.

Who to contact: Phone (206)886-0148 or write to 23700 Flamingo Geyser, Auburn, WA 98002.

Location: Drive 28 miles east of Tacoma on Highway 410 to Enumclaw, then go northeast on Farman Road for 11 miles, and you'll see the park.

Trip note: This wooded campground offers private campsites set along the Green River. In summer, the river is ideal for rafting and kayaking. In winter, it attracts a nice run of steelhead. Year-round you can explore the area's hiking trails.

GREEN RIVER GORGE RESORT
Site **3**
on Green River

Campsites, facilities: There are 60 tent sites. Piped water, sewer hookups and picnic tables are provided. Flush toilets, sanitary services, a laundromat, ice and a playground are available. Electricity, showers and firewood can be obtained for an extra fee. Pets and motorbikes are permitted.

Reservations, fee: Reservations accepted; $8-10 fee per night; MasterCard and Visa accepted. Open all year.

Who to contact: Phone (206)886-2302 or write to 29500 Green River Gorge Road, Enumclaw, WA 98022.

Location: Drive 28 miles east of Tacoma on Highway 410 to Enumclaw, then go eight miles north on Highway 169 to Black Diamond Road and four miles east on Green River Gorge Road to the resort.

Trip note: This nice spot is not far from the Tacoma-Seattle metroplex. The resort is set along the Green River, where you can raft or fish. Nearby recreation options include marked hiking trails and tennis courts.

Site 4   FIR ACRES MOTORHOME AND RV PARK
near Tacoma

Campsites, facilities: There are 14 sites for trailers or motor homes of any length. Electricity, piped water, sewer hookups are provided. Flush toilets, showers and a laundromat are available. Bottled gas, sanitary services, a store, a cafe and ice are located within one mile. Pets are permitted.

Reservations, fee: Reservations accepted; $13 fee per night. Open all year.

Who to contact: Phone (206)588-7894 or write to 12623 Bridgeport Way SW, Tacoma, WA 98499.

Location: Take exit 125 off Interstate 5 near Tacoma and drive one-quarter mile east to the park.

Trip note: Nearby recreation options include an 18-hole golf course and a full-service marina. See the trip note for Site 1 for a list of attractions in Tacoma.

Site 5   KARWAN VILLAGE MOTORHOME AND RV PARK
near Tacoma

Campsites, facilities: There are six sites for trailers or motor homes up to 32 feet long in this adults only campground. Electricity, piped water and sewer hookups are provided. Flush toilets, showers, a laundromat, bottled gas, sanitary services, a store, a cafe and ice are available. Pets are permitted.

Reservations, fee: Reservations accepted; $10 fee per night. Open all year.

Who to contact: Phone (206)588-2501 or write to 2621 South 84th Street, Tacoma, WA 98409.

Location: Take exit 128 off Interstate 5 near Tacoma and drive one-eighth mile west on 84th Street to the park.

Trip note: Nearby recreation options include an 18-hole golf course and Wapato Park. See the trip note for Site 1 for a list of attractions in Tacoma.

Site 6   MAJESTIC MOBILE MANORE
on Puyallup River

Campsites, facilities: There are five tent sites and 123 sites (some drive-through) for trailers or motor homes of any length. Electricity, piped water and sewer hookups are provided. Flush toilets, bottled gas, sanitary services, showers, a recreation hall, a store, a laundromat, ice and a swimming pool are available. A cafe is located within one mile. Pets and motorbikes are permitted.

Reservations, fee: Reservations accepted; $10-14 fee per night. Open all year.

Who to contact: Phone (206)845-3144 or write to 7022 River Road, Puyallup, WA 98371.

Location: Take exit 135 off Interstate 5 near Tacoma and drive four miles east on Highway 167 (River Road) to the park.

Trip note: This park is set along the Puyallup River. Nearby recreation options include an 18-hole golf course, a full-service marina and tennis courts. For information on the attractions in Tacoma, see the trip note for Site 1.

Site 7   LAKE EASTON STATE PARK
on Lake Easton

Campsites, facilities: There are 91 sites for tents, trailers or motor homes and 45 sites for motor homes with full hookups. Picnic tables, fire grills are provided. Flush toilets, sanitary disposal station, a playground, electricity, piped water, sewer hookups, showers and firewood are available. A cafe and ice are located within one mile. Some facilities are wheelchair accessible. Leashed pets are permitted. Boat launching facilities and floats are located on Lake Easton.

Reservations, fee: No reservations necessary; $7.50-10.50 fee per night. Open all year.

Who to contact: Phone (206)656-2230 or write to P.O. Box 26, Easton, WA 98925.

Location: This state park is about 80 miles east of Tacoma. To get there, take Highway 18 to Interstate 90 and head east for 45 miles to Easton. The park is one mile west of town on Interstate 90.

Trip note: This campground offers a multitude of recreational opportunities. For starters, it is set along the shore of Lake Easton, with Kachess Lake and Keechelus Lake just a short drive. The park provides opportunities for both summer and winter recreation, including swimming, fishing, boating, cross-country skiing and snowmobiling. Nearby recreation options include an 18-hole golf course and hiking trails.

Site **8**

McKEAN'S TRAILER PARK
near Yakima River

Campsites, facilities: There are 15 sites for trailers or motor homes. Electricity, piped water, sewer hookups and picnic tables are provided. A cafe is available. Bottled gas, sanitary services, a store, a laundromat and ice are located within one mile. Pets are permitted.

Reservations, fee: Reservations accepted; $9 fee per night. Open March to late December.

Who to contact: Phone (509)674-2254 or write to 1011 East 1st Street, Cle Elum, WA 98922.

Location: This park is in Cle Elum at 1011 East 1st Street.

Trip note: You can rent rafts and canoes in Cle Elum and take a 16-mile raft trip down the Yakima River to Thorp, where they offer to pick you up and bring you back to Cle Elum. Cle Elum is the Indian word for "swift water". The Cle Elum Historical Telephone Museum is also in town. Sites 7 and 9 are also set near the Yakima River.

Site **9**

TRAILER CORRAL
on Yakima River

Campsites, facilities: There are 30 sites for trailers or motor homes of any length. Electricity, piped water, sewer hookups and picnic tables are provided. Flush toilets, sanitary services, showers, firewood, a laundromat and ice are available. A store is located within one mile. Pets are permitted. Boat launching facilities are nearby.

Reservations, fee: Reservations accepted; $10 fee per night. Open all year.

Who to contact: Phone (509)674-2433 or write to 8C61 Box 4081 Cle Elum, WA 98922.

Location: From Cle Elum, drive one mile east on Interstate 90 to exit 85, then head east on Highway 970 for one mile to the park.

Trip note: This wooded campground is set along the Yakima River. See the trip note for Site 8 for river rafting information. Nearby recreation options include an 18-hole golf course, marked hiking trails and tennis courts.

Site 10
TANEUM
on Taneum Creek
WENATCHEE NATIONAL FOREST

Campsites, facilities: There are 11 tent sites and 13 sites for trailers or motor homes up to 21 feet long. Picnic tables are provided. Piped water and firewood are available. Some facilities are wheelchair accessible. Pets are permitted.

Reservations, fee: No reservations necessary; $4 fee per night. Open May to late November.

Who to contact: Phone Wenatchee National Forest at (509)674-4411 or write to Cle Elum Ranger District, West 2nd Street, Cle Elum, WA 98922.

Location: From Cle Elum, drive nine miles southeast on Interstate 90 to exit 93. Cross the freeway and drive south on Thorpe Prairie Road to Taneum Road. Turn right and drive west to Forest Service Road 33. Drive four miles and look for campground on left.

Trip note: This rustic spot, set along Taneum Creek, is just far enough out of the way to keep it from getting much use.

Site 11
BUCK MEADOWS
on Taneum Creek
WENATCHEE NATIONAL FOREST

Campsites, facilities: There are five sites for tents, trailers or motor homes up to 14 feet long. Picnic tables are provided. Pit toilets are available, but there is **no piped water.** Pets are permitted.

Reservations, fee: No reservations necessary; no fee. Open June to mid-November.

Who to contact: Phone Wenatchee National Forest at (509)674-4411 or write to Cle Elum Ranger District, West 2nd Street, Cle Elum, WA 98922.

Location: From Ellensburg, drive 24 miles west on Manastash Road, (becomes Forest Service Road 31) to the campground.

Trip note: This park is set along Taneum Creek and is an option to nearby Site 10. It doesn't get heavy use because few out-of-towners know of it.

Site 12
COACH POST TRAILER PARK
near Olympia

Campsites, facilities: There are 20 drive-through sites for trailers or motor homes of any length. Electricity, piped water, sewer hookups and picnic tables are provided. Flush toilets, showers and a laundromat are available. Bottled gas, a store, a cafe and ice are located within one mile. Pets are permitted.

Reservations, fee: Reservations accepted; $9 fee per night. Open all year.

Who to contact: Phone (206)754-7580 or write to 3633 7th Avenue SW, Olympia, WA 98502.

Location: Take the Decatur Street exit off US 101 in Olympia and turn left at the fourth stop light. Drive one mile to the campground.

Trip note: This wooded park is in a rural area just west of Olympia. Nearby recreation options include an 18-hole golf course, a full-service marina, a riding stable and tennis courts.

Site 13
BLACK LAKE RV PARK
on Black Lake

Campsites, facilities: There are ten tent sites and 42 sites (some drive-through) for trailers or motor homes of any length. Electricity, piped water, sewer hookups and picnic tables are provided. Flush toilets, bottled gas, sanitary services, a recreation hall, a store, ice, showers and firewood are available. A cafe is located within one mile. Pets are permitted. Boat docks, launching facilities and rentals are nearby.

Reservations, fee: Reservations accepted; $8-12 fee per night. Open all year.

Who to contact: Phone (206)357-6775 or write to 4325 Black Lake-Belmore Road, Olympia, WA 98502.

Location: Heading north, take exit 102 (Tumwater-Black Lake) off Interstate 5 in Tumwater and take Trosper Road to Black Lake. Follow signs to park. Heading south, take the Black Lake Boulevard exit off US 101 and follow the signs to the park.

Trip note: Here's a good spot for campers traveling Interstate 5 who don't want to get stuck in a hotel for the night. This campground is set along the shore of Black Lake. Nearby recreation options include an 18-hole golf course and a full-service marina.

Site **14**   **COLUMBUS PARK**
                     on Black Lake

Campsites, facilities: There are 76 drive-through sites for trailers or motor homes of any length. Electricity, piped water, sewer hookups and picnic tables are provided. Flush toilets, sanitary services, a recreation hall, a store, a laundromat, ice, showers, firewood and a playground are available. Bottled gas and a cafe are located within one mile. Pets are permitted. Boat docks and launching facilities are nearby.

Reservations, fee: Reservations required; $9 fee per night. Open all year.

Who to contact: Phone (206)786-9460 or write to 5700 Black Lake Boulevard, Olympia, WA 98502.

Location: Take the US 101 exit in Olympia and go northwest on US 101 for 1.7 miles, then go south on Black Lake Boulevard for 3.5 miles to park.

Trip note: This spot is an option to Sites 13 and 15. It is a wooded area set along the shore of Black Lake. Nearby recreation options include an 18-hole golf course and a full-service marina.

Site **15**   **SALMON SHORES RESORT**
                     on Black Lake

Campsites, facilities: There are 20 tent sites and 45 drive-through sites for trailers or motor homes of any length. Electricity, piped water, sewer hookups and picnic tables are provided. Flush toilets, bottled gas, sanitary services, showers, a store, a laundromat, ice, firewood and a playground are available. A cafe is located within one mile. Boat docks, launching facilities and rentals are nearby on Black Lake.

Reservations, fee: Reservations accepted; $9 fee per night; MasterCard and Visa accepted. Open all year.

Who to contact: Phone (206)357-8618 or write to 5446 Black Lake Boulevard, Olympia, WA 98502.

Location: Take the US 101 exit in Olympia and go northwest on US 101 for 1.7 miles, then go south on Black Lake Boulevard for 3.5 miles to the resort.

Trip note: This resort is set along the shore of Black Lake. Nearby recreation options include an 18-hole golf course, a full-service marina and a riding stable. This is one of three camps in the immediate vicinity.

Site **16**
PORTER CREEK
on Porter Creek
CAPITOL FOREST

Campsites, facilities: There are 14 primitive campsites for tents or small trailers. Picnic tables, fire grills and tent pads are provided. Pit toilets, piped water and horse-loading ramps are available. Motorbikes and leashed pets are permitted.

Reservations, fee: No reservations necessary; no fee. Open all year.

Who to contact: Phone the Department of Natural Resources at (800)527-3305 or write to Department of Natural Resources AW-11, 1065 South Capitol Way, Olympia, WA 98504.

Location: Sixteen miles south of Olympia on Interstate 5, take US 12 west and drive 21 miles to Porter. Go northeast on Porter Creek Road for three miles and then continue straight for another one-half mile. the campground is on your left.

Trip note: This primitive, rustic campground is less than 20 miles from Olympia. It is in Capitol Forest and is managed by the Department of Natural Resources. Set along the shore of Porter Creek, it offers trails for hiking, horseback riding or motorbiking.

Site **17**
NORTH CREEK
on Cedar Creek

Campsites, facilities: There are five primitive campsites for tents or small trailers. Picnic tables, fire grills and tent pads are provided. Pit toilets and piped water are available. Leashed pets are permitted.

Reservations, fee: No reservations necessary; no fee. Open all year.

Who to contact: Phone the Department of Natural Resources at (800)527-3305 or write to Department of Natural Resources AW-11, 1065 South Capitol Way, Olympia, WA 98504.

Location: Sixteen miles south of Olympia off Interstate 5, take US 12 west for 12 miles to Oakville. Continue 2.5 miles west of Oakville on US 12 to D-Line Road then head east for two miles. Take the fork that goes to the right and drive three miles. You'll see the camp on your right.

Trip note: This little-known, wooded campground is set along Cedar Creek and is managed by the Department of Natural Resources. There are trails for hikers only. An option is visiting Chehalis River, a short drive to the west. A canoe launch off US 12 is available north of Oakville.

Site **18**
SHERMAN VALLEY
on Cedar Creek
CAPITOL FOREST

Campsites, facilities: There are seven primitive campsites for tents or small trailers. Picnic tables, fire grills and tent pads are provided. Pit toilets and piped water are available. Leashed pets are permitted.

Reservations, fee: No reservations necessary; no fee. Open all year.

Who to contact: Phone the Department of Natural Resources at (800)527-3305 or write Department of Natural Resources AW-11, 1065 South Capitol Way, Olympia, WA 98504.

Location: Sixteen miles south of Olympia off Interstate 5, take US 12 west for 12 miles to Oakville. Continue west on US 12 for 2.5 miles to D-Line Road and turn east. Go 1.6 miles and take the fork on the right, then go 4.5 miles to the campground which will be on the right.

Trip note: This is one of nine secluded camp spots set in the Capitol Forest, which is managed by the Department of Natural Resources. It is set along the shore of Porter Creek and there are hiking trails nearby.

Site **19**   **MIMA FALLS TRAILHEAD**
near Mima Falls

Campsites, facilities: There are five primitive campsites for tents or small trailers. Picnic tables, fire grills and tent pads are provided. Pit toilets, piped water and a horse-loading ramp are available. Leashed pets are permitted.

Reservations, fee: No reservations necessary; no fee. Open all year.

Who to contact: Phone the Department of Natural Resources at (800)527-3305 or write to Department of Natural Resources AW-11, 1065 South Capitol Way, Olympia, WA 98504.

Location: South of Olympia, take the Highway 121 exit off Interstate 5 and drive four miles to Littlerock. Go west for one mile, turn left on Mima Road and drive 1.5 miles, then turn right on Bordeaux Road and go one-half mile. At Marksman Road, turn right and continue two-thirds of a mile. Turn left and the campground is about 200 yards away.

Trip note: A highlight here is the trail that leads to Mima Falls. It is excellent for hikers or horseback riders. The campground is very quiet.

Site **20**   **MARGARET McKENNY**
CAPITOL FOREST

Campsites, facilities: There are 12 primitive campsites for tents or small trailers. Picnic tables, fire grills and tent pads are provided. Pit toilets, piped water, campfire circle, and a horse-loading ramp are available. Leashed pets are permitted.

Reservations, fee: No reservations necessary; no fee. Open all year.

Who to contact: Phone the Department of Natural Resources at (800)527-3305 or write Department of Natural Resources AW-11, 1065 South Capitol Way, Olympia, WA 98504.

Location: Take the Highway 121 exit off Interstate 5 south of Olympia and drive four miles to Littlerock. Go west for one mile and turn right on Waddell Creek Road. Drive 2.5 miles, then turn left and drive about 200 yards to the campground.

Trip note: This streamside campground is in the Capitol Forest and managed by the Department of Natural Resources. There are trails nearby that can be used by hikers or horseback riders.

Site **21**   **MIDDLE WADDELL**
on Waddell Creek
CAPITOL FOREST

Campsites, facilities: There are three primitive campsites for tents or small trailers. Picnic tables, fire grills and tent pads are provided. Pit toilets are available, but there is **no piped water.** Motorbikes and pets on leashes are permitted.

Reservations, fee: No reservations necessary; no fee. Open all year.

Who to contact: Phone the Department of Natural Resources at (800)527-3305 or write to Department of Natural Resources AW-11, 1065 South Capitol Way, Olympia, WA 98504.

Location: Take the Highway 121 exit off Interstate 5 south of Olympia and drive four miles to Littlerock. Continue west for one mile and turn right on Waddell

Creek Road. Drive three miles, turn left and go 100 yards. You'll see the campsite on your left.

Trip note: This wooded campground is set along Waddell Creek in the Capitol Forest. The trails are used primarily for motorbikes. Remember that no piped water is available here.

Site 22

YEW TREE
on Waddell Creek
CAPITOL FOREST

Campsites, facilities: There are three primitive campsites for tents or small trailers. Picnic tables, fire grills and tent pads are provided. Pit toilets are available, but there is **no piped water.** Motorbikes and pets on leashes are permitted.

Reservations, fee: No reservations necessary; no fee. Open all year.

Who to contact: Phone the Department of Natural Resources at (800)527-3305 or write to Department of Natural Resources AW-11, 1065 South Capitol Way, Olympia, WA 98504.

Location: Take the Highway 121 exit off Interstate 5 south of Olympia and drive four miles to Littlerock. Go west for one mile and then turn right on Waddell Creek Road. From there, go 3.5 miles, turn left and drive 100 yards to the campsites, which are on the left.

Trip note: This wooded camp is set along Waddell Creek in Capitol Forest. The trails are used primarily by motorbikers.

Site 23

MOUNT MOLLY
near Waddell Creek

Campsites, facilities: There are ten primitive campsites for tents or small trailers. Picnic tables, fire grills and tent pads are provided. Pit toilets are available, but there is **no piped water.** Motorbikes are permitted.

Reservations, fee: No reservations necessary; no fee. Open all year.

Who to contact: Phone the Department of Natural Resources at (800)527-3305 or write to Department of Natural Resources AW-11, 1065 South Capitol Way, Olympia, WA 98504.

Location: Start four miles west of Olympia at the Mud Bay exit off US 101 and go south on Delphi Road for six miles. Drive straight on Waddell Creek Road for three miles, turn right and go 1.5 miles. Take the left fork and drive one mile to the campsites on the left.

Trip note: This campground is set in the forest. The nearby trails are used primarily for motorbiking. Week days are often quiet. The campground is managed by the Department of Natural Resources.

Site 24

FALL CREEK
on Fall Creek
CAPITOL FOREST

Campsites, facilities: There are eight primitive campsites for tents or small trailers. Picnic tables, fire grills and tent pads are provided. Pit toilets, piped water and a horse-loading ramp are available. Leashed pets are permitted.

Reservations, fee: No reservations necessary; no fee. Open all year.

Who to contact: Phone the Department of Natural Resources at (800)527-3305 or write to Department of Natural Resources AW-11, 1065 South Capitol Way, Olympia, WA 98504.

Location: Start four miles west of Olympia at the Mud Bay exit off US 101 and go south on Delphi Road for six miles. Continue straight on Waddell Creek Road for three miles, turn right and go 1.5 miles. Take the left fork and drive two miles on C-Line Road and then turn left onto Road C 4000 and drive 2.5 miles. Turn right and go 200 yards to the campground.

Trip note: A good option to Sites 21-23, since the trails here are for hikers and horseback riders only. This wooded campground is set along Fall Creek in Capitol Forest.

Site **25**   **MARTIN WAY MOTORHOME AND RV PARK**
in Olympia

Campsites, facilities: There are 11 drive-through sites for trailers or motor homes of any length in this adult-only campground. Electricity, piped water and sewer hookups are provided. Flush toilets, showers and a laundromat are available. Bottled gas, sanitary services, a store, a cafe and ice are located within one mile.

Reservations, fee: No reservations necessary; $10 fee per night. Open all year.

Who to contact: Phone (206)491-6840 or write to 8103 Martin Way SE, Olympia, WA 98506.

Location: From Interstate 5 in Olympia, take exit 111 and drive three-quarters of a mile south to Martin Way, turn west and go one-quarter mile to the park.

Trip note: This park is in urban Olympia. Nearby recreation options include an 18-hole golf course, a full-service marina, tennis courts and the Nisqually National Wildlife Refuge. The refuge offers seven miles of foot trails along which you may view a great variety of plant and animal life.

Site **26**   **NISQUALLY PLAZA RV PARK**
near Nisqually National Wildlife Refuge

Campsites, facilities: There are 60 sites (eight drive-through) for trailers or motor homes of any length. Electricity, piped water, sewer hookups, telephone, cable TV hookups and picnic tables are provided. Flush toilets, bottled gas, sanitary services, a store, a cafe, a laundromat, ice, a playground and a swimming pool are available. Showers and firewood can be obtained for an extra fee. Pets are permitted. Boat launching facilities are nearby.

Reservations, fee: Reservations accepted; $7-20 fee per night. Open all year.

Who to contact: Phone (206)491-3831 or write to 10220 Martin Way East, Olympia, WA 98503.

Location: Heading north on Interstate 5 in Olympia, take exit 114 and turn right. Go 200 feet, turn right onto Martin Way, and you'll see the campground.

Trip note: Nearby recreation options include an 18-hole golf course and Nisqually National Wildlife Refuge, which offers seven miles of foot trails, along which you may view a great variety of flora and fauna.

Site **27**   **PLEASANT ACRES RESORT**
on Long Lake

Campsites, facilities: There are 20 tent sites and 60 drive-through sites for trailers or motor homes of any length. Electricity, piped water, sewer hookups and picnic tables are provided. Flush toilets, sanitary services, showers, a recreation hall, a store, a cafe and a laundromat are available. Firewood is available for an extra fee. Bottled gas and ice are available within one mile. Pets and motorbikes are permitted. Boat docks, launching facilities and rentals are available nearby.

Reservations, fee: Reservations accepted; $6-10.78 fee per night. Open all year.

Who to contact: Phone (206)491-3660 or write to 7225 14th Avenue SE, Olympia, WA 98503.

Location: From Interstate 5 in Olympia, take exit 109 and drive one mile east on Martin Way, then turn south and go 1.5 miles on Carpenter Road. Turn east on 14th Avenue and drive to the resort.

Trip note: A nice layover spot for Interstate 5 travelers, this wooded park is set along the shore of Long Lake, a narrow, 4.5-mile long lake. The best fishing is at either end of the lake. Nearby recreation options include an 18-hole golf course, hiking trails, marked bike trails and a full-service marina.

Site **28**   STAN'S RV PARK
                   near Olympia

Campsites, facilities: There are 41 pull-through sites for trailers or motor homes of any length. Electricity, piped water and picnic tables are provided. Flush toilets, showers and sanitary services are available. Bottled gas, a store and cafe are located within one mile. Pets are permitted.

Reservations, fee: Reservations accepted; $10-14 fee per night. Open all year.

Who to contact: Phone (206)943-3614 or write to 2430 93rd Avenue SW, Olympia, WA 98502.

Location: From Olympia, drive five miles south on Interstate 5 to exit 99. The park is on the northeast corner of the junction.

Trip note: This convenient spot is set just off the highway. Nearby recreation options include an 18-hole golf course and tennis courts.

Site **29**   OLYMPIA CAMPGROUND
                   near Olympia

Campsites, facilities: There are 105 sites for tents, trailers or motor homes of any length. Piped water and picnic tables are provided. Flush toilets, bottled gas, sanitary services, showers, a recreation hall, television hookups, a store, a laundromat, ice, a playground, a heated swimming pool, electricity, sewer hookups and firewood are available. A cafe is available within one mile. Pets and motorbikes are permitted.

Reservations, fee: Reservations accepted; $14-19 fee per night; MasterCard and Visa accepted. Open all year.

Who to contact: Phone (206)352-2551 or write to 1441 83rd Avenue SW, Olympia, WA 98502.

Location: From Olympia on Interstate 5, take exit 101 and go east for one-quarter mile on Airdustrial Way. Turn right on Center, go one mile to 83rd Avenue and turn right again. The campground is one-eighth of a mile down the road.

Trip note: This wooded campground has all the comforts. Nearby recreation options include an 18-hole golf course, hiking trails, marked bike trails and tennis courts. It is one of three sites (28,29,30) in the immediate area.

Site **30**   AMERICAN HERITAGE CAMPGROUND
                   near Olympia

Campsites, facilities: There are 33 tent sites and 72 sites for trailers or motor homes of any length. Piped water and picnic tables are provided. Flush toilets, bottled gas, sanitary services, showers, a recreation hall, recreation programs , a store, a cafe, a laundromat, ice, a playground, a heated swimming pool, electricity, sewer hookups and firewood are available. Pets and motorbikes are permitted.

Reservations, fee: Reservations accepted; $15-19 fee per night; MasterCard and

Visa accepted. Open mid-May to mid-September.

Who to contact: Phone (206)943-8778 or write to 9610 Kimmie Street SW, Olympia, WA 98502.

Location: From Olympia, drive five miles south on Interstate 5 to exit 99 east and go one-half mile east to Kimmie Street. At Kimmie Street, turn south and go one-quarter mile to the campground.

Trip note: This spacious, wooded campground is near an 18-hole golf course, hiking trails, marked bike trails and tennis courts. In addition, it's not far from the highway to boot.

Site **31**   **DEEP LAKE RESORT**
near Deep Lake

Campsites, facilities: There are five tent sites and 43 sites for trailers or motor homes up to 35 feet long. Electricity, piped water, sewer hookups and picnic tables are provided. Flush toilets, sanitary services, a recreation hall, a store, a cafe, a laundromat, ice, bicycle rentals, a playground, showers and firewood are available. Pets and motorbikes are permitted. Boat docks, launching facilities and rentals are nearby at the resort.

Reservations, fee: Reservations accepted; $10 fee per night; MasterCard and Visa accepted. Open mid-April to late September.

Who to contact: Phone (206)352-7388 or write to 12405 Tilley South, Olympia, WA 98502.

Location: Take exit 95 off Interstate 5 in south Olympia and drive east on Maytown Road for 2.5 miles, then turn north on Tilley Road and go one-half mile to the park.

Trip note: This wooded, well-maintained campground is set along the shore of Deep Lake near Millersylvania State Park, and offers swimming, fishing and boating opportunities. Other nearby recreation options include an 18-hole golf course and marked bike trails.

Site **32**   **MILLERSYLVANIA STATE PARK**
on Deep Lake

Campsites, facilities: There are 139 sites for tents or self-contained motor homes and 52 sites for trailers or motor homes up to 35 feet long. Picnic tables and fire grills are provided. Flush toilets, a sanitary disposal station, a playground, electricity, piped water, showers and firewood are available. A store, a restaurant and ice are located within one mile. Some facilities are wheelchair accessible. Pets are permitted. Boat docks and launching facilities are nearby on Deep Lake.

Reservations, fee: No reservations necessary; $7.50-10.50 fee per night. Open all year.

Who to contact: Phone (206)753-1519 or write to 1224 Tilley Road South, Olympia, WA 98502.

Location: Drive ten miles south of Olympia on Interstate 5 and take exit 95. Go east on Maytown Road and then one-half mile north on Tilly Road to the park.

Trip note: This is a popular park, not too far from Olympia, yet it offers a lot of choices. It is set along the shore of Deep Lake where you can go swimming or trout fishing. There are hiking trails and a fitness trail in among the old growth trees.

Site 33
PEPPERTREE WEST RV PARK
in Centralia

Campsites, facilities: There are 20 tent sites and 40 drive-through sites for trailers or motor homes of any length. Electricity, piped water and sewer hookups are provided. Flush toilets, sanitary services, showers, a recreation hall, a laundromat, ice, a swimming pool, bottled gas, a store and cafe are available. Pets and motorbikes are permitted. Boat launching facilities are available nearby.

Reservations, fee: Reservations accepted; $11 fee per night; MasterCard and Visa accepted. Open all year.

Who to contact: Phone (206)736-9362 or write to 1208 Alder Street, Centralia, WA 98531.

Location: Take exit 81 off Interstate 5 in Centralia (about 23 miles south of Olympia) and drive to the southeast corner of town. You'll see the park.

Trip note: If you're driving Interstate 5 and looking for a stopover, this spot, along with Site 34, offers a good layover for tent campers or motor homes. Surrounded by Chehalis Valley farmland, this campground is near an 18-hole golf course, hiking trails and tennis courts.

Site 34
TRAILER VILLAGE
in Centralia

Campsites, facilities: There are 16 drive-through sites for trailers or motor homes of any length. Electricity, piped water, sewer hookups and picnic tables are provided. Flush toilets and showers are available. Bottled gas, sanitary services, a store, a cafe, a laundromat and ice are located within one mile. Pets are permitted.

Reservations, fee: Reservations accepted; $10 fee per night. Open all year.

Who to contact: Phone (206)736-9260 or write to 1313 Harrison, Centralia, WA 98531.

Location: Take exit 82 (Harrison) off Interstate 5 in Centralia (about 23 miles south of Olympia) and go four blocks northwest on Harrison to the park.

Trip note: This is an option to Site 33, but for motor homes only. This park is in urban Centralia. Nearby recreation options include an 18-hole golf course.

Site 35
OFFUT LAKE RESORT
on Offut Lake

Campsites, facilities: There are nine tent sites and 35 drive-through sites for trailers or motor homes of any length. Electricity, piped water, sewer hookups and picnic tables are provided. Flush toilets, bottled gas, sanitary services, firewood, a recreation hall, a store, a cafe, a laundromat, ice and a playground are available. Showers can be obtained for an extra fee. Pets and motorbikes are permitted. Boat docks and rentals are nearby.

Reservations, fee: Reservations accepted; $10-12 fee per night; MasterCard and Visa accepted. Open year-round.

Who to contact: Phone (206)264-2438 or write to 4005 120th SE, Tenino, WA 98589.

Location: Take Highway 507 east off Interstate 5 about 16 miles south of Olympia and drive eight miles to exit 88A (Tenino). Go north on Old Highway 99 for four miles and then turn east on Offut Lake Road.

Trip note: This wooded campground is on Offut Lake. Just enough off the beaten track to provide a bit of seclusion, yet not a long drive from Interstate 5.

Site **36**
ALDER LAKE
on Alder Lake

Campsites, facilities: There are 25 campsites for tents or small trailers. Picnic tables, fire grills and tent pads are provided. Pit toilets, piped water, a group shelter and a boat launch are available. Leashed pets are permitted.

Reservations, fee: No reservations necessary; no fee. Open all year.

Who to contact: Phone the Department of Natural Resources at (800)527-3305 or write to Department of Natural Resources AW-11, 1065 South Capitol Way, Olympia, WA 98504.

Location: Take Highway 7 and drive south of Elbe for two miles, then turn right on Pleasant Valley Road and go 3.5 miles. Bear left on a paved, one lane road for 100 yards and you'll see the campground on your right.

Trip note: This campground is set along the shore of Alder Lake in an area managed by the Department of Natural Resources. One option is the Mount Rainier Scenic Railroad excursion that travels from Elbe through the forests to Mineral Lake.

Site **37**
ELBE HILLS
near Elbe

Campsites, facilities: There are three primitive campsites for tents or small trailers. Picnic tables, fire grills and tent pads are provided. Pit toilets and a group shelter are available, but there is **no piped water.** Leashed pets are permitted.

Reservations, fee: No reservations necessary; no fee. Open all year.

Who to contact: Phone the Department of Natural Resources at (800)527-3305 or (206)825-1631 or write Department of Natural Resources AW-11, 1065 South Capitol Way, Olympia, WA 98504.

Location: From Elbe, go east on Highway 706 for six miles, then turn left on a dead end road and go three miles. Keep right and continue one-half mile, then turn left and drive about 100 yards to the four-wheel drive trailhead.

Trip note: Here's a spot for four-wheel drive cowboys. The Department of Natural Resources manages this wooded campground and provides eight miles of trails for short wheelbase four-wheel drive vehicles. Beware. Trucks often get stuck here or can't make it up the hills when it is wet and slippery. Make sure yours can.

Site **38**
EAGLE'S NEST ALDER LAKE
on Alder Lake

Campsites, facilities: There are eight sites for trailers or motor homes up to 25 feet long. Electricity, piped water and sewer hookups are provided. Sanitary services and firewood are available. Pets are permitted. Boat launching facilities are located on Alder Lake.

Reservations, fee: Reservations accepted; $8 fee per night; MasterCard and Visa accepted. Open all year.

Who to contact: Phone (206)569-2533 or write to 52120 Mountain Highway East, Eatonville, WA 98328.

Location: From Tacoma, drive 29 miles south on Highway 7 and you'll see the turn-off for the park.

Trip note: This wooded RV park, set on the shore of Alder Lake, is a cozy, little spot with all amenities.

Site 39
ELBE TRAILER PARK
near Alder Lake

Campsites, facilities: There are ten tent sites and 14 sites for trailers or motor homes of any length. Electricity, piped water and sewer hookups are provided. Bottled gas, a store, a cafe and ice are available within one mile. Pets are permitted. Boat launching facilities are located nearby.

Reservations, fee: No reservations necessary; $7 fee per night. Open all year.

Who to contact: Write to Star Route, Elbe, WA 98330.

Location: From Tacoma, drive 37 miles south on Highway 7 to Elbe. The park is in town.

Trip note: This campground is near Alder Lake. The Mount Rainier Scenic Railroad leaves from Elbe regularly and makes its way through the forests to Mineral Lake. It features open deck cars, live music and restored passenger cars.

Site 40
ALDER LAKE PARK
on Alder Lake

Campsites, facilities: There are 20 tents sites and 15 sites for trailers or motor homes of any length. Electricity and piped water are provided. Vault toilets are available. Boat docks and launching facilities are located on Alder Lake.

Reservations, fee: No reservations; $4 to $6 fee per night. Open all year with limited facilities in the winter.

Who to contact: Phone (206)569-2778 or write 50324 School Road, Eatonville WA 98330.

Location: From Tacoma, drive 35 miles south on Highway 7 to Alder Lake. Go left to the park.

Trip note: This municipal park is set along the shore of Alder Lake. It's a very decent spot to spend a weekend.

Site 41
TANWAX LAKE RESORT
on Tanwax Lake

Campsites, facilities: There are three tent sites and 28 sites for trailers or motor homes of any length. Electricity, piped water, sewer hookups and picnic tables are provided. Flush toilets, showers, a cafe, a laundromat are available. Bottled gas, a store and ice are located within one mile. Boat docks, launching facilities and rentals are nearby.

Reservations, fee: Reservations accepted; $8-12 fee per night. Open year-round.

Who to contact: Phone (206)879-5533 or write to 34023 Tanwax Court East, Eatonville, WA 98328.

Location: From Tacoma, drive 27 miles south on Highway 7, then turn east to Eatonville on Highway 161. From there, drive seven miles north to Tanwax Drive. Go east on Tanwax Drive for one-half mile and you'll see the resort.

Trip note: This wooded resort is set along the shore of Tanwax Lake. "Northwest Trek," which is open from Memorial Day through Labor Day, is about one mile south of the turn-off to Tanwax Lake on Highway 161. It is a guided tram trip through a 600-acre wildlife preserve where you can see bison, caribou and many other animals in their natural habitat.

Site 42
RAINBOW RESORT
on Tanwax Lake

Campsites, facilities: There are ten tent sites and 50-70 drive-through sites for trailers or motor homes up to 30 feet long. Electricity, piped water, sewer hookups and picnic tables are provided. Flush toilets, bottled gas, firewood, a recreation hall, showers, a store, a laundromat, ice and a playground are available. A cafe is located within one mile. Boat docks, launching facilities and rentals are nearby.

Reservations, fee: Reservations accepted; $7-12 fee per night. Open all year.

Who to contact: Phone (206)879-5115 or write to 34217 Tanwax Lake Court East, Eatonville, WA 98328.

Location: From Tacoma, drive 27 miles south on Highway 7, then turn east to Eatonville on Highway 161 and drive seven miles north to Tanwax Drive. Turn and drive east to the resort on Lake Tanwax.

Trip note: This wooded park is set along the shore of Lake Tanwax. There is good fishing on the lake. Nearby recreation options include a riding stable. See the trip note for Site 41 for information about Northwest Trek.

Site 43   GATEWAY INN AND RV PARK
near Mount Rainier National Park

Campsites, facilities: There are 18 sites for trailers or motor homes of any length. Electricity, piped water and picnic tables are provided. Bottled gas, a laundromat, firewood, sanitary services, a cafe and ice are available. Pets are permitted.

Reservations, fee: Reservations accepted; $10 fee per night; MasterCard, Visa and American Express accepted. Open April to November.

Who to contact: Phone (206)569-2506 or write to 38820 SR 706 East, Ashford, WA 98304.

Location: This park is located near the southwestern entrance to Mount Rainier National Park, about 12 miles east of Elbe on Highway 706.

Trip note: This wooded park is very close to Mount Rainier National Park, one of the most spectacular mountains in the hemisphere. After entering at the Nisqually (southwestern) entrance to the park and driving on Nisqually Paradise Road, you will find the Longmire Visitor Center about five miles into the park. It offers general park information and exhibits on the plants and geology of the area. Continuing into the park for ten more miles, you will arrive at the Paradise Visitor Center, which has more exhibits and an observation deck. This is the only road into the park that is open all year.

Site 44   MOUNTHAVEN AT CEDAR PARK
near Mount Rainier National Park

Campsites, facilities: There are 20 sites for trailers or motor homes of any length. Electricity, piped water, sewer hookups and picnic tables are provided. Flush toilets, showers, a laundromat, firewood, a cafe, ice and a playground are available. Pets are permitted.

Reservations, fee: Reservations accepted; $12 fee per night; MasterCard and Visa accepted. Open all year.

Who to contact: Phone (206)569-2594 or write to 38210 Highway 706 East, Ashford, WA 98304.

Location: This park is located near the southwestern entrance to Mount Rainier National Park, about 11 miles east of Elbe on Highway 706.

Trip note: This wooded campground is near the Nisqually entrance to Mount Rainier National Park. See the trip note for Site 43 for information about nearby sights at the National Park.

EVANS CREEK

Site **45**

on Evans Creek

MOUNT BAKER-SNOQUALMIE NATIONAL FOREST

Campsites, facilities: There are 27 tent sites. Picnic tables and fire grills are provided. Pit toilets and firewood are available, but there is **no piped water.** Pets are permitted.

Reservations, fee: No reservations necessary; no fee. Open mid-June to late September.

Who to contact: Phone Mount Baker-Snoqualmie National Forest at (206)825-6585 or write to the White River Ranger District, 857 Roosevelt Avenue East, Enumclaw, WA 98022.

Location: Drive eight miles east of Tacoma on Highway 167, then continue east on Highway 410 to Buckley. Go 11 miles south on Highway 165 and turn left on Forest Service Road 7930. Drive 1.5 miles to the campground.

Trip note: This primitive campground is set near Evans Creek in an off-road vehicle area near the northwestern corner of Mount Rainier National Park. The two nearby roads that lead into the park are secondary or gravel roads and provide access to several other primitive campgrounds and backcountry trails in the park. A National Forest map details the back roads and hiking trails.

SUNSHINE POINT

Site **46**

MOUNT RAINIER NATIONAL PARK

Campsites, facilities: There are 18 sites for tents or motor homes up to 25 feet long. Picnic tables are provided. Piped water and pit toilets are available. Some facilities are wheelchair accessible. Leashed pets are permitted.

Reservations, fee: No reservations necessary; $4 fee per night. Open all year.

Who to contact: Phone Mount Rainier National Park at (206)569-2211 or write to Mount Rainier National Park, Tahoma Woods, Ashford, WA 98304.

Location: Drive 12 miles east of Elbe on Highway 706 and you'll see the entrance to the park. The campground is just inside the park entrance.

Trip note: This is one of just five campgrounds in Mount Rainier National Park, set near the Nisqually entrance. Sites 47-50 are also located in the park. See the trip note for Site 43 for information about the nearby sights and facilities.

COUGAR ROCK

Site **47**

MOUNT RAINIER NATIONAL PARK

Campsites, facilities: There are 200 sites for tents or motor homes up to 30 feet long. A group camp is also available. Picnic tables are provided. Flush toilets, piped water, camp store and a sanitary disposal station are available. Some facilities are wheelchair accessible. Leashed pets are permitted.

Reservations, fee: No reservations necessary; $5 fee per night. Open mid-June to mid-October.

Who to contact: Phone Mount Rainier National Park at (206)569-2211 or write to Mount Rainier National Park, Tahoma Woods, Ashford, WA 98304.

Location: Drive about 12 miles east of Elbe on Highway 706 and enter the park. You'll see the campground entrance on the left about two miles past the Longmire Visitor Center.

Trip note: This camp is at 3,180 feet elevation. The park provides a recreation program, and trout fishing is allowed without a permit. See the trip note for Site 43 for information on the nearby park sights and visitor centers.

Site **48**
IPSUT
near Carbon River
MOUNT RAINIER NATIONAL PARK

Campsites, facilities: There are 29 sites for tents or motor homes up to 20 feet long, and a group camp is also available. Picnic tables are provided. Pit toilets and piped water are available. Leashed pets are permitted.

Reservations, fee: No reservations necessary; $5 fee per night. Open Memorial Day to Labor Day.

Who to contact: Phone Mount Rainier National Park at (206)569-2211 or write to Mount Rainier National Park, Tahoma Woods, Ashford, WA 98304.

Location: Drive eight miles east of Tacoma on Highway 167, then continue east on Highway 410 for 13 miles to Buckley. From there, head southeast on Highway 165 for about 13 miles to the Carbon River Park entrance. The campground is five miles into the park.

Trip note: This camp is at the end of Carbon River Road and at the beginning of several trails that lead into the backcountry of Mount Rainier National Park, past lakes, glaciers, waterfalls and many other wonders. Obtain a map from the National Park Service for details, and get a permit if you plan to do some overnight backpacking.

Site **49**
WHITE RIVER
on White River
MOUNT RAINIER NATIONAL PARK

Campsites, facilities: There are 117 sites for tents or motor homes up to 20 feet long. Picnic tables and fire grills are provided. Flush toilets and piped water are available. Some facilities are wheelchair accessible. Leashed pets are permitted.

Reservations, fee: No reservations necessary; $6 fee per night. Open mid-June to mid-September.

Who to contact: Phone Mount Rainier National Park at (206)569-2211 or write to Mount Rainier National Park, Tahoma Woods, Ashford, WA 98304.

Location: From Enumclaw, drive 27 miles southeast on Highway 410 to the White River entrance into the park. Take White River Road to the right and drive about seven miles to the campground.

Trip note: This campground is set on the White River at 4,400 feet elevation. A trail near camp leads a short distance to the Sunrise Visitor Center. From there, you can take several trails that lead to backcountry lakes and glaciers. You name it, you got it.

Site **50**
OHANAPECOSH
on Ohanapecosh River
MOUNT RAINIER NATIONAL PARK

Campsites, facilities: There are 232 sites for tents or motor homes up to 30 feet long. Picnic tables are provided. Flush toilets, piped water and a sanitary disposal station are available. Some facilities are wheelchair accessible. Leashed pets are permitted.

Reservations, fee: No reservations necessary; $6 fee per night. Open mid-May to November.

Who to contact: Phone Mount Rainier National Park at (206)569-2211 or write to Mount Rainier National Park, Tahoma Woods, Ashford, WA 98304.

Location: Drive 11 miles northeast of Packwood on US 12 and Highway 123 to the Ohanapecosh entrance to the park. The camp is next to the visitor center as you enter the park.

Trip note: This campground is set along the Ohanapecosh River. The nearby visitor center provides exhibits on the history of the forest and visitor information. Highway 706, heading east, is closed by snowfall in winter.

Site 51 HATCHERY RV CAMP
on Ohanapecosh River
GIFFORD PINCHOT NATIONAL FOREST

Campsites, facilities: There are 30 sites for tents, trailers or motor homes up to 21 feet long. Picnic tables are provided. Pit toilets and firewood are available, but there is **no piped water.** Some facilities are wheelchair accessible. Pets are permitted.

Reservations, fee: No reservations necessary; $2 fee per night. Open late May to late September.

Who to contact: Phone Gifford Pinchot National Forest at (206)494-5515 or write to Packwood Ranger District, Packwood, WA 98361.

Location: From Packwood, drive seven miles northeast on US 12, then go one mile west on Forest Service Road 1272.

Trip note: This campground is set along the Ohanapecosh River about six miles south of the Ohanapecosh Hot Springs and the southeastern entrance to Mount Rainier National Park. There is a Forest Service information center about a mile from the camp. A National Forest map details the backcountry roads and trails.

Site 52 LA WIS WIS
GIFFORD PINCHOT NATIONAL FOREST

Campsites, facilities: There are 100 sites for tents, trailers or motor homes up to 18 feet long. Picnic tables are provided. Flush and pit toilets, piped water and firewood are available. Pets are permitted.

Reservations, fee: No reservations necessary; $8 fee per night. Open late May to late September.

Who to contact: Phone Gifford Pinchot National Forest at 206-494-5515 or write to Packwood Ranger District, Packwood, WA 98361.

Location: From Packwood, drive seven miles northeast on US 12, then go one-half mile west on Forest Service Road 1272.

Trip note: This campground is set along the Ohanapecosh River and offers nature trails. It is about seven miles south of the entrance to Mount Rainier National Park and the Ohanapecosh Hot Springs.

Site 53 SODA SPRINGS
on Summit Creek
GIFFORD PINCHOT NATIONAL FOREST

Campsites, facilities: There are eight primitive tent sites. Picnic tables are provided. Pit toilets and firewood are available, but there is **no piped water.** Pets are permitted.

Reservations, fee: No reservations necessary; no fee. Open mid-June to early September.

Who to contact: Phone Gifford Pinchot National Forest at 206-494-5515 or write to Packwood Ranger District, Packwood, WA 98361.

Location: From Packwood, drive ten miles northeast on US 12. Turn north on Forest

Service Road 4510 and drive about seven miles to the end of the road.

Trip note: This campground is set along Summit Creek, a good base camp for a backpacking expedition or daily hiking trips in the Cascade Range. There are many trails and lakes to choose from as destinations. Obtain a Forest Service map for details.

Site 54 SUMMIT CREEK
on Summit Creek
GIFFORD PINCHOT NATIONAL FOREST

Campsites, facilities: There are seven primitive tent sites. Picnic tables are provided. Pit toilets and firewood are available, but there is **no piped water.** Pets are permitted.

Reservations, fee: No reservations necessary; no fee. Open mid-June to early September.

Who to contact: Phone Gifford Pinchot National Forest at (206)494-5515 or write to Packwood Ranger District, Packwood, WA 98361.

Location: From Packwood, drive ten miles northeast on US 12. Turn north on Forest Service Road 4510 and drive about three miles to the campground.

Trip note: Set along Summit Creek, this campground is another good base camp for trips into the Cascade Range backcountry. See the trip note for Site 53.

Site 55 THE DALLES
on White River
MOUNT BAKER-SNOQUALMIE NATIONAL FOREST

Campsites, facilities: There are 19 tent sites and 26 sites for tents, trailers or motor homes up to 21 feet long. Picnic tables and fire grills are provided. Piped water, vault toilets and firewood are available. Leashed pets are permitted.

Reservations, fee: No reservations necessary; $7 fee per night. Open mid-May to late September.

Who to contact: Phone Mount Baker-Snoqualmie National Forest at (206)825-6585 or write to White River Ranger District, 857 Roosevelt Avenue East, Enumclaw, WA 98022.

Location: Drive to Enumclaw, 21 miles east of Tacoma. From there, go 25.5 miles southeast on Highway 410 and you'll see the campground on your right.

Trip note: This campground is set along the White River. There is a nature trail nearby, and the White River entrance to Mount Rainier National Park is about 14 miles south on Highway 410.

Site 56 SILVER SPRINGS
on White River
MOUNT BAKER-SNOQUALMIE NATIONAL FOREST

Campsites, facilities: There are 16 tent sites and 40 sites for trailers or motor homes up to 21 feet long. Picnic tables and fire grills are provided. Vault toilets, piped water and firewood are available. A store, a cafe and ice are located within one mile. Pets are permitted.

Reservations, fee: No reservations necessary; $7 fee per night. Open mid-May to late September.

Who to contact: Phone Mount Baker-Snoqualmie National Forest at (206)825-6585 or write to White River Ranger District, 857 Roosevelt Avenue East, Enumclaw, WA 98022.

Location: Drive to Enumclaw, 21 miles east of Tacoma. From there, go 31 miles southeast on Highway 410 and you will see the campground entrance on your right.

Trip note: This campground is set along the White River about eight miles from the White River entrance to Mount Rainier National Park. A Forest Service information center is nearby.

Site 57   CORRAL PASS
MOUNT BAKER-SNOQUALMIE NATIONAL FOREST

Campsites, facilities: There are 20 tent sites. Picnic tables and fire grills are provided. Vault toilets, a horse-loading ramp and firewood are available, but there is **no piped water.** Pets are permitted.

Reservations, fee: No reservations necessary; no fee. Open July to late September.

Who to contact: Phone Mount Baker-Snoqualmie National Forest at (206)825-6585 or write to White River Ranger District, Enumclaw, WA 98022.

Location: Drive to Enumclaw, 21 miles east of Tacoma. From there, go 31 miles southeast on Highway 410, then six miles east on Forest Service Road 7174. It is a winding, dirt road.

Trip note: This is the most remote of the campgrounds in the area. Primitive, quiet and an ideal base camp for a hiking trip, this campground is at 5,600 feet elevation. There are several trails near camp that lead to backcountry fishing lakes and streams. See a Forest Service map for details. In late summer and fall, visitors can find wild berries in the area.

Site 58   COTTONWOOD
on Naches River
WENATCHEE NATIONAL FOREST

Campsites, facilities: There are 16 sites for tents, trailers or motor homes up to 21 feet long. No piped water is available. Picnic tables are provided. Pit toilets, firewood, sanitary disposal station, a store, a cafe and ice are available nearby. Leashed pets are permitted.

Reservations, fee: No reservations necessary; $4 fee per night. Open April to December.

Who to contact: Phone Wenatchee National Forest at (509)653-2205 or write to Naches Ranger District, 510 Highway 12, Naches, WA 98937.

Location: From Yakima, drive 13 miles northwest on US 12 to Naches. From there, go 4.5 miles west on US 12, then 17.5 miles northwest on Highway 410 to the campground.

Trip note: This campground is set along the Naches River. Sites 59-62 and 67 provide nearby options if this one doesn't grab your fancy.

Site 59   HALFWAY FLAT
on Naches River
WENATCHEE NATIONAL FOREST

Campsites, facilities: There are 12 sites for tents, trailers or motor homes up to 15 feet long. Picnic tables are provided. Pit toilets and firewood are available, but there is **no piped water.** Leashed pets are permitted.

Reservations, fee: No reservations necessary; no fee. Open April to late November.

Who to contact: Phone Wenatchee National Forest at (509)653-2205 or write to Naches Ranger District, 510 Highway 12, Naches, WA 98937.

Location: From Yakima, drive 13 miles northwest on US 12 to Naches. From there, go 4.5 miles west on US 12, 21 miles northwest on Highway 410, then three miles northwest on Forest Service Road 1704 to the campground.

Trip note: This campground is set along the Naches River. A trail leads from the campground into the backcountry of the William O. Douglas Wilderness, which can also be reached by car. Try hoofing it.

Site **60**   **SAWMILL FLAT**
on Naches River
WENATCHEE NATIONAL FOREST

Campsites, facilities: There are 27 sites for tents, trailers or motor homes up to 21 feet long. Piped water and picnic tables are provided. Pit toilets and firewood are available. Some facilities are wheelchair accessible. Pets are permitted.

Reservations, fee: No reservations necessary; $4 fee per night. Open April to December.

Who to contact: Phone Wenatchee National Forest at (509)653-2205 or write to Naches Ranger District, 510 Highway 12, Naches, WA 98937.

Location: From Yakima, drive 13 miles northwest on US 12 to Naches. From there, drive 4.5 miles west on US 12, then 23.5 miles northwest on Highway 410 to the campground.

Trip note: This campground is set on the Naches River near the Halfway Flat (Site 59). It's not quite all the way flat, just sorta flat.

Site **61**   **CROW CREEK**
on Naches River
WENATCHEE NATIONAL FOREST

Campsites, facilities: There are 15 sites for tents, trailers or motor homes up to 16 feet long. Picnic tables and fire grills are provided. Pit toilets and firewood are available, but the is **no piped water.** Leashed pets are permitted.

Reservations, fee: No reservations necessary; no fee. Open mid-April to late November.

Who to contact: Phone Wenatchee National Forest at (509)653-2205 or write to Naches Ranger District, 510 Highway 12, Naches, WA 98937.

Location: From Yakima, drive 13 miles northwest on US 12 to Naches. From there, go 4.5 miles west on US 12, 24.5 miles northwest on Highway 410, 2.5 miles northwest on Forest Service Road 1900, then turn west on Forest Service Road 1902 and go one-half mile to the campground.

Trip note: This campground is set along the Naches River. A trail from the campground leads into the backcountry and then forks in several directions. One way leads to the American River, another follows West Quartz Creek and another goes along Fife's Ridge into the Norse Peak Wilderness. See a Forest Service map for details. There is good hunting and fishing in season in this area.

Site **62**   **KANER FLAT**
near Naches River
WENATCHEE NATIONAL FOREST

Campsites, facilities: There are 41 sites for tents, trailers or motor homes up to 21 feet long. Piped water and picnic tables are provided. Pit toilets and firewood are available. Leashed pets are permitted.

Reservations, fee: No reservations necessary; $4 fee per night, $30 per night for group reservations. Open mid-April to late November.

Who to contact: Phone Wenatchee National Forest at (509)653-2205 or write to

Naches Ranger District, 510 Highway 12, Naches, WA 98937.

Location: From Yakima, drive 13 miles northwest on US 12 to Naches. From there, go 4.5 miles west on US 12, then 25 miles northwest on Highway 410, and 2.5 miles northwest on Forest Service Road 1900 and you'll see the campground.

Trip note: This campground is on the site of an old wagon trail campsite on the Old Naches Trail. It is set near the Naches River. Motorcycle trails are available in the area.

Site 63
INDIAN FLAT
on American River
WENATCHEE NATIONAL FOREST

Campsites, facilities: There are 11 sites for tents, trailers or motor homes up to 16 feet long. Piped water and picnic tables are provided. Pit toilets and firewood are available. Leashed pets are permitted.

Reservations, fee: No reservations necessary; $4 fee per night. Open late May to mid-September.

Who to contact: Phone Wenatchee National Forest at (509)653-2205 or write to Naches Ranger District, 510 Highway 12, Naches, WA 98937.

Location: From Yakima, drive 13 miles northwest on US 12 to Naches. From there, go 4.5 miles west on US 12, then drive 27 miles northwest on Highway 410.

Trip note: This campground is set along the American River. A trail from the camp leads into the backcountry, west along Fife's Ridge and further north to the West Quartz Creek drainage. A Forest Service map details the adventures.

Site 64
AMERICAN FORKS
on Bumping and American Rivers
WENATCHEE NATIONAL FOREST

Campsites, facilities: There are 15 sites for tents, trailers or motor homes up to 21 feet long. Piped water is provided. Pit toilets are available. Leashed pets are permitted.

Reservations, fee: No reservations necessary; $4 fee per night. Open late May to mid-September.

Who to contact: Phone Wenatchee National Forest at (509)653-2205 or write to Naches Ranger District, 510 Highway 12, Naches, WA 98937.

Location: From Yakima, drive 13 miles northwest on US 12 to Naches. From there, go 4.5 miles west on US 12, 28 miles northwest on Highway 410, then turn southwest and go 200 yards on Forest Service Road 1800 to the campground.

Trip note: This campground is set at the confluence of the Bumping and American Rivers. A trail from nearby Cedar Springs campground is one of several in the area that lead into the backcountry. See a Forest Service map for details.

Site 65
PINE NEEDLE
on American River
WENATCHEE NATIONAL FOREST

Campsites, facilities: There are eight sites for tents, trailers or motor homes. Picnic tables are provided. Pit toilets and firewood are available, but there is **no piped water.** Leashed pets are permitted.

Reservations, fee: No reservations necessary; no fee. Open late April to mid-September.

Who to contact: Phone Wenatchee National Forest at (509)653-2205 or write to Naches Ranger District, 510 Highway 12, Naches, WA 98937.

Location: From Yakima, drive 13 miles northwest on US 12 to Naches. From there, go 4.5 miles west on US 12, 30.5 miles northwest on Highway 410 to the campground.

Trip note: This campground is set along the American River. It is easy to reach, rustic and beautiful.

Site **66**

PLEASANT VALLEY
on American River
WENATCHEE NATIONAL FOREST

Campsites, facilities: There are 19 sites for tents, trailers or motor homes up to 21 feet long. Piped water, picnic tables and fire grills are provided. Pit toilets and firewood are available. Leashed pets are permitted.

Reservations, fee: No reservations necessary; no fee. Open mid-June to late November.

Who to contact: Phone Wenatchee National Forest at (509)653-2205 or write to Naches Ranger District, 510 Highway 12, Naches, WA 98937.

Location: From Yakima, drive 13 miles northwest on US 12 to Naches. From there, go 4.5 miles west on US 12, then drive 37 miles northwest on Highway 410.

Trip note: This campground is set along the American River and is a good base camp for a hiking trip. A trail from the camp follows Kettle Creek up to the American Ridge and Kettle Lake in the William O. Douglas Wilderness. It joins another trail there that follows the ridge and then drops down to Bumping Lake. A Forest Service map is essential.

Site **67**

LITTLE NACHES
on Little Naches River
WENATCHEE NATIONAL FOREST

Campsites, facilities: There are 23 sites for tents, trailers or motor homes up to 15 feet long. Piped water, picnic tables and fire grills are provided. Pit toilets and firewood are available. Leashed pets are permitted.

Reservations, fee: No reservations necessary; $4 fee per night. Open late May to late November.

Who to contact: Phone Wenatchee National Forest at (509)653-2205 or write to Naches Ranger District, 510 Highway 12, Naches, WA 98937.

Location: From Yakima, drive 13 miles northwest on US 12 to Naches. From there, go 4.5 miles west on US 12, 25 miles northwest on Highway 410, and then 100 yards northwest on Forest Service Road 1900 to the campground.

Trip note: This campground is set on the Little Naches River near the American River. It is set just one-tenth of a mile off the highway, making the easy access a major attraction for highway cruisers.

Site **68**

CEDAR SPRINGS
on Bumping River
WENATCHEE NATIONAL FOREST

Campsites, facilities: There are 15 sites for tents, trailers or motor homes up to 21 feet long. **No piped water** is available. Picnic tables are provided. Pit toilets and firewood are available. Pets are permitted.

Reservations, fee: No reservations necessary; no fee. Open late May to late November.

Who to contact: Phone Wenatchee National Forest at (509)653-2205 or write to Naches Ranger District, 510 Highway 12, Naches, WA 98937.

Location: From Yakima, drive 13 miles northwest on US 12 to Naches. From there, go 4.5 miles west on US 12, 28.5 miles northwest on Highway 410, then turn and go one-half mile southwest on County Road 1800 to the campground.

Trip note: This campground is set along the Bumping River a short distance from American Forks. If you continue driving southwest for 11 miles on Forest Service Road 174, you will get to Bumping Lake.

Site 69   COUGAR FLAT
on Bumping River
WENATCHEE NATIONAL FOREST

Campsites, facilities: There are 12 sites for tents, trailers or motor homes up to 16 feet long. Piped water and picnic tables are provided. Pit toilets and firewood are available. Leashed pets are permitted.

Reservations, fee: No reservations necessary; $4 fee per night. Open late May to mid-September.

Who to contact: Phone Wenatchee National Forest at (509)653-2205 or write to Naches Ranger District, 510 Highway 12, Naches, WA 98937.

Location: From Yakima, drive 13 miles northwest on US 12 to Naches. From there, go 4.5 miles west on US 12, 28.5 miles northwest on Highway 410, then six miles southwest on County Road 1800 to the campground.

Trip note: This campground is set along the Bumping River. A trail from the camp follows the river and then heads up the tributaries. It is one of several camps in immediate vicinity on Forest Service Road 174. See the map for Zone 6.

Site 70   BUMPING CROSSING
on Bumping River
WENATCHEE NATIONAL FOREST

Campsites, facilities: There are 12 sites for tents, trailers or motor homes up to 15 feet long. Picnic tables are provided. Pit toilets and firewood are available, but there is **no piped water.** A store, a cafe and ice are located within one mile. Pets are permitted. Boat docks, launching facilities and rentals are nearby on Bumping Lake.

Reservations, fee: No reservations necessary; no fee. Open late May to late November.

Who to contact: Phone Wenatchee National Forest at (509)653-2205 or write to Naches Ranger District, 510 Highway 12, Naches, WA 98937.

Location: From Yakima, drive 13 miles northwest on US 12 to Naches. From there, go 4.5 miles west on US 12, 28.5 miles northwest on Highway 410, and then drive ten miles southwest on County Road 1800 to the campground.

Trip note: This campground is set along the Bumping River about a mile from the boat landing at Bumping Lake. It's a very good spot for a weekend.

Site 71   BUMPING DAM
on Bumping Lake
WENATCHEE NATIONAL FOREST

Campsites, facilities: There are 28 sites for tents, trailers or motor homes up to 16 feet long. Picnic tables and fire grills are provided. Pit toilets and firewood are available, but there is **no piped water.** A store is located within one mile. Leashed pets are permitted. Boat docks, launching facilities and rentals are nearby.

Reservations, fee: No reservations necessary; $4 fee per night. Open mid-May to late November.

Who to contact: Phone Wenatchee National Forest at (509)653-2205 or write to Naches Ranger District, 510 Highway 12, Naches, WA 98937.

Location: From Yakima, drive 13 miles northwest on US 12 to Naches. From there, go 4.5 miles west on US 12, 28 miles northwest on Highway 410, then drive 11 miles southwest on County Road 1800.

Trip note: This campground is next to the dam on Bumping Lake, a popular lake for fishing, swimming and waterskiing.

Site **72**   BUMPING LAKE AND BOAT LANDING
on Bumping Lake
WENATCHEE NATIONAL FOREST

Campsites, facilities: There are 45 sites for tents, trailers or motor homes up to 21 feet long. Piped water and picnic tables are provided. Pit toilets and firewood are available. Pets are permitted. Boat docks, launching facilities and rentals are nearby.

Reservations, fee: No reservations necessary; $4 fee per night. Open mid-May to late November.

Who to contact: Phone Wenatchee National Forest at (509)653-2205 or write to Naches Ranger District, 510 Highway 12, Naches, WA 98937.

Location: From Yakima, drive 13 miles northwest on US 12 to Naches. From there, go 4.5 miles west on US 12, 28.5 miles northwest on Highway 410, then drive 11 miles southwest on County Road 1800.

Trip note: Woods and water, this spot has them both. A variety of water activities are allowed at Bumping Lake, including waterskiing, fishing and swimming. There are also several hiking trails that go into the wilderness area surrounding the lake.

Site **73**   HELLS CROSSING
on American River
WENATCHEE NATIONAL FOREST

Campsites, facilities: There are 18 sites for tents, trailers or motor homes up to 16 feet long. Piped water and picnic tables are provided. Pit toilets and firewood are available. Leashed pets are permitted.

Reservations, fee: No reservations necessary; $4 fee per night. Open late May to late November.

Who to contact: Phone Wenatchee National Forest at (509)653-2205 or write to Naches Ranger District, 510 Highway 12, Naches, WA 98937.

Location: From Yakima, drive 13 miles northwest on US 12 to Naches. From there, go 4.5 miles west on US 12, then drive 33.5 miles northwest on Highway 410.

Trip note: This campground is set along the American River. A steep trail from the camp leads up to Goat Peak and follows the American Ridge in the William O. Douglas Wilderness. Other trails join the ridgetop trail and connect with lakes and streams. A Forest Service map details the backcountry.

Site **74**   LODGE POLE
on American River
WENATCHEE NATIONAL FOREST

Campsites, facilities: There are 34 sites for tents, trailers or motor homes up to 21 feet long. Piped water and picnic tables are provided. Pit toilets and firewood are available. Leashed pets are permitted.

Reservations, fee: No reservations necessary; $4 fee per night. Open mid-June to mid-September.

Who to contact: Phone Wenatchee National Forest at (509)653-2205 or write to Naches Ranger District, 510 Highway 12, Naches, WA 98937.

Location: From Yakima, drive 13 miles northwest on US 12 to Naches. From there, go 4.5 miles west on US 12, then drive 40.5 miles northwest on Highway 410 to the campground.

Trip note: This campground is set along the American River about seven miles west of the western boundary of Mount Rainier National Park. See the trip note for Site 43 for information on Mount Rainier.

Site 75   SODA SPRINGS
on Bumping Creek
WENATCHEE NATIONAL FOREST

Campsites, facilities: There are 26 sites for tents, trailers or motor homes. Piped water and picnic tables are provided. Pit toilets and firewood are available. Pets are permitted.

Reservations, fee: No reservations necessary; $4 fee per night. Open May to late November.

Who to contact: Phone Wenatchee National Forest at (509)653-2205 or write to Naches Ranger District, 510 Highway 12, Naches, WA 98937.

Location: From Yakima, drive 13 miles northwest on US 12 to Naches. From Naches, continue 4.5 miles west on US 12, then go 28.5 miles northwest on Highway 410. Turn and go five miles southwest on County Road 1800.

Trip note: This campground is set along Bumping Creek and offers natural mineral springs and a nature trail.

Site 76   SQUAW ROCK RESORT
near the Naches River

Campsites, facilities: There are 25 tent sites and 60 drive-through sites for trailers or motor homes of any length. Electricity, piped water and picnic tables are provided. Flush toilets, bottled gas, sanitary services, showers, a recreation hall, a store, a cafe, a laundromat, ice, a playground and a swimming pool are available. Sewer hookups can be obtained for an extra fee. Pets and motorbikes are permitted.

Reservations, fee: Reservations accepted; $12.50 fee per night; MasterCard and Visa accepted. Open all year.

Who to contact: Phone (509)658-2926 or write to 15690 Highway 410, Naches, WA 98937.

Location: From Yakima, drive 13 miles northwest on US 12 to Naches. From there, go five miles west on US 12, 15 miles northwest on Highway 410.

Trip note: This park is near the Naches River. Nearby recreation options include hiking trails, marked bike trails and a riding stable. The nearby town of Nile, located southeast of the campground on Highway 410, offers all services.

Site 77   SILVER COVE RESORT
on Rimrock Lake

Campsites, facilities: There are ten tent sites and 35 sites for trailers or motor homes. Electricity, piped water, sewer hookups and picnic tables are provided. Bottled gas, a cafe, ice, boat docks, launching facilities and rentals are available. A store is located within one mile. Pets and motorbikes are permitted.

Reservations, fee: Reservations accepted; $8 fee per night. Open all year with limited winter facilities.

Who to contact: Write to P.O. Box 985, Yakima, WA 98907.

Location: From Yakima, go 40 miles west on US 12 and you'll see the resort on Rimrock Lake.

Trip note: This resort is set along the shore of Rimrock Lake and is one of several camps in the immediate area. See the Zone 6 map. Nearby recreation options include hiking trails, marked bike trails, a full-service marina and a riding stable.

Site 78   TWELVE WEST RESORT
on Rimrock Lake

Campsites, facilities: There are 34 sites for trailers or motor homes up to 32 feet long. Picnic tables are provided. Flush toilets, bottled gas, electricity, piped water, showers, firewood, a cafe and ice are available. Pets are permitted. Boat docks, launching facilities and rentals are nearby.

Reservations, fee: Reservations accepted; $10 fee per night. Open all year with limited winter facilities.

Who to contact: Write to Star Route, Box 206, Naches, WA 98937.

Location: From Yakima, go 42 miles west on US 12 and you'll see the resort on Rimrock Lake.

Trip note: This resort is set along the shore of Rimrock Lake. Nearby recreation options include hiking trails, marked bike trails, a full-service marina and a riding stable.

Site 79   HAUSE CREEK
on Tieton River
WENATCHEE NATIONAL FOREST

Campsites, facilities: There are 42 sites for tents, trailers or motor homes up to 21 feet long. Piped water and picnic tables are provided. Flush toilets and firewood are available. Some facilities are wheelchair accessible. Leashed pets are permitted. Boat docks, launching facilities and rentals are located on Rimrock Lake.

Reservations, fee: No reservations necessary; $5 fee per night. Open late May to late November.

Who to contact: Phone Wenatchee National Forest at (509)653-2205 or write to Naches Ranger District, 510 Highway 12, Naches, WA 98937.

Location: Drive 22 miles southwest of Naches on US 12 to the campground.

Trip note: This campground is set along the Tieton River, where several creeks converge. The Tieton Dam, which creates Rimrock Lake, is just upstream.

Site 80   RIVER BEND
on Tieton River
WENATCHEE NATIONAL FOREST

Campsites, facilities: There are six sites for tents, trailers or motor homes up to 15 feet long. Piped water and picnic tables are provided. Pit toilets and firewood are available. Pets are permitted. Boat docks, launching facilities and rentals are located on Rimrock Lake.

Reservations, fee: No reservations necessary; $4 fee per night. Open April to mid-September.

Who to contact: Phone Wenatchee National Forest at (509)653-2205 or write to

Naches Ranger District, 510 Highway 12, Naches, WA 98937.

Location: Drive 22 miles southwest of Naches on US 12 to the campground.

Trip note: This campground is located near Site 79. It is set on the Tieton River about five miles from Rimrock Lake.

Site 81
WILD ROSE
on Tieton River
WENATCHEE NATIONAL FOREST

Campsites, facilities: There are eight sites for tents, trailers or motor homes up to 31 feet long. Picnic tables are provided. Piped water, pit toilets and firewood are available. Leashed pets are permitted.

Reservations, fee: No reservations necessary; no fee. Open April to late November.

Who to contact: Phone Wenatchee National Forest at (509)653-2205 or write to Naches Ranger District, 510 Highway 12, Naches, WA 98937.

Location: Drive 20.5 miles southwest of Naches on US 12 to the campground.

Trip note: This campground is set along the Tieton River. It's an option to Sites 79, 80, 82, 83 and 85.

Site 82
WILLOWS
on Tieton River
WENATCHEE NATIONAL FOREST

Campsites, facilities: There are 16 sites for tents, trailers or motor homes up to 16 feet long. Picnic tables are provided. Piped water, pit toilets and firewood are available. Pets are permitted.

Reservations, fee: No reservations necessary; $4 fee per night. Open April to late November.

Who to contact: Phone Wenatchee National Forest at (509)653-2205 or write to Naches Ranger District, 510 Highway 12, Naches, WA 98937.

Location: Drive 20 miles southwest of Naches on US 12 to the campground.

Trip note: This campground is set along the Tieton River. The site is primitive and beautiful and has easy access.

Site 83
SOUTH FORK
on South Fork Tieton River
WENATCHEE NATIONAL FOREST

Campsites, facilities: There are 15 sites for tents, trailers or motor homes up to 16 feet long. Picnic tables are provided. Pit toilets and firewood are available, but there is **no piped water.** Leashed pets are permitted. Boat docks are nearby.

Reservations, fee: No reservations necessary; no fee. Open late May to mid-September.

Who to contact: Phone Wenatchee National Forest at (509)653-2205 or write to Naches Ranger District, 510 Highway 12, Naches, WA 98937.

Location: From Yakima, drive 13 miles northwest on US 12 to Naches. From Naches, continue 22.5 miles west on US 12, then go four miles south on County Road 1200. Turn south on Forest Service Road 1203 and drive one-half mile to the campground.

Trip note: This campground is set along the South Fork of the Tieton River, less than a mile from where it empties into Rimrock Lake. This is often a good spot for trout fishing and swimming.

Site **84**
PENINSULA
on Rimrock Lake
WENATCHEE NATIONAL FOREST

Campsites, facilities: There are 19 sites for tents, trailers or motor homes up to 15 feet long. Picnic tables are provided. Pit toilets and firewood are available, but there is **no piped water.** Pets are permitted. Boat docks and launching facilities are nearby.

Reservations, fee: No reservations necessary; no fee. Open mid-April to late November.

Who to contact: Phone Wenatchee National Forest at (509)653-2205 or write to Naches Ranger District, 510 Highway 12, Naches, WA 98937.

Location: From Yakima, drive 13 miles northwest on US 12 to Naches. From Naches, continue 22.5 miles west on US 12, then go three miles south on County Road 1200. At Forest Service Road 1382, turn west and drive one more mile.

Trip note: This campground is set along the shore of Rimrock Lake. It is one of several on the lake. Swimming, fishing and waterskiing are all allowed.

Site **85**
WINDY POINT
on Tieton River
WENATCHEE NATIONAL FOREST

Campsites, facilities: There are 15 sites for tents, trailers or motor homes up to 21 feet long. Piped water and picnic tables are provided. Pit toilets and firewood are available. Leashed pets are permitted.

Reservations, fee: No reservations necessary; $4 fee per night. Open April to late November.

Who to contact: Phone Wenatchee National Forest at (509)653-2205 or write to Naches Ranger District, 510 Highway 12, Naches, WA 98937.

Location: Drive 13 miles west of Naches on US 12 to the campground.

Trip note: This campground, set along the Tieton River, is more isolated than the camps set westward toward Rimrock Lake. Piped water is a bonus.

Site **86**
INDIAN CREEK
on Rimrock Lake
WENATCHEE NATIONAL FOREST

Campsites, facilities: There are 39 sites for tents, trailers or motor homes up to 21 feet long. Piped water and picnic tables are provided. Pit toilets, firewood, a cafe, a store and ice are available. Leashed pets are permitted. Boat docks, launching facilities and rentals are available nearby.

Reservations, fee: No reservations necessary; $5 fee per night. Open late May to mid-September.

Who to contact: Phone Wenatchee National Forest at (509)653-2205 or write to Naches Ranger District, 510 Highway 12, Naches, WA 98937.

Location: Drive 31.5 miles west of Naches on US 12 and you'll see the entrance.

Trip note: This campground is set along the shore of Rimrock Lake. Fishing, swimming and waterskiing are allowed.

Site **87**
CLEAR LAKE NORTH
on Clear Lake
WENATCHEE NATIONAL FOREST

Campsites, facilities: There are 35 sites for tents, trailers or motor homes up to 21

feet long. Picnic tables are provided. Pit toilets and firewood are available, but there is **no piped water.** Pets are permitted. Boat docks, launching facilities and rentals are nearby.

Reservations, fee: No reservations necessary; $4. Open mid-April to late November.

Who to contact: Phone Wenatchee National Forest at (509)653-2205 or write to Naches Ranger District, 510 Highway 12, Naches, WA 98937.

Location: From Yakima, drive 13 miles northwest on US 12 to Naches. From Naches, continue 35.5 miles west on US 12, then go one mile south on County Road 1200. Continue one-half mile south on Forest Service Road 1200-840.

Trip note: This campground is set along the shore of Clear Lake, which is the forebay for Rimrock Lake. No swimming is allowed, only fishing.

Site **88**   **CLEAR LAKE SOUTH**
WENATCHEE NATIONAL FOREST

Campsites, facilities: There are 26 sites for tents, trailers or motor homes up to 21 feet long. Piped water and picnic tables are provided. Pit toilets and firewood are available, but there is **no piped water.** Pets are permitted. Boat docks, launching facilities and rentals are nearby.

Reservations, fee: No reservations necessary; $4. Open mid-April to late November.

Who to contact: Phone Wenatchee National Forest at (509)653-2205 or write to Naches Ranger District, 510 Highway 12, Naches, WA 98937.

Location: From Yakima, drive 13 miles northwest on US 12 to Naches. From Naches, continue 35.5 miles west on US 12, then go one mile south on County Road 1200 to Forest Service Road 1200-800.

Trip note: This campground is located on Clear Lake, which is the forebay for Rimrock Lake. Only fishing is allowed, no swimming.

Site **89**   **DOG LAKE**
on Dog Lake
WENATCHEE NATIONAL FOREST

Campsites, facilities: There are eight sites for tents, trailers or motor homes up to 16 feet long. Picnic tables are provided. Pit toilets and firewood are available, but there is **no piped water.** Pets are permitted. Boat docks and launching facilities are nearby.

Reservations, fee: No reservations necessary; no fee. Open late May to late November.

Who to contact: Phone Wenatchee National Forest at (509)653-2205 or write to Naches Ranger District, 510 Highway 12, Naches, WA 98937.

Location: From Packwood, drive 22 miles northeast on US 12.

Trip note: This campground is on the shore of Dog Lake. Nearby trails lead into the William O. Douglas Wilderness. See a Forest Service map for details.

Site **90**   **WHITE PASS LAKE**
on Leech Lake
WENATCHEE NATIONAL FOREST

Campsites, facilities: There are 16 sites for tents, trailers or motor homes up to 15 feet long. Picnic tables are provided. Pit toilets and firewood are available, but there is **no piped water.** A store, a cafe, a laundromat and ice are located within one mile. Pets are permitted. Boat docks and launching facilities are nearby.

Reservations, fee: No reservations necessary; no fee. Open June to late November.

Who to contact: Phone Wenatchee National Forest at (509)653-2205 or write to

Naches Ranger District, 510 Highway 12, Naches, WA 98937.

Location: From Packwood, drive 19 miles northeast on US 12, then turn north on Forest Service Road and drive 200 yards to Leech Lake.

Trip note: This campground is on the shore of Leech Lake. Nearby trails lead into the Goat Rock Wilderness to the south and the William O. Douglas Wilderness to the north. The trailhead to the Pacific Crest Trail is nearby.

Site **91**
BIG CREEK
on Big Creek
GIFFORD PINCHOT NATIONAL FOREST

Campsites, facilities: There are 30 sites for tents, trailers or motor homes up to 21 feet long. Piped water and picnic tables are provided. Pit toilets and firewood are available. Some facilities are wheelchair accessible. Pets are permitted.

Reservations, fee: No reservations necessary; $5 fee per night. Open late May to early September.

Who to contact: Phone Gifford Pinchot National Forest at (206)494-5515 or write to Packwood Ranger District, Packwood, WA 98361.

Location: From the junction of Highways 7 and 706 at Elbe, drive east about six miles to Ashford. Continue 2.5 miles east on Highway 706, 1.5 miles south on a County Road, then continue one-half miles east on Forest Service Road 152.

Trip note: This campground is on the shore of Big Creek, just a short drive east to Mount Rainier National Park. See the trip note for Site 46 for details about Mount Rainier.

Site **92**
PACKWOOD TRAILER AND RV PARK
in Packwood

Campsites, facilities: There are 15 tent sites and 57 drive-through sites for trailers or motor homes of any length. Electricity, piped water, sewer hookups and picnic tables are provided. Flush toilets, sanitary services, showers, bottled gas, a store, a cafe, a laundromat and ice are available. Pets and motorbikes are permitted.

Reservations, fee: Reservations accepted; $10 fee per night; MasterCard and Visa accepted. Open all year.

Who to contact: Phone (206)494-5145 or write to P.O. Box 309, Packwood, WA 98361.

Location: This park is in Packwood, 25 miles south of Mount Rainier National Park.

Trip note: Nearby recreation options include a riding stable and tennis courts.

Site **93**
MAPLE GROVE CAMPGROUND AND RV PARK
on Cowlitz River

Campsites, facilities: There are ten tent sites and 64 plus drive-through sites for trailers or motor homes of any length. Electricity, piped water and picnic tables are provided. Flush toilets, sanitary services, firewood, a recreation hall, a store, a cafe, a laundromat, showers, bottled gas, ice and a playground are available. Pets are permitted.

Reservations, fee: Reservations accepted; $8-13 fee per night. Open year-round with limited winter facilities.

Who to contact: Phone (206)497-2741 or write to P.O. Box 205, Randle, WA 98377.

Location: This park is located in Randle, 16 miles east of Packwood on US 12.

Trip note: This RV park is set along the shore of the Cowlitz River. Nearby recreation options include hiking trails. One good drive is along winding Highway 26, which starts at Randle and heads up to Strawberry Mountain (5,464 feet). It's a good lookout point towards Mount St. Helens to the west.

Site **94**   REDMON'S RV PARK
near Riffe Lake

Campsites, facilities: There are ten tent sites and six drive-through sites for trailers or motor homes of any length. Electricity, piped water and sewer hookups are provided. Flush toilets, bottled gas, sanitary services, a cafe, a store and ice are available. Pets are permitted.

Reservations, fee: Reservations accepted; $12 fee per night; MasterCard and Visa accepted. Open all year.

Who to contact: Phone (206)498-5425 or write to 8136 Highway 12, Glenoma, WA 98336.

Location: Drive 14 miles south of Centralia on Interstate 5 to the junction with US 12, then go east for 50 miles to the park.

Trip note: Recreation options include visiting huge Riffe Lake to the southeast, or driving up Strawberry Mountain or to the edge of Mount St. Helens National Park—from Randle, drive south on Highway 26.

Site **95**   HARMONY LAKESIDE RV PARK
near Mayfield Lake

Campsites, facilities: There are 14 tent sites and 60 drive-through sites for trailers or motor homes of any length. Electricity, piped water, sewer hookups and picnic tables are provided. Flush toilets, sanitary services, showers, firewood, a recreation hall and ice are available. Pets and motorbikes are permitted. Boat docks and launching facilities are nearby.

Reservations, fee: Reservations accepted; $9-12 fee per night. Open March to late October.

Who to contact: Phone (206)983-3804 or write to 563 Harmony Road, Silver Creek, WA 98585.

Location: Drive 14 miles south of Centralia on Interstate 5 to the junction with US 12, then go east for 18 miles. From there, drive 2.5 miles north on Harmony Road to the park.

Trip note: This park is set between three lakes. Sites 96, 97 and 98 provide nearby options.

Site **96**   LAKE MAYFIELD MARINA RESORT
on Mayfield Lake

Campsites, facilities: There are 50 tent sites and 100 drive-through sites for trailers or motor homes of any length. Electricity, piped water, sewer hookups and picnic tables are provided. Flush toilets, sanitary services, showers, a recreation hall, firewood, a store, a cafe and ice are available. A laundromat is located within seven miles. Pets are permitted. Boat docks and launching facilities are nearby.

Reservations, fee: Reservations accepted; $8-12 fee per night. Open all year.

Who to contact: Phone (206)985-2357 or write to 350 Lake Mayfield Resort, Mossy Rock, WA 98564.

Location: Drive 14 miles south of Centralia on Interstate 5 to the junction with US 12, then go east for 15 miles. From there, go one or two miles south on Winston Creek Road to the resort.

Trip note: This wooded resort is on the shore of Mayfield Reservoir. Nearby recreation options include hiking trails, marked bike trails and a riding stable.

Site **97**
WINSTON CREEK
near Mayfield Lake

Campsites, facilities: There are 11 primitive campsites for tents or small trailers.
Picnic tables, fire grills and tent pads are provided. Pit toilets and piped water
are available. Leashed pets are permitted.

Reservations, fee: No reservations necessary; no fee. Open all year.

Who to contact: Phone the Department of Natural Resources at (800)527-3305 or
write Department of Natural Resources AW-11, 1065 South Capitol Way,
Olympia, WA 98504.

Location: Drive 14 miles south of Centralia on Interstate 5 to the junction with US
12, then go east for 15 miles. From there, go 3.5 miles south on Winston Creek
Road. Turn left on Longbell Road and drive one mile. The camp is on the right.

Trip note: This campground is on the shore of Winston Creek, a primitive, quiet
spot. Mayfield Lake is across US 12, about four miles away, providing an
side-trip option. See the trip note for Site 98.

Site **98**
IKE KINSAWA STATE PARK
at Mayfield Lake

Campsites, facilities: There are 60 sites for tents or self-contained motor homes,
and 41 sites with full hookups for trailers. Picnic tables and fire grills are
provided. Flush toilets, a sanitary disposal station, a store, a cafe, a playground,
piped water, showers and firewood are available. Some facilities are wheelchair
accessible. Leashed pets are permitted. Boat docks and launching facilities are
nearby.

Reservations, fee: Reservations accepted; $7.50-10.50 fee per night. Open all year.

Who to contact: Phone (206)983-3402 or write to 873 Harmony Road, Silver Lake,
WA 98585.

Location: This state park is on Mayfield Lake, just north of Mossyrock, which is
18 miles east of Interstate 5 on US 12.

Trip note: This campground is on the shore of Mayfield Reservoir, an option to Site
97. This site provides more amenities. Nearby recreation options include hiking
trails. Fishing for rainbow trout is a year-round affair here, and can be quite
good. Two fish hatcheries are located nearby.

Site **99**
LEWIS & CLARK STATE PARK
near Chehalis

Campsites, facilities: There are 25 sites for tents or motor homes. Picnic tables and
fire grills are provided. Flush toilets, piped water, firewood and a playground
are available. Leashed pets are permitted.

Reservations, fee: No reservations necessary; $7 fee per night. Open all year.

Who to contact: Phone (206)864-2643 or write to 4583 Jackson Highway, Winlock,
WA 98596.

Location: From Chehalis, drive 12 miles southeast on Jackson Highway 99 and
you'll see the park.

Trip note: This state park has an interpretive center for Mount St. Helens. There is
also a kids' fishing pond stocked with trout and a 1.5-mile nature trail.

Site **100**
FROST ROAD TRAILER PARK
near Lewis and Clark State Park

Campsites, facilities: There are 15 tent sites and 20 drive-through sites for trailers

or motor homes of any length. Electricity, piped water, sewer hookups and picnic tables are provided. Flush toilets, bottled gas, sanitary services, showers, a recreation hall and ice are available. Pets are permitted.

Reservations, fee: Reservations accepted; $7-9 fee per night; MasterCard and Visa accepted. Open all year.

Who to contact: Phone (206)785-3616 or write to 762 Frost Road, Winlock, WA 98596.

Location: Take exit 63 off Interstate 5 near Winlock, drive three-quarters of a mile east, 1.5 mile north and one-half mile west and you'll see the park.

Trip note: The Lewis and Clark State Park is nearby. See the trip note for Site 99.

Site **101**   **STAN HEDWALL PARK**
on Chehalis River

Campsites, facilities: There are 30 sites for trailers or motor homes of any length. Electricity, piped water and picnic tables are provided. Flush toilets, showers, sanitary services and a playground are available. Bottled gas, a store, a cafe and a laundromat are available within one mile. Pets are permitted.

Reservations, fee: Reservations accepted; $7 fee per night. Open March to November.

Who to contact: Phone (206)748-0271 or write to P.O. Box 871, Chehalis, WA 98532.

Location: Take exit 76 off Interstate 5, near Chehalis, and drive one-eighth mile south on Rice Road.

Trip note: This park, set along the Chehalis River, is a possible layover for Interstate 5 travelers. Nearby recreation options include an 18-hole golf course and hiking trails.

Site **102**   **RAINBOW FALLS STATE PARK**
on Chehalis River

Campsites, facilities: There are 50 sites for tents or motor homes up to 32 feet long. Picnic tables are provided. Flush toilets, piped water, sanitary disposal station, showers, firewood and a playground are available. Pets are permitted.

Reservations, fee: No reservations necessary; $7 fee per night. Open all year.

Who to contact: Phone (206)291-3767 or write to 4008 Highway 6, Chehalis, WA 98532.

Location: Take Highway 6 west off Interstate 5 in Chehalis, travel 22 miles west on Highway 6 and you'll see the park entrance.

Trip note: Although this campground is only about a 25-minute drive from Interstate 5, out-of-towners pass it every time. It's a nice spot, with a swinging bridge over the Chehalis River, a pool at the base of Rainbow Falls for swimming, trout fishing opportunities and a self-guided nature trail through the old growth forest.

MOUNT SAINT HELENS

♦

SOME HIGHLIGHTS

59 CAMPGROUNDS

Mount St. Helens

Gifford Pinchot National Forest

Columbia River

Mount Adams

Cispus River

Indian Heaven Wilderness

Big Lava Bed

Goat Rocks Wilderness

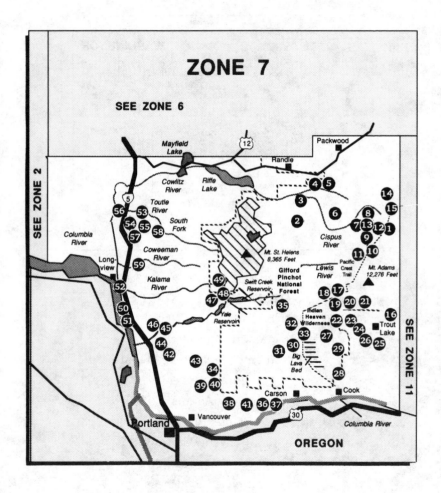

Site **1**

KEENE'S HORSE CAMP
on the South Fork of Spring Creek
GIFFORD PINCHOT NATIONAL FOREST

Campsites, facilities: There are 15 sites for tents, trailers or motor homes up to 21 feet long. Picnic tables and fire grills are provided. Pit toilets, firewood and horse corrals are available, but there is **no piped water.** Leashed pets are permitted.

Reservations, fee: No reservations necessary; no fee. Open July to mid-September.

Who to contact: Phone Gifford Pinchot National Forest at (206)497-7565 or write to Randle Ranger District, Randle, WA 98377.

Location: Take County Road 3 off US 12 in Randle and drive two miles south, then go 29 miles southeast on Forest Service Road 23. Turn northeast on Forest Service Road 2329 and go seven miles, then turn west on Forest Service Road 82 and drive 100 yards to the campground. A Forest Service map is essential.

Trip note: This campground is set at 4,200 feet elevation along the South Fork of Spring Creek on the northwest flank of Mount Adams (elevation 12,276 feet). The Pacific Crest Trail passes within a couple of miles of the camp. There are a number of trails from the camp leading into the backcountry and to several alpine meadows. The meadows are fragile, so it is best to walk along their outer edges, just where they meet the forest.

Site **2**

POLE PATCH
near French Butte
GIFFORD PINCHOT NATIONAL FOREST

Campsites, facilities: There are eight tent sites and four sites for trailers or motor homes up to 21 feet long. Picnic tables are provided. Pit toilets and firewood are available, but there is **no piped water.** Leashed pets are permitted.

Reservations, fee: No reservations necessary; no fee. Open July to mid-September.

Who to contact: Phone Gifford Pinchot National Forest at (206)497-7565 or write to Randle Ranger District, Randle, WA 98377.

Location: Take County Road 3 south off US 12 in Randle and go two miles. At Forest Service Road 25 continue south for 20 miles, then go east on Forest Service Road 28 for three miles. Turn north on Forest Service Road 77 (dirt road) and go six miles to the campground. A Forest Service map is essential.

Trip note: This primitive camp is at 4,400 feet elevation and is in an isolated alpine area near French Butte. Before taking your first step, you should obtain a map of the Gifford Pinchot National Forest, which details all backcountry roads, trails, lakes and streams. In season, there is good berry picking in the area.

Site **3**

IRON CREEK
on Cispus River
GIFFORD PINCHOT NATIONAL FOREST

Campsites, facilities: There are 98 sites for tents, trailers or motor homes. Piped water and picnic tables are provided. Pit toilets and firewood are available. Leashed pets are permitted.

Reservations, fee: No reservations necessary; $5 fee per night. Open mid-May to late October.

Who to contact: Phone Gifford Pinchot National Forest at (206)497-7565 or write to Randle Ranger District, Randle, WA 98377.

Location: Take County Road 3 south off US 12 in Randle and go two miles. Continue south for 7.5 miles on Forest Service Road 25 and you'll see the campground entrance.

Trip note: This is one of the more popular Forest Service campgrounds. This spot is set along the Cispus River near its confluence with Iron Creek. A Forest Service Visitors Center is nearby which provides information about the Mount St. Helens-Mount Adams area. The camp is located along the access route to the best viewing areas for Mount St. Helens.

Site 4
TOWER ROCK
on Cispus River
GIFFORD PINCHOT NATIONAL FOREST

Campsites, facilities: There are 22 sites for tents, trailers or motor homes up to 21 feet long. Piped water and picnic tables are provided. Pit toilets and firewood are available. Leashed pets are permitted.

Reservations, fee: No reservations necessary; $5 fee per night. Open mid-May to late September.

Who to contact: Phone Gifford Pinchot National Forest at (206)497-7565 or write to Randle Ranger District, Randle, WA 98377.

Location: Take County Road 3 off US 12 in Randle and drive south for two miles, then head southeast on Forest Service Road 23 for 5.5 miles. Turn south on Forest Service Road 28 and drive 1.5 miles, then go two miles west on Forest Service Road 76 to the campground. A Forest Service map is essential.

Trip note: This campground is set along the Cispus River. An option to nearby Sites 3 and 5.

Site 5
NORTH FORK
on Cispus River
GIFFORD PINCHOT NATIONAL FOREST

Campsites, facilities: There are 33 sites for tents, trailers or motor homes up to 31 feet long. Piped water and picnic tables are provided. Pit toilets and firewood are available. Leashed pets are permitted.

Reservations, fee: No reservations necessary; $5 fee per night. Open mid-May to late September.

Who to contact: Phone Gifford Pinchot National Forest at (206)497-7565 or write to Randle Ranger District, Randle, WA 98377.

Location: Take County Road 3 off US 12 in Randle and drive south for two miles, then turn southeast on Forest Service Road 23 and drive nine miles to the campground.

Trip note: This campground is set along the North Cispus River. In addition to fishing, there are nature trails and bike paths. A National Forest map details the backcountry.

Site 6
BLUE LAKE CREEK
near Blue Lake
GIFFORD PINCHOT NATIONAL FOREST

Campsites, facilities: There are 12 sites for tents, trailers or motor homes up to 31 feet long. Picnic tables are provided. Pit toilets, piped water and firewood are available. Leashed pets are permitted.

Reservations, fee: No reservations necessary; $3 fee per night. Open mid-May to late September.

Who to contact: Phone Gifford Pinchot National Forest at (206)497-7565 or write to Randle Ranger District, Randle, WA 98377.

Location: Take County Road 3 off US 12 in Randle and drive south for two miles, then turn southeast on Forest Service Road 23 and drive 13 miles to the campground.

Trip note: This is a classic Washington hideaway. The campground is set along Blue Lake Creek, a good base camp for the two-mile hike to Blue Lake. The trailhead is about one-half mile from the camp.

Site **7**
ADAMS FORK
on Cispus River
GIFFORD PINCHOT NATIONAL FOREST

Campsites, facilities: There are 33 sites for tents, trailers or motor homes up to 21 feet long. Piped water and picnic tables are provided. Pit toilets and firewood are available. Boat docks and launching facilities are nearby on the Upper Cispus River. Leashed pets are permitted.

Reservations, fee: No reservations necessary; $3 fee per night. Open mid-May to late September.

Who to contact: Phone Gifford Pinchot National Forest at (206)497-7565 or write to Randle Ranger District, Randle, WA 98377.

Location: Take County Road 3 off US 12 in Randle and drive south for two miles, then turn southeast on Forest Service Road 23 and go 16 miles. Turn southeast on Forest Service Road 20 and drive five miles, then turn east and go 200 yards on Forest Service Road 56 to the campground.

Trip note: This is an option to Site 6, which is about a mile away. This campground is set along the upper Cispus River near Adams Creek and at the foot of Mount Adams (2,600 feet elevation). A nearby trail leads north to Blue Lake, about a half-mile walk from the camp.

Site **8**
CAT CREEK
on Cat Creek and Cispus River
GIFFORD PINCHOT NATIONAL FOREST

Campsites, facilities: There are six sites for tents, trailers or motor homes up to 15 feet long. Picnic tables and fire grills are provided. Pit toilets and firewood are available, but there is **no piped water.** Leashed pets are permitted.

Reservations, fee: No reservations necessary; no fee. Open mid-May to late September.

Who to contact: Phone Gifford Pinchot National Forest at (206)497-7565 or write to Randle Ranger District, Randle, WA 98377.

Location: Take County Road 3 off US 12 in Randle and drive south for two miles, then turn southeast on Forest Service Road 23 and go 16 miles. Turn east on Forest Service Road 21 and drive six miles to the campground.

Trip note: A pretty spot, this campground is set along Cat Creek at its confluence with the Cispus River about ten miles from the summit of Mount Adams. A trail starts less than a mile from the camp and leads up along Blue Lake Ridge to Blue Lake. See a Forest Service map for details.

Site **9**
OLALLIE LAKE
on Olallie Lake
GIFFORD PINCHOT NATIONAL FOREST

Campsites, facilities: There are six sites for tents, trailers or motor homes up to 21 feet long. Picnic tables are provided. Pit toilets and firewood are available, but there is **no piped water.** Boat docks and launching facilities are nearby. Leashed pets are permitted.

Reservations, fee: No reservations necessary; no fee. Open July to mid-September.

Who to contact: Phone Gifford Pinchot National Forest at (206)497-7565 or write to Randle Ranger District, Randle, WA 98377.

Location: Take County Road 3 off US 12 in Randle and drive south for two miles, then turn southeast on Forest Service Road 23 and go 29 miles. Turn north on Forest Service Road 2329 and drive one mile, then continue north on Forest Service Road 5601 for one-half mile to the campground. A Forest Service map is essential.

Trip note: This campground is set along the shore of Olallie Lake at 4,000 feet elevation. This small alpine lake is one of several in the area fed by streams coming off the glaciers on nearby Mount Adams (elevation 12,326 feet). A word to the wise: Mosquitos can be a problem in the spring and early summer. See the chapter about protection against insects.

Site **10**   TAKHLAKH
on Takhlakh Lake
GIFFORD PINCHOT NATIONAL FOREST

Campsites, facilities: There are 54 sites for tents, trailers or motor homes up to 21 feet long. Piped water and picnic tables are provided. Pit toilets and firewood are available. Boat docks and launching facilities are nearby on the lake. Leashed pets are permitted.

Reservations, fee: No reservations necessary; $5 fee per night. Open mid-June to late September.

Who to contact: Phone Gifford Pinchot National Forest at (206)497-7565 or write to Randle Ranger District, Randle, WA 98377.

Location: Take County Road 3 off US 12 in Randle and drive south for two miles, then turn southeast on Forest Service Road 23 and go 29 miles. Go north on Forest Service Road 2329 for 1.5 miles to the campground.

Trip note: This campground is set along the shore of Takhlakh Lake. This is one of five lakes in the area, all accessible by car. It is a beautiful place, but alas, mosquitos abound until late July.

Site **11**   COUNCIL LAKE
on Council Lake
GIFFORD PINCHOT NATIONAL FOREST

Campsites, facilities: There are 11 sites for tents, trailers or motor homes up to 15 feet long. Picnic tables are provided. Pit toilets and firewood are available, but there is **no piped water.** Carry-in boat launching. Leashed pets are permitted.

Reservations, fee: No reservations necessary; no fee. Open July to mid-September.

Who to contact: Phone Gifford Pinchot National Forest at (206)497-7565 or write to Randle Ranger District, Randle, WA 98377.

Location: Take County Road 3 off US 12 in Randle and drive south for two miles, then turn southeast on Forest Service Road 23 and go 30 miles. Turn west on Forest Service Road 2334 and drive one mile to the campground.

Trip note: This campground is set along the shore of Council Lake on the northwest flank of Mount Adams at about 4,000 feet elevation. It is one of three lakeside campgrounds in the area. The others are Sites 9 and 10.

Site 12
KILLEN CREEK
near Mount Adams
GIFFORD PINCHOT NATIONAL FOREST

Campsites, facilities: There are six tent sites and eight sites for trailers or motor homes up to 21 feet long. Picnic tables are provided. Pit toilets and firewood are available, but there is **no piped water.** Leashed pets are permitted.

Reservations, fee: No reservations necessary; no fee. Open July to mid-September.

Who to contact: Phone Gifford Pinchot National Forest at (206)497-7565 or write to Randle Ranger District, Randle, WA 98377.

Location: Take County Road 3 off US 12 in Randle and drive south for two miles, then turn southeast on Forest Service Road 23 and go 29 miles. Turn southeast on Forest Service Road 2329 and go six miles, then go 200 yards west on Forest Service Road 72.

Trip note: This campground is set along Killen Creek at the foot of Mount Adams (elevation 12,326 feet). A trail from the camp leads up the mountain and connects with the Pacific Crest Trail, about a three-mile hike. It's worth the effort.

Site 13
HORSESHOE LAKE
on Horseshoe Lake
GIFFORD PINCHOT NATIONAL FOREST

Campsites, facilities: There are ten sites for tents, trailers or motor homes up to 16 feet long. Picnic tables are provided. Pit toilets and firewood are available, but there is **no piped water.** Boat docks and primitive launching facilities are located on the lake. Leashed pets are permitted.

Reservations, fee: No reservations necessary; no fee. Open mid-June to late September.

Who to contact: Phone Gifford Pinchot National Forest at (206)497-7565 or write to Randle Ranger District, Randle, WA 98377.

Location: Take County Road 3 off US 12 in Randle and drive south for three miles, then turn southeast on Forest Service Road 23 and go 29 miles. Turn northeast on Forest Service Road 2329 and drive 6.5 miles, then turn west and go 1.5 miles on Forest Service Road 78.

Trip note: This campground is set along the shore of Horseshoe Lake. A trail from the camp goes up nearby Green Mountain (elevation 5,000 feet). Another trail heads up the north flank of Mount Adams. See a Forest Service map for details.

Site 14
WALUPT LAKE
on Walupt Lake
GIFFORD PINCHOT NATIONAL FOREST

Campsites, facilities: There are 44 sites for tents, trailers or motor homes up to 21 feet long. Picnic tables are provided. Piped water, pit and vault toilets, and firewood are available. Some facilities are wheelchair accessible. Boat docks are located nearby on Walupt Lake. Leashed pets are permitted.

Reservations, fee: No reservations necessary; $5 per night. Open mid-June to early September.

Who to contact: Phone Gifford Pinchot National Forest at (206)494-5515 or write to Packwood Ranger District, Packwood, WA 98361.

Location: Drive 2.5 miles southwest of Packwood on US 12, then go southeast on Forest Service Road 1302 for 16.5 miles. Head east on Forest Service Road

1114 for 4.5 miles and you'll arrive at the campground.

Trip note: This is a good base-camp for a multi-day vacation. For starters, the camp is set along the shore of Walupt Lake. In addition, several nearby trails lead into the backcountry and other smaller alpine lakes. See a Forest Service map for details.

Site **15**   **WALUPT LAKE HORSE CAMP**
near Goat Rocks Wilderness
GIFFORD PINCHOT NATIONAL FOREST

Campsites, facilities: There are six sites for tents, trailers or motor homes up to 18 feet long. Picnic tables are provided. Pit toilets and firewood are available, but there is **no piped water.**

Reservations, fee: No reservations necessary; no fee. Open mid-June to early September.

Who to contact: Phone Gifford Pinchot National Forest at (206)494-5515 or write to Packwood Ranger District, Packwood, WA 98361.

Location: Drive 2.5 miles southwest of Packwood on US 12, then go southeast on Forest Service Road 2100 for 16.5 miles. Head east on Forest Service Road 2160 for 3.5 miles to the campground.

Trip note: Walupt Lake is just a mile away from the camp, where you can fish or use the boat dock. Several trails lead from Walupt Lake into the backcountry of southern Goat Rocks Wilderness, which has 85 miles of trails that can be used by horses. If you have planned a multi-day horsepack trip, you need to bring in your own feed for the horses.

Site **16**   **MORRISON CREEK**
on Morrison Creek
GIFFORD PINCHOT NATIONAL FOREST

Campsites, facilities: There are 12 tent sites. Picnic tables are provided. Pit toilets and firewood are available, but there is **no piped water.** Leashed pets are permitted.

Reservations, fee: No reservations necessary; no fee. Open July to late September.

Who to contact: Phone Gifford Pinchot National Forest at (509)395-2501 or write to Mount Adams Ranger District, Trout Lake, WA 98650.

Location: From the town of Trout Lake, drive 200 yards southeast on Highway 141, then go north on County Road 17 for two miles. Continue north on Forest Service Road 8000 for 3.5 miles, then head six miles north on Forest Service Road 8040.

Trip note: Here is a prime, yet little-known spot. It is set along Morrison Creek at an elevation of 4,600 feet near the southern slopes of Mount Adams, the second highest mountain in Washington (Rainier is higher). Nearby trails will take you to the ice fields and alpine meadows of the Mount Adams Wilderness.

Site **17**   **SADDLE**
near Mosquito Lakes
GIFFORD PINCHOT NATIONAL FOREST

Campsites, facilities: There are 12 tent sites and two sites for trailers or motor homes up to 15 feet long. Picnic tables are provided. Pit toilets and firewood are available, but there is **no piped water.** Leashed pets are permitted.

Reservations, fee: No reservations necessary; no fee. Open mid-June to late September.

Who to contact: Phone Gifford Pinchot National Forest at (509)395-2501 or write to Mount Adams Ranger District, Trout Lake, WA 98650.

Location: From the town of Trout Lake, drive 5.5 miles southwest on Highway 141, then turn northwest on Forest Service Road 2400 and go 19 miles. Take Forest Service Road 2480 north for one mile to the campground.

Trip note: There are two lakes nearby called Big and Little Mosquito Lakes which are fed by Mosquito Creek. So, while we're on the subject...mosquito attacks in late spring and early summer can be like squadrons of World War II bombers moving in. The Pacific Crest Trail passes right by camp. The area is known for premium huckleberry picking in August and early September.

Site 18   TILLICUM
near Meadow Lake
GIFFORD PINCHOT NATIONAL FOREST

Campsites, facilities: There are four tent sites and 37 sites for tents, trailers or motor homes up to 16 feet long. Piped water and picnic tables are provided. Pit toilets and firewood are available. Leashed pets are permitted.

Reservations, fee: No reservations necessary; no fee. Open mid-June to late September.

Who to contact: Phone Gifford Pinchot National Forest at (509)395-2501 or write to Mount Adams Ranger District, Trout Lake, WA 98650.

Location: From the town of Trout Lake, drive 5.5 miles southwest on Highway 141, then turn northwest on Forest Service Road 2400 and drive 19 miles to the campground.

Trip note: A trail from the camp leads southwest past little Meadow Lake to Squaw Butte, then over to Big Creek. Give it a try, it's a nice hike. A premium area for picking huckleberries in August and early September.

Site 19   SURPRISE LAKES
on Surprise Lakes
GIFFORD PINCHOT NATIONAL FOREST

Campsites, facilities: There are nine tent sites and six sites for trailers or motor homes up to 15 feet long. Picnic tables are provided. Pit toilets and firewood are available, but there is **no piped water.** Leashed pets are permitted.

Reservations, fee: No reservations necessary; no fee. Open mid-June to late September.

Who to contact: Phone Gifford Pinchot National Forest at (509)395-2501 or write to Mount Adams Ranger District, Trout Lake, WA 98650.

Location: From the town of Trout Lake, drive 5.5 miles southwest on Highway 141, then turn northwest on Forest Service Road 2400 and drive 16 miles to the campground.

Trip note: This camp is set near a cluster of small lakes called the Surprise Lakes. The Pacific Crest Trail passes by camp and continues south into the Indian Heaven Wilderness area which is accessible only by foot path. This is an historical Native American site. Mosquito repellent is advised in early summer.

Site 20   COLD SPRINGS
near Pacific Crest Trail
GIFFORD PINCHOT NATIONAL FOREST

Campsites, facilities: There are nine sites for tents, trailers or motor homes up to

15 feet long. Picnic tables are provided. Pit toilets and firewood are available, but there is **no piped water.** Leashed pets are permitted.

Reservations, fee: No reservations necessary; no fee. Open mid-June to late September.

Who to contact: Phone Gifford Pinchot National Forest at (509)395-2501 or write to Mount Adams Ranger District, Trout Lake, WA 98650.

Location: From the town of Trout Lake, drive 5.5 miles southwest on Highway 141, then turn northwest on Forest Service Road 2400 and go 15 miles. Turn northeast on Forest Service Road 220 and go one mile to camp.

Trip note: If you like to hike to remote mountain lakes, this is a great jump-off point. This camp is about a mile from the Pacific Crest Trail, which travels south through the Indian Heaven Wilderness. There you will find over 100 small lakes and ponds.

Site **21**   **MEADOW CREEK**
near Pacific Crest Trail
GIFFORD PINCHOT NATIONAL FOREST

Campsites, facilities: There are eight tent sites. Picnic tables and fire grills are provided. Pit and vault toilets and firewood are available. **No piped water** is available. Leashed pets are permitted.

Reservations, fee: No reservations necessary; no fee. Open mid-June to late September.

Who to contact: Phone Gifford Pinchot National Forest at (509)395-2501 or write to Mount Adams Ranger District, Trout Lake, WA 98650.

Location: From the town of Trout Lake, drive 5.5 miles southwest on Highway 141, then turn northwest on Forest Service Road 2400 and drive 14 miles to the campground.

Trip note: This campground is one mile south of Site 19. A map of Gifford Pinchot National Forest details back roads, trails, lakes and streams.

Site **22**   **CULTUS CREEK**
near Indian Heaven Wilderness
GIFFORD PINCHOT NATIONAL FOREST

Campsites, facilities: There are 51 sites for tents, trailers or motor homes up to 32 feet long. Piped water and picnic tables are provided. Pit toilets and firewood are available. Some facilities are wheelchair accessible. Leashed pets are permitted.

Reservations, fee: No reservations necessary; no fee. Open mid-June to late September.

Who to contact: Phone Gifford Pinchot National Forest at (509)395-2501 or write to Mount Adams Ranger District, Trout Lake, WA 98650.

Location: From the town of Trout Lake, drive 5.5 miles southwest on Highway 141, then turn northwest on Forest Service Road 2400 and drive 12.5 miles to the campground.

Trip note: This campground is set at an elevation of 4,000 feet along Cultus Creek and on the edge of Indian Heaven Wilderness. Nearby trails will take you into this backcountry area, which has numerous small meadows and lakes among the stands of firs and pines.

LITTLE GOOSE
Site **23**
on Little Goose Creek
GIFFORD PINCHOT NATIONAL FOREST

Campsites, facilities: There are 20 sites for tents, trailers or motor homes up to 18 feet long. Piped water and picnic tables are provided. Pit toilets and firewood are available. Leashed pets are permitted.

Reservations, fee: No reservations necessary; no fee. Open June to late October.

Who to contact: Phone Gifford Pinchot National Forest at (509)395-2501 or write to Mount Adams Ranger District, Trout Lake, WA 98650.

Location: From the town of Trout Lake, drive 5.5 miles southwest on Highway 141, then turn northwest on Forest Service Road 2400 and drive ten miles to the campground.

Trip note: This campground is near Little Goose Creek and the backcountry of the Indian Heaven Wilderness. See Sites 15-21 for details of the area. Since this camp has piped water available, it gets heavier use that most of the others in the immediate vicinity. Huckleberry picking is quite good in August and early September in the area.

SMOKEY CREEK CAMPGROUND
Site **24**
near Indian Heaven Wilderness
GIFFORD PINCHOT NATIONAL FOREST

Campsites, facilities: There are three sites for trailers or motor homes up to 21 feet long. Picnic tables are provided. Pit toilets and firewood are available, but there is **no piped water.** Leashed pets are permitted.

Reservations, fee: No reservations necessary; no fee. Open June to late October.

Who to contact: Phone Gifford Pinchot National Forest at (509)395-2501 or write to Mount Adams Ranger District, Trout Lake, WA 98650.

Location: From the town of Trout Lake, drive 5.5 miles southwest on Highway 141, then turn northwest on Forest Service Road 2400 and drive seven miles to the campground.

Trip note: This primitive, little-used campground is set along Smokey Creek. A trail leading into the Indian Heaven Wilderness passes through camp. See the trip notes for Sites 15-20 for details of the recreation options of the immediate area.

ICE CAVE
Site **25**
GIFFORD PINCHOT NATIONAL FOREST

Campsites, facilities: There are seven sites for tents, trailers or motor homes up to 18 feet long. Picnic tables are provided. Pit toilets and firewood are available, but there is **no piped water.**

Reservations, fee: No reservations necessary; no fee. Open June to late October.

Who to contact: Phone Gifford Pinchot National Forest at (509)395-2501 or write to Mount Adams Ranger District, Trout Lake, WA 98650.

Location: From the town of Trout Lake, drive 5.5 miles southwest on Highway 141, then turn west on Forest Service Road 2400 and go one mile. Turn south on Forest Service Road 31 and go 200 yards to the campground.

Trip note: This campground is located near 400-foot deep Ice Cave, one of the many lava tubes in the area. It looks like a different planet out here. This is the closest campground to the town of Trout Lake.

Site 26

PETERSON PRAIRIE
near town of Trout Lake
GIFFORD PINCHOT NATIONAL FOREST

Campsites, facilities: There are 30 sites for tents, trailers or motor homes up to 32 feet long. Piped water, picnic tables and fire grills are provided. Pit toilets and firewood are available. Some facilities are wheelchair accessible.

Reservations, fee: No reservations necessary; $6 fee per night, $8 for a double unit. Open mid-May to late September.

Who to contact: Phone Gifford Pinchot National Forest at (509)395-2501 or write to Mount Adams Ranger District, Trout Lake, WA 98650.

Location: From the town of Trout Lake, drive 5.5 miles southwest on Highway 141, then turn west on Forest Service Road 2400 and drive 2.5 miles to the campground.

Trip note: A good base camp if you want to have a short ride to town as well as access to the nearby wilderness areas. The nearby Sno-park area provides winter recreation, including snowmobiling and cross-country skiing tracks.

Site 27

GOOSE LAKE
on Goose Lake
GIFFORD PINCHOT NATIONAL FOREST

Campsites, facilities: There are 25 tent sites and one site for trailers or motor homes up to 18 feet long. Picnic tables and fire grills are provided. Pit toilets and firewood are available, but there is **no piped water.** A boat ramp is nearby. Leashed pets are permitted.

Reservations, fee: No reservations necessary, no fee. Open mid-June to late September.

Who to contact: Phone Gifford Pinchot National Forest at (509)395-2501 or write to Mount Adams Ranger District, Trout Lake, WA 98650.

Location: From the town of Trout Lake, drive 5.5 miles southwest on Highway 141, then turn west on Forest Service Road 2400 and drive 2.5 miles. At Forest Service Road 6000 go southwest for five more miles.

Trip note: This campground is set at an elevation of 3,200 feet along the shore of Goose Lake. The northern edge of Big Lava Bed and nearby crater are adjacent to camp. See the trip note for Site 33 for details.

Site 28

MOSS CREEK
on White Salmon River
GIFFORD PINCHOT NATIONAL FOREST

Campsites, facilities: There are 18 tent sites and eight sites for trailers or motor homes up to 31 feet long. Piped water, fire grills and picnic tables are provided. Pit toilets, a store, ice and firewood are available. Some facilities are wheelchair accessible. Leashed pets are permitted.

Reservations, fee: No reservations necessary; $4 fee per night. Open mid-May to mid-September.

Who to contact: Phone Gifford Pinchot National Forest at (509)395-2501 or write to Mount Adams Ranger District, Trout Lake, WA 98650.

Location: From Cook on Highway 14, go north on County Road 1800 for eight miles and you'll see the campground.

Trip note: This campground is set along the Little White Salmon River, a short distance from Willard and Big Cedars County Park.

Site 29
OKLAHOMA
on White Salmon River
GIFFORD PINCHOT NATIONAL FOREST

Campsites, facilities: There are 23 tent sites and nine sites for trailers or motor homes up to 21 feet long. Piped water, fire grills and picnic tables are provided. Pit toilets and firewood are available. Some facilities are wheelchair accessible. Leashed pets are permitted.

Reservations, fee: No reservations necessary; $4 fee per night. Open mid-May to mid-October.

Who to contact: Phone Gifford Pinchot National Forest at (509)395-2501 or write to Mount Adams Ranger District, Trout Lake, WA 98650.

Location: From Cook on Highway 14, go north on County Road 1800 for 14 miles and you'll see the campground entrance.

Trip note: This campground is set along the little Little White Salmon River. Big Lava Bed is just west and detailed in the trip note for Site 33. As to why they named this camp "Oklahoma," who knows? Guess they had to name it something.

Site 30
PANTHER CREEK
on Panther Creek
GIFFORD PINCHOT NATIONAL FOREST

Campsites, facilities: There are 33 sites for tents, trailers or motor homes up to 25 feet long. Piped water and picnic tables are provided. Pit toilets and firewood are available. Leashed pets are permitted.

Reservations, fee: No reservations necessary; $6 fee per night. Open mid-May to mid-September.

Who to contact: Phone Gifford Pinchot National Forest at (509)427-5645 or write to Wind River Ranger District, Carson, WA 98610.

Location: From Carson on Highway 14, go nine miles northwest on County Road 92135. Turn east on Forest Service Road 6517 and go 1.5 miles, then turn south on Forest Service Road 65 and drive 100 yards to the campground.

Trip note: This campground is set along Panther Creek, several miles from the Wind River Ranger Station. Just west of the ranger station is the Wind River Nursery, a tree nursery that has the capacity to produce 27 million seedlings per year. Tours are available.

Site 31
BEAVER
on Wind River
GIFFORD PINCHOT NATIONAL FOREST

Campsites, facilities: There are 24 sites for tents, trailers or motor homes up to 25 feet long. Piped water, fire grills, and picnic tables are provided. Pit toilets and firewood are available. Some facilities are wheelchair accessible. Group camping facilities are also available. Leashed pets are permitted.

Reservations, fee: No reservations necessary; $8 fee per night. For groups, fee is $20 to $60 per night. Open mid-May to late October.

Who to contact: Phone Gifford Pinchot National Forest at (509)427-5645 or write to Wind River Ranger District, Carson, WA 98610.

Location: From Carson on Highway 14, go 12 miles northwest on County Road 92135 and you'll see the campground entrance.

Trip note: This campground is set along Wind River about four miles from Trapper

Creek Wilderness. It's a nice spot, small and remote, yet it has piped water—the perfect combination.

Site **32**   **PARADISE CREEK**
on Paradise Creek and Wind River
GIFFORD PINCHOT NATIONAL FOREST

Campsites, facilities: There are 42 sites for tents, trailers or motor homes up to 25 feet long. Piped water, fire grills and picnic tables are provided. Pit toilets and firewood are available. Some facilities are wheelchair accessible. Leashed pets are permitted.

Reservations, fee: No reservations necessary; $6 fee per night. Open mid-May to mid-September.

Who to contact: Phone Gifford Pinchot National Forest at (509)427-5645 or write to Wind River Ranger District, Carson, WA 98610.

Location: From Carson on Highway 14, go 13 miles northwest on County Road 92135, then turn north on Forest Service Road 30 and go six miles.

Trip note: This is an option to Site 31; this campground is set deeper in the Gifford Pinchot National Forest. It's located at the confluence of Paradise Creek and the Wind River. Lava Butte is a short distance from the camp and accessible by trail.

Site **33**   **FALLS CREEK-CREST HORSE CAMP**
near Pacific Crest Trail
GIFFORD PINCHOT NATIONAL FOREST

Campsites, facilities: There are 14 sites for tents, trailers or motor homes up to 15 feet long. Picnic tables and fire grills are provided. Pit toilets and firewood are available, but there is **no piped water.** Leashed pets are permitted.

Reservations, fee: No reservations necessary; no fee. Open mid-June to late September.

Who to contact: Phone Gifford Pinchot National Forest at (509)427-5645 or write to Wind River Ranger District, Carson, WA 98610.

Location: From Carson on Highway 14, go 13 miles northwest on County Road 92135, 1.5 miles east on Forest Service Road 6517, and then 12.5 miles north on Forest Service Road 65 to the campground.

Trip note: This camp is set along the Pacific Crest Trail and adjacent to the Big Lava Bed near the crater. How big is Big Lava Bed? About 12,000 acres, with lava tubes and other strange formations. The Forest Service cautions: "No trails or roads traverse the lava field, generally limiting exploration to the perimeter. If you choose to explore the interior, choose your route carefully. Compasses are not always reliable due to local magnetic influences in the vast expanse of rock." The southern boundary of Indian Heaven Wilderness is two miles north of the camp and is accessible by the Pacific Crest Trail.

Site **34**   **SUNSET**
on the East Fork of Lewis River
GIFFORD PINCHOT NATIONAL FOREST

Campsites, facilities: There are ten sites for tents, trailers or motor homes up to 22 feet long. Well water and picnic tables are provided. Pit toilets and firewood are available. Leashed pets are permitted.

Reservations, fee: No reservations necessary; $4 fee per night. Open April through October.

Who to contact: Phone Gifford Pinchot National Forest at (509)427-5645 or write to Wind River Ranger District, Carson, WA 98610.

Location: From Highway 503 near Rock Creek (four miles north of Battle Ground), take County Road 12 and drive 15 miles east to the campground.

Trip note: This campground is set at 1,000 feet elevation along the East Fork of the Lewis River. There are a number of trails in the area for fishing, huckleberry picking, and mushroom hunting.

Site **35**   **LOWER LEWIS RIVER FALLS**
on Lewis River
GIFFORD PINCHOT NATIONAL FOREST

Campsites, facilities: There are 20 sites for tents, trailers or motor homes up to 20 feet long. **No piped water** is available. Picnic tables are provided. Pit toilets and firewood are available. Leashed pets are permitted.

Reservations, fee: No reservations necessary; no fee. Open May to October.

Who to contact: Phone Gifford Pinchot National Forest at (509)247-5743 or write to Mount St. Helens National Volcanic Monument, Amboy, WA 98601.

Location: From Interstate 5 at Woodland, take Highway 503 to Cougar. Drive east on Forest Service Road 90 for 28 miles to the campground.

Trip note: This is one of the great spots in the Pacific Northwest. The camp is set in the primary viewing area for three major waterfalls on the Lewis River. The spectacular Lewis River trail is available for hiking or horseback riding. The elevation is 1,300 feet.

Site **36**   **BEACON ROCK TRAILER PARK**
on Columbia River

Campsites, facilities: There are six tent sites and 15 drive-through sites for trailers or motor homes of any length. Electricity, piped water, sewer hookups and picnic tables are provided. Flush toilets, bottled gas, sanitary services, showers, firewood, a store, a cafe, a recreation hall, a laundromat and ice are available. Pets are permitted. Boat launching facilities are located nearby on the Columbia River.

Reservations, fee: Reservations accepted; $6-10 fee per night. Open all year.

Who to contact: Phone (509)427-8473 or write to Beacon Rock Trailer Park, Skamania, WA 98648.

Location: Drive 15 miles west of Carson on Highway 14 to milepost 34, and you will see the park in Skamania, at the corner of Highway 14 and Moorage Road.

Trip note: This trailer park is set along the Columbia River, a short distance from Beacon Rock State Park. See the trip note for Site 37 for details. Nearby recreation options include an 18-hole golf course.

Site **37**   **BEACON ROCK STATE PARK**
on Columbia River

Campsites, facilities: There are 33 sites for tents or motor homes up to 50 feet long. Picnic tables and fire grills are provided. Flush toilets, sanitary disposal station, and a playground are available. Showers and firewood are available for an extra fee. Some facilities are wheelchair accessible. Boat docks, launching facilities and rentals are nearby.

Reservations, fee: No reservations necessary; $7.50-10.50 fee per night. Open all year with limited winter facilities.

Who to contact: Phone (509)427-8265 or write to MP34 83L, State Road 14,

Skamania, WA 98648.

Location: Drive 35 miles east of Vancouver, Washington, on Highway 14 and you'll see the park entrance.

Trip note: This state park is set along the Columbia River with hiking trails heading inland. One trail leads to Beacon Rock, the second largest monolith in the world, which overlooks the Columbia River Gorge. If you like to fish, sturgeon are plentiful in the Columbia. Remember, there is a six-foot maximum size limit for Mr. Sturgeon. A riding stable is nearby.

Site 38   JONES CREEK
near Columbia River

Campsites, facilities: There are nine campsites for tents or small trailers. Picnic tables, fire grills and tent pads are provided. Pit toilets and piped water are available. Motorbikes are permitted. Leashed pets are also permitted.

Reservations, fee: No reservations necessary; no fee. Open all year.

Who to contact: Phone the Department of Natural Resources at (800)527-3305 or write to Department of Natural Resources AW-11, 1065 South Capitol Way, Olympia, WA 98504.

Location: Drive six miles east of Vancouver, Washington, on Highway 14 to Camas. From the junction of Highway 14 and Highway 500, go north on Highway 500 for four miles to Fern Prairie. Turn right on 19th Street and go one mile. Turn left on 292 Avenue and go two miles, then turn right on Ireland Drive and go about 200 yards. Turn left on Lessard Road and go two miles, then continue straight on Winters Road for 1.5 miles and you'll arrive at the campground.

Trip note: A lot of folks cruising the Columbia River Highway miss this spot, but it's worth a look. It is set along Jones Creek. A motorbike trail adjacent to camp makes a seven-mile loop through the nearby area.

Site 39   COLD CREEK
on Cold Creek

Campsites, facilities: There are six campsites for tents or small trailers. Picnic tables, fire grills and tent pads are provided. Pit toilets and piped water are available. Leashed pets are permitted.

Reservations, fee: No reservations necessary; no fee. Open all year.

Who to contact: Phone the Department of Natural Resources at (800)527-3305 or write to Department of Natural Resources AW-11, 1065 South Capitol Way, Olympia, WA 98504.

Location: Start five miles north of Vancouver, Washington, at exit 9 off Interstate 5. Go east on NE 179th Street for 5.5 miles. Turn right on Highway 503 and go 1.5 miles. Turn left on NE 159th Street and go three miles before turning right on 182nd Avenue. From there, drive one mile, then turn left on NE 139th (Road L 1400) and go eight miles, and then turn left on Road L 1000 and drive three miles. Make another left and go about one mile to the campground.

Trip note: Okay, the directions are complicated, but few things worth remembering come easy, right? This campground is set along Cold Creek. There are trails nearby for hiking and horseback riding. It gets minimal use although it has piped water.

Site 40   ROCK CREEK
on Rock Creek

Campsites, facilities: There are 19 campsites for tents or small trailers. Picnic tables, fire grills and tent pads are provided. Pit toilets and piped water are available. A horse loading ramp is nearby. Leashed pets are permitted.

Reservations, fee: No reservations necessary; no fee. Open all year.

Who to contact: Phone the Department of Natural Resources at (800)527-3305 or write to Department of Natural Resources AW-11, 1065 South Capitol Way, Olympia, WA 98504.

Location: Start five miles north of Vancouver, Washington, at exit 9 off Interstate 5. Go east on NE 179th Street for 5.5 miles, turn right on Highway 503 and go 1.5 miles. Turn left on NE 159th Street and go three miles, and then turn right on 182nd Avenue and drive one mile. Turn left on NE 139th (Road L 1400) and go eight miles, then turn left on Road L 1000 and drive 3.5 miles. (You'll pass Cold Creek—Site 39—after three miles.) Turn left on Road L 1200 and go about 200 yards to the campground, which will be on your right.

Trip note: A nearby option to Site 39, also managed by the Department of Natural Resources. This camp is set in a wooded area along Rock Creek. Nearby trails are for use by hikers and horseback riders.

Site 41   DOUGAN CREEK
near Washougal River

Campsites, facilities: There are seven campsites for tents or small trailers. Picnic tables, fire grills and tent pads are provided. Pit toilets and piped water are available. Leashed pets are available.

Reservations, fee: No reservations necessary; no fee. Open all year.

Who to contact: Phone the Department of Natural Resources at (800)527-3305 or write to Department of Natural Resources AW-11, 1065 South Capitol Way, Olympia, WA 98504.

Location: Drive 20 miles east of Vancouver, Washington, on Highway 14, turn north on Highway 140 and go five miles to Washougal River Road. Turn right on Washougal River Road and go about seven miles until you see the campground on your right.

Trip note: This campground is set along Dougan Creek where it empties into the Washougal River. It's small, remote and has piped water.

Site 42   BIG FIR CAMPGROUND
near Paradise Point State Park

Campsites, facilities: There are 100 tent sites and 28 sites for trailers or motor homes of any length. Electricity, piped water, sewer hookups and picnic tables are provided. Flush toilets, sanitary services, showers, a recreation hall, a store and ice are available. Pets and motorbikes are permitted. Boat launching facilities are located nearby.

Reservations, fee: Reservations accepted; $13 fee per night. Open all year.

Who to contact: Phone (206)887-8970 or write to 5515 NE 259th Street, Ridgefield, WA 98642.

Location: Take the Ridgefield exit 14 off Interstate 5 and drive four miles east. Follow the signs to the campground.

Trip note: This wooded campground is in a rural area not far from Paradise Point State Park. See the trip note for Site 44 for details.

Site 43   BATTLE GROUND LAKE STATE PARK
on Battle Ground Lake

Campsites, facilities: There are 35 sites for tents or self-contained motor homes up to 50 feet long. An additional 15 primitive campsites are also available. Piped water, fire grills and picnic tables are provided. Flush toilets, sanitary disposal station, showers, a store, firewood, a restaurant and playground are available. Some facilities are wheelchair accessible. Leashed pets are permitted. Boat launching facilities and rentals are nearby.

Reservations, fee: No reservations necessary; $7.50-10.50 fee per night. Open all year.

Who to contact: Phone (206)687-4621 or write to 17612 NE Palmer Road, Battleground, WA 98604.

Location: Drive 21 miles northeast of Vancouver, Washington, on Highway 503 until you get to the Battle Ground crossroads. Head east for three miles, turn north and go 1.5 miles to the lake.

Trip note: This state park has horseback riding trails and some primitive campsites that will accommodate campers with horses. It is a good lake for swimming as well as fishing and it has a nice beach area. If you are traveling on Interstate 5 and looking for a quiet layover, this is ideal and only about a 15-minute drive from the highway.

Site **44**   **PARADISE POINT STATE PARK**
on the East Fork of Lewis River

Campsites, facilities: There are 70 sites for tents or self-contained motor homes up to 45 feet long. An additional nine primitive campsites are available. Piped water, fire grills and picnic tables are provided. Flush toilets, sanitary services, firewood and showers are available. Leashed pets are permitted. Boat launching facilities are located nearby on the East Fork of the Lewis River.

Reservations, fee: No reservations necessary; $7.50-10.50 fee per night. Open all year.

Who to contact: Phone (206)263-2350 or write to Route 1, Box 33914, Ridgefield, WA 98642.

Location: Drive 15 miles north of Vancouver, Washington, on Interstate 5. The park is east of the freeway.

Trip note: This campground is set along the East Fork of the Lewis River. Nearby recreation options include an 18-hole golf course and a two-mile hiking trail. This is a good motor home layover spot for Interstate 5 travelers.

Site **45**   **WOODLAND**
near Woodland

Campsites, facilities: There are ten campsites for tents or small trailers. Picnic tables, fire grills and tent pads are provided. Pit toilets, piped water, firewood and a children's playground are available. Some facilities are wheelchair accessible. Leashed pets are permitted.

Reservations, fee: No reservations necessary; no fee. Open all year.

Who to contact: Phone the Department of Natural Resources at (800)527-3305 or write to Department of Natural Resources AW-11, 1065 South Capitol Way, Olympia, WA 98504.

Location: Take exit 21 off Interstate 5 in Woodland and go 100 yards east on Highway 503. Turn right to East CC Street and go just south of the bridge. Turn right on County Road 1 and drive 300 yards. Then turn left on County Road 38 and drive 2.5 miles and you'll see the campground to your left.

Trip note: This is an optimum spot for people who are touring Washington on Interstate 5 but want a quiet setting along the way. This campground is nestled in a forest area that is managed by the Department of Natural Resources. It's quiet, near the main highways and has playground equipment for the kids.

Site **46**   **LEWIS RIVER RV PARK**
                               on Lewis River

Campsites, facilities: There are 90 sites for tents, trailers or motor homes of any length. Electricity, piped water, sewer hookups and picnic tables are provided. Flush toilets, bottled gas, firewood, sanitary services, showers, bathhouse, a store, a cafe, a laundromat, ice and a swimming pool are available. Pets are permitted. Boat docks, launching facilities and rentals are nearby on the Lewis River. Discounts are given for Good Sam members.

Reservations, fee: Reservations accepted; $12.50-14 per night; MasterCard and Visa accepted. Open all year.

Who to contact: Phone (206)225-9556 or write to 3125 Lewis River Road, Woodland, WA 98674.

Location: Take exit 21 off Interstate 5 in Woodland and drive four miles east on Highway 503-Lewis River Road to 3125 Lewis River Road.

Trip note: This park is set along the Lewis River, where the salmon and the steelhead can run thick in season. Nearby recreation options include an 18-hole golf course.

Site **47**   **VOLCANO VIEW CAMPGROUND**
                              near Mount St. Helens

Campsites, facilities: There are 28 tent sites and 47 sites for trailers or motor homes of any length. Electricity, piped water, sewer hookups and picnic tables are provided. Flush toilets, sanitary services, showers, a recreation hall, firewood, a store, a cafe and ice are available. Pets and motorbikes are permitted.

Reservations, fee: Reservations accepted; $6-10.50 fee per night. Open all year.

Who to contact: Phone (206)231-4329 or write to 230 Highway 503, Ariel, WA 98603.

Location: Take exit 21 off Interstate 5 in Woodland and drive 23 miles east to Jack's Restaurant, then turn south and go one mile to campground.

Trip note: This campground is close to Mount St. Helens and along the edge of Yale Reservoir. Merrill Lake and Swift Creek Reservoir are nearby.

Site **48**   **LONE FIR RESORT**
                               near Yale Lake

Campsites, facilities: There are five tent sites and 32 sites for trailers or motor homes of any length. Electricity, piped water, sewer hookups and picnic tables are provided. Flush toilets, a laundromat, showers, ice and a swimming pool are available. Bottled gas, sanitary services, a store and a cafe are located within one mile. Pets and motorbikes are permitted. Boat docks and launching facilities are nearby.

Reservations, fee: Reservations accepted; $10.50-12 fee per night; MasterCard and Visa accepted. Open all year.

Who to contact: Phone (206)238-5210 or write to Lone Fir Resort, Cougar, WA 98616.

Location: Take exit 21 off Interstate 5 in Woodland and drive 29 miles east on Highway 503 (Lewis River Road) and you'll see the resort.

Trip note: This campground is near Yale Lake, the smallest of four lakes in the area. This private camp is designed primarily for motor home use.

Site **49**
LAKE MERRILL
near Mount St. Helens

Campsites, facilities: There are 11 campsites for tents or small trailers. Picnic tables, fire grills and tent pads are provided. Pit toilets, firewood and piped water are available. Boat launching facilities are located on Lake Merrill. Leashed pets are permitted.

Reservations, fee: No reservations necessary; no fee. Open all year.

Who to contact: Phone the Department of Natural Resources at (800)527-3305 or write to Department of Natural Resources AW-11, 1065 South Capitol Way, Olympia, WA 98504.

Location: Take exit 21 off Interstate 5 in Woodland and drive 29 miles east on Highway 503 to Cougar. Go north on Cougar Road for 5.5 miles, then turn left on Forest Service Road 81 and drive 4.5 miles. Turn left on the access road to the campground.

Trip note: This is the best choice in the area for campers seeking a primitive, quiet setting. This wooded campground is nestled on the shore of Lake Merrill, very near Mount St. Helens.

Site **50**
LOUIS RASMUSSEN RV PARK
on Columbia River

Campsites, facilities: There are 50 tent sites and 22 drive-through sites for trailers or motor homes of any length. Electricity, piped water and sewer hookups are provided. Flush toilets, showers and sanitary services are available. Bottled gas, a store, a cafe, a laundromat and ice are located within one mile. Pets and motorbikes are permitted. Boat docks and launching facilities are nearby.

Reservations, fee: Reservations accepted; $8 fee per night. Open all year.

Who to contact: Phone (206)673-2626 or write to P.O. Box 7, Kalama, WA 98625.

Location: Take exit 30 off Interstate 5 near Kalama and drive 100 feet west then go south for one-half mile to the RV park.

Trip note: This park is in an urban area along the shore of the Columbia River. Nearby recreation options include a full-service marina and tennis courts. It's a good motor home stopover for Interstate 5 travelers.

Site **51**
CAMP KALAMA CAMPGROUND
on Columbia River

Campsites, facilities: There are 30 tent sites and 75 drive-through sites for trailers or motor homes of any length. Electricity, piped water, sewer hookups and picnic tables are provided. Flush toilets, bottled gas, sanitary services, a store, a cafe, showers, firewood, a laundromat, ice and playground are available. Pets and motorbikes are permitted. Boat launching facilities are located nearby.

Reservations, fee: Reservations accepted; $11 fee per night; MasterCard and Visa accepted. Open all year.

Who to contact: Phone (206)673-2456 or write to 5055 North Meeker Drive, Kalama, WA 98625.

Location: Take exit 32 off Interstate 5 near Kalama, drive one block south of the frontage road and you'll see the campground.

Trip note: An option to Site 50 with a more rustic setting and some accommodations for tent campers. It is set along the Columbia River. Nearby recreation options include a full-service marina.

Site 52   OAKS TRAILER AND RV PARK
in Commerce

Campsites, facilities: There are 62 drive-through sites for trailers or motor homes of any length. Electricity, piped water, sewer hookups and picnic tables are provided. Flush toilets, sanitary services, showers, a laundromat, ice and playground are available. Bottled gas, a store and a cafe are located within one mile. Pets are permitted.

Reservations, fee: Reservations accepted; $11 fee per night; MasterCard and Visa accepted. Open all year.

Who to contact: Phone (206)425-2708 or write to 636 California Way, Longview, WA 98632.

Location: Take exit 36 off Interstate 5 near Longview and drive west on Highway 432 for 3.5 miles to Commerce. Go one block south and then turn southeast.

Trip note: This park is in an urban area near Longview. Nearby recreation options include an 18-hole golf course, marked bike trails and a full-service marina.

Site 53   SILVER LAKE MOTEL AND RESORT
on Silver Lake

Campsites, facilities: There are 13 tent sites and 22 sites for trailers or motor homes of any length. Electricity, piped water, sewer hookups and picnic tables are provided. Flush toilets, a store, showers, ice and playground are available. Sanitary services and a cafe are located within one mile. Pets and motorbikes are permitted. Boat docks, launching facilities and rentals are nearby.

Reservations, fee: Reservations accepted; $9-12 fee per night; MasterCard and Visa accepted. Open all year.

Who to contact: Phone (206)274-6141 or write to 3201 Spirit Lake Highway, Silver Lake, WA 98645.

Location: Take exit 49 off Interstate 5 and go 6.5 miles east on Highway 504 to the park.

Trip note: This park is set along the shore of Silver Lake, one of Washington's better bass fishing lakes.

Site 54   MERMAC STORE AND RV PARK
near Toutle River

Campsites, facilities: There are ten tent sites and 13 drive-through sites for trailers or motor homes of any length. Electricity, piped water, sewer hookups and picnic tables are provided. Flush toilets, showers, firewood, a store and ice are available. Pets and motorbikes are permitted. Boat launching facilities are nearby.

Reservations, fee: Reservations accepted; $6-10 fee per night; MasterCard and Visa accepted. Open all year.

Who to contact: Phone (206)274-6785 or write to 112 Burma Road, Castle Rock, WA 98611.

Location: Take exit 52 off Interstate 5 at Castle Rock and drive 100 yards east to the park.

Trip note: This wooded park is about 400 yards from the Toutle River and one-half mile from the Cowlitz River. Take your pick.

Site 55
TOUTLE VILLAGE
on Silver Lake

Campsites, facilities: There are six tent sites and ten drive-through sites for trailers or motor homes of any length. Electricity, piped water, sewer hookups and picnic tables are provided. Flush toilets, sanitary services, a store, showers, a recreation hall, a cafe, a laundromat and ice are available. Pets and motorbikes are permitted. Boat docks, launching facilities and rentals are nearby.

Reservations, fee: Reservations accepted; $10 fee per night. Open all year.

Who to contact: Phone (206)274-7343 or write to 5037 Spirit Lake Highway, Toutle, WA 98649.

Location: Take exit 49 off Interstate 5 and drive ten miles east on Highway 504 and you'll see the park.

Trip note: This campground is set on the shore of Silver Lake. Nearby recreation options include a full-service marina. Bass fishing can be quite good in early summer, when they pop out of their winter doldrums.

Site 56
RIVER OAKS CAMPGROUND
on Cowlitz River

Campsites, facilities: There are 50 tent sites and 24 drive-through sites for trailers or motor homes of any length. Piped water and picnic tables are provided. Flush toilets, electricity, showers, sanitary services and ice are available. Bottled gas, a store, a cafe and a laundromat are located within one mile. Pets and motorbikes are permitted. Boat launching facilities are nearby.

Reservations, fee: Reservations accepted; $7-11.50 fee per night. Open all year.

Who to contact: Phone (206)864-2895 or write to 491 Highway 506, Toledo, WA 98591.

Location: Take exit 59 off Interstate 5 near Castle Rock and drive west on Highway 506 for one-half mile to the campground.

Trip note: This camp is set right on the Cowlitz River. Every spring the river is the site of a big smelt run. They come thick. Using a dip net, you can fill a five-gallon bucket with just a couple of dips.

Site 57
SEQUEST STATE PARK
near Silver Lake

Campsites, facilities: There are 79 sites for tents and self-contained motor homes, and 16 additional sites for trailers or motor homes with full hookups. Picnic tables are provided. Flush toilets, playground, piped water, a sanitary disposal station, showers and firewood are available. A store is available within one mile. Some facilities are wheelchair accessible.

Reservations, fee: No reservations necessary; $6 fee per night. Open all year.

Who to contact: Phone (206)274-8633 or write to Box 3030, Spirit Lake Highway, Castle Rock, WA 98611.

Location: Take exit 49 off Interstate 5 and drive seven miles east on Highway 504 to the park.

Trip note: This state park is located across from Silver Lake, and is considered to be one of western Washington's finest bass fishing lakes.

Site 58
VOLCANO VIEW RESORT
on Silver Lake

Campsites, facilities: There are 15 tent sites and 26 drive-through sites for trailers

or motor homes of any length. Electricity, piped water, sewer hookups and picnic tables are provided. Sanitary services, a cafe and ice are available. Bottled gas, a store and a laundromat are located within one mile. Pets and motorbikes are permitted. Boat docks, launching facilities and rentals are obtained on Silver Lake.

Reservations, fee: Reservations accepted; $6.50-12.50 fee per night; MasterCard and Visa accepted. Open all year.

Who to contact: Phone (206)274-7087 or write to 4220 Spirit Lake Highway, Silver Lake, WA 98645.

Location: Take exit 49 off Interstate 5 and drive nine miles east on Highway 504 to the resort.

Trip note: This resort is set along the shore of Silver Lake, one of three campgrounds on the lake. The others are Sites 53 and 55.

Site **59**

THE CEDARS RV PARK
near Coweeman River

Campsites, facilities: There are seven tent sites and 20 drive-through sites for trailers or motor homes of any length. Electricity, piped water and picnic tables are provided. Flush toilets, Bottled gas, showers, sanitary services, a laundromat and ice are available. Pets and motorbikes are permitted.

Reservations, fee: Reservations accepted; $7.50-9 fee per night. Open April to November.

Who to contact: Phone (206)274-7019 or write to 115 Beauvals Road, Kelso, WA 98626.

Location: Take exit 46 off Interstate 5 and drive east to the first service road, then go north to the park.

Trip note: This private park provides a good stopover for Interstate 5 travelers looking for a spot near Kelso. The nearby Coweeman River is a highlight, along with the park's natural setting.

WENATCHEE

♦

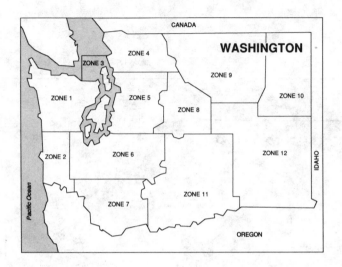

SOME HIGHLIGHTS

61 CAMPGROUNDS

Wenatchee National Forest

Glacier Peak Wilderness

Entiat River

Chiwawa River

Lake Chelan

Wenatchee River

Alpine Lakes Wilderness

Cle Elum River

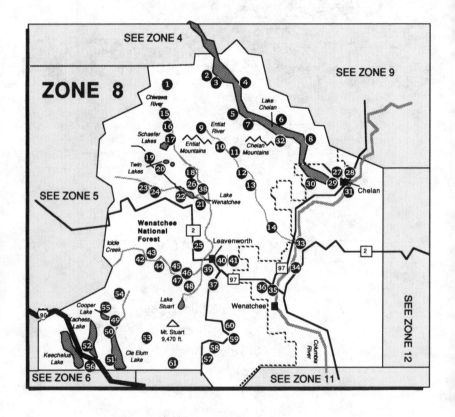

ZONE 8

SEE ZONE 4

SEE ZONE 9

SEE ZONE 5

SEE ZONE 6

SEE ZONE 11

SEE ZONE 12

Chiwawa River

Lake Chelan

Schaefer Lakes

Entiat River

Entiat Mountains

Chelan Mountains

Twin Lakes

Lake Wenatchee

Wenatchee National Forest

Icicle Creek

Leavenworth

Cooper Lake

Lake Stuart

Wenatchee

Kachess Lake

Mt. Stuart 9,470 ft.

Keechelus Lake

Cle Elum Lake

Columbia River

Chelan

HOLDEN
Site **1**   near Glacier Peak Wilderness, boat-in or ferry only
WENATCHEE NATIONAL FOREST

Campsites, facilities: There are eight primitive tent sites that are accessible only by boat or ferry. Picnic tables are provided. Pit toilets and firewood are available, but there is **no piped water.**

Reservations, fee: No reservations necessary; no fee. Open mid-June to late September.

Who to contact: Phone Wenatchee National Forest at (509)682-2576 or write to Chelan Ranger District, Chelan, WA, 98816.

Location: Take the 8:30 a.m. ferry from Chelan, Manson or Fields Point Landing and go to Lucerne, 41 miles from the town of Chelan. (This spectacular voyage costs $18 or less for a round trip, depending on your destination. For more information call (509)682-2224). From Lucerne take the bus 12 miles west to Holden. The campground is at the end of the road.

Trip note: Getting there is half the fun, with a ferry boat and bus rides. Several trails to lakes in the Glacier Peak Wilderness are accessible from a trail next to the campground, which is set along Railroad Creek. Since this area is along the eastern slope of the Cascade Range, it is drier than the western slopes and not as heavily forested. However, there is no shortage of glacier-fed streams and lakes in the area. See a Forest Service map for details. Less than a mile from the campground is the Holden Mine site, which was Washington's largest gold, copper and zinc mine until it closed in 1957. Many of the buildings from the mining town have been preserved and Holden Village offers housing and meals for travelers.

LUCERNE
Site **2**   on Lake Chelan, boat-in or ferry only
WENATCHEE NATIONAL FOREST

Campsites, facilities: There are two tent sites accessible only by boat. Piped water, fire grills and picnic tables are provided. Pit toilets and firewood are available. A cafe is located within one mile. Boat docks are nearby.

Reservations, fee: No reservations necessary; no fee. Open May to late October.

Who to contact: Phone Wenatchee National Forest at (509)682-2576 or write to Chelan Ranger District, Chelan, WA, 98816.

Location: Take the 8:30 a.m ferry from Chelan, Manson or Fields Point Landing and go to Lucerne, 41 miles from the town of Chelan. See Site 1 for ferry information.

Trip note: This campground is set along the shore of Lake Chelan, a 55-mile long lake. It's the second deepest lake in North America, with a depth of 1,500 feet. Mountains reaching to 8,000 feet flank each side of the lake. See the trip note for Site 1 for information on the Holden Mine and Village.

DOMKE LAKE
Site **3**   near Glacier Peak Wilderness, boat-in or ferry only
WENATCHEE NATIONAL FOREST

Campsites, facilities: There are six tent sites accessible only by boat. Picnic tables are provided. Pit toilets and firewood are available, but there is **no piped water.** Boat docks and rentals are nearby.

Reservations, fee: No reservations necessary; no fee. Open May to late October.

Who to contact: Phone Wenatchee National Forest at (509)682-2576 or write to Chelan Ranger District, Chelan, WA, 98816.

Location: Take the 8:30 a.m ferry from Chelan, Manson or Fields Point Landing and get off at Lucerne, 41 miles from Chelan. Hike about one mile to Domke Lake and the campground. See Site 1 for additional ferry information.

Trip note: Little known and little used, this is a perfect jump-off for a wilderness backpacking trip. Domke Lake is about one mile long and one-half mile wide. The trail continues past the lake into Glacier Peak Wilderness. See a Forest Service map for details.

Site **4**

PRINCE CREEK
on Lake Chelan, boat-in or ferry only
WENATCHEE NATIONAL FOREST

Campsites, facilities: There are five tent sites accessible only by boat. Picnic tables are provided. Pit toilets and firewood are available, but there is **no piped water.** Boat docks are nearby.

Reservations, fee: No reservations necessary; no fee. Open May to mid-November.

Who to contact: Phone Wenatchee National Forest at (509)682-2576 or write to Chelan Ranger District, Chelan, WA, 98816.

Location: Take the 8:30 a.m ferry from Chelan, Manson or Fields Point Landing and get off at Prince Creek, 35 miles from Chelan. See Site 1 for additional ferry information.

Trip note: This camp is set along the shore of Lake Chelan at the mouth of Prince Creek. A trail from camp follows Prince Creek into the Lake Chelan-Sawtooth Wilderness, and then connects to a network of other trails—all of which lead to various lakes and streams. A Forest Service map details the options.

Site **5**

GRAHAM HARBOR CREEK
on Lake Chelan, boat-in or ferry only
WENATCHEE NATIONAL FOREST

Campsites, facilities: There are five tent sites accessible only by boat. Picnic tables are provided. Pit toilets and firewood are available, but there is **no piped water.** Boat docks are nearby.

Reservations, fee: No reservations necessary; no fee. Open all year.

Who to contact: Phone Wenatchee National Forest at (509)682-2576 or write to Chelan Ranger District, Chelan, WA, 98816.

Location: Take the 8:30 a.m ferry from Chelan, Manson or Fields Point Landing and get off at Graham Harbor Creek, 31 miles from Chelan. See Site 1 for additional ferry information.

Trip note: This campground is set along Lake Chelan at the mouth of Graham Harbor Creek. It is one of 12 campgrounds on giant Chelan.

Site **6**

DEER POINT
on Lake Chelan, boat-in or ferry only
WENATCHEE NATIONAL FOREST

Campsites, facilities: There are four tent sites accessible only by boat. Picnic tables are provided. Pit toilets and firewood are available, but there is **no piped water.** Boat docks are nearby.

Reservations, fee: No reservations necessary; $2 fee per night. Open May to late October.

Who to contact: Phone Wenatchee National Forest at (509)682-2576 or write to

Chelan Ranger District, Chelan, WA, 98816.

Location: Take the 8:30 a.m ferry from Chelan, Manson or Fields Point Landing and get off at Deer Point, 22 miles from Chelan. See Site 1 for additional ferry information.

Trip note: Another little known spot set along the shore of Chelan Lake. If you want to camp on the remote east shore, this is one of three camps. The others are Sites 4 and 8.

Site 7
BIG CREEK
on Lake Chelan, boat-in or ferry only
WENATCHEE NATIONAL FOREST

Campsites, facilities: There are four primitive tent sites accessible only by boat. Picnic tables are provided. Pit toilets and firewood are available, but there is **no piped water.** Boat docks are nearby.

Reservations, fee: No reservations necessary; no fee. Open May to late October.

Who to contact: Phone Wenatchee National Forest at (509)682-2576 or write to Chelan Ranger District, Chelan, WA, 98816.

Location: Take the 8:30 a.m ferry from Chelan, Manson or Fields Point Landing and get off at Big Creek, 27 miles from Chelan. See Site 1 for additional ferry information.

Trip note: This is another in the series of camps on Chelan. If you decide to camp here or any other boat campsite during the late fall or early winter, be advised that the water level often drops, putting the docks out of reach.

Site 8
MITCHELL CREEK
Lake Chelan, boat-in or ferry only
WENATCHEE NATIONAL FOREST

Campsites, facilities: There are ten tent sites accessible only by boat. Picnic tables are provided. Pit toilets and firewood are available, but there is **no piped water.** Boat docks are nearby.

Reservations, fee: No reservations necessary; no fee. Open May to late October.

Who to contact: Phone Wenatchee National Forest at (509)682-2576 or write to Chelan Ranger District, Chelan, WA, 98816.

Location: Take the 8:30 a.m ferry from Chelan, Manson or Fields Point Landing and get off at Mitchell Creek, 15 miles from Chelan.

Trip note: This campground is set along the shore of Lake Chelan. Fishing, swimming, boating, hiking and waterskiing are all options here.

Site 9
COTTONWOOD
on Entiat River
WENATCHEE NATIONAL FOREST

Campsites, facilities: There are 25 tent sites and two additional sites for tents or small motor homes. Piped water, fire grills and picnic tables are provided. Pit toilets and firewood are available. Leashed pets are permitted.

Reservations, fee: No reservations necessary; $4 fee per night. Open early June to mid-October.

Who to contact: Phone Wenatchee National Forest at (509)784-1511 or write to Entiat Ranger District, Box 476, Entiat, WA, 98822.

Location: From Entiat, drive 1.5 miles southwest on US 97, then turn northwest on County Road 371 and go 25 miles. Continue northwest on Forest Service Road 317 for 13 miles to the campground.

Trip note: At 3,100 feet elevation, this campground is at a major trailhead leading into the Glacier Peak Wilderness. It is set along the Entiat River. A Forest Service map details the back country. A bonus is good berry picking in season.

Site 10

NORTH FORK
on Entiat River
WENATCHEE NATIONAL FOREST

Campsites, facilities: There are seven tent sites and one site for a small motor home. Piped water, fire grills and picnic tables are provided. Pit toilets and firewood are available. Leashed pets are permitted.

Reservations, fee: No reservations necessary; $3 fee per night. Open mid-May to mid-November.

Who to contact: Phone Wenatchee National Forest at (509)784-1511 or write to Entiat Ranger District, Box 476, Entiat, WA, 98822.

Location: From Entiat, drive 1.5 miles southwest on US 97, then turn northwest on County Road 371 and go 25 miles. Turn northwest on Forest Service Road 317 and drive 8.5 miles to the campground.

Trip note: This is one of the six campgrounds nestled along the Entiat River. This one is set near the confluence of the Entiat and the North Fork of the Entiat Rivers. Entiat Falls is nearby.

Site 11

SILVER FALLS
on Entiat River
WENATCHEE NATIONAL FOREST

Campsites, facilities: There are 30 tent sites and 31 sites for tents, trailers or motor homes up to 21 feet long. Piped water, fire grills and picnic tables are provided. Pit toilets and firewood are available. Leashed pets are permitted.

Reservations, fee: No reservations necessary; $5 fee per night. Open mid-May to mid-November.

Who to contact: Phone Wenatchee National Forest at (509)784-1511 or write to Entiat Ranger District, Box 476, Entiat, WA, 98822.

Location: From Entiat, drive 1.5 miles southwest on Highway 97, then turn northwest on County Road 371 and go 25 miles. Turn northwest on Forest Service Road 317 and drive 5.5 miles to the campground.

Trip note: This campground, an enchanted spot, is set at the confluence of Silver Creek and the Entiat River. A trail from camp leads one-half mile to the base of Silver Falls.

Site 12

LAKE CREEK
Entiat River
WENATCHEE NATIONAL FOREST

Campsites, facilities: There are 16 tent sites. Piped water, picnic tables and fire grills are provided. Pit toilets and firewood are available. Leashed pets are permitted.

Reservations, fee: No reservations necessary; $3 fee per night. Open May to late October.

Who to contact: Phone Wenatchee National Forest at (509)784-1511 or write to Entiat Ranger District, Box 476, Entiat, WA, 98822.

Location: From Entiat, drive 1.5 miles southwest on US 97, then turn northwest on County Road 371 and go 25 miles. Turn northwest on Forest Service Road 317 and drive three miles to the campground.

Trip note: This camp is set at the confluence of Lake Creek and the Entiat River. It is at a trail crossroads, one heads northeast up to Lake Creek Basin in the Chelan Mountains, and several others head south and west into the Entiat Mountains. See a Forest Service map for details. Site 13 is a nearby spot with piped water.

Site **13**   **FOX CREEK**
on Entiat River
WENATCHEE NATIONAL FOREST

Campsites, facilities: There are 19 tent sites. Piped water, fire grills and picnic tables are provided. Pit toilets and firewood are available. Leashed pets are permitted.

Reservations, fee: No reservations necessary; $3 fee per night. Open May to early November.

Who to contact: Phone Wenatchee National Forest at (509)784-1511 or write to Entiat Ranger District, Box 476, Entiat, WA, 98822.

Location: From Entiat, drive 1.5 miles southwest on US 97, then turn northwest on County Road 371 and go 25 miles. Turn northwest on Forest Service Road 317 and drive two miles to campground.

Trip note: This camp is set along the Entiat River near Fox Creek. It is a good alternative to Site 12 but without the traffic. During the winter, some of the snow-covered logging roads in the area are open for use by snowmobiles and cross-country skiers. Contact the Forest Service for details.

Site **14**   **PINE FLAT**
on Mad River
WENATCHEE NATIONAL FOREST

Campsites, facilities: There are eight tent sites and one site for a trailer or motor home. Picnic tables are provided. Pit toilets and firewood are available, but there is **no piped water.** Leashed pets are permitted.

Reservations, fee: No reservations necessary; no fee. Open mid-April to early November.

Who to contact: Phone Wenatchee National Forest at (509)784-1511 or write to Entiat Ranger District, Box 476, Entiat, WA, 98822.

Location: From Entiat, drive 1.5 miles southwest on US 97, then turn northwest on County Road 371 and go ten miles. Turn northwest on Forest Service Road 2710 and go 3.5 miles to campground.

Trip note: You get guaranteed quiet around these parts. This camp is set along the Mad River at a major backpacking trailhead that provides access to several areas in the Entiat Mountains. The trail that follows the Mad River provides shelters along the route. Contact the Forest Service for details. Motorcycle and horse trails are also available in the area.

Site **15**   **PHELPS CREEK**
on Chiwawa River
WENATCHEE NATIONAL FOREST

Campsites, facilities: There are seven tent sites. Picnic tables and fire grills are provided. Pit toilets and firewood are available, but there is **no piped water.** Leashed pets are permitted.

Reservations, fee: No reservations necessary; no fee. Open mid-June to mid-October.

Who to contact: Phone Wenatchee National Forest at (509)782-1413 or write to Leavenworth Ranger District, 600 Sherbourne, Leavenworth, WA, 98826.

Location: From Leavenworth, drive 16 miles northwest on US 2, turn north on Highway 207 and go four miles. Turn east on County Road 22 and go one mile, then head northwest on Forest Service Road 311 for 21 miles to the campground.

Trip note: This campground is set at the confluence of Phelps Creek and the Chiwawa River. There's a key trailhead for backpackers nearby provides access to Glacier Peak Wilderness. It's advisable to obtain a Forest Service map.

Site 16   ATKINSON FLAT
on Chiwawa River
WENATCHEE NATIONAL FOREST

Campsites, facilities: There are six primitive, undeveloped sites for tents, trailers or motor homes up to 21 feet long. No toilets and **no piped water** are available. Pets are permitted.

Reservations, fee: No reservations necessary; no fee. Open mid-June to mid-October.

Who to contact: Phone Wenatchee National Forest at (509)782-1413 or write to Leavenworth Ranger District, 600 Sherbourne, Leavenworth, WA, 98826.

Location: From Leavenworth, drive 16 miles northwest on US 2, turn north on Highway 207 and go four miles. Turn east on County Road 22 and go one mile, then head northwest on Forest Service Road 311 for 15 miles to the campground.

Trip note: This is one of several "minimum maintenance" campgrounds provided by the Forest Service in this area. Minimum maintenance means that minimum impact camping techniques are a necessity. It is set along the Chiwawa River.

Site 17   SCHAEFER CREEK
on Chiwawa River
WENATCHEE NATIONAL FOREST

Campsites, facilities: There are five primitive, undeveloped sites for tents, trailers or motor homes. No toilets and **no piped water** are available. Pets are permitted.

Reservations, fee: No reservations necessary; no fee. Open mid-June to mid-October.

Who to contact: Phone Wenatchee National Forest at (509)782-1413 or write to Leavenworth Ranger District, 600 Sherbourne, Leavenworth, WA, 98826.

Location: From Leavenworth, drive 16 miles northwest on US 2, turn north on Highway 207 and go four miles. Turn east on County Road 22 and go one mile, then head northwest on Forest Service Road 311 for 14 miles to the campground.

Trip note: Like Site 16, this is a "minimum maintenance" campground. It is set along the Chiwawa River and less than a mile north of Rock Creek, where two major recreation trails intersect. See a Forest Service map for details.

Site 18   MEADOW CREEK
near Chiwawa River
WENATCHEE NATIONAL FOREST

Campsites, facilities: There are seven primitive, undeveloped sites for tents, trailers or motor homes. No toilets and **no piped water** are available. Pets are permitted.

Reservations, fee: No reservations necessary; no fee. Open May to late October.

Who to contact: Phone Wenatchee National Forest at (509)782-1413 or write to Leavenworth Ranger District, 600 Sherbourne, Leavenworth, WA, 98826.

Location: From Leavenworth, drive 16 miles northwest on US 2, turn north on Highway 207 and go four miles. Turn east on County Road 22 and go one mile, then head northeast on Forest Service Road 311 for 2.5 miles to the campground.

Trip note: This is a "go-for-it" spot. There's nobody keeping track of you, but plenty of recreation options. This minimum maintenance campground is set near the confluence of Meadow Creek and the Chiwawa River. Both Fish Lake and Lake Wenatchee are within five miles of camp.

Site 19   WHITE RIVER FALLS
on White River
WENATCHEE NATIONAL FOREST

Campsites, facilities: There are five tent sites. Picnic tables are provided. Pit toilets and firewood are available, but there is **no piped water.** Leashed pets are permitted.

Reservations, fee: No reservations necessary; $2 fee per night. Open June to mid-October.

Who to contact: Phone Wenatchee National Forest at (509)782-1413 or write to Leavenworth Ranger District, 600 Sherbourne, Leavenworth, WA, 98826.

Location: From Leavenworth, drive 16 miles northwest on US 2, then turn north on Highway 207 and go 8.5 miles. Head northwest on County Road 22 for one mile, then continue northwest on Forest Service Road 293 for nine miles.

Trip note: This campground is set close to the White River Falls on the White River. It is located at a major trailhead that connects to a network of hiking trails into the Glacier Peak Wilderness. Quiet and beautiful, you get your money's worth.

Site 20   NAPEEQUA
on White River
WENATCHEE NATIONAL FOREST

Campsites, facilities: There are three tent sites and two sites for trailers or motor homes up to 31 feet long. Picnic tables are provided. Pit toilets and firewood are available, but there is **no piped water.** Leashed pets are permitted.

Reservations, fee: No reservations necessary; $2 fee per night. Open mid-May to late October.

Who to contact: Phone Wenatchee National Forest at (509)782-1413 or write to Leavenworth Ranger District, 600 Sherbourne, Leavenworth, WA, 98826.

Location: From Leavenworth, drive 16 miles northwest on US 2, then turn north on Highway 207 and go eight miles. Head northwest on County Road 22 for one mile, then continue northwest on Forest Service Road 293 for six miles and you'll arrive at the campground.

Trip note: This campground is set along the White River. A trail from camp heads east for about two miles to Twin Lakes in Glacier Peak Wilderness. Worth the hike.

Site 21   NASON CREEK
near Lake Wenatchee
WENATCHEE NATIONAL FOREST

Campsites, facilities: There are 27 tent sites and 41 sites for tents, trailers or motor homes up to 31 feet long. Piped water, fire grills and picnic tables are provided. Flush toilets, sanitary disposal station and a laundromat are available within one mile. Boat docks, launching facilities and rentals are nearby.

Reservations, fee: No reservations necessary; $5 fee per night. Open May to late October.

Who to contact: Phone Wenatchee National Forest at (509)763-3103 or write to Wenatchee Ranger District, Star Route Box 109, Leavenworth, WA, 98826.

Location: From Leavenworth, drive 16 miles northwest on US 2, turn northeast on Highway 207 and go 3.5 miles. Head west on County Road 290 for 100 yards to the campground.

Trip note: This campground is on Nason Creek near Lake Wenatchee. Recreation activities include swimming, fishing and waterskiing. Horse rentals are available just one mile from the campground.

Site **22**
GLACIER VIEW
on Lake Wenatchee
WENATCHEE NATIONAL FOREST

Campsites, facilities: There are 20 tent sites. Piped water, fire grills and picnic tables are provided. Pit toilets and firewood are available. Boat docks are nearby. Leashed pets are permitted.

Reservations, fee: No reservations necessary; $4 fee per night. Open mid-May to mid-October.

Who to contact: Phone Wenatchee National Forest at (509)763-3103 or write to Wenatchee Ranger District, Star Route Box 109, Leavenworth, WA, 98826.

Location: From Leavenworth, drive 16 miles northwest on US 2, turn northeast on Highway 207 and go 3.5 miles. Turn west on County Road 290 and go four miles, then continue west on Forest Service Road 290 for 1.5 miles to the campground.

Trip note: This campground is on the southwestern shore of Lake Wenatchee, one of the quieter camps on the lake. It's a popular spot for boating, swimming, fishing and waterskiing.

Site **23**
LAKE CREEK
on Wenatchee River
WENATCHEE NATIONAL FOREST

Campsites, facilities: There are eight tent sites. Picnic tables and fire grills are provided, but **no piped water** is available. Pit toilets and firewood are available.

Reservations, fee: No reservations necessary; no fee. Open May to early November.

Who to contact: Phone Wenatchee National Forest at (509)763-3103 or write to Wenatchee Ranger District, Star Route Box 109, Leavenworth, WA, 98826.

Location: From Leavenworth, drive 16 miles northwest on US 2, turn north on Highway 207 and go 8.5 miles. Turn west on County Road 22 and go 1.5 miles, then continue west on Forest Service Road 283 for ten miles to the campground.

Trip note: This camp is set along the Wenatchee River. It is a remote and primitive spot. Berry picking is a bonus sidelight in late summer.

Site **24**
SODA SPRINGS
on Wenatchee River
WENATCHEE NATIONAL FOREST

Campsites, facilities: There are five tent sites. Picnic tables and fire grills are provided. Pit toilets and firewood are available, but there is **no piped water.**

Reservations, fee: No reservations necessary; no fee. Open May to late October.

Who to contact: Phone Wenatchee National Forest at (509)763-3103 or write to Wenatchee Ranger District, Star Route Box 109, Leavenworth, WA, 98826.

Location: From Leavenworth, drive 16 miles northwest on US 2, turn north on Highway 207 and go 8.5 miles. Turn west on County Road 22 and go 1.5 miles, then west on Forest Service Road 283 for 7.5 miles to the campground.

Trip note: This campground is set along the Wenatchee River. It's a small, quiet closer-to-civilization option to Site 25, without piped water.

Site 25   TUMWATER
near Alpine Lakes Wilderness
WENATCHEE NATIONAL FOREST

Campsites, facilities: There are 27 tent sites and 53 sites for tents, trailers or motor homes up to 22 feet long. Piped water, fire grills and picnic tables are provided. Flush toilets and firewood are available. Leashed pets are permitted.

Reservations, fee: No reservations necessary; $6 fee per night. Open May to late October.

Who to contact: Phone Wenatchee National Forest at (509)782-1413 or write to Leavenworth Ranger District, 600 Sherbourne, Leavenworth, WA, 98826.

Location: From Leavenworth, drive ten miles northwest on US 2 and you'll see the campground entrance.

Trip note: This large, popular camp provides a little bit of both worlds. It is a good layover for campers cruising US 2. But there are also two Forest Service roads nearby, each less than a mile long, which end at trailheads that provide access to the Alpine Lakes Wilderness. If you don't like to hike, no problem. The camp is on the Wenatchee River in the Tumwater Canyon.

Site 26   LAKE WENATCHEE STATE PARK
on Lake Wenatchee

Campsites, facilities: There are 197 sites for tents, trailers or motor homes of any length. Piped water, fire grills and picnic tables are provided. Flush toilets, sanitary disposal station, a store, ice, showers, firewood, a restaurant, a playground, and horse rentals are available. Some facilities are wheelchair accessible. Boat docks, launching facilities and rentals are nearby. Leashed pets are permitted.

Reservations, fee: No reservations necessary; $7 fee per night. Open all year.

Who to contact: Phone (509)763-3101 or write to Highway 207, Leavenworth, WA, 98826.

Location: From Leavenworth, drive 22 miles north on Highway 207 and you'll see the park entrance.

Trip note: This park is set in a nice spot, the drive-in sites are spaced just right, so you can expect plenty of company. The secluded campsites are near the Wenatchee River, which offers opportunities for canoeing, kayaking, swimming, fishing and horseback riding.

Site 27   PARADISE RESORT
on Wapato Lake

Campsites, facilities: There are ten tent sites and 23 drive-through sites for trailers or motor homes. Electricity, piped water and picnic tables are provided. Flush toilets, showers, firewood and ice are available. Pets and motorbikes are permitted. Boat launching facilities and rentals are nearby.

Reservations, fee: Reservations accepted; $10-11 fee per night. Open mid-April to mid-October.

Who to contact: Phone (509)687-3444 or write to Route 1, Box 198, Manson, WA,

98831.

Location: From Chelan, drive seven miles west on Highway 150, then turn northwest on Wapato Lake Road and go three miles to East Lake Road.

Trip note: This campground is set along the shore of Wapato Lake about two miles from Lake Chelan. The town of Chelan offers a history museum and a downtown area with many restored buildings from the early days.

Site 28   KAMEI RESORT
on Lake Wapato

Campsites, facilities: There are 40 sites for trailers or motor homes of any length. Electricity, piped water, sewer hookups and picnic tables are provided. Flush toilets, showers and ice are available. Pets and motorbikes are permitted. Boat docks, launching facilities and rentals are nearby.

Reservations, fee: Reservations accepted; $9-10 fee per night. Open late April to August.

Who to contact: Phone (509)687-3690 or write to Route 1, Box 238, Manson, WA, 98831.

Location: From Chelan, drive seven miles west on Highway 150, then turn north on Wapato Lake Road and drive three miles to the resort.

Trip note: This resort is on Lake Wapato, about two miles from Lake Chelan. If you have an extra day, take the ferry boat ride on Lake Chelan, which is detailed in Site 1.

Site 29   LAKEVIEW PARK
on Lake Chelan

Campsites, facilities: There are 50 sites for trailers or motor homes of any length. Electricity, piped water and sewer hookups are provided. Flush toilets, sanitary services, showers, a playground, bottled gas, a store, a cafe, a laundromat and ice are available. Pets are permitted. Boat docks and launching facilities are nearby.

Reservations, fee: Reservations accepted; $10-14 fee per night. Open April to November.

Who to contact: Phone (509)687-3612 or write to P.O. Box 324, Manson, WA, 98831.

Location: From Chelan, drive 5.2 miles northwest on Highway 150 and you'll see the park on the right.

Trip note: This developed park for motor homes and trailers is set along the shore of Lake Chelan. Nearby recreation options include an 18-hole golf course.

Site 30   LAKE CHELAN STATE PARK
on Lake Chelan

Campsites, facilities: There are 27 sites for tents or self-contained motor homes, and 17 sites for trailers or motor homes with full hookups. Picnic tables are provided. Flush toilets, sanitary disposal station, a store, a restaurant, ice, a playground, electricity, piped water, sewer hookups, showers and firewood are available. Some facilities are wheelchair accessible. Boat docks and launching facilities are nearby.

Reservations, fee: Reservations accepted; $7.50-10.50 fee per night. Open April to late October.

Who to contact: Phone (509)687-3710 or write to Route 1, Box 90, Chelan, WA, 98816.

Location: Drive nine miles west of Chelan off US 97. The park is on the south side of the lake.

Trip note: This is the recreation headquarters for Lake Chelan. See the trip notes for Sites 1-7 for some of the options available. Water sports include fishing, swimming, scuba diving and waterskiing.

Site **31**   **LAKESHORE TRAILER PARK AND MARINA**
on Lake Chelan

Campsites, facilities: There are 160 drive-through sites for trailers or motor homes of any length. Electricity, piped water, sewer hookups and picnic tables are provided. Flush toilets, sanitary services, showers, a store, a cafe, a laundromat, ice, a playground, bottled gas are available within one mile. Boat docks and launching facilities are nearby.

Reservations, fee: Reservations accepted; $18 fee per night. Open March to November.

Who to contact: Phone (509)682-5031 or write to P.O. Box 1669, Chelan, WA, 98816.

Location: From the center of Chelan, drive one mile north on US 97 to Highway 150.

Trip note: This municipal park and marina on Lake Chelan serves all members of the family. Nearby recreation options include an 18-hole golf course, a miniature golf course and lighted tennis courts. A visitor center is nearby.

Site **32**   **TWENTY-FIVE MILE CREEK STATE PARK**
near Lake Chelan

Campsites, facilities: There are 52 tent sites and 33 sites for trailers or motor homes up to 60 feet long. Picnic tables are provided. Rest rooms, piped water, electricity, sewer hookups and a swimming pool are available. A boat dock is nearby.

Reservations, fee: No reservations; $6 fee per night. Open early April to late October.

Who to contact: Phone (509)687-3710 or write c/o Lake Chelan State Park, Route 1, Box 90, Chelan, WA 98816.

Location: Drive 18 miles north of Chelan on the South Shore Road and you'll see the park at the end of the road.

Trip note: This campground is located on Twenty-Five Mile Creek near where it empties into Lake Chelan. Forest Service Road 5900, which heads west from the park, accesses several trailheads leading into the Forest Service lands of the Chelan Mountains. Obtain a Wenatchee National Forest Service map for details.

Site **33**   **ENTIAT CITY PARK**
near Columbia River

Campsites, facilities: There are 100 tent sites and 31 sites for trailers or motor homes. Electricity, piped water and picnic tables are provided. Flush toilets, sanitary services, showers, a playground, bottled gas, a store, a cafe, a laundromat and ice are available. Motorbikes are permitted. Boat docks and launching facilities are nearby.

Reservations, fee: Reservations accepted; $10 fee per night. Open April to mid-September.

Who to contact: Phone (509)784-1500 or write to P.O. Box 228, Entiat, WA, 98822.

Location: Drive 16 miles north of Wenatchee on US 97 to Entiat. The park is set along the shore of Lake Entiat.

Trip note: Lake Entiat is actually a dammed portion of the Columbia River. Rocky Reach Dam, located ten miles south, is the closest to this campground. This is a good camping spot for boaters because of the launching facilities nearby.

Site 34   LINCOLN ROCK STATE PARK
on Lake Entiat

Campsites, facilities: There are 27 sites for tents or self-contained motor homes, and 67 sites with full hookups for trailers or motor homes of any length. Picnic tables and fire grills are provided. Flush toilets, a sanitary disposal station, a playground, showers and firewood are available. Some facilities are wheelchair accessible. Boat docks and launching facilities are located on Lake Entiat. Leashed pets are permitted.

Reservations, fee: No reservations necessary; $7.50-10.50 fee per night. Open all year.

Who to contact: Phone (509)884-3044 or write to Route 3, P.O. Box 3137, East Wenatchee, WA, 98801.

Location: From East Wenatchee, drive six miles north on US 2 and you'll see the park.

Trip note: An option to nearby Site 33, this park is ideal for families with motor homes or trailers. It's set adjacent to the Rocky Reach Dam along the shore of Lake Entiat. Water sports include swimming, boating and waterskiing.

Site 35   TOWN AND COUNTRY TRAILER PARK
on Wenatchee River

Campsites, facilities: There are 12 drive-through sites for trailers or motor homes up to 25 feet long. Electricity, piped water, sewer hookups and picnic tables are provided. Flush toilets, showers, ice and a swimming pool are available. Bottled gas, a store and a cafe are located within one mile. Motorbikes are permitted. Boat docks and launching facilities are nearby.

Reservations, fee: Reservations accepted; $10 fee per night; MasterCard and Visa accepted. Open all year.

Who to contact: Phone (509)663-5157 or write to 2921 School Street, Wenatchee, WA, 98801.

Location: From the town of Wenatchee, drive three miles west via US 2 and US 97.

Trip note: This is a good layover for cross-country travelers who reach the junction of US 2 and US 97. The park is set in an urban area along the Wenatchee River. Nearby recreation options include hiking trails, marked bike trails, a full-service marina and tennis courts.

Site 36   WENATCHEE RIVER COUNTY PARK
on Wenatchee River

Campsites, facilities: There are 25 tent sites and 64 drive-through sites for trailers or motor homes. Electricity, piped water, sewer hookups and picnic tables are provided. Flush toilets, showers, sanitary services and a playground are available. A store, a cafe and ice are available within one mile. Pets and motorbikes are permitted. Boat launching facilities are available nearby.

Reservations, fee: No reservations necessary; $10 fee per night. Open April to late October.

Who to contact: Phone (509)662-2525 or write to P.O. Box 254, Monitor, WA, 98836.

Location: From Wenatchee, drive six miles northwest on US 2. The park is near Monitor.

Trip note: This municipal park is set along the Wenatchee River. It's the only option for tent campers in immediate area.

Site **37**   **BLU SHASTIN RV PARK**
near Penshastin Creek

Campsites, facilities: There are 20 tent sites and 50 drive-through sites for trailers or motor homes of any length. Electricity, piped water, sewer hookups and picnic tables are provided. Flush toilets, sanitary services, showers, a recreation hall, firewood, a laundromat, ice, a playground and a swimming pool are available. Bottled gas, a store and a cafe are located within one mile. Pets and motorbikes are permitted.

Reservations, fee: Reservations accepted; $11-15 fee per night; MasterCard and Visa accepted. Open all year.

Who to contact: Phone (509)548-4184 or write to 3300 US 97, Leavenworth, WA, 98826.

Location: From Leavenworth, go three miles southeast on US 2 to the junction with US 97, then go seven miles south on US 97 to the park.

Trip note: This park is set in a mountainous area near Penshastin Creek. Nearby recreation options include hiking trails and marked bike trails.

Site **38**   **MIDWAY VILLAGE GROCERY AND RV PARK**
on Wenatchee River

Campsites, facilities: There are 20 tent sites and 23 sites for trailers or motor homes of any length. Electricity, piped water, sewer hookups and picnic tables are provided. Bottled gas, a store, showers, firewood, a cafe, a laundromat, ice and a playground are available. Pets and motorbikes are permitted. Boat docks, launching facilities and rentals are nearby.

Reservations, fee: Reservations accepted; $9 fee per night. Open all year.

Who to contact: Phone (509)763-3344 or write to 14193 Chiwawa, Leavenworth, WA, 98826.

Location: From Winton, drive one mile northwest on US 2 to Highway 207 and then go four miles north to the bridge over the Wenatchee River. Head east for one mile and you'll see the park.

Trip note: This private campground is a short distance from Lake Wenatchee State Park (Site 26) and is set along the Wenatchee River. Nearby recreation options include waterskiing, swimming, boating, fishing, hiking and bike riding.

Site **39**   **ICICLE RIVER RANCH**
on Icicle Creek

Campsites, facilities: There are 30 tent sites and 41 drive-through sites for trailers or motor homes of any length. Electricity, piped water, sewer hookups and picnic tables are provided. Flush toilets and bottled gas are available. Showers and firewood are available for an extra fee. Pets and motorbikes are permitted.

Reservations, fee: Reservations accepted; $11 fee per night. Open April to late October.

Who to contact: Phone (509)548-5420 or write to 7305 Icicle Road, Leavenworth, WA, 98826.

Location: Take Icicle Road south off US 2 in Leavenworth and drive three miles to the campground.

Trip note: This is one of three campgrounds in immediate area. The others are Sites 40 and 41. This wooded spot is set along Icicle Creek. Nearby recreation options include an 18-hole golf course and hiking trails.

Site 40   KOA PINE VILLAGE
near Wenatchee River

Campsites, facilities: There are 40 tent sites and 60 drive-through sites for trailers or motor homes of any length. Picnic tables are provided. Flush toilets, sanitary services, showers, firewood, a recreation hall, a store, a laundromat, ice, a playground, a wading pool, a heated swimming pool, electricity, piped water and sewer hookups are available. Bottled gas and a cafe are located within one mile. Pets and motorbikes are permitted.

Reservations, fee: Reservations accepted; $16-21 fee per night; American Express, MasterCard and Visa accepted. Open April to November.

Who to contact: Phone (509)548-7709 or write to Pine Village KOA, 11401 River Bend Drive, Leavenworth, WA, 98826.

Location: Drive one-quarter mile east of Leavenworth on US 2 to River Bend Drive, then go north one-half mile to the campground.

Trip note: This campground is set among pines with access to the Wenatchee River. Nearby recreation options include an 18-hole golf course and hiking trails.

Site 41   CHALET TRAILER PARK
on Wenatchee River

Campsites, facilities: There are 40 tent sites and 24 sites for trailers or motor homes of any length. Electricity, piped water, sewer hookups and picnic tables are provided. Flush toilets, sanitary services and showers are available. Bottled gas, a store, a cafe, a laundromat and ice are available within one mile. Pets and motorbikes are permitted.

Reservations, fee: Reservations accepted; $10 fee per night. Open May to early October.

Who to contact: Phone (509)548-4578 or write to 6504 NE 171st Place, Bothel, WA, 98155.

Location: From Leavenworth, drive one-half mile southeast on US 2 to the campground.

Trip note: This park is set along the Wenatchee River near Leavenworth. Nearby recreation options include an 18-hole golf course.

Site 42   BLACKPINE CREEK HORSECAMP
near Alpine Lakes Wilderness
WENATCHEE NATIONAL FOREST

Campsites, facilities: There are six tent sites and two sites for tents, trailers or motor homes up to 21 feet long. Piped water, fire grills and picnic tables are provided. Pit toilets, firewood and riding facilities are available. Leashed pets are permitted.

Reservations, fee: No reservations necessary; $3 fee per night. Open mid-May to late October.

Who to contact: Phone Wenatchee National Forest at (509)782-1413 or write to Leavenworth Ranger District, 600 Sherbourne, Leavenworth, WA, 98826.

Location: From Leavenworth, drive one-half mile southeast on US 2, then turn south on Highway 71 and drive three miles. Turn northwest on Forest Service Road 2451 and drive 15 miles to the campground.

Trip note: This campground is set on Black Pine Creek near Icicle Creek at a major trailhead leading into the Alpine Lakes Wilderness. It is one of seven rustic camp spots on the creek.

Site **43**
ROCK ISLAND
near Alpine Lakes Wilderness
WENATCHEE NATIONAL FOREST

Campsites, facilities: There are 12 tent sites for tents and ten sites for tents, trailers or motor homes up to 21 feet long. Piped water, fire grills and picnic tables are provided. Pit toilets and firewood are available. Leashed pets are permitted.

Reservations, fee: No reservations necessary; $4 fee per night. Open May to late October.

Who to contact: Phone Wenatchee National Forest at (509)782-1413 or write to Leavenworth Ranger District, 600 Sherbourne, Leavenworth, WA, 98826.

Location: From Leavenworth, drive one-half mile southeast on US 2, then turn south on Highway 71 and drive three miles. Turn northwest on Forest Service Road 2451 and drive 14 miles to campground.

Trip note: This campground is set along Icicle Creek about a mile from the trailhead that accesses the Alpine Lakes Wilderness.

Site **44**
CHATTER CREEK
near Alpine Lakes Wilderness
WENATCHEE NATIONAL FOREST

Campsites, facilities: There are nine tent sites and three sites for tents, trailers or motor homes up to 21 feet long. Piped water, fire grills and picnic tables are provided. Pit toilets and firewood are available. Leashed pets are permitted.

Reservations, fee: No reservations necessary; $4 fee per night. Open May to late October.

Who to contact: Phone Wenatchee National Forest at (509)782-1413 or write to Leavenworth Ranger District, 600 Sherbourne, Leavenworth, WA, 98826.

Location: From Leavenworth, drive one-half mile southeast on US 2, then turn south on Highway 71 and drive three miles. Turn northwest on Forest Service Road 2451 and drive 12.5 miles to campground.

Trip note: This campground is set along Icicle Creek and Chatter Creek. Trails lead out in several directions from the camp into the Alpine Lakes Wilderness.

Site **45**
IDA CREEK
on Icicle Creek
WENATCHEE NATIONAL FOREST

Campsites, facilities: There are five tent sites and five sites for tents, trailers or motor homes up to 21 feet long. Piped water, fire grills and picnic tables are provided. Pit toilets and firewood are available. Leashed pets are permitted.

Reservations, fee: No reservations necessary; $4 fee per night. Open May to late October.

Who to contact: Phone Wenatchee National Forest at (509)782-1413 or write to Leavenworth Ranger District, 600 Sherbourne, Leavenworth, WA, 98826.

Location: From Leavenworth, drive one-half miles southeast on US 2, then turn south on Highway 71 and drive three miles. Turn northwest on Forest Service Road 2451 and drive ten miles to campground.

Trip note: This campground is one of several small, quiet campgrounds set along Icicle Creek and Ida Creek.

Site **46**   **JOHNNY CREEK**
on Icicle Creek
WENATCHEE NATIONAL FOREST

Campsites, facilities: There are eight tent sites and eight sites for tents, trailers or motor homes up to 21 feet long. Piped water, fire grills and picnic tables are provided. Pit toilets and firewood are available. Leashed pets are permitted.

Reservations, fee: No reservations necessary; $4 fee per night. Open May to late October.

Who to contact: Phone Wenatchee National Forest at (509)782-1413 or write to Leavenworth Ranger District, 600 Sherbourne, Leavenworth, WA, 98826.

Location: From Leavenworth, drive one-half mile southeast on US 2, then turn south on Highway 71 and drive three miles. Turn northwest on Forest Service Road 2451 and drive eight miles to campground.

Trip note: This campground is set along Icicle Creek and Johnny Creek.

Site **47**   **BRIDGE CREEK**
on Icicle Creek
WENATCHEE NATIONAL FOREST

Campsites, facilities: There are six tent sites. Piped water, fire grills and picnic tables are provided. Pit toilets and firewood are available. Leashed pets are permitted.

Reservations, fee: No reservations necessary; $4 fee per night. Open mid-April to late October.

Who to contact: Phone Wenatchee National Forest at (509)782-1413 or write to Leavenworth Ranger District, 600 Sherbourne, Leavenworth, WA, 98826.

Location: From Leavenworth, drive one-half mile southeast on US 2, then turn south on Highway 71 and drive three miles. Turn northwest on Forest Service Road 2451 and drive 5.5 miles to campground.

Trip note: This is a small, quiet spot set along Icicle Creek and Bridge Creek. About one mile south of the camp at Eightmile Creek is a trail that accesses the Alpine Lakes Wilderness. See a Forest Service map for details.

Site **48**   **EIGHTMILE**
near Alpine Lakes Wilderness
WENATCHEE NATIONAL FOREST

Campsites, facilities: There are 13 tent sites and 12 sites for tents, trailers or motor homes up to 21 feet long. Piped water, fire grills, and picnic tables are provided. Pit toilets and firewood are available. Leashed pets are permitted.

Reservations, fee: No reservations necessary; $4 fee per night. Open mid-April to late October.

Who to contact: Phone Wenatchee National Forest at (509)782-1413 or write to Leavenworth Ranger District, 600 Sherbourne, Leavenworth, WA, 98826.

Location: From Leavenworth, drive one-half mile southeast on US 2, then turn south on Highway 71 and drive three miles. Turn west on Forest Service Road 2451 and drive four miles to campground.

Trip note: This campground is set along Icicle Creek and Eightmile Creek. A key trailhead for backpackers is located here that provides access to many lakes and streams in the Alpine Lakes Wilderness.

Site **49**
SALMON LA SAC
on Cle Elum River
WENATCHEE NATIONAL FOREST

Campsites, facilities: There are 30 tent sites and 80 sites for tents, trailers or motor homes up to 21 feet long. A horse-use camp is also available. Piped water, fire grills and picnic tables are provided. Flush toilets and firewood are available. Some facilities are wheelchair accessible. Leashed pets are permitted.

Reservations, fee: No reservations necessary; $4 fee per night. Open late May to late October.

Who to contact: Phone Wenatchee National Forest at (509)674-4411 or write to Cle Elum Ranger District, West 2nd Street, Cle Elum, WA, 98922.

Location: From Cle Elum, drive 11 miles northwest on Highway 903, then continue northwest on County Road 903 for 10.5 miles to campground.

Trip note: This is an ideal base camp for backpackers and day hikers. The camp is set along the Cle Elum River at a major trailhead. Hikers can follow creeks heading off in several directions, including into the Alpine Lakes Wilderness. A Forest Service map details the possibilities.

Site **50**
RED MOUNTAIN
on Cle Elum River
WENATCHEE NATIONAL FOREST

Campsites, facilities: There are two tent sites and 13 sites for tents, trailers or motor homes up to 15 feet long. Picnic tables and fire grills are provided. Pit toilets and firewood are available, but there is **no piped water.** Boat docks are nearby. Leashed pets are permitted.

Reservations, fee: No reservations necessary; no fee. Open mid-May to mid-November.

Who to contact: Phone Wenatchee National Forest at (509)674-4411 or write to Cle Elum Ranger District, West 2nd Street, Cle Elum, WA, 98922.

Location: From Cle Elum, drive 11 miles northwest on Highway 903, then continue northwest on County Road 903 for eight miles to campground.

Trip note: This option to nearby Site 51 has two big differences. This site has no piped water and is not on Cle Elum Lake. The campground is set along the Cle Elum River a mile from the lake, just above where the river feeds into it.

Site **51**
WISH POOSH
on Cle Elum Lake
WENATCHEE NATIONAL FOREST

Campsites, facilities: There are 17 tent sites and 22 for tents, trailers or motor homes up to 21 feet long. Piped water, fire grills and picnic tables are provided. Flush toilets, firewood, a restaurant and ice are available. Boat docks and launching facilities are located on Cle Elum Lake. Leashed pets are permitted but are not allowed in swimming areas.

Reservations, fee: No reservations necessary; $6 fee per night. Open mid-May to mid-November.

Who to contact: Phone Wenatchee National Forest at (509)674-4411 or write to Cle Elum Ranger District, West 2nd Street, Cle Elum, WA, 98922.

Location: From Cle Elum, drive ten miles northwest on Highway 903, then turn west on Forest Service Road 112 and go about 100 yards to the campground.

Trip note: This campground is set along the shore of Cle Elum Lake, where waterskiing, fishing and swimming are among recreation possibilities. Note that dogs are not allowed in swimming areas—too many juicy legs to tempt them.

Site 52   KACHESS
on Kachess Lake
WENATCHEE NATIONAL FOREST

Campsites, facilities: There are 133 tent sites and 26 sites for trailers or motor homes up to 32 feet long. A group site is also available. Piped water, fire grills and picnic tables are provided. Rest rooms, sanitary disposal station, firewood and a store are available. Boat docks, launching facilities and rentals are located on Kachess Lake. Leashed pets are permitted but are not allowed in swimming areas.

Reservations, fee: No reservations necessary; $6 fee per night. Open late May to October.

Who to contact: Phone Wenatchee National Forest at (509)674-4411 or write to Cle Elum Ranger District, West 2nd Street, Cle Elum, WA, 98922.

Location: From Cle Elum, drive 21 miles northwest on Highway 190, then turn northeast on County Road 49 and drive 5.5 miles to the campground.

Trip note: This is the only campground on the shore of Kachess Lake and it is a winner. Recreation opportunities include waterskiing, fishing, hiking and bicycling. A trail from camp heads north into the Alpine Lakes Wilderness. See a Forest Service map for details. The Kachess Sno-Park is about a mile south of the campground, which provides parking and access to Forest Service Roads and open areas which are ideal for snowmobiling and cross-country skiing.

Site 53   BEVERLY
on the North Fork of Teanaway River
WENATCHEE NATIONAL FOREST

Campsites, facilities: There are 13 tent sites and three sites for trailers or motor homes up to 21 feet long. Picnic tables and fire grills are provided. Pit toilets are available, but there is **no piped water.** Leashed pets are permitted.

Reservations, fee: No reservations necessary; no fee. Open June to mid-November.

Who to contact: Phone Wenatchee National Forest at (509)674-4411 or write to Cle Elum Ranger District, West 2nd Street, Cle Elum, WA, 98922.

Location: From Cle Elum, drive eight miles east on Highway 970, turn north on County Road 107, then go north on Forest Service Road 9737 for four miles to campground.

Trip note: This primitive campground is set along the North Fork of the Teanaway River. There are several trails near camp leading up nearby creeks and into the Alpine Lakes Wilderness.

Site 54   FISH LAKE
on Tucquala Lake
WENATCHEE NATIONAL FOREST

Campsites, facilities: There are ten tent sites. Picnic tables and fire grills are provided. Pit toilets and firewood are available, but there is **no piped water.** Leashed pets are permitted.

Reservations, fee: No reservations necessary; no fee. Open July to October.

Who to contact: Phone Wenatchee National Forest at (509)674-4411 or write to Cle

Elum Ranger District, West 2nd Street, Cle Elum, WA, 98922.

Location: From Cle Elum, drive 11 miles northwest on Highway 903, then 10.5 miles northwest on County Road 903, and turn northeast on Forest Service Road 4330 and go 11 miles to campground. This access road is rough: no trailers.

Trip note: This campground is way out there, just a short jaunt to the Alpine Lakes Wilderness. There are numerous opportunities to access trails into the backcountry. This camp is nestled along the shore of tiny Tucquala Lake, a jewel near the headwaters of Cle Elum Creek.

Site **55**
OWHI
on Cooper Lake
WENATCHEE NATIONAL FOREST

Campsites, facilities: There are 22 tent sites. Picnic tables and fire grills are provided. Pit toilets and firewood are available, but there is **no piped water.** Boat docks and launching facilities are nearby. Leashed pets are permitted.

Reservations, fee: No reservations necessary; no fee. Open mid-June to mid-October.

Who to contact: Phone Wenatchee National Forest at (509)674-4411 or write to Cle Elum Ranger District, West 2nd Street, Cle Elum, WA, 98922.

Location: From Cle Elum, go 11 miles northwest on Highway 903, then 9.5 miles northwest on County Road 903. Turn northwest on Forest Service Road 228 and go five miles, then north on Forest Service Road 235 for about 300 yards to campground.

Trip note: This spot has everything. Well, everything but piped water. It is located on the shore of Cooper Lake, near the boundary of Alpine Lakes Wilderness. A nearby trailhead provides access to several lakes in the Wilderness and extends to the Pacific Crest Trail. See a Forest Service map for details. Fishing, swimming and boating are all popular at Cooper Lake.

Site **56**
CRYSTAL SPRINGS
near Kachess and Keechelus Lakes
WENATCHEE NATIONAL FOREST

Campsites, facilities: There are 20 tent sites and ten sites for tents, trailers or motor homes up to 21 feet long. Piped water, fire grills and picnic tables are provided. Pit toilets and firewood are available. Boat docks and rentals are nearby. Leashed pets are permitted.

Reservations, fee: No reservations necessary; $4 fee per night. Open mid-May to mid-November.

Who to contact: Phone Wenatchee National Forest at (509)674-4411 or write to Cle Elum Ranger District, West 2nd Street, Cle Elum, WA, 98922.

Location: From Cle Elum, go 20.5 miles northwest on Interstate 90, then turn northwest on Forest Service Road 212 and drive one-half mile to the campground.

Trip note: This campground is just off Interstate 90 and a short drive from Kachess Lake and Keechelus Lake. There are boat ramps at both lakes. For winter sports, there are also several Sno-parks in the area, which provide parking and access to Forest Service roads and open areas which are available for snowmobiling and cross-country skiing. The Pacific West Ski Area is at the north end of Keechelus Lake.

Site 57

MINERAL SPRINGS
on Medicine Creek
WENATCHEE NATIONAL FOREST

Campsites, facilities: There are five tent sites and seven sites for tents, trailers or motor homes up to 21 feet long. Piped water and picnic tables are provided. Flush toilets, showers, a store, a restaurant, a laundromat and a gas station are available.

Reservations, fee: No reservations necessary; $4 fee per night. Open mid-April to late November.

Who to contact: Phone Wenatchee National Forest at (509)674-4411 or write to Cle Elum Ranger District, West 2nd Street, Cle Elum, WA, 98922.

Location: From Cle Elum, go southeast for four miles on Highway 10, then turn northeast on US 97 and drive 14 miles to the campground.

Trip note: This campground is set at the confluence of Medicine Creek and Swauk Creek. It is one of five campgrounds along US 97. Fishing, berry picking and hunting are good in season in this area.

Site 58

SWAUK
on Swauk Creek
WENATCHEE NATIONAL FOREST

Campsites, facilities: There are 23 sites for tents, trailers or motor homes. Piped water, fire grills and picnic tables are provided. Pit toilets and firewood are available. Leashed pets are permitted.

Reservations, fee: No reservations necessary; $5 fee per night. Open mid-April to late November.

Who to contact: Phone Wenatchee National Forest at (509)674-4411 or write to Cle Elum Ranger District, West 2nd Street, Cle Elum, WA, 98922.

Location: From Cle Elum, go southeast for four miles on Highway 10, then turn northeast on US 97 and drive 18 miles to the campground.

Trip note: This campground is set along Swauk Creek. It is a prime spot, particularly during winter months. About three miles east of the campground is Swauk Sno-Park, which provides a parking area and access to Forest Service Roads and open areas for snowmobiling and cross-country skiing.

Site 59

TRONSEN
on Tronsen Creek
WENATCHEE NATIONAL FOREST

Campsites, facilities: There are 13 tent sites and 12 sites for tents, trailers or motor homes up to 21 feet long. Piped water, fire grills and picnic tables are provided. Pit toilets and firewood are available. Leashed pets are permitted.

Reservations, fee: No reservations necessary; $4 fee per night. Open mid-May to late October.

Who to contact: Phone Wenatchee National Forest at (509)782-1413 or write to Leavenworth Ranger District, 600 Sherbourne, Leavenworth, WA, 98826.

Location: From Leavenworth, drive 4.5 miles southeast on US 2, then turn south on US 97 and drive 18 miles to the campground.

Trip note: This campground is set along Tronsen Creek. Like Site 58, it's a good winter layover. About a mile away is the Swauk Sno-park, which provides parking and access to Forest Service roads and open areas for snowmobiling and cross-country skiing.

Site **60**
BONANZA
on Tronsen Creek
WENATCHEE NATIONAL FOREST

Campsites, facilities: There are four tent sites and one site for tents, trailers or motor homes up to 15 feet long. Piped water, fire grills and picnic tables are provided. Pit toilets and firewood are available. Leashed pets are permitted.

Reservations, fee: No reservations necessary; $4 fee per night. Open mid-April to late November.

Who to contact: Phone Wenatchee National Forest at (509)782-1413 or write to Leavenworth Ranger District, 600 Sherbourne, Leavenworth, WA, 98826.

Location: From Leavenworth, drive 4.5 miles southeast on US 2, then turn south on US 97 and drive 13 miles to the campground.

Trip note: This campground is just off US 97 and is set along Tronsen Creek. If this camp is full, a nearby option is Site 59, which is south, about ten miles from Site 60.

Site **61**
INDIAN CAMP
on the Middle Fork of Teenaway River

Campsites, facilities: There are nine campsites for tents or small trailers. Picnic tables, fire grills and tent pads are provided. Pit toilets are available, but there is **no piped water.** Leashed pets are permitted.

Reservations, fee: No reservations necessary; no fee. Open all year.

Who to contact: Phone the Department of Natural Resources at (800)527-3305 or write Department of Natural Resources AW-11, 1065 South Capitol Way, Olympia, WA 98504.

Location: In Cle Elum, take exit 85 off Interstate 90 and drive east on Highway 970 for seven miles. Turn left on Teanaway Road and go 7.5 miles, then turn left of West Fork Teanaway Road and drive one-half mile. Go right on Middle Fork Teanaway Road and drive four miles to the campground, which will be on your left.

Trip note: This campground is set along the Middle Fork of the Teanaway River. Bet you didn't know about it.

COLVILLE
♦

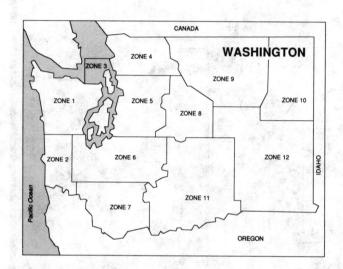

86 CAMPGROUNDS

Colville National Forest

Okanogan National Forest

Sinlahekin Habitat Management Area

Coulee Dam National Recreation Area

Columbia River

Chewack River

Methow River

Curlew Lake

Conconully Lake

Okanogan River

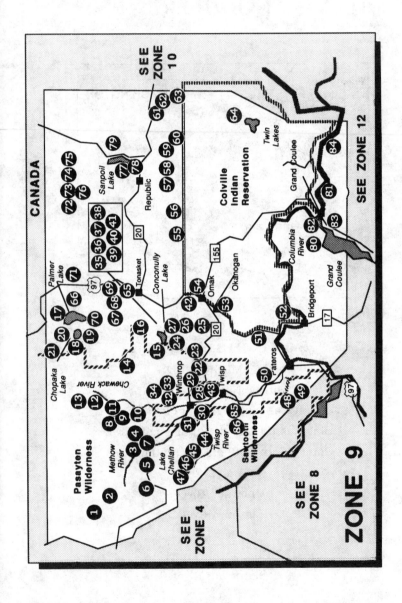

Site **1**
HARTS PASS
near Pasayten Wilderness
OKANOGAN NATIONAL FOREST

Campsites, facilities: There are five tent sites. Picnic tables are provided. Vault toilets are available, but there is **no piped water.** Leashed pets are permitted.

Reservations, fee: No reservations necessary; no fee. Open mid-July to late September.

Who to contact: Phone the Okanogan National Forest at (509)996-2266 or write to Winthrop Ranger District, Box 579 Winthrop, WA 98862.

Location: From Winthrop, drive 13 miles northwest on Highway 20, then continue northwest on County Road 1163 for seven miles. Go 12.5 miles northwest on Forest Service Road 5400 and you'll arrive at the campground. Be aware that this last stretch of road is not suitable for trailers or RVs.

Trip note: This campground is set at the edge of the Pasayten Wilderness, which offers 500 miles of trails to alpine meadows, glacier-fed lakes and streams, and along ridges to spectacular mountain heights. Contact the district Ranger for details. The Pacific Crest Trail passes near camp, and nearby Slate Peak, at 7,500 feet elevation, offers a great view of the northern Cascade Range.

Site **2**
MEADOWS
near Pacific Crest Trail
OKANOGAN NATIONAL FOREST

Campsites, facilities: There are 14 tent sites. Picnic tables are provided. Vault toilets are available, but there is **no piped water.** Leashed pets are permitted.

Reservations, fee: No reservations necessary; no fee. Open mid-July to late September.

Who to contact: Phone the Okanogan National Forest at (509)996-2266 or write to Winthrop Ranger District, Winthrop, Box 579 WA 98862.

Location: From Winthrop, drive 13 miles northwest on Highway 20, then continue northwest on County Road 1163 for seven miles. Go 12.5 miles northwest on Forest Service Road 5400, then turn south of Forest Service Road 500 and drive one mile to the campground.

Trip note: This campground is about one mile from Site 1 and offers the same opportunities. It is adjacent to the Pacific Crest Trail.

Site **3**
RIVER BEND
on Methow River
OKANOGAN NATIONAL FOREST

Campsites, facilities: There are three tent sites and three sites for tents, trailers or motor homes. Piped water and picnic tables are provided. Vault toilets are available and leashed pets are permitted.

Reservations, fee: No reservations necessary; $3 fee per night. Open June to late September.

Who to contact: Phone the Okanogan National Forest at (509)996-2266 or write to Winthrop Ranger District, Box 579, Winthrop, WA 98862.

Location: From Winthrop, drive 13 miles northwest on Highway 20, then continue northwest on County Road 1163 for seven miles. Go 2.5 miles northwest on Forest Service Road 5400, then head west on Forest Service Road 60 and drive one-half mile to the campground.

Trip note: This campground is set along the Methow River about two miles from the boundary of the Pasayten Wilderness. There are several trails near camp that provide access to the Wilderness, as well as one that follows the Methow River west for about eight miles before hooking up with the Pacific Crest Trail near Azurite Peak; a Forest Service map will show you the options. If you are interested in traveling with pack animals or horses there is a Forest Service camp nearby that provides facilities. See the trip note for Site 4 for further details.

Site **4**
BALLARD
near Methow River
OKANOGAN NATIONAL FOREST

Campsites, facilities: There are six tent sites and one site for a tent, trailer or motor home up to 21 feet long. **No piped water** is available. Picnic tables and fire grills are provided. Pit toilets are available and leashed pets are permitted.

Reservations, fee: No reservations necessary; no fee. Open June to late September.

Who to contact: Phone the Okanogan National Forest at (509)996-2266 or write to Winthrop Ranger District, Box 579, Winthrop, WA 98862.

Location: From Winthrop, drive 13 miles northwest on Highway 20, then continue northwest on County Road 1163 for seven miles. Go two miles northwest on Forest Service Road 5400 until you see the campground.

Trip note: This campground is set at 2,600 feet elevation, about one-half mile from Site 3. Facilities for horsepacking, including a hitch rail, truck dock and water, are available at a primitive camp less than a mile northeast of Ballard.

Site **5**
KLIPCHUCK
on Early Winters Creek
OKANOGAN NATIONAL FOREST

Campsites, facilities: There are six tent sites and 40 sites for tents, trailers or motor homes up to 32 feet long. Piped water and picnic tables are provided. Flush and vault toilets are available, and leashed pets are permitted.

Reservations, fee: No reservations necessary; $5 fee per night. Open June to late September.

Who to contact: Phone the Okanogan National Forest at (509)996-2266 or write to Winthrop Ranger District, Box 579, Winthrop, WA 98862.

Location: From Winthrop, drive 17 miles northwest on Highway 20, then continue northwest on Forest Service Road 300 for one mile and you'll see the campground.

Trip note: This campground is set along Early Winters Creek at 3,000 feet elevation. A trail from the camp leads about five miles up and over Delancy Ridge to the Methow River. Another trail starts nearby on Forest Service Road 200 (Sandy Butte-Cedar Creek Road) and goes two miles up Cedar Creek to lovely Cedar Creek Falls. See a Forest Service map for details.

Site **6**
LONE FIR
on Early Winters Creek
OKANOGAN NATIONAL FOREST

Campsites, facilities: There are 28 tent sites and 13 sites for trailers or motor homes up to 21 feet long. Piped water, fire grills and picnic tables are provided. Vault toilets are available. Leashed pets are permitted.

Reservations, fee: No reservations necessary; $5 fee per night. Open June to late September.

Who to contact: Phone the Okanogan National Forest at (509)996-2266 or write to Winthrop Ranger District, Box 579, Winthrop, WA 98862.

Location: From Winthrop, drive 27 miles northwest on Highway 20 and you'll see the campground.

Trip note: This campground is set at 3,800 feet elevation, 800 feet higher on Early Winters Creek than Site 5. This spot is easier to reach than Site 5, and as a result, gets more traffic.

Site **7**

EARLY WINTERS
on Early Winters Creek/Methow River
OKANOGAN NATIONAL FOREST

Campsites, facilities: There are seven tent sites and six sites for tents, trailers or motor homes up to 16 feet long. Piped water, fire grills and picnic tables are provided. Vault toilets are available. Leashed pets are permitted.

Reservations, fee: No reservations necessary; $5 fee per night. Open June to late September.

Who to contact: Phone the Okanogan National Forest at (509)996-2266 or write to Winthrop Ranger District, Box 579, Winthrop, WA 98862.

Location: From Winthrop, drive 16 miles northwest on Highway 20 and you'll see the campground entrance.

Trip note: This campground is set at the confluence of Early Winters Creek and the Methow River. There are several trails that follow the streams in the area. A Forest Service information center is nearby.

Site **8**

HONEYMOON
on Eightmile Creek
OKANOGAN NATIONAL FOREST

Campsites, facilities: There are five sites for tents, trailers or motor homes. Picnic tables are provided. Vault toilets are available, but there is **no piped water.** Leashed pets are permitted.

Reservations, fee: No reservations necessary; no fee. Open June to late September.

Who to contact: Phone the Okanogan National Forest at (509)996-2266 or write to Winthrop Ranger District, Box 579, Winthrop, WA 98862.

Location: From Winthrop, drive 6.5 miles north on County Road 1213, continue north on Forest Service Road 51 for 2.5 miles, then turn northwest on Forest Service Road 5130 and drive nine miles to the campground.

Trip note: This campground is set at 3,500 feet elevation along Eightmile Creek. If you continue north seven miles to the end of Forest Service Road 5130, you will reach a trailhead that provides access to the Pasayten Wilderness. See a Forest Service map for details. As to why it is named Honeymoon, well, there are some things about camping that not even this book can answer.

Site **9**

NICE
on Eightmile Creek
OKANOGAN NATIONAL FOREST

Campsites, facilities: There are four tent sites. Picnic tables and fire grills are provided. Vault toilets are available, but there is **no piped water.** Leashed pets are permitted.

Reservations, fee: No reservations; no fee. Open June to late September.

Who to contact: Phone the Okanogan National Forest at (509)996-2266 or write to Winthrop Ranger District, Box 579, Winthrop, WA 98862.

Location: From Winthrop, drive 6.5 miles north on County Road 1213, continue north on Forest Service Road 51 for three miles, then turn northwest on Forest Service Road 5130 and drive four miles to the campground.

Trip note: This campground is set along Eightmile Creek about four miles from Buck Lake.

Site **10**
FLAT
on Eightmile Creek
OKANOGAN NATIONAL FOREST

Campsites, facilities: There are nine sites for tents, trailers or motor homes up to 15 feet long. Piped water and picnic tables are provided. Vault toilets are available. Leashed pets are permitted.

Reservations, fee: No reservations necessary; $3 fee per night. Open June to late September.

Who to contact: Phone the Okanogan National Forest at (509)996-2266 or write to Winthrop Ranger District, Box 579, Winthrop, WA 98862.

Location: From Winthrop, drive 6.5 miles north on County Road 1213, continue north on Forest Service Road 51 for three miles, then turn northwest on Forest Service Road 5130 for two miles to the campground.

Trip note: This campground is set along Eightmile Creek two miles from where it empties to the Chewack River. Buck Lake is about three miles away. This is the closest of six camps to County Road 1213.

Site **11**
FALLS CREEK
on Chewack River
OKANOGAN NATIONAL FOREST

Campsites, facilities: There are four sites for tents, trailers or motor homes up to 15 feet long. Piped water and picnic tables are provided. Vault toilets are available. Leashed pets are permitted.

Reservations, fee: No reservations necessary; $4 fee per night. Open June to late September.

Who to contact: Phone the Okanogan National Forest at (509)996-2266 or write to Winthrop Ranger District, Box 579, Winthrop, WA 98862.

Location: From Winthrop, drive 6.5 miles north on County Road 1213, continue north on Forest Service Road 5160 for five miles to the campground.

Trip note: This campground is set at the confluence of Falls Creek and the Chewack River, a quiet and pretty spot that is about a 20-minute drive out of Winthrop. Nearby Sites 12 and 13 do not have piped water, but this camp does.

Site **12**
CHEWACK
on Chewack River
OKANOGAN NATIONAL FOREST

Campsites, facilities: There are four tent sites. Picnic tables are provided. Vault toilets are available. There is **no piped water.** Leashed pets are permitted.

Reservations, fee: No reservations; no fee. Open June to late September.

Who to contact: Phone the Okanogan National Forest at (509)996-2266 or write to Winthrop Ranger District, Box 579, Winthrop, WA 98862.

Location: From Winthrop, drive 6.5 miles north on County Road 1213, continue northeast on Forest Service Road 5160 for 8.5 miles to the campground.

Trip note: This campground is set along the Chewack River. It's a more primitive option to nearby Site 11.

Site **13**
CAMP 4
on Chewack River
OKANOGAN NATIONAL FOREST

Campsites, facilities: There are five tent sites. Picnic tables are provided. Vault toilets are available. There is **no piped water.** Leashed pets are permitted.

Reservations, fee: No reservations necessary; no fee. Open June to late September.

Who to contact: Phone the Okanogan National Forest at (509)996-2266 or write to Winthrop Ranger District, Box 579, Winthrop, WA 98862.

Location: From Winthrop, drive 6.5 miles north on County Road 1213, then continue northeast on Forest Service Road 5160 for 11 miles to the campground.

Trip note: This campground is set along the Chewack River, the smallest and most primitive of three camps on the river. There are two horse and pack animal facilities five miles north of camp: one is at Lake Creek and the other at Andrews Creek. They both have corrals, hitching rails, truck docks and water for the stock. Trails leading into the Pasayten Wilderness leave from both locations. Contact the Forest Service for details.

Site **14**
TIFFANY SPRING
near Tiffany Lake
OKANOGAN NATIONAL FOREST

Campsites, facilities: There are six tent sites and six sites for trailers or motor homes up to 15 feet long. Picnic tables are provided. Vault toilets and firewood are available, but there is **no piped water.** Leashed pets are permitted.

Reservations, fee: No reservations necessary; no fee. Open July to late September.

Who to contact: Phone the Okanogan National Forest at (509)486-2186 or write to Tonasket Ranger District, Box 466, Tonasket, WA 98855.

Location: From Conconully, drive 1.5 miles southwest on County Road 2017, then turn northwest on Forest Service Road 364 and drive 21 miles. Turn northeast on Forest Service Road 370 and go 7.5 miles to the campground.

Trip note: This campground is set at 6,800 feet elevation and is less than a mile hike from Tiffany Lake. Tiffany Mountain rises 8,200 feet in the distance. No other campgrounds are in the vicinity, and it is advisable to obtain a Forest Service map of the area.

Site **15**
KERR
on Salmon Creek
OKANOGAN NATIONAL FOREST

Campsites, facilities: There are 13 sites for tents, trailers or motor homes up to 21 feet long. Picnic tables are provided. Vault toilets and firewood are available, but there is **no piped water.** Leashed pets are permitted.

Reservations, fee: No reservations necessary; no fee. Open mid-May to mid-September.

Who to contact: Phone the Okanogan National Forest at (509)486-2186 or write to Tonasket Ranger District, Box 466, Tonasket, WA 98855.

Location: From Conconully, drive two miles northwest on County Road 2361, then go northwest on Forest Service Road 38 for two miles to the campground.

Trip note: This campground is set along Salmon Creek about four miles north of the Conconully Lake. It's one of the many campgrounds located near the lake.

Site **16**
SUGARLOAF
on Conconully Lake
OKANOGAN NATIONAL FOREST

Campsites, facilities: There are four tent sites and one site for a tent, trailer or motor homes up to 21 feet long. Piped water and picnic tables are provided. Vault toilets and firewood are available. Leashed pets are permitted. Boat docks, launching facilities and rentals are nearby.

Reservations, fee: No reservations necessary; $3 fee per night. Open mid-May to mid-September.

Who to contact: Phone the Okanogan National Forest at (509)486-2186 or write to Tonasket Ranger District, Box 466, Tonasket, WA 98855.

Location: From Conconully, drive 4.5 miles northeast on County Road 4015 to the campground.

Trip note: At 2,400 feet elevation, this campground is set along the shore of Conconully Lake. This is the smallest, most private of the camps on the lake.

Site **17**
PALMER LAKE
on Palmer Lake

Campsites, facilities: There are six campsites for tents or small trailers. Picnic tables, fire grills and tent pads are provided. Pit toilets are available, but there is **no piped water.** Leashed pets are permitted.

Reservations, fee: No reservations necessary; no fee. Open all year.

Who to contact: Phone the Department of Natural Resources at (800)527-3305 or write to Department of Natural Resources AW-11, 1065 South Capitol Way, Olympia, WA 98504.

Location: Drive five miles north of Tonasket on County Road 9437, then head west to Loomis on County Road 9425. From Loomis, continue north on County Road 9425 for 8.5 miles, keep right, and you'll find the campground at the north end of the lake.

Trip note: This campground is set along the shore of Palmer Lake, the only camp at the lake. The winter range of the deer is in the Sinlahekin Valley to the south of Palmer Lake. There are numerous migration routes in the area. Wildlife (not for hunting) include the endangered Bighorn sheep, cougar, bald and golden eagles, black and brown bear and grouse. See Site 20 for information on fishing for Atlantic salmon in nearby Chopaka Lake.

Site **18**
NORTH FORK NINE MILE
on the North Fork of Touts Coulee Creek

Campsites, facilities: There are 11 campsites for tents or small trailers. Picnic tables, fire grills and tent pads are provided. Pit toilets and piped water are available. Leashed pets are permitted.

Reservations, fee: No reservations necessary; no fee. Open all year.

Who to contact: Phone the Department of Natural Resources at (800)527-3305 or write to Department of Natural Resources AW-11, 1065 South Capitol Way, Olympia, WA 98504.

Location: Drive five miles north of Tonasket on County Road 9437, then head west to Loomis on County Road 9425. From Loomis, continue north on County Road 9425 for two miles, then turn left on Touts Coulee Road. Go 5.5 miles to the lower camp. Continue 100 yards to the upper camp at the junction of Roads OMT 2000 and OMT 1000. Take Road OMT 1000 and drive 2.5 miles to the campground.

Trip note: This campground is set in the forest along the North Fork of Touts Coulee Creek and Nine Mile Creek. This area is frequented by the northwestern moose. It is advisable to obtain a map that details the area from the Department of Natural Resources.

Site **19**   TOUTS COULEE
on Touts Coulee Creek

Campsites, facilities: There are nine campsites for tents or small trailers. Picnic tables, fire grills and tent pads are provided. Pit toilets are available. There is **no piped water.** Leashed pets are permitted.

Reservations, fee: No reservations necessary; no fee. Open all year.

Who to contact: Phone the Department of Natural Resources at (800)527-3305 or write to Department of Natural Resources AW-11, 1065 South Capitol Way, Olympia, WA 98504.

Location: Drive five miles north of Tonasket on County Road 9437, then head west to Loomis on County Road 9425. From Loomis, continue north on County Road 9425 for two miles, then turn left on Touts Coulee Road. Go 5.5 miles to the lower camp. Continue 100 yards to the upper camp at the junction of Roads OMT 2000 and OMT 1000.

Trip note: This wooded camp is set along Touts Coulee Creek. Some moose are in the area. A road for snowmobile use follows the South Fork of Touts Coulee Creek swinging south, then heading east along Cecil Creek. Contact the Department of Natural Resources for details. This is one of three little-known camps in the vicinity.

Site **20**   CHOPAKA LAKE
on Chopaka Lake

Campsites, facilities: There are 15 campsites for tents or small trailers. Picnic tables, fire grills and tent pads are provided. Pit toilets, piped water and boat launching facilities are available. Leashed pets are permitted.

Reservations, fee: No reservations necessary; no fee. Open all year.

Who to contact: Phone the Department of Natural Resources at (800)527-3305 or write to Department of Natural Resources AW-11, 1065 South Capitol Way, Olympia, WA 98504.

Location: Drive five miles north of Tonasket on County Road 9437, then head west to Loomis on County Road 9425. From Loomis continue north on County Road 9425, for two miles, then turn left on Touts Coulee Road and go 1.5 miles. Turn right onto a steep, one lane road and drive 3.5 miles, keep left and drive 1.5 miles, then turn right and drive two miles to the campground.

Trip note: This campground is set along the western shore of Chopaka Lake. The lake is stocked with Atlantic salmon and only catch and release fly fishing with barbless hooks is allowed. It's a classic setting for the expert angler.

Site **21**   COLD SPRINGS
near Cold Creek

Campsites, facilities: There are nine campsites for tents or small trailers. Picnic tables, fire grills and tent pads are provided. Pit toilets and piped water are available. Horse stalls and feeder boxes are also available. Leashed pets are permitted.

Reservations, fee: No reservations necessary; no fee. Open all year.

Who to contact: Phone the Department of Natural Resources at (800)527-3305 or write to Department of Natural Resources AW-11, 1065 South Capitol Way, Olympia, WA 98504.

Location: Drive five miles north of Tonasket on County Road 9437, then head west to Loomis on County Road 9425. From Loomis, continue north on County Road 9425 for two miles, then turn left on Touts Coulee Road and drive 5.5 miles to the Touts Coulee campground at the junction of OMT-2000 and OMT-1000. Take OMT-1000 Road for two miles to Cold Creek Road (gravel) and turn right. Go one-half mile, keep right and continue for two miles. Then keep left and go two miles to the picnic area or three miles to the campground.

Trip note: There are trails here for horseback riding, hiking and snowmobiling. Because it is little known and remote, it is advisable to obtain a map of the area to aid directions. Some moose tromp around these parts.

Site 22
J. R.
on Frazier Creek
OKANOGAN NATIONAL FOREST

Campsites, facilities: There are six sites for tents, trailers or motor homes up to 16 feet long. Piped water and picnic tables are provided. Vault toilets and firewood are available. Leashed pets are permitted.

Reservations, fee: No reservations necessary; $4 fee per night. Open late May to early September.

Who to contact: Phone the Okanogan National Forest at (509)997-2131 or write to Twisp Ranger District, Box 188, Twisp, WA 98856.

Location: From Twisp, drive 12 miles east on Highway 20 to the campground.

Trip note: This campground is set along Frazier Creek near the Loup Loup summit and ski area. Some of the recreation options include fishing, hunting, cross-country skiing, snowmobiling, hiking and bicycling. This is a good layover for travelers looking for a spot on Highway 20.

Site 23
LOUP LOUP
near Loup Loup Ski Area
OKANOGAN NATIONAL FOREST

Campsites, facilities: There are four tent sites and 20 sites for tents, trailers or motor homes up to 21 feet long. Piped water and picnic tables are provided. Vault toilets and firewood are available. Pets are permitted.

Reservations, fee: No reservations necessary; $4 fee per night. Open late May to early September.

Who to contact: Phone the Okanogan National Forest at (509)997-2131 or write to Twisp Ranger District, Box 188, Twisp, WA 98856.

Location: From Twisp, drive 13 miles east on Highway 20, then turn north on Forest Service Road 42 and drive one mile to the campground.

Trip note: At 4,200 feet elevation, this campground is set next to the Loup Loup ski area which has facilities for both downhill and cross-country skiing. There are trails for hiking and horseback riding. It's just far enough off Highway 20 to be missed by many out-of-towners.

Site 24
CONCONULLY STATE PARK
on Conconully Reservoir

Campsites, facilities: There are 65 sites for tents or self-contained motor homes, and ten sites with water hookups for motor homes. Piped water, fire grills and picnic tables are provided. Flush toilets, sanitary disposal station, showers, firewood and a playground are available. A store, a cafe, a laundromat and ice are located within one mile. Pets are permitted. Boat launching facilities are nearby.

Reservations, fee: No reservations necessary; $7.50-10.50 fee per night. Open all year with limited winter facilities.

Who to contact: Phone (509)826-2108 or write to Box 95, Conconully, WA 98819.

Location: From Omak, drive 22 miles northwest on US 97 and you'll see the park entrance.

Trip note: This park is set along Conconully Reservoir, where there is a boat launch, beach access and swimming, and fishing and hiking opportunities. Of special interest is the Sinlahekin Habitat Management Area which is accessible via County Road 4015. This route heads northeast along the shore of Conconully Lake on the other side of US 97. The road is narrow at first, but then becomes wider as you enter the Habitat Management Area.

Site 25   LEADER LAKE
on Leader Lake

Campsites, facilities: There are 16 campsites for tents or small trailers. Picnic tables, fire grills and tent pads are provided. Pit toilets are available, but there is **no piped water.** Boat launching facilities are nearby. Leashed pets are permitted.

Reservations, fee: No reservations necessary; no fee. Open all year.

Who to contact: Phone the Department of Natural Resources at (800)527-3305 or write to Department of Natural Resources AW-11, 1065 South Capitol Way, Olympia, WA 98504.

Location: Take Highway 20 west from Okanogan and go 8.5 miles, then turn right on Leader Lake Road and drive 400 yards to the campground.

Trip note: This campground is set along the shore of Leader Lake, where trout fishing can be good in season. It gets missed by many because it is just far enough off the beaten path.

Site 26   ROCK CREEK
on Rock Creek and Loup Loup Creek

Campsites, facilities: There are six campsites for tents or small trailers. Picnic tables, fire grills and tent pads are provided. Pit toilets and piped water are available. Leashed pets are permitted.

Reservations, fee: No reservations necessary; no fee. Open all year.

Who to contact: Phone the Department of Natural Resources at (800)527-3305 or write to Department of Natural Resources AW-11, 1065 South Capitol Way, Olympia, WA 98504.

Location: Take Highway 20 west from Okanogan and go ten miles, then turn right on Loup Loup Canyon Road and drive four miles to the camp, which is on the left.

Trip note: This wooded campground is at the confluence of Rock Creek and Loup Loup Creek. There are hiking trails in the area. It's advisable to obtain a map detailing the area from the Department of Natural Resources.

Site 27   ROCK LAKES
on Rock Lake

Campsites, facilities: There are eight campsites for tents or small trailers. Picnic tables, fire grills and tent pads are provided. Pit toilets are available, but there is **no piped water.** Leashed pets are permitted.

Reservations, fee: No reservations necessary; no fee. Open all year.

Who to contact: Phone the Department of Natural Resources at (800)527-3305 or write to Department of Natural Resources AW-11, 1065 South Capitol Way, Olympia, WA 98504.

Location: Take Highway 20 west from Okanogan and go ten miles, then turn right on Loup Loup Canyon Road and drive five miles. Turn left on Rock Lakes Road and go six miles then turn left and drive 300 yards to the campground.

Trip note: This campground is set in a forested area along the shore of Rock Lake. Trout fishing can be good. A good bet is to combine a trip here with nearby Site 25 at Leader Lake.

Site **28**   **KOA METHOW RIVER**
                    on Methow River

Campsites, facilities: There are 30 tent sites and 72 drive-through sites for trailers or motor homes of any length. Piped water and picnic tables are provided. Flush toilets, electricity, firewood, sewer hookups, sanitary services, showers, a recreation hall, store, a laundromat, ice, a playground and swimming pool are available. Bottled gas and a cafe are located within one mile. Pets and motorbikes are permitted.

Reservations, fee: Reservations accepted; $13 fee per night; MasterCard and Visa accepted. Open mid-April to November.

Who to contact: Phone (509)996-2258 or write to P.O. Box 305, Winthrop, WA 98862.

Location: From Winthrop, drive one mile east on Highway 20 and you'll see it.

Trip note: This campground is set along the Methow River. Nearby, Liberty Bell Alpine Tours and River Rafting offers both whitewater and scenic tours on the Methow River; phone (509)996-2250 for information. Winthrop is an interesting town with many restored, turn-of-the-century buildings lining the main street, including the Shafer Museum, which displays lots of old items from that era. If you would like to observe wildlife, take a short, two-mile drive southeast out of Winthrop on County Road 9129, on the east side of the Methow River. Turn east on County Road 1631 into Davis Lake, and follow the signs to the Methow River Habitat Management Area Headquarters. Depending upon the time of year, you may see mule deer, porcupine, bobcat, mountain lion, snowshoe hare, black bear, red squirrel and many species of birds. However, if you are looking for something tamer, other nearby recreation options include an 18-hole golf course and tennis courts.

Site **29**   **PINE-NEAR TRAILER PARK**
                    on Methow River

Campsites, facilities: There are ten tent sites and 28 drive-through sites for trailers or motor homes of any length. Electricity, piped water, sewer hookups and picnic tables are provided. Flush toilets, sanitary services, showers, a laundromat and a playground are available. A store and a cafe are located within one mile. Pets and motorbikes are permitted.

Reservations, fee: Reservations accepted; $5-10 fee per night. Open all year.

Who to contact: Phone (509)996-2391 or write to P.O. Box 157, Winthrop, WA 98862.

Location: Drive east of Winthrop on Highway 20 on Coral and Castle and you'll see the park.

Trip note: This campground is set along the Methow River. See the trip note for Site 28 for information on the various activities available in the Winthrop area.

Site 30

BIG TWIN LAKE CAMPGROUND
on Twin Lakes

Campsites, facilities: There are 35 tent sites and 58 drive-through sites for trailers or motor homes of any length. Electricity, piped water, sewer hookups and picnic tables are provided. Flush toilets, sanitary services, showers, firewood, a laundromat, ice and a playground are available. Pets and motorbikes are permitted. Boat docks, launching facilities and rentals can be obtained on Big Twin Lake.

Reservations, fee: Reservations accepted; $10 fee per night. Open April to late October.

Who to contact: Phone (509)996-2650 or write to Big Twin Lake Road, Winthrop, WA 98862.

Location: From Winthrop, drive three miles south on Highway 20, then turn west on Big Twin Lake Road and drive two miles to the campground.

Trip note: This campground is set along the shore of Twin Lakes. See the trip note for Site 28 for information on the various activities available in the Winthrop area.

Site 31

ROCKING HORSE RANCH
in Methow River Valley

Campsites, facilities: There are 25 tent sites and ten drive-through sites for trailers or motor homes of any length. Electricity, piped water, sewer hookups and picnic tables are provided. Flush toilets, sanitary services, showers, firewood, a recreation hall and ice are available. Some facilities are wheelchair accessible. Pets and motorbikes are permitted.

Reservations, fee: Reservations accepted; $8 fee per night. Open April to late October.

Who to contact: Phone (509)996-2768 or write to Star Route, P.O. Box 35, Winthrop, WA 98862.

Location: From Winthrop, drive nine miles northwest on Highway 20-North Cascade and you'll see the entrance to the ranch.

Trip note: This ranch is set in the lovely Methow River Valley, which is flanked on both sides by national forest. There are numerous trails nearby and a horse stable at the ranch. Owen Wister, who wrote the novel, *The Virginian,* lived in the nearby town of Winthrop at the turn of the century. Portions of the novel were based on his experiences in this area.

Site 32

5-Y RESORT ON PEARRYGIN LAKE
on Pearrygin Lake

Campsites, facilities: There are 60 drive-through sites for tents, trailers or motor homes of any length. Electricity, piped water, sewer hookups and picnic tables are provided. Flush toilets, showers, firewood, a laundromat and a playground are available. Bottled gas, sanitary services, a store, a cafe and ice are located within one mile. Pets and motorbikes are permitted. Boat docks, launching facilities and rentals are nearby.

Reservations, fee: Reservations accepted; $10 fee per night. Open April to October.

Who to contact: Phone (509)996-2448 or write to Route 1, P.O. Box 308, Winthrop, WA 98862.

Location: From Winthrop, drive two miles northeast on Pearrygin Lake Road and you'll see the resort.

Trip note: This resort is in a wooded area along the shore of Pearrygin Lake. Nearby recreation options include an 18-hole golf course, hiking trails and a riding stable. See the trip note for Site 28 for information on other available activities in the Winthrop area.

Site **33**   **DERRY'S RESORT**
on Pearrygin Lake

Campsites, facilities: There are 90 tent sites and 64 drive-through sites for trailers or motor homes of any length. Electricity, piped water, sewer hookups and picnic tables are provided. Flush toilets, bottled gas, showers, firewood, sanitary services, a store, a laundromat, ice and a playground are available. A cafe is located within three miles. Pets and motorbikes are permitted. Boat docks, launching facilities and rentals are available on Pearrygin Lake.

Reservations, fee: Reservations accepted; $8.50-12 fee per night. Open mid-April to November.

Who to contact: Phone (509)996-2322 or write to Route 1, P.O. Box 307, Winthrop, WA 98862.

Location: From Winthrop, drive three miles northeast on Pearrygin Lake Road and you'll see the resort.

Trip note: This campground is also set along the shore of Pearrygin Lake. Nearby recreation options include an 18-hole golf course, hiking trails and a riding stable.

Site **34**   **PEARRYGIN LAKE STATE PARK**
on Pearrygin Lake

Campsites, facilities: There are 26 sites for tents or self-contained motor homes, and 57 sites, many with full hookups, for trailers or motor homes of any length. Picnic tables and fire grills are provided. Flush toilets and sanitary services, electricity, piped water, sewer hookups, showers and firewood are available. A store, a cafe and ice are located within one mile. Some facilities are wheelchair accessible. Leashed pets are permitted. Boat launching facilities are available.

Reservations, fee: Reservations accepted; $7.50-10.50 fee per night. Open May through November.

Who to contact: Phone (509)996-2370 or write to Route 1, Winthrop, WA 98862.

Location: From Winthrop, drive five miles north on Highway 20. The park is adjacent to the highway along the shore of Pearrygin Lake.

Trip note: This park has a sandy beach and facilities for swimming, boating, fishing and hiking. In the winter there are opportunities for snowmobiling, cross-country skiing and ice fishing. Nearby recreation options include an 18-hole golf course. There are several other camps in the immediate area.

Site **35**   **KOZY KABINS AND RV PARK**
near Conconully Lake

Campsites, facilities: There are six tent sites and 12 drive-through sites for trailers or motor homes of any length. Electricity, piped water, sewer hookups and picnic tables are provided. Flush toilets, showers and firewood are available. Bottled gas, sanitary services, a store, a cafe, a laundromat and ice are located within one mile. Pets and motorbikes are permitted. Cabin rentals, boat docks, launching facilities and rentals are nearby.

Reservations, fee: Reservations accepted; $7-10 fee per night. Open all year.

Who to contact: Phone (509)826-6780 or write to P.O. Box 38, Conconully, WA 98819.

Location: From Okanogan, drive northwest on the Conconully Highway to Conconully. The park is at the junction of "A" Avenue and Broadway.

Trip note: This park is in Conconully near the lake. Nearby recreation options include a full-service marina. If you continue northeast of town on County Road 4015, the road will get a bit narrow for awhile, but it will widen again when you enter the Sinlahekin Habitat Management Area, which is managed by the Department of Fish and Game. There are some primitive campsites in this valley, especially along the shores of the lakes in the area.

Site 36   THE OTHER PLACE
on Conconully Lake

Campsites, facilities: There are 25 drive-through sites for trailers or motor homes of any length. Electricity, piped water, sewer hookups and picnic tables are provided. Flush toilets and showers are available. Bottled gas, sanitary services, a store, a cafe, a laundromat and ice are located within one mile. Pets and motorbikes are permitted. Boat docks, launching facilities and rentals are nearby.

Reservations, fee: Reservations accepted; $8 fee per night. Open mid-April to late October.

Who to contact: Phone (509)826-4231 or write to 310 "A" Avenue, Conconully, WA 98819.

Location: From Okanogan, drive northwest on the Conconully Highway to Conconully. Turn east on "A" Avenue and drive one block to the park.

Trip note: This campground is set along the shore of Conconully Lake. See the trip note for Site 35 for nearby recreation options and ideas.

Site 37   JACK'S RV PARK
near Conconully Lake

Campsites, facilities: There are 20 tent sites and 64 drive-through sites for trailers or motor homes of any length. Electricity, piped water, sewer hookups and picnic tables are provided. Flush toilets, bottled gas, showers, firewood, a laundromat, cabin and trailer rentals, and a swimming pool are available. Sanitary services, a store, a cafe and ice are located within one mile. Pets and motorbikes are permitted. Boat docks, launching facilities and rentals are nearby.

Reservations, fee: Reservations accepted; $9-11 fee per night; MasterCard and Visa accepted. Open all year.

Who to contact: Phone (509)826-0132 or write to P.O. Box 98, Conconully, WA 98819.

Location: From Okanogan, drive 20 miles northwest on the Conconully Highway to Conconully. The park is in town.

Trip note: This park is in town, not far from Conconully Lake. Nearby recreation options include hiking trails and water sports at the lake.

Site 38   ANDY'S TRAILER PARK
near Conconully Lake

Campsites, facilities: There are 38 drive-through sites for trailers or motor homes

of any length. Electricity, piped water, sewer hookups and picnic tables are provided. Flush toilets, firewood, showers, a laundromat and a swimming pool are available. Bottled gas, sanitary services, a store, a cafe and ice are located within one mile. Pets are permitted. Boat docks, launching facilities and rentals are nearby.

Reservations, fee: Reservations accepted; $8 fee per night. Open April to mid-November.

Who to contact: Phone (509)826-0326 or write to P.O. Box 67, Conconully, WA 98819.

Location: From Omak, drive 18 miles northwest on the Conconully Highway and you'll find the park in Conconully.

Trip note: This park is in downtown Conconully, a short distance from the lake. Nearby recreation options include hiking trails.

Site **39**   **LIAR'S COVE RESORT**
on Conconully Lake

Campsites, facilities: There are 20 drive-through sites for trailers or motor homes of any length. Electricity, piped water, sewer hookups and picnic tables are provided. Flush toilets, showers, a laundromat and ice are available. Bottled gas, sanitary services, a store and a cafe are located within one mile. Pets and motorbikes are permitted. Boat docks, launching facilities and rentals are nearby.

Reservations, fee: Reservations accepted; $10 fee per night; MasterCard and Visa accepted. Open April to early November.

Who to contact: Phone (509)826-1288 or write to P.O. Box 72, Conconully, WA 98819.

Location: From Okanogan, drive 18 miles northwest on the Conconully Highway and you'll see the park.

Trip note: This park is set along the shore of the Conconully Lake. Nearby recreation options include hiking trails.

Site **40**   **SHADY PINES RESORT**
on Conconully Lake

Campsites, facilities: There are five tent sites and 24 drive-through sites for trailers or motor homes of any length. Electricity, piped water, sewer hookups and picnic tables are provided. Flush toilets, ice, showers and firewood are available. Bottled gas, sanitary services, a store, a cafe and a laundromat are located within one mile. Pets and motorbikes are permitted. Boat launching facilities and rentals are nearby.

Reservations, fee: Reservations accepted; $11 fee per night; MasterCard and Visa accepted. Open mid-April to late October.

Who to contact: Phone (509)826-2287 or write to P.O. Box 44, Conconully, WA 98819.

Location: From Okanogan, drive 20 miles northwest on Conconully Highway, then turn west at the state park and drive one mile to the resort.

Trip note: This campground is set along the shore of the Conconully Lake, near the state park (Site 24).

Site **41**   **FLEMMINGS RESORT AND RV PARK**
on Upper Conconully Lake

Campsites, facilities: There are 11 sites for trailers or motor homes of any length.

Electricity, piped water, sewer hookups and picnic tables are provided. Flush toilets, showers and ice are available. Bottled gas, sanitary services, a store, a cafe and a laundromat are available within one mile. Pets and motorbikes are permitted. Boat docks, launching facilities and rentals are nearby.

Reservations, fee: Reservations accepted; $12 fee per night. Open mid-April to late October.

Who to contact: Phone (509)826-0813 or write to P.O. Box 131, Conconully, WA 98819.

Location: From Omak, drive 17 miles northwest on the Conconully Highway and you'll see the resort.

Trip note: This resort is set along the shore of Conconully Lake. See the trip note for Site 35 for recreation options.

Site 42   LOG CABIN TRAILER COURT
on Okanogan River

Campsites, facilities: There are ten sites for trailers or motor homes. Electricity, piped water and sewer hookups are provided. Flush toilets, sanitary services, showers and a laundromat are available. Bottled gas, a store, a cafe and ice are located within one mile. Pets are permitted.

Reservations, fee: No reservations necessary; $8 fee per night. Open all year.

Who to contact: Phone (509)826-4462 or write to P.O. Box 1630, Omak, WA 98841.

Location: This trailer park is located in Omak, on Highway 215.

Trip note: This trailer court is located in rural Omak on the Okanogan River. Nearby recreation options include an 18-hole golf course and tennis courts.

Site 43   RIVER BEND TRAILER PARK
near Methow River

Campsites, facilities: There are ten tent sites and 56 drive-through sites for trailers or motor homes of any length. Picnic tables are provided. Flush toilets, sanitary services, firewood, a store, a laundromat, ice, a playground, electricity, piped water, sewer hookups and showers are available. Pets and motorbikes are permitted.

Reservations, fee: Reservations accepted; $9 fee per night; MasterCard and Visa accepted. Open mid-April to November.

Who to contact: Phone (509)997-3500 or write to Route 2, Box 30, Twisp, WA 98856.

Location: Drive two miles north of Twisp on Highway 20 and you'll see the campground.

Trip note: This campground is set along the shore of the Methow River. The trip note for Site 28 details the recreation possibilities available within ten miles.

Site 44   WAR CREEK
on Twisp River
OKANOGAN NATIONAL FOREST

Campsites, facilities: There are 11 sites for tents, trailers or motor homes up to 21 feet long. Piped water, fire grills and picnic tables are provided. Vault toilets and firewood are available. Leashed pets are permitted.

Reservations, fee: No reservations necessary; $4 fee per night. Open late May to early September.

Who to contact: Phone the Okanogan National Forest at (509)997-2131 or write to Twisp Ranger District, Box 188, Twisp, WA 98856.

Location: From Twisp, drive 11 miles west on County Road 9114, then continue west on Forest Service Road 44 for 3.5 miles to the campground.

Trip note: This campground is set along the Twisp River near the trailhead for trail 408, which follows War Creek west up to Lake Juanita, and then to War Creek Pass at 7,400 feet elevation. Backpackers can take this path down into the Lake Chelan National Recreation Area, finishing the trip at the shore of Lake Chelan at the Stehekin campground and the National Park Service outpost. It's a 15-mile trek, so contact the Forest Service for details. This area is also open in the winter for cross-country skiing and snowmobiling.

Site **45**   **POPLAR FLAT**
on Twisp River
OKANOGAN NATIONAL FOREST

Campsites, facilities: There are 15 sites for tents, trailers or motor homes up to 21 feet long. Piped water, fire grills and picnic tables are provided. Vault toilets and firewood are available. Some facilities are wheelchair accessible. Leashed pets are permitted.

Reservations, fee: No reservations necessary; $4 fee per night. Open late May to early September.

Who to contact: Phone the Okanogan National Forest at (509)997-2131 or write to Twisp Ranger District, Twisp, WA 98856.

Location: From Twisp, drive 11 miles west on County Road 9114, then head northwest on Forest Service Road 44 and drive 9.5 miles to the campground.

Trip note: This campground is set at 2,900 feet elevation along the Twisp River. There are many trails in the area that follow streams, in some cases providing access to small lakes in the backcountry, in other cases providing access to the Lake Chelan National Recreation Area. Trail 407 is a bicycle trail. South Creek campground (Site 46), about two miles northwest of this campground, has horse facilities. During the winter the roads are available for snowmobiling and cross-country skiing. See a Forest Service map for details.

Site **46**   **SOUTH CREEK**
on the North Fork of Twisp River
OKANOGAN NATIONAL FOREST

Campsites, facilities: There are four sites for tents or small trailers. **No piped water** is available. Picnic tables and fire grills are provided. Vault toilets and firewood are available. Leashed pets are permitted. Horse facilities are also available.

Reservations, fee: No reservations necessary; no fee. Open late May to early September.

Who to contact: Phone the Okanogan National Forest at (509)997-2131 or write to Twisp Ranger District, Box 188, Twisp, WA 98856.

Location: From Twisp, drive 11 miles west on County Road 9114, then continue west on Forest Service Road 44 for 11 miles to the campground.

Trip note: This site is small, quiet and little-known, yet with piped water and good recreation options. It is set at the confluence of the North Fork of the Twisp River and South Creek at a major trailhead that accesses Lake Chelan National Recreation Area and North Cascades National Park. See a Forest Service map for details. This area is also open in the winter for cross-country skiing and snowmobiling.

Site **47**
ROADS END
on North Fork Twisp River
OKANOGAN NATIONAL FOREST

Campsites, facilities: There are four sites for tents or small trailers. **No piped water** is available. Picnic tables and fire grills are provided. Vault toilets and firewood are available. Leashed pets are permitted.

Reservations, fee: No reservations necessary; no fee. Open late May to early September.

Who to contact: Phone the Okanogan National Forest at (509)997-2131 or write to Twisp Ranger District, Twisp, WA 98856.

Location: From Twisp, drive 11 miles west on County Road 9114, then continue west on Forest Service Road 44 for 13.5 miles to the campground.

Trip note: This campground is set along the North Fork of the Twisp River at a major trailhead that provides access to the backcountry and North Cascades National Park. The trail intersects with the Pacific Crest Trail about nine miles from the camp. A Forest Service map is essential. This area is also open in the winter for cross-country skiing and snowmobiling.

Site **48**
ALTA LAKE STATE PARK
on Alta Lake

Campsites, facilities: There are 164 sites for tents or self-contained motor homes, and 16 additional sites with water and electrical hookups for trailers or motor homes up to 20 feet long. Picnic tables and fireplaces are provided. Flush toilets, piped water, showers, electricity, firewood and sanitary services are available. A store, a cafe and ice are available within one mile. Some facilities are wheelchair accessible. Pets are permitted. Boat launching facilities are nearby.

Reservations, fee: No reservations necessary; $7.50-10.50 fee per night. Open all year.

Who to contact: Phone (509)923-2473 or write to Star Route 40, Pateros, WA 98846.

Location: Take Highway 153 off US 97 just south of Pateros and drive two miles to Alta Lake Road. Turn southwest on Alta Lake Road and drive three miles to the park.

Trip note: This state park is set among the pines along the shore of Alta Lake, where a half-mile long swimming beach and boat launch are available. Nearby recreation options include an 18-hole golf course and a riding stable.

Site **49**
WHISTLIN' PINE RESORT
on Alta Lake

Campsites, facilities: There are 60 tent sites and ten sites for trailers or motor homes up to 30 feet long. Electricity, piped water, sewer hookups and picnic tables are provided. Flush toilets, showers, firewood and ice are available. Sanitary services are available within one mile. Pets and motorbikes are permitted. Boat docks, launching facilities and rentals are nearby.

Reservations, fee: Reservations accepted; $9 fee per night. Open April to October.

Who to contact: Phone (509)923-2548 or write to P.O. Box 284, Pateros, WA 98846.

Location: From Pateros at the junction of US 97 and Highway 153, drive two miles northwest on Highway 153 to Alta Lake Road, turn southwest on Alta Lake Road and drive three miles to the resort.

Trip note: This campground is set along the shore of Alta Lake. See the trip note for Site 48 for listing of lake recreation activities.

Site 50   SUPERSTOP RV PARK AND MARINA
on Columbia River

Campsites, facilities: There are six tent sites and 20 sites for trailers or motor homes of any length. Electricity, piped water and sewer hookups are provided. Flush toilets, bottled gas, sanitary services, a store, a cafe, a laundromat and ice are available. Pets and motorbikes are permitted. Boat docks and launching facilities are nearby.

Reservations, fee: Reservations accepted; $13 fee per night; MasterCard and Visa accepted. Open all year.

Who to contact: Phone (509)923-2200 or write to P.O. Box 147, Pateros, WA 98846.

Location: This park is at the south end of Pateros on US 97.

Trip note: This park and marina is set along the shore of the Columbia River. Nearby recreation options include an 18-hole golf course, hiking trails, a riding stable and tennis courts.

Site 51   BREWSTER MOTEL AND RV PARK
near the Columbia River

Campsites, facilities: There are six drive-through sites for trailers or motor homes of any length. Electricity, piped water and picnic tables are provided. Flush toilets, sanitary services, showers, ice and a swimming pool are available. Sewer hookups are available for an extra fee. Bottled gas, a store, a cafe and a laundromat are available within one mile. Pets and motorbikes are permitted. Boat docks and launching facilities are nearby on the Columbia River.

Reservations, fee: Reservations accepted; $10 fee per night; MasterCard and Visa accepted. Open all year.

Who to contact: Phone (509)689-2625 or write to P.O. Box 632, Brewster, WA 98812.

Location: The park is in Brewster (on US 97) at 806 Bridge Street.

Trip note: This park is near the Columbia River. Nearby recreation options include an 18-hole golf course, a full-service marina and tennis courts.

Site 52   BRIDGEPORT STATE PARK
on Rufus Woods Lake

Campsites, facilities: There are ten sites for tents or self-contained motor homes, and 20 sites with water and electrical hookups for trailers or motor homes up to 45 feet. Piped water, fire grills and picnic tables are provided. Flush toilets, showers, firewood and a sanitary disposal station are available. A store, a cafe and ice are located within one mile. Leashed pets are permitted. Boat docks and launching facilities are nearby on both the upper and lower portions of the reservoir.

Reservations, fee: No reservations necessary; $7.50-10.50 fee per night. Open April to late October.

Who to contact: Phone (509)686-7231 or write to P.O. Box 846, Bridgeport, WA 98813.

Location: Drive 21 miles south of Okanogan on US 97, then head southeast on Highway 17 and drive eight miles until you see the sign to turn into the park.

Trip note: This park is set along the shore of Rufus Woods Lake, a reservoir on the Columbia River above the Chief Joseph Dam. There is beach access and a boat launch. There are also hiking trails, but the parks department warns that there are rattlesnakes in certain areas. Nearby recreation options include an 18-hole golf course.

Site 53   AMERICAN LEGION PARK
on Okanogan River

Campsites, facilities: There are 20 sites for trailers or motor homes of any length. Piped water and picnic tables are provided. Flush toilets and showers are available. A store, a cafe, a laundromat and ice are located within one mile.

Reservations, fee: No reservations necessary; $3 fee per night. Open all year.

Who to contact: Write to Okanogan City Hall, Okanogan, WA 98840.

Location: This park is located at the north end of Okanogan on Highway 215.

Trip note: This city park is set along the shore of the Okanogan River. There is an historical museum in town.

Site 54   EASTSIDE TRAILER PARK AND CAMPGROUND
on Okanogan River

Campsites, facilities: There are 50 tent sites and 68 drive-through sites for trailers or motor homes of any length. Electricity, piped water, sewer hookups and picnic tables are provided. Flush toilets, sanitary services, showers, swimming pool and a playground are available. A store, a cafe, a laundromat and ice are located within one mile. Pets are permitted. Boat launching facilities are nearby.

Reservations, fee: No reservations necessary; $8 fee per night. Open April to late October.

Who to contact: Phone (509)826-1170 or write to P.O. Box 72, Omak, WA 98841.

Location: This campground is located just east of Omak on Highway 155 between the Okanogan River and US 97.

Trip note: This city park is in town, along the shore of the Okanogan River. Nearby recreation options include an 18-hole golf course.

Site 55   CRAWFISH LAKE
on Crawfish Lake
OKANOGAN NATIONAL FOREST

Campsites, facilities: There are 17 sites for tents, trailers or motor homes up to 31 feet long. Picnic tables and fire grills are provided. Vault toilets are available, but there is **no piped water**. Pets are permitted. Boat docks and launching facilities are located on the lake.

Reservations, fee: No reservations necessary; no fee. Open mid-May to mid-September.

Who to contact: Phone the Okanogan National Forest at (509)486-2186 or write to Tonasket Ranger District, Box 466, Tonasket, WA 98855.

Location: From Riverside, drive 17.5 miles east on County Road 9320, then head south on Forest Service Road 30 for 1.5 miles. Next, turn southeast on Forest Service Road 30100 and drive 400 yards to the campground.

Trip note: This campground is set along the shore of Crawfish Lake, where fishing and crawdad hunting are popular. For the latter, just put a small piece of chicken on a hook and wait 'til the little critters get their pinchers on it.

Site 56   LYMAN LAKE
on Lyman Lake
OKANOGAN NATIONAL FOREST

Campsites, facilities: There are four sites for tents, trailers or motor homes up to 31 feet long. Picnic tables and fire grills are provided. Vault toilets are available, but there is **no piped water**. Leashed pets are permitted.

Reservations, fee: No reservations necessary; no fee. Open mid-May to mid-September.

Who to contact: Phone the Okanogan National Forest at (509)486-2186 or write to Tonasket Ranger District, Box 466, Tonasket, WA 98855.

Location: From Tonasket, drive 12.5 miles east on Highway 20, then turn southeast on County Road 9455 and go 13 miles. Turn south on County Road 3785 and drive 2.5 miles to the campground entrance.

Trip note: This campground is set along the shore of little Lyman Lake. Little known and little used, it is an idyllic setting for those wanting guaranteed quiet.

Site **57**
SWAN LAKE
on Swan Lake
COLVILLE NATIONAL FOREST

Campsites, facilities: There are seven tent sites and 18 sites for trailers or motor homes up to 31 feet long. Piped water, fire grills and picnic tables are provided. Firewood is available. Leashed pets are permitted. Boat docks and launching facilities are available.

Reservations, fee: No reservations necessary; $6 fee per night. Open May to late September.

Who to contact: Phone the Colville National Forest at (509)775-3305 or write to Republic Ranger District, Republic, WA 99166.

Location: From Republic, drive seven miles south on Highway 21, then turn southwest on Forest Service Road 53 and go eight miles to the campground.

Trip note: This campground is set along the shore of Swan Lake, elevation 3,600 feet. Swimming, boating, fishing and hiking are some of the possibilities here. It's a good out-of-the-way spot for motor home cruisers seeking a rustic setting.

Site **58**
FERRY LAKE
on Ferry Lake
COLVILLE NATIONAL FOREST

Campsites, facilities: There are nine sites for tents, trailers or motor homes up to 21 feet long. Piped water, fire grills and picnic tables are provided. Pit toilets and firewood are available. Leashed pets are permitted. Boat docks and launching facilities are nearby.

Reservations, fee: No reservations necessary; $5 fee per night. Open mid-May to late September.

Who to contact: Phone the Colville National Forest at (509)775-3305 or write to Republic Ranger District, Republic, WA 99166.

Location: From Republic, drive seven miles south on Highway 21, then turn southwest on Forest Service Road 53 and go six miles. Turn north on Forest Service Road 5330 and drive one mile, then continue north on Forest Service Road 100 for 500 yards to the campground.

Trip note: This is one of three fishing lakes within a four-square mile area. The others are Sites 57 and 59. Most campers are not aware that these three spots are available.

Site **59**
LONG LAKE
on Long Lake
COLVILLE NATIONAL FOREST

Campsites, facilities: There are 12 sites for tents, trailers or motor homes up to 21 feet long. Piped water, fire grills and picnic tables are provided. Vault toilets and firewood are available. Pets are permitted. Boat docks and launching facilities are nearby.

Reservations, fee: No reservations necessary; $5 fee per night. Open late May to early September.

Who to contact: Phone the Colville National Forest at (509)775-3305 or write to Republic Ranger District, Republic, WA 99166.

Location: From Republic, drive seven miles south on Highway 21, then turn southwest on Forest Service Road 53 and go eight miles. Turn south on Forest Service Road 400 and drive 1.5 miles to the campground.

Trip note: This is the third and smallest of the three lakes in this area. No motorboats are allowed on the lake, only fly fishing. Expert fishermen can get a quality angling experience here.

Site **60**

TEN MILE
on Sanpoil River
COLVILLE NATIONAL FOREST

Campsites, facilities: There are 13 sites for tents, trailers or motor homes up to 21 feet long. Piped water and picnic tables are provided. Pit toilets and firewood are available. Leashed pets are permitted.

Reservations, fee: No reservations necessary; no fee. Open mid-May to mid-October.

Who to contact: Phone the Colville National Forest at (509)775-3305 or write to Republic Ranger District, Republic, WA 99166.

Location: From Republic, drive ten miles south on Highway 21 and you'll see the campground entrance.

Trip note: This campground is set along the Sanpoil River. It is about four miles from the lakes at Sites 57, 58 and 59. A good choice is a multi-day trip, visiting each of the lakes.

Site **61**

KETTLE RANGE
at Sherman Pass
COLVILLE NATIONAL FOREST

Campsites, facilities: There are nine sites for tents, trailers or motor homes up to 21 feet long. Piped water, fire grills and picnic tables are provided. Pit toilets and firewood are available. Leashed pets are permitted.

Reservations, fee: No reservations necessary; no fee. Open mid-May to late September.

Who to contact: Phone the Colville National Forest at (509)738-6111 or write to Kettle Falls Ranger District, 255 West 11th Street, Kettle Falls, WA 99141.

Location: From Republic, drive 2.5 miles east on Highway 21, then go east on Highway 20 for 18 miles to the campground.

Trip note: This roadside campground is located at Sherman Pass. Several trails pass through camp that provide access to various peaks and vistas in the area. No other campgrounds are in the immediate vicinity.

Site **62**

CANYON CREEK
near East Portal Historical Site
COLVILLE NATIONAL FOREST

Campsites, facilities: There are 12 sites for tents, trailers or motor homes up to 30 feet long. Well water, fire grills and picnic tables are provided. Vault toilets are available. Leashed pets are permitted.

Reservations, fee: No reservations necessary; no fee. Open mid-April to late October.

Who to contact: Phone the Colville National Forest at (509)738-6111 or write to Kettle Falls Ranger District, 255 West 11th Street, Kettle Falls, WA 99141.

Location: From the town of Kettle Falls, drive 3.5 miles northwest of US 395. Head south on Highway 20 for 11 miles, then go south on Forest Road 2000 for one-third mile to the campground.

Trip note: This roadside campground is located near Bangs Mountain Driving Tour and within hiking distance of East Portal Historical Site.

Site 63   NE LAKE ELLEN
on Lake Ellen
COLVILLE NATIONAL FOREST

Campsites, facilities: There are 11 sites for tents, trailers or motor homes up to 21 feet long in this adult-only campground. Piped water and picnic tables are provided. Pit toilets and firewood are available. Leashed pets are permitted. A boat dock is nearby.

Reservations, fee: No reservations necessary; no fee. Open mid-April to mid-October.

Who to contact: Phone the Colville National Forest at (509)738-6111 or write to Kettle Falls Ranger District, 255 West 11 Street, Kettle Falls, WA 99141.

Location: From the town of Kettle Falls, drive 3.5 miles northwest on US 395, then head south on Highway 20 for four miles. Turn southwest on County Road 2014 and drive 4.5 miles, and continue southwest on Forest Service Road 2014 for 5.5 miles to the campground.

Trip note: Fishing and swimming are both permitted on this good-sized lake, located about three miles west of the Columbia River and the Coulee Dam National Recreation Area.

Site 64   RAINBOW BEACH RESORT
on Twin Lakes Reservoir

Campsites, facilities: There are ten tent sites and 100 drive-through sites for trailers or motor homes of any length. Electricity, piped water, sewer hookups and picnic tables are provided. Flush toilets, bottled gas, sanitary services, a shower, firewood, recreation hall, a store, a cafe, a laundromat, ice and a playground are available. Pets and motorbikes are permitted. Boat docks, launching facilities and rentals are nearby.

Reservations, fee: Reservations required; $8 fee per night; MasterCard and Visa accepted. Open all year.

Who to contact: Phone (509)722-5901 or write to Star Route B, Inchelium, WA 99138.

Location: From Inchelium, drive ten miles west on Bridge Creek-Twin Lakes County Road to the resort.

Trip note: This resort is set along the shore of Twin Lakes Reservoir. Nearby recreation options include hiking trails, marked bike trails, a full-service marina and tennis courts. You get a unique chance at a quality campground set in the Colville Indian Reservation.

Site 65   RIVERVIEW MARKET AND TRAILER COURT
on Okanogan River

Campsites, facilities: There are six sites for trailers or motor homes of any length in this adult-only campground. Electricity, piped water, sewer hookups and picnic tables are provided. A store, a cafe and ice are available. Bottled gas, sanitary services and a laundromat are located within one mile.

Reservations, fee: Reservations accepted; $10 fee per night. Open all year.

Who to contact: Phone (509)486-2491 or write to 305 West 4th Street, Tonasket, WA 98855.

Location: In Tonasket, drive north on US 97 to 4th Street, then turn west and drive to the bridge and you'll see the trailer court.

Trip note: Nearby recreation options include marked bike trails and tennis courts. This trailer court is set along the Okanogan River.

Site 66   SUN COVE RESORT GUEST RANCH
on Wannacut Lake

Campsites, facilities: There are 22 tent sites and 28 drive-through sites for trailers or motor homes of any length. Electricity, piped water, sewer hookups and picnic tables are provided. Flush toilets, sanitary services, a recreation hall, a store, a cafe, a laundromat, ice, a playground and swimming pool are available. Showers are available for an extra fee. Pets and motorbikes are permitted. Boat docks, launching facilities and rentals are available.

Reservations, fee: Reservations accepted; $11 fee per night; MasterCard and Visa accepted. Open late April to November.

Who to contact: Phone (509)476-2223 or write to Route 2, Box 1294, Oroville, WA 98844.

Location: Drive eight miles north of Tonasket on US 97 to Ellisforde. Turn west to Wannacut Lake and follow the signs to the resort.

Trip note: This resort is a nice little spot that doesn't get much traffic. It's set along the shore of Wannacut Lake. Nearby recreation options include hiking trails and a riding stable.

Site 67   SPECTACLE LAKE RESORT
on Spectacle Lake

Campsites, facilities: There are 15 tent sites and 40 drive-through sites for trailers or motor homes of any length. Electricity, piped water, sewer hookups and picnic tables are provided. Flush toilets, bottled gas, sanitary services, showers, a store, a laundromat, ice, a playground and swimming pool are available. Pets and motorbikes are permitted. Boat docks, launching facilities and rentals are also available.

Reservations, fee: Reservations accepted; $9 fee per night. Open mid-April to late November.

Who to contact: Phone (509)223-3433 or write to 10 McCammon, Tonasket, WA 98855.

Location: From Tonasket, drive 12 miles northwest on Loomis Highway and you'll see the resort.

Trip note: This resort is set along the shore of long, narrow Spectacle Lake. Nearby recreation options include swimming, fishing, hunting and horseback riding. A riding stable is nearby.

Site 68   RAINBOW RESORT
on Spectacle Lake

Campsites, facilities: There are 20 tent sites and 40 drive-through sites for trailers or motor homes of any length. Electricity, piped water, sewer hookups and picnic tables are provided. Flush toilets, showers, firewood and ice are available. Pets and motorbikes are permitted. Boat docks, launching facilities and rentals are nearby.

Reservations, fee: Reservations accepted; $10 fee per night. Open April to late October.

Who to contact: Phone (509)223-3700 or write to 761 Loomis Highway, Tonasket, WA 98855.

Location: From Tonasket, drive 14 miles northwest on Loomis Highway and you'll see the resort.

Trip note: This resort is set along the shore of Spectacle Lake. Nearby recreation options include swimming, fishing, hunting and tennis.

Site 69   SPECTACLE FALLS RESORT
on Spectacle Lake

Campsites, facilities: There are ten tent sites and 28 drive-through sites for trailers or motor homes of any length. Electricity, piped water, sewer hookups and picnic tables are provided. Flush toilets, sanitary services, showers and ice are available. Pets and motorbikes are permitted. Boat docks, launching facilities and rentals are nearby.

Reservations, fee: Reservations accepted; $9 fee per night. Open mid-April to late October.

Who to contact: Phone (509)223-4141 or write to 879 Loomis Highway, Tonasket, WA 98855.

Location: From Tonasket, drive 15 miles northwest on Loomis Highway and you'll see the resort.

Trip note: This resort is set along the shore of Spectacle Lake. Nearby recreation options include hiking, swimming, fishing, horseback riding, and tennis. A riding stable is nearby.

Site 70   STAGE STOP AT SULL'S RV
near Chopaka Lake

Campsites, facilities: There are ten tent sites and 20 drive-through sites for trailers or motor homes. Electricity, piped water, sewer hookups and picnic tables are provided. Bottled gas, a store, a cafe, ice and a playground are available. Pets and motorbikes are permitted.

Reservations, fee: Reservations accepted; $8 fee per night. Open all year.

Who to contact: Phone (509)223-3275 or write to P.O. Box 5, Loomis, WA 98826.

Location: From Tonasket, drive 20 miles northwest on Loomis Highway to Loomis. The park is in town on Palmer Road.

Trip note: This campground is in rural Loomis, less than five miles from Chopaka Lake, Palmer Lake and Spectacle Lake. Nearby recreation options include hiking trails, a riding stable, a full-service marina and tennis courts.

Site 71   OSOYOOS STATE PARK
on Osoyoos Lake

Campsites, facilities: There are 80 sites for tents, trailer, or motor homes up to 45 feet long. Picnic tables and fire grills are provided. Flush toilets, piped water, sanitary services, a store, a cafe, showers, firewood and a playground are available. A laundromat and ice are located within one mile. Leashed pets are permitted. Boat launching facilities are nearby.

Reservations, fee: No reservations necessary; $7.50-10.50 fee per night. Open all year.

Who to contact: Phone (509)476-3321 or write to Route 1, P.O. Box 102 A, Oroville, WA 98844.

Location: Drive one mile north of Oroville on US 97 and you'll see the park.

Trip note: Many years ago, this area was the site of the annual Okanogan, which means "rendezvous," of the Washington and British Columbia Indians. They would gather and share supplies of fish and game for the year. The park is set along the shore of Osoyoos Lake, where swimming, fishing and waterskiing are all possibilities. Osoyoos Lake is a winter nesting area for geese. Nearby recreation options include an 18-hole golf course.

Site **72**   **BONAPARTE LAKE RESORT**
                         on Bonaparte Lake

Campsites, facilities: There are ten tent sites and 35 drive-through sites for trailers or motor homes of any length. Electricity, piped water, sewer hookups and picnic tables are provided. Flush toilets, bottled gas, sanitary services, showers, firewood, a recreation hall, a store, a cafe, a laundromat, ice and a playground are available. Leashed pets and motorbikes are permitted. Boat docks, launching facilities and rentals are also available.

Reservations, fee: Reservations accepted; $7-8.50 fee per night; MasterCard and Visa accepted. Open all year.

Who to contact: Phone (509)486-2828 or write to 695 Bonaparte, Tonasket, WA 98855.

Location: From Tonasket, drive 19 miles east on Highway 20 to Bonaparte Road. Turn north and drive six miles to the resort.

Trip note: This resort is set along the southeast shore of Bonaparte Lake, where fishing is popular. Nearby recreation options include hiking and hunting in the nearby Forest Service lands. In the winter, the area is open for snowmobiling and cross-country skiing.

Site **73**   **BONAPARTE LAKE**
                         on Bonaparte Lake
                     OKANOGAN NATIONAL FOREST

Campsites, facilities: There are 29 sites for tents, trailers or motor homes up to 31 feet long. Piped water, fire grills and picnic tables are provided. Vault toilets, a store, a cafe and ice are available. Sanitary services are located within one mile. Leashed pets are permitted. Boat docks, launching facilities and rentals are also available.

Reservations, fee: No reservations necessary; $5 fee per night. Open mid-May to mid-September.

Who to contact: Phone the Okanogan National Forest at (509)486-2186 or write to Tonasket Ranger District, Box 466, Tonasket, WA 98855.

Location: From Tonasket, drive 20 miles east on Highway 20 to Forest Service Road 32. Turn north and drive 5.5 miles to the campground.

Trip note: This campground is set along the southern shore of Bonaparte Lake. See the trip note for Site 72 for lake recreation information. There are several trails nearby that provide access to Mount Bonaparte Lookout and the roadless area west of the lake. See a Forest Service map for details.

Site **74**

LOST LAKE
on Lost Lake
OKANOGAN NATIONAL FOREST

Campsites, facilities: There are 18 sites for tents, trailers or motor homes up to 31 feet long. Piped water and picnic tables are provided. Vault toilets are available and leashed pets are permitted. Boat docks and launching facilities are nearby.

Reservations, fee: No reservations necessary; $5 fee per night. Open mid-May to mid-September.

Who to contact: Phone the Okanogan National Forest at (509)486-2186 or write to Tonasket Ranger District, Box 466, Tonasket, WA 98855.

Location: From Tonasket, drive 20 miles east on Highway 20 to Forest Service Road 32. Turn north and drive 10.5 miles, then turn northwest on Forest Service Road 33 and drive 6.5 miles to the campground.

Trip note: This site is set along the shore of Lost Lake where fishing, swimming, hiking, hunting and horseback riding are some of the possibilities. It is about a mile from the Big Tree Botanical Area. This area is open for snowmobiling and cross-country skiing in the winter.

Site **75**

BEAVER LAKE
on Beaver Lake
OKANOGAN NATIONAL FOREST

Campsites, facilities: There are 13 sites for tents, trailers or motor homes up to 21 feet long. Piped water and picnic tables are provided. Vault toilets are available. Leashed pets are permitted.

Reservations, fee: No reservations necessary; $4 fee per night. Open mid-May to mid-September.

Who to contact: Phone the Okanogan National Forest at (509)486-2186, write to Tonasket Ranger District, Box 466, Tonasket, WA 98855.

Location: From Tonasket, drive 20 miles east on Highway 20 to Forest Service Road 32. Turn north and drive 11 miles, then continue northeast on Forest Service Road 32 for three miles to the campground.

Trip note: This campground is set along the southeastern shore of long, narrow Beaver Lake, one of several lakes in this area. Fishing, swimming, hunting and hiking are all possibilities here. See the trip notes for Sites 73 and 74 for information on the other lakes.

Site **76**

BETH LAKE
on Beth Lake
OKANOGAN NATIONAL FOREST

Campsites, facilities: There are 14 sites for tents, trailers or motor homes up to 31 feet long. Piped water and picnic tables are provided. Vault toilets are available, and pets are permitted. Boat launching facilities are available.

Reservations, fee: No reservations necessary; $5 fee per night. Open mid-May to mid-September.

Who to contact: Phone the Okanogan National Forest at (509)486-2186 or write to Tonasket Ranger District, Box 466, Tonasket, WA 98855.

Location: From Tonasket, drive 20 miles west on Highway 20 to Forest Service Road 32. Turn north and drive 11 miles, then continue northeast on Forest Service Road 32 for three miles. From there, go northwest on County Road 9840 to the campground.

Trip note: This campground is set along little Beth Lake, which is adjacent to Beaver Lake (Site 75).

Site **77**   **TIFFANY'S RESORT**
                          on Curlew Lake

Campsites, facilities: There are ten tent sites and 16 sites for trailers or motor homes of any length. Electricity, piped water, sewer hookups and picnic tables are provided. Flush toilets, showers, firewood, a store, a laundromat, ice and a playground are available. Pets and motorbikes are permitted. Boat docks, launching facilities and rentals are nearby.

Reservations, fee: Reservations accepted; $8 fee per night. Open all year.

Who to contact: Phone (509)775-3152 or write to 1026 Tiffany, Republic, WA 99166.

Location: Drive ten miles north of Republic on Highway 21, then turn north on West Curlew Lake Road and drive five miles to the resort.

Trip note: This resort is set along the western shore of Curlew Lake, where fishing can be good.

Site **78**   **BLACK'S BEACH RESORT**
                          on Curlew Lake

Campsites, facilities: There are 151 drive-through sites for trailers or motor homes of any length. Electricity, piped water, sewer hookups and picnic tables are provided. Flush toilets, bottled gas, sanitary services, showers, firewood, recreation hall, a store, a cafe, a laundromat, ice and a playground are available. Pets and motorbikes are permitted. Boat docks, launching facilities and rentals are located nearby.

Reservations, fee: Reservations accepted; $9.50-11.50 fee per night. Open all year.

Who to contact: Phone (509)775-3989 or write to 848 Blacks Beach, Republic, WA 99166.

Location: Drive north of Republic on West Curlew Lake Drive and you will see the entrance to the resort on the lake.

Trip note: This is another resort set along Curlew Lake. Waterskiing, swimming and fishing are all options here.

Site **79**   **CURLEW LAKE STATE PARK**
                          on Curlew Lake

Campsites, facilities: There are 64 sites for tents and self-contained motor homes, and 18 sites with full hookups for trailers or motor homes up to 30 feet long. Picnic tables are provided. Flush toilets, sanitary services, electricity, piped water, sewer hookups, showers and firewood are available. Some facilities are wheelchair accessible. Pets are permitted. Boat launching facilities are also available.

Reservations, fee: No reservations necessary; $7.50-10.50 fee per night. Open April to late October.

Who to contact: Phone (509)775-3592 or write to 974 Curlew Lake Street, Republic, WA 99166.

Location: Drive ten miles north of Republic on Highway 21 and you'll see the park entrance.

Trip note: This park is set along the eastern shore of Curlew Lake. There is beach access, fishing, swimming, waterskiing and hiking. Nearby recreation options include an 18-hole golf course, and in the winter, snowmobiling.

Site **80**
SPRING CANYON
on Franklin Roosevelt Lake
COULEE DAM NATIONAL RECREATION AREA

Campsites, facilities: There are 87 sites for tents, trailers or self-contained motor homes up to 26 feet long. Piped water, fire grills and picnic tables are provided. Flush toilets, sanitary services, a cafe and a playground are available. Some facilities are wheelchair accessible. Leashed pets are permitted. Boat docks and launching facilities are nearby.

Reservations, fee: No reservations necessary; $6 fee per night. Open all year.

Who to contact: Phone the Coulee Dam National Recreation Area at (509)633-1360 or write to P.O. Box 37, Coulee Dam, WA 99116.

Location: Drive three miles east of Grand Coulee on Highway 174 and you'll see the campground entrance.

Trip note: Fishing for bass, walleye, trout and sunfish are popular at the Franklin Roosevelt Lake. And, if you don't like to fish, try waterskiing. The campground is not far from the Grand Coulee Dam, which has a visitor center. There are also hiking trails in the area.

Site **81**
LAKEVIEW TERRACE MOBILE PARK
near Franklin Roosevelt Lake

Campsites, facilities: There are 20 tent sites and 15 drive-through sites for trailers or motor homes of any length. Electricity, piped water, sewer hookups and picnic tables are provided. Flush toilets, showers, a laundromat and a playground are available. Pets and motorbikes are permitted. Boat docks, launching facilities and rentals are nearby.

Reservations, fee: Reservations accepted; $8 fee per night. Open all year.

Who to contact: Phone (509)633-2169 or write to Highway 174, Grand Coulee, WA 99133.

Location: Drive 3.5 miles east of Grand Coulee on Highway 174 and you'll see the park entrance.

Trip note: This resort is set near Franklin Roosevelt Lake, which is created by the Grand Coulee Dam. See the trip note for Site 80 for water recreation options. A full-service marina and tennis courts are nearby.

Site **82**
CURLEY'S TRAILER PARK
on Grand Coulee Reservoir

Campsites, facilities: There are ten tent sites and 20 drive-through sites for trailers or motor homes of any length. Electricity, piped water, sewer hookups and picnic tables are provided. Flush toilets, bottled gas, a store, a cafe, a laundromat and ice are available within one mile. Pets and motorbikes are permitted. Boat docks, launching facilities and rentals are nearby.

Reservations, fee: Reservations accepted; $8-12.50 fee per night. Open all year.

Who to contact: Phone (509)633-0750 or write to P.O. Box 61, Grand Coulee, WA 99133.

Location: Drive one-half mile northwest of Grand Coulee on Highway 174 and you'll see the park.

Trip note: This park is set along the shore of the Grand Coulee Reservoir, a short distance from the Grand Coulee Dam. Nearby recreation options include an 18-hole golf course and tennis courts.

Site **83**

COULEE PLAYLAND RESORT
near Grand Coulee Dam

Campsites, facilities: There are 70 sites for tents, trailers or motor homes of any
length. Electricity, piped water, sewer hookups and picnic tables are provided.
Flush toilets, sanitary services, a store, a laundromat, showers, firewood, ice
and a playground are available. Bottled gas and a cafe are located within one
mile. Pets and motorbikes are permitted. Boat docks, launching facilities and
rentals are nearby.

Reservations, fee: Reservations accepted; $8-11 fee per night; MasterCard and Visa
accepted. Open all year.

Who to contact: Phone (509)633-2671 or write to P.O. Box 457, Electric City, WA
99123.

Location: Drive two miles south of Grand Coulee on Highway 155 to Electric City.
This spot is in town.

Trip note: Nearby recreation options include hiking trails, marked bike trails, a
full-service marina and tennis courts.

Site **84**

KELLER FERRY
on Franklin Roosevelt Lake
COULEE DAM NATIONAL RECREATION AREA

Campsites, facilities: There are 50 sites for tents, trailers or motor homes up to 16
feet long. Piped water, fire grills and picnic tables are provided. Flush toilets,
sanitary services, ice and a playground are available. A cafe is located within
one mile. Leashed pets are permitted. Boat docks, launching facilities, fuel and
marine dump station are also available nearby.

Reservations, fee: No reservations necessary; $6 fee per night. Open all year.

Who to contact: Phone the Coulee Dam National Recreation Area at (509)633-1360
or write to P.O. Box 37, Coulee Dam, WA 99116.

Location: Drive 14 miles north of Wilbur on Highway 21 and you'll see the
campground.

Trip note: This campground is set along the shore of Franklin Roosevelt Lake, a
large reservoir created by the Grand Coulee Dam, about 15 miles west of camp.
Waterskiing, fishing and swimming are all options here.

Site **85**

WISHING TREE CAMPGROUND
on Methow River

Campsites, facilities: There are ten tent sites and 12 drive-through sites for trailers
or motor homes of any length. Electricity, piped water and sewer hookups are
provided. Flush toilets, sanitary services and showers are available. Bottled
gas, a store, a cafe, a laundromat and ice are located within one mile. Motorbikes
are permitted. Boat launching facilities are nearby.

Reservations, fee: Reservations accepted; $10 fee per night; MasterCard and Visa
accepted. Open April to late November.

Who to contact: Phone (509)997-0833 or write to P.O. Box 117, Carlton, WA 98814.

Location: Take Highway 153 off US 97 just south of Pateros and drive northwest
for 26 miles to Carlton. The campground is located in the town on Highway
153.

Trip note: This nice, little out-of-the-way place for motor homes is set along the
Methow River. A good side trip is to explore westward up Libby Creek, a
tributary to the Methow.

FOGGY DEW
Site **86**
on Foggy Dew Creek
OKANOGAN NATIONAL FOREST

Campsites, facilities: There are 13 sites for tents, trailers or motor homes. Picnic tables and fire grills are provided. Vault toilets and firewood are available, but there is **no piped water.** Pets are permitted.

Reservations, fee: No reservations necessary; no fee. Open late May to early September.

Who to contact: Phone the Okanogan National Forest at (509)997-2131 or write to Twisp Ranger District, Box 466, Twisp, WA 98856.

Location: From Carlton, drive four miles south on Highway 153, then continue south on County Road 1029 for one mile. Next, turn west on Forest Service Road 4340 and drive four miles to the campground.

Trip note: This campground is set at the confluence of Foggy Dew Creek and the North Fork of Gold Creek. There are several trails nearby that provide access to various backcountry lakes and streams. To get to the trailheads, just follow the Forest Service Roads near camp. Bicycles are allowed on Trails 417, 429 and 431. In the winter the area is open for both cross-country skiing and snowmobiling. See a Forest Service map for options.

SPOKANE
♦

SOME HIGHLIGHTS

76 CAMPGROUNDS

Coulee Dam National Recreation Area

Franklin Roosevelt Lake

Colville National Forest

Lake Sullivan

Medical Lake

Pend Oreille River

Little Pend Oreille Habitat Management Area

Sherman Creek Habitat Management Area

Waitts Lake

Spokane Mountain

Banks Mountain

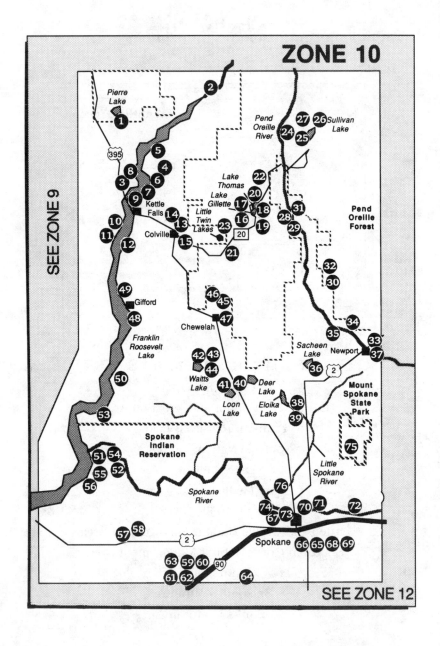

ZONE 10

Pierre Lake

Pend Oreille River

Sullivan Lake

SEE ZONE 9

Kettle Falls

Lake Thomas
Lake Gillette
Little Twin Lakes

Colville

Pend Oreille Forest

Gifford

Franklin Roosevelt Lake

Chewelah

Sacheen Lake

Newport

Mount Spokane State Park

Waitts Lake

Deer Lake

Loon Lake

Eloika Lake

Spokane Indian Reservation

Little Spokane River

Spokane River

Spokane

SEE ZONE 12

Site **1**

PIERRE LAKE
on Pierre Lake
COLVILLE NATIONAL FOREST

Campsites, facilities: There are 15 sites for tents, trailers or motor homes up to 32 feet long. Piped water, fire grills and picnic tables are provided. Pit toilets and firewood are available. A store and ice are located within one mile. Leashed pets are permitted. Boat docks and launching facilities are nearby.

Reservations, fee: No reservations necessary; no fee. Open mid-April to mid-October.

Who to contact: Phone the Colville National Forest at (509)738-6111 or write to Republic Ranger Station, Republic, WA 99166.

Location: From Colville, drive about 31 miles north on US 395 to Orient. From Orient, drive four miles east on County Road 1510, then turn north on County Road 1500 and drive three miles to the campground.

Trip note: This campground is set along the shore of Pierre Lake, a quiet, little-known jewel near the Canadian border. This is only short drive from US 395, yet the campground gets relatively little use.

Site **2**

SHEEP CREEK
on Sheep Creek

Campsites, facilities: There are 11 campsites for tents or small trailers. Picnic tables, fire grills and tent pads are provided. Pit toilets, piped water and a group shelter are available. Leashed pets are permitted.

Reservations, fee: No reservations necessary; no fee. Open all year.

Who to contact: Phone the Department of Natural Resources at (800)527-3305 or write to Department of Natural Resources AW-11, 1065 South Capitol Way, Olympia, WA 98504.

Location: From Northport, drive north on Highway 25 for one mile, then turn left on Sheep Creek Road and go four miles. Turn right into the campground.

Trip note: This campground is set in a forested area along Sheep Creek, about four miles from the Columbia River, and very close to the Canadian border. It's a primitive camp, yet it has piped water.

Site **3**

WHISPERING PINE RV PARK
on Columbia River

Campsites, facilities: There are 15 tent sites and 40 drive-through sites for trailers or motor homes of any length. Electricity, sewer hookups and picnic tables are provided. Flush toilets, sanitary services, a laundromat, a playground, piped water, showers and firewood are available. Pets are permitted.

Reservations, fee: Reservations accepted; $6-11 fee per night. Open April to November.

Who to contact: Phone (509)738-2593 or write to P.O. Box 778, Kettle Falls, WA 99141.

Location: From the town of Kettle Falls, drive 6.5 miles north on US 395, then turn east at the sign for the campground and drive 300 yards to the entrance.

Trip note: This campground is a good layover for US 395 motor home cruisers. It is set along the shore of the Columbia River. Nearby recreation options include marked bike trails, a full-service marina and tennis courts. A good side trip is to Colville National Forest East Portal Interpretive Area, which is less than ten miles away. To reach it, drive south to the junction of Highway 20 and go southwest for about six miles. There's a nature trail and the Bangs Mountain Auto Tour, a five-mile drive that takes you through old-growth forest to Bangs Mountain Vista, which overlooks the Columbia River-Kettle Falls area.

Site 4
WILLIAMS LAKE
on Williams Lake

Campsites, facilities: There are eight campsites for tents or small trailers. Picnic tables, fire grills and tent pads are provided. Pit toilets, piped water and a boat launch are available. Leashed pets are permitted.
Reservations, fee: No reservations necessary; no fee. Open all year.
Who to contact: Phone the Department of Natural Resources at (800)527-3305 or write to Department of Natural Resources AW-11, 1065 South Capitol Way, Olympia, WA 98504.
Location: From Colville, drive west on US 395 for 1.5 miles, then head north on Williams Lake Road for 15 miles. Turn left and then immediately left again.
Trip note: With a plethora of camps set on nearby Franklin Roosevelt Lake, this secluded spot provides a good alternative. It is set along the shore of Williams Lake, where the trout fishing is good. In winter, ice fishing is an option.

Site 5
NORTH GORGE
on Franklin Roosevelt Lake
COULEE DAM NATIONAL RECREATION AREA

Campsites, facilities: There are ten sites for tents, trailers or motor homes. Piped water, fire grills and picnic tables are provided. Pit toilets are available, and pets are permitted. Boat docks and launching facilities are nearby.
Reservations, fee: No reservations necessary; no fee. Open all year.
Who to contact: Phone the Coulee Dam National Recreation Area at (509)633-9441 or write to Kettle Falls Ranger District, Route 1, Box 537, Kettle Falls, WA 99141.
Location: From the town of Kettle Falls, drive about 20 miles north on Highway 25 and you'll see the campground entrance.
Trip note: This is the first of many campgrounds we discovered along the shore of 130-mile long Franklin Roosevelt Lake, which was formed by damming the Columbia River at Coulee. Recreation options include waterskiing and swimming. There is also fishing for walleye, trout, bass and sunfish. During winter, the lake level is drawn down and a unique trip is to walk along the barren lake's edge.

Site 6
EVANS
on Franklin Roosevelt Lake
COULEE DAM NATIONAL RECREATION AREA

Campsites, facilities: There are 46 sites for tents, trailers or motor homes up to 26 feet long. Piped water, fire grills and picnic tables are provided. Flush toilets, a sanitary disposal station, a store and a playground are available. Leashed pets are permitted. Boat docks and launching facilities are nearby. Some facilities are wheelchair accessible.
Reservations, fee: No reservations necessary; $6 fee per night. Open year-round with limited facilities in winter.
Who to contact: Phone the Coulee Dam National Recreation Area at (509)633-9441 or write to Kettle Falls Ranger District, Route 1, Box 537, Kettle Falls, WA 99141.

Location: Drive eight miles north of the town of Kettle Falls on Highway 25 and you'll see the campground entrance.

Trip note: Like Site 5, this campground is set along the shore of Franklin Roosevelt Lake. Fishing, swimming and waterskiing are all options here.

Site 7

MARCUS ISLAND
on Franklin Roosevelt Lake
COULEE DAM NATIONAL RECREATION AREA

Campsites, facilities: There are 20 sites for tents, trailers or motor homes up to 20 feet long. Piped water, fire grills and picnic tables are provided. Pit toilets are available. A store is located within one mile. Leashed pets are permitted. A boat dock is nearby.

Reservations, fee: No reservations necessary; no fee. Open all year.

Who to contact: Phone the Coulee Dam National Recreation Area at (509)633-9441 or write to Kettle Falls Ranger District, Route 1, Box 537, Kettle Falls, WA 99141.

Location: Drive four miles north of the town of Kettle Falls and you'll see the campground entrance.

Trip note: This campground is set just south of Site 6 and is quite similar to that camp, including being nestled along the lake's edge. Waterskiing, fishing and swimming are the primary recreation options.

Site 8

KAMLOOPS
on Franklin Roosevelt Lake
COULEE DAM NATIONAL RECREATION AREA

Campsites, facilities: There are 14 tent sites. Picnic tables and fire grills are provided. Pit toilets are available, but there is **no piped water.** Leashed pets are permitted. Boat docks are nearby.

Reservations, fee: No reservations necessary; no fee. Open all year.

Who to contact: Phone the Coulee Dam National Recreation Area at (509)633-9441 or write to Kettle Falls Ranger District, Route 1, Box 537, Kettle Falls, WA 99141.

Location: From the town of Kettle Falls, drive seven miles west and north on US 395 to the campground.

Trip note: This is one of the few primitive campsites of the many located along Franklin Roosevelt Lake. It is set at Kamloops Island, an optimum area for waterskiing and fishing. See the trip note for Site 3 for side trip information.

Site 9

KETTLE FALLS
on Franklin Roosevelt Lake
COULEE DAM NATIONAL RECREATION AREA

Campsites, facilities: There are 77 sites for tents, trailers or motor homes up to 26 feet long. Piped water, fire grills and picnic tables are provided. Flush toilets, a sanitary disposal station, firewood, a cafe and a playground are available. A store is available within one mile. Some facilities are wheelchair accessible. Leashed pets are permitted. Boat docks, fuel and launching facilities are nearby.

Reservations, fee: No reservations necessary; $6 fee per night. Open year-round with limited facilities in winter.

Who to contact: Phone the Coulee Dam National Recreation Area at (509)738-6266 or write to Kettle Falls Ranger District, Route 1, Box 537, Kettle Falls, WA 99141.

Location: Drive two miles west of the town of Kettle Falls and you'll see the campground entrance.

Trip note: This is a modern, developed campground that attracts fairly heavy use in summer months. It is set along the shore of Franklin Roosevelt Lake, where waterskiing, swimming and fishing are all options. In the summer there is a lifeguard on duty, and the rangers offer campfire programs in the evenings. The park headquarters is nearby.

Site 10   SHERMAN CREEK
on Franklin Roosevelt Lake, boat-in only
COULEE DAM NATIONAL RECREATION AREA

Campsites, facilities: There are six tent sites at this campground, accessible only by boat. Piped water, picnic tables, and fire grills are provided. Pit toilets and boat docks are available.

Reservations, fee: No reservations necessary; no fee. Open all year with limited winter facilities.

Who to contact: Phone the Coulee Dam National Recreation Area at (509)633-9441 or write to Kettle Falls Ranger District, Route 1, Box 537, Kettle Falls, WA 99141.

Location: This campground is located opposite the town of Kettle Falls on the other side of Franklin Roosevelt Lake.

Trip note: This is one of the few campgrounds east of the Cascade Range that is accessible only by boat. It is located in an idyllic setting where Sherman Creek enters Franklin Roosevelt Lake (Columbia River). It is within the boundaries of the Sherman Creek Habitat Management Area, an 8,000-acre area that provides critical winter deer habitat and a year-round habitat for many little critters.

Site 11   HAAG COVE
on Franklin Roosevelt Lake
COULEE DAM NATIONAL RECREATION AREA

Campsites, facilities: There are 18 sites for tents, trailers or motor homes up to 26 feet long. Piped water, fire grills and picnic tables are provided. Pit toilets and boat docks are available. Pets are permitted.

Reservations, fee: No reservations necessary; no fee. Open all year.

Who to contact: Phone the Coulee Dam National Recreation Area at (509)633-9441 or write to Kettle Falls Ranger District, Route 1, Box 537, Kettle Falls, WA 99141.

Location: From Republic, drive 25 miles east on Highway 30, then turn south on County Road 3 and drive five miles to the campground.

Trip note: This campground is tucked away in a cove along the shore of Franklin Roosevelt Lake (Columbia River). A good side trip is to the Sherman Creek Habitat Management Area, located just north of camp. It is rugged and steep, but a good place to see and photograph wildlife.

Site 12   BRADBURY BEACH
on Franklin Roosevelt Lake
COULEE DAM NATIONAL RECREATION AREA

Campsites, facilities: There are five tent sites. Picnic tables and fire grills are provided. Pit toilets and piped water are available. Pets are permitted. Boat docks and launching facilities are nearby.

Reservations, fee: No reservations necessary; no fee. Open all year with limited winter facilities.

Who to contact: Phone the Coulee Dam National Recreation Area at (509)633-9441 or write to Kettle Falls Ranger District, Route 1, Box 537, Kettle Falls, WA 99141.

Location: From the town of Kettle Falls, drive ten miles south on Highway 25 to the campground.

Trip note: Quiet, small and pretty, the availability of piped water makes this spot a winner. It is one of the smallest camps set along Franklin Roosevelt Lake. See the trip note for Site 5 for recreation possibilities.

Site 13   ROADHOUSE LODGE INCORPORATED
near Colville National Forest

Campsites, facilities: There are 14 sites for tents, trailers or motor homes. Electricity, piped water, sewer hookups and picnic tables are provided. Flush toilets, sanitary services, showers, bathhouse, firewood and a cafe are available. Bottled gas, a store, a laundromat and ice are located within one mile. Some facilities are wheelchair accessible. Pets and motorbikes are permitted.

Reservations, fee: Reservations accepted; $7-9 fee per night; MasterCard and Visa accepted. Open all year, but call ahead in winter.

Who to contact: Phone (509)684-3021 or write to Route 3, Box 16, Colville, WA 99114.

Location: This park is located in Colville, 64 miles north of Spokane, on US 395.

Trip note: This a good layover for motor home cruisers who want to stay in Colville. Nearby recreation options include an 18-hole golf course, hiking trails and tennis courts. The main headquarters for Colville National Forest is in town at 795 South Main Street. You can purchase a Forest Service map there for $2, which details nearby backcountry roads and hiking trails.

Site 14   DOUGLAS FALLS
on Mill Creek

Campsites, facilities: There are ten campsites for tents or small trailers. Picnic tables, fire grills and tent pads are provided. Pit toilets and piped water are available. A baseball field is nearby. Leashed pets are permitted.

Reservations, fee: No reservations necessary; no fee. Open all year.

Who to contact: Phone the Department of Natural Resources at (800)527-3305 or write to Department of Natural Resources AW-11, 1065 South Capitol Way, Olympia, WA 98504.

Location: Drive to the eastern edge Colville on Highway 20. Take Aladdin Road north off Highway 20 and drive two miles, then continue straight for five miles. You'll see the parking area on the left.

Trip note: This campground is set in a wooded area along Mill Creek near Douglas Falls, just outside of town. It is one of the only campgrounds in the Pacific Northwest that has a baseball field.

Site 15   ROCKY LAKE
on Rocky Lake

Campsites, facilities: There are seven campsites for tents or small trailers. Picnic tables, fire grills and tent pads are provided. Pit toilets, piped water and a boat launch are available. Leashed pets are permitted.

Reservations, fee: No reservations necessary; no fee. Open all year.

Who to contact: Phone the Department of Natural Resources at (800)527-3305 or write to Department of Natural Resources AW-11, 1065 South Capitol Way, Olympia, WA 98504.

Location: Take Highway 20 off US 395 in Colville and drive six miles east, then turn right on Rocky Lake Road and go three miles and turn right again onto a one-lane gravel road. Go about 100 yards and stay left, then continue another 300 yards to the campground.

Trip note: This is not exactly paradise, but it has remarkable recreational diversity nearby. Rocky Lake is a shallow, weedy pond lined with a lot of rocks. That is where the campground is set. But if you backtrack a bit on Rocky Lake Road you'll see the entrance signs for the nearby Little Pend Oreille Habitat Management Area. This is a premium area for hiking, fishing, hunting, and photographing wildlife.

Site **16**   **CARNEY'S BLACK LAKE RESORT**
Black Lake

Campsites, facilities: There are 12 tent sites and six sites for trailers or motor homes of any length. Piped water and picnic tables are provided. Flush toilets, sanitary services, ice, electricity, showers and firewood are available. Pets are permitted. Boat docks, launching facilities and rentals are located nearby.

Reservations, fee: Reservations accepted; $7 fee per night. Open April to late October. Closed in 1991.

Who to contact: Phone (509)684-2093 or write to 1971 Black Lake Road, Colville, WA 99114.

Location: From Colville, drive 18 miles east on Highway 20, then turn north on Black Lake Road and drive two miles to the resort.

Trip note: This resort is set along the shore of Black Lake, a narrow, one-mile-long natural lake. The area is very private, with good fishing in May and June for brook trout. If you dislike roughing it, a cabin that sleeps six is available for rental, and includes boat dock facilities. An excellent side trip is seven miles northeast to a chain of lakes, all with good fishing. See the trip note for Site 15 for information on the nearby Little Pend Oreille Habitat Management Area.

Site **17**   **BEAVER LODGE RESORT**
on Lake Thomas

Campsites, facilities: There are 30 tent sites and 25 drive-through sites for trailers or motor homes of any length. Electricity, piped water, sewer hookups and picnic tables are provided. Flush toilets, bottled gas, showers, firewood, a recreation hall, a store, a cafe, ice and a playground are available. Sanitary services are located within one mile. Pets and motorbikes are permitted. Boat docks, launching facilities and rentals are nearby.

Reservations, fee: Reservations accepted; $6.50-10.00 fee per night; MasterCard and Visa accepted. Open all year.

Who to contact: Phone (509)684-5657 or write to 2430 Highway 20 East, Colville, WA 99114.

Location: From Colville, drive 25 miles east on Highway 20 to the lodge.

Trip note: This developed camp is set along the shore of Lake Thomas, one in a chain of seven lakes. At the southern end of the chain, Little Pend Oreille information is available. At the northern end of the lake chain, at Lake Leo, there is a nordic ski trail during winter. Nearby recreation options include hiking trails and marked bike trails.

Site 18 LAKE THOMAS
on Lake Thomas
COLVILLE NATIONAL FOREST

Campsites, facilities: There are 15 tent sites. Piped water, fire grills and picnic tables are provided. Pit toilets and firewood are available. Sanitary services are located within one mile. Leashed pets are permitted. Boat docks, launching facilities and rentals are nearby.

Reservations, fee: No reservations necessary; $5 fee per night. Open mid-May to mid-September.

Who to contact: Phone the Colville National Forest at (509)684-4557 or write to Colville Ranger District, 755 South Main, Colville, WA 99114.

Location: Drive four miles south of Ione on Highway 31, then turn southwest on Highway 20 and drive 11 miles. Go east on County Road 200 for one mile to the campground.

Trip note: This campground is set along the shore of Lake Thomas. See the trip note for Site 17 for recreation information.

Site 19 EAST GILLETTE
on Lake Gillette
COLVILLE NATIONAL FOREST

Campsites, facilities: There are 39 single family and five multiple family sites for tents, trailers or motor homes up to 31 feet long. Piped water, fire grills and picnic tables are provided. Pit toilets, sanitary services and firewood are available. A store and ice are located within one mile. Some facilities are wheelchair accessible. Leashed pets are permitted. Boat docks, launching facilities and rentals are nearby.

Reservations, fee: No reservations necessary; $10 fee per night. Open mid-May to mid-September.

Who to contact: Phone the Colville National Forest at (509)684-4557 or write to Colville Ranger District, 795 South Main, Colville, WA 99114.

Location: Drive four miles south of Ione on Highway 31, then turn southwest on Highway 20 and drive 11 miles. Go east on County Road 200 for one-half mile to the campground.

Trip note: This campground is set along the shore of Lake Gillette, just south of Sites 17 and 18 and part of the chain of lakes. See the trip note for Site 17 for recreation information.

Site 20 LAKE LEO
on Lake Leo
COLVILLE NATIONAL FOREST

Campsites, facilities: There are eight sites for tents, trailers or motor homes up to 15 feet long. Piped water and picnic tables are provided. Pit toilets and firewood are available. Leashed pets are permitted. Boat docks, launching facilities and rentals are nearby.

Reservations, fee: No reservations necessary; $5 fee per night. Open mid-May to mid-September.

Who to contact: Phone the Colville National Forest at (509)684-4557 or write to Colville Ranger District, 795 South Main, Colville, WA 99114.

Location: Drive four miles south of Ione on Highway 31, then turn southwest on Highway 20 and drive seven miles to the campground.

Trip note: Lake Leo is the northernmost camp on the chain of lakes. This is the quietest of the camps in the immediate vicinity. Frater and Nile Lakes, both quite small, are set a mile north. In winter, there is a nordic ski trail that starts adjacent to the camp.

Site 21   FLODELLE CREEK
on Flodelle Creek

Campsites, facilities: There are eight campsites for tents or small trailers. Picnic tables, fire grills and tent pads are provided. Pit toilets and piped water are available. Motorbikes are permitted. Leashed pets are permitted.

Reservations, fee: No reservations necessary; no fee. Open all year.

Who to contact: Phone the Department of Natural Resources at (800)527-3305 or write to Department of Natural Resources AW-11, 1065 South Capitol Way, Olympia, WA 98504.

Location: Take Highway 20 out of Colville and drive east for 20 miles. Turn right on a two-lane gravel road and go 300 yards, then go left and drive 100 yards to the campground entrance.

Trip note: This little-known campground is set along the shore of Flodelle Creek, where hiking, hunting and fishing are quite good. It is advisable to obtain a detailed map of the area from the Department of Natural Resources.

Site 22   IONE TRAILER PARK AND MOTEL
on Pend Oreille River

Campsites, facilities: There are three tent sites and 19 sites for trailers or motor homes of any length. Electricity, piped water, sewer hookups and picnic tables are provided. Flush toilets, bottled gas, sanitary services, showers, a laundromat and a playground are available. A store, a cafe and ice are located within one mile. Motorbikes are permitted. Boat docks and launching facilities are nearby.

Reservations, fee: Reservations accepted; $9 fee per night. Open all year.

Who to contact: Phone (509)442-3213 or write to P.O. Box 517, Ione, WA 99139.

Location: This park is in Ione on Highway 31.

Trip note: This is a good layover for campers with motor homes or trailers who want to stay in town. The park is set along the shore of the Pend Oreille River. Nearby recreation options include marked bike trails.

Site 23   LITTLE TWIN LAKES
on Little Twin Lakes
COLVILLE NATIONAL FOREST

Campsites, facilities: There are 20 sites for tents, trailers or motor homes up to 16 feet long. Piped water, fire grills and picnic tables are provided. Pit toilets and firewood are available. Pets are permitted. Boat docks, launching facilities and rentals are located nearby.

Reservations, fee: No reservations necessary; no fee. Open mid-May to mid-September.

Who to contact: Phone the Colville National Forest at (509)684-4557 or write to Colville Ranger District, 795 South Main, Colville, WA 99114.

Location: Drive 12.5 miles east of Colville on Highway 20, then turn northeast on County Road 4915 and drive 1.5 miles. Turn north on Forest Service Road 4939 and drive 4.5 miles to the campground.

Trip note: This campground is set along the shore of Little Twin Lakes. See the trip note for Site 15 for side trip information.

Site **24**

EDGEWATER
on Pend Oreille River
COLVILLE NATIONAL FOREST

Campsites, facilities: There are 23 sites for tents, trailers or motor homes up to 21 feet long. Piped water, fire grills and picnic tables are provided. Pit toilets are available and leash pets are permitted. Boat docks are nearby.

Reservations, fee: No reservations necessary; no fee. Open late May to early September.

Who to contact: Phone the Colville National Forest at (509)446-2681 or write to Sullivan Lake Ranger District, Metaline Falls, WA 99153.

Location: Drive one mile south of Ione on Highway 31, then turn east on County Road 9345 for 300 yards. Turn north on County Road 3669 and go two miles, then turn west to the campground.

Trip note: This campground is set along the shore of the Pend Oreille River, about two miles downstream from the Box Canyon Dam. The camp is not far out of Ione, yet has a rustic feel to it.

Site **25**

NOISY CREEK
on Sullivan Lake
COLVILLE NATIONAL FOREST

Campsites, facilities: There are 19 tent sites and eight sites for trailers or motor homes up to 32 feet long. Piped water, fire grills and picnic tables are provided. Pit toilets are available. Leashed pets are permitted. Boat launching facilities are nearby.

Reservations, fee: No reservations necessary; $6-8 fee per night. Open late May to early September.

Who to contact: Phone the Colville National Forest at (509)446-2681 or write to Sullivan Land Ranger District, Metaline Falls, WA 99153.

Location: Drive one mile south of Ione on Highway 31, then turn and drive northeast on County Road 9345 for nine miles to the campground.

Trip note: This campground is situated in an idyllic setting, adjacent to where Noisy Creek pours into Sullivan Lake. Sullivan Lake is about 3.5 miles long and waterskiing is allowed. There is a trail from camp that heads east along Noisy Creek and then north up to Hall Mountain (elevation 6,323 feet), which is bighorn sheep country.

Site **26**

SULLIVAN LAKE
on Sullivan Lake
COLVILLE NATIONAL FOREST

Campsites, facilities: There are 35 sites for tents, trailers or motor homes up to 32 feet long. Piped water, fire grills and picnic tables are provided. Pit toilets are available. Sanitary services are located within one mile. Pets are permitted. Boat docks and launching facilities are nearby.

Reservations, fee: No reservations necessary; $6 fee per night. Open late May to early September.

Who to contact: Phone the Colville National Forest at (509)446-2681 or write to Sullivan Lake Ranger District, Metaline Falls, WA 99153.

Location: Drive 1.5 miles east of Metaline Falls on Highway 31, then go east for five miles on County Road 9345 to the campground.

Trip note: This campground is set along the north shore of Sullivan Lake. There are trails and roads leading to backcountry areas to the northeast, all of which is detailed on a Forest Service map.

Site **27**
MILL POND
near Sullivan Lake
COLVILLE NATIONAL FOREST

Campsites, facilities: There are ten sites for tents, trailers or motor homes up to 21 feet long. Piped water, fire grills and picnic tables are provided. Pit toilets are available. Sanitary services are located within one mile. Pets are permitted. Boat docks and launching facilities are nearby.

Reservations, fee: No reservations necessary; $5 fee per night. Open late May to early September.

Who to contact: Phone the Colville National Forest at (509)446-2681 or write to Sullivan Lake Ranger District, Metaline Falls, WA 99153.

Location: Drive 1.5 miles northeast of Metaline Falls on Highway 31, then go east for 3.5 miles on County Road 9345 to the campground.

Trip note: This campground is set along the shore of a small lake just north of Lake Sullivan. This is a good base camp for backpackers. A trail starts here and takes off into the backcountry.

Site **28**
BLUESIDE RESORT
on Pend Oreille River

Campsites, facilities: There are 20 tent sites and 34 drive-through sites for trailers or motor homes of any length. Electricity, piped water, sewer hookups and picnic tables are provided. Flush toilets, sanitary services, showers, a recreation hall, a store, a laundromat, ice, firewood, a playground and a swimming pool are available. Pets and motorbikes are permitted. Boat docks, launching facilities and rentals are nearby.

Reservations, fee: Reservations accepted; $8 fee per night. Open all year with limited winter facilities.

Who to contact: Phone (509)445-1327 or write to Route 2, P.O. Box 260, Usk, WA 99180.

Location: Drive ten miles south of Tiger on Highway 20. The resort is near mileage marker 400.

Trip note: This resort is set along the shore of the Pend Oreille River. Nearby recreation options include marked bike trails. The only other campground in the vicinity is Site 29.

Site **29**
THE OUTPOST RESORT
on Pend Oreille River

Campsites, facilities: There are 30 tent sites and 20 drive-through sites for trailers or motor homes of any length. Picnic tables are provided. Flush toilets, sanitary services, firewood, a store, a cafe, ice, a playground, electricity, piped water, sewer hookups and showers are available. Pets and motorbikes are permitted. Boat docks and launching facilities are nearby.

Reservations, fee: Reservations accepted; $8-12 fee per night. Open all year with limited winter facilities.

Who to contact: Phone (509)445-1317 or write to State Route 2, Box 145, Cusick, WA 99119.

Location: Drive 33 miles northwest of Newport on Highway 20. The resort is between mileage markers 305 and 306.

Trip note: This campground is set along the shore of the Pend Oreille River. If you are cruising Highway 20, Site 28 is located about five miles north, otherwise the nearest alternative is Site 35, about a half-hour's drive to the south.

Site **30**
SOUTH SKOOKUM LAKE
on South Skookum Lake
COLVILLE NATIONAL FOREST

Campsites, facilities: There are 15 sites for tents, trailers or motor homes up to 21 feet long. Piped water, fire grills and picnic tables are provided. Pit toilets and firewood are available. Leashed pets are permitted. Boat docks and launching facilities are nearby.

Reservations, fee: No reservations necessary; $6 fee per night. Open late May to early September.

Who to contact: Phone the Colville National Forest at (509)447-3129 or write to Newport Ranger District, Box 770, Newport, WA 99156.

Location: Drive 16 miles northwest of Newport on Highway 20 to the town of Usk. Take Forest Service Road 3389 northeast and drive 7.5 miles to the campground.

Trip note: This campground is set along the shore of South Skookum Lake, at the foot of Kings Mountain (4,383 feet elevation). Waterskiing is allowed. It is one of several lakes in the immediate area. You pass Kings Lake on Road 3389 about a mile before you get to the camp.

Site **31**
PANHANDLE CAMPGROUND
on Pend Oreille River
COLVILLE NATIONAL FOREST

Campsites, facilities: There are 11 sites for trailers or motor homes up to 30 feet long. Piped water, fire grills and picnic tables are provided. Vault toilets are available. Leashed pets are permitted.

Reservations, fee: No reservations necessary; no fee. Open mid-May to mid-September.

Who to contact: Phone the Colville National Forest at (509)447-3129 or write to Newport Ranger District, Box 770, Newport, WA 99156.

Location: Drive 16 miles northwest of Newport on Highway 20 to the town of Usk. Cross the Pend Oreille River and drive 16.2 miles north on County Road 9325.

Trip note: Here is a scenic setting along the shore of the Pend Oreille River. It is a good base camp for a fishing or waterskiing trip. The campground is located directly across the river from Site 29.

Site **32**
BROWNS LAKE
on Browns Lake
COLVILLE NATIONAL FOREST

Campsites, facilities: There are 17 sites for tents, trailers or motor homes up to 21 feet long. Piped water, fire grills and picnic tables are provided. Pit toilets and firewood are available. Pets are permitted. Boat docks and launching facilities are nearby.

Reservations, fee: No reservations necessary; $6 fee per night. Open late May to early September.

Who to contact: Phone the Colville National Forest at (509)447-3129 or write to Newport Ranger District, Box 770, Newport, WA 99156.

Location: Drive 16 miles northwest of Newport on Highway 20 to the town of Usk.

Take Forest Service Road 50 and go northeast for 6.5 miles, then turn north on Forest Service Road 5030 and go three miles to the campground.

Trip note: This campground is set along the shore of Browns Lake about five miles from Site 30. In addition to those two, the only other campground in the area on the east side of the Pend Oreille River is Site 34.

Site 33   PIONEER PARK
on Box Canyon Reservoir
COLVILLE NATIONAL FOREST

Campsites, facilities: There are 12 tent sites and 13 sites for trailers or motor homes up to 21 feet long. Piped water, fire grills and picnic tables are provided. Pit toilets and firewood are available. Some facilities are wheelchair accessible. Pets are permitted. Boat docks, launching facilities and rentals are nearby.

Reservations, fee: No reservations necessary; $6 fee per night. Open late May to early September.

Who to contact: Phone the Colville National Forest at (509)447-3129 or write to Newport Ranger District, Box 770, Newport, WA 99156.

Location: Drive one-half mile northeast of Newport on US 2, then go north on County Road 9305 for two miles to the campground.

Trip note: This campground is set along the shore of Box Canyon Reservoir on the Pend Oreille River near Newport. Waterskiing is allowed. This is a good motor home and tent park located just inside the Washington state border. Because it is set on the east side of the river, it is more secluded than Site 37.

Site 34   SKOOKUM CREEK
near Pend Oreille River

Campsites, facilities: There are ten campsites for tents or small trailers. Picnic tables, fire grills and tent pads are provided. Pit toilets and piped water are available. Leashed pets are permitted.

Reservations, fee: No reservations necessary; no fee. Open all year.

Who to contact: Phone the Department of Natural Resources at (800)527-3305 or write to Department of Natural Resources AW-11, 1065 South Capitol Way, Olympia, WA 98504.

Location: Drive 16 miles northwest of Newport on Highway 20 to the town of Usk. Go east across the bridge and turn right on LeClerc Road. Drive 2.5 miles then turn left and drive about 400 yards to the campground.

Trip note: This campground is in a wooded area along Skookum Creek, about a mile and a half from where it empties into the Pend Oreille River. It's a good canoeing spot, has piped water and gets little attention. You can't beat the price of admission.

Site 35   DALKENA'S HIDE-A-WAY RESORT
on Pend Oreille River

Campsites, facilities: There are ten tent sites and 30 sites for trailers or motor homes up to 30 feet long. Picnic tables are provided. Flush toilets, sanitary services, showers, a store, a cafe, ice, electricity, piped water and sewer hookups are available. Pets and motorbikes are permitted. Boat docks and launching facilities are nearby.

Reservations, fee: Reservations accepted; $5-7.50 fee per night. Open all year.

Who to contact: Phone (509)447-4174 or write to Route 1, Box 610, Newport, WA 99156.

Location: Drive 11 miles north of Newport on Highway 20 and you'll see the resort entrance.

Trip note: This resort is set along the shore of the Pend Oreille River near Dalkena. It's a good layover for motor home cruisers on Highway 20. The nearest option is 16 miles in Newport at Site 37.

Site 36
CIRCLE MOON
on Sacheen Lake

Campsites, facilities: There are 50 tent sites and 34 sites for trailers or motor homes of any length. Electricity, piped water, sewer hookups and picnic tables are provided. Flush toilets, sanitary services, showers, firewood, a cafe and a playground are available. Pets and motorbikes are permitted. Boat docks and launching facilities are nearby.

Reservations, fee: Reservations accepted; $8 fee per night. Open May to November.

Who to contact: Phone (509)447-3735 or write to Route 3, Box 1038, Newport, WA 99156.

Location: Drive 12 miles southwest of Newport to the junction of US 2 with US 195 and Highway 211. Head northwest on Highway 211 for four miles to the campground.

Trip note: This campground is set along the shore of Sacheen Lake. It's a nice spot just a short drive off Highway 211, yet it is missed by almost all of the out-of-staters.

Site 37
R & R CAMPGROUND AND MOTORHOME PARK
near Pend Oreille River

Campsites, facilities: There are 25 tent sites and 50 sites for trailers or motor homes of any length. Electricity, piped water, sewer hookups and picnic tables are provided. Flush toilets, sanitary services and showers are available. Bottled gas, a store, a cafe, a laundromat and ice are available. Boat docks, launching facilities, cable TV, and propane gas are available. Pets and motorbikes are permitted.

Reservations, fee: Reservations accepted; $6.50-10 fee per night. Open mid-May to mid-October.

Who to contact: Phone (509)447-3663 or write to 701 North Newport Avenue, Newport, WA 99156.

Location: The campground is in Newport at the east edge of town, two blocks from US 2.

Trip note: This campground is near the Pend Oreille River, right in Newport. It is a major junction for this part of the country, where US 2 and Highway 20 intersect. If you want a more secluded spot, Site 33 is about a 15-minute drive away, on the east side of the river.

Site 38
WATERS EDGE CAMPGROUND
on Eloika Lake

Campsites, facilities: There are 15 tent sites and 30 drive-through sites for trailers or motor homes of any length. Electricity, piped water, sewer hookups and picnic tables are provided. Flush toilets, sanitary services, firewood, showers, a laundromat and ice are available. Bottled gas, a store and a cafe are available within one mile. Pets and motorbikes are permitted. Boat docks, launching facilities and rentals are nearby.

Reservations, fee: Reservations accepted; $9 fee per night. Open April to late

September.

Who to contact: Phone (509)292-2111 or write to Eloika Lake, Elk, WA 99009.

Location: Drive 28 miles north of Spokane on US 2, then go west on Bridges Road for one mile and you'll see the campground.

Trip note: This campground is set along the shore of Eloika Lake, considered one of the better lakes for fishing in the region. Trout fishing can be excellent as soon as the ice is off the lake in spring. During the hot days of summer, crappie fishing turns on.

Site **39**   **JERRY'S LANDING**
on Eloika Lake

Campsites, facilities: There are five tent sites and 20 drive-through sites for trailers or motor homes of any length. Picnic tables are provided. Flush toilets, sanitary services, a store, a cafe, ice, electricity, piped water, sewer hookups, showers and firewood are available. Bottled gas is available within one mile. Pets and motorbikes are permitted. Boat docks, launching facilities and rentals are nearby.

Reservations, fee: Reservations accepted; $9.50-10.50 fee per night. Open April to November.

Who to contact: Phone (509)292-2337 or write to North 41114 Lakeshore Drive, Elk, WA 99009.

Location: Drive 23 miles north of Spokane on US 2, then head west on Oregon Road for one mile to the campground.

Trip note: This campground is also set along the shore of Eloika Lake. See the trip note for Site 38 for details.

Site **40**   **GRANITE POINT ROCK**
on Loon Lake

Campsites, facilities: There are 68 sites for trailers or motor homes of any length. Electricity, piped water, sewer hookups and picnic tables are provided. Flush toilets, showers, a recreation hall, a store, a cafe, a laundromat, ice and a playground are available. Bottled gas is located within one mile. Pets are not permitted. Boat docks, launching facilities and rentals are nearby.

Reservations, fee: Reservations accepted; $12 fee per night. Open mid-April to mid-September.

Who to contact: Phone (509)233-2100 or write to Route 1, Box 254, Loon Lake, WA 99148.

Location: Drive 26 miles north of Spokane on US 395.

Trip note: This campground is set along the shore of Loon Lake, a clear, clean, spring-fed lake. In the spring, the Mackinaw trout range from four to 30 pounds and can be taken by deep water trolling, downriggers suggested. Easier to catch are Kokanee salmon and rainbow trout in the 12- to 14-inch class. A sprinkling of perch, sunfish and bass come out of their doldrums when the weather heats up.

Site **41**   **SHORE ACRES**
on Loon Lake

Campsites, facilities: There are 14 tent sites and 21 drive-through sites for trailers or motor homes up to 30 feet long. Electricity, piped water, sewer hookups and picnic tables are provided. Flush toilets, sanitary services, a store, a cafe, showers, firewood, ice and a playground are available. Pets and motorbikes are permitted. Boat docks, launching facilities and rentals are nearby.

Reservations, fee: Reservations accepted; $10-12 fee per night. Open mid-April to late October.

Who to contact: Phone (509)233-2474 or write to Route 1, Box 166, Loon Lake, WA 99148.

Location: Drive 30 miles north of Spokane on US 395, then go west on Highway 292 to the northwest edge of Loon Lake.

Trip note: Set along the shore of Loon Lake, this campground offers a long expanse of beach and is an option to Site 40. See the trip note for Site 40 for details about the fishing.

Site **42**   **WINONA BEACH RESORT AND RV PARK**
on Waitts Lake

Campsites, facilities: There are ten tent sites and 36 drive-through sites for trailers or motor homes of any length. Electricity, piped water, sewer hookups and picnic tables are provided. Flush toilets, sanitary services, firewood, a recreation hall, a store, a cafe and ice are available. Bottled gas is located within one mile. Pets and motorbikes are permitted. Boat docks, launching facilities and rentals are nearby.

Reservations, fee: Reservations accepted; $10-13 fee per night. Open mid-April to late October.

Who to contact: Phone (509)937-2231 or write to Route 1, Box 38, Valley, WA 99181.

Location: Drive 42 miles north of Spokane on US 395, then turn west on Waitts Lake Road and drive five miles to the resort.

Trip note: This resort is set along the shore of Waitts Lake. In the spring, the fishing for brown trout and rainbow trout can be quite good. In summer, the trout head to deeper water, and bluegills and perch are easier to catch.

Site **43**   **TEAL'S WAITTS LAKE**
on Waitts Lake

Campsites, facilities: There are 15 tent sites and 27 sites for trailers or motor homes of any length. Electricity, piped water, sewer hookups and picnic tables are provided. Flush toilets, bottled gas, sanitary services, showers, a recreation hall, a store, firewood, a cafe, a laundromat and ice are available. Pets are permitted. Boat docks, launching facilities and rentals are nearby.

Reservations, fee: Reservations required; $10 fee per night; MasterCard and Visa accepted. Open early April to late October.

Who to contact: Phone (509)937-2400 or write to Route 1, Box 50, Valley, WA 99181.

Location: Drive 42 miles north of Spokane on US 395, then turn north on Highway 232 for 1.5 miles and head west on Highway 231 to Waitts Lake.

Trip note: This resort is set along the shore of Waitts Lake. See the trip note for Site 42 for information about the lake.

Site **44**   **SILVER BEACH RESORT**
on Waitts Lake

Campsites, facilities: There are 53 sites for trailers or motor homes of any length. Electricity, piped water, sewer hookups and picnic tables are provided. Flush toilets, bottled gas, sanitary services, a recreation hall, a store, showers, a restaurant, a laundromat, ice and a playground are available. Pets are permitted.

Boat docks, launching facilities and rentals are available.

Reservations, fee: Reservations accepted; $13 fee per night. Open late April to late October.

Who to contact: Phone (509)937-2811 or write to Route 1, Box 75, Valley, WA 99181.

Location: Drive 38 miles north of Spokane on US 395 to the Valley exit, then head west for six miles until you get to Waitts Lake. The resort is on the lake.

Trip note: This resort offers grassy sites set along the shore of Waitts Lake where fishing and waterskiing are popular. See the trip note for Site 42 for information about the lake.

Site 45   FORTY-NINER MOTEL AND CAMPGROUND
near Chewelah

Campsites, facilities: There are 15 tent sites and 28 drive-through sites for trailers or motor homes of any length. Electricity, piped water, sewer hookups and picnic tables are provided. Flush toilets, sanitary services, showers, a recreation hall, ice and a swimming pool are available. Bottled gas, a store, a cafe and a laundromat are located within one mile. Pets are permitted.

Reservations, fee: Reservations accepted; $6-10 fee per night; MasterCard and Visa accepted. Open all year.

Who to contact: Phone (509)935-8613 or write to P.O. Box 124, Chewelah, WA 99109.

Location: Drive 44 miles north of Spokane on US 395, then follow the signs to the campground.

Trip note: This is in the heart of the mining country. Nearby recreation options include an 18-hole golf course, hiking trails and marked bike trails. This is a good deal for motor home cruisers: a rustic setting only five miles from town.

Site 46   CHEWELAH GOLF AND COUNTRY CLUB
near Waitts Lake

Campsites, facilities: There are 41 drive-through sites for trailers or motor homes of any length. Electricity, piped water, sewer hookups and picnic tables are provided. Sanitary services and a cafe are available. A laundromat is located within one mile. Pets are permitted.

Reservations, fee: Reservations required; $8 fee per night; MasterCard and Visa accepted. Open April to November.

Who to contact: Phone (509)935-6807 or write to P.O. Box 315, Chewelah, WA 99109.

Location: Drive 44 miles north of Spokane on US 395 to Chewelah. Then go north on Sand Canyon Road for three miles, and follow the signs to the club.

Trip note: Nearby recreation options include an 18-hole golf course, hiking trails and marked bike trails. A good side trip is to Waitts Lake, detailed in the trip note for Site 42.

Site 47   CHEWELAH CITY PARK
on Chewelah Creek

Campsites, facilities: There are 50 tent sites and 40 sites for trailers or motor homes of any length. Electricity, piped water and picnic tables are provided. Flush toilets and a playground are available. A store, a cafe, a laundromat and ice are located within one mile. Pets are permitted.

Reservations, fee: No reservations necessary; no fee. Open all year.

Who to contact: Write to Chewelah City Park, Chewelah, WA 99109.

Location: Drive 44 miles north of Spokane on US 395 to Chewelah. The park is on the north edge of town.

Trip note: This is a good option to nearby Sites 45 and 46, and the price doesn't come any cheaper. It is set along Chewelah Creek. Nearby recreation options include an 18-hole golf course, marked bike trails and tennis courts.

Site **48**
GIFFORD
on Franklin Roosevelt Lake
COULEE DAM NATIONAL RECREATION AREA

Campsites, facilities: There are 47 sites for tents, trailers or motor homes up to 20 feet long. Piped water, fire grills and picnic tables are provided. Pit toilets are available. Leashed pets are permitted. Boat docks and launching facilities are nearby.

Reservations, fee: No reservations necessary; $6 fee per night. Open all year with limited winter facilities.

Who to contact: Phone the Coulee Dam National Recreation Area at (509)633-9441 or write to P.O. Box 37, Coulee Dam, WA 99116.

Location: This campground is located about three miles south of Gifford on Highway 25.

Trip note: This campground is set along the shore of Franklin Roosevelt Lake (Columbia River). Fishing and waterskiing are some of the recreation options here. For a more detailed description of Roosevelt Lake, see the trip note for Site 5.

Site **49**
CLOVER LEAF
on Franklin Roosevelt Lake
COULEE DAM NATIONAL RECREATION AREA

Campsites, facilities: There are eight tent sites. Piped water, fire grills and picnic tables are provided. Pit toilets are available. Leashed pets are permitted. A boat dock is available.

Reservations, fee: No reservations necessary; no fee. Open all year with limited winter facilities.

Who to contact: Phone the Coulee Dam National Recreation Area at (509)633-9441 or write to P.O. Box 37, Coulee Dam, WA 99116.

Location: This campground is located about two miles south of Gifford on Highway 25.

Trip note: It's free, it's small and it's quite primitive. In this particular area of Roosevelt Lake, waterskiing is not advised, fishing is. See the trip note for Site 5 for recreation details.

Site **50**
HUNTERS PARK
on Franklin Roosevelt Lake
COULEE DAM NATIONAL RECREATION AREA

Campsites, facilities: There are 42 sites for tents, trailers or motor homes up to 26 feet long. Piped water, fire grills and picnic tables are provided. Flush toilets, a store and ice are available within one mile. Leashed pets are permitted. Boat docks and launching facilities are nearby.

Reservations, fee: No reservations necessary; $6 fee per night. Open May through October.

Who to contact: Phone the Coulee Dam National Recreation Area at (509)633-9441

or write to Fort Spokane, Star Route, Box 30, Davenport, WA 99122.
Location: This campground is located two miles west of Hunters on an access road off Highway 25.
Trip note: This campground is set on a shoreline point along Roosevelt Lake (Columbia River). It's a good spot for swimming, fishing or waterskiing. See the trip note for Site 5.

Site 51
FORT SPOKANE
on Franklin Roosevelt Lake
COULEE DAM NATIONAL RECREATION AREA

Campsites, facilities: There are 67 sites for tents, trailers or motor homes up to 26 feet long. Piped water, picnic tables and fire grills are provided. Flush toilets, sanitary services and a playground are available. A store and ice are located within one mile. Some facilities are wheelchair accessible. Leashed pets are permitted. Boat docks, launching facilities and a marine dump station are nearby.
Reservations, fee: No reservations necessary; $6 fee per night. Open all year with limited winter facilities.
Who to contact: Phone the Coulee Dam National Recreation Area at (509)633-9441 or write to Fort Spokane, Star Route, Box 30, Davenport, WA 99122.
Location: Drive 26 miles north of Davenport on Highway 25 and you'll see the campground.
Trip note: This modern campground is set along the shore of Roosevelt Lake. A lifeguard is on duty during the summer and the rangers offer evening campfire programs. This is one of 16 campgrounds on 130-mile-long Roosevelt Lake.

Site 52
PORCUPINE BAY
on Franklin Roosevelt Lake
COULEE DAM NATIONAL RECREATION AREA

Campsites, facilities: There are 31 sites for tents, trailers or motor homes up to 20 feet long. Piped water, picnic tables and fire grills are provided. Flush toilets and a playground are available. Leashed pets are permitted. Boat docks and launching facilities are nearby. Some facilities are wheelchair accessible.
Reservations, fee: No reservations necessary; $6 fee per night. Open May through October.
Who to contact: Phone the Coulee Dam National Recreation Area at (509)725-2715 or write to Fort Spokane, Star Route, Box 30, Davenport, WA 99122.
Location: Drive 20 miles north of Davenport on Highway 25, and then head north on a county road and you'll see the campground.
Trip note: This is a good spot for campers with boats because of its proximity to a nearby dock and launch. A swimming beach is adjacent to the campground and a lifeguard is on duty during the summer months.

Site 53
ENTERPRISE
on Franklin Roosevelt Lake, boat-in only
COULEE DAM NATIONAL RECREATION AREA

Campsites, facilities: There are 12 tent sites, accessible only by boat. Picnic tables and fire grills are provided, but **no piped water** is available. Pets are permitted. Boat docks are nearby.
Reservations, fee: No reservations necessary; no fee. Open all year.
Who to contact: Phone the Coulee Dam National Recreation Area at (509)725-2715

or write to Fort Spokane, Star Route, Box 30, Davenport, WA 99122.

Location: This camp is located ten miles north of Fort Spokane and is accessible only by boat.

Trip note: This is one of the few boat-in camps anywhere east of the Cascade Range, and one of two on Roosevelt Lake. The other is at Site 10. (Another boat-in site is Site 54 on the Spokane River.) This is quite a pretty spot, situated adjacent to where Wilmont Creek empties into the lake.

Site 54   DETILLON
on Spokane River
COULEE DAM NATIONAL RECREATION AREA

Campsites, facilities: There are 12 tent sites. Picnic tables and fire grills are provided, but **no piped water** is available. Pets are permitted. Boat docks and a marine dump station are nearby.

Reservations, fee: No reservations necessary; no fee. Open all year.

Who to contact: Phone the Coulee Dam National Recreation Area at (509)725-2715 or write to Fort Spokane, Star Route, Box 30, Davenport, WA 99122.

Location: This camp is located six miles northeast of Fort Spokane and is accessible only by boat.

Trip note: This is a secluded, primitive spot that gets very little traffic. It is set along the shore of the Spokane River, which, like Roosevelt Lake, has its water backed up by the Grand Coulee Dam. Waterskiing, fishing and swimming are all options at this quiet spot.

Site 55   SEVEN BAYS RESORT
on Franklin Roosevelt Lake

Campsites, facilities: There are 20 tent sites and 70 drive-through sites for trailers or motor homes of any length. Electricity, piped water, sewer hookups and picnic tables are provided. Flush toilets, bottled gas, sanitary services, showers, a store, a cafe, a laundromat and ice are available. Pets and motorbikes are permitted. Boat docks and launching facilities are nearby.

Reservations, fee: Reservations accepted; $10 fee per night. Open March to October.

Who to contact: Phone (509)725-5794 or write to Route 1, Box 62L, Davenport, WA 99122.

Location: Drive five miles southwest of Miles on Creston Road and you'll see the resort.

Trip note: This resort is set along the shore of Roosevelt Lake, and is an option to Sites 51 and 56. A full-service marina sets this spot apart from the others.

Site 56   HAWK CREEK
on Franklin Roosevelt Lake
COULEE DAM NATIONAL RECREATION AREA

Campsites, facilities: There are 16 sites for tents or trailers and motor homes up to 16 feet long. Picnic tables, fire grills and piped water are provided. Pit toilets are available. Leashed pets are permitted. Boat docks and launching facilities are nearby.

Reservations, fee: No reservations necessary; no fee. Open all year with limited winter facilities.

Who to contact: Phone the Coulee Dam National Recreation Area at (509)633-9441 or write to P.O. Box 37, Coulee Dam, WA 99116.

Location: This campground is located about ten miles southwest of Miles on Creston

Road at the mouth of Hawk Creek.

Trip note: This is a pleasant spot set along the shore of Roosevelt Lake (Columbia River), adjacent to the mouth of Hawk Creek. It gets less use than the other campgrounds at Roosevelt Lake, but is an idyllic spot.

Site 57 MICK'S EXXON AND RV PARK
in Davenport

Campsites, facilities: There are 12 drive-through sites for trailers or motor homes. Electricity, piped water and sewer hookups are provided. Flush toilets, bottled gas and sanitary services are available. A store, a cafe, a laundromat and ice are located within one mile. Pets are permitted.

Reservations, fee: Reservations accepted; $7 fee per night; MasterCard and Visa accepted. Open all year.

Who to contact: Phone (509)725-0015 or write to P.O. Box 242, Davenport, WA 99122.

Location: The park is located in Davenport on US 2 at the eastern edge of town.

Trip note: This is one of two motor home parks in Davenport. Nearby recreation options include tennis courts. This is an okay layover point for motor home travelers on US 2. The nearest alternatives are on the outskirts of Spokane.

Site 58 DIAMOND S MOTEL AND RV PARK
in Davenport

Campsites, facilities: There are nine drive-through sites for trailers or motor homes of any length. Electricity, piped water and sewer hookups are provided. Bottled gas, sanitary services, a store, a cafe, a laundromat and ice are available within one mile. Pets are permitted.

Reservations, fee: Reservations accepted; $7 fee per night; MasterCard and Visa accepted. Open May to November.

Who to contact: Phone (509)725-7742 or write to P.O. Box 106, Davenport, WA 99122.

Location: The park is located in Davenport on US 2 at the eastern edge of town.

Trip note: This is a good stopover site in Davenport. Nearby recreation options include tennis courts.

Site 59 WEST MEDICAL LAKE RESORT
on West Medical Lake

Campsites, facilities: There are 20 tent sites and 18 sites for trailers or motor homes. Picnic tables are provided. Flush toilets, showers, a cafe and ice are available. Electricity, piped water and sewer hookups can be obtained for an extra fee. Pets and motorbikes are permitted. Boat docks, launching facilities and rentals are nearby.

Reservations, fee: Reservations required; $7.50-10.50 fee per night. Open mid-April to July.

Who to contact: Phone (509)299-3921 or write to P.O. Box 216, Medical Lake, WA 99022.

Location: Take exit 264 off Highway 90 near Medical Lake and drive 4.5 miles north on Salnave Road, then turn west on Faucher and go one-half mile to the resort.

Trip note: This resort is set along the shore of Medical Lake, one of five campgrounds on the lake. It is a popular spot for Spokane locals making the half-hour drive. There are actually two lakes: West Medical is the larger of the two and also has the better fishing, with boat rentals available. Medical Lake is just a quarter-mile wide and a half-mile long and boating is restricted to rowboats, canoes, kayaks and sailboats. The lakes got their names from the wondrous medical powers once attributed to these waters.

Site 60   CONNIE'S COVE CAMPGROUND
on Medical Lake

Campsites, facilities: There are five tent sites and 16 sites for trailers or motor homes of any length. Electricity, piped water, sewer hookups and picnic tables are provided. Showers, flush toilets, a cafe and ice are available. Pets are permitted. Boat docks, launching facilities and rentals are nearby.

Reservations, fee: Reservations accepted; $9.25 fee per night. Open mid-April to late September.

Who to contact: Phone (509)299-3717 or write to South 12514 Clear Lake Road, Medical Lake, WA 99022.

Location: Take exit 264 off Highway 90 near Medical Lake and drive 300 feet west on Salnave Road, then turn north on Clear Lake Road and follow the signs.

Trip note: This resort is set along the shore of Medical Lake. Nearby recreation options include marked bike trails and tennis courts. See the trip note for Site 59 for more details about the lake.

Site 61   PICNIC PINES ON SILVER LAKE
on Medical Lake

Campsites, facilities: There are ten tent sites and 29 drive-through sites for trailers or motor homes of any length. Electricity, piped water, sewer hookups and picnic tables are provided. Flush toilets, showers, a recreation hall, a store, a cafe, ice and a playground are available. Bottled gas and a laundromat are located within one mile. Pets and motorbikes are permitted. Boat docks, launching facilities and rentals are nearby.

Reservations, fee: Reservations accepted; $9 fee per night; MasterCard and Visa accepted. Open all year.

Who to contact: Phone (509)299-3223 or write to Route 1, Box 90-1, Medical Lake, WA 99022.

Location: Take exit 270 off Highway 90 near Spokane and drive three miles west on Medical Lake Road to the park.

Trip note: This resort is set along the shore of Medical Lake. Nearby recreation options include marked bike trails, a full-service marina and tennis courts.

Site 62   BERNIE'S LAST RESORT
on Medical Lake

Campsites, facilities: There are 20 tent sites and 35 drive-through sites for trailers or motor homes up to 32 feet long. Picnic tables are provided. Flush toilets, sanitary services, showers, a recreation hall, a store, a cafe, a laundromat, ice, a playground, bottled gas, electricity, piped water and sewer hookups are available. Pets and motorbikes are permitted. Boat docks, launching facilities and rentals are nearby.

Reservations, fee: Reservations accepted; $10 fee per night. Open mid-April to late September.

Who to contact: Phone (509)299-7273 or write to Route 1, Box 267, Medical Lake, WA 99022.

Location: Take exit 270 off Highway 90 near Spokane and drive three miles west on Medical Lake Road to the resort.

Trip note: This resort is set along the shore of Medical Lake and is one of five camps at the lake.

Site **63**
BARBER'S RESORT
on Medical Lake

Campsites, facilities: There are 35 tent sites and 50 drive-through sites for trailers or motor homes of any length. Electricity, piped water and picnic tables are provided. Flush toilets, bottled gas, sanitary services, showers, a cafe, ice and a playground are available. Pets and motorbikes are permitted. Boat docks, launching facilities and rentals are nearby.

Reservations, fee: Reservations accepted; $9-10 fee per night. Open mid-April to late September.

Who to contact: Phone (509)299-3830 or write to Route 1, Box 64, Cheney, WA 99004.

Location: Take exit 264 off Highway 90 near Cheney and drive two miles west on Salnave Road and follow the signs to the resort.

Trip note: This resort is set along the shore of Medical Lake. Nearby recreation options include marked bike trails, a riding stable and tennis courts.

Site **64**
MYERS PARK AND RESORT
on Fish Lake

Campsites, facilities: There are 20 tent sites and 30 sites for trailers or motor homes of any length. Electricity, piped water, sewer hookups and picnic tables are provided. Flush toilets, showers, a restaurant and lounge, ice and a playground are available. Pets and motorbikes are permitted. Boat docks, launching facilities and rentals are nearby.

Reservations, fee: Reservations accepted; $7.50 fee per night. Open April to late September.

Who to contact: Phone (509)235-6367 or write to Route 4, Box 233, Cheney, WA 99004.

Location: Take the Tyler exit off Interstate 90 near Cheney and drive to Cheney. Turn right at the Farmers and Merchants Bank and drive three miles to the resort.

Trip note: This resort is set along the shore of Fish Lake, a 47-acre fishing lake that offers seasonal fishing for brook trout. Nearby recreation options include tennis courts.

Site **65**
TOVERLAND STATION
near Eloika Lake

Campsites, facilities: There are 40 tent sites and 32 drive-through sites for trailers or motor homes of any length. Electricity, piped water, sewer hookups and picnic tables are provided. Flush toilets, showers, a store, a cafe, a laundromat, ice and a playground are available. Pets and motorbikes are permitted.

Reservations, fee: Reservations accepted; $8-13 fee per night. Open all year.

Who to contact: Phone (509)747-1703 or write to Route 14, Box 586, Spokane, WA 99204.

Location: Take exit 272 off Highway 90 in Spokane. The park is on the northeast corner of the intersection.

Trip note: This is one of seven campgrounds located in the immediate Spokane area. A number of side trips are available to learn the history of the area, including the Cheney Cowles Memorial Museum and the Museum of Native American Cultures. Riverfront Park is the site of the 1974 World Exposition and it now offers a science center and planetarium, opera house, Japanese garden, gondola ride, carousel, ice-skating rink and five-screen theater. The closest lake with good fishing is Eloika Lake, described in the trip note for Sites 38 and 39.

Site 66   SMOKEY TRAIL CAMPGROUND
in Spokane

Campsites, facilities: There are 40 tent sites and 30 drive-through sites for trailers or motor homes up to 30 feet long. Picnic tables are provided. Flush toilets, sanitary services, showers, firewood, a store, a laundromat, ice and a playground are available. Electricity, piped water and sewer can be obtained for an extra fee. Pets and motorbikes are permitted.

Reservations, fee: Reservations accepted; $9 fee per night. Open mid-May to late September.

Who to contact: Phone (509)747-9415 or write to Rural Route 14, Box 650, Spokane, WA 99204.

Location: Take exit 272 off Highway 90 in Spokane and drive one mile east on Hallett. Then turn south on Mallon and drive one-half mile to the campground.

Trip note: This park is in a wooded, rural area. Nearby recreation options include an 18-hole golf course and hiking trails are nearby. See the trip note for Site 65.

Site 67   SUNSET CAMP
near Spokane

Campsites, facilities: There are ten tent sites and 29 drive-through sites for trailers or motor homes of any length. Electricity, piped water, sewer hookups and picnic tables are provided. Flush toilets, sanitary services, showers, a laundromat and ice are available. A store and a cafe are within one mile. Pets and motorbikes are permitted.

Reservations, fee: Reservations accepted; $11 fee per night. Open May to late October.

Who to contact: Phone (509)747-9467 or write to South 4110 Fosseen, Spokane, WA 99204.

Location: Take exit 276 (Geiger Field) off Highway 90, go five miles west of Spokane and drive to the campground.

Trip note: Nearby recreation options include an 18-hole golf course and a riding stable. See the trip note for Site 65 for information on attractions in Spokane.

Site 68   TRAILER INNS
in Spokane

Campsites, facilities: There are 158 drive-through sites for trailers or motor homes of any length. Electricity, piped water, sewer hookups and picnic tables are provided. Flush toilets, bottled gas, showers, a recreation hall, tanning beds, color TV, a swimming pool, a laundromat, ice and a playground are available. Sanitary services, a store and a cafe are within one mile. Pets and motorbikes are permitted.

Reservations, fee: Reservations accepted; $15-19 fee per night; MasterCard and Visa accepted. Open all year.

Who to contact: Phone (509)535-1811 or write to 6021 East 4th Avenue, Spokane, WA 99212.

Location: If you are eastbound, take exit 283B off Highway 90 in Spokane and drive east on 3rd Avenue. Follow the signs to the campground.

Trip note: Nearby recreation options include an 18-hole golf course and tennis courts. See the trip note for Site 65 for information on attractions in Spokane.

Site 69   EL RANCHO MOTEL AND TRAILER PARK
in Spokane

Campsites, facilities: There are eight tent sites and eight sites for trailers or motor homes of any length. Electricity, piped water, sewer hookups and picnic tables are provided. Flush toilets, sanitary services, showers, a laundromat, ice and a swimming pool are available. Bottled gas, a store and a cafe are located within one mile. Pets are permitted.

Reservations, fee: Reservations accepted; $15-18 fee per night; American Express, MasterCard and Visa accepted. Open April to November.

Who to contact: Phone (509)455-9400 or write to 3000 West Sunset, Spokane, WA 99204.

Location: In Spokane, take the Maple Street exit off Highway 90 and drive one mile west on Business 90 to 3000 West Sunset.

Trip note: Nearby recreation options include an 18-hole golf course, hiking trails, marked bike trails and tennis courts. See the trip note for Site 65 for information on attractions in Spokane.

Site 70   NORTH VIEW MOBILE PARK AND CAMPGROUNDS
in Spokane

Campsites, facilities: There are 21 drive-through sites for trailers or motor homes of any length. Electricity, piped water, sewer hookups and picnic tables are provided. Flush toilets, sanitary services, showers, a recreation hall, bottled gas, a store, a cafe, a laundromat and ice are available. Pets are permitted.

Reservations, fee: Reservations accepted; $15 fee per night. Open all year.

Who to contact: Phone (509)467-9512 or write to N 8004 Division, Spokane, WA 99208.

Location: Take the Division Street north off Highway 90 in Spokane and drive five miles to Lincoln Street, then go east one block and you're there.

Trip note: Nearby recreation options include an 18-hole golf course, marked bike trails and tennis courts. See the trip note for Site 65 for information on attractions in Spokane.

Site 71   SHADOWS MOTEL AND TRAILER PARK
in Spokane

Campsites, facilities: There are 20 tent sites and 60 drive-through sites for trailers or motor homes of any length. Electricity, piped water and sewer hookups are provided. Flush toilets, sanitary services, showers and a laundromat are available. Bottled gas, a store, a cafe and ice are located within one mile. Pets and motorbikes are permitted.

Reservations, fee: Reservations accepted; $6-16 fee per night; MasterCard and Visa accepted. Open May to mid-October.

Who to contact: Phone (509)467-6951 or write to N 9025 Division, Spokane, WA 99208.

Location: Take Division Street north off Highway 90 in Spokane and drive five miles to N 9025 Division Street.

Trip note: Nearby recreation options include an 18-hole golf course, hiking trails, marked bike trails and tennis courts. See the trip note for Site 65 for information on attractions in Spokane.

Site 72   KOA SPOKANE
on Spokane River

Campsites, facilities: There are 50 tent sites and 190 drive-through sites for trailers or motor homes of any length. Piped water and picnic tables are provided. Flush toilets, sanitary services, showers, a recreation hall, a store, a laundromat, ice, a playground and a swimming pool, electricity and sewer hookups are available. A cafe is located within one mile. Pets are permitted.

Reservations, fee: Reservations accepted; $14-17 fee per night; MasterCard and Visa accepted. Open all year.

Who to contact: Phone (509)924-4722 or write to 3025 North Barker, Otis Orchards, WA 99027.

Location: Go 13 miles east of Spokane on Highway 90 and take exit 293. Drive north on Barker for 1.5 miles to the campground.

Trip note: This campground is set along the shore of the Spokane River. Nearby recreation options include an 18-hole golf course and tennis courts. See the trip note for Site 65 for information on attractions in Spokane.

Site 73   RIVERSIDE STATE PARK
near Spokane

Campsites, facilities: There are 101 sites for tents or self-contained motor homes up to 45 feet long. Picnic tables and fire grills are provided. Flush toilets, a playground, showers and firewood are available. A store, a restaurant, and ice are available within one mile. Leashed pets are permitted. Boat launching facilities are located on the Spokane River.

Reservations, fee: No reservations necessary; $6 fee per night. Open all year.

Who to contact: Phone (509)456-3964 or write to Riverside State Park, Spokane, WA 99205.

Location: Drive six miles northwest of Spokane on Riverside Park Drive to the junction with Highway 291. The park entrance is there.

Trip note: This is a good option for people looking for a more rural alternative to the camps set on the outskirts of Spokane. This large state park provides an interpretive center, riding stable, and trails for hiking, horseback riding, and off-road vehicles. Nearby recreation options include an 18-hole golf course.

Site 74   LONG LAKE CAMP AND PICNIC AREA
on Spokane River

Campsites, facilities: There are seven campsites for tents or small trailers. Picnic tables, fire grills and tent pads are provided. Pit toilets and piped water are available.

Reservations, fee: No reservations necessary; no fee. Open all year.

Who to contact: Phone the Department of Natural Resources at (800)527-3305 or write to Department of Natural Resources AW-11, 1065 South Capitol Way, Olympia, WA 98504.

Location: Drive 21 miles west of Spokane on US 2 to Reardan. Go north on Highway 231 for 14 miles, then turn right on Long Lake Dam Road. Drive five miles and turn right into the campground.

Trip note: This is a secret spot that Spokaners should take advantage of. It's about a 45-minute drive out of Spokane and you get a small, quiet spot set along the Spokane River. It comes free.

Site **75**   **MOUNT SPOKANE STATE PARK**
             on Mount Spokane

Campsites, facilities: There are 12 sites for tents or self-contained motor homes up to 30 feet long. Piped water, fire grills and picnic tables are provided. Flush toilets and a cafe are available. A laundromat is located within one mile. Pets are permitted.

Reservations, fee: No reservations necessary; $7.50 fee per night. Open all year with limited winter facilities.

Who to contact: Phone (509)456-4169 or write to Route 1, Box 336, Mead, WA 99021.

Location: This park is located 30 miles northeast of Spokane on Highway 206.

Trip note: This is a prime hideaway on the slopes of 5,878-foot Mount Spokane. Mount Kit Carson (5,180 feet) sits alongside, its little brother. Nearby recreation options include marked hiking trails, a riding stable and tennis courts. This is one of the better short trips available out of Spokane.

Site **76**   **DRAGOON CREEK**
             near Little Spokane River

Campsites, facilities: There are 22 campsites for tents or small trailers. Picnic tables, fire grills and tent pads are provided. Pit toilets and piped water are available. Leashed pets are permitted.

Reservations, fee: No reservations necessary; no fee. Open all year.

Who to contact: Phone the Department of Natural Resources at (800)527-3305 or write to Department of Natural Resources AW-11, 1065 South Capitol Way, Olympia, WA 98504.

Location: From the junction of US 2 and US 395 in Spokane, drive north on US 395 for ten miles. Turn left on Dragoon Creek Road and drive one-half mile to the campground entrance.

Trip note: Out-of-towners just plain don't know about this one. It's not far from US 395, but it's quiet, rustic and set along Dragoon Creek, a tributary to the Little Spokane River. The Department of Natural Resources offers a map that details the area.

YAKIMA

◆

SOME HIGHLIGHTS

25 CAMPGROUNDS

Dalles Dam

Yakima River

Moses Lake State Park

Potholes Reservoir

Klickitat Habitat Management Area

Columbia Wildlife Refuge

Darland Mountain

Umatilla National Wildlife Refuge

Goldendale Observatory

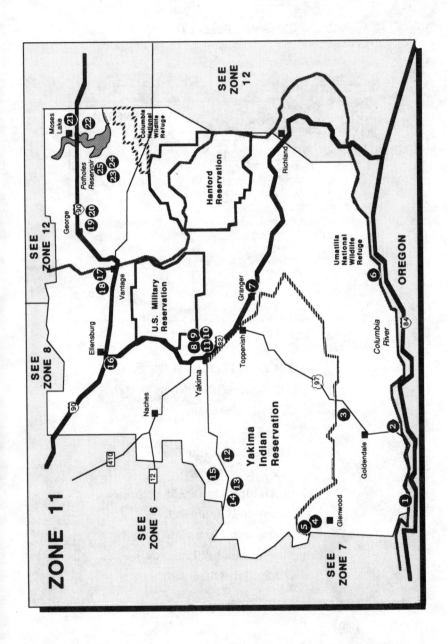

HORSETHIEF LAKE STATE PARK
Site **1**   near Dalles Dam

Campsites, facilities: There are 12 sites for tents or self-contained motor homes up to 30 feet long. Piped water, fire grills and picnic tables are provided. Flush toilets, showers, firewood and sanitary services are available. A store and a cafe are located within one mile. Pets are permitted. Boat launching facilities are located on both the lake and the river.

Reservations, fee: No reservations necessary; $7.50 fee per night. Open April to late October.

Who to contact: Phone (509)767-1159 or write to Route 677, P.O. Box 27 A, Goldendale, WA 98620.

Location: From Goldendale, drive 28 miles west on Highway 14 to the park.

Trip note: This is a good spot to camp if you are driving along the Columbia River Highway. This state park is set along the shore of Horsethief Lake adjacent to the Dalles Dam. There are hiking trails and access both to the lake and the Columbia River. Only non-powered boats are allowed, and fishing is for trout and bass. See the trip note for Site 2 for information on other recreation options in the area.

MARYHILL STATE PARK
Site **2**   on Columbia River

Campsites, facilities: There are 50 sites with full hookups for trailers or motor homes up to 50 feet long. Picnic tables are provided. Flush toilets, sanitary services, a store and a cafe are available. Electricity, piped water, sewer hookups, showers and firewood can be obtained for an extra fee. Some facilities are wheelchair accessible. Pets are permitted. Boat docks and launching facilities are nearby.

Reservations, fee: No reservations necessary; $10.50 fee per night. Open all year.

Who to contact: Phone (509)773-5007 or write to Route 677, P.O. Box 27 A, Goldendale, WA 98620.

Location: From Goldendale, drive 12 miles south on US 97 to the park.

Trip note: This park is set along the Columbia River and the recreation opportunities include fishing, waterskiing and windsurfing. The climate here is very pleasant from March through mid-November. There are two interesting spots near Maryhill, one is a replica of Stonehenge, which is located on a bluff overlooking the Columbia River, and the other is the Maryhill Museum—phone (509)773-3733 for details. A great side trip, 30 miles northwest, is the Klickitat Habitat Management Area. It is run by the Department of Game and has some primitive camping spots and a boat launch along the Klickitat River, where you can enjoy boating, fishing, hunting or observing wildlife. To get there drive 11 miles west of Goldendale on Highway 142, then continue northwest on Glendale Road for five miles and look for the headquarters on your left. The public areas beyond the wildlife refuge headquarters are easier to get to. Another treat at the refuge is Stinson Flat, a good steelhead fishing spot.

BROOKS MEMORIAL STATE PARK
Site **3**   near Goldendale Observatory

Campsites, facilities: There are 22 sites for tents or self-contained motor homes and 23 sites with water and electrical hookups for trailers or motor homes up to 50 feet long. Picnic tables and fire grills are provided. Flush toilets, sanitary services and a playground are available. Electricity, piped water, sewer hookups, showers and firewood can be obtained for an extra fee. A store is located within one mile. Leashed pets are permitted.

Reservations, fee: No reservations necessary; $7.50-10.50 fee per night. Open all year with limited winter facilities.

Who to contact: Phone (509)773-4611 or write to Route 1, Box 136, Goldendale, WA 98620.

Location: From Goldendale, drive 15 miles northeast on US 97 to the park.

Trip note: There is only one other campground (Site 2) within 25 miles. This forested park is set at nearly 3,000 feet elevation. There are several miles of hiking trails and a 1.5 mile long nature trail. A unique side trip is for birdwatching at Toppenish National Wildlife Refuge, 28 miles north of the park on US 97; phone the refuge at (509)865-2405 for details. If you like star gazing, the Goldendale Observatory is located just one mile north of Goldendale. It houses one of the largest telescopes in the world that is available for public use; phone (509)773-3141 for hours of operation.

Site **4**
BIRD CREEK
near Mount Adams Wilderness

Campsites, facilities: There are eight campsites for tents or small trailers. Picnic tables, fire grills and tent pads are provided. Pit toilets are available, but there is **no piped water.** Leashed pets are permitted.

Reservations, fee: No reservations necessary; no fee. Open all year.

Who to contact: Phone the Department of Natural Resources at (800)527-3305 or write to Department of Natural Resources AW-11, 1065 South Capitol Way, Olympia, WA 98504.

Location: Drive 34 miles west of Goldendale to Glenwood. From the post office in Glenwood, drive 300 yards west then turn right on Bird Creek Road and drive one mile. Turn left, then right on a dirt road and drive one mile. Stay left on Road K 3000 and drive 300 yards, cross a gravel road, stay right for the next two miles, and then turn right into the campground.

Trip note: This campground is set in a forested area along Bird Creek, one of two camps in the immediate area. (The other is Site 5, also a primitive site.) This spot is just east of the Mount Adams Wilderness area. See the trip note for Site 2 for information on the nearby Klickitat Habitat Management Area.

Site **5**
ISLAND CAMP
on Bird Creek

Campsites, facilities: There are six campsites for tents or small trailers. Picnic tables, fire grills and tent pads are provided. Pit toilets are available, but there is **no piped water.** Leashed pets are permitted.

Reservations, fee: No reservations necessary; no fee. Open all year.

Who to contact: Phone the Department of Natural Resources at (800)527-3305 or write to Department of Natural Resources AW-11, 1065 South Capitol Way, Olympia, WA 98504.

Location: Drive 34 miles west of Goldendale to Glenwood. From the post office in Glenwood, drive 300 yards west then turn right on Bird Creek Road and drive one mile. Turn left, then right on a dirt road and drive one mile. Stay left on Road K 3000 and drive 300 yards, cross a gravel road, stay right for the next two miles, go past the Bird Creek camp entrance, and continue on Road K 3000 for 1.5 miles. Stay right for 1.5 miles then turn right into the campground.

Trip note: This campground is set in a forested area along Bird Creek. There are lava tubes and blow holes nearby. In the winter the roads are used for snowmobiling. See the trip note for Site 2 for information on boating and fishing in the nearby Klickitat Habitat Management Area.

Site **6**
CROW BUTTE STATE PARK
on Columbia River

Campsites, facilities: There are 50 sites with full hookups for trailers or motor homes up to 50 feet long. Fire grills and picnic tables are provided. Flush toilets, showers and sanitary disposal station are available. Some facilities are wheelchair accessible. Boat launching facilities are nearby. Leashed pets are permitted.

Reservations, fee: No reservations necessary; $10.50 fee per night. Open all year with limited winter facilities.

Who to contact: Phone (509)875-2644 or write to P.O. Box 277, Paterson, WA 99345.

Location: From the town of McNary Dam, drive 14 miles west on Highway 14 to the park.

Trip note: This state park is set along the Columbia River, the only campground in a 25-mile radius. Recreation options include waterskiing, fishing, swimming and hiking. The Umatilla National Wildlife Refuge is adjacent to the park and allows fishing and hunting in specified areas.

Site **7**
GRANGER MOBILE VILLA AND RV PARK
near Yakima River

Campsites, facilities: There are 45 tent sites and 45 drive-through sites for trailers or motor homes of any length. Electricity, piped water and sewer hookups are provided. Flush toilets, sanitary services, showers and a laundromat are available. Bottled gas, a store, a cafe and ice are located within one mile. Pets and motorbikes are permitted. Discounts are given for Good Sam members.

Reservations, fee: Reservations accepted; $10 fee per night. Open all year.

Who to contact: Phone (509)854-1300 or write to P.O. Box 695, Granger, WA 98932.

Location: Drive 25 miles south of Yakima on Interstate 82 to Granger. Take the Highway 223 exit in Granger and you'll see the park.

Trip note: This park is near the Yakima River. A unique side trip can be made to the Toppenish Wildlife Refuge, which is particularly good for birdwatching. It is 15 miles away, south of Toppenish on US 97. Call for information at (509)865-2405.

Site **8**
KOA YAKIMA
on Yakima River

Campsites, facilities: There are 50 tent sites and 90 drive-through sites for trailers or motor homes of any length. Picnic tables are provided. Flush toilets, bottled gas, sanitary services, showers, a recreation hall, A store, a laundromat, ice, a playground, electricity, piped water, sewer hookups and firewood are available. A cafe is located within one mile. Pets and motorbikes are permitted. Boat rentals, including paddleboats, are available.

Reservations, fee: Reservations accepted; $13-16 fee per night. Open all year.

Who to contact: Phone (509)248-5882 or write to 1500 Keyes Road, Yakima, WA 98901.

Location: Take the Highway 24 exit off Interstate 82 in Yakima and drive one-half mile east. Turn north on Keys Road and drive 300 yards to the campground.

Trip note: This campground offers well-maintained, shaded sites. It is set along the Yakima River. Some points of interest in Yakima are the Yakima Valley Museum and the Yakima Trolley Lines which offer rides on restored trolley cars originally built in 1906. Indian Rock Paintings State Park is five miles west of Yakima on US 12. Nearby recreation options include an 18-hole golf course, hiking trails, marked bike trails and tennis courts.

Site 9   CIRCLE H RV RANCH
in Yakima

Campsites, facilities: There are 25 tent sites and 36 drive-through sites for trailers or motor homes of any length. Electricity, piped water, sewer hookups and picnic tables are provided. Flush toilets, showers, a recreation hall, a laundromat, a playground and a swimming pool are available. Bottled gas, sanitary services, a store, a cafe and ice are located within one mile. Pets and motorbikes are permitted.

Reservations, fee: Reservations accepted; $11 fee per night; MasterCard and Visa accepted. Open all year.

Who to contact: Phone (509)457-3683 or write to 1107 South 18th Street, Yakima, WA 98901.

Location: Take exit 34 off Interstate 82 in Yakima and drive 300 yards west to 18th Street. Turn north and drive 300 yards to the park.

Trip note: Nearby recreation options include an 18-hole golf course, hiking trails, marked bike trails and a riding stable. See the trip note for Site 8 for information on points of interest in Yakima.

Site 10   TRAILER INN RV PARK
AND RECREATION CENTER
in Yakima

Campsites, facilities: There are 101 drive-through sites for trailers or motor homes of any length. Electricity, piped water, sewer hookups and picnic tables are provided. Flush toilets, bottled gas, sanitary services, showers, a recreation hall, a laundromat, ice, a swimming pool, a whirlpool, a sauna and a playground are available. A store and a cafe are located within one mile. Pets are permitted.

Reservations, fee: Reservations accepted; $13.50 fee per night; MasterCard and Visa accepted. Open all year.

Who to contact: Phone (509)452-9561 or write to 1610 North 1st Street, Yakima, WA 98901.

Location: Take exit 31 off Interstate 82 in Yakima and drive three blocks south on North 1st Street to the park.

Trip note: Nearby recreation options include an 18-hole golf course, hiking trails, marked bike trails and tennis courts. See the trip note for Site 8 for information on some of the points of interest in Yakima.

Site 11   YAKIMA SPORTSMEN'S STATE PARK
on Yakima River

Campsites, facilities: There are 28 sites for tents or self-contained motor homes and 36 drive-through sites with full hookups for trailers or motor homes of any length. Picnic tables and fire grills are provided. Flush toilets, sanitary services and a playground are available. Showers and firewood can be obtained for an extra fee. A store and ice are available within one mile. Leashed pets are permitted.

Reservations, fee: No reservations necessary; $7.50-10.50 fee per night. Open all year.

Who to contact: Phone (509)575-2774 or write to Route 9, P.O. Box 498, Yakima, WA 98901.

Location: Take Interstate 82 east out of Yakima and drive one mile to the park.

Trip note: This park is set along the Yakima River. There is also a pond in the park for children to fish in. Nearby recreation options include an 18-hole golf course and hiking trails. See the trip note for Site 8 for information on other points of interest in Yakima.

Site 12   AHTANUM CAMP
on Ahtanum Creek

Campsites, facilities: There are 11 campsites for tents or small trailers. Picnic tables, fire grills and tent pads are provided. Pit toilets and piped water are available. Leashed pets are permitted.

Reservations, fee: No reservations necessary; no fee. Open all year.

Who to contact: Phone the Department of Natural Resources at (800)527-3305 or write to Department of Natural Resources AW-11, 1065 South Capitol Way, Olympia, WA 98504.

Location: Drive two miles south of Yakima on Interstate 82 to Union Gap. Go west on Ahtanum Road to Tampico. Continue west on Road A 2000 (middle fork) and drive 9.5 miles to the campground, which will be on the left.

Trip note: This campground is set along Ahtanum Creek, one of four primitive campsites in a ten-mile vicinity. A good side trip is to continue driving on Road A 2000 Road for 14 miles, where you will reach the Darland Mountain viewpoint at 6,900 feet elevation. The road gets very steep near the lookout and is not suitable for motor homes or trailers. In the winter, this area offers 60 miles of groomed trails for snowmobilers. A snow shelter with firewood is provided at Site 13. Contact the Department of Natural Resources for a map.

Site 13   TREE PHONES
on Middle Fork Ahtanum Creek

Campsites, facilities: There are 14 campsites for tents or small trailers. Picnic tables, fire grills and tent pads are provided. Pit toilets are available, but there is **no piped water**. Motorbikes are permitted. Saddlestock facilities are also available. Leashed pets are permitted.

Reservations, fee: No reservations necessary; no fee. Open all year.

Who to contact: Phone the Department of Natural Resources at (800)527-3305 or write to Department of Natural Resources AW-11, 1065 South Capitol Way, Olympia, WA 98504.

Location: Drive two miles south of Yakima on Interstate 82 to Union Gap. Go west on Ahtanum Road to Tampico. Continue west on Road A 2000 (middle fork) and drive 15 miles, then go left and drive 100 yards to the campground.

Trip note: This forested campground is set along the Middle Fork of Ahtanum Creek. The nearby trails are used by motorbike riders, hikers and horseback riders. During summer months, there are beautiful wildflower displays. See the trip note for Site 12 for snowmobiling information.

Site 14
CLOVER FLATS
near Goat Rocks Wilderness

Campsites, facilities: There are nine campsites for tents or small trailers. Picnic tables, fire grills and tent pads are provided. Pit toilets and piped water are available. Leashed pets are permitted.

Reservations, fee: No reservations necessary; no fee. Open all year.

Who to contact: Phone the Department of Natural Resources at (800)527-3305 or write to Department of Natural Resources AW-11, 1065 South Capitol Way, Olympia, WA 98504.

Location: Drive two miles south of Yakima on Interstate 82 to Union Gap. Go west on Ahtanum Road to Tampico. Continue west on Road A 2000 (middle fork).

Trip note: This campground is in the sub-alpine zone on the slope of Darland Mountain, which peaks at 6,982 feet. There are trails that connect this area with Goat Rocks Wilderness, six miles to the west. Contact the Department of Natural Resources or Wenatchee National Forest for details. See the trip note for Site 12 for information on winter snowmobiling.

Site 15
SNOW CABIN
on the North Fork of Ahtanum Creek

Campsites, facilities: There are eight campsites for tents or small trailers. Picnic tables, fire grills and tent pads are provided. Pit toilets are available, but there is **no piped water.** Saddlestock facilities are available. Leashed pets are permitted.

Reservations, fee: No reservations necessary; no fee. Open all year.

Who to contact: Phone the Department of Natural Resources at (800)527-3305 or write to Department of Natural Resources AW-11, 1065 South Capitol Way, Olympia, WA 98504.

Location: Drive two miles south of Yakima on Interstate 82 to Union Gap. Go west on Ahtanum Road to Tampico. Continue west on Road A 2000 (middle fork) and drive ten miles to Ahtanum Camp. From there, take the North Fork Ahtanum Road (A 3000) and drive 4.5 miles. Keep left and drive 2.5 miles to the campground, which will be on your left.

Trip note: Most remote of the four campgrounds in the area, this spot is set in a wooded area along the North Fork of the Ahtanum Creek. Green Lake is about two miles from the camp and is accessible by car. See the trip note for Site 12 for information on winter snowmobiling.

Site 16
KOA ELLENSBURG
on Yakima River

Campsites, facilities: There are 50 tent sites and 100 drive-through sites for trailers or motor homes of any length. Piped water and picnic tables are provided. Flush toilets, sanitary services, showers, a recreation hall, a store, a laundromat, ice, a playground, wading pool and a swimming pool are available. Electricity and sewer hookups can be obtained for an extra fee. Bottled gas and a cafe are located within one mile. Pets and motorbikes are permitted.

Reservations, fee: Reservations accepted; $14-19 fee per night; MasterCard and Visa accepted. Open April to November.

Who to contact: Phone (509)925-9319 or write to Route 1, P.O. Box 252, Ellensburg, WA 98926.

Location: Take exit 106 off Interstate 90 near Ellensburg and you'll see the campground.

Trip note: This is the only campground in a 25-mile radius. It offers well-maintained, shaded campsites set along the Yakima River. The Kittitas County Historical Museum is in town at 3rd and Pine Streets. Nearby recreation options include an 18-hole golf course and tennis courts.

Site **17**   GINKGO-WANAPUM STATE PARK
on Columbia River and Wanapum Lake

Campsites, facilities: There are 50 sites with full hookups for trailers or motor homes of any length. Picnic tables and fire grills are provided. Flush toilets are provided and electricity, piped water, sewer hookups, showers and firewood are available for an extra fee. Pets are permitted. Boat docks and launching facilities are nearby.

Reservations, fee: No reservations necessary; $6 fee per night. Open all year.

Who to contact: Write to Ginkgo-Wanapum State Park, Vantage, WA 98950.

Location: Drive 29 miles east of Ellensburg on Interstate 90, then take the Vantage exit and drive south to the park.

Trip note: This state park is set along Wanapum Lake and the Columbia River. It is the site of an ancient petrified forest and there is an interpretive center and trail. Recreation options include hiking, swimming, boating, waterskiing and fishing.

Site **18**   KOA VANTAGE
on Columbia River

Campsites, facilities: There are 25 tent sites and 100 sites for trailers or motor homes of any length. Picnic tables are provided. Flush toilets, bottled gas, sanitary services, showers, a recreation hall, a laundromat, ice, a playground, a swimming pool, a sauna and a whirlpool are available. Electricity, piped water and sewer hookups can be obtained for an extra fee. A store and a cafe are located within one mile. Pets and motorbikes are permitted. Boat docks and launching facilities are nearby.

Reservations, fee: Reservations accepted; $12.50-16.50 fee per night; MasterCard and Visa accepted. Open all year.

Who to contact: Phone (509)856-2230 or write to P.O. Box 36, Vantage, WA 98950.

Location: Drive 29 miles east of Ellensburg on Interstate 90 to Vantage, then take exit 136 and drive north for one-half mile to the park.

Trip note: This campground offers pleasant, grassy sites overlooking the Columbia River, a short distance from the state park (see Site 17). This is the only campground in the immediate area that provides space for tent camping. The next closest is 12 miles away at Site 20 in George.

Site **19**   GEORGE EXXON
near Frenchman Hills Lakes

Campsites, facilities: There are ten drive-through sites for trailers or motor homes of any length. Electricity, piped water and sewer hookups are provided. Sanitary services, a store and ice are available. Bottled gas and a cafe are located within one mile. Pets are permitted. Boat launching facilities are nearby.

Reservations, fee: Reservations accepted; $5 fee per night; MasterCard and Visa accepted. Open all year.

Who to contact: Phone (509)785-4511 or write to P.O. Box 5098, George, WA 98824.

Location: Drive 41 miles east of Ellensburg on Interstate 90 to George. Take exit 149 and drive 300 yards southwest to the park.

Trip note: This roadside park is in a desert-like area. A good side trip is to take the county road south out of town to the sand dunes north of Frenchman Hills Lake.

Site **20**   **SHADY TREE RV PARK**
                   near Frenchman Hills Lakes

Campsites, facilities: There are five tent sites and 44 drive-through sites for trailers or motor homes of any length. Electricity, piped water, sewer hookups and picnic tables are provided. Flush toilets, showers and a laundromat are available. Sanitary services are located within one mile. Pets and motorbikes are permitted.

Reservations, fee: Reservations accepted; $10 fee per night. Open all year.

Who to contact: Phone (509)785-2851 or write to P.O. Box 5306, George, WA 98824.

Location: Drive 41 miles east of Ellensburg on Interstate 90 to George. Go to the intersection of Highways 281 and 283 and you'll see the park.

Trip note: This is an oasis in a desert-like area. A good side trip is to Frenchman Hills Lakes, bordered by sand dunes.

Site **21**   **BIG SUN RESORT**
                   near Moses Lake State Park

Campsites, facilities: There are ten tent sites and 50 drive-through sites for trailers or motor homes of any length. Electricity, piped water, sewer hookups and picnic tables are provided. Flush toilets, a recreation hall, a laundromat, ice and a playground are available. Showers can be obtained for an extra fee. Bottled gas, sanitary services, a store and a cafe are located within one mile. Pets and motorbikes are permitted. Boat docks, launching facilities and rentals are nearby.

Reservations, fee: Reservations accepted; $8-12 fee per night. Open all year.

Who to contact: Phone (509)765-8294 or write to 2300 West Marina, Moses Lake, WA 98837.

Location: Take exit 176 off Interstate 90 in the town of Moses Lake and drive one-half mile on Broadway to Burress Avenue. Turn west on Burress and go one block to the park.

Trip note: This park is a short distance from Moses Lake State Park, which is open for day-use only. You will find shady picnic spots with tables and fire grills, beach access and moorage floats. Waterskiing is allowed on the lake.

Site **22**   **WILLOWS TRAILER VILLAGE**
                   near Moses Lake State Park

Campsites, facilities: There are 20 tent sites and 64 drive-through sites for trailers or motor homes of any length. Electricity, piped water, sewer hookups and picnic tables are provided. Flush toilets, bottled gas, showers, a store, a laundromat and ice are available. Pets and motorbikes are permitted.

Reservations, fee: Reservations accepted; $10-14.50 fee per night. Open all year.

Who to contact: Phone (509)765-7531 or write to Route 3, P.O. Box 53, Moses Lake, WA 98837.

Location: Take exit 179 off Interstate 90 in the town of Moses Lake and drive 2.5 miles south on Highway 17, then go 300 yards southwest on "M" Road to the park.

Trip note: This is one of four campgrounds set in the area. See the trip notes for Sites 21 and 24 for information on recreation spots in this area.

Site **23**
MAR-DON RESORT
near Potholes Reservoir

Campsites, facilities: There are 160 drive-through sites for tents, trailers or motor homes of any length. Electricity, piped water, sewer hookups and picnic tables are provided. Flush toilets, bottled gas, sanitary services, showers, a recreation hall, a store, a laundromat, ice and a playground are available. Pets and motorbikes are permitted. Boat docks, rentals and launching facilities are nearby.

Reservations, fee: No reservations necessary; $12 fee per night; American Express, MasterCard and Visa accepted. Open all year.

Who to contact: Phone (509)765-5061 or write to 800 O'Sullivan, Othello, WA 99344.

Location: Take exit 179 off Interstate 90 in the town ofMoses Lake and drive 1.5 miles south on Highway 17. Head south on O'Sullivan Dam Road and drive about 15 miles to the west end of the dam. From there, you'll see the resort.

Trip note: See the trip note for Site 24 for information on the area. Nearby recreation options include hiking trails and marked bike trails.

Site **24**
FISH HAVEN RESORT
on Potholes Reservoir

Campsites, facilities: There are 40 tent sites and 90 drive-through sites for trailers or motor homes of any length. Electricity, piped water and sewer hookups are provided. Flush toilets, showers, a store, firewood and ice are available. Bottled gas, sanitary services and a cafe are located within one mile. Pets and motorbikes are permitted. Boat launching facilities are nearby.

Reservations, fee: No reservations necessary; $10 fee per night. Open March to late October.

Who to contact: Phone (509)346-2447 or write to 691 O'Sullivan Dam Road, Othello, WA 99344.

Location: Take exit 179 off Interstate 90 in the town ofMoses Lake and drive 1.5 miles south on Highway 17. Turn southwest on O'Sullivan Road and drive about 14 miles to 691 O'Sullivan Dam Road.

Trip note: This park is set along the Potholes Reservoir, a unique lake formed in a desert area by the O'Sullivan Dam. The area gets very little rainfall. The nearby Columbia Wildlife Refuge is populated with many types of birds and is used most heavily as a wintering range from November through January. The numerous sloughs and small lakes formed by seepage from the reservoir provide the best fishing spots.

Site **25**
POTHOLES STATE PARK
on Potholes Reservoir

Campsites, facilities: There are 66 sites for tents or self-contained motor homes, and 60 sites with full hookups for trailers or motor homes up to 50 feet long. Picnic tables and fire grills are provided. Flush toilets, sanitary services, a store and a playground are available. Electricity, piped water, sewer hookups, showers and firewood can be obtained for an extra fee. Leashed pets are permitted. Boat launching facilities and rentals are nearby.

Reservations, fee: No reservations necessary; $6 fee per night. Open all year.

Who to contact: Phone (509)765-7271 or write to Royal Star Route, Othello, WA 99344.

Location: Drive 24 miles southwest of the town of Moses Lake on Highway 170.

Trip note: See the trip note for Site 24 for a description of this unique area. Waterskiing, fishing, and hiking are some of the options here. A side trip to the Columbia Wildlife Refuge is recommended.

SOUTHEASTERN PLAINS

◆

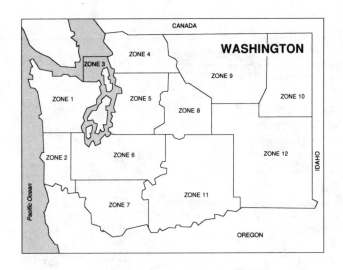

SOME HIGHLIGHTS

48 CAMPGROUNDS

Umatilla National Forest

Snake River

Columbia River

Lake Lenore Caves State Park

Sacajawea State Park

Sun Lakes State Park

McNary National Wildlife Refuge

Turnbull National Wildlife Refuge

Summer Falls State Park

Palouse River

Lewis and Clark Trail

Blue Lake

Sprague Lake

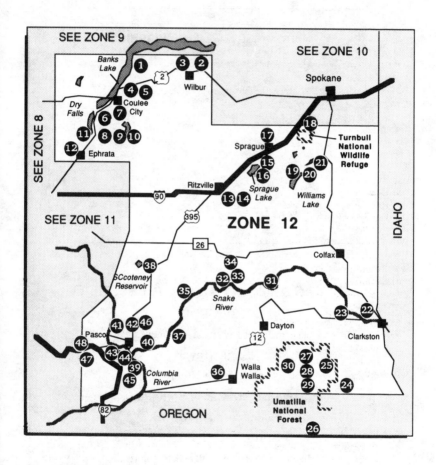

SEE ZONE 9

SEE ZONE 10

Banks Lake

Spokane

Wilbur

Dry Falls

Coulee City

SEE ZONE 8

Ephrata

Sprague

Turnbull National Wildlife Refuge

Ritzville

Sprague Lake

Williams Lake

SEE ZONE 11

ZONE 12

Colfax

SCcoteney Reservoir

Snake River

Dayton

Clarkston

Pasco

Columbia River

Walla Walla

Umatilla National Forest

OREGON

IDAHO

STEAMBOAT ROCK STATE PARK
Site 1   on Banks Lake

Campsites, facilities: There are five sites for tents or self-contained motor homes and 100 sites with full hookups for trailers or motor homes of any length. Picnic tables and fire grills are provided. Flush toilets, a cafe and a playground are available. Electricity, piped water, sewer hookups and showers can be obtained for an extra fee. Some facilities are wheelchair accessible. Pets are permitted. Boat launching facilities are nearby.

Reservations, fee: Reservations accepted; $7.50-10.50 fee per night. Open all year with limited winter facilities.

Who to contact: Phone (509)633-1304 or write to P.O. Box 352, Electric City, WA 99123.

Location: Drive eight miles south of Grand Coulee on Highway 155.

Trip note: This state park is set along the shores of Banks Lake, a reservoir a few miles down from the Grand Coulee Dam. There is a swimming beach, and fishing and waterskiing are popular. Horse trails are available in nearby Northrup Canyon. During the winter, the park is used by snowmobilers, cross-country skiers and ice fishermen.

BELLS TRAILER PARK
Site 2   near Grand Coulee Dam

Campsites, facilities: There are two tent sites and ten sites for trailers or motor homes of any length. Electricity, piped water, sewer hookups and picnic tables are provided. Showers, flush toilets, a laundromat and ice are available. Bottled gas, sanitary services, a store and a cafe are located within one mile. Pets and motorbikes are permitted.

Reservations, fee: Reservations accepted; $10 fee per night. Open all year.

Who to contact: Phone (509)647-5888 or write to Route 1, Box 75, Wilbur, WA 99185.

Location: This park is located on the eastern edge of Wilbur on US 2.

Trip note: This private park is in the small town of Wilbur, about 20 miles south of the Grand Coulee Dam. Nearby recreation options include an 18-hole golf course and tennis courts. A good side trip is to take Highway 21 north for 20 minutes to Roosevelt Lake.

WILBUR CAMPGROUND AND MOTEL
Site 3   near Grand Coulee Dam

Campsites, facilities: There are 20 tent sites and 20 sites for trailers or motor homes of any length. Piped water, sewer hookups and picnic tables are provided. Flush toilets, sanitary services, electricity and showers are available. Bottled gas, a store, a cafe, a laundromat and ice are located within one mile. Pets and motorbikes are permitted.

Reservations, fee: Reservations accepted; $7 fee per night. Open mid-March to mid-November.

Who to contact: Phone (509)647-5608 or write to P.O. Box 538, Wilbur, WA 99185.

Location: This park is located on the west side of Wilbur on US 2.

Trip note: The camp is an option to Site 2 and has the same recreational possibilities.

Site 4
BLUE TOP TRAILER PARK
near Banks Lake

Campsites, facilities: There are seven sites for trailers or motor homes of any length. Electricity, piped water and sewer hookups are provided. Bottled gas, sanitary services, a store, a cafe, a laundromat and ice are available within one mile. Pets are permitted. Boat docks and launching facilities are nearby.

Reservations, fee: Reservations accepted; $8 fee per night; MasterCard and Visa accepted. Open all year.

Who to contact: Phone (509)632-5596 or write to P.O. Box 836, Coulee City, WA 99115.

Location: This park is located in Coulee City. Drive there on US 2, then turn south on 4th Street and drive 300 yards to Walnut Street. You'll see the park.

Trip note: This is one of two campgrounds in the immediate area. The other is Site 5. Both are located at the southern end of Banks Lake, near Dry Falls Dam. Nearby recreation options include hiking trails, marked bike trails, a riding stable and tennis courts. Several side trips are possible from here. Dry Falls is four miles southwest, just off Highway 17, where you will find the remnants of a huge, 3.5-mile wide waterfall from the last ice age and an interpretive center that describes its history. Summer Falls State Park, located seven miles south of town, is known for a big set of waterfalls. Another option are the mineral waters at Soap Lake, 26 miles to the south on Highway 17.

Site 5
COULEE CITY PARK
on Banks Lake

Campsites, facilities: There are 75 tent sites and 34 drive-through sites for trailers or motor homes up to 24 feet long. Electricity, piped water, sewer hookups and picnic tables are provided. Flush toilets, sanitary services, showers and a playground are available. Bottled gas, firewood, a store, a cafe, a laundromat and ice are located within one mile. Boat docks and launching facilities are nearby.

Reservations, fee: No reservations necessary; $7 fee per night. Open mid-April to October.

Who to contact: Phone (509)632-5331 or write to P.O. Box 398, Coulee City, WA 99115.

Location: This park is located in Coulee City on US 2.

Trip note: This park is set along the south shore of 30-mile-long Banks Lake, where boating, fishing and waterskiing are popular. Nearby recreation options include an 18-hole golf course. See the trip note for Site 4 for more details on the area.

Site 6
SUN LAKES STATE PARK
on Park Lake

Campsites, facilities: There are 175 sites for tents or self-contained motor homes and 18 sites with full hookups for trailers or motor homes up to 50 feet long. Picnic tables are provided. Flush toilets, sanitary disposal station, a cafe, a laundromat, ice, a swimming pool, electricity, piped water, sewer hookups, showers and firewood are available. A store is located within one mile. Some facilities are wheelchair accessible. Pets are permitted. Boat docks, launching facilities and rentals are nearby.

Reservations, fee: No reservations necessary; $7.50-10.50 fee per night. Open all year.

Who to contact: Phone (509)632-5583 or write to Star Route 1, P.O. Box 136, Coulee City, WA 99115.

Location: Drive seven miles southwest of Coulee City on Highway 17 and you'll find the park.

Trip note: Sun Lakes State Park is set along the shore of Park Lake, which is used primarily by boaters and water-skiers. The Lake Lenore Caves can be reached by a trail at the north end of the lake. Dry Falls and the interpretive center are also within the park boundaries. See the trip note for Site 4 for description of Dry Falls. Nearby recreation options include an 18-hole golf course, hiking trails and a riding stable.

Site 7
SUN LAKES PARK RESORT
SUN LAKES STATE PARK

Campsites, facilities: There are 112 drive-through sites for trailers or motor homes of any length. Electricity, piped water, sewer hookups and picnic tables are provided. Flush toilets, bottled gas, sanitary services, a store, showers, firewood, a cafe, a laundromat, ice, a playground and a swimming pool are available. Pets are permitted. Boat docks, launching facilities and rentals are nearby.

Reservations, fee: Reservations accepted; $12 fee per night; MasterCard and Visa accepted. Open mid-April to November.

Who to contact: Phone (509)632-5291 or write to Star Route 1, P.O. Box 141, Coulee City, WA 99115.

Location: Drive seven miles southwest of Coulee City on Highway 17 and you'll come to the park.

Trip note: This is the concession that operates within Sun Lakes State Park. See the trip note for Site 6.

Site 8
BLUE LAKE RESORT AND RV PARK
on Blue Lake

Campsites, facilities: There are 100 tent sites and 66 drive-through sites for trailers or motor homes of any length. Electricity, piped water, sewer hookups and picnic tables are provided. Flush toilets, bottled gas, sanitary services, firewood, showers, a store, ice and a playground are available. Pets and motorbikes are permitted. Boat docks, launching facilities and rentals are nearby.

Reservations, fee: Reservations accepted; $8-9.30 fee per night. Open April to October.

Who to contact: Phone (509)632-5364 or write to HCR-1, P.O. Box 158, Coulee City, WA 99115.

Location: Drive 11 miles southwest of Coulee City on Highway 17 and you'll come to the park.

Trip note: This park is set along the shore of Blue Lake between Sun Lakes State Park and Lake Lenore Caves State Park. See the trip note for Site 6.

Site 9
LAURENT'S SUN VILLAGE RESORT
on Blue Lake

Campsites, facilities: There are six tent sites and 105 drive-through sites for trailers or motor homes of any length. Electricity, piped water, sewer hookups and picnic tables are provided. Flush toilets, bottled gas, sanitary services, a store, a cafe, a laundromat, ice and a playground are available. Showers and firewood can be obtained for an extra fee. Pets and motorbikes are permitted. Boat docks, launching facilities and rentals are nearby.

Reservations, fee: Reservations accepted; $10 fee per night; MasterCard and Visa accepted. Open mid-April to October.

Who to contact: Phone (509)632-5664 or write to Star Route 1, P.O. Box 151, Coulee City, WA 99115.

Location: Drive ten miles southwest of Coulee City on Highway 17 to Blue Lake. Head east for one-half mile. The resort is at the north end of the lake.

Trip note: Like Site 8, this campground is set along the shore of Blue Lake. See the trip note for Site 6 for information on the nearby state parks and other recreation options.

Site 10　　COULEE LODGE RESORT
on Blue Lake

Campsites, facilities: There are 14 tent sites and 30 drive-through sites for trailers or motor homes of any length. Electricity, piped water, sewer hookups and picnic tables are provided. Flush toilets, bottled gas, sanitary services, a store, showers, firewood, a laundromat and ice are available. A cafe is located within one mile. Some facilities are wheelchair accessible. Pets and motorbikes are permitted. Boat docks, launching facilities and rentals are nearby.

Reservations, fee: Reservations accepted; $8.50-10 fee per night; MasterCard and Visa accepted. Open mid-April to October.

Who to contact: Phone (509)632-5565 or write to HCR-1, P.O. Box 156, Coulee City, WA 99115.

Location: Drive eight miles south of Coulee City on Highway 17 to Blue Lake. The resort is at the north end of the lake.

Trip note: This is one of five camps in the general area and one of three in the immediate vicinity. See the trip note for Site 6 for details.

Site 11　　SMOKIAM RV PARK
on Soap Lake

Campsites, facilities: There are 20 tent sites and 50 drive-through sites for trailers or motor homes. Electricity, piped water, sewer hookups and picnic tables are provided. Flush toilets, sanitary services and showers are available. Bottled gas, a store, a cafe, a laundromat and ice are located within one mile. Pets and motorbikes are permitted.

Reservations, fee: Reservations accepted; $7 fee per night. Open March to early November.

Who to contact: Phone (509)246-1366 or write to P.O. Box 591, Soap Lake, WA 98851.

Location: Drive 25 miles southwest of Coulee City on Highway 17 to the town of Soap Lake. The park is at the north end of town.

Trip note: "Smokiam" is the Indian word for "healing waters" and is the name the Indians gave to what is now called Soap Lake. Nearby recreation options include hot mineral baths, an 18-hole golf course, hiking trails, marked bike trails and tennis courts.

Site 12　　OASIS PARK
near Soap Lake

Campsites, facilities: There are 38 tent sites and 66 drive-through sites for trailers or motor homes of any length. Picnic tables are provided. Flush toilets, golf course, bottled gas, sanitary services, a store, propane gas, a laundromat, ice and a swimming pool. A fishing pond for children is available. Electricity, piped water, sewer hookups and showers can be obtained for a 25 cent fee. A cafe is located within one mile. Pets and motorbikes are permitted.

Reservations, fee: Reservations accepted; $7-10.50 fee per night; MasterCard and Visa accepted. Open all year.

Who to contact: Phone (509)754-5102 or write to 2541 Basin SW, Ephrata, WA 98823.

Location: This park is located 1.5 miles south of Ephrata on Highway 28.

Trip note: This can be a warm, arid area in the summer, but fortunately, this park offers shaded sites. There are two fishing ponds: one has bass and crappie, while the other is for kids. Nearby recreation options include an 18-hole golf course. See the trip note for Site 11 for information on mineral baths seven miles north of this park.

Site 13   COTTAGE MOTEL AND TRAILER PARK
in Ritzville

Campsites, facilities: There are 26 drive-through sites for trailers or motor homes of any length. Electricity, piped water and sewer hookups are provided. Flush toilets, sanitary services and showers are available. Bottled gas, a store, a cafe, a laundromat and ice are located within one mile. Pets and motorbikes are permitted.

Reservations, fee: Reservations accepted; $10 fee per night. Open all year.

Who to contact: Phone (509)659-0721 or write to 508 East First, Ritzville, WA 99169.

Location: Drive on Interstate 90 to Ritzville. Take exit 220 and drive to 508 East First Street on the eastern edge of town.

Trip note: This is one of two parks in Ritzville, which is set in the middle of the Washington plains country. The other is Site 14. This park is 56 miles from Spokane. Nearby recreation options include an 18-hole golf course.

Site 14   COMFORT INN MOTEL AND RV PARK
in Ritzville

Campsites, facilities: There are 30 plus drive-through sites for tents, trailers or motor homes of any length. Electricity, piped water, sewer hookups and picnic tables are provided. Flush toilets, sanitary services, showers, a laundromat, ice, a playground and a swimming pool are available. Bottled gas, a store and a cafe are located within one mile. Pets and motorbikes are permitted.

Reservations, fee: Reservations accepted; $8-13 fee per night; American Express, MasterCard and Visa accepted. Open March to late October.

Who to contact: Phone (509)659-1007 or write to 1405 Smitty's Boulevard, Ritzville, WA 99169.

Location: Drive on Interstate 90 to Ritzville. Take exit 221 and you'll see the motel one-half block off the freeway.

Trip note: If all you have is a tent, well, this is the only site within a radius of 25 miles. The nearest fishing is at Sprague Lake, 30 miles north on Highway 395. Burroughs Historical Museum is a possible side trip in town. Nearby recreation options include an 18-hole golf course and tennis courts.

Site 15
BOB LEE CAMPGROUND
on Sprague Lake

Campsites, facilities: There are 25 tent sites and 30 drive-through sites for trailers or motor homes. Electricity, piped water, sewer hookups and picnic tables are provided. Flush toilets, sanitary services, showers, firewood, ice, a playground and a swimming pool are available. Pets and motorbikes are permitted. Boat docks, launching facilities and rentals are nearby.

Reservations, fee: Reservations accepted; $9 fee per night. Open mid-April to October.

Who to contact: Phone (509)257-2332 or write to Route 1, Box 41, Sprague, WA 99032.

Location: Take exit 231 off Interstate 90 in Sprague. Head east on Keystone and follow the signs to the campground.

Trip note: This campground is set along the shore of Sprague Lake. The fishing is best in May and June for rainbow trout, with some bass in spring and fall. Because there is an abundance of natural feed in the lake, the fish reach larger sizes here than in neighboring lakes. In late July through August, a fair algae bloom is a turnoff for swimmers and water-skiers.

Site 16
SPRAGUE LAKE RESORT
on Sprague Lake

Campsites, facilities: There are 50 tent sites and 30 drive-through sites for trailers or motor homes of any length. Electricity, piped water, sewer hookups and picnic tables are provided. Flush toilets, sanitary services, a store, a laundromat, showers, ice and a playground are available. Pets are permitted. Boat docks, launching facilities and rentals are nearby.

Reservations, fee: Reservations accepted; $10-13 fee per night. Open April to mid-October.

Who to contact: Phone (509)257-2864 or write to Route 1, Box 5, Sprague, WA 99032.

Location: Get off Interstate 90 at the Sprague business center exit. Follow the signs and drive two miles to the resort.

Trip note: This campground is set along the shore of Sprague Lake, about 35 miles from Spokane. See the trip note for Site 15.

Site 17
LAST ROUNDUP MOTEL AND RV PARK
near Sprague Lake

Campsites, facilities: There are 15 tent sites and 15 drive-through sites for trailers or motor homes. Electricity, piped water, sewer hookups and picnic tables are provided. Flush toilets, showers, a laundromat and ice are available. Bottled gas, sanitary services, a store and a cafe are located within one mile. Pets and motorbikes are permitted.

Reservations, fee: Reservations accepted; $8-11 fee per night; MasterCard and Visa accepted. Open April to November.

Who to contact: Phone (509)257-2583 or write to Route 1, Box C-1, Sprague, WA 99032.

Location: Take exit 245 off Interstate 90 in Sprague and drive one-half mile south on Highway 23.

Trip note: The camp is set just on the outskirts of Sprague. The best game in town is at nearby Sprague Lake. See the trip note for Site 15.

Site 18
PEACEFUL PINES CAMPGROUND
near Turnbull National Wildlife Refuge

Campsites, facilities: There are 20 tent sites and 18 sites for trailers or motor homes of any length. Electricity, piped water, sewer hookups and picnic tables are provided. Flush toilets, sanitary services and showers are available. A store, a cafe, a laundromat and ice are located within one mile. Pets and motorbikes are permitted.

Reservations, fee: Reservations accepted; $8.50-10.50 fee per night. Open all year.

Who to contact: Phone (509)235-4966 or write to West 13314-SR904, Cheney, WA 99004.

Location: Drive 17 miles southwest of Spokane on Interstate 90. Take the Highway 904 exit to Cheney. Drive one mile southwest of Cheney on Highway 904 and you'll see the campground.

Trip note: This campground is a short distance from Turnbull National Wildlife Refuge, an expanse of marsh and pine that is a significant stopover point for migratory birds on the Pacific Flyway. You can pick up a map and bird checklist at the refuge headquarters. This prime spot is only a 45-minute drive out of Spokane, yet relatively few know of it.

Site 19
WILLIAMS LAKE RESORT
on Williams Lake

Campsites, facilities: There are 15 tent sites and 60 sites for trailers or motor homes of any length. Electricity, piped water and picnic tables are provided. Flush toilets, bottled gas, sanitary services, firewood, a store, a cafe, a restaurant, showers, ice and a playground are available. Pets and motorbikes are permitted. Boat docks, launching facilities and rentals are available.

Reservations, fee: Reservations accepted; $10-12 fee per night. Open mid-April to October.

Who to contact: Phone (509)235-2391 or write to West 18617 Williams Lake Road, Cheney, WA 99004.

Location: Drive 11.5 miles south of Cheney on Cheney Lake Road, then head north on Williams Lake Road and drive 3.5 miles to the campground.

Trip note: This resort is set along the shore of Williams Lake. The lake is just under three miles long and is popular for swimming and waterskiing. It is also one of the top fishing lakes in the region for rainbow and cutthroat trout. The lake is bordered in some areas by rocky cliffs. See the trip note for Site 18 for information on nearby Turnbull National Wildlife Refuge.

Site 20
LEWIS BROTHERS RESORT
on Williams Lake

Campsites, facilities: There are 25 tent sites and 62 sites for trailers or motor homes of any length. Electricity, piped water, sewer hookups and picnic tables are provided. Flush toilets, bottled gas, sanitary services, a store, a cafe, showers, a laundromat, ice and a playground are available. Pets and motorbikes are permitted. Boat docks, launching facilities and rentals are nearby.

Reservations, fee: Reservations accepted; $8 fee per night. Open mid-April to late September.

Who to contact: Phone (509)235-4144 or write to Route 3, Box 330, Cheney, WA 99004.

Location: Drive 12 miles south of Cheney on Williams Lake Road and follow the signs to the resort.

Trip note: This resort is set along the shore of Williams Lake and is a more developed option to Site 19.

Site **21**
BUNKERS RESORT
on Williams Lake

Campsites, facilities: There are 35 drive-through sites for trailers or motor homes of any length. Electricity, piped water and picnic tables are provided. Flush toilets, bottled gas, sanitary services, recreation hall, cabins, a restaurant, a store, a cafe and ice are available. Pets are permitted. Boat docks, fishing docks, launching facilities and rentals are nearby.

Reservations, fee: Reservations accepted; $12 fee per night; MasterCard and Visa accepted. Open mid-April to October.

Who to contact: Phone (509)235-5212 or write to S36402 Bunker Landing Road, Cheney, WA 99004.

Location: Drive 14 miles south of Cheney and follow the signs to the resort.

Trip note: This campground is set along the shore of Williams Lake. See the trip note for Site 19 for information on the lake and trip note for Site 18 for information on nearby Turnbull National Wildlife Refuge.

Site **22**
NOBLE'S MOBILE HOME PARK
near Snake River

Campsites, facilities: There are ten sites for trailers or motor homes of any length. Electricity, piped water and sewer hookups are provided. Sanitary services and a laundromat are available. Bottled gas, a store, a cafe and ice are located within one mile. Pets are permitted. Boat docks, launching facilities and rentals are nearby.

Reservations, fee: Reservations accepted; $5 fee per night. Open all year.

Who to contact: Phone (509)758-7031 or write to 1432 Tenth Street, Clarkston, WA 99403.

Location: Drive one mile south of US 12 in Clarkston to 10th Street. The park is at 1432 10th Street.

Trip note: This camp is set just inside the Washington state border. Nearby recreation options include swimming, fishing and boating on the Snake River. There is also an 18-hole golf course and tennis courts. There are outfitters in Clarkston that will take you sightseeing up the Grand Canyon of the Snake River. Call the Chamber of Commerce at (509)758-7712 for details.

Site **23**
CHIEF TIMOTHY STATE PARK
on Snake River

Campsites, facilities: There are 33 sites for tents or self-contained motor homes and 33 sites with water and electrical hookups for trailers or motor homes of any length. Picnic tables and fire grills are provided. Flush toilets, sanitary services and a playground are available. Electricity, piped water, sewer hookups, showers and firewood can be obtained for an extra fee. Some facilities are wheelchair accessible. Pets are permitted. Boat docks and launching facilities are nearby.

Reservations, fee: No reservations necessary; $7.50-9.75 fee per night. Open all year.

Who to contact: Phone (509)758-9580 or write to Highway 12, Clarkston, WA 99403.

Location: Drive eight miles southwest of Clarkston on US 12 to the park.

Trip note: This unique state park is set on a bridged island in the Snake River. It offers all water sports, docks for boating campers, a beach area and an interpretive center. It is one of three camps within a 30-mile radius.

Site **24**   **FIELDS SPRING STATE PARK**
                         near Puffer Butte

Campsites, facilities: There are 20 sites for tents or self-contained trailers or motor homes up to 30 feet long. Piped water, picnic tables and fire grills are provided. Flush toilets, a sanitary disposal station and a playground are available. Showers and firewood can be obtained for an extra fee. A store, a restaurant and ice are located within one mile. Some facilities are wheelchair accessible. Pets are permitted.

Reservations, fee: No reservations necessary; $7.50 fee per night. Open all year.

Who to contact: Phone (509)256-3332 or write to Box 86, Anatone, WA 99401.

Location: Drive 4.5 miles south of Anatone on Highway 129.

Trip note: Just about nobody knows about this spot, and it's a good one, tucked away in the southeast corner of the state. This park is noted for its variety of bird life and wildflowers. A hiking trail leads up to Puffer Butte at 4,500 feet elevation, which offers a panoramic view of the Snake River Canyon, the Wallowa Mountains and Idaho, Oregon and Washington. Two day-use areas with boat launches, managed by the Department of Fish and Game, are within about 25 miles of the park. One is called the Snake River Access, 22.5 miles south of Asotin on Snake River Road; the other is the Grand Ronde River Access, 24 miles south of Asotin on the same road. During the winter, this state park is open for snowmobiling and cross-country skiing.

Site **25**   **WICKIUP**
                    UMATILLA NATIONAL FOREST

Campsites, facilities: There are five sites for tents, trailers or motor homes up to 15 feet long. Picnic tables and fire grills are provided. Pit toilets are available, but there is **no piped water.** A cold water spring is available 100 yards from the campground. Leashed pets are permitted.

Reservations, fee: No reservations necessary; $2 fee per night. Open mid-June to late October.

Who to contact: Phone Umatilla National Forest at (509)843-1891 or write to Umatilla Ranger Station, Asotin, WA 99402.

Location: From Pomeroy, follow County Road 128 to the "Y." Continue straight on to Forest Road 40. At Troy Junction, about 17 miles, follow Road 44 for three miles. Wickiup is at the intersection of Roads 44 and 43. From Asotin, take road leading west through Cloverland and onto Forest Road 43. Continue to the intersection at Road 44, where the camp is located.

Trip note: This is a primitive Forest Service campground that gets very little camping pressure. It is a good jump-off for summer backpacking trips or a fall hunting trip. A Forest Service map details backcountry roads and trails.

Site **26**   **GODMAN**
                 near Wenaha-Tucannon Wilderness
                    UMATILLA NATIONAL FOREST

Campsites, facilities: There are eight sites for tents, trailers or motor homes up to 15 feet long. Picnic tables and fire grills are provided. Pit toilets and firewood

are available, but there is **no piped water.** Leashed pets are permitted. Facilities
are available for horses, including hitching rails, feed mangers and a spring.

Reservations, fee: No reservations necessary; no fee. Open mid-June to late October.

Who to contact: Phone Umatilla National Forest at (509)843-1891 or write to
Umatilla Ranger Station, Asotin, WA 99402.

Location: Drive 14 miles southeast of Dayton on County Road 118, then head south
on Forest Service Road 46 (Kendall Skyline Road) for 11 miles to the
campground.

Trip note: This tiny, little-known spot borders a wilderness area. There are several
trails nearby that provide access to the Wenaha-Tucannon Wilderness for hikers
and horseback riders. In the winter the trails and roads are used for
snowmobiling.

Site **27**   **ALDER THICKET**
UMATILLA NATIONAL FOREST

Campsites, facilities: There are six sites for tents, trailers or motor homes up to 15
feet long. Picnic tables and fire grills are provided. Pit toilets and firewood are
available, but there is **no piped water.** Pets are permitted.

Reservations, fee: No reservations necessary; no fee. Open mid-May to
mid-November.

Who to contact: Phone Umatilla National Forest at (509)843-1891 or write to
Umatilla Ranger Station, Pomeroy, WA 99347.

Location: Drive nine miles south of Pomeroy on Highway 128, then head south on
County Road 107 and drive eight miles. Turn south on Forest Service Road 40
and drive 3.5 miles to the campground.

Trip note: This is probably the first time you've heard of this spot. Hardly anybody
knows about it, including people who live relatively nearby in Walla Walla. It
is a prime base camp for a backcountry hiking adventure in summer or a
jump-off point for a hunting trip in the fall. A National Forest map details the
possibilities.

Site **28**   **TEAL**
UMATILLA NATIONAL FOREST

Campsites, facilities: There are ten sites for tents, trailers or motor homes up to 15
feet long. **No piped water** is available. Picnic tables and fire grills are provided.
Vault toilets and firewood are available. Leashed pets are permitted.

Reservations, fee: No reservations necessary; $2 fee per night. Open June to
mid-November.

Who to contact: Phone Umatilla National Forest at (509)843-1891 or write to
Umatilla Ranger Station, Pomeroy, WA 99347.

Location: Drive ten miles south of Pomeroy on Highway 128. At the "Y," continue
straight to mountain Road 40 and enter the National Forest boundary. Drive
nine miles to the Clearwater lookout tower; the campground turnoff is about a
half-mile past the tower.

Trip note: This is one of several small, primitive camps in the area. It has piped
water, a valuable asset. A National Forest map details the backcountry roads,
trails and streams.

Site **29**   **BIG SPRINGS**
UMATILLA NATIONAL FOREST

Campsites, facilities: There are 15 tent sites. Picnic tables are provided. Pit toilets and firewood are available, but there is **no piped water.** Leashed pets are permitted.

Reservations, fee: No reservations necessary; no fee. Open mid-May to mid-November.

Who to contact: Phone Umatilla National Forest at (509)843-1891 or write to Umatilla Ranger Station, Pomeroy, WA 99347.

Location: From Pomeroy, drive ten miles southeast on Highway 128 to the "Y," then continue straight to mountain Road 40. Pass the National Forest boundary and continue nine miles to the Clearwater lookout tower. Turn left on Road 42 and continue for three miles, then turn left on Road 4225 to the campground. From Clarkson, drive on County Road 128 for 20 miles, then turn left on Iron Springs Road (County Road 42). Continue for about five miles, turning right on Forest Service Road 4225 to the campground.

Trip note: This is a more primitive, remote option to Site 28. In the fall, it is used primarily by hunters. In the summer, it is a possible base camp for a backpacking trip. It's advisable to obtain a Forest Service map of the area. This is a nice, cool spot in the summer.

Site **30**   **TUCANNON**
UMATILLA NATIONAL FOREST

Campsites, facilities: There are 13 sites for tents, trailers or motor homes up to 15 feet long. Picnic tables and fire grills are provided. Pit toilets and firewood are available, but there is **no piped water.** Pets are permitted.

Reservations, fee: No reservations necessary; no fee. Open May to late November.

Who to contact: Phone Umatilla National Forest at (509)843-1891 or write to Umatilla Ranger Station, Pomeroy, WA 99347.

Location: Drive 17 miles southwest of Pomeroy on County Road 101, then head southwest on Forest Service Road 47 for four miles. Turn south on Forest Service Road 160 and drive 200 yards to the campground.

Trip note: For people willing to rough it, this backcountry camp in Umatilla National Forest is the place. There is plenty of hiking, fishing and hunting all in a rugged setting.

Site **31**   **CENTRAL FERRY STATE PARK**
on Snake River

Campsites, facilities: There are 60 sites with full hookups for trailers or motor homes up to 45 feet long. Picnic tables and fire grills are provided. Flush toilets, a sanitary service station, a store, restaurant, electricity, piped water, sewer hookups, showers and firewood are available. Some facilities are wheelchair accessible. Pets are permitted. Boat docks, launching facilities and a fishing pier are nearby.

Reservations, fee: No reservations necessary; $10.50 fee per night. Open all year.

Who to contact: Phone (509)549-3551 or write to Route 3, Box 99, Pomeroy, WA 99347.

Location: This park is reached by driving 34 miles southwest of Colfax on Highways 26 and 127.

Trip note: This is the only campground within a 20-mile radius. It is set along the shore of the Snake River and has a beach. Waterskiing, boating, swimming and fishing for bass and catfish are all options here.

Site 32
LYON'S FERRY STATE PARK
on Snake River

Campsites, facilities: There are 52 sites for tents, self-contained trailers or motor homes. Picnic tables and fire grills are provided. Flush toilets, sanitary services, showers and firewood are available. Some facilities are wheelchair accessible. Pets are permitted. Boat docks and launching facilities are nearby.

Reservations, fee: No reservations necessary; $7.50 fee per night. Open April to late September.

Who to contact: Phone (509)646-3252 or write to P.O. Box 217, Starbuck, WA 99359.

Location: This park is reached by driving 39 miles west of Pomeroy on US 12 and Highway 261.

Trip note: This state park is set at the confluence of the Snake and Palouse Rivers. Fishing, hiking, swimming, waterskiing and boating are all options here. A riding stable is nearby.

Site 33
LYONS FERRY MARINA
on Snake River

Campsites, facilities: There are 40 tent sites and 18 sites for trailers or motor homes of any length. Picnic tables are provided. Flush toilets, showers, a store, a cafe, a laundromat, ice, electricity, piped water and sewer hookups are available. Sanitary services are available within one mile. Pets are permitted. Boat docks and launching facilities are nearby.

Reservations, fee: No reservations necessary; $7.50-10 fee per night. Open all year with limited winter facilities.

Who to contact: Phone the Army Corps of Engineers at (509)399-2387 or write to P.O. Box 387, Starbuck, WA 99359.

Location: This park and marina is reached by driving 37 miles west of Pomeroy on US 12 and Highway 261 or 33 miles north of Dayton on US 12 and Highway 261.

Trip note: The highlight here is eight miles of shoreline access to the Snake River. Unique elements include a 200-foot gorge, basalt bluffs and lava terraces.

Site 34
PALOUSE FALLS STATE PARK
on Snake and Palouse Rivers

Campsites, facilities: There are ten primitive campsites for tents, self-contained trailers or motor homes up to 40 feet long. Picnic tables and fire grills are provided. Pit toilets are available.

Reservations, fee: No reservations necessary; $3.50-5 fee per night. Open April to late September.

Who to contact: Phone (509)646-3252 or write to Route 3, P.O. Box 99, Pomeroy WA 99347.

Location: This park is reached by driving 45 miles west of Pomeroy on US 12 and Highway 261.

Trip note: This state park is set at the confluence of the Snake and Palouse Rivers, just enough off the beaten path to be missed by many. Spectacular 190-foot Palouse Falls is worth the trip. A riding stable is nearby.

Site 35
WINDUST
on Sacajawea Lake

Campsites, facilities: There are ten primitive tent sites and ten sites for trailers or motor homes. Picnic tables and fire grills are provided. Flush toilets and a playground are available. Pets and motorbikes are permitted. Boat docks and launching facilities are nearby.

Reservations, fee: No reservations necessary; no fee. Open all year.

Who to contact: Phone the Army Corps of Engineers at (509)399-2387 or write to P.O. Box 387, Starbuck, WA 99359.

Location: Drive 30 miles northeast of Pasco on Pasco-Kahlotus Road, then head south on Burr Canyon Road for five miles to the campground.

Trip note: This is the only game in town, with no other campgrounds within a 20-mile radius. This campground is set along the shore of Sacajawea Lake near the Lower Monumental Dam on the Snake River. Swimming and fishing are popular.

Site 36
LEWIS AND CLARK TRAIL STATE PARK
on Lewis and Clark Trail

Campsites, facilities: There are 30 sites for tents or self-enclosed trailers or motor homes up to 28 feet long. Picnic tables and fire grills are provided. Flush toilets, showers, firewood and sanitary services are available. A store, a cafe and ice are located within one mile. Pets are permitted.

Reservations, fee: No reservations necessary; $7.50 fee per night. Open all year.

Who to contact: Phone (509)337-6457 or write to Route 1, P.O. Box 90, Dayton, WA 99328.

Location: Drive five miles west of Dayton on US 12 and you'll see the park entrance.

Trip note: If it's getting late and you need a spot, you'd better pick this one. There are no other campgrounds within 20 miles. It is not a bad choice, since it's set along the original Lewis and Clark Trail. During the summer, the rangers offer campfire programs where they share the details of this site's history.

Site 37
FISHHOOK PARK
on Snake River

Campsites, facilities: There are 35 tent sites and 41 drive-through sites for trailers or motor homes of any length. Picnic tables and fire grills are provided. Flush toilets, sanitary services, showers and a playground are available. Some facilities are wheelchair accessible. Pets are permitted. Boat docks and launching facilities are nearby.

Reservations, fee: No reservations necessary; $7 fee per night. Open April to late September.

Who to contact: Phone the Army Corps of Engineers at (509)547-7781 or write to P.O. Box 2427, Tri-Cities, WA 99302.

Location: Drive four miles southeast of Pasco on US 395, then go 15 miles northeast on Highway 124. Turn northwest on Page Road and drive four miles to the park.

Trip note: If you are driving along Highway 124 and you need a spot for the night, make the turn on Page Road and check out this park. It is set along the Snake River and has a beach. Fishing, swimming and waterskiing are all options here.

Site 38
CHARBONNEAU PARK
on Snake River

Campsites, facilities: There are 69 drive-through sites for tents, trailers or motor homes of any length. Picnic tables and fire grills are provided. Flush toilets, sanitary services, showers, a playground, electricity, piped water and sewer hookups are available. Some facilities are wheelchair accessible. Pets are permitted. Boat docks, launching facilities and a marine dump station are nearby.

Reservations, fee: No reservations necessary; $8 fee per night. Open all year.

Who to contact: Phone the Army Corps of Engineers at (509)547-7781 or write to P.O. Box 2427, Tri-Cities, WA 99302.

Location: Drive four miles southeast of Pasco on US 395, then go eight miles northeast on Highway 124. Turn north on Sun Harbor Road and drive two miles to the park.

Trip note: This campground is set along the shore of the Snake River, just below Ice Harbor Dam. It has a good swimming beach. Fishing, hunting, swimming and waterskiing are options here.

Site 39
SCOOTENEY PARK
on Scooteney Reservoir

Campsites, facilities: There are 21 drive-through sites for trailers or motor homes of any length. Picnic tables are provided. Flush toilets, showers and a playground are available. Pets are permitted. Boat docks and launching facilities are nearby.

Reservations, fee: No reservations necessary; $2 fee per night. Open April to November.

Who to contact: Phone (509)545-3514 or write to Courthouse, Pasco, WA 99301.

Location: Drive 24 miles north of Pasco on US 395 to Mesa, then go north on Highway 17 for seven miles to the park.

Trip note: This county park is set along the shore of the Scooteney Reservoir, a waterskiing and swimming lake. There are no other campgrounds in the area.

Site 40
McNARY HABITAT MANAGEMENT AREA
near Columbia River

Campsites, facilities: There are 24 primitive sites for tents, trailers or motor homes. No piped water is available. Boat launching facilities are nearby.

Reservations, fee: No reservations necessary; no fee. Open all year.

Who to contact: Phone Department of Fish and Game at (509)456-4082 or write to North 8702 Division Street, Spokane, WA 99218.

Location: Drive ten miles southeast of Pasco on US 395. The area is located between the Snake and the Walla Walla Rivers.

Trip note: This premium spot is only a ten-minute drive from Pasco. This area adjoins the McNary National Wildlife Refuge, accessible by foot or horseback. Seven miles of stream frontage along the Columbia River is accessible. Fishing on the adjacent wildlife refuge is good for bass, bluegill, bullhead and carp. Some hunting is allowed in season.

Site 41
HOOD PARK
on Columbia River

Campsites, facilities: There are 69 drive-through sites for tents, trailers or motor homes of any length. Piped water, fire grills and picnic tables are provided. Flush toilets, sanitary services, showers, electricity and a playground are available. A cafe is available within one mile. Some facilities are wheelchair accessible. Pets are permitted. Boat docks and launching facilities are nearby.

Reservations, fee: No reservations necessary; $8 fee per night. Open April to late October.

Who to contact: Phone the Army Corps of Engineers at (509)547-7781 or write to P.O. Box 2427, Tri-Cities, WA 99302.

Location: Drive four miles southeast of Pasco on US 395, then head northeast.

Trip note: A more developed, nearby alternative to Site 44, this park also has beach access for swimming and river access for waterskiing. Other recreation options include volleyball and horseshoes. McNary Wildlife Refuge and Sacajawea State Park are nearby.

Site 42   GREENTREE RV PARK
in Pasco

Campsites, facilities: There are 70 sites for trailers or motor homes of any length. Electricity, piped water and sewer hookups are provided. A laundromat and showers are available. Bottled gas, a store, a cafe and ice are located within one mile. Pets and motorbikes are permitted. Boat docks, launching facilities and rentals are nearby.

Reservations, fee: Reservations accepted; $12 fee per night. Open all year.

Who to contact: Phone (509)547-6220 or write to 2103 North Fifth Avenue #69, Pasco, WA 99301.

Location: This park is located in Pasco. Take exit 13 off Interstate 182 and you'll see it on the southwest corner.

Trip note: This park is in urban Pasco. Nearby recreation options include an 18-hole golf course, hiking trails, a full-service marina and tennis courts. The Franklin County Historical Museum, which is located in town, and the Sacajawea State Park Museum and Interpretive Center, located three miles southeast of town, both offer extensive collections of Indian artifacts.

Site 43   ARROWHEAD RV PARK
near Columbia River

Campsites, facilities: There are 20 tent sites and 70 drive-through sites for trailers or motor homes of any length. Electricity, piped water, sewer hookups and picnic tables are provided. Flush toilets, showers, a laundromat and ice are available. A store and a cafe are located within one mile. Pets and motorbikes are permitted.

Reservations, fee: Reservations accepted; $13 fee per night. Open all year.

Who to contact: Phone (509)545-8206 or write to 3120 Commercial, Pasco, WA 99301.

Location: This park is located on the eastern edge of Pasco at 3120 Commercial Street.

Trip note: This is an okay layover spot in Pasco. See the trip note for Site 42 for information on Pasco. Nearby recreation options include an 18-hole golf course, a full-service marina and tennis courts.

Site 44   COLUMBIA PARK CAMPGROUND
on Columbia River

Campsites, facilities: There are 22 tent sites and 18 drive-through sites for trailers

or motor homes. Electricity, piped water and picnic tables are provided. Flush toilets, sanitary services, ice and a playground are available. Showers and firewood can be obtained for an extra fee. A store and a cafe are located within one mile. Pets and motorbikes are permitted. Boat docks and launching facilities are nearby.

Reservations, fee: Reservations accepted; $8 fee per night. Open mid-April to mid-October.

Who to contact: Phone (509)783-3711 or write to 6601 SE Columbia, Richland, WA 99352.

Location: This campground is located between Richland and Kennewick. Take the Columbia Center exit north off US 12 and drive one mile east to the campground.

Trip note: The campground is set on the Columbia River, adjacent to Columbia Park. Nearby recreation options include waterskiing on the Columbia River, an 18-hole golf course, hiking trails, marked bike trails and tennis courts. The sun can feel like a branding iron during the summer out here.

Site **45**   **DESERT GOLD RV PARK**
near Columbia River

Campsites, facilities: There are 84 sites (30 drive-through) for trailers or motor homes of any length in this adult-only campground. Electricity, piped water, sewer hookups and picnic tables are provided. Flush toilets, showers, rest rooms, showers, sanitary services, a store, a laundromat, ice and a swimming pool are available. Bottled gas and a cafe are located within one mile. Pets are permitted. Boat docks and launching facilities are nearby on the Columbia River.

Reservations, fee: Reservations accepted; $13.50 fee per night; American Express, MasterCard and Visa accepted. Open all year with limited winter facilities.

Who to contact: Phone (509)627-1000 or write to 611 SE Columbia Drive, Richland, WA 99352.

Location: This park is located in Richland. Take Columbia Drive west for one-quarter mile to 611 Columbia Drive SE.

Trip note: This is a nice motor home park set about a mile from the Columbia River. Nearby recreation options include an 18-hole golf course, hiking trails, a full-service marina, tennis courts or a visit to the Department of Energy public information center at the Hanford Science Center.

Site **46**   **TRAILER CITY PARK**
near Columbia River

Campsites, facilities: There are 100 plus sites for trailers or motor homes of any length. Electricity, piped water and sewer hookups are provided. A laundromat and a swimming pool are available. Bottled gas, a store, a cafe and ice are located within one mile. Boat docks and launching facilities are nearby.

Reservations, fee: Reservations accepted; $10 fee per night. Open all year.

Who to contact: Phone (509)783-2513 or write to 7120 W Bonnie, Kennewick, WA 99336.

Location: This park is located in Kennewick. Take the Columbia Center Boulevard exit off US 12 and go south, following the signs.

Trip note: This urban park is near a number of recreation options including an 18-hole golf course, a state park and museum (see the trip note for Site 42), a wildlife refuge (Site 40) and a full-service marina.

Site 47
RIVIERA TRAILER VILLAGE
near Columbia River

Campsites, facilities: There are six sites for trailers or motor homes of any length. Electricity, piped water and sewer hookups are provided. Flush toilets, showers, a recreation hall, a laundromat and a swimming pool are available. Bottled gas, a store, a cafe and ice are located within one mile. Pets are permitted. Boat docks and launching facilities are nearby.

Reservations, fee: Reservations accepted; $6.50 fee per night. Open all year.

Who to contact: Phone (509)547-3521 or write to Lot 90 Riviera, Pasco, WA 99301.

Location: Take the Court Street exit off US 395 in Pasco, turn left on Road 34 and drive to the park.

Trip note: This small motor home park is located just one-half mile from the Columbia River and provides easy access to the highway. See the trip note for Site 42 for information on some of the sights in Pasco. Nearby recreation options include an 18-hole golf course, marked bike trails, a full-service marina and tennis courts.

Site 48
BEACH RV PARK
on Yakima River

Campsites, facilities: There are six tent sites and 38 drive-through sites for trailers or motor homes of any length. Electricity, piped water, sewer hookups and picnic tables are provided. Flush toilets, showers, a laundromat and ice are available. Bottled gas, sanitary services, a store and a cafe are located within one mile. Pets and motorbikes are permitted. Boat launching facilities are nearby.

Reservations, fee: Reservations accepted; $8 tent fee; call ahead for motor home fees. Open all year.

Who to contact: Phone (509)588-5959 or write to Route 2, Box 2094 C, Benton City, WA 99320.

Location: Take the Benton City exit off Interstate 82 and drive one block north, then turn west on Abby Street to the park at 113 Abby Street.

Trip note: If you are heading west on Interstate 182 and it is getting late, you'd best stop here. There is nowhere else to stop for a long stretch. This park is set along the shore of the Yakima River. Nearby recreation options include an 18-hole golf course, a full-service marina and tennis courts.

GUIDE TO THE
OREGON
CAMPING AREAS

TILLAMOOK

◆

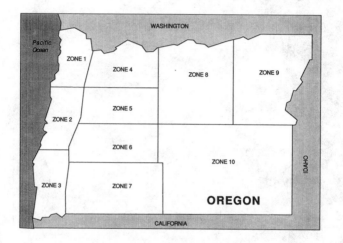

SOME HIGHLIGHTS

37 CAMPGROUNDS

Fort Stevens State Park

Columbia River

Saddle Mountain

Tillamook Bay

Netarts Bay

Siuslaw National Forest

Fogerty Creek State Park

Cape Meares State Park

Cape Kiwanda State Park

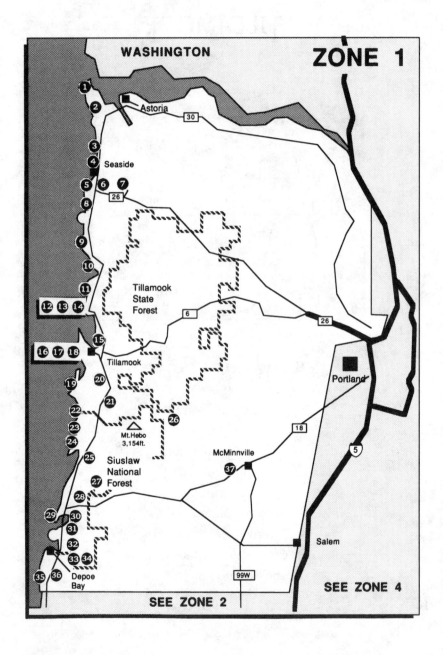

Site **1**   **FORT STEVENS STATE PARK**
                    at the mouth of Columbia River

Campsites, facilities: There are 262 tent sites, 343 sites with full or partial hookups
for trailers or motor homes of any length and a special camping area for hikers
and bicyclists. Picnic tables and fire grills are provided. Flush toilets, sanitary
disposal station, showers, firewood, a laundromat and a playground are
available. Some facilities are wheelchair accessible. Leashed pets are
permitted. Boat docks and launching facilities are nearby.

Reservations, fee: Reservations accepted; $9-11 fee per night in summer season,
$6-8 off-season. Open all year.

Who to contact: Phone (503)861-1671 or write to Hammond, OR 97121.

Location: From Astoria, cross the Klaskanine River west on Highway 30. Take the
Hammond exit and drive four miles to the park.

Trip note: This is a classic spot, set at the northern tip of Oregon, right where the
Columbia River enters the Pacific Ocean. This large state park offers five miles
of ocean frontage, three miles of Columbia River frontage and several small
lakes. Fishing is best out at the point, swimming is best in the small lakes. There
are bike paths, hiking trails and the trailhead for the Oregon Coast Trail.

Site **2**   **KAMPERS WEST CAMPGROUND**
                    near Fort Stevens State Park

Campsites, facilities: There are 50 tent sites and 200 drive-through sites for trailers
or motor homes of any length. Electricity, piped water and picnic tables are
provided. Flush toilets, bottled gas, sanitary services, showers, a laundromat
and ice are available. A store and a cafe are available. Pets and motorbikes are
permitted.

Reservations, fee: Reservations accepted; $9-13 fee per night. Open May to October.

Who to contact: Phone (503)861-1814 or write to 1140 NW Warrenton Drive,
Warrenton, OR 97146.

Location: From Gearhart, take US 101 north to the Warrenton Drive exit. Go north
on Warrenton Drive to the park, located at 1140 NW Warrenton Drive.

Trip note: Located just four miles from Fort Stevens State Park, this privately-run
site offers full RV services. Nearby recreation options include an 18-hole golf
course, hiking trails, marked bike trails and a riding stable.

Site **3**   **BUD'S CAMPGROUND**
                    on the Pacific Ocean

Campsites, facilities: There are eight tent sites and 24 sites for trailers or motor
homes of any length. Electricity, piped water, sewer hookups and picnic tables
are provided. Flush toilets, showers, a store, a laundromat and ice are available.
Bottled gas and a cafe are located within one mile. Pets and motorbikes are
permitted. Boat docks, launching facilities and rentals are nearby.

Reservations, fee: Reservations accepted; $9-13 fee per night. Open all year.

Who to contact: Phone (503)738-6855 or write to 4412 Highway 101 North,
Gearhart, OR 97138.

Location: From Gearhart, drive one mile north on US 101 and you'll see the
campground entrance.

Trip note: This private campground is set along the ocean, about four miles north
of Seaside (see the trip notes for Sites 4 and 5). Nearby recreation options
include an 18-hole golf course, hiking trails and a riding stable.

Site **4**

PINE COVE RV PARK
near the Pacific Ocean

Campsites, facilities: There are 23 tent sites and 21 sites for trailers or motor homes of any length. Electricity, piped water and sewer hookups are provided. Flush toilets, showers, a laundromat, firewood and a playground are available. A store, a cafe and ice are located within one mile. Leashed pets are permitted.

Reservations, fee: Reservations accepted; $12 fee per night; MasterCard and Visa accepted. Open all year.

Who to contact: Phone (503)738-5243 or write to 2481 Highway 101 N, Seaside, OR 97138.

Location: Take US 101 to Seaside. Go north about one mile past Seaside on US 101. The park is located at 2481 Highway 101 North.

Trip note: This park and motel is set among the pines about a mile from Seaside. It is a good spot for fishing, both in the ocean and in the two rivers that run through town, where you can fish from the bridges. Crabbing is good on calm spring days in the ocean. Nearby recreation options include an 18-hole golf course and hiking trails. See the trip note for Site 5 for more information about Seaside.

Site **5**

VENICE RV PARK
on Neawanna River

Campsites, facilities: There are 26 drive-through sites for trailers or motor homes of any length. Electricity, piped water, sewer hookups and picnic tables are provided. Flush toilets, bottled gas, showers, a laundromat and ice are available. A store and a cafe are located within one mile. Leashed pets are permitted.

Reservations, fee: Reservations accepted; $13 fee per night. Open all year.

Who to contact: Phone (503)738-8851 or write to 1032 24th Avenue, Seaside, OR 97138.

Location: Take US 101 to the north end of Seaside, turn on 24th Avenue and drive to the campground at 1032 24th Avenue.

Trip note: This park is set along the Neawanna River, one of two rivers that run through Seaside. Seaside offers beautiful ocean beaches for fishing and surfing, moped and bike rentals, shops and a theatre. The city has provided swings and volleyball nets on the beach. An 18-hole golf course is available nearby

Site **6**

RIVERSIDE LAKE RV AND TRAILER PARK
on Necanicum River

Campsites, facilities: There are eight tent sites and 37 drive-through sites for trailers or motor homes of any length. Electricity, piped water and picnic tables are provided. Flush toilets, showers, firewood, a laundromat and ice are available. Sewer hookups can be obtained for an extra fee. Bottled gas, sanitary services, a store and a cafe are located within one mile. Pets and motorbikes are permitted. Boat launching facilities are nearby.

Reservations, fee: Reservations accepted; $9 fee per night. Open all year.

Who to contact: Phone (503)738-6779 or write to Hamlet Route, Box 255, Seaside, OR 97138.

Location: From Seaside, go 1.5 miles south on US 101, then follow the signs to the park. It is just north of the junction of Highway 26 and US 101.

Trip note: This park is set along the shore of the Necanicum River, which attracts a steelhead run every winter. It is low during the summer but provides many pools for swimming. Boating is allowed. There is a small scenic lake in the campground that attracts wildlife. No swimming or boating is allowed on the campground lake, but it is stocked with trout, a practice that began in 1988. Nearby recreation options include an 18-hole golf course and a riding stable.

Site 7 SADDLE MOUNTAIN STATE PARK
on Saddle Mountain

Campsites, facilities: There are nine primitive tent sites. Picnic tables and fire grills are provided. Flush toilets and firewood are available. Leashed pets are permitted.

Reservations, fee: No reservations necessary; $8 fee per night. Open mid-April to late October.

Who to contact: Phone (503)861-1671 or write to Cannon Beach, OR 97110.

Location: From the town of Cannon Beach, go nine miles east on US 26, then eight miles northeast on the entrance road to the park.

Trip note: This is a good alternative to the many beach front parks in Zone 3. A three-mile trail climbs to the top of Saddle Mountain, a great lookout on clear days. This park is a real find for the naturalist interested in rare and unusual varieties of plants, many of which have evolved along the slopes of this isolated mountain.

Site 8 RV RESORT AT CANNON BEACH
near Ecola State Park

Campsites, facilities: There are 100 sites (11 are drive-through) for trailers or motor homes of any length. Electricity, piped water, sewer hookups and picnic tables are provided. Flush toilets, bottled gas, showers, firewood, a recreation hall, a store, a cafe, a laundromat, ice, a playground and a swimming pool are available. Leashed pets are permitted.

Reservations, fee: Reservations accepted; $17-22 fee per night; American Express, MasterCard and Visa accepted. Open all year.

Who to contact: Phone (503)436-2231 or write to P.O. Box 219, Cannon Beach, OR 97110.

Location: Driving north on Highway 101, take the second right-hand exit for the town of Cannon Beach and you'll see the signs for the resort.

Trip note: This private resort is located about seven blocks from one of the nicest beaches in the region. From the town of Cannon Beach you can walk for miles in either direction. Ecola State Park is just two miles north. Nearby recreation options include marked bike trails, a riding stable and tennis courts.

Site 9 OSWALD WEST STATE PARK
on the Pacific Ocean, walk-in only

Campsites, facilities: There are 36 primitive walk-in tent sites. Picnic tables and fire grills are provided. Piped water, flush toilets and firewood are available. Leashed pets are permitted.

Reservations, fee: No reservations necessary; $8 fee per night. Open mid-March to late October.

Who to contact: Phone (503)368-5943 or write to 8300 3rd Street, Nehalem, OR 97130.

Location: This park is located ten miles south of the town of Cannon Beach on US 101. Walk one-quarter mile to the campground.

Trip note: This state park is set along a dramatic section of the Oregon Coast with rugged cliffs rising high above the ocean. This is not beach-walking territory,

but the park does offer 15 miles of hiking trails, including the Oregon Coast
Trail, a small beach, and several fishing streams.

Site 10 — NEHALEM BAY STATE PARK
on the Pacific Ocean

Campsites, facilities: There are 291 sites for trailers or motor homes of any length
and a special camping area for hikers and bicyclists. Electricity, piped water,
picnic tables and fire grills are provided. Flush toilets, sanitary disposal station,
showers, firewood and a laundromat are available. Some facilities are
wheelchair accessible. Leashed pets are permitted. Boat launching facilities
are located nearby on Nehalem Bay.

Reservations, fee: No reservations necessary; $10 fee per night in summer, $7
off-season. Open year-round.

Who to contact: Phone (503)368-5943 or write to 8300 3rd Street, Nehalem, OR
97131.

Location: From the town of Cannon Beach, drive 17 miles south on US 101 to
Nehalem, then head west on the entrance road for 1.5 miles to the park.

Trip note: This state park is located on a sandy point that separates the Pacific Ocean
and Nehalem Bay. It offers six miles of beach frontage. The Oregon Coast Trail
passes through the park.

Site 11 — JETTY FISHERY RV PARK
on Nehalem Bay

Campsites, facilities: There are six tent sites and 30 drive-through sites for trailers
or motor homes of any length. Electricity, piped water and picnic tables are
provided. Flush toilets, bottled gas, firewood, a store, showers, a cafe and ice
are available. Leashed pets are permitted. Boat docks, launching facilities and
rentals are nearby.

Reservations, fee: Reservations accepted; $6-10 fee per night; MasterCard and Visa
accepted. Open all year.

Who to contact: Phone (503)368-5746 or write to 27550 Highway 101 North,
Rockaway, OR 97136.

Location: From Rockaway, drive three miles north on US 101 and you will see the
park entrance.

Trip note: This small park is located at the base of a mile-long jetty, which extends
out into Nehalem Bay and the ocean. Fishing and crabbing are good off the
jetty, but sometimes the snags bite good too. There is a small beach on the bay
side of the jetty, a popular spot for kids. For boaters, a full-service marina is
nearby.

Site 12 — SHOREWOOD TRAVEL TRAILER VILLAGE
on the Pacific Ocean

Campsites, facilities: There are 30 drive-through sites for trailers or motor homes
of any length. Electricity, piped water, and picnic tables are provided. Flush
toilets, bottled gas, sanitary services, cable TV hookups, showers, firewood, a
laundromat, ice and a playground are available. A store and a cafe are located
within one mile. Leashed pets are permitted.

Reservations, fee: Reservations accepted; $11-12 fee per night. Open all year.

Who to contact: Phone (503)355-2278 or write to 17600 Ocean Boulevard,
Rockaway, OR 97136.

Location: From Rockaway, travel two miles south on US 101, then follow the signs to the park.

Trip note: This park is set along a beach that is ideal for surf fishing for perch or beachcombing during low tides. The 1.5-mile hike to Tillamook Bay jetty is a good side trip. An 18-hole golf course is located a short drive from the park.

Site **13**   **BARVIEW JETTY COUNTY PARK**
near Girabaldi

Campsites, facilities: There are 200 tent sites and 40 drive-through sites for trailers or motor homes of any length. Electricity, piped water, sewer hookups and picnic tables are provided. Flush toilets, sanitary services, showers and a playground are available. Bottled gas, a store, a cafe and ice are located within one mile. Leashed pets are permitted.

Reservations, fee: Reservations accepted; $9 fee per night. Open all year.

Who to contact: Phone (503)322-3522 or write to PO Box 633, Garibaldi, OR 97118.

Location: From Garibaldi, go two miles north on US 101, then one-quarter mile west to campground.

Trip note: This park is near the beach, yet set in a wooded area. Nearby recreation options include an 18-hole golf course, hiking trails, bike trails and a full-service marina.

Site **14**   **BIAK-BY-THE-SEA TRAILER COURT**
on Tillamook Bay

Campsites, facilities: There are 45 drive-through sites for trailers or motor homes of any length. Electricity, piped water and sewer hookups are provided. Flush toilets, showers and a laundromat are available. Bottled gas, a store, a cafe and ice are located within one mile. Pets and motorbikes are permitted. Boat docks, launching facilities and rentals are nearby.

Reservations, fee: Reservations accepted; $5-10 fee per night; MasterCard and Visa accepted. Open all year.

Who to contact: Phone (503)322-3206 or write to Box 507, Garibaldi, OR 97118.

Location: This trailer park is located at the northern edge of Garibaldi on Fisherman's Wharf.

Trip note: This park is set along the shore of Tillamook Bay. The deep sea fishing, crabbing, clamming, surf fishing, scuba diving and beachcombing make it a prime retreat. The nearby town of Tillamook offers a cheese factory and a historical museum. A good side trip is Cape Meares State Park, where you can hike through a national wildlife preserve and see where the seabirds nest along the cliffs.

Site **15**   **PACIFIC CAMPGROUND
AND OVERNIGHT TRAILER PARK**
on Tillamook Bay

Campsites, facilities: There are 20 tent sites and 28 drive-through sites for trailers or motor homes of any length. Electricity, piped water, sewer hookups and picnic tables are provided. Flush toilets, cable TV, showers, firewood and ice are available. A store and a cafe are located within one mile. Pets and motorbikes are permitted.

Reservations, fee: Reservations accepted; $7-12 fee per night. Open all year.

Who to contact: Phone (503)842-5201 or write to 1950 Suppress Road North, Tillamook, OR 97141.

Location: From Tillamook, drive 2.5 miles north on US 101. The campground entrance is across from the Tillamook Cheese factory.

Trip note: This campground is set at the southern end of Tillamook Bay, not far from the Wilson River. The Tillamook Cheese factory is just south of the park, and an 18-hole golf course is also nearby. See the trip note for Site 14 for more information about the area.

Site 16
HAPPY CAMP RESORT
on Netarts Bay

Campsites, facilities: There are 70 sites for trailers or motor homes of any length. Electricity, piped water and picnic tables are provided. Flush toilets, bottled gas, sanitary services, showers, firewood, a store, sewer hookups, cable TV, a cafe, a laundromat, ice and a playground are available. Leashed pets are permitted. Boat docks, launching facilities and rentals are nearby.

Reservations, fee: Reservations accepted; $12 fee per night. Open all year.

Who to contact: Phone (503)842-4012 or write to Box 82, Netarts, OR 97143.

Location: From Tillamook, drive seven miles west on Netarts Highway and you'll see the campground entrance.

Trip note: Netarts Bay offers sheltered waters, perfect for small boaters to take advantage of excellent crabbing. Shoreliners can discover good crabbing and fair perch fishing. Crabbing gear, boat rentals, and crab cooking are available. The camp is set along the shore of Netarts Bay, a short drive from Cape Lookout State Park (Site 19), Cape Meares State Park and national wildlife refuge (Site 14).

Site 17
BIG SPRUCE TRAILER PARK
on Netarts Bay

Campsites, facilities: There are 23 drive-through sites for trailers or motor homes of any length. Electricity, piped water, sewer hookups and picnic tables are provided. Flush toilets, bottled gas, cable TV, showers and a laundromat are available. A store, a cafe and ice are located within one mile. Leashed pets are permitted. Boat docks and launching facilities are nearby.

Reservations, fee: Reservations accepted; $11 fee per night. Open all year.

Who to contact: Phone (503)842-7443 or write to 4850 Netarts Highway West, Tillamook, OR 97141.

Location: From Tillamook, go 6.5 miles west on Cape Lookout-Netarts Highway.

Trip note: This trailer park is one block from the boat launch on Netarts Bay. See the trip note for Site 16 for details on the fishing here.

Site 18
BAY SHORE RV PARK
on Netarts Bay

Campsites, facilities: There are 54 drive-through sites for trailers or motor homes of any length. Electricity, piped water, sewer hookups and picnic tables are provided. Flush toilets, bottled gas, showers, firewood, a recreation hall, a laundromat and ice are available. A store and a cafe are located within one mile. Leashed pets are permitted. Boat docks, launching facilities and rentals are nearby.

Reservations, fee: Reservations accepted; $13.50 fee per night; MasterCard and Visa accepted. Open all year.

Who to contact: Phone (503)842-7774 or write to P.O. Box 218, Netarts, OR 97413.

Location: From US 101 in Tillamook, go six miles west on the Cape Lookout-Netarts Highway and you will see the park entrance.

Trip note: This is one of three camps set on the east shore of Netarts Bay. See the trip note for Site 16 for more information about the fishing here.

Site **19**   **CAPE LOOKOUT STATE PARK**
                           near Netarts Bay

Campsites, facilities: There are 197 tent sites, 53 sites with full hookups for trailers or motor homes of any length, and a special camping area for hikers and bicyclists. Picnic tables and fire grills are provided. Flush toilets, sanitary services, showers, firewood and a laundromat are available. A restaurant is located within one mile. Some facilities are wheelchair accessible. Leashed pets are permitted.

Reservations, fee: Reservations accepted; $9-11 fee per night in summer, $6-8 off-season. Open all year.

Who to contact: Phone (503)842-4981 or write to 13000 Whiskey Creek Road West, Tillamook, OR 97141.

Location: From Tillamook, travel 11 miles southwest on Netarts Road and you'll see the park entrance.

Trip note: This unique park offers an assortment of walks. One trail leads out along a ridge to headlands high above the ocean. Another walk will take you out through a variety of estuarine habitats along the five-mile sand spit that extends between the ocean and Netarts Bay.

Site **20**   **KOA TILLAMOOK**
                          on Tillamook River

Campsites, facilities: There are 12 tent sites and 71 drive-through sites for trailers or motor homes of any length. Piped water and picnic tables are provided. Flush toilets, bottled gas, sanitary services, showers, firewood, a recreation hall, electricity, sewer hookups, a store, a laundromat, ice and a playground are available. Leashed pets are permitted.

Reservations, fee: Reservations accepted; $12 fee per night; MasterCard and Visa accepted. Open all year.

Who to contact: Phone (503)842-4779 or write to 11880 Highway 101 South, Tillamook, OR 97141.

Location: From Tillamook, drive six miles south on Highway 101 and you'll see the campground entrance.

Trip note: This campground is set along the Tillamook River. Boat launching facilities are available nearby.

Site **21**   **CAMPER COVE PARK**
                          on Beaver Creek

Campsites, facilities: There are two tent sites and 15 drive-through sites for trailers or motor homes up to 31 feet long. Electricity, piped water, sewer hookups and picnic tables are provided. Flush toilets, bottled gas, sanitary services, showers, firewood, a recreation hall, a laundromat and ice are available. Leashed pets are permitted.

Reservations, fee: Reservations accepted; $6-11 fee per night. Open year-round.

Who to contact: Phone (503)398-5334 or write to Box 42, Beaver, OR 97108.

Location: From Beaver, go 2.5 miles north on US 101 and you will see the park entrance.

Trip note: This small, wooded campground is set along Beaver Creek, just far enough off the highway to provide quiet. The park can be used as a base camp for fishermen, with steelhead and salmon fishing in season in the nearby Nestucca River.

Site 22
SAND BEACH
SIUSLAW NATIONAL FOREST

Campsites, facilities: There are 101 sites for tents, trailers or motor homes up to 30 feet long. (If filled, the east and west parking lots provide additional sites for trailers or motor homes.) Picnic tables and fire grills are provided. Piped water, flush toilets and sanitary services are available. Leashed pets are permitted. Boat docks are nearby.

Reservations, fee: Some reservations available through MISTIX by phoning (800)283-CAMP; $7 fee per night. Open mid-May to early September.

Who to contact: Phone at (503)392-3161 or write to Hebo Ranger District, Siuslaw National Forest, Hebo, OR 97122.

Location: In Pacific City at the blinking red light, turn west and drive over the bridge. Make a sharp right and go past Cape Kiwanda and drive about nine miles to the Sand Lake store. Turn left on Gallaway Road and drive to the end to the campground.

Trip note: This area is known for its large sand dunes, which are open to off-road vehicles. The campground is set along the shore of Sand Lake, which is actually more like an estuary, since the ocean is just around the bend.

Site 23
CAPE KIWANDA RV PARK
on the Pacific Ocean

Campsites, facilities: There are 12 tent sites and 130 sites for trailers or motor homes of any length. Electricity, piped water, sewer hookups and picnic tables are provided. Flush toilets, sanitary services, showers, firewood, a recreation hall, a laundromat and a playground are available. Bottled gas, a store, a cafe and ice are located within one mile. Pets and motorbikes are permitted. Boat docks, launching facilities and rentals are nearby.

Reservations, fee: Reservations accepted; $8-13.50 fee per night. Open all year.

Who to contact: Phone (503)965-6230 or write to Box 129, Pacific City, OR 97135.

Location: From US 101 in Pacific City, drive three miles west on Pacific City Loop Road, then cross the bridge and travel one mile north and you'll see the park entrance.

Trip note: This park is set along the ocean, a short distance from Cape Kiwanda State Park, which is open for day-use only. There is a boat launch there and hiking trails that lead out to the cape. A recreation option is four miles south at Nestucca Spit, where there is another day-use park. The point extends about three miles and is a good spot for birdwatching.

Site 24
RAINES RESORT AND RV PARK
on Nestucca River

Campsites, facilities: There are 12 sites for trailers or motor homes of any length. Electricity, piped water, sewer hookups and picnic tables are provided. Flush toilets, sanitary services, showers, a store and a laundromat are available. Bottled gas, a cafe and ice are located within one mile. Pets and motorbikes are permitted. Boat docks, launching facilities and rentals are nearby.

Reservations, fee: Reservations accepted; $9-12 fee per night; MasterCard and Visa accepted. Open all year.

Who to contact: Phone (503)965-6371 or write to P.O. Box 777, Pacific City, OR

97135.

Location: From Pacific City, drive 1.5 miles north on Brooten Road, then one block west on Woods Bridge and you'll see the campground entrance.

Trip note: This campground is set along the Nestucca River, which attracts a king salmon run from late August through Thanksgiving. Nearby recreation options include a full-service marina.

Site 25
HEBO LAKE
on Hebo Lake
SIUSLAW NATIONAL FOREST

Campsites, facilities: There are ten tent sites and six sites for trailers or motor homes up to 16 feet long. Picnic tables and fire grills are provided. Piped water, and vault toilets are available. A store, a cafe and ice are located within five miles. Leashed pets are permitted. Boats without motors are permitted on the lake.

Reservations, fee: No reservations necessary; $4 fee per night. Open mid-April to mid-October.

Who to contact: Phone the Siuslaw National Forest at (503)392-3161 or write to Hebo Ranger District, Hebo, OR 97122.

Location: From Hebo, drive one-quarter mile east on Highway 22 to Forest Service Road 14. Turn left, and drive east on Road 14 for five miles to the campground.

Trip note: This Forest Service campground is set along the shore of little Hebo Lake. This is a secluded campground where the campsites are nestled under trees. There is a shaded group shelter area with tables and a large barbecue. A nearby trail leads eight miles to South Lake in the backcountry. The trail around the lake is barrier-free.

Site 26
ROCKY BEND
on Nestucca River
SIUSLAW NATIONAL FOREST

Campsites, facilities: There are seven tent sites. **No piped water** is available. Picnic tables, and fire grills are provided. Vault toilets available. Leashed pets are permitted.

Reservations, fee: No reservations necessary; no fee. Open mid-April to mid-October.

Who to contact: Phone the Siuslaw National Forest at (503)392-3161 or write to Hebo Ranger District, Hebo, OR 97122.

Location: At Beaver, turn east on County Road 858 and drive 15.5 miles east to the campground.

Trip note: This campground is set along the Nestucca River, a little-known, secluded spot that provides a guarantee for peace and quiet.

Site 27
CASTLE ROCK
on Three Rivers
SIUSLAW NATIONAL FOREST

Campsites, facilities: There are four tent sites. Picnic tables are provided and pit toilets are available, but there is **no piped water.** Leashed pets are permitted.

Reservations, fee: No reservations necessary; no fee. Open all year.

Who to contact: Phone the Siuslaw National Forest at (503)392-3161 or write to Hebo Ranger District, OR 97122.

Location: This campground is located about five miles southeast of Hebo on Highway 22.

Trip note: This tiny spot provides an alternative for tent campers to the large beachfront RV parks popular on the Oregon coast. It is set along Three Rivers.

Site 28   NESKOWIN CREEK
on Neskowin Creek
SIUSLAW NATIONAL FOREST

Campsites, facilities: There are 12 primitive tent sites. Picnic tables and fire grills are provided. Pit toilets are available, but there is **no piped water.** Leashed pets are permitted.

Reservations, fee: No reservations necessary; no fee. Open mid-April to mid-October.

Who to contact: Phone the Siuslaw National Forest at (503)392-3161 or write to Hebo Ranger District, Hebo, OR 97122.

Location: From Neskowin, go 1.5 miles south on US 101, then 4.5 miles southeast on County Road 12. Campground entrance is signed on Road 12.

Trip note: This campground is set along Neskowin Creek, in the Cascade Head Scenic Area, a rustic setting. If you take Forest Service Road 1861 west from the camp for five miles, you will come to trailheads which provide hiking access to meadows overlooking the coast. See a Forest Service map for details.

Site 29   KOA LINCOLN CREEK
on the Pacific Ocean

Campsites, facilities: There are 41 tent sites and 45 drive-through sites for trailers or motor homes of any length. Picnic tables are provided. Flush toilets, bottled gas, sanitary services, showers, firewood, a recreation hall, a store, a cafe, a laundromat, ice and a playground are available. Electricity, piped water, sewer, and cable TV hookups are located for an extra fee. Pets and motorbikes are permitted. Boat launching facilities are nearby. Cabin rentals are also available for $20 a night.

Reservations, fee: Reservations accepted; $11.50-16.50 fee per night; MasterCard and Visa accepted. Open all year.

Who to contact: Phone (503)994-2961 or write to 5298 NE Park Lane, Route 2, Box 255, Otis, OR 97368.

Location: From Lincoln City, go 1.2 miles north on US 101, then one mile east on East Devil's Lake Road and you're there.

Trip note: This area offers opportunity for beachcombing, tidepooling and fishing along a seven-mile stretch of beach. Two stops to consider if you're going into Lincoln City for supplies: the Premier Market, which has smoked salmon, and the Colonial Bakery, which carries the best pastries west of Paris. Nearby recreation options include an 18-hole golf course and tennis courts.

Site 30   DEVIL'S LAKE STATE PARK
on Devil's Lake

Campsites, facilities: There are 68 tent sites and 32 sites with full hookups for trailers or motor homes of any length. Picnic tables and fire grills are provided. Flush toilets, showers, firewood, a store, a restaurant, a laundromat and ice are available. Some facilities are wheelchair accessible. Leashed pets are permitted. Boat docks and launching facilities are nearby.

Reservations, fee: Reservations accepted; $9-11 fee per night in summer, $6-8 off-season. Open mid-April to late October.

Who to contact: Phone (503)994-2002 or write to 1542 Northeast 6th, Lincoln City,

OR 97367.

Location: This park is in Lincoln City, just off US 101.

Trip note: This is a take-your-pick deal. At Devil's Lake, you can swim, fish or water-ski. An alternative is to head west and explore the seven miles of beaches. Lincoln City also has a number of art and craft galleries in town.

Site 31
TREE N' SEA TRAILER PARK
on the Pacific Ocean

Campsites, facilities: There are seven sites for trailers or motor homes of any length. Electricity, piped water and sewer hookups are provided. Flush toilets and showers are available. A store, a cafe and a laundromat are available within one mile. Leashed pets are permitted.

Reservations, fee: Reservations preferred; $12 fee per night. Open all year.

Who to contact: Phone (503)996-3801 or write to 1015 Southwest 51st Street, Lincoln City, OR 97367.

Location: In Lincoln City, turn west off US 101 onto Southwest 51st Street and drive one block to the park.

Trip note: This park is set along the ocean in Lincoln City. See the trip notes for Sites 29 and 30 for recreation options.

Site 32
SPORTSMAN'S LANDING RV PARK
on Siletz River

Campsites, facilities: There are 30 sites for trailers or motor homes of any length. Electricity, piped water and sewer hookups are provided. Flush toilets, bottled gas, sanitary services, showers, a store, a cafe, a laundromat, ice and a playground are available. Leashed pets are permitted. Boat docks, launching facilities and rentals are nearby.

Reservations, fee: Reservations accepted; $7 fee per night; MasterCard and Visa accepted. Open all year.

Who to contact: Phone (503)996-4225 or write to Kernville Route, Lincoln City, OR 97367.

Location: From Lincoln City, go two miles south on US 101, then four miles east on Highway 229 and you'll see the park entrance.

Trip note: This area offers a number of backcountry trips. The park is set along the shore of the Siletz River. If you head farther east on Highway 229, you will discover several Forest Service roads that lead into the Siuslaw National Forest and provide access to a number of creeks. See a Forest Service map for details.

Site 33
HOLIDAY HILLS
near Fogerty Creek State Park

Campsites, facilities: There are 22 sites for trailers or motor homes of any length. Electricity, piped water, sewer hookups and picnic tables are provided. Flush toilets, sanitary services, showers, a laundromat and a playground are available. Bottled gas, a store, a cafe and ice are located within one mile. Pets and motorbikes are permitted.

Reservations, fee: Reservations accepted; $11 fee per night. Open all year.

Who to contact: Phone (503)764-2430 or write to HC63, Box 77, Depoe Bay, OR 97341.

Location: From the town of Depoe Bay, travel four miles north on US 101 and you will see the entrance.

Trip note: Fogerty Creek State Park, just two miles away, is a prime side trip. It offers beach access, wooded hiking trails and fishing in Fogerty Creek. An 18-hole golf course is nearby.

Site **34**   **SEA AND SAND OVERNIGHT PARK**
near Siletz Bay

Campsites, facilities: There are 85 drive-through sites for trailers or motor homes of any length. Electricity, piped water, sewer hookups and picnic tables are provided. Flush toilets, showers, sanitary services, firewood and a laundromat are available. A store, a cafe and ice are located within one mile. Leashed pets are permitted.

Reservations, fee: Reservations accepted; $15 fee per night. Open all year.

Who to contact: Phone (503)764-2313 or write to HC63, Box 79, Depoe Bay, OR 97341. In January, 1991, the new address will be 4985 N. Highway 101, Gleneden Beach, OR 97388.

Location: From the town of Depoe Bay, drive four miles north on US 101 and you'll see the campground entrance.

Trip note: Beachcombing is popular at this park, set near the ocean near Gleneden Beach on Siletz Bay. The Siletz River and numerous small creeks are in the area.

Site **35**   **BOILER BAY TRAILER PARK**
near Fogerty Creek State Park

Campsites, facilities: There are 17 drive-through sites for trailers or motor homes of any length. Electricity, piped water, sewer hookups and picnic tables are provided. Flush toilets, showers, a laundromat and a playground are available. Bottled gas, sanitary services, a store, a cafe and ice are located within one mile. Pets and motorbikes are permitted. Boat docks, launching facilities and rentals are nearby.

Reservations, fee: No reservations necessary; $10 fee per night. Open all year.

Who to contact: Phone (503)765-2548 or write to HC 63 Box 7, Depoe Bay, OR 97341.

Location: From the town of Depoe Bay, drive 1.5 miles north on US 101 and you will see the park entrance.

Trip note: This camp is set near a local landmark, the Boiler Bay Wayside, where the water spouts through the blowholes and over the road during storms or high tides. Fogerty Creek State Park is also nearby. Nearby recreation options include marked bike trails and a full-service marina.

Site **36**   **HOLIDAY RV PARK**
near Depoe Bay State Park

Campsites, facilities: There are 110 sites for trailers or motor homes of any length. Electricity, piped water, sewer hookups and picnic tables are provided. Flush toilets, bottled gas, showers, a recreation hall, a store, a cafe, a laundromat, ice, a playground and swimming pool are available. Pets are permitted.

Reservations, fee: Reservations accepted; $12-20 fee per night; MasterCard and Visa accepted. Open all year.

Who to contact: Phone (503)765-2302 or write to P.O. Box 433, Depoe Bay, OR 97341.

Location: This park is located on US 101 at the north edge of the town of Depoe Bay.

Trip note: This is a scenic stretch of coastline and some of the prime side trips include Depoe State Park and Depoe Creek. Nearby recreation options include an 18-hole golf course, tennis courts and a public aquarium.

Site **37**
MULKEY O RV PARK
near South Yamhill River

Campsites, facilities: There are 40 sites for tents, trailers or motor homes of any length. Electricity, piped water, sewer hookups and picnic tables are provided. Flush toilets, showers and a laundromat are available. Pets and motorbikes are permitted.

Reservations, fee: Reservations accepted; $8-12 fee per night. Open all year.

Who to contact: Phone (503)472-2475 or write to 14325 SW Highway 18, McMinnville, OR 97128.

Location: From McMinnville, travel 3.5 miles southwest on Highway 18 and you will see the park entrance.

Trip note: If you are in the area and looking for a camping spot, you had best stop here--there are no other campgrounds within 30 miles. This wooded park is set near the South Yamhill River. Nearby recreation options include an 18-hole golf course, tennis courts and the Western Deer Park and Arboretum, which has a playground.

UMPQUA

◆

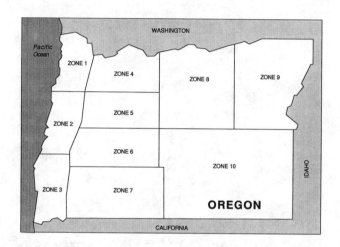

SOME HIGHLIGHTS

65 CAMPGROUNDS

Yaquina Bay

Siuslaw National Forest

Willamette River

Seal Rock State Park

Alsea River

Oregon Dunes National Recreation Area

Siuslaw River

Umpqua River

Coos Bay

Sea Lion Caves

Siltcoos Lake

Cape Perpetua Scenic Area

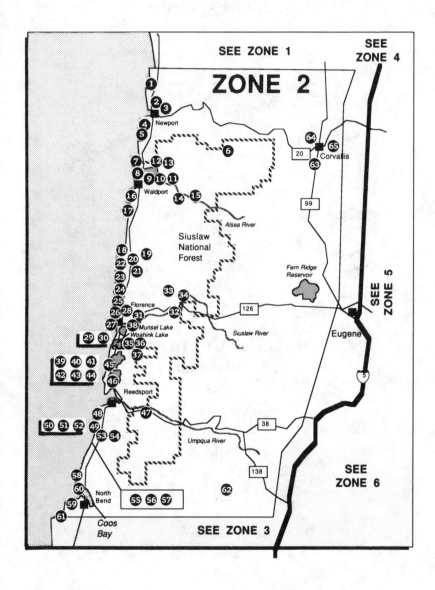

SEE ZONE 1

SEE ZONE 4

ZONE 2

Newport

Corvallis

20

Waldport

99

Alsea River

Siuslaw
National
Forest

Fern Ridge
Reservoir

SEE ZONE 5

Florence

126

Siuslaw River

Munsel Lake
Woahink Lake

Eugene

Reedsport

47

38

Umpqua River

5

138

SEE
ZONE 6

North
Bend

Coos
Bay

SEE ZONE 3

Site 1   BEVERLY BEACH STATE PARK
on the Pacific Ocean

Campsites, facilities: There are 152 tent sites, 127 sites with full hookups for trailers or motor homes of any length and a special camping area reserved for hikers and bicyclists. Picnic tables and fire grills are provided. Piped water, flush toilets, showers and a sanitary disposal station are available. There is a coffee shop in the park. Some facilities are wheelchair accessible. Leashed pets are permitted.

Reservations, fee: Reservations accepted; $9-11 fee per night in summer, $6-8 off-season. Open all year.

Who to contact: Phone (503)265-9278 or write to Star Route North, Box 684, Newport, OR 97365.

Location: From Newport, go seven miles north on US 101 and you'll see the park entrance.

Trip note: This beautiful campground is set in a wooded, grassy area on the east side of US 101. Like magic, you walk through a tunnel under the roadway and emerge on the beach. Just a mile to the north is a small, day-use state park called Devil's Punchbowl, so-called because of the unusual bowl-shaped rock formation which has caverns under it where the waves rumble about. For some great ocean views, head north one more mile to the Otter Crest Wayside.

Site 2   AGATE BEACH TRAILER AND RV PARK
near the Pacific Ocean

Campsites, facilities: There are 32 sites (12 drive-through) for trailers or motor homes of any length. Electricity, piped water, sewer hookups and picnic tables are provided. Flush toilets, sanitary services, showers and a laundromat are available. A store and ice are located within one mile. Leashed pets are permitted.

Reservations, fee: Reservations accepted; $11-12.50 fee per night. Open all year.

Who to contact: Phone (503)265-7670 or write to 6138 North Coast Highway, Newport, OR 97365.

Location: This park is off US 101 in Newport at the north end of town.

Trip note: This park is a short distance from Agate Beach Wayside, a small state park with beach access. Agate hunting can be good. Sometimes the agates are covered by a layer of sand and you have to dig a bit. But other times, wave action will clear the sand, unveiling the agates at low tides.

Site 3   HARBOR VILLAGE RV PARK
on Yaquina Bay

Campsites, facilities: There are 140 sites for trailers or motor homes of any length. Electricity, piped water, sewer hookups and picnic tables are provided. Flush toilets, showers, a laundromat and ice are available. Bottled gas, a store and a cafe are located within one mile. Boat docks, launching facilities and rentals are nearby.

Reservations, fee: Reservations accepted; $10.50 fee per night; MasterCard and Visa accepted. Open all year.

Who to contact: Phone (503)265-5088 or write to 923 Southeast Bay Boulevard, Box 6, Newport, OR 97365.

Location: From Newport, go east one-half mile on US 20, then one-half mile south on John Moore Road to the bay. Turn left and you'll see the entrance to the trailer park.

Trip note: This park is set right along the shore of Yaquina Bay. See the trip note for Site 4 for information on attractions in Newport. Nearby recreation options include an 18-hole golf course, hiking trails and a full-service marina.

Site 4   SOUTH BEACH MARINA AND RV PARK
on Yaquina Bay

Campsites, facilities: There are 38 sites for trailers or motor homes. Electricity, piped water and sewer hookups are provided. Flush toilets, showers, a store, a cafe, a laundromat, ice and playground are available. Pets and motorbikes are permitted. Boat docks and launching facilities are nearby.

Reservations, fee: Reservations accepted; $10 fee per night; MasterCard and Visa accepted. Open all year.

Who to contact: Phone (503)867-3321 or write to P.O. Box 1343, Newport, OR 97365.

Location: From Newport, travel one-quarter mile south on US 101, then one-half mile east on Marine Science Drive and you'll see the park entrance.

Trip note: This park is set along the shore of Yaquina Bay, near Newport, a resort town which offers a variety of attractions. Among them are ocean fishing, a museum and aquarium at the nearby Hatfield Marine Science Center, the Undersea Garden, the Waxworks, Ripley's Believe It or Not and the Lincoln County Historical Society Museum. Nearby recreation options include an 18-hole golf course, hiking trails, a full-service marina and tennis courts.

Site 5   SOUTH BEACH STATE PARK
on the Pacific Ocean

Campsites, facilities: There are 257 sites with water and electrical hookups for trailers or motor homes of any length, and a special camping area for hikers and bicyclists. Fire grills and picnic tables are provided. Flush toilets, sanitary disposal station, showers, firewood and a laundromat are available. Some facilities are wheelchair accessible. Leashed pets are permitted.

Reservations, fee: Reservations accepted; $2-10 fee per night. Open mid-April to late October.

Who to contact: Phone (503)867-7451 or write to Box 1350, Newport, OR 97365.

Location: From Newport, go south on US 101 for two miles and you'll see the park entrance.

Trip note: This park is set along the beach and offers opportunities for hiking, beachcombing and fishing. The Oregon Coast Trail goes through the park and there is a primitive hike-in campground available. See the trip note for Site 4 for information on attractions in Newport.

Site 6   BIG ELK
on Elk Creek
SIUSLAW NATIONAL FOREST

Campsites, facilities: There are ten sites for tents, trailers or motor homes up to 20 feet long. Picnic tables and fire grills are provided. Piped water and vault toilets are available. Leashed pets are permitted.

Reservations, fee: No reservations necessary; $3 fee per night. Open all year.

Who to contact: Phone (503)487-5811 or write to Siuslaw National Forest, Alsea Ranger District, Alsea, OR 97324.

Location: From Philomath, just west of Corvallis, drive 15.5 miles west on Highway

20 to Burnt Woods, then turn south on County Road 547 and drive eight miles to Harlan. From there, take County Road 538 west for 1.5 miles to the campground entrance.

Trip note: This out-of-the-way spot is just an hour's drive from Corvallis. It is set along Elk Creek. A National Forest map details the backcountry roads and trails in the area.

Site 7   **SEAL ROCKS TRAILER COVE**
near Seal Rock State Park

Campsites, facilities: There are 26 drive-through sites for trailers or motor homes of any length. Electricity, piped water, sewer hookups and picnic tables are provided. Flush toilets, sanitary services and showers are available. Firewood, a store, a cafe and ice are located within one mile.

Reservations, fee: No reservations necessary; $10 fee per night. Open all year.

Who to contact: Phone (503)563-3955 or write to Box 71, Seal Rock, OR 97376.

Location: From Seal Rock, travel one-quarter mile south on US 101 and you'll see the park entrance.

Trip note: This trailer park is set along the rugged coastline near Seal Rock State Park, which is open for day-use only. There you can see seals, sea lions and a variety of birds.

Site 8   **ALSEA BAY TRAILER PARK**
on Alsea Bay

Campsites, facilities: There are 50 sites for trailers or motor homes of any length. Electricity, piped water and sewer hookups are provided. Flush toilets, showers and a recreation hall are available. Bottled gas, sanitary services, a store, a cafe, a laundromat and ice are located within one mile. Leashed pets are permitted. Boat docks, launching facilities and rentals are nearby.

Reservations, fee: Reservations accepted; $10-12 fee per night. Open all year.

Who to contact: Phone (503)563-2250 or write to P.O. Box 397, Waldport, OR 97394.

Location: This park is located in Waldport, off US 101 near the north end of the Alsea Bay Bridge.

Trip note: This area is a favorite for fishermen because Alsea Bay has sandy and rocky shorelines. The crabbing and clamming can also be quite good. Ona Beach State Park is about five miles north on US 101 and offers additional fishing opportunities and a boat ramp along Beaver Creek. It is open for day-use only. Other nearby recreation options include hiking trails, marked bike trails and a marina.

Site 9   **CHINOOK TRAILER PARK**
on Alsea River

Campsites, facilities: There are 15 sites for trailers or motor homes of any length in this adults-only campground. Electricity, piped water and sewer hookups are provided. Flush toilets, showers and a laundromat are available. Bottled gas, a store, a cafe and ice are located within one mile. Pets and motorbikes are permitted. Boat docks are nearby.

Reservations, fee: Reservations accepted; $8-12 fee per night. Open all year.

Who to contact: Phone (503)563-3485 or write to 3299 Highway 34, Waldport, OR 97394.

Location: From Waldport, travel 3.5 miles east on Highway 34 and you'll see the entrance.

Trip note: This trailer park is set along the shore of the Alsea River. For more information on the area, see the trip note for Site 8.

Site **10**   DRIFT CREEK LANDING
                        on Alsea River

Campsites, facilities: There are 60 drive-through sites for trailers or motor homes of any length. Electricity, piped water and sewer hookups are provided. Flush toilets, bottled gas, showers, a recreation hall, store, a cafe and a laundromat are available. Leashed pets are permitted. Boat docks, launching facilities and rentals are nearby.

Reservations, fee: Reservations accepted; $9 fee per night. Open all year.

Who to contact: Phone (503)563-3610 or write to 3850 Highway 34, Waldport, OR 97394.

Location: From Waldport, travel 3.5 miles east on Highway 34, and you'll see the campground.

Trip note: This campground is set along the shore of the Alsea River. An 18-hole golf course is located nearby. For more information on the area, see the trip note for Site 8.

Site **11**   FISHIN' HOLE TRAILER PARK
                        on Alsea River

Campsites, facilities: There are five tent sites and 33 sites for trailers or motor homes of any length. Electricity, piped water, sewer hookups and picnic tables are provided. Flush toilets, showers, a store, a cafe and a laundromat are available. Bottled gas is located within one mile. Leashed pets are permitted. Boat docks, launching facilities and rentals are nearby.

Reservations, fee: Reservations accepted; $10 fee per night. Open all year.

Who to contact: Phone (503)563-3401 or write to 3900 Highway 34, Waldport, OR 97394.

Location: Drive four miles east of Waldport on Highway 34 and you'll see the entrance.

Trip note: This is one of several campgrounds set along the shore of the Alsea River here. For information on the area, see the trip note for Site 8.

Site **12**   TAYLOR'S LANDING
                        on Alsea River

Campsites, facilities: There are six tent sites and 28 sites for trailers or motor homes of any length. Electricity, piped water, sewer hookups and picnic tables are provided. Flush toilets, bottled gas, showers, a cafe and a laundromat are available. Pets and motorbikes are permitted. Boat docks, launching facilities and rentals are nearby.

Reservations, fee: Reservations accepted; $10 fee per night; MasterCard and Visa accepted. Open all year.

Who to contact: Phone (503)528-3388 or write to 4250 Highway 34, Waldport, OR 97394.

Location: From Waldport, go seven miles east on Highway 34 to the entrance.

Trip note: This campground is set along the Alsea River. For more information on the area, see the trip notes for Sites 8 and 13.

Site 13
KOZY KOVE MARINA
on Alsea River

Campsites, facilities: There are 15 tent sites and 27 sites for trailers or motor homes of any length. Electricity, piped water, sewer hookups and picnic tables are provided. Flush toilets, bottled gas, sanitary services, showers, a store, a cafe, a laundromat and ice are available. Pets and motorbikes are permitted. Boat docks, launching facilities and rentals are nearby.

Reservations, fee: Reservations accepted; $12 fee per night for motor homes; MasterCard and Visa accepted; call ahead for tent fee. Open all year.

Who to contact: Phone (503)528-3251 or write to 4800 LC Highway, Tightwater, OR 97394.

Location: From Waldport, drive 9.5 miles east on Highway 34 to the entrance.

Trip note: This campground is set along the Alsea River about ten miles from Waldport. Nearby Forest Service roads provide access to the various creeks and streams in the surrounding mountains. Consult a Siuslaw National Forest map for details.

Site 14
CANAL CREEK
on Canal Creek
SIUSLAW NATIONAL FOREST

Campsites, facilities: There are seven sites for tents only and ten sites for tents or small motor homes. Picnic tables and fire grills are provided. Piped water and vault toilets are available. A picnic shelter and a play area are also available.

Reservations, fee: No reservations; no fee. Open all year.

Who to contact: Phone (503)563-3211 or write to Siuslaw National Forest, Waldport Ranger District, Waldport, OR 97394.

Location: Drive about seven miles east of Waldport on Highway 34 to Forest Service Road 3462, then turn south and go three miles to the campground.

Trip note: This pleasant little campground is off the beaten path in a large, wooded, open area along Canal Creek. The climate here is relatively mild, with 13 degrees Fahrenheit being the coldest winter temperature recorded in recent years. On the other hand, there is the rain ... lots of it.

Site 15
BLACKBERRY
on Alsea River
SIUSLAW NATIONAL FOREST

Campsites, facilities: There are 32 sites for tents, trailers or motor homes. Picnic tables and fire grills are provided. Piped water and flush toilets are available. There is no firewood. A boat ramp is on the site.

Reservations, fee: Reservations available for some sites through MISTIX by phoning (800)283-CAMP; $5 fee per night. Open May through November.

Who to contact: Phone (503)487-5811 or write to Siuslaw National Forest, Alsea Ranger District, Alsea, OR 97324.

Location: From Waldport, drive about 15 miles east on Highway 34 to the campground entrance. From Alsea, drive 22.2 miles west on Highway 34 to the campground.

Trip note: This is a good base camp for a fishing trip on the Alsea River. The Forest Service provides boat launches and picnic areas at several spots along this stretch of river. Often there will be a "camp host," who can give you inside information on nearby recreational opportunities.

Site **16**

BEACHSIDE STATE PARK
near Alsea Bay

Campsites, facilities: There are 60 sites for tents or self-contained motor homes, and 20 sites with water and electrical hookups for trailers or motor homes up to 30 feet long. Picnic tables and fire grills are provided. Flush toilets, sanitary disposal station, showers, firewood and a laundromat are available. Some facilities are wheelchair accessible. Leashed pets are permitted.
Reservations, fee: Reservations accepted; $9-10 fee per night in summer, $6-7 off-season. Open year-round.
Who to contact: Phone (503)563-3023 or write to Box 1350, Newport, OR 97365.
Location: From Waldport, travel four miles south on US 101 to the park entrance.
Trip note: This state park offers a half-mile long beach and is not far from Alsea Bay and the Alsea River. See the trip note for Sites 8 and 13 for more information on the fishing opportunities in the area.

Site **17**

TILLICUM BEACH
on the Pacific Ocean
SIUSLAW NATIONAL FOREST

Campsites, facilities: There are 60 sites for tents, trailers or motor homes up to 32 feet long. Picnic tables and fire grills are provided. Flush toilets and piped water are available. Leashed pets are permitted.
Reservations, fee: No reservations necessary; $7 fee per night. Open all year.
Who to contact: Phone (503)563-3211 or write to Siuslaw National Forest, Waldport Ranger District, Waldport, OR 97394.
Location: Drive 4.5 miles south of Waldport on US 101 and you'll see the campground entrance on your right.
Trip note: You get ocean view campsites, and that may be just what you're looking for. This campground is set along the ocean, just south of Beachside State Park. Nearby Forest Service roads provide access to streams in the mountains east of the beach area. A Forest Service map details the possibilities. In the summer, rangers offer campfire programs.

Site **18**

CAPE PERPETUA
on Cape Creek

Campsites, facilities: There are 37 sites for tents, trailers or motor homes up to 22 feet long. Picnic tables and fire grills are provided. Flush toilets, piped water and sanitary services are available. Leashed pets are permitted.
Reservations, fee: No reservations necessary; $6-8 fee per night. Open mid-May to late September.
Who to contact: Phone (503)563-3211 or write to Cape Perpetua Visitor Center, P.O. Box 274, Yachats, OR 97498.
Location: From Yachats, go three miles south on US 101 and you'll see the entrance on the left.
Trip note: This Forest Service campground is set along Cape Creek in the Cape Perpetua Scenic Area. The visitor information center here provides hiking and driving maps to guide you through this spectacular area. A movie is available for viewing which explains this unique area. Maps also highlight the tide pool and picnic areas. The coastal cliffs can be perfect for whale watching from December through March. Neptune State Park is just south and offers additional rugged coastline vistas.

Site **19**
TENMILE CREEK
near Cummins Creek and Rock Creek
SIUSLAW NATIONAL FOREST

Campsites, facilities: There are four sites for tents, small trailers or motor homes. Fire grills and picnic tables are provided. Vault toilets are available, but there is **no piped water.**

Reservations, fee: No reservations necessary; no fee. Open all year.

Who to contact: Phone (503)563-3211 or write to Siuslaw National Forest, Waldport Ranger District, Waldport, OR 97394.

Location: Drive 4.5 miles south of Cape Perpetua on US 101. Turn east on Forest Service Road 56 for 5.5 miles and you'll see the campground entrance.

Trip note: This small, secluded spot is only 15 or 20 minutes from the highway, yet it remains a virtual secret. A map of Siuslaw National Forest details the surrounding backcountry. Bring your own drinking water or a water filter.

Site **20**
ROCK CREEK
on Rock Creek
SIUSLAW NATIONAL FOREST

Campsites, facilities: There are seven picnic sites and nine sites for tents, trailers or motor homes up to 22 feet long. Fire grills and picnic tables are provided. Flush toilets and piped water are available. Leashed pets are permitted.

Reservations, fee: No reservations necessary; $6 fee per night. Open late May to mid-September.

Who to contact: Phone (503)563-3211 or write to Siuslaw National Forest, Waldport Ranger District, Waldport, OR 97394.

Location: Drive ten miles south of Yachats on US 101 and you'll see the campground entrance on your left.

Trip note: This little out-of-the-way campground is set along Rock Creek, just one-quarter mile from the ocean. It's a premium spot for coast highway travelers.

Site **21**
LANHAM BIKE CAMP
SIUSLAW NATIONAL FOREST

Campsites, facilities: There are ten primitive tent sites at this bike-in, hike-in campground. Picnic tables and fire grills are provided. Vault toilets are available. There is **no piped water.**

Reservations, fee: No reservations necessary; no fee. Open all year.

Who to contact: Phone (503)563-3211 or write to Siuslaw National Forest, Waldport Ranger District, Waldport, OR 97394.

Location: Ride ten miles south of Yachats on US 101 past Rock Creek and hike in from there.

Trip note: This is a good layover spot for bikers working their way along the coast highway. And you can't beat the price.

Site **22**
SEA PERCH
near Cape Perpetua

Campsites, facilities: There are ten drive-through sites for tents, trailers or motor homes of any length. Electricity, piped water, sewer hookups and picnic tables are provided. Flush toilets, bottled gas, sanitary services, showers, firewood, a recreation hall, a store, a cafe, a laundromat, ice and a playground are available. Pets and motorbikes are permitted.

Reservations, fee: Reservations accepted; $10 fee per night; MasterCard and Visa accepted. Open all year.

Who to contact: Phone (503)547-3505 or write to 95480 Highway 101, Yachats, OR 97498.

Location: From Yachats, go 6.5 miles south on US 101 to mile-marker 171.

Trip note: This is one of the most scenic areas on the Oregon coast and Sea Perch is right in the middle of it. This private camp is set just south of Cape Perpetua. For more information, see the trip note for Site 18.

Site 23   CARL G. WASHBURNE STATE PARK
on the Pacific Ocean

Campsites, facilities: There are eight tent sites and 58 sites with full hookups for trailers or motor homes up to 45 feet long. A special area is available for hikers and bicyclists. Picnic tables are provided. Flush toilets, showers, firewood and a laundromat are available. Leashed pets are permitted.

Reservations, fee: No reservations necessary; $9-11 fee per night in summer, $6-8 off-season. Open all year.

Who to contact: Phone (503)238-7488 or write to Florence, OR 97439.

Location: From Florence, drive 14 miles north on US 101, then one mile west on the park entrance road.

Trip note: This park is located in a unique area with a variety of exciting trips. Short hikes lead from the campground to a two-mile long beach and extensive tide pools along the base of the cliffs. The inland sections of this park are frequented by elk, which are commonly spotted by campers. Just three miles south of the park are the Sea Lion Caves, where there is an elevator to take visitors down into the cavern, providing an insider's view of the life of a sea lion.

Site 24   ALDER LAKE
near Alder Lake
OREGON DUNES NATIONAL RECREATION AREA

Campsites, facilities: There are 39 sites for tents, trailers or motor homes up to 30 feet long. Picnic tables and fire grills are provided. Flush toilets and piped water are available. Leashed pets are permitted.

Reservations, fee: Reservations are available for 20 sites through MISTIX by phoning (800)283-CAMP, other sites are taken on first come, first served basis; $6 fee per night. Open mid-May to mid-September.

Who to contact: Phone (503)268-4473 or write to Mapleton Ranger District, Mapleton, OR 97453.

Location: From Florence, drive seven miles north on US 101 and you'll see the campground.

Trip note: This campground is set near three lakes, Alder Lake (quite small), Sutton Lake (larger) and Mercer Lake (largest). A boat launch is available at Sutton Lake. An option is exploring the expansive sand dunes in the area by foot. No off-road vehicle access here. See the trip note for Site 26 for other information on the area.

Site 25   SUTTON CREEK, B LOOP
near Sutton Lake
OREGON DUNES NATIONAL RECREATION AREA

Campsites, facilities: There are four campgrounds with 79 sites for tents, trailers or motor homes up to 22 feet long. Picnic tables and fire grills are provided. Flush toilets and piped water are available. Leashed pets are permitted.

Reservations, fee: No reservations necessary; $6 fee per night. Open all year.

Who to contact: Phone (503)268-4473 or write to Mapleton Ranger District, Mapleton, OR 97453.

Location: From Florence, drive six miles north on US 101, then 1.5 miles northwest on Forest Service Road 794. From there, go one-quarter mile northeast on Forest Service Road 793 and you'll see the campground entrance.

Trip note: This campground is located adjacent to Sutton Creek, not far from Sutton Lake. Swimming and fishing are both popular. A hiking trail leads from camp out to the dunes. There is no off-road vehicle access here.

Site 26   LANE COUNTY HARBOR VISTA PARK
near Florence

Campsites, facilities: There are 27 sites for tents, trailers or motor homes up to 32 feet long. Picnic tables are provided. Flush toilets, sanitary services, showers, piped water and a playground are available. Pets and motorbikes are permitted.

Reservations, fee: No reservations necessary; $6 fee per night. Open all year, but facilities are limited during the winter.

Who to contact: Phone (503)997-8721 or write to P.O. Box 700, Florence, OR 97439.

Location: From Florence, travel three miles north on Rhododendron Drive, then take Harbor Vista Road to 87658 Harbor Vista Road.

Trip note: This county park is set out among the dunes near the entrance to the harbor and offers a great lookout point from the observation deck. There are a number of side trips available, including Darlington State Park, Jessie M. Honeyman Memorial State Park (see the trip note for Site 38) and the Indian Forest, just four miles north of Florence. Florence also has displays of Indian dwellings and crafts.

Site 27   RHODODENDRON TRAILER PARK
near Florence

Campsites, facilities: There are 18 drive-through sites for trailers or motor homes of any length. Electricity, piped water and sewer hookups are provided. Flush toilets, showers and a laundromat are available. Bottled gas, a store, a cafe and ice are located within one mile. Leashed pets are permitted. Boat docks are nearby.

Reservations, fee: Reservations accepted; $9 fee per night. Open all year.

Who to contact: Phone (503)997-2206 or write to 87735 Highway 101, Florence, OR 97439.

Location: From Florence, go three miles north on US 101 and you'll see the park.

Trip note: See the trip note for Site 26 for side trip possibilities. Nearby recreation options include an 18-hole golf course, a riding stable and tennis courts.

Site 28   MERCER LAKE RESORT
on Mercer Lake

Campsites, facilities: There are 15 drive-through sites for trailers or motor homes of any length. Electricity, piped water, sewer hookups and picnic tables are provided. Flush toilets, bottled gas, sanitary services, showers, a store, a laundromat, ice and a playground are available. Leashed pets are permitted. Boat docks, launching facilities and rentals are nearby.

Reservations, fee: Reservations accepted; $8 fee per night; MasterCard and Visa accepted. Open all year.

Who to contact: Phone (503)997-3633 or write to 88875 Bay Berry, Florence, OR 97439.

Location: From Florence, go five miles north on US 101, then one mile east on Mercer Lake Road. Go north on Resort Road to the campground.

Trip note: This resort is set along the shore of Mercer Lake, one of a number of lakes that have formed among the ancient dunes in this area.

Site 29   WAYSIDE MOBILE AND RV PARK
near Florence

Campsites, facilities: There are 32 sites for trailers or motor homes of any length. Electricity, piped water, sewer hookups and picnic tables are provided. Flush toilets, sanitary services, showers and a laundromat are available. Bottled gas, a store, a cafe and ice are located within one mile. Leashed pets are permitted. Boat launching facilities are nearby.

Reservations, fee: Reservations accepted; $12 fee per night. Open all year.

Who to contact: Phone (503)997-6451 or write to 3760 Highway 101 North, Florence, OR 97439.

Location: In Florence, from the junction of Highway 126 and US 101, travel 1.8 miles north on US 101 to the park.

Trip note: See the trip notes for Sites 26 and 30 for side trip ideas. Nearby recreation options include an 18-hole golf course, a riding stable and tennis courts.

Site 30   PORT OF SIUSLAW RV AND MARINA
on Siuslaw River

Campsites, facilities: There are 80 tent sites and 78 sites for trailers or motor homes of any length. Electricity, piped water, sewer hookups and picnic tables are provided. Flush toilets, bottled gas, sanitary services, showers, firewood, a recreation hall, a store, a laundromat and ice are available. A cafe is located within one mile. Leashed pets are permitted. Boat docks and launching facilities are nearby.

Reservations, fee: Reservations accepted; $6-11 fee per night. Open all year.

Who to contact: Phone (503)997-3040 or write to P.O. Box 1638, Florence, OR 97439.

Location: In Florence, turn off US 101 and go about one-half mile east on First Street to Harbor Street and you'll see the marina.

Trip note: This resort is set along the Siuslaw River in Florence. Fishermen with boats will find the Highway 101 bridge support pilings make good spots to fish for perch and flounder.

Site 31   COAST MARINA AND RV PARK
on Siuslaw River

Campsites, facilities: There are seven sites for trailers or motor homes up to 26 feet long. Electricity, piped water, sewer hookups and picnic tables are provided. Flush toilets, bottled gas, showers, a recreation hall, a store, a cafe, a laundromat and ice are available. Pets and motorbikes are permitted. Boat docks, launching facilities and rentals are located nearby.

Reservations, fee: Reservations accepted; $14-20 fee per night; call ahead for availability of overnight rentals. Open all year.

Who to contact: Phone (503)997-3031 or write to 07790 Highway 126, Florence,

OR 97439.

Location: From Florence, travel 5.5 miles east on Highway 126 and you'll see the entrance to the park.

Trip note: This privately-owned, rural park is set along the shore of the Siuslaw River mid-way between Florence and Mapleton, and offers boat rentals and facilities. Fishing can be excellent in season, but it's advisable to phone for the latest report.

Site **32**   **ARCHIE KNOWLES**
                      on Knowles Creek

Campsites, facilities: There are nine sites for tents, trailers or motor homes up to 16 feet long. Picnic tables and fire grills are provided. Flush toilets and piped water are available. Leashed pets are permitted.

Reservations, fee: No reservations necessary; $5 fee per night. Open May to early September.

Who to contact: Phone (503)268-4473 or write to Siuslaw National Forest, Mapleton Ranger District, Mapleton, OR 97453.

Location: From Mapleton, go three miles east on Highway 126 and you'll see the campground entrance.

Trip note: This little campground is set along Knowles Creek about three miles from the Siuslaw River. This is a more rustic alternative to Site 31.

Site **33**   **NORTH FORK SIUSLAW**
                      on the North Fork of Siuslaw River
                      SIUSLAW NATIONAL FOREST

Campsites, facilities: There are five tent sites. Picnic tables and fire grills are provided. Pit toilets are available, but there is **no piped water.** Leashed pets are permitted.

Reservations, fee: No reservations necessary; no fee. Open May to early September.

Who to contact: Phone (503)268-4473 or write to Siuslaw National Forest, Mapleton Ranger District, Mapleton, OR 97453.

Location: From Florence, drive one mile east on Highway 36, then 13.5 miles northeast on County Road 5070 and you'll see the campground.

Trip note: Little known and little used, this can be the ideal hideaway. It is set along the North Fork of the Siuslaw River. A dirt road opposite the camp follows Wilhelm Creek for about two miles. See a Forest Service map for other trip possibilities.

Site **34**   **MAPLE LAKE TRAILER PARK-MARINA**
                      on Siuslaw River

Campsites, facilities: There are 46 sites for tents, trailers or motor homes of any length. Electricity, piped water and sewer hookups are provided. Flush toilets, bottled gas, sanitary services and showers are available. A store, a cafe and ice are located within one mile. Pets and motorbikes are permitted. Boat docks and launching facilities are nearby.

Reservations, fee: Reservations accepted; $5-9 fee per night. Open all year.

Who to contact: Phone (503)268-4822 or write to 10730 Highway 126, Mapleton, OR 97453.

Location: This park is located in Mapleton on Highway 126 behind the Forest Service station.

Trip note: This park is set along the shore of the Siuslaw River in Mapleton. There are boat rentals and hiking trails nearby. The general area is surrounded by Siuslaw National Forest land. A Forest Service map details nearby backcountry trip ideas.

Site 35   LAKESHORE TRAILER PARK
on Woahink Lake

Campsites, facilities: There are 25 drive-through sites for trailers or motor homes of any length. Electricity, piped water and sewer hookups are provided. Flush toilets, cable TV, showers, a store and a laundromat are available. A cafe is located within one mile. Leashed pets are permitted. Boat docks are nearby.

Reservations, fee: Reservations accepted; $12 fee per night. Open all year.

Who to contact: Phone (503)997-2741 or write to 83763 Highway 101, Florence, OR 97439.

Location: From Florence, go four miles south on US 101 and you'll see the park.

Trip note: This is a prime area for vacationers. This park is set along the shore of Woahink Lake, a popular spot to fish for trout, perch, catfish, crappie, bluegill and bass. It is adjacent to Jessie M. Honeyman Memorial State Park and the Oregon Dunes National Recreation Area. Off-road vehicle access to the dunes can be found four miles northeast of the park. Hiking trails through the dunes can be found at Honeyman Memorial State Park. If you set out across the dunes off the trail, note your path: People going off the trail commonly get lost out here.

Site 36   SILTCOOS LAKE RESORT MOTEL
on Siltcoos River

Campsites, facilities: There are four tent sites and six drive-through sites for trailers or motor homes up to 32 feet long. Electricity, piped water, cable TV, sewer hookups and picnic tables are provided. Flush toilets, showers, a recreation hall and a playground are available. Bottled gas, a store, a cafe, a laundromat and ice are located within one mile. Pets and motorbikes are permitted. Boat docks, launching facilities and rentals are nearby.

Reservations, fee: Reservations accepted; $10 fee per night; MasterCard and Visa accepted. Open all year.

Who to contact: Phone (503)997-3741 or write to Box 36, Westlake, OR 97493.

Location: From Florence, go six miles south on US 101, then one-quarter mile east on Westlake turnoff and you'll see the motel.

Trip note: This resort is set along the Siltcoos River adjacent to Siltcoos Lake, which is a large lake with many inlets, ideal for fishing. Just across the highway, you will find off-road vehicle and hiking access to the Oregon Dunes National Recreation Area.

Site 37   DARLINGS RESORT
on Siltcoos Lake

Campsites, facilities: There are 35 sites for tents, trailers or motor homes of any length. Electricity, piped water, sewer hookups and picnic tables are provided. Flush toilets, showers, firewood, a store, a cafe and a laundromat are available. Leashed pets are permitted. Boat docks, launching facilities and rentals are nearby.

Reservations, fee: Reservations accepted; $10 fee per night. Open all year.

Who to contact: Phone (503)997-2841 or write to 4879 Darling Loop, Florence, OR 97439.

Location: From Florence, go five miles south on US 101, then one-half mile east on North Beach Road to the resort.

Trip note: This park is set in a rural area along the north shore of Siltcoos Lake, adjacent to the extensive Oregon Dunes National Recreation Area. An access point to the dunes for hikers and off-road vehicles is just across the highway. There is a full-service marina at the lake.

Site **38**
JESSIE M. HONEYMAN MEMORIAL STATE PARK
on Cleowax Lake

Campsites, facilities: There are 240 sites for tents or self-contained motor homes, 141 sites with full or partial hookups for trailers or motor homes of any length, and a special camping area for hikers and bicyclists. Picnic tables and fire grills are provided. Flush toilets, sanitary services, showers, firewood and a laundromat are available. Some facilities are wheelchair accessible. Leashed pets are permitted. Boat docks and launching facilities are nearby.

Reservations, fee: Reservations accepted; $9-11 fee per night in summer, $6-8 off-season, $2 for hikers' sites. Open all year.

Who to contact: Phone (503)997-3851 or write to 84505 Highway 101, Florence, OR 97439.

Location: From Florence, drive three miles south on US 101 and you'll see the park entrance.

Trip note: This is a popular state park set along the shore of Cleowax Lake and adjacent to the dunes of the Oregon Dunes National Recreation Area. Many good hiking trails are available in the park. For off-road vehicle access to the dunes, head about three miles north on the main highway. Boating, fishing and swimming are popular at either of the two lakes within the park.

Site **39**
DRIFTWOOD II
near Siltcoos Lake
OREGON DUNES NATIONAL RECREATION AREA

Campsites, facilities: There are 70 sites for tents, trailers or motor homes up to 22 feet long. Picnic tables and fire grills are provided. Piped water and flush and pit toilets are available. A sanitary disposal station is available within five miles. Some facilities are wheelchair accessible. Leashed pets are permitted. Boat docks, launching facilities and rentals are located about four miles away on Siltcoos Lake.

Reservations, fee: No reservations necessary; $4 fee per night. Open all year.

Who to contact: Phone (503)271-3611 or write to Oregon Dunes National Recreation Area, 855 Highway Avenue, Reedsport, OR 97467.

Location: From Florence, go seven miles south on US 101, then 1.5 miles west on Siltcoos Beach and Dune Access Road and you'll see the campground.

Trip note: This is primarily a campground for off-road vehicles. It is set near the ocean in the Oregon Dunes National Recreation Area and has off-road vehicle access. Several small lakes, the Siltcoos River and Siltcoos Lake are nearby.

Site **40**
LAGOON
near Siltcoos Lake
OREGON DUNES NATIONAL RECREATION AREA

Campsites, facilities: There are 51 sites for tents, trailers or motor homes up to 22 feet long. Picnic tables and fire grills are provided. Piped water and flush and pit toilets are available. Sanitary services are located within five miles. Leashed pets are permitted. Boat docks, launching facilities and rentals are nearby on Siltcoos Lake.

Reservations, fee: No reservations necessary; $6 fee per night. Open June to late September.

Who to contact: Phone (503)271-3611 or write to Oregon Dunes National Recreation Area, 855 Highway Avenue, Reedsport, OR 97467.

Location: From Florence, go seven miles south on US 101, then 1.3 miles west on Siltcoos Beach and Dune Access Road and you're there.

Trip note: This is one of several campgrounds in this area. This one is set along the lagoon about one mile from Siltcoos Lake. There are hiking trails nearby and off-road vehicle access about one-half of a mile away at Driftwood (Site 39).

Site **41**
TYEE
on Siltcoos Lake
OREGON DUNES NATIONAL RECREATION AREA

Campsites, facilities: There are 15 sites for tents, trailers or motor homes up to 22 feet long. Picnic tables and fire grills are provided. Piped water, pit toilets and a store are available. Leashed pets are permitted. Boat docks, launching facilities and rentals are nearby.

Reservations, fee: No reservations necessary; $6 fee per night. Open all year.

Who to contact: Phone (503)271-3611 or write to Oregon Dunes National Recreation Area, 855 Highway Avenue, Reedsport, OR 97467.

Location: From Florence, go six miles south on US 101, then 100 yards southeast on Forest Service Road 1068 and you'll see the campground.

Trip note: This campground is set along the shore of Siltcoos Lake, an option to nearby Sites 39 and 40. Swimming, fishing and waterskiing are permitted at the lake. Off-road vehicle access to the dunes is available from Site 39 and there are hiking trails.

Site **42**
WAXMYRTLE
near Siltcoos Lake
OREGON DUNES NATIONAL RECREATION AREA

Campsites, facilities: There are 53 sites for tents, trailers or motor homes up to 22 feet long. Picnic tables and fire grills are provided. Piped water and flush toilets are available. Leashed pets are permitted. Boat docks, launching facilities and rentals are nearby on Siltcoos Lake.

Reservations, fee: Reservations available through MISTIX at (800)283-CAMP; $6 fee per night. Open June to late September.

Who to contact: Phone (503)271-3611 or write to Oregon Dunes National Recreation Area, 855 Highway Avenue, Reedsport, OR 97467.

Location: From Florence, travel seven miles south on US 101, then 1.3 miles west on Siltcoos Beach and Dune Access Road and you'll see the campground on your left.

Trip note: This is one of four camps in the immediate vicinity. It is set adjacent to Site 40 and less than a mile from Site 39, which has off-road vehicle access to the dunes. The campground is set near the lagoon, about a mile from Siltcoos Lake, a good-sized lake with boating facilities where waterskiing, fishing and swimming are permitted. There are hiking trails in the area.

Site 43

LODGEPOLE
on Siltcoos River
OREGON DUNES NATIONAL RECREATION AREA

Campsites, facilities: There are three sites for tents, trailers or motor homes up to 16 feet long. Picnic tables and fire grills are provided. Piped water and pit toilets are available. Leashed pets are permitted. Boat docks, launching facilities and rentals are nearby on Siltcoos Lake.

Reservations, fee: No reservations necessary; $4 fee per night. Open June to late September.

Who to contact: Phone (503)271-3611 or write to Oregon Dunes National Recreation Area, 855 Highway Avenue, Reedsport, OR 97467.

Location: From Florence, travel seven miles south on US 101, then turn west on Siltcoos Beach and Dune Access Road and you'll see the campground.

Trip note: This is the smallest, most private camp and the fastest one to fill up in the Siltcoos Lake area. This campground is set along the Siltcoos River and offers good fishing. It is within a mile of the previous four camps. Site 39 has off-road vehicle access to the dunes. Siltcoos Lake has complete boating facilities.

Site 44

CARTER LAKE
on Carter Lake
OREGON DUNES NATIONAL RECREATION AREA

Campsites, facilities: There are 24 sites for tents, trailers or motor homes up to 22 feet long. Picnic tables and fire grills are provided. Piped water and pit toilets are available. Leashed pets are permitted.

Reservations, fee: Fifteen of the campsites are available through reservation by calling MISTIX at (800)283-CAMP; $6 fee per night. Open all year.

Who to contact: Phone (503)271-3611 or write to Oregon Dunes National Recreation Area, 855 Highway Avenue, Reedsport, OR 97467.

Location: From Florence, drive 8.5 miles south on US 101, then 200 yards west on Forest Service Road 1086 and you're there.

Trip note: This campground is set along the north shore of Carter Lake. Boating, swimming and fishing are permitted on this long, narrow lake, which is set among dunes overgrown with vegetation. Hiking is allowed in the dunes, but there is no off-road vehicle access here. If you want ORV access then head north one mile to Siltcoos Road, turn west and drive 1.3 miles to Driftwood (Site 39).

Site 45

TAHKENITCH LANDING
near Tahkenitch Lake
OREGON DUNES NATIONAL RECREATION AREA

Campsites, facilities: There are about 15 sites for tents, trailers or motor homes up to 22 feet long. Picnic tables are provided and pit toilets are available. There is **no piped water.** Leashed pets are permitted. Boat launching facilities and a floating dock are available.

Reservations, fee: No reservations necessary; $4 fee per night. Open June to late September.

Who to contact: Phone (503)271-3611 or write to Oregon Dunes National Recreation Area, 855 Highway Avenue, Reedsport, OR 97467.

Location: From Reedsport, drive seven miles north on US 101 and you'll see the campground on the east side of the road.

Trip note: This camp overlooks Tahkenitch Lake and has easy access for fishing or swimming. There is no piped water here, but there is water nearby at Tahkenitch Lake (Site 46).

Site **46**   **TAHKENITCH**
                   near Tahkenitch Lake
            OREGON DUNES NATIONAL RECREATION AREA

Campsites, facilities: There are 35 sites for tents, trailers or motor homes up to 22 feet long. Picnic tables and fire grills are provided. Piped water, and flush and pit toilets are available. Leashed pets are permitted. Boat docks and launching facilities are on the lake.

Reservations, fee: No reservations necessary; $6 fee per night. Open June to late September.

Who to contact: Phone (503)271-3611 or write to Oregon Dunes National Recreation Area, 855 Highway Avenue, Reedsport, OR 97467.

Location: From Reedsport, travel seven miles north on US 101. The campground entrance is on the left.

Trip note: This campground is set in a wooded area across the highway from Tahkenitch Lake, which offers numerous coves and backwater areas for fishing and swimming. There is a hiking trail nearby that goes through the dunes out to the beach, and also to Threemile Lake. If this camp is filled, Site 45 provides nearby space.

Site **47**   **SALBASGEON INN & RV PARK**
                        on Umpqua River

Campsites, facilities: There are ten sites for trailers or motor homes of any length. Electricity, piped water, sewer hookups and picnic tables are provided. Flush toilets, showers, firewood, a store and ice are available. Leashed pets are permitted. Boat docks and launching facilities are nearby.

Reservations, fee: Reservations accepted; $10 fee per night. Open all year.

Who to contact: Phone (503)271-2025 or write to Route 4, Box 27, Reedsport, OR 97467.

Location: From Reedsport, drive 7.5 miles east on Highway 38 and you'll see the park.

Trip note: This wooded park is set along the Umpqua River near an elk preserve. Fishing for salmon and steelhead can be outstanding in season. In summer, Highway 38 is one of the prettiest drives in the western U.S.

Site **48**   **UMPQUA LIGHTHOUSE STATE PARK**
                        on Umpqua River

Campsites, facilities: There are 41 sites for tents or self-contained motor homes, and 22 sites with full hookups for trailers or motor homes up to 45 feet long. Electricity, piped water, sewer hookups and picnic tables are provided. Flush toilets, showers, firewood and a laundromat are available. Leashed pets are permitted. Boat docks and launching facilities are on the Umpqua River.

Reservations, fee: No reservations necessary; $9-11 fee per night in summer, $6-8 off-season. Open mid-April to late October.

Who to contact: Phone (503)271-4118 or write to Box 94, Winchester Bay, OR 97467.

Location: Drive six miles south of Reedsport on US 101 and you'll see the park entrance.

Trip note: This park is set near the mouth of the Umpqua River, a unique area where the dunes are as high as 500 feet. Hiking trails lead out from the park south into Umpqua Dunes Scenic Area. The park offers over two miles of beach access on the ocean and one-half mile along the Umpqua River.

Site 49   WILLIAM M. TUGMAN STATE PARK
on Eel Lake

Campsites, facilities: There are 115 sites with water and electrical hookups for trailers or motor homes up to 50 feet long, and a special camping area for hikers and bicyclists. Electricity, piped water and picnic tables are provided. Flush toilets, sanitary services, showers, firewood and a laundromat are available. Some facilities are wheelchair accessible. Leashed pets are permitted. Boat docks and launching facilities are nearby.

Reservations, fee: No reservations necessary; $7.50-10.50 fee per night, $2 per person for hikers' sites. Open mid-April to late October.

Who to contact: Phone (503)271-4118 or write c/o Umpqua Lighthouse State Park, P.O. Box 94, Winchester Bay, OR 97467.

Location: From Reedsport, travel eight miles south on US 101 and you'll see the park entrance.

Trip note: This campground is set along the shore of Eel Lake, which offers almost five miles of shoreline for swimming and trout fishing. There is a boat ramp, but there is a 10-mph speed limit for boats. Across the highway is the Oregon Dunes National Recreation Area.

Site 50   SURFWOOD CAMPGROUND & RV PARK
on Winchester Bay

Campsites, facilities: There are 22 tent sites and 141 drive-through sites for trailers or motor homes. Electricity, piped water, sewer hookups and picnic tables are provided. Flush toilets, sanitary services, showers, firewood, a store, a cafe, a laundromat, ice, a playground and a swimming pool are available. Pets and motorbikes are permitted. Boat docks and launching facilities are nearby.

Reservations, fee: Reservations accepted; $8 fee per night. Open all year.

Who to contact: Phone (503)271-4020 or write to HC 4, Box 268, Reedsport, OR 97467.

Location: Travel one-half mile north of Winchester Bay on US 101 and you'll see the park entrance.

Trip note: The pull-through sites are separated by shrubs, which helps privacy. This park is a half-mile drive from the marina at Winchester Bay. Fishing is the focal point, but there are other possibilities in the area. There are many trails nearby, leading west across the dunes to the ocean and east to lakes in wooded areas. Some ten miles east, an elk preserve is located adjacent to Highway 38.

Site 51   UMPQUA BEACH RESORT
on Winchester Bay

Campsites, facilities: There are 50 drive-through sites for trailers or motor homes of any length. Electricity, piped water, sewer hookups and picnic tables are provided. Flush toilets, bottled gas, showers, a store, a cafe, a laundromat and ice are available. Sanitary services are located within one mile. Pets and motorbikes are permitted. Boat docks and launching facilities are nearby.

Reservations, fee: Reservations accepted; $10 fee per night; MasterCard and Visa accepted. Open all year.

Who to contact: Phone (503)271-3443 or write to HC 4, Box 242, Reedsport, OR 97467.

Location: Take the Windy Cove exit off US 101 near Winchester Bay and drive 1.5 miles west to the resort.

Trip note: This resort is set on the shore of Winchester Bay in a fishing village near the mouth of the Umpqua River. For details on nearby recreation options, see the trip note for Site 50.

Site 52   WINDY COVE COUNTY PARK
on the Pacific Ocean

Campsites, facilities: There are 29 tent sites and 75 sites for trailers or motor homes up to 30 feet long. Electricity, piped water, sewer hookups and picnic tables are provided. Flush toilets, showers and a playground are available. Bottled gas, sanitary services, a store, a cafe, a laundromat and ice are located within one mile. Pets and motorbikes are permitted. Boat docks, launching facilities and rentals are nearby.

Reservations, fee: No reservations necessary; $7.35-10 fee per night. Open all year.

Who to contact: Phone (503)271-4138 or (for tent sites) write to P.O. Box 265, Winchester Bay, OR 97467. For RV sites, write to P.O. Box 224, Winchester Bay, OR 97467.

Location: Drive south of Reedsport on Highway 101 to Winchester Bay and take the Windy Cove exit to the park.

Trip note: This county park is set on the ocean and offers boat rentals and fishing equipment. Nearby recreation options include an 18-hole golf course and tennis courts.

Site 53   NORTH LAKE RESORT & MARINA
on Tenmile Lake

Campsites, facilities: There are 112 sites for trailers or motor homes of any length. Picnic tables are provided. Flush toilets, bottled gas, sanitary services, showers, firewood, a store, ice, a playground, electricity, piped water and sewer hookups are available. A cafe and a laundromat are located within one mile. Leashed pets are permitted. Boat docks, launching facilities and rentals are nearby.

Reservations, fee: Reservations accepted; $9.50-13 fee per night; MasterCard and Visa accepted. Open all year.

Who to contact: Phone (503)759-3515 or write to 2090 North Lake Avenue, Lakeside, OR 97449.

Location: Take the Lakeside exit off US 101, then go three-quarters of a mile east to North Lake Avenue and one-half mile east to the resort.

Trip note: This resort is set along the shore of Tenmile Lake, which has a full-service marina.

Site 54   SEADRIFT MOTEL & CAMPGROUND
near Tenmile Lake

Campsites, facilities: There are 42 drive-through sites for trailers or motor homes of any length. Picnic tables are provided. Flush toilets, bottled gas, sanitary services, showers and a playground are available. A store, a cafe and a laundromat are located within one mile. Leashed pets are permitted. Boat docks, launching facilities and rentals are nearby. Discounts are given for Good Sam members.

Reservations, fee: Reservations accepted; $11 fee per night; MasterCard and Visa accepted. Open all year.

Who to contact: Phone (503)271-3611 or write to Oregon Dunes National Recreation Area, 855 Highway Avenue, Reedsport, OR 97467.

Location: From Reedsport, drive 12 miles south on US 101. The campground entrance is on the right.

Trip note: This campground is set along Eel Creek, near both Eel Lake and Tenmile Lake. Waterskiing is allowed on Tenmile Lake but not on Eel Lake. There are hiking trails nearby that access the Umpqua Dunes Scenic Area. Access for off-road vehicles is available at Site 57.

Site **55**

NORTH EEL CREEK
near Eel Lake
OREGON DUNES NATIONAL RECREATION AREA

Campsites, facilities: There are 52 sites for tents, trailers or motor homes up to 22 feet long. Picnic tables and fire grills are provided. Piped water, and flush and pit toilets are available. Leashed pets are permitted. Boat docks, launching facilities and rentals are nearby.

Reservations, fee: No reservations necessary; $6 fee per night. Open June to late September.

Who to contact: Phone (503)271-3611 or write to Oregon Dunes National Recreation Area, 855 Highway Avenue, Reedsport, OR 97467.

Location: From Reedsport, travel 12 miles southwest on US 101 and you'll see the campground entrance on your right.

Trip note: This campground is set along Eel Creek, near both Eel Lake, and Tenmile Lake. Waterskiing is allowed at Tenmile Lake, but not at Eel Lake. There are trails nearby that access the Umpqua Dunes Scenic Area. Access for off-road vehicles is available at Site 57.

Site **56**

MID EEL
on Eel River
OREGON DUNES NATIONAL RECREATION AREA

Campsites, facilities: There are 27 sites for tents, trailers or motor homes up to 16 feet long. Picnic tables and fire grills are provided. Flush toilets and piped water are available. Leashed pets are permitted. Boat docks, launching facilities and rentals are nearby.

Reservations, fee: No reservations necessary; $6 fee per night. Open June to late September.

Who to contact: Phone (503)271-3611 or write to Oregon Dunes National Recreation Area, 855 Highway Avenue, Reedsport, OR 97467.

Location: From Reedsport, go 12 miles southwest on US 101, then about 100 yards west on Forest Service Road 1093.

Trip note: This campground is set very near Site 55 and offers the same opportunities.

Site **57**

SPINREEL
on Tenmile Lake
OREGON DUNES NATIONAL RECREATION AREA

Campsites, facilities: There are 37 sites for tents, trailers or motor homes up to 22 feet long. Piped water and flush toilets are available. Picnic tables and fire grills are provided. Firewood, a store and a laundromat are available. Leashed pets are permitted. Boat docks, launching facilities and rentals are located on Tenmile Lake.

Reservations, fee: No reservations necessary; $6 fee per night. Open all year.

Who to contact: Phone (503)271-3611 or write to Oregon Dunes National Recreation Area, 855 Highway Avenue, North Bend, OR 97459.

Location: From North Bend, go eight miles north on US 101 and you'll see a sign directing you to Spinreel Campground. Drive one mile northwest to the campground.

Trip note: This campground is set at the outlet of Tenmile Lake, in the Oregon Dunes National Recreation Area. Boating facilities are located near the camp. There are hiking trails and off-road vehicle access to the dunes. Off-road vehicle rentals are available adjacent to the camp.

Site **58**
BLUEBILL LAKE
on Bluebill Lake
OREGON DUNES NATIONAL RECREATION AREA

Campsites, facilities: There are 19 sites for tents, trailers or motor homes up to 22 feet long. Picnic tables and fire grills are provided. Flush toilets and piped water are available. Leashed pets are permitted.

Reservations, fee: No reservations necessary; $6 fee per night. Open all year.

Who to contact: Phone (503)271-3611 or write to Oregon Dunes National Recreation Area, 855 Highway Avenue, Reedsport, OR 97467.

Location: From North Bend, travel four miles north on US 101, then three-quarters of a mile west on Horsefall Dunes and Beach Access Road. From there, go 2.5 miles northwest on Horsefall Road and you'll see the campground entrance.

Trip note: This campground gets very little camping pressure. It is set next to little Bluebill Lake, so small it dries up during the summer. It is a short distance from Horsefall Lake, which is surrounded by private property. If you continue west on the Forest Service road you will come to a picnicking and parking area near the beach that has off-road vehicle access to the dunes.

Site **59**
KELLEY'S RV PARK
near Coos Bay

Campsites, facilities: There are 38 drive-through sites for trailers or motor homes of any length. Electricity, piped water, sewer hookups and picnic tables are provided. Flush toilets, sanitary services, a laundromat and ice are available. Bottled gas, a store and a cafe are located within one mile. Leashed pets are permitted. Boat docks and launching facilities are nearby.

Reservations, fee: Reservations accepted; $8 fee per night; MasterCard and Visa accepted. Open all year.

Who to contact: Phone (503)888-6531 or write to 555 South Empire Boulevard, Coos Bay, OR 97420.

Location: In Coos Bay, take the Charleston exit off US 101 and go 4.5 miles to 555 South Empire Boulevard.

Trip note: This RV park is in the town of Coos Bay, well-known for its salmon, deep sea fishing and lumber. Nearby recreation options include a full-service marina.

Site **60**
HORSEFALL
OREGON DUNES NATIONAL RECREATION AREA

Campsites, facilities: There are 125 sites for trailers or motor homes of any length.

Piped water, showers and flush toilets are available. Leashed pets are permitted.

Reservations, fee: No reservations necessary; $6 fee per night. Open all year.

Who to contact: Phone (503)271-3611 or write to Oregon Dunes National Recreation Area, 855 Highway Avenue, Reedsport, OR 97467.

Location: Drive north out of North Bend on US 101 for four miles, then turn west on Horsefall Road and continue three miles to the campground.

Trip note: This campground is actually a nice, large paved area for parking motor homes. It is the staging area for off-road vehicle access into the southern section of Oregon Dunes National Recreation Area.

Site 61   SUNSET BAY STATE PARK
near Sunset Bay

Campsites, facilities: There are 109 sites for tents or self-contained motor homes, and 29 sites with full hookups for trailers or motor homes up to 47 feet long. Picnic tables and fire grills are provided. Flush toilets, showers, firewood and a laundromat are available. A restaurant is located within one mile. Some facilities are wheelchair accessible. Leashed pets are permitted.

Reservations, fee: Reservations accepted; $9-11 in summer, $6-8 off-season. Open year-round.

Who to contact: Phone (503)888-4902 or write to 13030 Cape Argo Highway, Coos Bay, OR 97420.

Location: From Coos Bay, travel 12 miles southwest on the Cape Argo Highway and you'll see the park entrance.

Trip note: This campground is set near Sunset Bay, which is a small, enclosed and well-protected bay with a nice beach for swimming.

Site 62   TYEE
on Umpqua River

Campsites, facilities: There are 11 sites for tents, trailers or motor homes. Piped water, fire grills and picnic tables are provided. Vault toilets and firewood are available. A store is located within one mile. Leashed pets are permitted.

Reservations, fee: No reservations necessary; $4 fee per night. Open May to late October.

Who to contact: Phone (503)672-4491 or write to Bureau of Land Management, 777 NW Garden Valley Boulevard, Roseburg, OR 97470.

Location: From Sutherlin, go 12 miles northwest on Highway 138 and you'll see the campground entrance.

Trip note: Here is a classic spot, set along the Umpqua River with great fishing in season, yet very few people know of it. It is managed by the Bureau of Land Management, which rarely publicizes its campgrounds.

Site 63   WILLAMETTE CITY PARK
on Willamette River

Campsites, facilities: There are 25 sites for tents, trailers or motor homes of any length. Vault toilets, piped water, a covered outdoor kitchen area, picnic tables and a small playground are available. Bottled gas, a store, a cafe, a laundromat and ice are within one mile. There is a dump station at the Texaco on 9th Street in the center of town, three miles away. Pets and motorbikes are permitted. Boat docks and launching facilities are located two miles away.

Reservations, fee: No reservations necessary; $4 fee per night. Open April to late October.

Who to contact: Phone (503)757-6918 or write to Corvallis Department of Parks and Recreation, P.O. Box 1083, Corvallis, OR 97339.

Location: From Corvallis, go one mile south on Highway 99W, then go one-half mile east on SE Goodnight Road to the park.

Trip note: This 40-acre city park is set along the banks of the Willamette River, just outside Corvallis. The camping area is actually a large clearing near the entrance to the park, which has been left in its natural state. There are trails leading down to the river, and the birdwatching is good here. Trout fishing can be a winner on the Willamette.

Site 64   CORVALLIS MOTORHOME PARK
in Corvallis

Campsites, facilities: There are ten sites for trailers or motor homes. Electricity, piped water and sewer hookups are provided. Flush toilets, showers, a store, a cafe, a laundromat and ice are available. Bottled gas and sanitary services are located within one mile. Pets and motorbikes are permitted.

Reservations, fee: Reservations accepted; $15 fee per night. Open all year.

Who to contact: Phone (503)752-2334 or write to 200 Northwest 53rd Street, Corvallis, OR 97330.

Location: From Corvallis, go 2.5 miles west on US 20, then turn north on 53rd Street and travel 1.3 mile to the park.

Trip note: This is a decent layover spot on your way to and from the coast. Nearby recreation options include an 18-hole golf course, hiking trails and a riding stable.

Site 65   SOUTH CORVALLIS TRAILER COURT
in Corvallis

Campsites, facilities: There are 12 sites for trailers or motor homes of any length. Electricity, piped water and sewer hookups are provided. Flush toilets, showers and a laundromat are available. Bottled gas, a store, a cafe and ice are located within one mile. Leashed pets are permitted.

Reservations, fee: Reservations accepted; $8 fee per night. Open all year.

Who to contact: Phone (503)753-3334 or write to 245 Southwest Twin Oak, Corvallis, OR 97330.

Location: From Corvallis, drive south on Highway 99W one block south of the bridge. The trailer court is located one block west of there.

Trip note: This park is in Corvallis, home of Oregon State University. Nearby recreation options include an 18-hole golf course, hiking trails, a riding stable and tennis courts.

SISKIYOU

♦

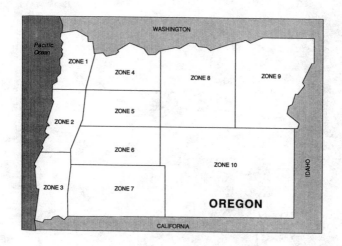

SOME HIGHLIGHTS
---

53 CAMPGROUNDS

Sixes River

Siskiyou National Forest

Coquille River

Rogue River

Chetco River

Illinois River

Oregon Caves National Monument

West Coast Game Park Walk-Through Safari

Humbug Mountain

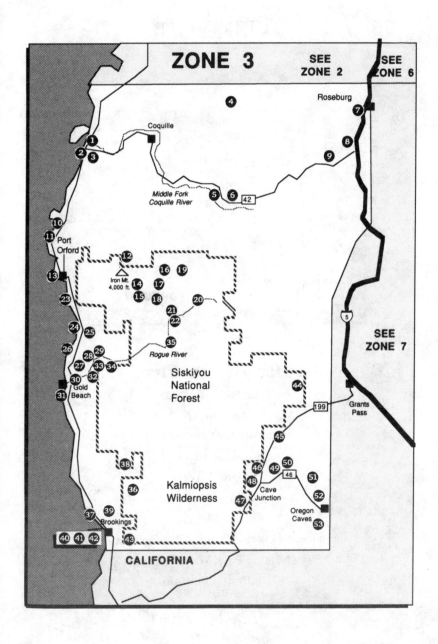

ZONE 3

SEE
ZONE 2

SEE
ZONE 6

Roseburg

Coquille

Middle Fork
Coquille River

42

Port
Orford

Iron Mt.
4,000 ft.

Rogue River

Siskiyou
National
Forest

Grants
Pass

199

SEE
ZONE 7

Gold
Beach

Kalmiopsis
Wilderness

Cave
Junction

46

Oregon
Caves

Brookings

CALIFORNIA

BULLARDS BEACH
Site **1**

on Coquille River

Campsites, facilities: There are 192 sites with full or partial hookups for trailers or motor homes. A special area for horses is also available, as well as an area reserved for hikers and bicyclists. Piped water, picnic tables and fire grills are provided. Flush toilets, sanitary disposal station, showers, firewood, a store, a cafe, a laundromat and a loading ramp for horses are available. Some facilities are wheelchair accessible. Leashed pets are permitted. Boat docks and launching facilities are located in the park on the Coquille River.

Reservations, fee: No reservations necessary; $10-11 during summer months, $7-8 off-season. Open all year.

Who to contact: Phone (503)347-2209 or write to P.O. Box 25, Bandon, OR 97411.

Location: Drive north of Bandon on US 101 for about one mile and you'll see the park entrance on the west side of the road.

Trip note: The Coquille River is the centerpiece for this park. It offers good fishing in season, both for boaters and bankers, with four miles of shore access. If fishing isn't your thing, the park has several hiking trails. A historic lighthouse built in 1896 provides a side trip option.

DRIFTWOOD SHORES RV PARK
Site **2**

near Bandon State Park

Campsites, facilities: There are 40 drive-through sites for trailers or motor homes of any length. Electricity, piped water and sewer hookups are provided. Flush toilets, sanitary services, showers, a store, a cafe, a laundromat and ice are available. Bottled gas is located within one mile. Leashed pets are permitted. Boat docks and launching facilities are nearby.

Reservations, fee: Reservations accepted; $8 fee per night. Open all year.

Who to contact: Phone (503)347-4122 or write to 935 East 2nd Street, Bandon, OR 97411.

Location: From US 101 in Bandon, take Highway 42S and travel one block south and you'll see the park entrance.

Trip note: This is an in-town motor home park that can be a base point for many adventures. Rockhounds will enjoy beachcombing for agates and other semi-precious stones hidden along the beaches. Kids will enjoy the West Coast Game Park Walk-Through Safari petting zoo seven miles south of town, and Bandon State Park, which is four miles south of town and offers a good wading spot in the creek at the north end of the park. Nearby recreation opportunities include an 18-hole golf course, riding stable and tennis courts.

BLUE JAY CAMPGROUND
Site **3**

near the Pacific Ocean

Campsites, facilities: There are 19 tent sites and 22 sites for trailers or motor homes up to 30 feet long. Electricity, piped water and picnic tables are provided. Flush toilets, bottled gas, sanitary services, showers, firewood, a store, a cafe, a laundromat, ice and a playground are available. Pets and motorbikes are permitted. Boat launching facilities are nearby.

Reservations, fee: Reservations accepted; $7 fee per night. Open all year.

Who to contact: Phone (503)347-3258 or write to P.O. Box 281, Bandon, OR 97411.

Location: Drive two miles south of Bandon on US 101, then go one-half mile west on Beach Loop Road and you'll see the campground entrance.

Trip note: The trip note for Site 2 offers side trip information in Bandon. This park is near the beach and close to an 18-hole golf course and hiking trails.

Site 4
PARK CREEK
near Coquille

Campsites, facilities: There are 12 sites for tents, small trailers or camping vans. Picnic tables and fire grills are provided. Pit toilets are available. There is **no piped water.** Leashed pets are permitted.

Reservations, fee: No reservations necessary; no fee. Open all year.

Who to contact: Phone (503)756-0100 or write to Bureau of Land Management, 1300 Airport Lane, North Bend, OR 97459.

Location: Follow Middle Canyon Road east from Coquille for 24 miles to the campground.

Trip note: You want to be by yourself? You came to the right place. This pretty little campground is set along Park Creek out in the middle of nowhere.

Site 5
REMOTE CAMPGROUND
near Coos Bay

Campsites, facilities: There are 16 sites for tents, trailers or motor homes of any length. Electricity, piped water, sewer hookups and picnic tables are provided. Showers, a store and a laundromat are available. Pets and motorbikes are permitted.

Reservations, fee: Reservations accepted; $8-11 fee per night. Open all year.

Who to contact: Phone (503)572-5105 or write to Box 13, Highway 42, Remote, OR 97468.

Location: This campground is located east of Remote on Highway 42.

Trip note: This is a good layover for the motor home cruiser between Roseburg and Coos Bay. It is a quiet, pretty spot, set along the Middle Fork of the Coquille River.

Site 6
BEAR CREEK
on the Middle Fork of Coquille River

Campsites, facilities: There are nine tent sites and eight sites for trailers or motor homes up to 16 feet long. Picnic tables and fire grills are provided. Pit toilets and piped water are available. Leashed pets are permitted.

Reservations, fee: No reservations necessary; no fee. Open all year.

Who to contact: Phone (503)756-0100 or write to Bureau of Land Management, 1300 Airport Lane, North Bend, OR 97459.

Location: From Coquille, go 26 miles southeast on Highway 42 to the campground.

Trip note: This spot is a rustic camping option to Site 5, and the price is right. It is set along Bear Creek near where it empties into the Middle Fork of the Coquille River. It's a nice little spot.

Site 7
JOHN P. AMACHER COUNTY PARK
on Umpqua River

Campsites, facilities: There are ten sites for tents, and 30 sites for trailers or motor homes up to 30 feet long. Electricity, piped water, sewer hookups and picnic tables are provided. Flush toilets, showers, and a playground are available. Bottled gas, a store, a cafe, a laundromat and ice are located within one mile. Pets and motorbikes are permitted. Boat launching facilities are nearby.

Reservations, fee: No reservations necessary; $7-9 fee per night. Open all year.

Who to contact: Phone (503)672-4901 or write to P.O. Box 800, Winchester, OR 97495.

Location: This campground is five miles north of Roseburg.

Trip note: This is a prime layover spot for Interstate 5 motor home cruisers. It is a wooded county park set along the banks of the Umpqua River, just enough off the beaten track to be missed by most out-of-towners. Nearby recreation options include an 18-hole golf course and tennis courts.

Site 8   WILDLIFE SAFARI RV PARK
near Roseburg

Campsites, facilities: There are 39 drive-through sites for trailers or motor homes. Electricity is provided. A store and a cafe are available. Pets and motorbikes are permitted.

Reservations, fee: No reservations necessary; $3-5 fee per night. Open all year.

Who to contact: Phone (503)679-6761 or write to P.O. Box 1600, Winston, OR 97496.

Location: In Winston, take exit 119 off Interstate 5 and continue 3.5 miles southwest on Highway 42 to the park.

Trip note: This park is adjacent to the Wildlife Safari Park in Winston (near Roseburg), which offers a walk-through, petting zoo. Nearby recreation options include an 18-hole golf course, hiking trails and marked bike trails.

Site 9   TWIN RIVERS VACATION PARK
near Umpqua River

Campsites, facilities: There are ten tent sites and 75 drive-through sites for trailers or motor homes of any length. Electricity, piped water, sewer hookups, picnic tables, fire pits and firewood are provided. Flush toilets, bottled gas, showers, firewood, a store, a laundromat, ice and a playground are available. Pets and motorbikes are permitted. Boat launching facilities are nearby at River Fork Park.

Reservations, fee: Reservations accepted; $12.50 fee per night. Open all year.

Who to contact: Phone (503)673-3811 or write to 433 River Forks Park, Roseburg, OR 97470.

Location: Near Roseburg, take exit 125 off Interstate 5 and follow it five miles west to Old Garden Valley Road, then turn south for 1.5 miles to the campground.

Trip note: This country park is set next to River Fork Park, a 100-acre day-use park situated where the North and South Forks of the Umpqua River meet. In season, salmon and steelhead migrate through here. It has a playground for children that includes a fort, tepees, totem poles and a wading pool.

Site 10   KOA PINE SPRINGS
near Elk River

Campsites, facilities: There are 46 tent sites and 26 drive-through sites for trailers or motor homes of any length. Picnic tables are provided. Flush toilets, bottled gas, sanitary services, showers, firewood, a recreation hall, a store, a cafe, a laundromat, ice, a playground, electricity, piped water and sewer hookups are available. Pets and motorbikes are permitted. Cabins are available for $20 per night.

Reservations, fee: Reservations accepted; $11-15 fee per night; MasterCard and Visa accepted. Open all year.

Who to contact: Phone (503)348-2358 or write to 46612 Highway 101, Langlois,

OR 97450.

Location: This campground is located about ten miles north of Port Orford on US 101.

Trip note: This spot is often considered to be just a layover camp, but it offers large, secluded sites set among big trees and coastal ferns. It is minutes away from Elk River and Sixes River, where the fishing can be good. Cape Blanco State Park is just a few miles away.

Site 11   CAPE BLANCO STATE PARK
near Sixes River

Campsites, facilities: There are 58 sites with water and electrical hookups for tents, trailers or motor homes of any length. A special camping area is reserved for hikers and bicyclists. Picnic tables, piped water, electrical hookups and fire grills are provided. Firewood, flush toilets, showers, a laundromat and sanitary disposal station are available. Leashed pets are permitted. Some facilities are wheelchair accessible.

Reservations, fee: No reservations necessary; $10 in summer, $7 off-season. Open from mid-April to late September.

Who to contact: Phone (503)332-2971 or write to P.O. Box 299, Sixes, OR 97476.

Location: Travel four miles north of Port Orford on US 101, then head northwest on the road to the park. Drive five miles to the campground.

Trip note: This large park is named for the white ("blanco") chalk appearance of the sea cliffs, which rise 200 feet above the ocean. Sea lions inhabit the offshore rocks, and there are trails and a road that leads to the black sand beach below the cliffs. There is good access to the Sixes River, which runs for over two miles through the meadows and forests of the park. Of historical interest are the lighthouse and Hughes House Museum, both located within the park.

Site 12   SIXES RIVER
on Sixes River

Campsites, facilities: There are 19 sites for tents, trailers or motor homes up to 16 feet long. Picnic tables and fire grills are provided. Pit toilets are available. There is **no piped water.** Leashed pets are permitted.

Reservations, fee: No reservations necessary; no fee. Open all year.

Who to contact: Phone (503)756-0100 or write to Bureau of Land Management, 1300 Airport Lane, North Bend, OR 97459.

Location: Drive on US 101 to Sixes, then head east on Highway 184 for 11.5 miles to the campground. The last one-half mile is unpaved.

Trip note: This is a primitive, secluded campground for people who want quiet and a free, rustic spot. It is set along the banks of Sixes River.

Site 13   PORT ORFORD TRAILER VILLAGE
near Elk and Sixes Rivers

Campsites, facilities: There are seven tent sites and 49 drive-through sites for trailers or motor homes of any length. Electricity, piped water, sewer hookups and picnic tables are provided. Flush toilets, bottled gas, sanitary services, showers, a recreation hall, a store, a cafe, a laundromat and ice are available. Pets and motorbikes are permitted. Boat docks and launching facilities are nearby.

Reservations, fee: Reservations accepted; $7-12 fee per night. Open all year.

Who to contact: Phone (503)332-1041 or write to P.O. Box 697, Port Orford, OR 97465.

Location: In Port Orford, drive one block east on Madrona Avenue, then one-half mile north on Port Orford Loop.

Trip note: This is a friendly, Mom-and-Pop campground in Port Orford, where the hosts make you feel at home. An informal group campfire and happy hour is scheduled each evening. There is a small gazebo where you can get coffee in the morning and a patio where you can sit. Fishing is good during the fall and winter on the nearby Elk and Sixes Rivers, and the campground has a smokehouse, freezer and cleaning table.

Site **14**
BUTLER BAR
on Elk River
SISKIYOU NATIONAL FOREST

Campsites, facilities: There are 16 sites for tents, trailers or motor homes up to 16 feet long. Picnic tables and fire grills are provided. Piped water, pit toilets and firewood are available. Leashed pets are permitted.

Reservations, fee: No reservations necessary; $2 fee per night. Open late May to late September.

Who to contact: Phone the Siskiyou National Forest at (503)439-3011 or write to Powers Ranger District, Port Orford, OR 97465.

Location: From Port Orford, go three miles north on US 101, then 7.5 miles southeast on County Road 208. From there, take Forest Service Road 325 southeast and drive 11 miles to the campground. The road is paved all the way to the campground.

Trip note: This campground is set back from the shore of the Elk River and is surrounded by old growth forest, with some reforested areas nearby. Across the river is the Grassy Knob Wilderness Area, but it has no trails and is too rugged to hike. Elk River has native trout and steelhead in the winter.

Site **15**
LAIRD LAKE
on Laird Lake
SISKIYOU NATIONAL FOREST

Campsites, facilities: There are undeveloped, dispersed tent sites available. There is **no piped water.** Leashed pets are permitted.

Reservations, fee: No reservations necessary; no fee. Open late May to late September.

Who to contact: Phone the Siskiyou National Forest at (503)439-3011 or write to Powers Ranger District, Powers, OR 97466.

Location: From Port Orford, go three miles north on US 101, then 7.5 miles southeast on County Road 208. From there, take Forest Service Road 325 southeast and drive 15.5 miles to the campground. The road is paved all the way to the campground.

Trip note: This secluded campground is set along the shore of Laird Lake in a very private and scenic spot. Most campers have no idea that such a spot is available here.

Site **16**
MYRTLE GROVE
on the South Fork of Coquille River
SISKIYOU NATIONAL FOREST

Campsites, facilities: There are eight tent sites and four sites for trailers or motor homes. Picnic tables and fire grills are provided. Pit toilets and firewood are available. There is **no piped water.** Leashed pets are permitted.

Reservations, fee: No reservations necessary; no fee. Open late May to late September.

Who to contact: Phone the Siskiyou National Forest at (503)439-3011 or write to Powers Ranger District, Powers, OR 97466.

Location: From Powers, take Highway 242 for 4.3 miles, then go 4.5 miles south on Forest Service Road 33, and you'll see the campground. The road is paved all the way to the campground.

Trip note: This Forest Service campground is set along the South Fork of the Coquille River, a little downstream from Site 17 and in similar surroundings. Big Tree Recreation Site is a few miles away; there is a huge Port Orford cedar there. A prime hike can be made on the trail that runs adjacent to Elk Creek.

Site **17**   **DAPHNE GROVE**
                        on the South Fork of Coquille River
                        SISKIYOU NATIONAL FOREST

Campsites, facilities: There are 17 sites for tents, trailers or motor homes up to 15 feet long. Picnic tables and fire grills are provided. Pit toilets, piped water and firewood are available. Leashed pets are permitted.

Reservations, fee: No reservations necessary; $4 fee per night. Open late May to late September.

Who to contact: Phone the Siskiyou National Forest at (503)439-3011 or write to Powers Ranger District, Powers, OR 97466.

Location: From Powers, go 4.5 miles southeast on Highway 242, then 10.5 miles south on Forest Service Road 33, and you'll see the campground entrance. The road is paved all the way to the campground.

Trip note: This prime spot is far enough out of the way that it attracts little attention. It is set along the South Fork of the Coquille River and is surrounded by old growth Douglas fir and cedar. The road is paved all the way to the campground.

Site **18**   **ROCK CREEK**
                        near the South Fork of Coquille River
                        SISKIYOU NATIONAL FOREST

Campsites, facilities: There are six tent sites and two sites for trailers or motor homes. Picnic tables and fire grills are provided. Pit toilets and firewood are available. There is **no piped water.** Leashed pets are permitted.

Reservations, fee: No reservations necessary; $2 fee per night. Open late May to late September.

Who to contact: Phone the Siskiyou National Forest at (503)439-3011 or write to Powers Ranger District, Powers, OR 97466.

Location: From Powers, go 4.5 miles on Highway 242 to Forest Service Road 33. Go south on Forest Service Road 33 for 13 miles, then 1.5 miles southwest on Forest Service Road 3347 to the campground. The road is paved all the way.

Trip note: This little-known camp is set along Rock Creek, just upstream from its confluence with the South Fork of the Coquille River. It is surrounded by old growth forest and some reforested areas. One good side trip here is the one-mile climb to Azalea Lake, which is stocked with trout. There are some hike-in campsites at the lake, but there is no piped drinking water. In July, the Azalea blooms can be spectacular.

SQUAW LAKE
Site **19**
on Squaw Lake
SISKIYOU NATIONAL FOREST

Campsites, facilities: There are no developed sites, but rather dispersed sites for tents only. Pit toilets are provide. **No piped water** is available.

Reservations, fee: No reservations necessary; $2 fee per night. Open late May to late September.

Who to contact: Phone the Siskiyou National Forest at (503)439-3011 or write to Powers Ranger District, Powers, OR 97466.

Location: From Powers, take Highway 242 southeast for 4.5 miles. At Forest Service Road 33 go south for 12.5 miles, then southeast on Forest Service Road 3348 for 4.5 miles. Turn east on Forest Service Road 3342 and drive for one mile and you'll see the campground. The road is paved for all but the last one-half mile.

Trip note: This campground is set along the shore of five-acre Squaw Lake, set in rich, old-growth forest. The trailheads for Panther Ridge Trail and Coquille River Falls Trail are a ten-minute drive from the campground. It is strongly advised that you obtain a Forest Service map that details the backcountry roads and trails.

TUCKER FLAT
Site **20**
on Rogue River

Campsites, facilities: There are ten primitive tent sites. Picnic tables and fire grills are provided. Piped water, pit toilets and firewood are available. Leashed pets are permitted.

Reservations, fee: No reservations necessary; no fee. Open May to late October.

Who to contact: Phone (503)779-2351 or write to Bureau of Land Management, 3040 Biddle Road, Medford, OR 97501.

Location: Travel 20 miles west of Glendale on Cow Creek Road, then five miles southwest on Marial Road to the campground.

Trip note: This campground is set in the Zane Grey Bureau of Land Management tract, covering 18,460 acres. The Rogue River passes through the tract, and the Rogue River Trail runs alongside the river for 26 miles. This is rugged country, with steep canyons and many small waterfalls. There is a riding stable nearby.

FOSTER BAR
Site **21**
on Rogue River
SISKIYOU NATIONAL FOREST

Campsites, facilities: There are several dispersed sites for tents, trailers or motor homes up to 16 feet long, though access is difficult for motor homes and trailers. Fire rings and picnic tables are provided. Pit toilets and firewood are available, but there is **no piped water.** Leashed pets are permitted. Boat launching facilities are available.

Reservations, fee: No reservations necessary; no fee. Open year-round.

Who to contact: Phone the Siskiyou National Forest at (503)247-6651 or write to Gold Beach Ranger District, P.O. Box 548, Gold Beach, OR 97444.

Location: From the town of Gold Beach, take Agness-Gold Beach Road east for 30 miles to the turn-off to Agness. Turn right on Illahe-Agness Road and drive three miles to the campground.

Trip note: This campground is located on the banks of the Rogue River, a popular put-in spot for the eight-mile inner tube ride to Agness. Life jackets are mandatory because of rough rapids. A day permit is required from the Forest Service in order to put a boat into the water here. People also fish from the river bar. Sites 22 and 35 provide nearby options.

Site 22
ILLAHE
on Rogue River
SISKIYOU NATIONAL FOREST

Campsites, facilities: There are 23 sites for tents, trailers or motor homes up to 21 feet long. Piped water, fire rings and picnic tables are provided. Flush toilets and firewood are available. A store is located within five miles. Leashed pets are permitted. Boat docks are nearby (Site 21).

Reservations, fee: No reservations necessary; no fee. Open mid-May to mid-October.

Who to contact: Phone the Siskiyou National Forest at (503)247-6651 or write to Gold Beach Ranger District, P.O. Box 548, Gold Beach, OR 97444.

Location: From Agness, travel five miles north on County Road 375 and you'll see the campground entrance.

Trip note: This campground is quiet and isolated, yet boating and fishing opportunities are just a mile away at Foster Bar campground (Site 21).

Site 23
HUMBUG MOUNTAIN STATE PARK
near the Pacific Ocean

Campsites, facilities: There are 75 tent sites and 30 sites with full hookups for trailers or motor homes of any length. A special camping area is reserved for hikers and bicyclists. Fire grills and picnic tables are provided. Flush toilets, showers, firewood and a laundromat are available. Leashed pets are permitted.

Reservations, fee: No reservations necessary; $9-11 in summer months, $6-8 off-season. Open mid-April to late October.

Who to contact: Phone (503)332-6774 or write to Port Orford, OR 97465.

Location: From Port Orford, go six miles south on US 101 and you'll see the park entrance.

Trip note: This park is named after the mountain that towers almost 2,000 feet above the nearby coastline. A three-mile trail leads to its peak. This is a special place because both the Pacific Ocean and nearby Bush Creek are accessible. You can fish in either.

Site 24
ARIZONA BEACH CAMPGROUND
near Gold Beach

Campsites, facilities: There are 31 tent sites and 96 drive-through sites for trailers or motor homes of any length. Electricity, piped water, sewer hookups and picnic tables are provided. Flush toilets, bottled gas, sanitary services, showers, firewood, a recreation hall, a store, a laundromat, ice and a playground are available. Pets and motorbikes are permitted.

Reservations, fee: Reservations accepted; $8-12 fee per night, $14 for a full hookup in the summer; MasterCard and Visa accepted. Open all year.

Who to contact: Phone (503)332-6491 or write to P.O. Box 621, Gold Beach, OR 97444.

Location: Drive 15 miles north of the town of Gold Beach on US 101 and you'll see the campground.

Trip note: This pleasant campground offers grassy, tree-lined sites set along a half mile of ocean beach frontage. A creek runs through the campground and people swim at the mouth of it in the summer. The elk and deer roam nearby. An 11-unit motel is available for campers who need some cleanup time.

Site 25   HONEYBEAR CAMPGROUND
near Gold Beach

Campsites, facilities: There are 20 tent sites and 58 drive-through sites for trailers or motor homes of any length. Picnic tables are provided. Flush toilets, electricity, piped water, cable TV, sanitary services, showers, firewood, a recreation hall, a store, a laundromat, ice and a playground are available. Pets and motorbikes are permitted.

Reservations, fee: Reservations accepted; $9 fee per night; MasterCard and Visa accepted. Open May to late October.

Who to contact: Phone (503)247-2765 or write to P.O. Box 97, Ophir, OR 97464.

Location: From the town of Gold Beach, go nine miles north on US 101 to Ophir Road. The campground is two miles north on Ophir Road.

Trip note: This campground offers wooded sites with ocean views. The owners have built a huge, authentic chalet which contains a German deli, a recreation area and a big dance floor. Six nights a week during the summer, they hold dances with live music provided by a European band.

Site 26   NESIKA BEACH TRAILER PARK
near Gold Beach

Campsites, facilities: There are ten tent sites and 27 sites for trailers or motor homes of any length. Electricity, piped water, sewer hookups and picnic tables are provided. Flush toilets, sanitary services, showers, a store, a cafe, a laundromat and ice are available. Pets and motorbikes are permitted.

Reservations, fee: Reservations accepted; $8-12.50 fee per night. Open all year.

Who to contact: Phone (503)247-6077 or write to 32887 Nesika Road, Gold Beach, OR 97444.

Location: Take US 101 six miles north of the town of Gold Beach to Nesika Road. From there, go one-half mile west on Nesika Road to the campground.

Trip note: This campground is next to Nesika Beach, a good layover spot for Highway 101 cruisers. An 18-hole golf course is available nearby.

Site 27   FOUR SEASONS RV RESORT
on Rogue River

Campsites, facilities: There are 45 drive-through sites for trailers or motor homes up to 35 feet long. Electricity, piped water, sewer hookups and picnic tables are provided. Flush toilets, bottled gas, sanitary services, showers, firewood, a recreation hall, a store, a laundromat and ice are available. Pets and motorbikes are permitted. Boat docks and launching facilities are nearby.

Reservations, fee: Reservations accepted; $10.50-14 fee per night. Open all year.

Who to contact: Phone (503)247-7959 or write to 96526 North Bank Rogue, Gold Beach, OR 97444.

Location: Drive one mile north of the town of Gold Beach on US 101, then three miles northeast on Rogue River Road. From there, follow the signs on North Bank Rogue Road to the campground.

Trip note: This resort is set along the shore of the Rogue River. Nearby recreation options include an 18-hole golf course, a riding stable and boat trips on the wild and scenic Rogue—on anything from a raft to a jet boat.

Site **28**
KIMBALL CREEK BEND
on Rogue River

Campsites, facilities: There are 13 tent sites and 56 drive-through sites for trailers or motor homes of any length. Electricity, piped water, sewer hookups and picnic tables are provided. Flush toilets, bottled gas, sanitary services, showers, a recreation hall, a store, a cafe, a laundromat, ice and a playground are available. Leashed pets are permitted. Boat docks and launching facilities are nearby.

Reservations, fee: Reservations accepted; $9-15 fee per night; MasterCard and Visa accepted. Open all year.

Who to contact: Phone (503)247-7580 or write to 32051 Watson, Gold Beach, OR 97444.

Location: From the town of Gold Beach, go one mile north on US 101, then 3.5 miles northeast on Rogue River Road to North Bank Rogue Road and head 4.5 miles southeast to the campground.

Trip note: This campground is set along the scenic Rogue River, just far enough from the coast to provide quiet and its own distinct character. Nearby recreation options include an 18-hole golf course, hiking trails and boating facilities.

Site **29**
LUCKY LODGE RV PARK
on Rogue River

Campsites, facilities: There are seven tent sites and 36 drive-through sites for trailers or motor homes of any length. Electricity, piped water, sewer hookups and picnic tables are provided. Flush toilets, bottled gas, sanitary services, showers, firewood, a recreation hall and a laundromat are available. Pets and motorbikes are permitted. Boat docks and rentals are nearby.

Reservations, fee: Reservations accepted; $9-10 fee per night. Open all year.

Who to contact: Phone (503)247-7618 or write to 32040 Watson Lane, Gold Beach, OR 97444.

Location: Go one mile north of Gold Beach on US 101. At Rogue River Road, go northeast 3.5 miles to North Bank Rogue Road and follow it 4.5 more miles.

Trip note: Nearby recreation options include hiking trails and a riding stable.

Site **30**
INDIAN CREEK RECREATION PARK
on Rogue River

Campsites, facilities: There are 25 tent sites and 100 drive-through sites for trailers or motor homes of any length. Electricity, piped water, sewer hookups and picnic tables are provided. Flush toilets, showers, firewood, a recreation hall, a store, sauna, a cafe, a laundromat, ice and a playground are available. Bottled gas is located within one mile. Pets and motorbikes are permitted. Boat docks, launching facilities and rentals are nearby.

Reservations, fee: Reservations accepted; $12 fee per night; MasterCard and Visa accepted. Open all year.

Who to contact: Phone (503)247-7704 or write to 94680 Jerry's Flat, Gold Beach, OR 97444.

Location: Look for Jerry's Flat Road in Gold Beach, drive one-half mile down the road and you'll find the campground.

Trip note: This campground is set along the Rogue River on the outskirts of the town of Gold Beach. Nearby recreation options include a riding stable and boat trips on the Rogue.

Site 31

OCEANSIDE CAMP RV
on the Pacific Ocean

Campsites, facilities: There are four tent sites and 60 drive-through sites for trailers or motor homes of any length. Electricity, piped water, sewer hookups and picnic tables are provided. Flush toilets, showers, cable TV hookups, firewood and ice are available. Bottled gas, sanitary services, a store, a cafe and a laundromat are located within one mile. Pets and motorbikes are permitted. Boat docks, launching facilities and rentals are nearby.

Reservations, fee: Reservations accepted; $10-14 fee per night; MasterCard and Visa accepted. Open April to mid-October.

Who to contact: Phone (503)247-2301 or write to P.O. Box 1107, Gold Beach, OR 97444.

Location: This park is in the town of Gold Beach, at the south jetty of the Port of Gold Beach.

Trip note: This park is set right on the ocean. Nearby recreation options include beachcombing, marked bike trails and boating facilities.

Site 32

ANGLERS TRAILER VILLAGE
on Rogue River

Campsites, facilities: There are 36 drive-through sites for trailers or motor homes of any length. Electricity, piped water and sewer hookups are provided. Flush toilets, showers, a recreation hall, a store, a laundromat and ice are available. Pets and motorbikes are permitted.

Reservations, fee: Reservations accepted; $12 fee per night. Open all year.

Who to contact: Phone (503)247-7922 or write to 95706 Jerry's Flat, Gold Beach, OR 97444.

Location: In Gold Beach, turn east at the south end of Rogue River Bridge, then go 3.5 miles north on Jerry's Flat Road to the campground.

Trip note: This is one of seven campgrounds set along the lower Rogue River.

Site 33

LOBSTER CREEK
on Rogue River
SISKIYOU NATIONAL FOREST

Campsites, facilities: There are five sites for tents, trailers or motor homes up to 21 feet long. Piped water, fire rings and picnic tables are provided. Flush toilets are available. Leashed pets are permitted. A boat launch is also available.

Reservations, fee: No reservations necessary; no fee. Open April to late October.

Who to contact: Phone the Siskiyou National Forest at (503)247-6651 or write to Gold Beach Ranger District, P.O. Box 548, Gold Beach, Beach, OR 97444.

Location: From Gold Beach, take County Road 375 for 4.5 miles northeast, then go 5.5 miles northeast on Forest Service Road 33 to the campground.

Trip note: This tiny, little-known campground is set on a river bar along the Rogue River, about a 15-minute drive from Gold Beach. It's a good base camp for a fishing trip.

Site 34

QUOSATANA
on Rogue River
SISKIYOU NATIONAL FOREST

Campsites, facilities: There are 44 sites for tents, trailers or motor homes up to 32 feet long. Piped water, fire grills and picnic tables are provided. Flush toilets, firewood, and a sanitary disposal station are available. Leashed pets are permitted. A boat ramp is available.

Reservations, fee: No reservations necessary; $5 fee per night. Open April to late October.

Who to contact: Phone the Siskiyou National Forest at (503)247-6651 or write to Gold Beach Ranger District, P.O. Box 548, Gold Beach, Beach, OR 97444.

Location: From the town of Gold Beach, go 4.5 miles northeast on County Road 595, then ten miles northeast on Forest Service Road 33 to the campground.

Trip note: This campground is set along the banks of the Rogue River, upriver from much smaller Site 33. This is a good base camp for a fishing trip.

Site **35**   **AGNESS RV PARK**
on Rogue River
SISKIYOU NATIONAL FOREST

Campsites, facilities: There are five tent sites and 91 drive-through sites for trailers or motor homes of any length. Electricity, piped water, sewer hookups and picnic tables are provided. Flush toilets, bottled gas, sanitary services, showers and a laundromat are available. A store, a cafe and ice are located within one mile. Pets and motorbikes are permitted. Boat launching facilities are nearby.

Reservations, fee: Reservations accepted; $10-12 fee per night; MasterCard and Visa accepted. Open all year.

Who to contact: Phone (503)247-2813 or write to 04215 Agness Road, Agness, OR 97406.

Location: From Gold Beach, drive 28 miles east on Jerry's Flat Road and you'll see the entrance to the campground.

Trip note: This is a destination campground set along the scenic Rogue River, in the middle of the Siskiyou National Forest. Fishing is the main focus here. Boating is sharply limited because the nearest pullout is 12 miles downstream. It is advisable to obtain a Forest Service map, which details the backcountry.

Site **36**   **LOEB STATE PARK**
near Chetco River

Campsites, facilities: There are 53 sites with water and electrical hookups for trailers or motor homes up to 50 feet long. Picnic tables and fire grills are provided. Flush toilets and firewood are available. Leashed pets are permitted.

Reservations, fee: No reservations necessary; $10 fee per night in summer, $7 off-season. Open all year.

Who to contact: Phone (503)469-2021 or write c/o Harris Beach State Park, 1655 Highway 101, Brookings, OR 97415.

Location: From Brookings, drive eight miles northeast on a county road that goes along the Chetco River and you'll see the entrance to the park.

Trip note: This park is located in a canyon formed by the Chetco River, and is adjacent to Siskiyou National Forest. There are hiking trails in the forest. A Forest Service map details trailheads.

Site **37**   **HARRIS BEACH STATE PARK**
on the Pacific Ocean

Campsites, facilities: There are 66 sites for tents or self-contained motor homes, and 85 sites with full or partial hookups for trailers or motor homes up to 50 feet long. There is a special camping area for hikers and bicyclists. Picnic tables and fire grills are provided. Electricity, piped water, sewer hookups, flush toilets, sanitary services, showers, firewood and a laundromat are available. Some facilities are wheelchair accessible. Leashed pets are permitted.

Reservations, fee: Reservations accepted; $9-11 in summer months, $6-8 off-season, $2 per person in the hikers' and bicyclists' camp. Open all year.

Who to contact: Phone (503)469-2021 or write to 1655 Highway 101, Brookings, OR 97415.

Location: Drive two miles north of Brookings on US 101 and you'll see the park entrance.

Trip note: This state park is set along the beach. Goat Rock, a migratory bird sanctuary is just offshore. There are numerous trout streams in the area. For details, pick up a Siskiyou Forest Service map in Brookings at 555 Fifth Street. In the fall and winter, the nearby Chetco River attracts good runs of salmon and steelhead, respectively.

Site **38**   **LITTLE REDWOOD**
on Chetco River
SISKIYOU NATIONAL FOREST

Campsites, facilities: There are 16 sites for tents, trailers or motor homes up to 16 feet long. Picnic tables and fire grills are provided. Pit toilets and firewood are available. Leashed pets are permitted.

Reservations, fee: No reservations necessary; $4 fee per night. Open late May to mid-September.

Who to contact: Phone the Siskiyou National Forest at (503)469-2196 or write to Chetco Ranger District, P.O. Box 730, Brookings, OR 97415.

Location: Go south for one-half mile on US 101 from Brookings to County Road 784, then turn northeast on County Road 784 and continue 7.5 miles. At Forest Service Road 376, turn northeast and drive six miles to the campground.

Trip note: This campground is set among old-growth fir trees near the bank of the Chetco River. The primary water sport here in summer is swimming, although there is some trout worth fishing for. In winter, this is a prime base camp for a steelhead trip. The camp is also on the main western access route to the Kalmiopsis Wilderness, which is about 20 miles away. If this and nearby Site 39 are full, the Forest Service offers a number of small, alternative sites. If you are stuck, call them for details.

Site **39**   **RIVER BEND RV PARK**
on Chetco River

Campsites, facilities: There are eight tent sites and 120 drive-through sites for trailers or motor homes of any length. Electricity, piped water, sewer hookups and picnic tables are provided. Flush toilets, bottled gas, sanitary services, showers, a recreation hall with exercise equipment, a store, a cafe, a laundromat, cable TV, ice and a playground are available. Pets and motorbikes are permitted. Boat launching facilities are also available.

Reservations, fee: Reservations accepted; $10 fee per night. Open all year.

Who to contact: Phone (503)469-3356 or write to 98203 South Bank Chetco, Brookings, OR 97415.

Location: In Brookings, drive 1.5 miles east on Chetco River Road and follow the signs to the park.

Trip note: This campground is set along the banks of the Chetco River and offers complete fishing services including guided salmon and steelhead trips on the Chetco in fall and winter. Deep sea trips for salmon or rockfish are available in the summer. Bait, tackle and a free fishing class for campers is offered. There is a beach for sunbathing and swimming.

Site **40**   **CHETCO RV PARK**
near Chetco River

Campsites, facilities: There are 117 drive-through sites for trailers or motor homes of any length. Electricity, piped water, sewer hookups and picnic tables are provided. Flush toilets, bottled gas, sanitary services, showers, a recreation hall, a store, a cafe, a laundromat and ice are available. Pets are permitted. Boat docks, launching facilities and rentals are nearby.

Reservations, fee: Reservations accepted; $11-14 fee per night; MasterCard and Visa accepted. Open all year.

Who to contact: Phone (503)469-3863 or write to 16117 Highway 101S, Brookings, OR 97415.

Location: In Brookings, go one mile south of the Chetco River bridge on US 101 and you'll see the park entrance.

Trip note: This park is near both the Chetco River, known for its winter steelhead run, and the beach. Whale watching is good from January through May. Nature trails are a good side trip; they are located a short drive up the river road.

Site **41**   **DRIFTWOOD TT RETREAT**
on Chetco River

Campsites, facilities: There are a few tent sites and 108 drive-through sites for trailers or motor homes of any length. Electricity, piped water, sewer hookups and picnic tables are provided. Flush toilets, showers, a recreation hall and a laundromat are available. Bottled gas, sanitary services, a store, a cafe and ice are located within one mile. Leashed pets are permitted. Boat docks, launching facilities and rentals are nearby.

Reservations, fee: Reservations accepted; $9 fee per night. Open all year.

Who to contact: Phone (503)469-3213 or write to Box 2066, Harbor, OR 97415.

Location: Go to the south end of the Chetco River bridge in Brookings, then follow Lower Harbor Road to camp.

Trip note: This park is set along the beach near the mouth of the Chetco River. Nearby recreation options include bike trails, hiking trails and a full-service marina.

Site **42**   **SEA BIRD RV**
on the Pacific Ocean

Campsites, facilities: There are 60 drive-through sites for trailers or motor homes of any length. Electricity, piped water, sewer hookups and picnic tables are provided. Flush toilets, bottled gas, sanitary services, showers, a recreation hall, a store, a cafe, a laundromat and ice are available. Pets and motorbikes are permitted. Boat docks, launching facilities and rentals are nearby.

Reservations, fee: Reservations accepted; $8 fee per night. Open all year.

Who to contact: Phone (503)469-3512 or write to P.O. Box 1026, Brookings, OR 97415.

Location: In Brookings, drive one-quarter mile south of the Chetco River bridge on US 101 and you'll see the park entrance.

Trip note: This is one of several campgrounds set along the beach here. Nearby recreation options include marked bike trails, a full-service marina and tennis courts.

Site 43

WINCHUCK
on Winchuck River
SISKIYOU NATIONAL FOREST

Campsites, facilities: There are five tent sites and eight sites for trailers or motor homes up to 16 feet long. Picnic tables and fire grills are provided. Pit toilets, piped water and firewood are available. Leashed pets are permitted.

Reservations, fee: No reservations necessary; $4 fee per night. Open late May to mid-September.

Who to contact: Phone the Siskiyou National Forest at (503)469-2196 or write to Chetco Ranger District, P.O. Box 730, Brookings, OR 97415.

Location: From Brookings, go 5.5 miles south on US 101, then six miles east on County Road 896. From there, take Forest Service Road 3907 and go one mile east to the campground.

Trip note: This forested campground is set along the banks of the Winchuck River, an out-of-the-way stream that out-of-towners don't have a clue about. It's quiet, remote and not that far from the coast, although it feels like it's a long way.

Site 44

BIG PINE
near Grants Pass
SISKIYOU NATIONAL FOREST

Campsites, facilities: There are 14 tent sites. Picnic tables and fire grills are provided. Pit toilets and firewood are available. There is **no piped water.** Leashed pets are permitted.

Reservations, fee: No reservations necessary; $2 fee per night. Open late May to mid-September.

Who to contact: Phone the Siskiyou National Forest at (503)476-3830 or write to Galice Ranger District, P.O. Box 1131, Grants Pass, OR 97526.

Location: Go 3.5 miles north of Grants Pass on Interstate 5, then turn northwest on County Road 2-6 and drive 12.5 miles. At Forest Service Road 355 head southwest for 12.8 miles to the campground.

Trip note: This little campground is in an isolated area west of Grants Pass, set in a valley of old-growth pine and Douglas fir. A small creek is about one mile from camp. It is advisable to obtain a National Forest map.

Site 45

THE LAST RESORT
on Lake Selmac

Campsites, facilities: There are 18 tent sites and 25 sites for trailers or motor homes of any length. Electricity, piped water, sewer hookups and picnic tables are provided. Flush toilets, bottled gas, sanitary services, showers, firewood, a recreation hall, a store, a cafe, a laundromat, ice and a playground are available. Pets and motorbikes are permitted. Boat docks, launching facilities and rentals are nearby.

Reservations, fee: Reservations accepted; $9 fee per night. Open all year.

Who to contact: Phone (503)597-4989 or write to 2700 Lake Shore Drive, Selma, OR 97538.

Location: Near Selma, take the Lake Selmac exit off US 199, then go two miles east on Lake Selmac Road to the resort.

Trip note: This resort is set along the shore of Lake Selmac. A golf course is nearby. A unique tour is available at Oregon Caves National Monument, about 30 miles away. To get there, drive 20 miles east of Cave Junction on Highway 46. This road gets narrow near the end and is not recommended for trailers. A 75-minute guided tour is available. The caves are a long, winding trail through a series of amazing caverns. Dress warmly, it can be cold and clammy.

Site 46   KERBY TRAILER PARK AND CAMPGROUND
near Illinois River

Campsites, facilities: There are ten tent sites and 14 drive-through sites for trailers or motor homes of any length. Electricity, piped water, sewer hookups and picnic tables are provided. Flush toilets, bottled gas, showers and a laundromat are available. A store and ice are located within one mile. Pets and motorbikes are permitted.

Reservations, fee: Reservations accepted; $6-9 fee per night. Open all year.

Who to contact: Phone (503)592-2897 or write to 24542 Redwood Highway, Kerby, OR 97531.

Location: This campground is about 400 yards south of Kerby on US 199.

Trip note: This small campground is set near the Illinois River, a good stream during the summer for swimming. See the trip note for Site 45 for side trip information. Other recreation options include an 18-hole golf course, hiking trails and tennis courts.

Site 47   SHADY ACRES
on Illinois River

Campsites, facilities: There are four tent sites and 27 drive-through sites for trailers or motor homes of any length. Electricity, piped water, sewer hookups and picnic tables are provided. Flush toilets, bottled gas, sanitary services, showers and firewood are available. A store, a cafe, a laundromat and ice are located within one mile. Pets are permitted.

Reservations, fee: Reservations accepted; $8-10 fee per night. Open all year.

Who to contact: Phone (503)592-3702 or write to 27550 Redwood Highway, Cave Junction, OR 97523.

Location: From Cave Junction, go one mile south on US 199 and you'll see the entrance.

Trip note: This park is set in a forested area on the banks of the Illinois River. See the trip note for Site 45 for information on Oregon Caves National Monument.

Site 48   TRAILS END RV PARK & CAMPGROUND
on Illinois River

Campsites, facilities: There are 25 tent sites and 16 drive-through sites for trailers or motor homes of any length. Electricity, piped water, sewer hookups and picnic tables are provided. Flush toilets, bottled gas, sanitary services, showers and a playground are available. A store, a cafe, a laundromat and ice are located within one mile. Pets and motorbikes are permitted.

Reservations, fee: Reservations accepted; $10 fee per night. Open all year.

Who to contact: Phone (503)592-3354 or write to 336 Burch Drive, Cave Junction, OR 97523.

Location: Go south on US 199 from Cave Junction for 2.5 miles, then turn west on Burch Drive and travel about 400 yards to the campground entrance.

Trip note: This campground is set along the Illinois River, about 20 miles from Oregon Caves National Monument. See the trip note for Site 45 for details. The Kerbyville Historical Museum is two miles south of Cave Junction. Nearby recreation options include hiking trails, bike trails and a riding stable.

Site 49   CAVES HIGHWAY TRAILER PARK
near Oregon Caves National Monument

Campsites, facilities: There are two tent sites and 20 drive-through sites for trailers or motor homes of any length. Electricity, piped water, sewer hookups and picnic tables are provided. Flush toilets, bottled gas, sanitary services, showers and a playground are available. A store, a cafe, a laundromat and ice are located within one mile. Pets and motorbikes are permitted.

Reservations, fee: Reservations accepted; $7-10 fee per night. Open all year.

Who to contact: Phone (503)592-3338 or write to 977 Caves Highway, Cave Junction, OR 97523.

Location: From Cave Junction, take Highway 46 one mile east to the campground.

Trip note: See the trip note for Site 45 for additional information on the nearby Oregon Caves National Monument. Nearby recreation options include an 18-hole golf course, hiking trails, marked bike trails and tennis courts.

Site 50   WOODLAND ECHOES RESORT
near Oregon Caves National Monument

Campsites, facilities: There are 20 drive-through sites for trailers or motor homes of any length. Picnic tables are provided. Flush toilets, showers, firewood, a cafe and ice are available. Leashed pets are permitted.

Reservations, fee: Reservations accepted; $7 fee per night; MasterCard and Visa accepted. Open all year.

Who to contact: Phone (503)592-3406 or write to 7901 Caves Highway, Cave Junction, OR 97523.

Location: From Cave Junction, take Highway 46 east for eight miles.

Trip note: See the trip note for Site 45 for information about the nearby Oregon Caves National Monument.

Site 51   GRAYBACK
near Oregon Caves National Monument
SISKIYOU NATIONAL FOREST

Campsites, facilities: There are 35 sites for tents, trailers or motor homes up to 22 feet long. Picnic tables and fire grills are provided. Flush toilets and piped water are available. Leashed pets are permitted.

Reservations, fee: No reservations necessary; $4 fee per night. Open May through September.

Who to contact: Phone the Siskiyou National Forest at (503)592-2166 or write to Illinois Valley Ranger District, P.O. Box 389, Cave Junction, OR 97523.

Location: From Cave Junction, go 12 miles east on Highway 46.

Trip note: This wooded campground is set along the banks of Sucker Creek, about ten miles from Oregon Caves National Monument. It is a good spot to camp if you're planning to visit the caves.

Site 52   CAVE CREEK
near Oregon Caves National Monument
SISKIYOU NATIONAL FOREST

Campsites, facilities: There are 18 tent sites. Piped water, pit toilets, picnic tables are provided. Firewood is available. Showers are located within five miles. Leashed pets are permitted.

Reservations, fee: No reservations necessary; $4 fee per night. Open June to mid-September.

Who to contact: Phone the Siskiyou National Forest at (503)592-2166 or write to Illinois Valley Ranger District, P.O. Box 389, Cave Junction, OR 97523.

Location: Take Highway 46 east of Cave Junction for 16 miles, then go one mile south on Forest Service Road 4032.

Trip note: This Forest Service camp is just four miles from the Oregon Caves National Monument; no campground is closer. See the trip note for Site 45 for details on the Monument. The camp is set along Cave Creek, a small creek with some trout fishing opportunities. There are many hiking trails in the area.

Site **53**

BOLAN LAKE
on Bolan Lake
SISKIYOU NATIONAL FOREST

Campsites, facilities: There are 22 sites for tents, trailers or motor homes up to 16 feet long. Picnic tables and fire grills are provided. Pit toilets and firewood are available, but there is **no piped water.** Leashed pets are permitted. Boat docks and launching facilities are nearby.

Reservations, fee: No reservations necessary; $2 fee per night. Open July to November.

Who to contact: Phone the Siskiyou National Forest at (503)592-2166 or write to Illinois Valley Ranger District, P.O. Box 389, Cave Junction, OR 97523.

Location: From Cave Junction, take County Road 12 eight miles southeast, then go 14 miles southeast on County Road 4007. Located at Forest Service Road 408.

Trip note: This campground is set along the shore of 15-acre Bolan Lake. Very few out-of-towners know about this spot. A trail from the lake leads up to a lookout point and ties into miles of other trails. See a Forest Service map for more information.

MOUNT HOOD

◆

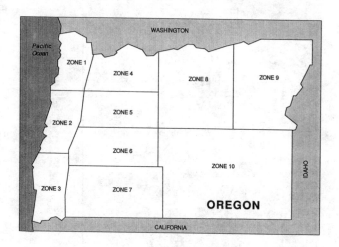

SOME HIGHLIGHTS

104 CAMPGROUNDS

Columbia River

Portland

Mount Hood National Forest

Cascade Range Wilderness

Hood River

Zigzag River

Sandy River

Pacific Crest Trail

Willamette National Forest

Breitenbush River

Olallie Lake

Clackamas River

Timothy Lake

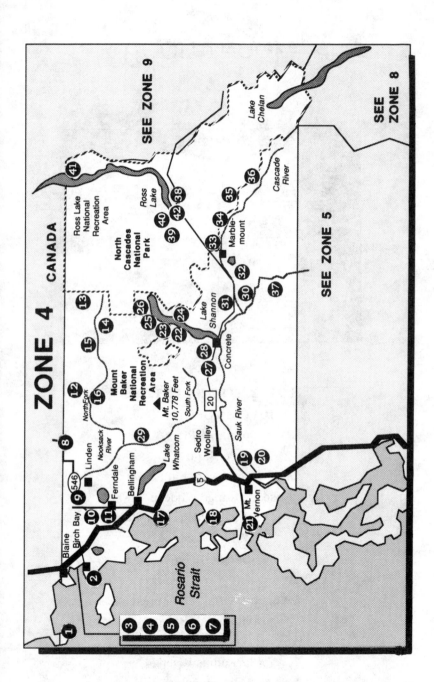

JANTZEN BEACH RV PARK
Site **1**
near Columbia River

Campsites, facilities: There are 164 sites for trailers or motor homes of any length. Electricity, piped water, sewer hookups and picnic tables are provided. Flush toilets, bottled gas, showers, a recreation hall, a store, a cafe, a laundromat, ice, a playground and a swimming pool are available. Pets are permitted. Boat docks, launching facilities and rentals are nearby.

Reservations, fee: Reservations accepted; $19-21.50 fee per night; MasterCard and Visa accepted. Open all year.

Who to contact: Phone (503)289-7626 or write to 1503 North Hayden Island Drive, Portland, OR 97217.

Location: Take Interstate 5 about four miles north of Portland and look for the Jantzen Beach exit, then go one-half mile west on Hayden Island Drive.

Trip note: This motor home campground is set near the banks of the Columbia River on the outskirts of Portland. Nearby recreation options include an 18-hole golf course, a riding stable and tennis courts.

PORTLAND MOBILE HOME PARK
Site **2**
near Columbia River

Campsites, facilities: There are 100 drive-through sites for trailers or motor homes of any length. Electricity, piped water and sewer hookups are provided. Flush toilets, bottled gas, sanitary services, showers, a store, a cafe, a laundromat and ice are available. Leashed pets are permitted. This park is due to open soon. Call ahead for fees and opening dates.

Reservations, fee: Reservations accepted; $14 fee per night. Open all year.

Who to contact: Phone (503)285-1617 or write to 9000 Northeast Union, Portland, OR 97211.

Location: Take exit 307 off Interstate 5 in Portland. Follow Northeast Union Avenue for 1.5 miles south to the campground.

Trip note: Many recreation opportunities are available in the Portland area. Numerous marinas on the Willamette and Columbia Rivers offer boat trips and rentals, and the city parks and nearby state parks—call (503)238-7488 for more information—offer hiking, bicycling and horseback riding possibilities. The Columbia River Highway (US 30) is a scenic drive. If golf is your game, Portland has 18 public golf courses. The winter ski areas at Mount Hood are an hour's drive away.

FIR GROVE RV & TRAILER PARK
Site **3**
near Columbia River

Campsites, facilities: There are five tent sites and 25 sites for trailers or motor homes of any length. Electricity, piped water and sewer hookups are provided. Flush toilets, showers and ice are available. Bottled gas, sanitary services, a store, a cafe and a playground are located within one mile. Pets and motorbikes are permitted.

Reservations, fee: Reservations accepted; $11-15 fee per night; MasterCard and Visa accepted. Open all year.

Who to contact: Phone (503)252-9993 or write to 5541 Northeast 72nd, Portland, OR 97218.

Location: In Portland off Interstate 205, go about 400 yards northeast on Columbia Boulevard, then one mile west on Northeast Killingsworth and you'll see the park entrance.

Trip note: This park is set near the banks of the Columbia River in the outskirts of Portland. See the trip note for Site 2 for information about the nearby recreation opportunities.

Site 4   SOUTH GATE MOBILE HOME & RV PARK
in Portland

Campsites, facilities: There are 24 sites for trailers or motor homes of any length in this adult only campground. Electricity, piped water and sewer hookups are provided. Flush toilets, showers and a laundromat are available. Bottled gas, sanitary services, a store, a cafe and ice are located within one mile. Motorbikes are permitted.

Reservations, fee: No reservations necessary; $7 fee per night. Open all year.

Who to contact: Phone (503)775-0456 or write to 7911 Southeast 82nd, Portland, OR 97266.

Location: In Portland off Interstate 205, take the Foster exit and go one-half mile west to 82nd Avenue. The park is one mile south.

Trip note: Motor home campers can use this for a base of operations for a Portland vacation. See the trip note for Site 2 for information about the recreation possibilities in the area.

Site 5   TALL FIRS RV & MOBILE HOME PARK
in Portland

Campsites, facilities: There are six sites for trailers or motor homes of any length. Electricity, piped water and sewer hookups are provided. Flush toilets, showers and a laundromat are available. Bottled gas, a store, a cafe and ice are located within one mile. Leashed pets are permitted.

Reservations, fee: No reservations necessary; $14 fee per night. Open all year.

Who to contact: Phone (503)761-8210 or write to 15656 Southeast Division Street, Portland, OR 97236.

Location: Take the Division Street exit off Interstate 205 in Portland and go east on Southeast Division.

Trip note: This small RV park is located in Portland. See the trip note for Site 2 for information about the recreation possibilities in the area.

Site 6   BELL ACRES MOBILE ESTATES
in Portland

Campsites, facilities: There are 12 drive-through sites for trailers or motor homes of any length in this adult-only campground. Electricity, piped water and sewer hookups are provided. Flush toilets, showers, a recreation hall and laundromat are available. Bottled gas, sanitary services, a store, a cafe and ice are located within one mile. Pets are permitted.

Reservations, fee: Reservations accepted; $14 fee per night. Open all year.

Who to contact: Phone (503)665-4774 or write to 2980 Northeast Division Street, Gresham, OR 97030.

Location: Take East Hogan Road off US 26 in Gresham and travel one-half mile north, then go one-half mile east on Northeast Division.

Trip note: This is an option for motor home campers in Portland. See the trip note for Site 2 for information on recreation opportunities in the area.

Site **7**   **CROWN POINT RV PARK**
near Columbia River

Campsites, facilities: There are 15 sites for trailers or motor homes of any length. Electricity, piped water and picnic tables are provided. Flush toilets, bottled gas, sanitary services, showers, a store, a laundromat and ice are available. Leashed pets are permitted.

Reservations, fee: Reservations accepted; $13 fee per night. Open April to late October.

Who to contact: Phone (503)695-5207 or write to 37000 East Crown Point Highway, Corbett, OR 97019.

Location: Take Interstate 84 east from Portland to exit 22 near Troutdale, then take US 30 (Crown Point Highway) southeast about 400 yards to the park.

Trip note: This little park is located near the Columbia River along scenic US 30. Crown Point State Park is nearby and is open during the day. It offers views of the Columbia River Gorge and the historical Vista House, a memorial built in 1918 to honor Oregon's pioneers.

Site **8**   **ROLLING HILLS MOBILE TERRACE**
near Columbia River

Campsites, facilities: There are 101 drive-through sites for trailers or motor homes of any length. Electricity, piped water, sewer hookups and picnic tables are provided. Flush toilets, bottled gas, showers, a recreation hall, a laundromat and a swimming pool are available. A store, a cafe and ice are located within one mile. Leashed pets are permitted.

Reservations, fee: Reservations accepted; $18 fee per night. Open all year.

Who to contact: Phone (503)666-7282 or write to 20145 Northeast Sandy, Troutdale, OR 97060.

Location: From Troutdale, take Interstate 84 West to Sandy Boulevard exit, then go three-quarters of a mile west on Sandy Boulevard to the motor home park.

Trip note: This full-service layover spot is about ten miles east of Portland, near the Columbia River. Nearby recreation options include an 18-hole golf course, a full-service marina and tennis courts.

Site **9**   **MULTNOMAH COUNTY CAMPGROUND/OXBOW**
on Sandy River

Campsites, facilities: There are 45 sites for tents, trailers or motor homes up to 35 feet long. Picnic tables are provided. Piped water, pit toilets, firewood and a playground are available. Boat launching facilities are nearby.

Reservations, fee: No reservations necessary; $6 fee per night. Open all year.

Who to contact: Phone (503)663-4708 or write to 3010 Southeast Oxbow Parkway, Gresham, OR 97030.

Location: In Gresham, take Southeast Division four miles east, then continue east four miles on Oxbow Parkway to the park.

Trip note: This 1,000-acre park is set along the Sandy River, a short distance from the Columbia River Gorge and has been designated a natural preservation area. Fishing, swimming and non-motored boating are permitted here.

Site **10**   **TRAILER PARK OF PORTLAND**
in Tualatin

Campsites, facilities: There are 100 drive-through sites for trailers or motor homes

of any length. Electricity, piped water, sewer hookups and picnic tables are provided. Flush toilets, sanitary services, showers, a laundromat and a playground are available. Bottled gas, a store, a cafe and ice are located within one mile. Pets and motorbikes are permitted.

Reservations, fee: Reservations accepted; $13 fee per night; MasterCard and Visa accepted. Open all year.

Who to contact: Phone (503)692-0225 or write to 6645 Southwest Nyberg Road, Tualatin, OR 97062.

Location: Take Interstate 5 south from Portland to Tualatin, then take exit 289 and follow Highway 212 east for about one-quarter mile to the park.

Trip note: This park is set just south of Portland. See the trip note for Site 2 for information about the recreation possibilities in the area.

Site 11   FOUR-U MOBILE PARK
near Portland

Campsites, facilities: There are nine sites for trailers or motor homes of any length. Electricity, piped water and sewer hookups are provided. Flush toilets, sanitary services, showers and a laundromat are available. A store, a cafe and ice are located within one mile. Leashed pets are permitted.

Reservations, fee: Reservations accepted; $10 fee per night. Open all year.

Who to contact: Phone (503)639-3350 or write to 18030 Southwest Lower Boones Ferry Road, Portland, OR 97223.

Location: Go 11 miles south of Portland on Interstate 5, take exit 290, then go west to Lower Boones Ferry Road.

Trip note: This is a good option for motor home campers visiting the Portland area who want a base camp outside the city. Nearby recreation options include an 18-hole golf course and marked bike trails.

Site 12   ISBERG RV PARK
near Aurora

Campsites, facilities: There are 84 sites for trailers or motor homes of any length. Electricity, piped water and sewer hookups are provided. Flush toilets, bottled gas, sanitary services, showers, a recreation hall, a store, a cafe, a laundromat and ice are available. Leashed pets are permitted.

Reservations, fee: Reservations accepted; $16 fee per night; MasterCard and Visa accepted. Open all year.

Who to contact: Phone (503)678-2646 or write to 21599 Dolores Northeast, Aurora, OR 97002.

Location: Take Interstate 5 north for about seven miles from Woodburn, then take exit 278 at Aurora and go about 200 yards to the park.

Trip note: This motor home campground is in a rural area just off the main highway and offers a recreation room, a jogging trail and a pitch-and-putt golf course.

Site 13   CHAMPOEG STATE PARK
on Willamette River

Campsites, facilities: There are 48 sites with water and electrical hookups for trailers or motor homes up to 50 feet long. Picnic tables and fire grills are provided. Flush toilets, sanitary disposal station, showers, firewood and laundromat are available. Some facilities are wheelchair accessible. Leashed pets are permitted. Boat docking facilities are nearby.

Reservations, fee: No reservations necessary; $10 fee per night in summer, $7 off-season. Open all year with limited winter facilities.

Who to contact: Phone (503)678-1251 or write to 7679 Champoeg Road NE, Saint Paul, OR 97137.

Location: Take the Champoeg-Aurora exit off Interstate 5 between Salem and Portland and drive eight miles west to the park.

Trip note: This state park is set along the banks of the Willamette River and offers an interpretive center, a botanical garden featuring native plants, and hiking and bike trails. In July, a historical pageant re-enacting the early history of the area is staged Thursday through Sunday evenings.

Site 14   MILO McIVER STATE PARK
on Collawash River

Campsites, facilities: There are 44 sites with water and electrical hookups for trailers or motor homes of any length. Picnic tables and fire grills are provided. Flush toilets, sanitary services, showers, firewood and laundromat are available. Some of the facilities are wheelchair accessible. Leashed pets are permitted. Boat launching facilities are nearby.

Reservations, fee: No reservations necessary; $10 fee per night in summer, $7 off-season. Open year-round.

Who to contact: Phone (503)630-7150 or write to 24101 South Entrance Road, Estacada, OR 97023.

Location: This state park is located five miles north of Estacada just off Highway 211.

Trip note: This park is not far from the Portland area, yet it is far enough off the beaten track to provide a feeling of separation from the metropolitan area. It is set along the banks of the Collawash River and has a boat ramp. Trails for hiking and horseback riding and a group picnic area are also accessible.

Site 15   NORTH FORK EAGLE CREEK
on the North Fork of Eagle Creek

Campsites, facilities: There are 18 tent sites and five drive-through sites for trailers or motor homes up to 20 feet long. Picnic tables are provided. Piped water and pit toilets are available. Leashed pets are permitted.

Reservations, fee: No reservations necessary; $4 fee per night. Open mid-May to late September.

Who to contact: Phone the Bureau of Land Management at (503)399-5646 or write to Box 3227, Salem, OR 97302.

Location: Take US 26 southeast from Portland 28 miles, then turn south on Firwood Road and continue five miles to the campground.

Trip note: This campground is set along the North Fork of Eagle Creek. It's a more primitive option than nearby Site 14 and known by few from outside the area.

Site 16   AINSWORTH STATE PARK
in Columbia River Gorge

Campsites, facilities: There are 45 sites with full hookups for trailers or motor homes of any length. Picnic tables and fire grills are provided. Flush toilets, showers, firewood and a laundromat are available. Leashed pets are permitted.

Reservations, fee: No reservations necessary; $11 fee per night in summer, $8 off-season. Open mid-April to late October.

Who to contact: Phone (503)695-2301 or write to Ainsworth State Park, Bonneville, OR 97014.

Location: Travel 37 miles east of Portland on US 30 to the park.

Trip note: This state park is set along the scenic Columbia River Gorge. A two-mile section of the Columbia River Gorge Trail connects this park with John Yeon State Park, which is open during the day. Fishermen should take a look at the Bonneville Fish Hatchery, where there's a giant sturgeon that's a unique sight.

Site 17   EAGLE CREEK
near Cascade Range Wilderness
MOUNT HOOD NATIONAL FOREST

Campsites, facilities: There are 20 sites for tents, trailers or motor homes up to 22 feet long. Picnic tables and fire grills are provided. Piped water, flush toilets and a sanitary disposal station are available. Leashed pets are permitted. Boat docks and launching facilities are nearby.

Reservations, fee: No reservations necessary; $5 fee per night. Open mid-May to October. Reservations required for groups.

Who to contact: Phone the Columbia Gorge Ranger District at (503)695-2276 or write to Mount Hood National Forest, 31520 SE Woodard Road, Troutdale, OR 97060.

Location: This campground is located two miles east of Bonneville off Interstate 84.

Trip note: This is a good base camp for a hiking trip. The Eagle Creek Trail leaves the campground and goes 14 miles to Wahtum Lake, where it intersects with the Pacific Crest Trail. There is a primitive campground at the 7.5-mile point. The upper seven miles of the trail pass through the Cascade Range wilderness.

Site 18   HERMAN HORSE CAMP
near Pacific Crest Trail
MOUNT HOOD NATIONAL FOREST

Campsites, facilities: There are seven sites for tents, trailers or motor homes up to 31 feet long. Piped water, fire grills and picnic tables are provided. Stock handling facilities are available. Sanitary services, showers, a store, a cafe, a laundromat and ice are nearby. Some facilities are wheelchair accessible. Leashed pets are permitted.

Reservations, fee: No reservations necessary; $5 fee per night. Open mid-May to October.

Who to contact: Phone the Columbia Gorge Ranger District at (503)695-2276 or write to Mount Hood National Forest, 31520 SE Woodard Road, Troutdale, OR 97060.

Location: Located about 1.5 miles east of Cascade Locks.

Trip note: This campground is located about one-half mile from Herman Creek, not far from the Pacific Crest Trail. This is one of three campgrounds in the immediate area.

Site 19   KOA CASCADE LOCKS
near Columbia River

Campsites, facilities: There are 25 tent sites and 74 sites for trailers or motor homes of any length. Electricity, piped water, sewer hookups and picnic tables are provided. Flush toilets, bottled gas, sanitary services, showers, firewood, heated hot tub, cable TV hookups, a recreation hall, a store, a laundromat, ice, a playground and a heated swimming pool are available. A cafe is located within one mile. Pets and motorbikes are permitted.

Reservations, fee: Reservations accepted; $13-16 fee per night; MasterCard and Visa accepted. Open all year.

Who to contact: Phone (503)374-8668 or write to Star Route, Box 660, Cascade Locks, OR 97014.

Location: Turn off Interstate 84 in Cascade Locks and travel two miles east on Forest Lane to the campground.

Trip note: This is a good layover for motor home campers touring the Columbia River corridor. Nearby recreation options include bike trails, hiking trails and tennis courts. The 200-acre Cascade Locks and Marine Park is nearby and offers everything from museums to boat trips.

Site 20   CASCADE LOCKS MARINE PARK
in Cascade Locks

Campsites, facilities: There are ten tent sites and 30 drive-through sites for trailers or motor homes of any length. Picnic tables are provided. Flush toilets, sanitary services, showers and a playground are available. Bottled gas, a store, a cafe, a laundromat and ice are located within one mile. Pets and motorbikes are permitted. Boat docks and launching facilities are nearby.

Reservations, fee: No reservations necessary; $7 fee per night. Open all year.

Who to contact: Phone (503)374-8619 or write to P.O. Box 307, Cascade Locks, OR 97014.

Location: In Cascade Locks, take exit 42 off Interstate 84 and follow it one-half mile east to the park.

Trip note: This riverfront park covers 200 acres and offers a museum and boat rides. Nearby recreation options include hiking trails and tennis courts.

Site 21   WYETH
on Gordon Creek
MOUNT HOOD NATIONAL FOREST

Campsites, facilities: There are 17 sites for tents, trailers or motor homes up to 26 feet long. Fire grills and picnic tables are provided. Piped water and flush toilets are available. Leashed pets are permitted.

Reservations, fee: No reservations necessary; $5 fee per night. Open mid-May to October.

Who to contact: Phone the Columbia Gorge Ranger District at (503)695-2276 or write to Mount Hood National Forest, 31520 SE Woodard Road, Troutdale, OR 97060.

Location: Travel seven miles east of Cascade Locks on Interstate 84 to the Wyeth exit, then go one-half mile on a county road and you'll see the campground entrance.

Trip note: This is a good layover spot for Columbia River corridor cruisers. It is set along Gordon Creek, near the Columbia.

Site 22   TUCKER PARK
on Hood River

Campsites, facilities: There are five tent sites and 29 sites for tents, trailers or motor homes of any length. Picnic tables are provided. Electricity, piped water, flush toilets, showers, firewood and a playground are available. A store, a cafe, laundromat and ice are located within one mile. Leashed pets and motorbikes are permitted.

Reservations, fee: Reservations accepted; $8 fee per night. Open April to November.

Who to contact: Phone (503)386-4477 or write to 2440 Dee Highway, Hood River, OR 97031.

Location: From the town of Hood River travel four miles south on Highway 281 to the park.

Trip note: This county park is set along the banks of the Hood River. It's just far enough out of the way to be missed by most of the tourist traffic.

Site 23   VIENTO STATE PARK
in Columbia River Gorge

Campsites, facilities: There are 17 tent sites and 58 sites with water and electrical hookups for trailers or motor homes up to 30 feet long. Picnic tables and fire grills are provided. Flush toilets, showers, firewood and a laundromat are available. Leashed pets are permitted.

Reservations, fee: No reservations necessary; $9-11 fee per night in summer, $6-8 off-season. Open mid-April to late October.

Who to contact: Phone (503)295-2215 or write to Hood River, OR 97031.

Location: Travel eight miles west on Interstate 84 from the town of Hood River and you'll see the park entrance.

Trip note: This park is set along the Columbia River Gorge and offers scenic hiking trails. Take the picturesque drive along old US 30, which skirts the Columbia River.

Site 24   MEMALOOSE STATE PARK
in Columbia River Gorge

Campsites, facilities: There are 67 tent sites and 43 sites with full hookups for trailers or motor homes of any length. Picnic tables and fire grills are provided. Flush toilets, sanitary services, showers and firewood are available. Some facilities are wheelchair accessible. Pets and motorbikes are permitted.

Reservations, fee: No reservations necessary; $9-11 in the summer, $6-8 off-season. Open mid-April to late October.

Who to contact: Phone (503)478-3336 or write to 5th & Washington, The Dalles, OR 97058.

Location: From The Dalles, go 11 miles west on Interstate 84 and you'll see the turn-off. Access is available traveling westbound only.

Trip note: This park is set along the scenic Columbia River Gorge and makes a prime layover spot for campers cruising the Oregon-Washington border.

Site 25   LONE PINE TRAVEL PARK
near Columbia River

Campsites, facilities: There are 22 drive-through sites for trailers or motor homes of any length. Electricity, piped water and sewer hookups are provided. Flush toilets, showers, a cafe, a laundromat, ice and a playground are available. Bottled gas and sanitary services are located within one mile. Leashed pets are permitted. Boat docks and launching facilities are nearby.

Reservations, fee: Reservations accepted; $15-17 fee per night; MasterCard and Visa accepted. Open all year.

Who to contact: Phone (503)296-9133 or write to 335 US 197, The Dalles, OR 97058.

Location: Near The Dalles, take exit 87 off Interstate 84 to US 197 and follow it to the park.

Trip note: This area gets hot weather and occasional winds shooting through the river canyon during summer months. Nearby recreation options include an 18-hole golf course and tennis courts.

Site 26
TOLL BRIDGE PARK
on the East Fork of Hood River

Campsites, facilities: There are 18 tent sites and 20 sites with hookups for trailers or motor homes up to 20 feet long. Picnic tables and fire grills are provided. Flush toilets, sanitary services, showers, firewood, a recreation hall and a playground are available. Bottled gas, a store, a cafe, laundromat and ice are located within one mile. Leashed pets and motorbikes are permitted.

Reservations, fee: Reservations accepted; $15-17 fee per night. Open April to November and some off-season weekends.

Who to contact: Phone (503)352-6300 or write to 7360 Toll Bridge Road, Parkdale, OR 97041.

Location: Travel on Highway 35 south from the town of Hood River for 16 miles. One mile south of the town of Mount Hood, go one-quarter mile southwest on the county road to 7360 Toll Bridge Road.

Trip note: This 100-acre county park is set along the East Fork of the Hood River and offers bike trails, hiking trails and tennis courts. The Mount Hood Wilderness area is located southwest of the park.

Site 27
GREEN CANYON
on Salmon River
MOUNT HOOD NATIONAL FOREST

Campsites, facilities: There are 15 sites for tents, trailers or motor homes up to 31 feet long. Picnic tables and fire grills are provided. Pit toilets and piped water are available. A store, a cafe and ice are located within five miles. Some facilities are wheelchair accessible. Leashed pets are permitted.

Reservations, fee: No reservations necessary; $5-7 fee per night. Open May to late September.

Who to contact: Phone the Zigzag Ranger District at (503)666-0704 or write Mount Hood National Forest, to 70220 East Highway 35, Zigzag, OR 97049.

Location: Just north of Zigzag on US 26, take Forest Service Road 2618 and drive 4.5 miles south to the campground.

Trip note: This winner is one that few out-of-towners know about. It is set along the banks of the Salmon River. There is a long trail nearby that parallels the Salmon River and passes several waterfalls. See a Forest Service map for details.

Site 28
CAMP CREEK
near Zigzag River
MOUNT HOOD NATIONAL FOREST

Campsites, facilities: There are 15 sites for tents, trailers or motor homes up to 22 feet long. Piped water, fire grills and picnic tables are provided. Flush toilets are available. Leashed pets are permitted.

Reservations, fee: No reservations necessary; $5-8 fee per night. Open late May to late September.

Who to contact: Phone the Zigzag Ranger District at (503)666-0704 or write to Mount Hood National Forest, 70220 East Highway 35, Zigzag, OR 97049.

Location: Travel southeast on US 26 from Rhododendron about three miles to camp.

Trip note: This campground is set along Camp Creek, not far from the Zigzag River.

Site 29
TOLL GATE
on Zigzag River
MOUNT HOOD NATIONAL FOREST

Campsites, facilities: There are 15 tent sites and nine sites for trailers or motor homes up to 22 feet long. Picnic tables and fire grills are provided. Piped water and pit toilets are available. Leashed pets are permitted.

Reservations, fee: No reservations necessary; $4-6 fee per night. Open late May to late September.

Who to contact: Phone the Zigzag Ranger District at (503)666-0704 or write to Mount Hood National Forest, 70220 East Highway 35, Zigzag, OR 97049.

Location: This campground is about 2.5 miles southeast of Zigzag on US 26.

Trip note: This campground is set along the banks of the Zigzag River near Rhododendron, the most primitive of the three camps in the immediate vicinity. The Mount Hood Wilderness is nearby and there are numerous trails in the area.

Site 30
McNEIL
on the Clear Fork of Sandy River
MOUNT HOOD NATIONAL FOREST

Campsites, facilities: There are 34 sites for tents, trailers or motor homes up to 22 feet long. Picnic tables are provided. There is **no piped water.** Leashed pets are permitted.

Reservations, fee: No reservations necessary; $4 fee per night. Open May to late September.

Who to contact: Phone the Zigzag Ranger District at (503)666-0704 or write to Mount Hood National Forest, 70220 East Highway 35, Zigzag, OR 97049.

Location: From Zigzag go 4.5 miles northeast on County Road 18, then one-half mile northeast on Forest Service Road 17. The camp is about 200 yards east on Forest Service Road 1825.

Trip note: This campground is set along the Clear Fork of the Sandy River near the western border of the Mount Hood Wilderness area. Several trails nearby provide access to the Wilderness backcountry. See a Forest Service map for options.

Site 31
RILEY HORSE CAMP
near the Clear Fork of Sandy River
MOUNT HOOD NATIONAL FOREST

Campsites, facilities: There are 14 sites for tents, trailers or motor homes up to 22 feet long. Piped water, fire grills and picnic tables are provided. Facilities for horses are available. Leashed pets are permitted.

Reservations, fee: No reservations necessary; $3 fee per night. Open May to late September.

Who to contact: Phone the Zigzag Ranger District at (503)666-0704 or write to Mount Hood National Forest, 70220 East Highway 35, Zigzag, OR 97049.

Location: Take County Road 18 northeast of Zigzag for four miles, then go one mile east on Forest Service Road 1825. The campground is about 100 yards south on Forest Service Road 382.

Trip note: This campground is near Site 30 and offers the same opportunities, except that this camp provides stock handling facilities.

Site 32
ALPINE
near Pacific Crest Trail
MOUNT HOOD NATIONAL FOREST

Campsites, facilities: There are 16 tent sites. Piped water, fire grills and picnic tables are provided. Leashed pets are permitted.

Reservations, fee: No reservations necessary; $5 fee per night. Open July to late September.

Who to contact: Phone the Zigzag Ranger District at (503)666-0704 or write to Mount Hood National Forest, 70220 East Highway 35, Zigzag, OR 97049.

Location: From Government Camp, take Highway 50 northeast 4.5 miles to the campground.

Trip note: This small, quiet campground is adjacent to the Mount Hood ski area on the south slopes of Mount Hood. The Pacific Crest Trail passes very close to camp and there are several trails nearby that offer access to the Mount Hood Wilderness area.

Site 33
STILL CREEK
on Still Creek
MOUNT HOOD NATIONAL FOREST

Campsites, facilities: There are 27 sites for tents, trailers or motor homes up to 30 feet long. Picnic tables and fire grills are provided. Pit toilets and piped water are available. Leashed pets are permitted.

Reservations, fee: No reservations necessary; $4 fee per night. Open mid-June to late September.

Who to contact: Phone the Zigzag Ranger District at (503)666-0704 or write to Mount Hood National Forest, 70220 East Highway 35, Zigzag, OR 97049.

Location: From Government Camp, go one mile east on US 26, then 500 yards south on Forest Service Road 2650.

Trip note: This primitive camp is set near the junction of US 26 and Highway 35, located along Still Creek where it pours off the south slope of Mount Hood.

Site 34
ROBINHOOD
on the East Fork of Hood River
MOUNT HOOD NATIONAL FOREST

Campsites, facilities: There are 24 tent sites. Piped water and picnic tables are provided. Leashed pets are permitted.

Reservations, fee: No reservations necessary; $5 fee per night. Open mid-May to early September.

Who to contact: Phone the Hood River Ranger District at (503)666-0701 or write to Mount Hood National Forest, 2955 NW Division Street, Gresham, OR 97030.

Location: From Parkdale, go three miles southeast on Highway P28, then 12 miles south on Highway 35 to the campground.

Trip note: This campground is set along the East Fork of the Hood River at the base of Mount Hood. A trail from the camp follows the river north for about four miles to Sherwood campground. From there, it joins a network of trails that provide access to the Mount Hood Wilderness.

Site 35
KNEBAL SPRINGS
near Knebal Springs
MOUNT HOOD NATIONAL FOREST

Campsites, facilities: There are four sites for tents and small trailers or motor homes. Picnic tables and fire grills are provided. Pit toilets are available. There is **no piped water.** Horse loading and tending facilities are available. Leashed pets are permitted.

Reservations, fee: No reservations necessary; no fee. Open July to early September.

Who to contact: Phone the Barlow Ranger District at (503)467-2291 or write to Mount Hood National Forest, P.O. Box 67, Dufur, OR 97021.

Location: Go 12 miles southwest of Dufur on County Road 1 and continue west on Forest Service Road 44. At Forest Service Road 4430 travel four miles north, then go southwest on Forest Service Road 1720 for one mile to the campground.

Trip note: This is in a semi-primitive area near Knebal Springs, an ephemeral water source. A trail from the camp provides access to a network of other trails in the area. A Forest Service map is advised.

Site 36
EIGHTMILE CROSSING
on Eightmile Creek
MOUNT HOOD NATIONAL FOREST

Campsites, facilities: There are 24 sites for tents, trailers or motor homes up to 16 feet long. **No piped water** is available. Picnic tables and fire grills are provided. Pit toilets are available. Leashed pets are permitted.

Reservations, fee: No reservations necessary; $4 fee per night. Open June to mid-October.

Who to contact: Phone the Barlow Ranger District at (503)467-2291 or write to Mount Hood National Forest, P.O. Box 67, Dufur, OR 97021.

Location: Go 12 miles southwest of Dufur on County Road 1 and continue west on Forest Service Road 44. At Forest Service Road 4430 travel north for one-half mile to the campground.

Trip note: This campground is set along Eightmile Creek and gets little camping pressure. There are some trails in the area. See a Forest Service map for options.

Site 37
PEBBLE FORD
MOUNT HOOD NATIONAL FOREST

Campsites, facilities: There are three sites for tents, trailers or motor homes up to 15 feet long. Picnic tables and fire grills provided. Pit toilets are available. There is **no piped water.** Leashed pets are permitted.

Reservations, fee: No reservations necessary; no fee. Open July to early September.

Who to contact: Phone the Barlow Ranger District at (503)467-2291 or write to Mount Hood National Forest, P.O. Box 67, Dufur, OR 97021.

Location: From Dufur, go 12 miles southwest on County Road 1, then five miles west on Forest Service Road 44. Turn south on Forest Service Road 131 and travel one-half mile and you'll see the campground.

Trip note: This is just a little camping spot by the side of the gravel Forest Service road. It is primitive and quiet.

BADGER LAKE
Site **38**
on Badger Lake
MOUNT HOOD NATIONAL FOREST

Campsites, facilities: There are 15 tent-only sites, accessible only by campers with four-wheel drive vehicles. Picnic tables and fire grills are provided. Pit toilets are available. There is **no piped water.** Leashed pets are permitted.

Reservations, fee: No reservations necessary; no fee. Open July to early September.

Who to contact: Phone the Barlow Ranger District at (503)467-2291 or write to Mount Hood National Forest, P.O. Box 67, Dufur, OR 97021.

Location: From the town of Mount Hood travel 19 miles south on Highway 35, then take a left onto Forest Service Road 3550 and drive 3.5 miles to Forest Service Road 3530. Turn left and drive one mile to Camp Windy. From there go two miles on Forest Service Road 4860, then make a hairpin left on Forest Service Road 140 and drive four miles to the lake. The last two miles require a four-wheel drive vehicle.

Trip note: This high country campground is set along the shore of Badger Lake. Boating is permitted. It is adjacent to the Badger-Jordon Wilderness area and numerous trails provide access to the backcountry. A Forest Service map details the backcountry roads and trails.

BONNEY MEADOWS
Site **39**
MOUNT HOOD NATIONAL FOREST

Campsites, facilities: There are five sites for tents or small trailers or motor homes. Picnic tables and fire grills are provided. Pit toilets are available. There is **no piped water.** Leashed pets are permitted.

Reservations, fee: No reservations necessary; no fee. Open July to early September.

Who to contact: Phone the Barlow Ranger District at (503)467-2291 or write to Mount Hood National Forest, P.O. Box 67, Dufur, OR 97021.

Location: From Tygh Valley on US 197, head west to Wamic. From Wamic, go six miles west on County Road 226, then continue south and west on Forest Service Road 48 for 14 miles. Next, go two miles north on Forest Service Road 4890, then continue four miles north on Forest Service Road 4891 to the campground.

Trip note: This high-elevation, primitive campground is located on the east side of the Cascade Range. As a result, there is little water in the area. Several trails are available, one of which travels 1.5 miles up to a group of small lakes. See a Forest Service map for details.

BARLOW CROSSING
Site **40**
on Barlow Creek
MOUNT HOOD NATIONAL FOREST

Campsites, facilities: There are five sites for tents. Picnic tables and fire grills are provided. Pit toilets are available. There is **no piped water.** Leashed pets are permitted.

Reservations, fee: No reservations necessary; no fee. Open mid-May to September.

Who to contact: Phone the Bear Springs Ranger District at (503)328-6211 or write to Mount Hood National Forest, Route 1, Box 65, Maupin, OR 97037.

Location: Take US 26 two miles east of Government Camp, then six miles east on Highway 35. The camp is located nine miles south on Forest Service Road 48.

Trip note: This small roadside campground is set along Barlow Creek and is not known by many folks.

Site **41**

BARLOW CREEK
on Barlow Creek
MOUNT HOOD NATIONAL FOREST

Campsites, facilities: There are five sites for tents. Picnic tables and fire grills are provided. Pit toilets are available, but there is **no piped water.** Leashed pets are permitted.

Reservations, fee: No reservations necessary; no fee. Open May to October.

Who to contact: Phone the Bear Springs Ranger District at (503)328-6211 or write to Mount Hood National Forest, Route 1, Box 65, Maupin, OR 97037.

Location: Go two miles east of Government Camp on US 26, then go 4.5 miles east on Highway 35. From there, go four miles southeast on Forest Service Road 3530.

Trip note: This campground is set along Barlow Creek on Old Barlow Road, which was the wagon trail for early settlers in this area. This is one of several primitive Forest Service camps in the immediate vicinity.

Site **42**

GRINDSTONE
near Barlow Creek
MOUNT HOOD NATIONAL FOREST

Campsites, facilities: There are five sites for tents. Picnic tables and fire grills are provided. Pit toilets are available, but there is **no piped water.** Leashed pets are permitted.

Reservations, fee: No reservations necessary; no fee. Open May to October.

Who to contact: Phone the Bear Springs Ranger District at (503)328-6211 or write to Mount Hood National Forest, Route 1, Box 65, Maupin, OR 97037.

Location: Drive two miles east of Government Camp on US 26, then go 4.5 miles east on Highway 35. From there, go two miles southeast on Forest Service Road 3530.

Trip note: This tiny campground is set a few miles upstream on Barlow Creek from Site 41, on Old Barlow Road. It's a little-known and little-used spot.

Site **43**

DEVIL'S HALF ACRE MEADOW
on Barlow Creek
MOUNT HOOD NATIONAL FOREST

Campsites, facilities: There are six sites for tents, trailers or motor homes up to 16 feet long. Picnic tables and fire grills are provided. Firewood and pit toilets are available. There is **no piped water.** Leashed pets are permitted.

Reservations, fee: No reservations necessary; no fee. Open May to October.

Who to contact: Phone the Bear Springs Ranger District at (503)328-6211 or write to Mount Hood National Forest, Route 1, Box 65, Maupin, OR 97037.

Location: Go two miles east of Government Camp on US 26, then go 4.5 miles east on Highway 35. From there, go one mile southeast on Forest Service Road 3530.

Trip note: This campground is set a few miles upstream on Barlow Creek from Site 42, which was the wagon trail for early settlers to this area. Several hiking trails are nearby, including the Pacific Crest Trail, which provide access to some small lakes in the area.

Site **44**
FROG LAKE
near Pacific Crest Trail
MOUNT HOOD NATIONAL FOREST

Campsites, facilities: There are 33 sites for tents, trailers or motor homes up to 16 feet long. Piped water and picnic tables are provided. Pit toilets are available. Leashed pets are permitted. Primitive launching facilities are nearby. No motorized boats allowed.

Reservations, fee: No reservations necessary; $6-8 fee per night. Open mid-June to October.

Who to contact: Phone the Bear Springs Ranger District at (503)328-6211 or write to Mount Hood National Forest, Route 1, Box 65, Maupin, OR 97037.

Location: From Government Camp, go seven miles southeast on US 26, then one mile southeast on Forest Service Road 2610. The camp is about 500 yards south on Forest Service Road 230.

Trip note: This classic spot in the Cascade Range is set on the shore of little Frog Lake, a short distance from the Pacific Crest Trail. Several other trails lead to nearby lakes.

Site **45**
TRILLIUM LAKE
on Trillium Lake
MOUNT HOOD NATIONAL FOREST

Campsites, facilities: There are 39 sites for tents, trailers or motor homes up to 30 feet long. Picnic tables and fire grills are provided. Pit toilets and piped water are available. Leashed pets are permitted. Some of the facilities are wheelchair accessible. Boat docks and launching facilities are available on the lake, but no motors are permitted.

Reservations, fee: No reservations necessary; $6-8 fee per night. Open late May to late September.

Who to contact: Phone the Zigzag Ranger District at (503)666-0704 or write to Mount Hood National Forest, 70220 East Highway 35, Zigzag, OR 97049.

Location: Take US 26 two miles southeast of Government Camp, then go south on Forest Service Road 2656 for 1.3 miles to the campground.

Trip note: This campground is set along the shores of Trillium Lake, which is about one-half mile long and one-quarter mile wide. It is a good lake for canoes and rafts.

Site **46**
CLEAR LAKE
near Pacific Crest Trail
MOUNT HOOD NATIONAL FOREST

Campsites, facilities: There are 28 sites for tents, trailers or motor homes up to 22 feet long. Picnic tables and fire grills are provided. Piped water and pit toilets are available. Leashed pets are permitted. Boat docks and launching facilities are nearby. Motorboats are allowed and there is no speed limit.

Reservations, fee: No reservations necessary; $6-8 fee per night. Open late May to early September.

Who to contact: Phone the Bear Springs Ranger District at (503)822-3381 or write to Mount Hood National Forest, Route 1, Box 65, Maupin, OR 97037.

Location: Travel nine miles southeast of Government Camp on US 26, then go one mile south on Forest Service Road 449.

Trip note: This campground is set along the shore of Clear Lake, a spot favored by fishermen, swimmers and windsurfers. A nearby trail heads north from the lake and provides access to the Pacific Crest Trail and Frog Lake.

Site 47
WHITE RIVER STATION
on White River
MOUNT HOOD NATIONAL FOREST

Campsites, facilities: There are five sites for tents, trailers or motor homes up to 16 feet long. Picnic tables and fire grills are provided. Pit toilets are available, but **no piped water** is available. Leashed pets are permitted.
Reservations, fee: No reservations necessary; no fee. Open May to October.
Who to contact: Phone the Bear Springs Ranger District at (503)328-6211 or write to Mount Hood National Forest, Route 1, Box 65, Maupin, OR 97037.
Location: Take US 26 two miles east of Government Camp, then go two miles east on Highway 35. Turn south on Forest Service Road 46 and travel nine miles southeast, and then turn south and drive one mile on Forest Service Road 3530.
Trip note: This tiny campground is set along the White River on Old Barlow Road, an original wagon trail used by early settlers. This is one of several small, secluded camps in the area.

Site 48
FOREST CREEK
on Forest Creek
MOUNT HOOD NATIONAL FOREST

Campsites, facilities: There are eight sites for tents, trailers or motor homes up to 16 feet long. **No piped water** is available. Picnic tables and fire grills are provided. Pit toilets are available. Leashed pets are permitted.
Reservations, fee: No reservations necessary; $2 fee per night. Open July to early September.
Who to contact: Phone the Barlow Ranger District at (503)467-2291 or write to Mount Hood National Forest, P.O. Box 67, Dufur, OR 97021.
Location: From Tygh Valley on US 197, head west to Wamic. Take County Road 226 six miles west of Wamic, then go 12.5 miles southwest on Forest Service Road 48. From there go one mile southeast on Forest Service Road 4885, then south for one-quarter mile on Forest Service Road 3530 to the campground.
Trip note: This is a very old camp set along Forest Creek on the original Barlow Trail. Early settlers used to camp here. You cross a small bridge to reach the camp.

Site 49
KEEPS MILL
on Clear Creek
MOUNT HOOD NATIONAL FOREST

Campsites, facilities: There are five sites for tents. The road to the campground is not good for trailers. Picnic tables and fire grills are provided. Pit toilets are available. There is **no piped water.** Leashed pets are permitted.
Reservations, fee: No reservations necessary; no fee. Open May to October.
Who to contact: Phone the Bear Springs Ranger District at (503)328-6211 or write to Mount Hood National Forest, Route 1, Box 65, Maupin, OR 97037.
Location: Take County Road 226 six miles west of Wamic, then go 12.5 miles southwest on Forest Service Road 48. From there go three miles southeast on Forest Service Road 4885, then turn right and drive one-quarter mile to the campground.
Trip note: This campground is located at the confluence of Clear Creek and the

White River. Hiking trails are in the area. A map of Mount Hood National Forest details the back roads and trails and is strongly advised.

Site 50
CLEAR CREEK
on Clear Creek
MOUNT HOOD NATIONAL FOREST

Campsites, facilities: There are five sites for tents, trailers or motor homes up to 16 feet long. Picnic tables and fire grills are provided. Pit toilets are available. There is **no piped water**. Leashed pets are permitted.

Reservations, fee: No reservations necessary; no fee. Open May to October.

Who to contact: Phone the Bear Springs Ranger District at (503)328-6211 or write to Mount Hood National Forest, Route 1, Box 65, Maupin, OR 97037.

Location: Drive 28 miles west of Maupin on Highway 216, then three miles north on Forest Service Road 2130. The camp is located about one-half mile east on Forest Service Road 260.

Trip note: This campground is set along the banks of Clear Creek. It's a secluded, little-known camp in Mount Hood National Forest. A Forest Service map details recreational options.

Site 51
BEAR SPRINGS
on Indian Creek
MOUNT HOOD NATIONAL FOREST

Campsites, facilities: There are 21 sites for tents, trailers or motor homes up to 16 feet long. Piped water, fire grills and picnic tables are provided. Pit toilets are available. Leashed pets are permitted.

Reservations, fee: No reservations necessary; $5 fee per night. Open June to October.

Who to contact: Phone the Bear Springs Ranger District at (503)328-6211 or write to Mount Hood National Forest, Route 1, Box 65, Maupin, OR 97037.

Location: Coming from the northwest on US 26, turn east on Highway 216 just before entering Warm Springs Indian Reservation. Continue on Highway 216 for five miles and look for the campground on the right.

Trip note: This campground is set along the banks of Indian Creek, just far enough east of US 26 to be missed by the highway cruisers.

Site 52
McCUBBINS GULCH
MOUNT HOOD NATIONAL FOREST

Campsites, facilities: There are six sites for tents, trailers or motor homes up to 16 feet long. Picnic tables and fire grills are provided. Pit toilets available. There is **no piped water**. Leashed pets are permitted.

Reservations, fee: No reservations necessary; no fee. Open May to October.

Who to contact: Phone the Bear Springs Ranger District at (503)328-6211 or write to Mount Hood National Forest, Route 1, Box 65, Maupin, OR 97037.

Location: Coming from the northwest on US 26, turn east on Highway 216 just before entering Warm Springs Indian Reservation. Continue on Highway 216 for six miles, then make a sharp left onto Forest Service Road 2110 and continue for 1.5 miles. Look for the campground entrance on the right side.

Trip note: This is a small, primitive camp that gets little attention from travelers.

Site **53**
ROCK CREEK RESERVOIR
on Rock Creek Reservoir
MOUNT HOOD NATIONAL FOREST

Campsites, facilities: There are 33 sites for tents, trailers or motor homes up to 22 feet long. Picnic tables and fire grills are provided. Pit toilets, piped water and firewood are available. Some facilities are wheelchair accessible. Leashed pets are permitted. There are boat docks nearby but no motorboats are allowed on the reservoir.

Reservations, fee: No reservations necessary; $5 fee per night. Open late April to early October.

Who to contact: Phone the Barlow Ranger District at (503)467-2291 or write to Mount Hood National Forest, P.O. Box 67, Dufur, OR 97021.

Location: Travel west on County Road 226 for six miles out of Wamic, then go one mile southwest on Forest Service Road 48. The campground is located about 200 yards west on Forest Service Road 4820.

Trip note: This campground is set along the shore of Rock Creek Reservoir. A loop trail is nearby.

Site **54**
BONNEY CROSSING
on Badger Creek
MOUNT HOOD NATIONAL FOREST

Campsites, facilities: There are eight sites for tents, trailers or motor homes up to 16 feet long. Picnic tables and fire grills are provided. Pit toilets are available. There is **no piped water.** Leashed pets are permitted.

Reservations, fee: No reservations necessary; no fee. Open late April to mid-October.

Who to contact: Phone the Barlow Ranger District at (503)467-2291 or write to Mount Hood National Forest, P.O. Box 67, Dufur, OR 97021.

Location: Drive six miles west of Wamic on County Road 226, then one mile west on Forest Service Road 48. From there, go 200 yards west on Forest Service Road 4810 to the campground.

Trip note: This campground is set along Badger Creek and is the trailhead for the Badger Creek Trail, which provides access to the Badger Creek Wilderness. See a Forest Service map for details.

Site **55**
CASCADE HYLANDS RESORT
on Pine Hollow Reservoir

Campsites, facilities: There are 35 tent sites and 75 sites for trailers or motor homes. Electricity, piped water, sewer hookups and picnic tables are provided. Flush toilets, bottled gas, sanitary services, showers, firewood, a store, a cafe, a laundromat and ice are available. Pets and motorbikes are permitted. Boat docks, launching facilities and rentals are nearby.

Reservations, fee: Reservations accepted; $9.50-12 fee per night; MasterCard and Visa accepted. Open all year.

Who to contact: Phone (503)544-2271 or write to 34 North Mariposa Drive, Wamic, OR 97063.

Location: Take the Tygh Valley Road exit off US 197, then go 4.5 miles west on Wamic Road to Pine Hollow Reservoir Road, and follow it north 3.5 miles.

Trip note: This resort is set along the shore of Pine Hollow Reservoir. It's the best game in town for motor home campers.

Site 56
WASCO COUNTY FAIRGROUNDS
on Badger Creek

Campsites, facilities: There are 50 tent sites and 150 drive-through sites for trailers or motor homes of any length. Electricity, piped water and picnic tables are provided. Flush toilets, a dump station, sanitary services and showers are available. A store, a cafe and ice are located within one mile. Leashed pets are permitted.

Reservations, fee: Reservations accepted; $3-7 fee per night. Open all year.

Who to contact: Phone (503)483-2288 or write to Route 1, Box 93, Tygh Valley, OR 97063.

Location: Take US 197 south from Maupin, at Tygh Valley Road go southwest for about 2 miles. The campground is located on Fairgrounds Road.

Trip note: This county campground is set near the confluence of Badger Creek and Tygh Creek. Nearby recreation options include hiking trails, marked bike trails and tennis courts.

Site 57
BEAVERTAIL
on Deschutes River

Campsites, facilities: There are 21 tent sites and 18 drive-through sites for trailers or motor homes up to 20 feet long. Picnic tables and fire grills are provided. Piped water and vault toilets are available. Leashed pets are permitted. Boat launching facilities are nearby.

Reservations, fee: No reservations necessary; $2 fee per night. Open all year.

Who to contact: Phone (503)447-4115, or write to Bureau of Land Management, P.O. Box 550, Prineville, OR 97754.

Location: This campground is located 17 miles northeast of Maupin along the Deschutes River Road.

Trip note: This isolated campground is set along the banks of the Deschutes River on BLM land. The Deschutes is one of the classic trout streams in the Pacific Northwest.

Site 58
KAH-NEE-TA RESORT
on Warm Springs Indian Reservation

Campsites, facilities: There are 90 drive-through sites for trailers or motor homes of any length. Electricity, piped water and sewer hookups are provided. Flush toilets, bottled gas, sanitary services, showers, a cafe, a laundromat, ice, a playground and a swimming pool are available. Pets and motorbikes are permitted.

Reservations, fee: Reservations accepted; $13-17 fee per night; American Express, MasterCard and Visa accepted. Open all year.

Who to contact: Phone (800)831-0100 or write to P.O. Box K, Warm Springs, OR 97761.

Location: From Warm Springs, drive 11 miles northeast on Highway 3 to Kah-Nee-Ta.

Trip note: This is the only public camp on the east side of the Warm Springs Indian Reservation; there are no other camps within 30 miles. Nearby recreation options include an 18-hole golf course, hiking trails, a riding stable and tennis courts.

Site **59**

LITTLE CRATER
on Crater Lake
MOUNT HOOD NATIONAL FOREST

Campsites, facilities: There are 16 sites for tents, trailers or motor homes up to 16 feet long. Picnic tables and fire grills are provided. Pit toilets and piped water are available. Leashed pets are permitted.

Reservations, fee: No reservations necessary; $4 fee per night. Open June to October.

Who to contact: Phone the Bear Springs Ranger District at (503)328-6211 or write to Mount Hood National Forest, Route 1, Box 65, Maupin, OR 97037.

Location: Travel 15 miles southeast from the town of Government Camp on US 26, then go six miles south on Highway 42. From there, go 2.5 miles northwest on Forest Service Road 58 to the campground.

Trip note: This camp is next to Crater Creek and scenic, Little Crater Lake. It's also alongside the Pacific Crest Trail about a mile from Timothy Lake. See the trip note for Site 60 for more information about Timothy Lake.

Site **60**

GONE CREEK
on Timothy Lake
MOUNT HOOD NATIONAL FOREST

Campsites, facilities: There are 50 sites for tents, trailers or motor homes up to 31 feet long. Piped water, fire grills and picnic tables are provided. Pit toilets are available. Leashed pets are permitted. Boat docks are nearby.

Reservations, fee: No reservations necessary; $6-8 fee per night. Open mid-May to mid-September.

Who to contact: Phone the Bear Springs Ranger District at (503)328-6211 or write to Mount Hood National Forest, Route 1, Box 65, Maupin, OR 97037.

Location: Take US 26 southeast of Government Camp for 15 miles, then go eight miles south on Forest Service Road 42. Turn on Forest Service Road 57 and drive about 500 yards west to the campground.

Trip note: This campground is set along the shore of Timothy Lake at 3,200 feet elevation. It is one of five camps at the lake. Timothy Lake provides good fishing for brook trout, cutthroat trout, rainbow trout and kokanee salmon. Boats with motors are allowed, but a ten-mph speed limit keeps it quiet. Several trails are in the area, including the Pacific Crest Trail, which provide access to several small mountain lakes.

Site **61**

HOODVIEW
on Timothy Lake
MOUNT HOOD NATIONAL FOREST

Campsites, facilities: There are 43 sites for tents, trailers or motor homes up to 31 feet long. Picnic tables and fire grills are provided. Piped water and pit toilets are available. Leashed pets are permitted. Boat docks are nearby.

Reservations, fee: No reservations necessary; $6-8 fee per night. Open mid-May to mid-September.

Who to contact: Phone the Bear Springs Ranger District at (503)328-6211 or write to Mount Hood National Forest, Route 1, Box 65, Maupin, OR 97037.

Location: Take US 26 southeast of Government Camp for 15 miles, then go eight miles south on Forest Service Road 42. Turn on Forest Service Road 57 and continue for another mile to the campground.

Trip note: This site is also set along the shore of Timothy Lake. See the trip note for Site 60 for details.

Site **62**
OAK FORK
on Timothy Lake
MOUNT HOOD NATIONAL FOREST

Campsites, facilities: There are 47 sites for tents, trailers or motor homes up to 22 feet long. Picnic tables and fire grills are provided. Piped water and pit toilets are available. Leashed pets are permitted. Boat docks and launching facilities are nearby.

Reservations, fee: No reservations necessary; $6-8 fee per night. Open June to October.

Who to contact: Phone the Bear Springs Ranger District at (503)328-6211 or write to Mount Hood National Forest, Route 1, Box 65, Maupin, OR 97037.

Location: Take US 26 southeast from Government Camp for 15 miles, then go eight miles south on Forest Service Road 42 and three miles west on Forest Service Road 57.

Trip note: This camp is set along the shore of Timothy Lake. See the trip note for Site 60 for details.

Site **63**
PINE POINT
on Timothy Lake
MOUNT HOOD NATIONAL FOREST

Campsites, facilities: There are 20 sites for tents, trailers or motor homes up to 31 feet long: ten single sites, ten double sites and five group campsites. Picnic tables and fire grills are provided. Piped water and pit toilets are available. Leashed pets are permitted. Boat docks and launching facilities are nearby.

Reservations, fee: No reservations necessary; $6-20 fee per night depending on type of campsite. Open late May to mid-September.

Who to contact: Phone the Bear Springs Ranger District at (503)328-6211 or write to Mount Hood National Forest, Route 1, Box 65, Maupin, OR 97037.

Location: From Government Camp, go 15 miles southeast on US 26, then eight miles south on Forest Service Road 42. The camp is located five miles west on Forest Service Road 57.

Trip note: This is one of five camps on Timothy Lake. See the trip note for Site 60 for details.

Site **64**
MEDITATION POINT
on Timothy Lake, boat-in or walk-in only
MOUNT HOOD NATIONAL FOREST

Campsites, facilities: There are four tent sites accessible by trail or by boat. Picnic tables and fire grills are provided. Pit toilets are available. There is **no piped water.** Leashed pets are permitted. Boat docks and launching facilities are nearby.

Reservations, fee: No reservations necessary; no fee. Open late May to mid-September.

Who to contact: Phone the Bear Springs Ranger District at (503)328-6211 or write to Mount Hood National Forest, Route 1, Box 65, Maupin, OR 97037.

Location: From Government Camp, go 15 miles southeast on US 26, then eight miles south on Forest Service Road 42. Park at Pine Point campground, located five miles west on Forest Service Road 57, and hike one mile or take a boat to the north shore of the lake.

Trip note: Accessible only by foot or boat, this offers a more secluded location along Timothy Lake than Sites 60-63. See the trip note for Site 60 for details about the lake.

Site **65**
CLACKAMAS LAKE
near Clackamas River
MOUNT HOOD NATIONAL FOREST

Campsites, facilities: There are 47 sites for tents, trailers or motor homes up to 16 feet long. Piped water, fire grills and picnic tables are provided. Pit toilets are available. Leashed pets are permitted. Boat docks and launching facilities are nearby.

Reservations, fee: No reservations necessary; $4 fee per night. Open June to October.

Who to contact: Phone the Bear Springs Ranger District at (503)328-6211 or write to Mount Hood National Forest, Route 1, Box 65, Maupin, OR 97037.

Location: From Government Camp, go 15 miles southeast on US 26, then go eight miles south on Forest Service Road 42. The camp is about 500 yards east on Forest Service Road 4270.

Trip note: Clackamas Lake is small and shallow, but not far from the Clackamas River. The Pacific Crest Trail passes nearby and Timothy Lake is little more than a one-mile hike from camp. See the trip note for Site 60 for information on Timothy Lake.

Site **66**
JOE GRAHAM HORSE CAMP
near Clackamas Lake
MOUNT HOOD NATIONAL FOREST

Campsites, facilities: There are 14 sites for tents, trailers or motor homes up to 31 feet long. Picnic tables, and fire grills are provided. Piped water, pit toilets and firewood are available. Leashed pets are permitted.

Reservations, fee: No reservations; $5 fee per night. Open mid-May to mid-September.

Who to contact: Phone the Bear Springs Ranger District at (503)328-6211 or write to Mount Hood National Forest, Route 1, Box 65, Maupin, OR 97037.

Location: From Government Camp, go 15 miles southeast on US 26, then eight miles south on Forest Service Road 42.

Trip note: This campground is set just north of tiny Clackamas Lake and is the only campground in the area that allows horses. See the trip note for Sites 65 for additional information. Timothy Lake (Sites 60-64) provides a nearby alternative to the northwest.

Site **67**
SUMMIT LAKE
on Summit Lake
MOUNT HOOD NATIONAL FOREST

Campsites, facilities: There are four tent sites. Fire grills and picnic tables are provided. Pit toilets and firewood are available. There is **no piped water.** Leashed pets are permitted. Boat docks are nearby, but no motorboats are allowed.

Reservations, fee: No reservations necessary; no fee. Open late May to October.

Who to contact: Phone the Bear Springs Ranger District at (503)328-6211 or write to Mount Hood National Forest, Route 1, Box 65, Maupin, OR 97037.

Location: From Government Camp, go 15 miles southeast on US 26, then go 13 miles south on Forest Service Road 42. Head west on Forest Service Road 141 (a dirt road) for one mile to the campground.

Trip note: This is an idyllic setting in a remote area along the western slopes of the Cascade Range. The camp is located on the shore of little Summit Lake. It's primitive, but it's a jewel.

Site **68** ### SHELLROCK CREEK
on Shellrock Creek
MOUNT HOOD NATIONAL FOREST

Campsites, facilities: There are five sites for tents, trailers or motor homes up to 16 feet long. Picnic tables and fire grills are provided. Pit toilets are available. There is **no piped water.** Leashed pets are permitted.

Reservations, fee: No reservations necessary; no fee. Open mid-June to early September.

Who to contact: Phone the Clackamas Ranger District at (503)630-4256 or write to Mount Hood National Forest, 61431 East Highway 224, Estacada, OR 97023.

Location: From Government Camp, go 15 miles southeast on US 26, then eight miles south on Forest Service Road 42. Turn west on Forest Service Road 57 and drive 15 miles to Forest Service Road 58. The campground is one mile south on Forest Service Road 58.

Trip note: This quiet little campground is at a nice spot on Shellrock Creek, good for "sneak fishing" for trout. It's advisable to obtain a Forest Service map that details the backcountry roads and trails.

Site **69** ### LAKE HARRIET
MOUNT HOOD NATIONAL FOREST

Campsites, facilities: There are 13 sites for tents, trailers or motor homes up to 22 feet long. Picnic tables and fire grills are provided. Piped water and vault toilets are available. Some facilities are wheelchair accessible. Leashed pets are permitted. Boat docks and launching facilities are located on the lake. No horses are allowed in the campground.

Reservations, fee: No reservations necessary; $5 fee per night. Open late April to late September.

Who to contact: Phone the Clackamas Ranger District at (503)630-4256 or write to Mount Hood National Forest, 61431 East Highway 224, Estacada, OR 97023.

Location: From Government Camp, go 15 miles southeast on US 26, then eight miles south on Forest Service Road 42. Turn west on Forest Service Road 57 and drive 15 miles to Forest Service Road 58. Drive one mile south on Forest Service Road 58, then west on Forest Service Road 4630 for two miles to the campground.

Trip note: This little lake has been formed by a dam on the Oak Grove Fork of the Clackamas River and is a popular spot during the summer. Rowboats and boats with small motors are permitted. The lake can provide good fishing for a variety of trout, including brown, brook, rainbow and cutthroat.

Site **70** ### HIDEAWAY LAKES
near Rocks Lake Basin
MOUNT HOOD NATIONAL FOREST

Campsites, facilities: There are nine sites for tents, small trailers or camper vans. Picnic tables and fire grills are provided. Pit toilets and piped water are available. Leashed pets are permitted.

Reservations, fee: No reservations necessary; $4 fee per night. Open mid-June to late September.

Who to contact: Phone the Clackamas Ranger District at (503)630-4256 or write to Mount Hood National Forest, 61431 East Highway 224, Estacada, OR 97023.

Location: From Estacada, go 27 miles southeast on Highway 224, then 7.5 miles east on Forest Service Road 57. From there, take Forest Service Road 58, and travel three miles north to Forest Service Road 5830, turn northwest and drive 5.5 miles to the campground.

Trip note: A jewel of a spot, this small, deep lake is set at 3,800 feet elevation. The campsites are separate and set around the lake. At the north end of the lake there is an 8.5-mile loop trail that goes past a number of lakes in the Rock Lakes Basin, all of which support populations of rainbow and brook trout. If you don't want to make the whole trip in a day, you can camp overnight at Serene Lake. See a Forest Service map for directions.

Site 71   HIGH ROCK SPRINGS
near Rock Lakes Basin
MOUNT HOOD NATIONAL FOREST

Campsites, facilities: There are six tent sites. Picnic tables and fire grills are provided. Pit toilets are available. There is no piped water. Leashed pets are permitted.

Reservations, fee: No reservations necessary; no fee. Open mid-June to late September.

Who to contact: Phone the Clackamas Ranger District at (503)630-4256 or write to Mount Hood National Forest, 61431 East Highway 224, Estacada, OR 97023.

Location: Take Highway 224 southeast of Estacada for 27 miles, then go 7.5 miles east on Forest Service Road 57. Turn northeast on Forest Service Road 58 and travel 10.5 miles to the campground.

Trip note: This small, remote campground is adjacent to High Rock. A half-mile climb offers a tremendous view of the surrounding area, including Mount Hood. About four miles east of the camp are trails that lead to some of the fishing lakes in Rock Lakes Basin. In August and September, ripe huckleberries are available in the area.

Site 72   LAZY BEND
on Clackamas River
MOUNT HOOD NATIONAL FOREST

Campsites, facilities: There are 21 sites for tents, trailers or motor homes up to 22 feet long. Picnic tables and fireplaces are provided. Piped water and flush toilets are available. Leashed pets are permitted.

Reservations, fee: No reservations necessary; $6 fee per night. Open late April through Labor Day.

Who to contact: Phone the Estacada Ranger District at (503)630-6861 or write to Mount Hood National Forest, 595 NW Industrial Way, Estacada, OR 97023.

Location: From Estacada, go 10.5 miles southeast on Highway 224 to the campground.

Trip note: This campground is set along the banks of the Clackamas River, near the large North Fork Reservoir. It is far enough off the highway to provide a secluded, primitive feeling.

Site **73**
FISH CREEK
on Clackamas River
MOUNT HOOD NATIONAL FOREST

Campsites, facilities: There are 24 sites for tents, trailers or motor homes. Picnic tables and fire grills are provided. Vault toilets and pump water are available. Leashed pets are permitted.

Reservations, fee: No reservations necessary; $6 fee per night. Open late May to early September.

Who to contact: Phone the Estacada Ranger District at (503)630-6861 or write to Mount Hood National Forest, 595 NW Industrial Way, Estacada, OR 97023.

Location: From Estacada, go 15.5 miles southeast on Highway 224 and you'll see the campground.

Trip note: This campground is set along the banks of the Clackamas River, not far from the Clackamas River Trail and the North Fork Reservoir. There is an amphitheater near the camp.

Site **74**
ARMSTRONG
on Clackamas River
MOUNT HOOD NATIONAL FOREST

Campsites, facilities: There are 12 sites for tents, trailers or motor homes up to 30 feet long. Picnic tables and fire rings are provided. Vault toilets and piped water are available. Some facilities are wheelchair accessible. Leashed pets are permitted.

Reservations, fee: No reservations necessary; $6 fee per night. Open late May to early September.

Who to contact: Phone the Estacada Ranger District at (503)630-6861 or write to Mount Hood National Forest, 595 NW Industrial Way, Estacada, OR 97023.

Location: Go 15 miles southeast of Estacada on Highway 224 and you'll see the campground entrance.

Trip note: This campground is set along the banks of the Clackamas River and offers good fishing access. This is one of four camps in the immediate area.

Site **75**
CARTER BRIDGE
on Clackamas River
MOUNT HOOD NATIONAL FOREST

Campsites, facilities: There are 15 sites for tents, trailers or motor homes up to 22 feet long. Picnic tables and fireplaces are provided. Vault toilets and piped water are available. Some facilities are wheelchair accessible. Leashed pets are permitted.

Reservations, fee: No reservations necessary; $6 fee per night. Open all year.

Who to contact: Phone the Estacada Ranger District at (503)630-6861 or write to Mount Hood National Forest, 595 NW Industrial Way, Estacada, OR 97023.

Location: Go 15 miles southeast of Estacada on Highway 224 and you'll see the campground.

Trip note: This campground is set along the banks of the Clackamas River.

Site **76**
LOCKABY
on Clackamas River
MOUNT HOOD NATIONAL FOREST

Campsites, facilities: There are 30 sites for tents, trailers or motor homes up to 30

feet long. Picnic tables, fireplaces, pump water and vault toilets are available. Leashed pets are permitted.

Reservations, fee: No reservations necessary; $6 fee per night. Open late May to early September.

Who to contact: Phone the Estacada Ranger District at (503)630-6861 or write to Mount Hood National Forest, 595 NW Industrial Way, Estacada, OR 97023.

Location: From Estacada, go 15 miles southeast on Highway 224.

Trip note: This campground is set along the banks of the Clackamas River. It is one of the many campgrounds set on or near Highway 224 in this area.

Site 77 — ROARING RIVER
on Roaring River
MOUNT HOOD NATIONAL FOREST

Campsites, facilities: There are 19 sites for tents, trailers or motor homes up to 16 feet long. Picnic tables, fireplaces, pump water and vault toilets are available. Leashed pets are permitted.

Reservations, fee: No reservations necessary; $6 fee per night. Open mid-May to mid-September.

Who to contact: Phone the Estacada Ranger District at (503)630-6861 or write to Mount Hood National Forest, 595 NW Industrial Way, Estacada, OR 97023.

Location: Drive 18 miles south of Estacada on Highway 224 to the campground.

Trip note: This campground is set along the banks of the Roaring River. It provides access to the Dry Ridge Trail and several other trails into the adjacent roadless area. See a Forest Service map for details.

Site 78 — SUNSTRIP
on Clackamas River
MOUNT HOOD NATIONAL FOREST

Campsites, facilities: There are nine sites for tents, trailers or motor homes up to 15 feet long. Picnic tables, fireplaces, pump water and vault toilets, are available. Leashed pets are permitted.

Reservations, fee: No reservations necessary; $6 fee per night. Open late May to early September.

Who to contact: Phone the Estacada Ranger District at (503)630-6861 or write to Mount Hood National Forest, 595 NW Industrial Way, Estacada, OR 97023.

Location: Take Highway 224 southeast from Estacada about 18 miles to the campground.

Trip note: This campground is set along the banks of the Clackamas River and offers fishing and rafting access. It is one of 15 campgrounds set along the Highway 224 corridor.

Site 79 — INDIAN HENRY
on Clackamas River
MOUNT HOOD NATIONAL FOREST

Campsites, facilities: There are 86 sites for tents, trailers or motor homes up to 22 feet long. Picnic tables and fire grills are provided. Flush toilets, a sanitary dump station and piped water are available. Some facilities are wheelchair accessible. Leashed pets are permitted.

Reservations, fee: Reservations accepted; $7 fee per night. Open late May to early September.

Who to contact: Phone the Estacada Ranger District at (503)630-6861 or write to

Mount Hood Ranger District at 595 NW Industrial Way, Estacada, OR 97023.

Location: From Estacada, take Highway 224 southeast for 23 miles, then go one-half mile southeast on Forest Service Road 53.

Trip note: This campground is set along the banks of the Clackamas River and offers a trail that can be traveled on by wheelchair. Group campsites and an amphitheater are available. The Clackamas River Trail is nearby.

Site **80**   **ALDER FLAT**
on Clackamas River, hike-in only
MOUNT HOOD NATIONAL FOREST

Campsites, facilities: There are six tent sites at this hike-in campground. Picnic tables and fire grills are provided. Pit toilets are available. There is **no piped water**. Pets are permitted.

Reservations, fee: No reservations necessary; no fee. Open late April to late September.

Who to contact: Phone the Clackamas Ranger District at (503)630-4256 or write to Mount Hood National Forest, 61431 East Highway 224, Estacada, OR 97023.

Location: Take Highway 224 southeast from Estacada for 26 miles to the Ripplebrook Ranger Station. Parking for the camp is about one-half mile west of the ranger station. Hike one mile to the campground.

Trip note: This secluded hike-in campground is set along the banks of the Clackamas River. If you want peace and quiet and don't mind the short walk to get it, this is the spot. Be sure to pack out whatever you bring in.

Site **81**   **RIPPLEBROOK**
on the Oak Grove Fork of Clackamas River
MOUNT HOOD NATIONAL FOREST

Campsites, facilities: There are 13 sites for trailers or motor homes up to 16 feet long. Picnic tables and fire grills are provided. Pit toilets and piped water are available. Leashed pets are permitted; horses are not allowed in campground.

Reservations, fee: No reservations necessary; $5 fee per night. Open late April to late September.

Who to contact: Phone the Clackamas Ranger District at (503)630-4256 or write to Mount Hood National Forest, 61431 East Highway 224, Estacada, OR 97023.

Location: Travel 26.5 miles southeast of Estacada on Highway 224 and you'll see the campground entrance.

Trip note: This campground is set along the banks of the Oak Grove Fork of the Clackamas River. There is a four-mile foot trail from the camp that follows the river south to Riverside campground, a nice walk in beautiful country.

Site **82**   **RAINBOW**
on the Oak Grove Fork of Clackamas River
MOUNT HOOD NATIONAL FOREST

Campsites, facilities: There are 17 sites for tents, trailers or motor homes up to 16 feet long. Piped water, fire grills and picnic tables are provided. Pit toilets are available. Leashed pets are permitted.

Reservations, fee: No reservations necessary; $5 fee per night. Open late April to late September.

Who to contact: Phone the Clackamas Ranger District at (503)630-4256 or write to Mount Hood National Forest, 61431 East Highway 224, Estacada, OR 97023.

Location: From Estacada, go 27 miles southeast on Highway 224 to Forest Service

Road 46. The camp is about 100 yards south on Forest Service Road 46.

Trip note: This campground is set along the banks of the Oak Grove Fork of the Clackamas River not far from where it empties into the Clackamas River. Nearby Ripplebrook campground provides an option.

Site 83
RIVERSIDE
on Clackamas River
MOUNT HOOD NATIONAL FOREST

Campsites, facilities: There are 16 sites for tents, trailers or motor homes up to 16 feet long. Picnic tables and fire grills are provided. Pit toilets are available. Piped water can usually be found here. Leashed pets are permitted; no horses are allowed in the campground.

Reservations, fee: No reservations necessary; $5 fee per night. Open mid-May to late September.

Who to contact: Phone the Clackamas Ranger District at (503)854-3366 or write to Mount Hood National Forest, 61431 East Highway 224, Estacada, OR 97023.

Location: Take Highway 224 southeast of Estacada 27 miles, then go 2.5 miles south on Forest Service Road 46 to the campground.

Trip note: This campground is set along the banks of the Clackamas River. A trail worth hiking leaves the camp and follows the river for four miles north to Ripplebrook campground.

Site 84
RIVERFORD
on Clackamas and Collawash Rivers
MOUNT HOOD NATIONAL FOREST

Campsites, facilities: There are ten sites for tents, trailers or motor homes up to 16 feet long. Picnic tables and fire grills are provided. Pit toilets are available. There is **no piped water** except at nearby Two Rivers Picnic Area. Leashed pets are permitted.

Reservations, fee: No reservations necessary; no fee. Open late April to late September.

Who to contact: Phone the Clackamas Ranger District at (503)630-4256 or write to Mount Hood National Forest, 61431 East Highway 224, Estacada, OR 97023.

Location: From Estacada, go 27 miles southeast on Highway 224, then 3.5 miles south on Forest Service Road 46 to the campground.

Trip note: This campground is set at the confluence of the Clackamas and the Collawash Rivers. Some nice swimming spots are available, but use care: some areas are rocky, swift and treacherous.

Site 85
RAAB
on Collawash River
MOUNT HOOD NATIONAL FOREST

Campsites, facilities: There are 27 sites for tents, trailers or motor homes up to 22 feet long. Picnic tables and fire grills are provided. Pit toilets are available. There is **no piped water** except one mile away at Two Rivers Picnic Area. Leashed pets are permitted.

Reservations, fee: No reservations necessary; no fee. Open late May to early September.

Who to contact: Phone the Clackamas Ranger District at (503)630-4256 or write to Mount Hood National Forest, 61431 East Highway 224, Estacada, OR 97023.

Location: Take Highway 224 southeast of Estacada 27 miles, then go four miles south on Forest Service Road 46 to the campground.

Trip note: This campground is set along the banks of the Collawash River, about a mile from its confluence with the Clackamas River.

Site **86**
KINGFISHER
on the Hot Springs Fork of Collawash River
MOUNT HOOD NATIONAL FOREST

Campsites, facilities: There are 23 sites for tents, trailers or motor homes up to 30 feet long. Picnic tables and fireplaces provided. Vault toilets and piped water are available. Leashed pets are permitted.

Reservations, fee: No reservations necessary; $5 fee per night. Open late May to early September.

Who to contact: Phone the Estacada Ranger District at (503)630-6861 or write to Mount Hood National Forest, 595 NR Industrial Way, Estacada, OR 97023.

Location: Take Highway 224 out of Estacada and go 26 miles southeast to Forest Service Road 46. Go 3.5 miles south on Forest Service Road 46, three miles south on Forest Service Road 63, then one mile west on Forest Service Road 70 to the campground.

Trip note: This campground is set along the banks of the Hot Springs Fork of the Collawash River, about three miles from Bagby Hot Springs, a Forest Service day-use area. It is an easy 1.5-mile hike to the hot springs from the day-use area.

Site **87**
ROUND LAKE
on Round Lake, walk-in only
MOUNT HOOD NATIONAL FOREST

Campsites, facilities: There are six tent sites at this hike-in campground. Picnic tables and fire grills are provided. Pit toilets are available. There is **no piped water.** Leashed pets are permitted.

Reservations, fee: No reservations necessary; no fee. Open mid-June to late September.

Who to contact: Phone the Clackamas Ranger District at (503)630-4256 or write to Mount Hood National Forest, 61431 East Highway 224, Estacada, OR 97023.

Location: From Estacada, go 27 miles southeast on Highway 224, then 3.5 miles south on Forest Service Road 46. Get on Forest Service Road 63 and go southeast for 12.5 miles, then continue southeast on Forest Service Road 6370 for 6.7 miles until you get to the campground parking area. Walk one-half mile to the campground.

Trip note: This is an idyllic spot, beautiful and secluded, set at the edge of Round Lake. It's well worth figuring out the maze of Forest Service roads and then making the half-mile hike. Try not to be discouraged by the cleared areas as you hike to the lake.

Site **88**
CAMP TEN
on Olallie Lake
MOUNT HOOD NATIONAL FOREST

Campsites, facilities: There are seven sites for tents, trailers or motor homes up to 16 feet long. Picnic tables and fire grills are provided. Pit toilets are available. There is **no piped water.** Leashed pets are permitted. A store that sells fishing tackle and other supplies is nearby. Boat docks, launching facilities and rentals are nearby.

Reservations, fee: No reservations necessary; no fee. Open mid-June to late September.

Who to contact: Phone the Clackamas Ranger District at (503)630-4256 or write to Mount Hood National Forest, 61431 East Highway 224, Estacada, OR 97023.

Location: Take Highway 224 southeast of Estacada for 27 miles, then go south on Forest Service Road 46 for about 22 miles. From there, travel on Forest Service Road 4690 southeast for 8.2 miles. When you reach Forest Service Road 4220, head south for six miles to the campground.

Trip note: This is one of several campgrounds set along the shore of Olallie Lake, a popular area. Boats without motors, such as canoes, kayaks and rafts, are permitted on the lake. Numerous smaller lakes in the area can be reached from trails nearby. A Forest Service map details the possibilities.

Site **89**
LOWER LAKE
near Olallie Lake
MOUNT HOOD NATIONAL FOREST

Campsites, facilities: There are nine tent sites. Picnic tables and fire grills are provided. Pit toilets are available. There is **no piped water.** Leashed pets are permitted. Boat docks, launching facilities and rentals are nearby at Olallie Lake.

Reservations, fee: No reservations necessary; no fee. Open mid-June to late September.

Who to contact: Phone the Clackamas Ranger District at (503)630-4256 or write to Mount Hood National Forest, 61431 East Highway 224, Estacada, OR 97023.

Location: Take Highway 224 southeast of Estacada for 27 miles, then go south on Forest Service Road 46 for about 22 miles. From there, travel on Forest Service Road 4690 southeast for 8.5 miles. When you reach Forest Service Road 4220, head south for 4.5 miles to the parking area. Hike one-half mile to the campground.

Trip note: This sunny, open campground is set along the shore of Lower Lake, a small, deep lake used for fishing and swimming. It is a short distance from Olallie Lake and near a network of trails that provide access to other nearby lakes. I advise you to obtain a Forest Service map that details the backcountry roads and trails.

Site **90**
OLALLIE MEADOWS
near Olallie Lake
MOUNT HOOD NATIONAL FOREST

Campsites, facilities: There are five sites for tents, trailers or motor homes up to 16 feet long. Picnic tables and fire grills are provided. Pit toilets are available. There is **no piped water.** Leashed pets are permitted. Boat docks, launching facilities and rentals are located about three miles away on Olallie Lake.

Reservations, fee: No reservations necessary; no fee. Open mid-June to late September.

Who to contact: Phone the Clackamas Ranger District at (503)630-4256 or write to Mount Hood National Forest, 61431 East Highway 224, Estacada, OR 97023.

Location: Take Highway 224 southeast of Estacada for 27 miles, then go south on Forest Service Road 46 for about 22 miles. From there, travel on Forest Service Road 4690 southeast for 8.2 miles. When you reach Forest Service Road 4220, head south for 1.5 miles to the campground.

Trip note: This campground is set at 4,500 feet elevation in a large, peaceful meadow about three miles from Olallie Lake. The Pacific Crest Trail passes very close to camp. Horses are permitted only at specified campsites. Contact the Forest Service for details.

Site **91**
PAUL DENNIS
on Olallie Lake
MOUNT HOOD NATIONAL FOREST

Campsites, facilities: There are 15 sites for tents or small campers (trailers are not recommended) and three hike-in tent sites. Picnic tables and fire grills are provided. Pit toilets are available. There is **no piped water**. A store and ice are nearby. Leashed pets are permitted. Boat docks, launching facilities and rentals are located on Olallie Lake.

Reservations, fee: No reservations necessary; no fee. Open mid-June to late September.

Who to contact: Phone the Clackamas Ranger District at (503)630-4256 or write to Mount Hood National Forest, 61431 East Highway 224, Estacada, OR 97023.

Location: Take Highway 224 southeast of Estacada for 27 miles, then go south on Forest Service Road 46 for about 22 miles. From there, travel on Forest Service Road 4690 southeast for 8.2 miles. When you reach Forest Service Road 4220, head south for 6.2 miles to the campground.

Trip note: This campground is set along the north shore of Olallie Lake. From here, you can see the reflection of Mount Jefferson (10,497 feet). Boats with motors are not permitted on the lake. Numerous smaller lakes in the area can be reached from nearby trails. It's advisable to obtain a Forest Service map.

Site **92**
PENINSULA
on Olallie Lake
MOUNT HOOD NATIONAL FOREST

Campsites, facilities: There are 35 sites for tents, trailers or motor homes up to 22 feet long, and six walk-in tent sites. Picnic tables and fire grills are provided. Pit toilets and piped water are available. Some facilities are wheelchair accessible. Leashed pets are permitted. Boat docks, launching facilities and rentals are nearby.

Reservations, fee: No reservations necessary; $5 fee per night. Open mid-June to late September.

Who to contact: Phone the Clackamas Ranger District at (503)630-4256 or write to Mount Hood National Forest, 61431 East Highway 224, Estacada, OR 97023.

Location: Take Highway 224 southeast of Estacada for 27 miles, then go south on Forest Service Road 46 for about 22 miles. From there, travel southeast on Forest Service Road 4690 for 8.2 miles. When you reach Forest Service Road 4220, head south for 6.5 miles to the campground.

Trip note: This is the largest of several campgrounds set along the shore of Olallie Lake. The amphitheater is near camp, and, during the summer, rangers present campfire programs. Boats without motors are permitted on the lake. Numerous smaller lakes in the area can be reached from trails nearby.

Site **93**
BREITENBUSH LAKE
on Breitenbush Lake
MOUNT HOOD NATIONAL FOREST

Campsites, facilities: There are 20 sites for tents or trailers. Picnic tables and fire grills are provided. Pit toilets are available. There is **no piped water**. A store and ice are located within five miles. Leashed pets are permitted. Boat docks, launching facilities and rentals are nearby.

Reservations, fee: No reservations necessary; no fee. Open mid-June to late September.

Who to contact: Phone the Clackamas Ranger District at (503)630-4256 or write to Mount Hood National Forest, 61431 East Highway 224, Estacada, OR 97023.

Location: From Estacada, drive 27 miles southeast on Highway 224, then 28.5 miles south on Forest Service Road 46, then turn east on Forest Service Road 4220 and drive 8.5 miles to the lake. Be aware that the access road to the lake is not maintained and can be pretty rough. A vehicle with clearance can be a help.

Trip note: This lakeside campground is set at 5,500 feet elevation on the western border of the Warm Springs Indian Reservation. Breitenbush is a large lake, which borders on the Jefferson Wilderness area. Numerous trails provide access to other lakes in the area, and horses are allowed in areas specified by the Forest Service. Ripe huckleberries can be found in the area in late August and September.

Site **94**   **BREITENBUSH**
on Breitenbush River
WILLAMETTE NATIONAL FOREST

Campsites, facilities: There are two tent sites and 28 sites for tents, trailers or motor homes up to 16 feet long (longer trailers may have difficulty parking and turning). Picnic tables and fire grills are provided. Piped water, vault toilets and a store are available. Some of the facilities are wheelchair accessible. Leashed pets are permitted.

Reservations, fee: No reservations necessary; $5 fee per night. Open all year with limited winter facilities.

Who to contact: Phone the Detroit Ranger District at (503)854-3366 or write to Willamette National Forest, HC 73 Box 320, Mill City, OR 97360.

Location: From Detroit, travel ten miles northeast on Forest Service Road 46 (Breitenbush Road) to the campground.

Trip note: This campground is set along the Breitenbush River and has fishing access available. South Breitenbush Gorge National Recreation Trail is three miles away. It is detailed on a map of Willamette National Forest.

Site **95**   **CLEATOR BEND**
near Breitenbush River
WILLAMETTE NATIONAL FOREST

Campsites, facilities: There are nine sites for tents, trailers or motor homes up to 16 feet long. Picnic tables, fire grills, piped water and vault toilets are available. Leashed pets are permitted.

Reservations, fee: No reservations necessary; $5 fee per night. Open mid-May to late September.

Who to contact: Phone the Detroit Ranger District at (503)854-3366 or write to Willamette National Forest, HC 73, Box 320, Mill City, OR 97360.

Location: From Detroit, travel nine miles northeast on Forest Service Road 46 (Breitenbush Road) to the campground.

Trip note: This camp is quite close to Site 94. See the trip note for recreation options.

Site 96

HUMBUG
on Breitenbush River
WILLAMETTE NATIONAL FOREST

Campsites, facilities: There are 22 sites for tents, trailers or motor homes up to 22 feet long. Picnic tables, fire grills, piped water and vault toilets are available. Leashed pets are permitted.

Reservations, fee: No reservations necessary; $5 fee per night. Open mid-April to late September.

Who to contact: Phone the Detroit Ranger District at 503-854-3366, or write Willamette National Forest, HC 73, Box 320, Mill City, OR 97360.

Location: From Detroit, travel five miles northeast on Forest Service Road 46 (Breitenbush Road) to the campground.

Trip note: This campground is set along the bank of Breitenbush River about four miles from where it empties into Detroit Lake (see Zone 5). Fishing and hiking are popular here.

Site 97

ELK LAKE
near Bull of the Woods Wilderness
WILLAMETTE NATIONAL FOREST

Campsites, facilities: There are 12 primitive tent sites. Picnic tables, fire grills and pit toilets are available. There is **no piped water.** Leashed pets are permitted. Primitive launching facilities are nearby.

Reservations, fee: No reservations necessary; no fee. Open July to mid-September.

Who to contact: Phone the Detroit Ranger District at (503)854-3366 or write to Willamette National Forest, HC 73, Box 320, Mill City, OR 97360.

Location: From Detroit, travel 4.5 miles north on Forest Service Road 46 (Breitenbush Road), then ten miles north on Forest Service Road 2209 (Elkhorn-Elk Lake Road) to the campground. The road is rough. High clearance vehicles are recommended.

Trip note: This remote campground is set along the shore of Elk Lake, where boating, fishing and swimming can be quite good in summer. Several trails are nearby that provide access to the Bull of the Wood Wilderness. Please pack out your garbage.

Site 98

SHADY COVE
North Santiam River
WILLAMETTE NATIONAL FOREST

Campsites, facilities: There are 11 primitive tent sites. Picnic tables, fire grills, and pit toilets are available. There is **no piped water.** Leashed pets are permitted.

Reservations, fee: No reservations necessary; no fee. Open mid-May to late September.

Who to contact: Phone the Detroit Ranger District at (503)854-3366, or write Willamette National Forest, HC 73, Box 320, Mill City, OR 97360.

Location: From Mehama, travel 19 miles northeast on Little North Santiam Road to the campground.

Trip note: This campground is set where Battle and Cedar Creeks meet to form the North Santiam River. To keep this a classic Cascades spot, Forest Service rangers urge campers to pack out their own garbage.

Site 99
ELKHORN VALLEY
on Elkhorn Creek

Campsites, facilities: There are 16 sites for tents, trailers or motor homes up to 18 feet long. Picnic tables, fire grills, pit toilets and piped water are available. Leashed pets are permitted.

Reservations, fee: No reservations necessary; $4 fee per night. Open mid-May to late November.

Who to contact: Phone (503)399-5646 or write to Bureau of Land Management, 1717 Fabry Road SE, Salem, OR 97306.

Location: This campground is located 25 miles east of Salem on Highway 22, then nine miles northeast on Elkhorn Road to the campground.

Trip note: This campground is set along Elkhorn Creek, not far from the North Fork of the Santiam River. This is an option to Site 98, which is located about ten miles to the east.

Site 100
SILVER FALLS STATE PARK
near Salem

Campsites, facilities: There are 51 tent sites and 53 sites with water and electrical hookups for trailers or motor homes up to 35 feet long. Picnic tables and fire grills are provided. Flush toilets, sanitary services, showers, firewood, a laundromat and a playground are available. Some facilities are wheelchair accessible. Leashed pets are permitted.

Reservations, fee: No reservations necessary; $9-10 in the summer, $6-7 off-season. Open mid-April to late October.

Who to contact: Phone (503)873-8681 or write to 20024 Silver Falls Highway, Sublimity, OR 97385.

Location: Take the Salem exit off Interstate 5 to Highway 22 and proceed southeast five miles, then go east 15 miles on Highway 214 to the park.

Trip note: This is Oregon's largest state park, covering more than 8,000 acres. Numerous trails are available here, including some that meander past waterfalls that are over 100 feet high, in the moist forest of Silver Creek Canyon. A stable is located near the park entrance.

Site 101
FOREST GLEN RV PARK
near Enchanted Forest

Campsites, facilities: There are 115 drive-through sites for tents, trailers or motor homes of any length. Electricity, piped water, sewer hookups and picnic tables are provided. Flush toilets, bottled gas, sanitary services, showers, a recreation hall, a laundromat, ice and a swimming pool are available. A cafe is within one mile. Pets and motorbikes are permitted. Camp Coast-to-Coast members and the public are welcome.

Reservations, fee: Reservations accepted; $15 fee per night. Open all year.

Who to contact: Phone (503)363-7616 or write to 8372 Enchanted Way, Turner, OR 97392.

Location: From Salem, travel seven miles south on Interstate 5 to exit 248, then one-half mile south on Enchanted Way.

Trip note: This is a good layover for motor home travelers on Interstate 5. It is just south of Salem. Nearby recreation options include an 18-hole golf course, tennis courts and the Enchanted Forest, a kids' tour with statues of storybook characters.

Site **102**   SALEM TRAILER PARK VILLAGE
near Willamette River

Campsites, facilities: There are 22 sites for trailers or motor homes of any length in this adults-only campground. Electricity, piped water and sewer hookups are provided. Flush toilets, showers and a laundromat are available. Bottled gas, a store, a cafe and ice are located within one mile. Pets are not permitted.

Reservations, fee: No reservations necessary; $12 fee per night. Open all year.

Who to contact: Phone (503)393-7424 or write to 4733 Portland Northeast, Salem, OR 97305.

Location: In Salem, take Highway 99E one-half mile east to the park.

Trip note: This park is set in the city of Salem, Oregon's capital. Several museums and parks are located in town, and the Willamette River flows nearby. Other recreation options include an 18-hole golf course, marked bike trails and a full-service marina.

Site **103**   CENTER STREET MOBILE PARK
in Salem

Campsites, facilities: There are 11 sites for trailers or motor homes up to 27 feet long. Electricity, piped water and sewer hookups are provided. A laundromat is available. Bottled gas, a store, a cafe and ice are located within one mile.

Reservations, fee: No reservations necessary; $14 fee per night. Open all year.

Who to contact: Phone (503)363-2684 or write to 4155 Center, Salem, OR 97301.

Location: Take the Market Street exit off Interstate 5 in Salem and drive east for one-quarter mile to Lancaster Drive, then turn south and travel one mile to Center Street. Head east and drive to 4155 Center Street.

Trip note: This park is in the center of Salem. See the trip note for Site 102 for information on Salem. An 18-hole golf course is nearby.

Site **104**   KOA SALEM
in Salem

Campsites, facilities: There are 30 tent sites and 190 drive-through sites for trailers or motor homes of any length. Picnic tables are provided. Flush toilets, bottled gas, sanitary services, showers, a recreation hall, a store, a laundromat, ice, a playground, electricity, piped water and sewer hookups are available. A cafe is located within one mile. Pets and motorbikes are permitted.

Reservations, fee: Reservations accepted; $8 fee per night; MasterCard and Visa accepted. Open all year.

Who to contact: Phone (503)581-6736 or write to 1595 Lancaster Drive Southeast, Salem, OR 97301.

Location: Take the 253 exit off Highway 22 in Salem and drive to Lancaster Drive. Turn south and drive to 1595 Lancaster Drive.

Trip note: This park is just off Interstate 5 in Salem (see the trip note for Site 102). Nearby recreation options include an 18-hole golf course, hiking trails, a riding stable and tennis courts.

WILLAMETTE

◆

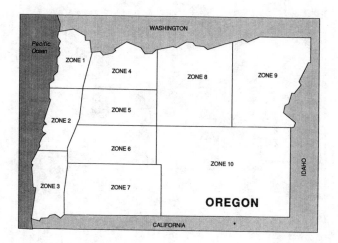

SOME HIGHLIGHTS

110 CAMPGROUNDS

Willamette River

Willamette National Forest

McKenzie River

Santiam River

Deschutes National Forest

Detroit Lake

Suttle Lake

Metolius River

McKenzie River National Recreation Trail

Lava Butte Geological Area

Lake Billy Chinook

Blue River Reservoir

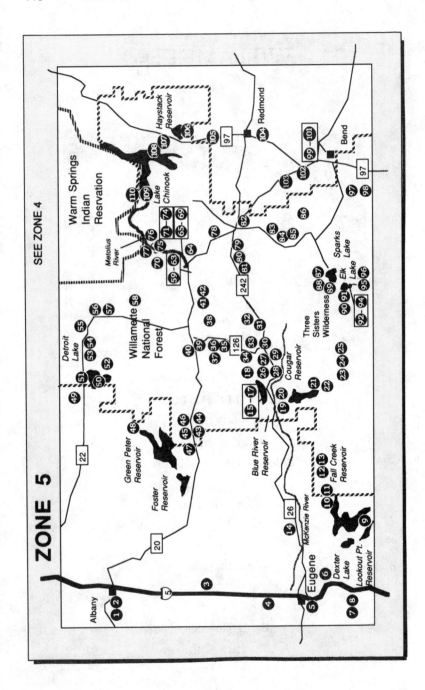

Site **1**
ALBANY TRAILER PARK
on Willamette River

Campsites, facilities: There are 13 drive-through sites for trailers or motor homes of any length. Electricity, piped water and sewer hookups are provided. Flush toilets, showers, a store, a laundromat and ice are available. Sanitary services are located within one mile. Leashed pets are permitted.

Reservations, fee: Reservations accepted; $13 fee per night. Open all year.

Who to contact: Phone (503)928-8532 or write to 1197 Century Drive, Albany, OR 97321.

Location: This camp is located in Albany at 1197 Century Drive.

Trip note: Albany is located at the confluence of the Willamette and the Calapooia Rivers. Nearby recreation options include a golf course and tennis courts.

Site **2**
THE VILLAGE ESTATE
in Albany

Campsites, facilities: There are 13 drive-through sites for trailers or motor homes of any length. Electricity, piped water and sewer hookups are provided. Flush toilets and showers are available. Sanitary services, a store, a cafe, a laundromat and ice are within one mile. Leashed pets are permitted.

Reservations, fee: Reservations accepted; $7 fee per night. Open all year.

Who to contact: Phone (503)926-3383 or write to 3246 Salem Avenue, Albany, OR 97321.

Location: This motor home park is located in Albany just off Interstate 5.

Trip note: This is an option to Site 1, also located in Albany. It's an okay layover spot for motor home campers traveling Interstate 5.

Site **3**
DIAMOND HILL RV PARK
in Willamette Valley

Campsites, facilities: There are 43 tent sites and 42 drive-through sites for trailers or motor homes of any length. Electricity, piped water, sewer hookups and picnic tables are provided. Flush toilets, bottled gas, sanitary services, showers, firewood, a store, a laundromat, ice, a playground and a swimming pool are available. A cafe is located within one mile. Pets and motorbikes are permitted.

Reservations, fee: Reservations accepted; $10 fee per night; MasterCard and Visa accepted. Open all year.

Who to contact: Phone (503)995-8050 or write to 32917 Diamond Hill, Harrisburg, OR 97446.

Location: Drive 15 miles north of Eugene on Interstate 5, then take exit 209 and the campground is about one block away.

Trip note: This private campground is located in the center of the Willamette Valley, just off the highway. No other campgrounds are in the area. Site 4 is the closest, about ten miles to the south.

Site **4**
KOA EUGENE
near Willamette River

Campsites, facilities: There are 30 tent sites and 114 drive-through sites for trailers or motor homes of any length. Electricity, piped water, sewer hookups and picnic tables are provided. Flush toilets, bottled gas, sanitary services, showers, a recreation hall, a store, a laundromat, ice and a playground are available. A cafe is located within one mile. Pets and motorbikes are permitted.

Reservations, fee: Reservations accepted; $12-16.50 fee per night; MasterCard and Visa accepted. Open all year.

Who to contact: Phone (503)343-4832 or write to Route 2, Box 353, Eugene, OR 97401.

Location: Go seven miles north of Eugene on Interstate 5. Take the Coburg exit and go 400 yards west to the campground.

Trip note: Eugene is one of Oregon's major cities, but it offers many riverside parks and hiking opportunities. Both the Willamette and McKenzie Rivers run right through town. The McKenzie, in particular, provides good trout fishing. Nearby recreation options include a golf course and tennis courts.

Site **5**   **EUGENE MOBILE VILLAGE**
near Willamette River

Campsites, facilities: There are 30 drive-through sites for trailers or motor homes of any length. Electricity, piped water and sewer hookups are provided. Flush toilets, sanitary services, showers, a recreation hall, a laundromat and a playground are available. Bottled gas, a store, a cafe and ice are located within one mile. Leashed pets are permitted.

Reservations, fee: Reservations accepted; $13 fee per night; MasterCard and Visa accepted. Open all year.

Who to contact: Phone (503)747-2257 or write to 4750 Franklin, Eugene, OR 97403.

Location: In Eugene, take exit 189 off Interstate 5, then go one mile on Franklin Boulevard to the park.

Trip note: This motor home park is in Eugene near the Willamette River (see the trip note for Site 4). Nearby recreation options include a golf course, bike paths, a full-service marina and tennis courts.

Site **6**   **CHALET VILLAGE MOBILE HOME PARK**
near Willamette and McKenzie Rivers

Campsites, facilities: There are 24 drive-through sites for trailers or motor homes of any length. Electricity, piped water and sewer hookups are provided. Flush toilets, sanitary services, showers, a recreation hall and a swimming pool are available. Bottled gas, a store, a cafe, a laundromat and ice are within one mile. Leashed pets are permitted.

Reservations, fee: Reservations accepted; $13 fee per night. Open all year.

Who to contact: Phone (503)747-8311 or write to 205 South 54th Street, Springfield, OR 97478.

Location: Take Interstate 5 to Springfield then go east to the park, located in town.

Trip note: Springfield is set on the outskirts of Eugene, close to the Willamette and McKenzie Rivers. Highway 126 heading east borders the McKenzie, known for good trout fishing and rafting opportunities.

Site **7**   **KOA SHERWOOD FOREST**
near Eugene

Campsites, facilities: There are 40 tent sites and 100 drive-through sites for trailers or motor homes of any length. Electricity, piped water, sewer hookups and picnic tables are provided. Flush toilets, sanitary services, showers, a recreation hall, a store, a laundromat, ice, a playground and a swimming pool are available. Bottled gas and a cafe are within one mile. Pets and motorbikes are permitted.

Reservations, fee: Reservations accepted; $9 fee per night; MasterCard and Visa accepted. Open all year.

Who to contact: Phone (503)895-4110 or write to 298 East Oregon, Creswell, OR 97426.

Location: Travel on Interstate 5 to Creswell and go west on Oregon Avenue for one-half block to the campground.

Trip note: This is a fairly good layover spot for motor home travelers heading north on Interstate 5. It is ten miles before Eugene. Nearby recreation options include a golf course, a riding stable and tennis courts.

Site **8**
TAYLOR'S TRAVEL PARK
near Willamette River

Campsites, facilities: There are ten tent sites and 24 drive-through sites for trailers or motor homes of any length. Electricity, piped water, sewer hookups and picnic tables are provided. Flush toilets, sanitary services, showers and a playground are available. Bottled gas, a store, a cafe, a laundromat and ice are within one mile. Pets and motorbikes are permitted.

Reservations, fee: Reservations accepted; $9 fee per night. Open all year.

Who to contact: Phone (503)895-4715 or write to 82149 Davisson, Creswell, OR 97426.

Location: Travel on Interstate 5 to Creswell, then go one-quarter mile west on Oregon Avenue and 1.2 miles south on Highway 99 to Davisson Road. From there, go one-half mile south to the park.

Trip note: This is an option to nearby Site 7. This wooded campground is set near the Willamette River. Nearby recreation options include a golf course, bike paths and a full-service marina.

Site **9**
WINBERRY
on Winberry Creek
WILLAMETTE NATIONAL FOREST

Campsites, facilities: There are five sites for tents, and two sites for trailers or motor homes up to 16 feet long. Picnic tables and fire grills are provided. Piped water, vault toilets and firewood are available. Leashed pets are permitted.

Reservations, fee: No reservations necessary; $3-5 fee per night. Open all year.

Who to contact: Phone the Lowell Ranger District at (503)937-2129 or write to Willamette National Forest, Lowell, OR 97452.

Location: From Lowell, go two miles north on County Road 6220, then six miles southeast on County Road 6245 (Winberry Road). Continue 3.5 miles on Forest Service Road 191 to the campground.

Trip note: This campground is located at the confluence of Winberry Creek and North Blanket Creek. A little inside knowledge: On the map, Lookout Point Reservoir appears to be about three miles away, but to get there, you have to drive nine miles to Lowell, at the north end of the reservoir. Elijah Barstow State Park, which is open for day use, is about five miles southwest of Lowell on Highway 58. Hiking and horseback riding trails are located there.

Site **10**
DOLLY VARDEN
on Fall Creek
WILLAMETTE NATIONAL FOREST

Campsites, facilities: There are three sites for tents and two sites for tents, trailers or motor homes up to 16 feet long. Picnic tables and fire grills are provided. Vault toilets are available. There is **no piped water.** Pets are permitted.

Reservations, fee: No reservations necessary; no fee. Open May to mid-September.

Who to contact: Phone the Lowell Ranger District at (503)937-2129 or write to Willamette National Forest, Lowell, OR 97452.

Location: From Lowell, go two miles north on County Road 6220, then ten miles east on County Road 6240 and Forest Service Road 18 (Fall Creek Road) to the campground.

Trip note: This campground is adjacent to Fall Creek and is at the lower trailhead for the scenic, 14-mile Fall Creek National Recreation Trail. Primitive campsites are located along this trail, which follows the creek and ranges between 960 to 1,385 feet elevation for the length of the trail.

Site **11**
BIG POOL
on Fall Creek
WILLAMETTE NATIONAL FOREST

Campsites, facilities: There are three tent sites and two sites for tents, trailers or motor homes up to 16 feet long. Picnic tables and fire grills are provided. Vault toilets, piped water and firewood are available. Leashed pets are permitted.

Reservations, fee: No reservations necessary; $4 fee per night. Open May to mid-September.

Who to contact: Phone the Lowell Ranger District at (503)937-2129 or write to Willamette National Forest, Lowell, OR 97452.

Location: From Lowell, drive two miles north on County Road 6220, then ten miles east on County Road 6240 and 1.5 miles on Forest Service Road 181 (Fall Creek Road) to the campground.

Trip note: This campground is set along Fall Creek at about 1,000 feet elevation. The scenic Fall Creek National Recreation Trail passes camp on the other side of the Creek. See the trip note for Site 10.

Site **12**
BEDROCK
on Bedrock Creek
WILLAMETTE NATIONAL FOREST

Campsites, facilities: There are 18 sites for tents, trailers or motor homes up to 22 feet long. Picnic tables and fire grills are provided. Vault toilets and piped water are available. Leashed pets are permitted.

Reservations, fee: No reservations necessary; $4 fee per night. Open May to late October.

Who to contact: Phone the Lowell Ranger District at (503)937-2129 or write to Willamette National Forest, Lowell, OR 97452.

Location: From Lowell, drive two miles north on County Road 6220, then ten miles east on County Road 6240 and four miles on Forest Service Road 18 (Fall Creek Road) to the campground.

Trip note: This campground is set along the banks of Bedrock Creek near its confluence with Fall Creek. It is one of the access points for the scenic Fall Creek National Recreation Trail. See the trip note for Site 10 for trail information. The campground is also adjacent to the Jones Trail, which heads north for about six miles before joining a forest service road.

Site **13**
PUMA CREEK
on Fall Creek
WILLAMETTE NATIONAL FOREST

Campsites, facilities: There are 11 sites for tents, trailers or motor homes up to 16 feet long. Picnic tables and fire grills are provided. Vault toilets and piped water are available. Leashed pets are permitted.

Reservations, fee: No reservations necessary; $4 fee per night. Open May to late October.

Who to contact: Phone the Lowell Ranger District at (503)937-2129 or write to Willamette National Forest, Lowell, OR 97452.

Location: From Lowell, travel two miles north on County Road 6220, then ten miles east on County Road 6240 and 6.5 miles east on Forest Service Road 18 (Fall Creek Road) to the campground.

Trip note: This campground is set along the banks of Fall Creek, across from the Fall Creek National Recreation Trail. It is one of four camps in the immediate area.

Site **14**   **VIDA-LEA MOBILE LODGE**
on McKenzie River

Campsites, facilities: There are two tent sites and five drive-through sites for trailers or motor homes of any length in this adult only campground. Electricity, piped water and sewer hookups are provided. Flush toilets, sanitary services, showers and a laundromat are available. Motorbikes are permitted. Boat docks and launching facilities are nearby.

Reservations, fee: Reservations accepted; $8 fee per night. Open all year.

Who to contact: Phone (503)896-3898 or write to 44221 McKenzie Highway, Leaburg, OR 97489.

Location: From Leaburg, go three miles east on Highway 126 to the park.

Trip note: This private resort is set along the banks of the scenic McKenzie River. Ben and Kay Dorris State Park, which is open for day use, is about six miles east of the campground on Highway 126 and is also set along the McKenzie River. Nearby recreation options include a golf course, hiking trails and bike paths.

Site **15**   **LAZY DAYS**
on McKenzie River

Campsites, facilities: There are 18 drive-through sites for trailers or motor homes of any length. Electricity, piped water, sewer hookups and picnic tables are provided. Flush toilets, bottled gas, showers, firewood and a laundromat are available. Leashed pets are permitted. Boat launching facilities are nearby.

Reservations, fee: Reservations accepted; $8 fee per night. Open all year.

Who to contact: Phone (503)822-3889 or write to 52511 McKenzie, Blue River, OR 97413.

Location: Go 1.5 miles east on Highway 126 from the town of Blue River.

Trip note: This motor home park is set along the banks of the McKenzie River, not far from Blue River Reservoir. This lake covers about 1,400 acres and offers opportunities for fishing, swimming and waterskiing. A golf course is fairly close.

Site **16**   **MAPLE LEAF RV PARK**
near McKenzie River

Campsites, facilities: There are three tent sites and 27 drive-through sites for trailers or motor homes of any length. Electricity, piped water, sewer hookups and picnic tables are provided. Flush toilets, bottled gas, showers, firewood and a laundromat are available. Leashed pets are permitted.

Reservations, fee: Reservations accepted; $10 fee per night. Open all year.

Who to contact: Phone (503)822-3912 or write to 52970 McKenzie, Blue River, OR 97413.

Location: Take Highway 126 east from the town of Blue River 2.5 miles and watch for signs.

Trip note: This wooded campground is set near the McKenzie River, not far from Blue River Reservoir. See the trip note for Site 15.

Site 17
DELTA
on McKenzie River
WILLAMETTE NATIONAL FOREST

Campsites, facilities: There are 39 sites for tents, trailers or motor homes up to 21 feet long. Picnic tables and fire grills are provided. Piped water and vault toilets are available. Some facilities are wheelchair accessible. Leashed pets are permitted.

Reservations, fee: No reservations necessary; $5-$10 fee per night. Open all year.

Who to contact: Phone the Blue River Ranger District at (503)822-3317 or write to Willamette National Forest, P.O. Box 199, Blue River, OR 97413.

Location: From the town of Blue River, travel five miles east to Forest Service Road 400 (Delta Road) and go one mile to the campground.

Trip note: This popular campground is set along the banks of the McKenzie River in a stand of old-growth Douglas fir. Blue River Reservoir and Cougar Lake are nearby, both of which offer trout fishing, waterskiing, and swimming.

Site 18
MONA
near Blue River Reservoir
WILLAMETTE NATIONAL FOREST

Campsites, facilities: There are 23 sites for tents, trailers or motor homes up to 21 feet long. Picnic tables and fire grills are provided. Piped water and flush toilets are available. Some facilities are wheelchair accessible. Leashed pets are permitted.

Reservations, fee: No reservations necessary; $5-7 fee per night. Open all year.

Who to contact: Phone the Blue River Ranger District at (503)822-3317 or write to Willamette National Forest, P.O. Box 199, Blue River, OR 97413.

Location: From the town of Blue River, travel about four miles east on Highway 126, then head north on Forest Service Road 15 for three miles to the campground.

Trip note: This campground is set along the banks of the Blue River, near its entrance to Blue River Reservoir. There is a boat ramp across the river from the campground. After launching a boat, campers can ground it near the campsite.

Site 19
RAINBOW MOBILE HOME & RV PARK
on the South Fork of McKenzie River

Campsites, facilities: There are ten tent sites and seven drive-through sites for trailers or motor homes of any length. Electricity, piped water, sewer hookups and picnic tables are provided. Flush toilets, showers, firewood, a store and a laundromat are available. Bottled gas and ice are within one mile. Leashed pets are permitted. Boat launching facilities are nearby.

Reservations, fee: Reservations accepted; $7-9 fee per night. Open all year.

Who to contact: Phone (503)822-3928 or write to 54665 McKenzie, Blue River, OR 97413.

Location: From the town of Blue River, travel six miles east on Highway 126, then one-half mile southeast on McKenzie River Drive.

Trip note: This campground is set along the banks of the South Fork of the McKenzie River, not far from Cougar Lake. See the trip note for Site 20 for recreation options.

Site **20**
PATIO TRAILER COURT
near South Fork of McKenzie River

Campsites, facilities: There are 66 sites for trailers or motor homes of any length in this adult-only campground. Electricity, piped water, sewer hookups and picnic tables are provided. Flush toilets, bottled gas, sanitary services, showers, firewood, a recreation hall and a laundromat are available. A store, a cafe and ice are within one mile. Leashed pets are permitted.

Reservations, fee: Reservations accepted; $10-12 fee per night. Open all year.

Who to contact: Phone (503)822-3596 or write to 55636 McKenzie, Blue River, OR 97413.

Location: Go six miles east on Highway 126 from the town of Blue River, then go two miles south on McKenzie River Drive.

Trip note: This motor home park is set near the banks of the South Fork of the McKenzie River, not far from Cougar Lake, which offers opportunities for fishing, swimming and waterskiing. Nearby recreation options include a golf course, hiking trails and bike paths.

Site **21**
SLIDE CREEK
on Cougar Lake
WILLAMETTE NATIONAL FOREST

Campsites, facilities: There are 16 sites for tents, trailers or motor homes. Picnic tables and fire grills are provided. Piped water, vault toilets and firewood are available. Pets are permitted. A boat ramp is nearby.

Reservations, fee: No reservations necessary; $3-5 fee per night. Open mid-May to mid-September.

Who to contact: Phone the Blue River Ranger District at (503)822-3317 or write to Willamette National Forest, P.O. Box 199, Blue River, OR 97413.

Location: Take US 126 east of the town of Blue River for 3.5 miles, then travel south on Forest Service Road 19 (Aufderheide Drive) for three miles. Take the Eastside Road 500 for about nine miles along the east side of Cougar Reservoir to the campground.

Trip note: This campground is on the banks of Cougar Lake, which covers about 1,300 acres and offers opportunities for fishing and swimming. The camp is west of Olallie Mountain near the Three Sisters Wilderness.

Site **22**
FRENCH PETE
on the South Fork of McKenzie River
WILLAMETTE NATIONAL FOREST

Campsites, facilities: There are 17 sites for tents, trailers or motor homes. Picnic tables and fire grills are provided. Piped water and vault toilets are available. Some facilities are wheelchair accessible. Leashed pets are permitted.

Reservations, fee: No reservations necessary; $5 fee per night. Open mid-May to mid-September.

Who to contact: Phone the Blue River Ranger District at (503)822-3317 or write to Willamette National Forest, P.O. Box 199, Blue River, OR 97413.

Location: Take US 126 east of the town of Blue River for 3.5 miles, then go south

on Forest Service Road 19 (Aufderheide Drive) for 12 miles to the campground.
Trip note: This quiet, wooded campground is on the banks of the South Fork of the McKenzie River and French Pete Creek. There is a trail across the road from the campground that provides access to the Three Sisters Wilderness. Three more primitive camps (Sites 23-25) are a few miles southeast on the same road.

Site **23**

HOMESTEAD
on South Fork McKenzie River
WILLAMETTE NATIONAL FOREST

Campsites, facilities: There are eight sites for tents, trailers or motor homes. Picnic tables and fire grills are provided. Vault toilets are available. There is **no piped water.** Leashed pets are permitted.

Reservations, fee: No reservations necessary; no fee. Open mid-May to mid-September.

Who to contact: Phone the Blue River Ranger District at (503)822-3317 or write to Willamette National Forest, P.O. Box 199, Blue River, OR 97413.

Location: Take US 126 east of the town of Blue River for 3.5 miles, then go south on Forest Service Road 19 (Aufderheide Drive) for 19 miles to the campground.

Trip note: This quiet little campground is set along the banks of the South Fork of the McKenzie River. It's little-known and free. Site 25 is nearby and has piped water.

Site **24**

TWIN SPRINGS
on South Fork McKenzie River
WILLAMETTE NATIONAL FOREST

Campsites, facilities: There are seven sites for tents, trailers or motor homes. Picnic tables and fire grills are provided. Vault toilets are available. There is **no piped water.** Leashed pets are permitted.

Reservations, fee: No reservations necessary; no fee. Open mid-May to mid-September.

Who to contact: Phone the Blue River Ranger District at (503)822-3317 or write to Willamette National Forest, P.O. Box 199, Blue River, OR 97413.

Location: Take US 126 east of the town of Blue River for 3.5 miles, then go south on Forest Service Road 19 (Aufderheide Drive) for 21 miles to the campground.

Trip note: This pretty little campground is set along the banks of the South Fork of the McKenzie River.

Site **25**

FRISSELL CROSSING
near Three Sisters Wilderness
WILLAMETTE NATIONAL FOREST

Campsites, facilities: There are 12 sites for tents, trailers or motor homes. Picnic tables and fire grills are provided. Piped water and vault toilets are available. Pets are permitted.

Reservations, fee: No reservations necessary; $3-5 fee per night. Open mid-May to mid-September.

Who to contact: Phone the Blue River Ranger District at (503)822-3317 or write to Willamette National Forest, P.O. Box 199, Blue River, OR 97413.

Location: Take US 126 east of the town of Blue River for 3.5 miles, then go south on Forest Service Road 19 (Aufderheide Drive) for 23 miles to the campground.

Trip note: This campground is at 2,600 feet elevation and is on the banks of the South Fork of the McKenzie River, adjacent to a trailhead that provides access to the backcountry of the Three Sisters Wilderness. This is the only camp in the immediate area that has piped water.

Site 26
McKENZIE BRIDGE
on McKenzie River
WILLAMETTE NATIONAL FOREST

Campsites, facilities: There are 20 sites for tents, trailers or motor homes up to 22 feet long. Picnic tables and fire grills are provided. Vault toilets, piped water and firewood are available. Leashed pets are permitted.

Reservations, fee: No reservations necessary; $4 fee per night. Open late May to early September.

Who to contact: Phone the McKenzie Ranger District at (503)822-3381 or write to Willamette National Forest, 7600 McKenzie Highway, McKenzie Bridge, OR 97413.

Location: From the town of McKenzie Bridge, travel one mile west on Highway 126 to the campground.

Trip note: This campground is set along the banks of the McKenzie River, near the town of McKenzie Bridge. There's good evening fly fishing for trout during summer on this stretch of river.

Site 27
HORSE CREEK GROUP CAMP
on Horse Creek
WILLAMETTE NATIONAL FOREST

Campsites, facilities: There are eight tent sites and 13 sites for trailers or motor homes up to 21 feet long. Picnic tables and fire grills are provided. Piped water, vault toilets and firewood are available. Leashed pets are permitted.

Reservations, fee: Reservations required; $30 fee per night. Open all year.

Who to contact: Phone the McKenzie Ranger District at (503)822-3381 or write to Willamette National Forest, 57600 McKenzie Highway, McKenzie Bridge, OR 97413.

Location: From the town of McKenzie Bridge on Highway 126, turn south on Horse Creek Road and drive three miles to the campground.

Trip note: This campground is reserved for groups. It is set along the banks of Horse Creek, near the town of McKenzie Bridge.

Site 28
THE HUB TRAILER PARK
near McKenzie River

Campsites, facilities: There are 54 sites for trailers or motor homes of any length. Electricity, piped water, cable TV, sewer hookups and picnic tables are provided. Flush toilets, bottled gas, sanitary services, showers, a recreation hall and a laundromat are available. A store, a cafe and ice are within one mile. Leashed pets are permitted.

Reservations, fee: Reservations accepted; $12.50 fee per night; MasterCard and Visa accepted. Open all year.

Who to contact: Phone (503)822-3514 or write to 56642 McKenzie Highway, McKenzie Bridge, OR 97413.

Location: This camp is located in the town of McKenzie Bridge on the south side of US 126, one-half mile past the 50-mile marker.

Trip note: This motor home park is set near the banks of the McKenzie River. The Forest Service office is in the town of McKenzie Bridge and has information on many of the recreation options in the area.

Site 29
PARADISE CREEK
on McKenzie River
WILLAMETTE NATIONAL FOREST

Campsites, facilities: There are 64 sites for tents, trailers or motor homes up to 22 feet long. Picnic tables and fire grills are provided. Flush toilets, piped water and firewood are available. Leashed pets are permitted.

Reservations, fee: No reservations necessary; $6-8 fee per night. Open late May to early September.

Who to contact: Phone the McKenzie Ranger District at (503)822-3381 or write to Willamette National Forest, 57600 McKenzie Highway, McKenzie Bridge, OR 97413.

Location: On Highway 126, drive 3.5 miles east of the town of McKenzie Bridge.

Trip note: This campground is set along the banks of the McKenzie River. Here, you get easy highway access with a rustic, streamside setting. Trout fishing can be good.

Site 30
LIMBERLOST
on Lost Creek
WILLAMETTE NATIONAL FOREST

Campsites, facilities: There are 12 sites for tents, trailers or motor homes. Picnic tables and fire grills are provided. Vault toilets and firewood are available. There is **no piped water.** Leashed pets are permitted.

Reservations, fee: No reservations necessary; no fee. Open late May to early September.

Who to contact: Phone the McKenzie Ranger District at (503)822-3381 or write to Willamette National Forest, 57600 McKenzie Highway, McKenzie Bridge, OR 97413.

Location: Take Highway 126 four miles east of the town of McKenzie Bridge, then go one-half mile on Highway 242 to the camp.

Trip note: This little campground is set along Lost Creek about two miles from where it empties into the McKenzie River. Hidden and secluded, it's a good base camp for a trout fishing trip.

Site 31
ALDER SPRINGS
WILLAMETTE NATIONAL FOREST

Campsites, facilities: There are six tent sites. **No piped water** is available. Picnic tables and fire grills are provided. Pit toilets are available. Leashed pets are permitted.

Reservations, fee: No reservations necessary; $2 fee per night. Open late May to early September.

Who to contact: Phone the McKenzie Ranger District at (503)822-3381 or write to Willamette National Forest, McKenzie Bridge, OR 97413.

Location: Travel east on Highway 126 for seven miles east of the town of McKenzie Bridge to Highway 242, then head east on Highway 242 for eight miles to the campground.

Trip note: This remote campground is set at 3,600 feet elevation and offers good hiking possibilities. A map of Willamette National Forest details the nearby back roads and trails.

Site **32**
SCOTT LAKE
on Scott Lake
WILLAMETTE NATIONAL FOREST

Campsites, facilities: There are 12 tent sites. Picnic tables and fire grills are provided. Pit toilets and firewood are available. There is **no piped water.** Leashed pets are permitted. Boat docks are located nearby.

Reservations, fee: No reservations necessary; no fee. Open late June to early September.

Who to contact: Phone the McKenzie Ranger District at (503)822-3381 or write to Willamette National Forest, 57600 McKenzie Highway, McKenzie Bridge, OR 97413.

Location: Travel east on Highway 126 for seven miles east of the town of McKenzie Bridge to Highway 242, then head east on Highway 242 for 14.5 miles to Forest Service Road 1532 and turn left to the campground.

Trip note: This campground offers hike-in sites set around Scott Lake. The elevation is 4,800 feet. Only non-motorized boats are allowed on the lake, and there are trails leading out from camp that provide access to several small lakes in the Mount Washington Wilderness.

Site **33**
BELKNAP WOODS RESORT
on McKenzie River

Campsites, facilities: There are six tent sites and 36 sites for trailers or motor homes of any length. Electricity, piped water, sewer hookups and picnic tables are provided. Flush toilets, showers, a laundromat and a swimming pool are available. Pets and motorbikes are permitted.

Reservations, fee: Reservations accepted; $8 fee per night; MasterCard and Visa accepted. Open April to late October.

Who to contact: Phone (503)822-3535 or write to Box 1, McKenzie Bridge, OR 97413.

Location: This camp is located in Belknap Springs on Belknap Springs Road.

Trip note: This campground is set along the banks of the McKenzie River. Nearby recreation options include hot springs, hiking trails and bike paths. This is one in a series of campgrounds on the slopes of the Cascade Range along this 20-mile stretch of Highway 126.

Site **34**
OLALLIE
on McKenzie River
WILLAMETTE NATIONAL FOREST

Campsites, facilities: There are 17 sites for tents, trailers or motor homes up to 22 feet long. Picnic tables and fire grills are provided. Vault toilets, piped water and firewood are available. Leashed pets are permitted.

Reservations, fee: No reservations necessary; $4 fee per night. Open late May to early September.

Who to contact: Phone the McKenzie Ranger District at (503)822-3381 or write to Willamette National Forest, 57600 McKenzie Highway, McKenzie Bridge, OR 97413.

Location: Travel 11 miles northeast of the town of McKenzie Bridge on Highway 126 to the campground.

Trip note: This campground is set along the banks of the McKenzie River and offers opportunities for boating, fishing and hiking. You get easy access from

Highway 126 and a jump-off point into the Willamette National Forest. A Forest Service map details back roads and trails.

Site **35**
TRAIL BRIDGE
on Trailbridge Reservoir
WILLAMETTE NATIONAL FOREST

Campsites, facilities: There are 20 sites for tents and 21 sites for trailers or motor homes. Picnic tables and fire grills are provided. Piped water, vault toilets and firewood are available. Pets are permitted. Boat docks are nearby.

Reservations, fee: No reservations necessary; $3-4 fee per night. Open late May to early September.

Who to contact: Phone the McKenzie Ranger District at (503)822-3381 or write to Willamette National Forest, 57600 McKenzie Highway, McKenzie Bridge, OR 97413.

Location: Drive on Highway 126 northeast of the town of McKenzie Bridge for 13 miles, then turn southwest at the turnoff at the north end of Trailbridge Reservoir and go 200 yards to the campground.

Trip note: This campground is set along the shore of Trailbridge Reservoir, where boating, fishing and hiking are recreation options. It's an exceptional spot for car campers.

Site **36**
LAKES END
on Smith Reservoir, boat-in only
WILLAMETTE NATIONAL FOREST

Campsites, facilities: There are 17 tent sites at this campground which is only accessible by boat. Picnic tables and fire grills are provided. Vault toilets and firewood are available. There is **no piped water.** Leashed pets are permitted. Boat docks are nearby.

Reservations, fee: No reservations necessary; no fee. Open late May to early September.

Who to contact: Phone the McKenzie Ranger District at (503)822-3381 or write to Willamette National Forest, 57600 McKenzie Highway, McKenzie Bridge, OR 97413.

Location: Drive northeast from the town of McKenzie Bridge on Highway 126 for 13 miles, then go three miles north on Forest Service Road 1477 to the boat ramp. Travel by boat for another two miles to the north end of Smith Reservoir where the campground is located.

Trip note: This secluded boat-in campground is set along the shore of Smith Reservoir. It is one of the few boat-in campgrounds in the entire state. Here, there are no cars, no traffic and the fishing can be good.

Site **37**
ICE CAP CREEK
on Carmen Reservoir
WILLAMETTE NATIONAL FOREST

Campsites, facilities: There are 11 tent sites and 11 sites for tents, trailers or motor homes up to 16 feet long. Picnic tables and fire grills are provided. Piped water, flush toilets and firewood are available. Leashed pets are permitted. Boat docks, launching facilities and rentals are nearby.

Reservations, fee: No reservations necessary; $5 fee per night. Open late May to early September.

Who to contact: Phone the McKenzie Ranger District at (503)822-3381 or write to

Willamette National Forest, 57600 McKenzie Highway, McKenzie Bridge, OR
97413.

Location: Drive on Highway 126 north of the town of McKenzie Bridge for 19
miles, then go 200 yards southwest on the entrance road to the campground.

Trip note: This campground is set along the shore of Carmen Reservoir, which was
created by a dam on the McKenzie River. The McKenzie River National
Recreation Trail passes by camp, and Koosah Falls and Sahalie Falls are nearby.

Site **38**
COLDWATER COVE
on Clear Lake
WILLAMETTE NATIONAL FOREST

Campsites, facilities: There are 34 sites for tents, trailers or motor homes up to 22
feet long. Picnic tables and fire grills are provided. Piped water, vault toilets,
firewood, a store and a cafe are available. Leashed pets are permitted. Some
facilities are wheelchair accessible. Boat docks, launching facilities and at
rentalsrentals are nearby.

Reservations, fee: No reservations necessary; $6 fee per night. Open late May to
early September.

Who to contact: Phone the McKenzie Ranger District at (503)822-3381 or write to
Willamette National Forest, 57600 McKenzie Highway, McKenzie Bridge, OR
97413.

Location: Take Highway 126 north of the town of McKenzie Bridge for 14 miles,
then go east on Forest Service Road 1372 to the campground.

Trip note: This campground is set along the south shore of Clear Lake. This
spring-fed lake is formed by a natural lava dam and is the source of the
McKenzie River. The northern section of the McKenzie River National
Recreation Trail passes by the camp.

Site **39**
FISH LAKE
near Clear Lake
WILLAMETTE NATIONAL FOREST

Campsites, facilities: There are seven sites for tents, trailers or motor homes up to
16 feet long. Picnic tables and fire grills are provided. Piped water, pit toilets
and firewood are available. Leashed pets are permitted.

Reservations, fee: No reservations necessary; no fee. Open late June to early
September.

Who to contact: Phone the McKenzie Ranger District at (503)822-3381 or write to
Willamette National Forest, 57600 McKenzie Highway, McKenzie Bridge, OR
97413.

Location: Travel on Highway 126 north of the town of McKenzie Bridge for 23
miles, then go 200 yards southwest on the entrance road to the campground.

Trip note: This campground is on the shore of Fish Lake. The "lake" though usually
dries up at the end of the summer. An interpretive display is set up at the guard
station nearby. Across the road is a trail that follows the Old Santiam Wagon
Road and the northern trailhead for the McKenzie River National Recreation
Trail. The Clear Lake picnic area is two miles south off Highway 126.

Site **40**
LOST PRAIRIE
on Hackleman Creek
WILLAMETTE NATIONAL FOREST

Campsites, facilities: There are eight tent sites and two sites for trailers or motor homes up to 22 feet long. Picnic tables and fire grills are provided. Piped water and vault toilets are available. Some facilities are wheelchair accessible. Leashed pets are permitted.

Reservations, fee: No reservations necessary; $5 fee per night, $10 for a double. Open mid-April to mid-November.

Who to contact: Phone the Sweet Home Ranger District at (503)367-5168 or write to Willamette National Forest, Sweet Home, OR 97386.

Location: From Albany, drive 40 miles east on US 20 to the camp. From Highway 126, turn west at the US 20 junction and look for the camp on the north side of the road.

Trip note: This campground is set along the banks of Hackleman Creek at 3,300 feet elevation. This is an option to nearby Site 39.

Site **41**
BIG LAKE
on Big Lake
WILLAMETTE NATIONAL FOREST

Campsites, facilities: There are 22 sites for tents, trailers or motor homes up to 16 feet long. Picnic tables and fire grills are provided. Piped water, vault toilets and firewood are available. Leashed pets are permitted. Boat docks and launching facilities are nearby.

Reservations, fee: No reservations necessary; $6-8 fee per night. Open late June to early September.

Who to contact: Phone the McKenzie Ranger District at (503)822-3381 or write to Willamette National Forest, Sisters, OR 97759.

Location: From Sisters, go 21 miles west on US 20, then 3.5 miles south on Forest Service Road 2690.

Trip note: This jewel of a spot is set on the north shore of Big Lake at 4,650 feet elevation. Fishing, swimming, waterskiing and hiking make it attractive. One of the better hikes is the five-mile loop trail that heads out from the south shore of the lake and cuts past a few small lakes before returning.

Site **42**
BIG LAKE WEST
on Big Lake, walk-in only
WILLAMETTE NATIONAL FOREST

Campsites, facilities: There are 13 walk-in tent sites. Picnic tables and fire grills are provided. Vault toilets and firewood are available. There is **no piped water** here, but there is at the Big Lake campground (Site 41). Leashed pets are permitted. Boat docks and launching facilities are nearby.

Reservations, fee: No reservations necessary; no fee. Open late June to early September.

Who to contact: Phone the McKenzie Ranger District at (503)822-3381 or write to Willamette National Forest, Sisters, OR 97759.

Location: Take US 20 west from Sisters for 21 miles, then 4.5 miles south on Forest Service Road 2690, then hike a short distance to the campground.

Trip note: This camp is set along the western shore of Big Lake and is a primitive option to Site 41.

Site **43**
HOUSE ROCK
on Santiam River
WILLAMETTE NATIONAL FOREST

Campsites, facilities: There are 17 tent sites. Picnic tables and fire grills are provided. Vault toilets and piped water are available. Leashed pets are permitted.

Reservations, fee: No reservations necessary; $5 fee per night, $10 for double. Open mid-April to mid-November.

Who to contact: Phone the Sweet Home Ranger District at (509)367-5168 or write to Willamette National Forest, Sweet Home, OR 97386.

Location: From Sweet Home, travel 26.5 miles east on US 20, then follow Forest Service Road 2044 southeast for a short distance to the campground.

Trip note: This campground is set where Sheep Creek and Squaw Creek meet to form the Santiam River. Trout fishing can be good, particularly during summer evenings. The elevation is 1,600 feet.

Site **44**   **FERNVIEW**
on Santiam River
WILLAMETTE NATIONAL FOREST

Campsites, facilities: There are 11 sites for tents, trailers or motor homes up to 22 feet long. Picnic tables and fire grills are provided. Piped water and vault toilets are available. Leashed pets are permitted.

Reservations, fee: No reservations necessary; $3-6 fee per night. Open mid-April to mid-November.

Who to contact: Phone the Sweet Home Ranger District at (509)367-5168 or write to Willamette National Forest, Sweet Home, OR 97386.

Location: From Sweet Home, go 23 miles east on US 20 to the campground.

Trip note: This campground is set at the confluence of Boulder Creek and the Santiam River. A three-mile trail connects this campground with Trout Creek (Site 45).

Site **45**   **TROUT CREEK**
on Santiam River
WILLAMETTE NATIONAL FOREST

Campsites, facilities: There are 24 sites for tents, trailers or motor homes up to 22 feet long. Picnic tables and fire grills are provided. Piped water and vault toilets are available. Leashed pets are permitted.

Reservations, fee: No reservations necessary; $5-10 fee per night. Open mid-April to mid-November.

Who to contact: Phone the Sweet Home Ranger District at (509)367-5168 or write to Willamette National Forest, Sweet Home, OR 97386.

Location: Travel 18.5 miles east of Sweet Home on US 20 to the campground.

Trip note: This campground is set along the banks of the Santiam River, about seven miles east of Cascadia. It is at the foot of the Menagerie Wilderness. Fishing and swimming are some of the possibilities here. A nearby trail travels east for about three miles to the Fernview campground (Site 44).

Site **46**   **YUKWAH**
on Santiam River
WILLAMETTE NATIONAL FOREST

Campsites, facilities: There are 20 sites for tents, trailers or motor homes up to 31 feet long. Picnic tables and fire grills are provided. Piped water and vault toilets are available. Leashed pets are permitted.

Reservations, fee: No reservations necessary; $5-10 fee per night. Open all year.

Who to contact: Phone the Sweet Home Ranger District at (503)367-5168 or write

to Willamette National Forest, Sweet Home, OR 97386.
Location: Travel 19 miles east of Sweet Home on US 20 to the campground.
Trip note: This campground is adjacent to Site 45 and offers the same recreation possibilities.

Site **47**　　CASCADIA STATE PARK
　　　　　on Santiam River

Campsites, facilities: There are 26 primitive sites for tents, trailers or motor homes up to 35 feet long. Picnic tables and fire grills are provided. Piped water, vault toilets and firewood are available. A store is located within one mile. Some facilities are wheelchair accessible. Leashed pets are permitted.
Reservations, fee: No reservations necessary; $8 fee per night. Open mid-April to late October.
Who to contact: Phone (503)343-7812 or write to P.O. Box 736, Cascadia, OR 97329.
Location: Travel 14 miles east of Sweet Home on US 20 to the park.
Trip note: This 258-acre park is set along the banks of the Santiam River.

Site **48**　　YELLOW BOTTOM
　　　　　on Quartzville Creek

Campsites, facilities: There are 12 tent sites and ten drive-through sites for trailers or motor homes up to 20 feet long. Picnic tables and fire grills are provided. Piped water and vault toilets are available. Leashed pets are permitted.
Reservations, fee: No reservations necessary; $4 fee per night. Open mid-May to late November.
Who to contact: Phone (503)399-5646 or write to Bureau of Land Management, 1717 Fabry Road SE, Salem, OR 97302.
Location: From Sweet Home, go 21 miles northeast on Quartzville Road.
Trip note: This campground is set along the banks of Quartzville Creek and it is always missed by out-of-town visitors. It is located on the edge of Willamette National Forest and the Middle Santiam Wilderness.

Site **49**　　DETROIT LAKE STATE PARK
　　　　　on Detroit Lake

Campsites, facilities: There are 134 tent sites and 177 sites with full or partial hookups for trailers or motor homes of any length. Fire grills and picnic tables are provided. Flush toilets, showers, firewood and a laundromat are available. Leashed pets are permitted. Boat docks and launching facilities are nearby.
Reservations, fee: Reservations accepted; $9-11 in the summer, $6-8 off-season. Open mid-April to late October.
Who to contact: Phone (503)854-3346 or write to Box 549, Detroit, OR 97342.
Location: From Detroit, travel two miles west on Highway 22 to the park.
Trip note: This campground is set along the shore of Detroit Lake at 1,600 feet elevation. Fishing, swimming and waterskiing are permitted. The lake is very crowded on the opening day of trout season in late April because it is heavily stocked.

Site **50**　　PIETY ISLAND BOAT-IN
　　　　　on Detroit Lake, boat-in only
　　　　WILLAMETTE NATIONAL FOREST

Campsites, facilities: There are 12 tent sites on this island campground which is accessible by boat only. Picnic tables and fire grills are provided. Pit toilets are available. Leashed pets are permitted. Boat docks, launching facilities and at rentalsrentals are nearby.

Reservations, fee: No reservations necessary; no fee. Open May to late September.

Who to contact: Phone the Detroit Ranger District at (503)854-3366 or write to Willamette National Forest, HC 73, Box 320, Mill City, OR 97360.

Location: This campground is located in the middle of Detroit Lake one mile southwest of Detroit.

Trip note: If you want to get away from the crowds at Detroit Lake State Park, this camp provides that possibility for boaters. Other campgrounds along the shore have piped water available.

Site **51**

UPPER ARM
on Detroit Lake
WILLAMETTE NATIONAL FOREST

Campsites, facilities: There are three tent sites and two sites for trailers or motor homes up to 16 feet long. Fire grills and picnic tables are provided. Pit toilets are available. There is **no piped water.** Leashed pets are permitted. Boat docks, launching facilities and rentals are nearby.

Reservations, fee: No reservations necessary; no fee. Open mid-April to late December.

Who to contact: Phone the Detroit Ranger District at (503)854-3366 or write to Willamette National Forest, HC 73, Box 320, Mill City, OR 97360.

Location: From Detroit, travel one mile northeast on Forest Service Road 46 (Breitenbush Road) to the campground.

Trip note: This little campground is set along the shore of the narrow upper arm of Detroit Lake, close to where the Breitenbush River empties into it. It's the smallest and most primitive camp in the area.

Site **52**

SOUTHSHORE
on Detroit Lake
WILLAMETTE NATIONAL FOREST

Campsites, facilities: There are seven tent sites and 23 sites for tents, trailers or motor homes up to 22 feet long. Fire grills and picnic tables are provided. Vault toilets and piped water are available. Leashed pets are permitted. Boat launching facilities are nearby.

Reservations, fee: No reservations necessary; $5 fee per night. Open mid-April to late September.

Who to contact: Phone the Detroit Ranger District at (503)854-3366 or write to Willamette National Forest, HC 73, Box 320, Mill City, OR 97360.

Location: Drive 2.5 miles southeast of Detroit on Highway 22, then four miles west on Forest Service Road 10 (Blow Out Road) to the campground.

Trip note: This campground is set along the south shore of Detroit Lake, where fishing, swimming and waterskiing are some of the recreation options. This is a popular place, particularly in late April when the trout season opens. The Stahlman Point trailhead is about 2.5 miles from camp.

Site **53**

HOOVER
on Detroit Lake
WILLAMETTE NATIONAL FOREST

Campsites, facilities: There are two tent sites and 34 sites for tents, trailers or motor homes up to 22 feet long. Picnic tables and fire grills are provided. Flush toilets and piped water are available. Leashed pets are permitted. Boat docks, launching facilities and rentals are nearby.

Reservations, fee: No reservations necessary; $5 fee per night. Open mid-April to mid-October.

Who to contact: Phone the Detroit Ranger District at (503)854-3356 or write to Willamette National Forest, HC 73, Box 320, Mill City, OR 97360.

Location: From Detroit, drive 2.5 miles southeast on Highway 22, then one mile northwest on Forest Service Road 10 (Blow Out Road) to the campground.

Trip note: This campground is along the eastern arm of Detroit Lake, near the mouth of the Santiam River. See the trip note for Site 52 for recreation details.

Site 54 — HOOVER GROUP CAMP
on Detroit Lake
WILLAMETTE NATIONAL FOREST

Campsites, facilities: This is a group camp that will accommodate up to 75 people. There are seven sites for tents, trailers or motor homes up to 15 feet long. Piped water and picnic tables are provided. Piped water, vault toilets and a group picnic shelter are available. Leashed pets are permitted. Boat docks, launching facilities and rentals are nearby.

Reservations, fee: Reservations required; $50 fee per night. Open mid-April to mid-October.

Who to contact: Phone the Detroit Ranger District at (503)854-3366 or write to Willamette National Forest, HC 73, Box 320, Mill City, OR 97360.

Location: From Detroit, drive 2.5 miles southwest on Highway 22, then one-half mile northwest on Forest Service Road 10 (Blow Out Road) to the campground.

Trip note: See the trip note for Site 52, which is also set at Detroit Lake.

Site 55 — WHISPERING FALLS
on Santiam River near Detroit Lake
WILLAMETTE NATIONAL FOREST

Campsites, facilities: There are 16 sites for tents, trailers or motor homes up to 22 feet long. Picnic tables and fire grills are provided. Piped water and vault toilets are available. A cafe is nearby. Leashed pets are permitted.

Reservations, fee: No reservations necessary; $5 fee per night. Open mid-April to late September.

Who to contact: Phone the Detroit Ranger District at (503)854-3366 or write to Willamette National Forest, HC 73, Box 320, Mill City, OR 97360.

Location: From Detroit, drive eight miles east on Highway 22 to the campground.

Trip note: This popular campground is set along the banks of the Santiam River. If the campsites at Detroit Lake are crowded, this provides a more secluded option and it's only about a ten-minute drive from the lake.

Site 56 — RIVERSIDE
on Santiam River
WILLAMETTE NATIONAL FOREST

Campsites, facilities: There are 37 sites for tents, trailers or motor homes up to 21 feet long. Picnic tables and fire grills are provided. Piped water and vault toilets are available. Leashed pets are permitted.

Reservations, fee: No reservations necessary; $5 fee per night. Open late April to late September.

Who to contact: Phone the Detroit Ranger District at (503)630-4256 or write to Willamette National Forest, HC 73, Box 320, Mill City, OR 97360.

Location: From Detroit, travel 14 miles southeast on Highway 22 to the campground.

Trip note: This campground is set along the banks of the Santiam River. The Mount Jefferson Wilderness is located directly to the east in Willamette National Forest.

Site **57**
MARION FORKS
on Santiam River
WILLAMETTE NATIONAL FOREST

Campsites, facilities: There are 15 sites for tents, trailers or motor homes up to 22 feet long. Picnic tables and fire grills are provided. Vault toilets and piped water are available. Leashed pets are permitted. There are additional eight sites with no piped water.

Reservations, fee: No reservations necessary; $5 fee per night. Open mid-May to mid-September.

Who to contact: Phone the Detroit Ranger District at (503)854-3366 or write to Willamette National Forest, HC 73, Box 320, Mill City, OR 97360.

Location: From Detroit, travel 16 miles southeast on Highway 22 to the campground.

Trip note: This campground is set at the confluence of Marion Creek and the Santiam River, adjacent to a Forest Service Ranger Station. Touring the nearby state fish hatchery is a possible side trip.

Site **58**
BIG MEADOWS
near Mount Jefferson Wilderness
WILLAMETTE NATIONAL FOREST

Campsites, facilities: There nine sites for tents, trailers or motor homes. Picnic tables, fire grills and a horse corral are provided at each site. Piped water and vault toilets are available.

Reservations, fees: No reservations necessary; $5 fee per night.

Who to contact: Phone Detroit Ranger District at (503)854-3366, or write Willamette National Forest HC-73, Box 320, Mill City, Or 97360.

Location: From Detroit, drive southeast on Highway 22 for 27 miles to Big Meadows Road (Forest Service Road 2267). Turn left and drive two miles, then turn left on Forest Service Road 2257 and drive one mile to the campground.

Trip note: Few people know of this spot. Why? Because it was only opened to the public in 1989! It was built by the Forest Service with the support of a horse club. It provides access to Big Meadows and the adjacent Mount Jefferson Wilderness.

Site **59**
BLUE LAKE RESORT
on Suttle Lake
WILLAMETTE NATIONAL FOREST

Campsites, facilities: There are 40 sites for tents, trailers or motor homes of any length. Picnic tables and fire grills are provided. Electricity, piped water, sewer hookups, flush toilets, bottled gas, sanitary disposal station, showers, firewood, a store, a cafe, ice and a playground are available. Leashed pets are permitted. Boat docks, launching facilities and rentals are nearby.

Reservations, fee: Reservations accepted; $10 fee per night; MasterCard and Visa accepted. Open all year.

Who to contact: Phone (503)595-6671 or write to Star Route, Sisters, OR 97759.

Location: From Sisters, travel 13 miles northwest on Highway 126, then 2.5 miles west on Suttle Lake Forest Highway.

Trip note: This 200-acre resort is set along the shore of Suttle Lake. It is one of five camps along the lake. Recreation options include fishing, swimming, hiking, bicycling and horseback riding.

Site **60**
SOUTH SHORE
on Suttle Lake
WILLAMETTE NATIONAL FOREST

Campsites, facilities: There are 38 sites for tents, trailers or motor homes up to 22 feet long. Picnic tables and fire grills are provided. Piped water and vault toilets are available. Leashed pets are permitted. Boat docks, launching facilities and rentals are nearby.

Reservations, fee: No reservations necessary; $7 fee per night. Open mid-April to late September.

Who to contact: Phone the Sisters Ranger District at (503)549-2111 or write Deschutes National Forest, P.O. Box 248, Sisters, OR 97759.

Location: Travel 14 miles northwest of Sisters on Highway 126 to Suttle Lake Forest Road and head west to the campground.

Trip note: This campground is located on the south shore of Suttle Lake, at 3,400 feet elevation. Rental boats and fishing supplies are available at the nearby resort. Waterskiing is permitted on the lake. A loop trail goes around the lake. A stable and horseback riding rentals are nearby.

Site **61**
LINK CREEK
on Suttle Lake
DESCHUTES NATIONAL FOREST

Campsites, facilities: There are 33 sites for tents, trailers or motor homes up to 22 feet long. Picnic tables and fire grills are provided. Piped water and vault toilets are available. Leashed pets are permitted. Boat docks, launching facilities and rentals are nearby.

Reservations, fee: No reservations necessary; $7 fee per night. Open mid-April to late September.

Who to contact: Phone the Sisters Ranger District at (503)549-2111 or write Deschutes National Forest, P.O. Box 248, Sisters, OR 97759.

Location: Travel 14 miles northwest of Sisters on Highway 126 to Suttle Lake Forest Road and head west to the campground.

Trip note: This campground is located at the west end of Suttle Lake. See the trip note for Site 60 for recreation details.

Site **62**
BLUE BAY
on Suttle Lake
DESCHUTES NATIONAL FOREST

Campsites, facilities: There are 25 sites for tents, trailers or motor homes up to 22 feet long. Picnic tables and fire grills are provided. Piped water and vault toilets are available. Leashed pets are permitted. Boat docks, launching facilities and rentals are nearby.

Reservations, fee: No reservations necessary; $7 fee per night. Open mid-April to late September.

Who to contact: Phone the Sisters Ranger District at (503)549-2111 or write Deschutes National Forest, P.O. Box 248, Sisters, OR 97759.

Location: Travel 14 miles northwest of Sisters on Highway 126 to Suttle Lake Forest Road and head west to the campground.

Trip note: This campground is set along the south shore of Suttle Lake. See the trip note for Site 60 for recreation details.

Site **63**
SCOUT LAKE
on Scout Lake
DESCHUTES NATIONAL FOREST

Campsites, facilities: There are 13 sites for tents, trailers or motor homes up to 22 feet long. Picnic tables and fire grills are provided. Vault toilets and piped water are available. Leashed pets are permitted.

Reservations, fee: Reservations accepted; $6 fee per night. Open mid-April to late September.

Who to contact: Phone the Sisters Ranger District at (503)549-2111 or write Deschutes National Forest, P.O. Box 248, Sisters, OR 97759.

Location: Travel 14 miles northwest of Sisters on Highway 126 to Suttle Lake Forest Road and head west, then turn and go south of Suttle Lake on Forest Service Road 2066 for a short distance to the campground.

Trip note: This campground is set about one-quarter mile from Suttle Lake along the shore of little Scout Lake. It is a good area for swimming and hiking. This campground is available for groups, but reservations need to be made in advance. Call the ranger district for details.

Site **64**
RIVERSIDE
on Metolius River
DESCHUTES NATIONAL FOREST

Campsites, facilities: There are 22 sites for tents, trailers or motor homes up to 21 feet long. Picnic tables and fire grills are provided. Vault toilets and piped water are available. Leashed pets are permitted.

Reservations, fee: No reservations necessary; no fee. Open mid-April to mid-October.

Who to contact: Phone the Sisters Ranger District at (503)549-2111 or write Deschutes National Forest, P.O. Box 248, Sisters, OR 97759.

Location: From the store in Camp Sherman, go two miles south on Forest Service Road 900 to the campground.

Trip note: This campground is set along the banks of the Metolius River, less than a mile from Metolius Springs at the base of Black Butte. It is just enough off the highway to be missed by most other people.

Site **65**
CAMP SHERMAN
on Metolius River
DESCHUTES NATIONAL FOREST

Campsites, facilities: There are 15 sites for tents, trailers or motor homes up to 22 feet long. Picnic tables and fire grills are provided. Vault toilets and piped water are available. Leashed pets are permitted.

Reservations, fee: No reservations necessary; $7 fee per night. Open May to October.

Who to contact: Phone the Sisters Ranger Station at (503)549-2111 or write to Deschutes National Forest, P.O. Box 248, Sisters, OR 97759.

Location: From the store in Camp Sherman, travel one-half mile north on Forest Service Road 1419 to the campground.

Trip note: This campground is set along the banks of the Metolius River, where you can fish for wild trout. This place is for expert fly fishermen seeking a quality angling experience. It's advisable to obtain a map of the Deschutes National Forest that details back roads, trails and streams. This is one of five camps in the immediate area.

Site 66 ALLINGHAM
on Metolius River
DESCHUTES NATIONAL FOREST

Campsites, facilities: There are ten sites for tents, trailers or motor homes up to 22 feet long. Picnic tables and fire grills are provided. Vault toilets and piped water are available. Leashed pets are permitted.

Reservations, fee: No reservations necessary; $7 fee per night. Open May to October.

Who to contact: Phone the Sisters Ranger Station at (503)549-2111 or write to Deschutes National Forest, P.O. Box 248, Sisters, OR 97759.

Location: From the store in Camp Sherman, travel one mile north to the campground.

Trip note: This campground is set along the banks of the Metolius River. It is one of five camps in the immediate area. See the trip note for Site 65.

Site 67 SMILING RIVER
on Metolius River
DESCHUTES NATIONAL FOREST

Campsites, facilities: There are 37 sites for tents, trailers or motor homes up to 22 feet long. Picnic tables and fire grills are provided. Vault toilets and piped water are available. Leashed pets are permitted.

Reservations, fee: No reservations necessary; $7 fee per night. Open May to October.

Who to contact: Phone the Sisters Ranger Station at (503)549-2111 or write to Deschutes National Forest, P.O. Box 248, Sisters, OR 97759.

Location: From the store in Camp Sherman, travel one mile north to the campground.

Trip note: This campground is set along the banks of the Metolius River. See the trip note for Site 65.

Site 68 PINE REST
on Metolius River
DESCHUTES NATIONAL FOREST

Campsites, facilities: There are eight tent sites. Picnic tables and fire grills are provided. Vault toilets and piped water are available. Leashed pets are permitted.

Reservations, fee: No reservations necessary; $7 fee per night. Open May to October.

Who to contact: Phone the Sisters Ranger Station at (503)549-2111 or write to Deschutes National Forest, P.O. Box 248, Sisters, OR 97759.

Location: From the store in Camp Sherman, travel 1.5 miles north to the campground.

Trip note: This campground is set along the banks of the Metolius River. See the trip note for Site 65.

Site 69
GORGE
on Metolius River
DESCHUTES NATIONAL FOREST

Campsites, facilities: There are 18 sites for tents, trailers or motor homes up to 22 feet long. Picnic tables and fire grills are provided. Vault toilets and piped water are available. Leashed pets are permitted.

Reservations, fee: No reservations necessary; $7 fee per night. Open May to October.

Who to contact: Phone the Sisters Ranger Station at (503)549-2111 or write to Deschutes National Forest, P.O. Box 248, Sisters, OR 97759.

Location: From the store in Camp Sherman, travel two miles north to the campground.

Trip note: This campground is set along the banks of the Metolius River. See the trip note for Site 65.

Site 70
JACK CREEK
near Mount Jefferson Wilderness
DESCHUTES NATIONAL FOREST

Campsites, facilities: There are 16 sites for tents, trailers or motor homes up to 15 feet long. Picnic tables and fire grills are provided. Vault toilets are available. There is **no piped water.** Leashed pets are permitted.

Reservations, fee: No reservations necessary; no fee. Open mid-April to mid-October.

Who to contact: Phone the Sisters Ranger Station at (503)549-2111 or write to Deschutes National Forest, P.O. Box 248, Sisters, OR 97759.

Location: This campground is located five miles northwest of Camp Sherman via Forest Service Roads 12 and 1230.

Trip note: This campground is set along the banks of Jack Creek where fishing and hiking are recreation options. A trail passes a mile east of camp heading nine miles south to Black Butte in one direction and northwest into the Mount Jefferson Wilderness in the other. This is a more primitive option to the other camps in the area.

Site 71
BLACK BUTTE MOTEL & RV PARK
on Metolius River

Campsites, facilities: There are 26 sites for trailers or motor homes of any length. Electricity, piped water, sewer hookups and picnic tables are provided. Flush toilets, showers, firewood and a laundromat are available. Bottled gas, sanitary services, a store, a cafe and ice are located within one mile. Pets and motorbikes are permitted.

Reservations, fee: Reservations accepted; $11 fee per night; MasterCard and Visa accepted. Open all year.

Who to contact: Phone (503)595-6514 or write to HCR 97736, Box 1250, Camp Sherman, OR 97730.

Location: From Camp Sherman, travel five miles north on Forest Service Road 14 to the park.

Trip note: This motor home park is set along the banks of the Metolius River. See the trip note for Site 65.

Site 72   COLD SPRINGS RESORT & RV PARK
near Metolius River

Campsites, facilities: There are 11 sites for trailers or motor homes of any length. Electricity, piped water and sewer hookups are provided. Bottled gas, a store, a cafe, a laundromat and ice are located within one mile. Pets and motorbikes are permitted.

Reservations, fee: Reservations accepted; $12 fee per night. Open mid-April to mid-October.

Who to contact: Phone (503)595-6271 or write to HCR, Box 1270, Camp Sherman, OR 97730.

Location: From Camp Sherman, travel five miles on Forest Service Road 14 to the park.

Trip note: This wooded motor home park is fairly close to the Metolius River. Nearby recreation options include a golf course, hiking trails, a riding stable and tennis courts.

Site 73   METOLIUS RIVER RESORT
near Metolius River

Campsites, facilities: There are ten drive-through sites for trailers or motor homes of any length. Electricity, piped water, sewer hookups and picnic tables are provided. Flush toilets, bottled gas, showers, a cafe and ice are available. A store and a laundromat are located within one mile. Leashed pets are permitted.

Reservations, fee: Reservations accepted; $10 fee per night; MasterCard and Visa accepted. Open all year.

Who to contact: Phone (503)595-6281 or write to Star Route, Box 1210, Camp Sherman, OR 97730.

Location: From Camp Sherman, travel five miles north on Forest Service Road 14 to the resort.

Trip note: This motor home resort is set near the banks of the Metolius River. Nearby recreation options include a golf course and hiking trails. Trout fishing can be good on the Metolius.

Site 74   ALLEN SPRINGS
on Metolius River
DESCHUTES NATIONAL FOREST

Campsites, facilities: There are four tent sites and 13 sites for tents, trailers or motor homes up to 22 feet long. Picnic tables and fire grills are provided. Vault toilets and piped water are available. A store, a cafe, a laundromat and ice are located within five miles. Leashed pets are permitted.

Reservations, fee: No reservations necessary; $7 fee per night. Open May to October.

Who to contact: Phone the Sisters Ranger Station at (503)549-2111 or write to Deschutes National Forest, P.O. Box 248, Sisters, OR 97759.

Location: From Camp Sherman, travel five miles north on Forest Service Road 14 to the campground.

Trip note: This campground is set along the banks of the Metolius River, where fishing and hiking can be good. The Wizard Falls Fish Hatchery is about a mile away, a good side trip.

Site 75
PIONEER FORD
on Metolius River
DESCHUTES NATIONAL FOREST

Campsites, facilities: There are two tent sites and 18 sites for tents, trailers or motor homes up to 22 feet long. Piped water and fire grills are provided. Piped water, vault toilets and firewood are available. Leashed pets are permitted.

Reservations, fee: No reservations necessary; $7 fee per night. Open May to October.

Who to contact: Phone the Sisters Ranger Station at (503)549-2111 or write to Deschutes National Forest, P.O. Box 248, Sisters, OR 97759.

Location: From Camp Sherman, travel seven miles north on Forest Service Road 14 to the campground.

Trip note: This campground is set along the banks of the Metolius River. See the trip notes for Sites 65 and 70 for recreation options.

Site 76
LOWER BRIDGE
on Metolius River
DESCHUTES NATIONAL FOREST

Campsites, facilities: There are 12 sites for tents, trailers or motor homes up to 22 feet long. Picnic tables and fire grills are provided. Vault toilets and piped water are available. Leashed pets are permitted.

Reservations, fee: No reservations necessary; $6 fee per night. Open May to October.

Who to contact: Phone the Sisters Ranger Station at (503)549-2111 or write to Deschutes National Forest, P.O. Box 248, Sisters, OR 97759.

Location: From Camp Sherman, travel nine miles north on Forest Service Road 14 to the entrance road to the campground. The last one-half mile of the road is dirt.

Trip note: This campground is set along the banks of the Metolius River. See the trip note for Site 65 for details about the area.

Site 77
SHEEP SPRINGS HORSE CAMP
near Mount Jefferson Wilderness
DESCHUTES NATIONAL FOREST

Campsites, facilities: There are 11 sites for tents, trailers or motor homes up to 15 feet long. Piped water and fire grills are provided. Vault toilets and box stalls for horses are available.

Reservations, fee: Reservations required; $5 fee per night. Open late May to mid-September.

Who to contact: Phone the Sisters Ranger Station at (503)549-2111 or write to Deschutes National Forest, P.O. Box 248, Sisters, OR 97759.

Location: Travel four miles north of Camp Sherman on Forest Service Road 1420, then one mile north on Forest Service Road 12. From there, drive 1.5 miles northwest on Forest Service Road 1230 to the campground.

Trip note: This equestrian camp is located near the trailhead for the Metolius-Windigo Horse Trail, which heads northeast into the Mount Jefferson Wilderness and south to Black Butte. Contact the Forest Service for details and maps of the backcountry.

Site 78

INDIAN FORD
on Squaw Creek
DESCHUTES NATIONAL FOREST

Campsites, facilities: There are 25 sites for tents, trailers or motor homes up to 22 feet long. Picnic tables and fire grills are provided. Vault toilets and piped water are available. Leashed pets are permitted.

Reservations, fee: No reservations necessary; $6 fee per night. Open May to October.

Who to contact: Phone the Sisters Ranger Station at (503)549-2111 or write to Deschutes National Forest, P.O. Box 248, Sisters, OR 97759.

Location: From Sisters, travel five miles northwest on US 20 to the campground.

Trip note: This campground is set along the banks of Squaw Creek. Stream fishing for trout can be good in the area. On the north side of nearby Black Butte is the spring which feeds the Metolius River. This can be a particularly good spot to fly fish for trout.

Site 79

COLD SPRINGS
on Trout Creek
DESCHUTES NATIONAL FOREST

Campsites, facilities: There are 23 sites for tents, trailers or motor homes up to 22 feet long. Picnic tables and fire grills are provided. Vault toilets and piped water are available. Leashed pets are permitted.

Reservations, fee: No reservations necessary; $6 fee per night. Open May to October.

Who to contact: Phone the Sisters Ranger Station at (503)549-2111 or write to Deschutes National Forest, P.O. Box 248, Sisters, OR 97759.

Location: From Sisters, travel five miles west on Highway 242 to the campground.

Trip note: This wooded campground is set at 3,400 feet elevation at the source of little Trout Creek. A trail passes near camp and extends north and south for miles. It is just far enough off the main drag to be missed by many campers.

Site 80

WHISPERING PINE
near Trout Creek Swamp
DESCHUTES NATIONAL FOREST

Campsites, facilities: There are nine primitive tent sites. Picnic tables and fire grills are provided. Pit toilets are available. There is **no piped water.** Leashed pets are permitted.

Reservations, fee: No reservations necessary; no fee. Open June to September.

Who to contact: Phone the Sisters Ranger Station at (503)549-2111 or write to Deschutes National Forest, P.O. Box 248, Sisters, OR 97759.

Location: From Sisters, travel 11 miles southwest via Highway 242 and Forest Service Road 1018 to the campground.

Trip note: This wooded campground is set at 4,400 feet elevation near Trout Creek Swamp. This is a primitive alternative to Site 79, near McKenzie Pass.

Site 81

LAVA CAMP LAKE
near Pacific Crest Trail
DESCHUTES NATIONAL FOREST

Campsites, facilities: There are two tent sites and ten sites for tents, trailers or motor homes up to 22 feet long. Picnic tables and fire grills are provided. Pit toilets are available. There is **no piped water.** Leashed pets are permitted.

Reservations, fee: No reservations necessary; no fee. Open June to September.

Who to contact: Phone the Sisters Ranger Station at (503)549-2111 or write to Deschutes National Forest, P.O. Box 248, Sisters, OR 97759.

Location: From Sisters, travel 17 miles west on Highway 242 to the campground.

Trip note: This wooded campground is set at 5,200 feet elevation in the McKenzie Pass, not far from the Pacific Crest Trail. Other trails provide hiking possibilities as well. A map of Deschutes National Forest details back roads, trails and streams.

Site 82   CIRCLE 5 TRAILER PARK
near Sisters

Campsites, facilities: There are three tent sites and 22 drive-through sites for trailers or motor homes of any length. Electricity, piped water, sewer hookups and picnic tables are provided. Flush toilets, bottled gas, sanitary services, showers and a laundromat are available. A store, a cafe and ice are located within one mile. Leashed pets are permitted.

Reservations, fee: Reservations accepted; $10 fee per night. Open all year.

Who to contact: Phone (503)549-3861 or write to P.O. Box 1360, Sisters, OR 97759.

Location: From Sisters, go one-half mile southeast on US 20 and you'll see the park entrance.

Trip note: This motor home camp is just outside Sisters. Nearby recreation options include a riding stable and tennis courts.

Site 83   BLACK PINE SPRING
near Three Creeks Lake
DESCHUTES NATIONAL FOREST

Campsites, facilities: There are seven sites for tents, trailers or motor homes up to 15 feet long. Picnic tables and fire grills are provided. Pit toilets are available. There is **no piped water.** Leashed pets are permitted.

Reservations, fee: No reservations necessary; no fee. Open mid-June to mid-October.

Who to contact: Phone the Sisters Ranger District at (503)549-2111 or write to Deschutes National Forest, P.O. Box 248, Sisters, OR 97759.

Location: Go nine miles south of Sisters on Forest Service Road 16.

Trip note: This primitive, remote campground is set at 4,400 feet elevation. Three Creeks Lake is about nine miles south on Forest Service Road 16. If this small, quiet spot is full, Sites 84 and 85 provide options.

Site 84   THREE CREEKS LAKE
on Three Creeks Lake
DESCHUTES NATIONAL FOREST

Campsites, facilities: There are ten sites for tents, trailers or motor homes up to 16 feet long. Picnic tables and fire grills are provided. Pit toilets are available. There is **no piped water.** Leashed pets are permitted. Boat docks, launching facilities and rentals are nearby. Boats with motors are not permitted.

Reservations, fee: No reservations necessary; $4 fee per night. Open mid-June to mid-September.

Who to contact: Phone the Sisters Ranger District at (503)549-2111 or write to Deschutes National Forest, P.O. Box 248, Sisters, OR 97759.

Location: From Sisters, travel 18 miles south on Forest Service Road 16 to the campground.

Trip note: This wooded campground is set along the shore of Three Creeks Lake in pretty spot. Fishing, swimming, hiking and non-motorized boating are the highlights.

Site **85**

DRIFTWOOD
on Three Creeks Lake
DESCHUTES NATIONAL FOREST

Campsites, facilities: There are six tent sites and 19 sites for tents, trailers or motor homes up to 16 feet long. Picnic tables and fire grills are provided. Pit toilets are available. There is **no piped water.** Leashed pets are permitted. Boat docks, launching facilities and rentals are nearby. Motorboats are not permitted.

Reservations, fee: No reservations necessary; $4 fee per night. Open mid-June to mid-September.

Who to contact: Phone the Sisters Ranger District at (503)549-2111 or write to Deschutes National Forest, P.O. Box 248, Sisters, OR 97759.

Location: From Sisters on Elm Street, travel 18 miles south on Forest Service Road 16 to the campground.

Trip note: This wooded campground is set along the shore of Three Creeks Lake and is hidden from outsiders. Fishing, swimming, hiking and non-motorized boating are some of the recreation options.

Site **86**

TUMALO FALLS
on Tumalo Creek
DESCHUTES NATIONAL FOREST

Campsites, facilities: There are four tent sites. Picnic tables and fire grills are provided. Vault toilets are available. There is **no piped water.** Leashed pets are permitted.

Reservations, fee: No reservations necessary; no fee. Open July to October.

Who to contact: Phone the Bend Ranger District at (503)388-5664 or write to Deschutes National Forest, 1230 NE Third Street, Bend, OR 97701.

Location: From Bend, travel 16 miles west on Forest Service Roads 4601 and 4603 to the campground.

Trip note: This secluded campground is set at 5,000 feet elevation along the banks of beautiful Tumalo Creek. Tumalo Falls, a 97-foot waterfall, is a short distance from the camp. The area surrounding the creek and camp was involved in a major fire in the 1970s, and young trees and vegetation are getting reestablished. There are many trails in the area. It's advisable to obtain a Forest Service map that details roads in the outback.

Site **87**

TODD LAKE
on Todd Lake
DESCHUTES NATIONAL FOREST

Campsites, facilities: There are eight tent sites. Picnic tables and fire grills are provided. Vault toilets are available. There is **no piped water.** Leashed pets are permitted.

Reservations, fee: No reservations necessary; no fee. Open July to October.

Who to contact: Phone the Bend Ranger District at (503)388-5664 or write to Deschutes National Forest, 1230 NE Third Street, Bend, OR 97701.

Location: From Bend, go 25 miles west on County Road 46, then about one mile north on the Forest Service entrance road. It is a short hike to the campground.

Trip note: This small campground is set along the shore of an alpine lake at 6,200 feet elevation. It is popular for canoeing, and offers great views. This is one of the numerous campsites in the area that offer a pristine mountain experience, yet can be reached by car.

Site **88**

DEVIL'S LAKE
on Devil's Lake, walk-in
DESCHUTES NATIONAL FOREST

Campsites, facilities: There are six tent sites. Picnic tables and fire grills are provided. Vault toilets are available. There is **no piped water.** Leashed pets are permitted. Boat docks are nearby.

Reservations, fee: No reservations necessary; no fee. Open July to October.

Who to contact: Phone the Bend Ranger District at (503)388-5664 or write to Deschutes National Forest, 1230 NE Third Street, Bend, OR 97701.

Location: From Bend, travel 27 miles west on Cascade Lakes Highway (Highway 46). Walk 200 yards to the campground.

Trip note: This walk-in campground is set along the shore of a scenic alpine lake with water that is an aqua-jade color. Devil's Lake is a popular rafting and canoeing spot, and there are several trailheads that lead from the lake into the wilderness.

Site **89**

SODA CREEK
near Sparks Lake
DESCHUTES NATIONAL FOREST

Campsites, facilities: There are four tent sites and eight sites for tents, trailers or motor homes up to 22 feet long. Picnic tables and fire grills are provided. Vault toilets are available. There is **no piped water.** Leashed pets are permitted. Boat docks are nearby.

Reservations, fee: No reservations necessary; no fee. Open July to October.

Who to contact: Phone the Bend Ranger District at (503)388-5664 or write to Deschutes National Forest, 1230 NE Third Street, Bend, OR 97701.

Location: From Bend, go 25 miles southwest on County Road 46, then about 100 yards south on Forest Service Road 400.

Trip note: This campground is located on the road to Sparks Lake, nestled between two meadows in a pastoral setting. Fishing and boating, particularly canoeing, are ideal here.

Site **90**

MALLARD MARSH
on Hosmer Lake
DESCHUTES NATIONAL FOREST

Campsites, facilities: There are 15 sites for tents, trailers or motor homes up to 22 feet long. Picnic tables and fire grills are provided. Vault toilets are available. There is **no piped water.** Leashed pets are permitted. Boat docks, launching facilities and rentals are nearby.

Reservations, fee: No reservations necessary; no fee. Open late May to late September.

Who to contact: Phone the Bend Ranger District at (503)388-5664 or write to Deschutes National Forest, 1230 NE Third Street, Bend, OR 97701.

Location: From Bend, go 31 miles southwest on Highway 46, then two miles southeast on Forest Service Road 4625 to the camp.

Trip note: This campground is set along the shore of Hosmer Lake, which is stocked with Atlantic Salmon and reserved for fly fishing only. It is a quiet campground and the lake is ideal for canoeing. You'll get a pristine, quality angling experience.

Site **91**
SOUTH
on Hosmer Lake
DESCHUTES NATIONAL FOREST

Campsites, facilities: There are 23 sites for tents, trailers or motor homes up to 22 feet long. Picnic tables and fire grills are provided. Vault toilets are available. There is **no piped water**. Leashed pets are permitted. Boat docks, launching facilities and rentals are nearby.

Reservations, fee: No reservations necessary; no fee. Open late May to late September.

Who to contact: Phone the Bend Ranger District at (503)388-5664 or write to Deschutes National Forest, 1230 NE Third Street, Bend, OR 97701.

Location: From Bend, go 31 miles southwest on County Road 46, then three miles southeast on Forest Service Road 4625 to the campground.

Trip note: This campground is set along the shore of Hosmer Lake. See the trip note for Site 90 for recreation details.

Site **92**
POINT
on Elk Lake
DESCHUTES NATIONAL FOREST

Campsites, facilities: There are nine sites for tents, trailers or motor homes up to 22 feet long, but be advised the sites are uneven and difficult for motor homes. Picnic tables and fire grills are provided. Vault toilets and piped water are available. Leashed pets are permitted. Boat docks, launching facilities and rentals are nearby.

Reservations, fee: No reservations necessary; $7 fee per night. Open late May to late September.

Who to contact: Phone the Bend Ranger District at (503)388-5664 or write to Deschutes National Forest, 1230 NE Third Street, Bend, OR 97701.

Location: From Bend, travel 33 miles southwest on County Road 46 to the campground entrance.

Trip note: This hidden campground is set along the shore of Elk Lake. Fishing can be good here; the same goes for hiking. A map of the Deschutes National Forest details the trails.

Site **93**
ELK LAKE
on Elk Lake
DESCHUTES NATIONAL FOREST

Campsites, facilities: There are 22 sites for tents, trailers or motor homes up to 22 feet long, but be advised the sites are uneven and difficult for motor homes. Picnic tables and fire grills are provided. Vault toilets and piped water are available. Leashed pets are permitted. Boat docks, launching facilities and rentals are nearby.

Reservations, fee: No reservations necessary; $7 fee per night. Open June to October.

Who to contact: Phone the Bend Ranger District at (503)388-5664 or write to Deschutes National Forest, 1230 NE Third Street, Bend, OR 97701.

Location: From Bend, travel 33 miles southwest on County Road 46 to Elk Lake.

The campground is on the southwest side of the lake.

Trip note: This campground is set along the shore of Elk Lake, adjacent to a private resort. See the trip note for Site 92 for recreation options.

Site **94**   ### LITTLE FAWN GROUP CAMP
on Elk Lake
DESCHUTES NATIONAL FOREST

Campsites, facilities: There are four tent sites and 27 sites for tents, trailers or motor homes up to 22 feet long. Picnic tables and fire grills are provided. Vault toilets are available. There is **no piped water**. Leashed pets are permitted. Boat docks, launching facilities and rentals are nearby on the southwest shore of the lake.

Reservations, fee: Reservations required; fee depends on group's size. Open June to October.

Who to contact: Phone the Bend Ranger District at (503)388-5664 or write to Deschutes National Forest, 1230 NE Third Street, Bend, OR 97701.

Location: Go 31 miles southwest of Bend on Highway 46, then two miles southeast on Forest Service Road 470. The campground is on the east side of Elk Lake.

Trip note: This campground is set along the eastern shore of Elk Lake. You can choose between sites on the lake's edge or nestled nearby in forest. There is a play area for children at one of the lake's inlets. See the trip note for Site 92 for recreation options.

Site **95**   ### LAVA LAKE
on Lava Lake
DESCHUTES NATIONAL FOREST

Campsites, facilities: There are 63 sites for tents, trailers or motor homes up to 22 feet long. Picnic tables and fire grills are provided. Vault toilets, piped water and sanitary disposal services are available. Leashed pets are permitted. Boat docks, launching facilities and at rentalsrentals are nearby.

Reservations, fee: No reservations necessary; $8 fee per night. Open June to October.

Who to contact: Phone the Bend Ranger District at (503)388-5664 or write to Deschutes National Forest, 1230 NE Third Street, Bend, OR 97701.

Location: From Bend, travel 38 miles southwest on Highway 46 to the entrance to Lava Lake. The campground is on the lake.

Trip note: This well-designed campground is set along the shore of pretty Lava Lake. Mount Bachelor and the Three Sisters are in the background, making a classic picture. Boating and fishing are popular here.

Site **96**   ### LITTLE LAVA LAKE
near Lava Lake
DESCHUTES NATIONAL FOREST

Campsites, facilities: There are 14 sites for tents, trailers or motor homes up to 22 feet long. Picnic tables and fire grills are provided. Vault toilets and piped water are available. Leashed pets are permitted. Boat docks, launching facilities and at rentalsrentals are nearby.

Reservations, fee: No reservations necessary; no fee. Open June to late September.

Who to contact: Phone the Bend Ranger District at (503)388-5664 or write to Deschutes National Forest, 1230 NE Third Street, Bend, OR 97701.

Location: From Bend, travel 38 miles southwest on Highway 46 to the entrance to Lava Lake. The campground is on Little Lava Lake.

Trip note: The campsites at this popular campground are not well marked, but the camping area is near the lakeshore. Boating, fishing, swimming and hiking are some of the recreation options.

Site 97
DILLON FALLS
on Deschutes River
DESCHUTES NATIONAL FOREST

Campsites, facilities: There are seven sites for tents, trailers or motor homes up to 30 feet long. Picnic tables and fire grills are provided. Vault toilets are available. There is **no piped water.** Leashed pets are permitted.
Reservations, fee: No reservations necessary; no fee. Open May to October.
Who to contact: Phone the Bend Ranger District at (503)388-5664 or write to Deschutes National Forest, 1230 NE Third Street, Bend, OR 97701.
Location: From Bend, travel 6.5 miles southwest on Highway 46, then drive three miles south on Forest Service Road 41. The camp is one mile further south on Forest Service Road 700.
Trip note: This campground is set in a deep gorge along the banks of the Deschutes River. It gets heavy day use because it is a take-out point for rafters and drift boaters. (Boaters should beware of Dillon Falls, located downstream). Some good day walks are available on trails along the river. They are detailed on a Forest Service map.

Site 98
BESSON CAMP
on Deschutes River
DESCHUTES NATIONAL FOREST

Campsites, facilities: There are two sites for tents, trailers or motor homes up to 16 feet long. Picnic tables and fire grills are provided. A pit toilet is available. There is **no piped water.** Leashed pets are permitted. A boat launch is nearby.
Reservations, fee: No reservations necessary; no fee. Open May to October.
Who to contact: Phone the Bend Ranger District at (503)388-5664 or write to Deschutes National Forest, 1230 NE Third Street, Bend, OR 97701.
Location: From Bend, travel 14.5 miles south on US 97, then 4.5 miles west on Sun River-Spring River Road (Forest Service Road 40). The camp is one-half mile further north on Forest Service Road 41.
Trip note: This secluded and unknown little spot is set along the bank of the Deschutes River. It has a boat launch and good trout fishing.

Site 99
BEND KEYSTONE RV PARK
near Deschutes River

Campsites, facilities: There are 29 sites for trailers or motor homes of any length. Electricity, cable TV, piped water and sewer hookups are provided. Flush toilets, showers and a laundromat are available. Bottled gas, sanitary services, a store, a cafe and ice are located within one mile. Leashed pets are permitted.
Reservations, fee: Reservations accepted; $12 fee per night. Open all year.
Who to contact: Phone (503)382-2335 or write to 305 Northeast Burnside, Bend, OR 97701.
Location: Travel one-half mile south of US 20 on US 97 in Bend. You'll see the turn-off for the park.
Trip note: Bend is a popular spot to use as a home base. The 100-mile Deschutes Forest Highway Loop connects here. Several state parks are within an hour's drive and several city-managed parks provide access to the Deschutes River.

Good side trips include the Oregon High Desert Museum, just six miles south of Bend on US 97. Just a few miles further is the Lava River Cave and the Lava Butte Geological Area.

Site **100**   **CROWN VILLA RV PARK**
near Bend

Campsites, facilities: There are 106 drive-through sites for trailers or motor homes of any length. Electricity, piped water, sewer hookups and picnic tables are provided. Flush toilets, showers, cable television, a laundromat, bottled gas, ice, sanitary disposal station and a playground are available. A store and a cafe are located within one mile. Leashed pets are permitted. Discounts given for Good Sam members.

Reservations, fee: Reservations accepted; $18 fee per night; MasterCard and Visa accepted. Open all year.

Who to contact: Phone (503)388-1131 or write to 60801 Brosterhous, Bend, OR 97702.

Location: Travel two miles south of Bend on US 97, then head east on Brosterhous Road to 60801 Brosterhous Road.

Trip note: This motor home park offers large, grassy sites. Nearby recreation options include horseback riding and golf. See the trip note for Site 99 for additional recreation information.

Site **101**   **JOHN'S RV AND TRAILER PARK**
near the Deschutes River

Campsites, facilities: There are ten tent sites and 35 drive-through sites for trailers or motor homes of any length. Electricity, piped water, picnic tables and sewer hookups are provided. Flush toilets, showers and a laundromat are available. Bottled gas, sanitary services, a store, a cafe and ice are located within one mile. Leashed pets are permitted.

Reservations, fee: Reservations accepted; $10-14 fee per night. Open all year.

Who to contact: Phone (503)382-6206 or write to 61415 South US 97, Bend, OR 97701.

Location: Travel one-half mile south of Bend on US 97 and you'll see the trailer park entrance.

Trip note: This park is set near the Deschutes River. Nearby recreation options include a golf course, a stable, bike paths and tennis courts. See the trip note for Site 99 for additional recreation information.

Site **102**   **KOA BEND**
near Bend

Campsites, facilities: There are 40 tent sites and 74 drive-through sites for trailers or motor homes of any length. Piped water and picnic tables are provided. Electricity, sewer hookups, flush toilets, showers, a laundromat, a store, a cafe, ice, firewood, a playground, a swimming pool, recreation room, bottled gas and sanitary disposal station are available. Leashed pets are permitted.

Reservations, fee: Reservations accepted; $14-18 fee per night; MasterCard and Visa accepted. Open all year.

Who to contact: Phone (503)382-7728 or write to 63615 North US 97, Bend, OR 97701.

Location: Travel two miles north of Bend on US 97 and you'll see the campground entrance.

Trip note: Nearby recreation options include a golf course, hiking trails, bike paths and tennis courts. See the trip note for Site 99 for additional recreation information.

Site **103**   TUMALO STATE PARK
on Deschutes River

Campsites, facilities: There are 68 sites for tents or self-contained motor homes and 20 sites with full hookups for trailers or motor homes up to 35 feet long. Electricity, piped water, sewer hookups, fire grills and picnic tables are provided. Flush toilets, showers, firewood, a laundromat and a playground are available. A store, a cafe and ice are located within one mile. Leashed pets are permitted.

Reservations, fee: No reservations necessary; $9-11 in the summer, $6-8 off-season. Open mid-April to late October.

Who to contact: Phone (503)388-6055 or write to Tumalo State Park, Bend, OR 97701.

Location: From Bend, go five miles northwest on US 20, then one mile west on the entrance road to the park.

Trip note: This campground is set along the banks of the Deschutes River. Trout fishing can be good. See the trip note for Site 99 for recreation information about the area.

Site **104**   DESERT TERRACE MOBILE ESTATES
near Redmond

Campsites, facilities: There are 20 drive-through sites for trailers or motor homes of any length. Electricity, piped water, sewer hookups and picnic tables are provided. Flush toilets, showers and a laundromat are available. Leashed pets are permitted.

Reservations, fee: Reservations accepted; $8-12 fee per night. Open all year.

Who to contact: Phone (503)548-2546 or write to 5063 South US 97, Redmond, OR 97756.

Location: Travel three miles south of Redmond on US 97 and you'll see the entrance.

Trip note: Nearby recreation options include a golf course, hiking trails, bike paths, tennis courts and Petersen's Rock Gardens. This motor home park is centrally located to many recreation opportunities. See the trip notes for Sites 99 and 107 for more details.

Site **105**   CROOKED RIVER RANCH RV PARK
near Smith Rock State Park

Campsites, facilities: There are 25 tent sites and 124 drive-through sites for trailers or motor homes of any length. Electricity, piped water and sewer hookups are provided. Flush toilets, sanitary services, showers, a store, a cafe, a laundromat, ice, a playground and a swimming pool are available. Pets and motorbikes are permitted.

Reservations, fee: Reservations accepted; $8-12 fee per night. Open mid-March to late October.

Who to contact: Phone (503)923-1441 or write to P.O. Box 1448, Crooked River Road, OR 97760.

Location: Drive six miles north of Redmond on US 97, then west at Terribone and follow the signs for 7.5 miles.

Trip note: This campground is a short distance from Smith Rock State Park, which offers unique and colorful volcanic formations overlooking the Crooked River Canyon. To the north is Lake Billy Chinook, which offers fishing for bass and panfish, and waterskiing. Nearby recreation options include a golf course and tennis courts.

Site 106 — HAYSTACK LAKE
on Haystack Reservoir
OCHOCHO NATIONAL FOREST

Campsites, facilities: There are 24 sites for tents, trailers or motor homes up to 22 feet long. Picnic tables and fire grills are provided. Flush toilets, piped water and firewood are available. A store, a cafe and ice are located within five miles. Leashed pets are permitted. Boat docks, launching facilities and rentals are nearby.

Reservations, fee: No reservations necessary; $5 fee per night. Open April to November.

Who to contact: Phone the Madras Ranger Station at (503)447-4120 or write to Ochocho National Forest, Madras, OR 97741.

Location: Drive on US 97 for nine miles south of Madras, then three miles southeast on County Road 6, then one-half mile north on Forest Service Road 1275.

Trip note: This campground is set along the shore of Haystack Reservoir, where waterskiing, swimming and fishing are some of the recreation options. The camping and fishing crowds are relatively light.

Site 107 — KOA MADRAS
near Lake Billy Chinook

Campsites, facilities: There are 21 tent sites and 68 drive-through sites for trailers or motor homes of any length. Electricity, piped water, sewer hookups and picnic tables are provided. Flush toilets, bottled gas, sanitary services, showers, firewood, a recreation hall, a store, a cafe, a laundromat, ice, a playground and a swimming pool are available. Pets and motorbikes are permitted. Boat docks and launching facilities are nearby.

Reservations, fee: Reservations accepted; $9 fee per night; MasterCard and Visa accepted. Open March to late November.

Who to contact: Phone (503)546-3073 or write to 2435 Southwest Jericho Lane, Culver, OR 97734.

Location: Travel nine miles south of Madras on US 97, then one-half mile east on Jericho Lane to the campground.

Trip note: This campground is about three miles from Lake Billy Chinook, a steep-sided reservoir formed where the Crooked River, Metolius River, Deschutes River and Squaw Creek all merge. Like much of the country east of the Cascades, it is a high desert area.

Site 108 — COVE PALISADES STATE PARK
on Lake Billy Chinook

Campsites, facilities: There are 94 sites for tents or self-contained motor homes and 178 sites with full hookups for trailers or motor homes of any length. Picnic tables and fire grills are provided. Flush toilets, sanitary services, showers, firewood, a store, a cafe, a laundromat and ice are available. Some facilities are wheelchair accessible. Leashed pets are permitted. Boat docks, launching facilities and rentals are nearby.

Reservations, fee: Reservations accepted; $9-11 during the summer, $6-8 off-season. Open mid-April to late October.

Who to contact: Phone (503)546-3412 or write to Route 1, Box 60 CP, Culver, OR 97734.

Location: From Madras, drive nine miles south on US 97 to Culver, then head west for five miles to the Park.

Trip note: This park is set along the shore of Lake Billy Chinook. Colorful rock formations rise from the canyon walls. See the trip notes for Sites 105 and 107 for recreation details.

Site **109**　　　**PERRY SOUTH**
on Lake Billy Chinook
DESCHUTES NATIONAL FOREST

Campsites, facilities: There are four tent sites and 59 sites for tents, trailers or motor homes up to 22 feet long. Picnic tables and fire grills are provided. Piped water and vault toilets are available. Leashed pets are permitted. Boat docks and launching facilities are nearby.

Reservations, fee: No reservations necessary; $7 fee per night. Open May to October.

Who to contact: Phone the Sisters Ranger District at (503)549-2111 or write to Deschutes National Forest, P.O. Box 248, Sisters, OR 97759.

Location: From Culver, drive 25 miles west and north on County Road 64 to the campground entrance.

Trip note: This campground is set near the shore of the Metolius arm of Lake Billy Chinook. See the trip note for Sites 105 and 107 for recreation details. This camp borders the Warm Springs Indian Reservation.

Site **110**　　　**MONTY**
on Metolius River
DESCHUTES NATIONAL FOREST

Campsites, facilities: There are 20 sites for tents, trailers or motor homes up to 22 feet long. Picnic tables and fire grills are provided. Piped water, firewood and vault toilets are available. Leashed pets are permitted. Boat docks and launching facilities are nearby.

Reservations, fee: No reservations necessary; $3 fee per night. Open May to October.

Who to contact: Phone the Sisters Ranger District at (503)549-2111 or write to Deschutes National Forest, P.O. Box 248, Sisters, OR 97734.

Location: From Culver, drive 30 miles west and north on County Road 64 to the campground entrance.

Trip note: This remote campground is set along the banks of the Metolius River near where it empties into Lake Billy Chinook. Trout fishing can be good. It's located just outside Warm Springs Indian Reservation.

CASCADE

◆

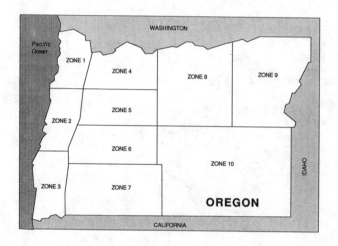

SOME HIGHLIGHTS
---

118 CAMPGROUNDS

Umpqua National Forest

Umpqua River

Diamond Peak Wilderness

Diamond Lake

Deschutes National Forest

Deschutes River

Crescent Lake

Odell Lake

Willamette National Forest

Willamette River

Crater Lake National Park

Winema National Forest

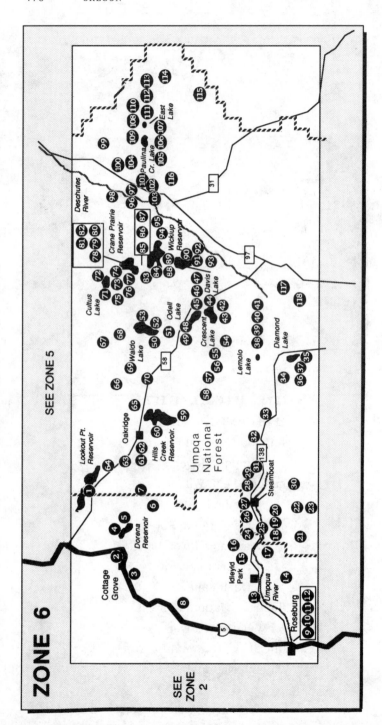

ZONE 6

SEE ZONE 5

SEE ZONE 2

Site 1   DEXTER SHORES MOTORHOME & RV PARK
near Lookout Point Reservoir

Campsites, facilities: There are ten sites for trailers or motor homes. Electricity, piped water, sewer hookups and picnic tables are provided. Flush toilets, sanitary services, showers, firewood, a laundromat and a playground are available. Bottled gas, a cafe and ice are within one mile. Pets and motorbikes are permitted. Boat docks and launching facilities are nearby.

Reservations, fee: Reservations accepted; $9 fee per night. Open all year.

Who to contact: Phone (503)937-3711 or write to P.O. Box 70, Dexter, OR 97431.

Location: Travel west on Highway 58 about 18 miles from Oakridge, then go southeast on Dexter Road for about one mile to the park.

Trip note: If you are traveling on Interstate 5, this motor home park is well worth the 15-minute drive out of Springfield. It is set near the shore of Lookout Point Reservoir, where fishing and boating are permitted. Swimming and waterskiing are allowed on nearby Dexter and Fall Creek Lakes.

Site 2   FRONTIER VILLAGE
near Willamette and Row Rivers

Campsites, facilities: There are six drive-through sites for trailers or motor homes up to 30 feet long. Electricity, piped water and sewer hookups are provided. Flush toilets, showers and a laundromat are available. Bottled gas, a store, a cafe and ice are within one mile.

Reservations, fee: Reservations accepted; $6 fee per night. Open all year.

Who to contact: Phone (503)942-3266 or write to 1557 Pacific Highway North, Cottage Grove, OR 97424.

Location: This campground is located in the north end of Cottage Grove.

Trip note: Cottage Grove is noted for its numerous recreation opportunities available along the Willamette and Row Rivers, which pass on either side of town. Dorena Reservoir is a short drive to the east. Nearby recreation options include a golf course and bike paths.

Site 3   PINE MEADOWS
on Cottage Grove Reservoir

Campsites, facilities: There are 93 sites for tents, trailers or motor homes of any length. Picnic tables and fire grills are provided. Flush toilets, sanitary services, showers and a playground are available. Pets and motorbikes are permitted. Boat docks and launching facilities are nearby.

Reservations, fee: No reservations necessary; $7.50 fee per night. Open Memorial Day to Labor Day.

Who to contact: Phone (503)942-5631 or write to Army Corps of Engineers Recreation Information, Cottage Grove, OR 97424.

Location: Travel south of Cottage Grove on Interstate 5, take exit 170, then go 3.5 miles south on London Road to the campground.

Trip note: This campground is set near the banks of Cottage Grove Reservoir, where boating, fishing, waterskiing and swimming are among the recreation options. It's an easy hop from Interstate 5, but a lot of vacationers don't realize it.

Site 4   SCHWARZ PARK
on Dorena Lake

Campsites, facilities: There are 155 tent sites and 35 drive-through sites for trailers

or motor homes of any length. Picnic tables and fire grills are provided. Flush toilets, sanitary services and showers are available. A store is within one mile. Pets and motorbikes are permitted. Boat docks and launching facilities are nearby.

Reservations, fee: No reservations necessary; $5.50 fee per night. Open mid-May to late September.

Who to contact: Phone (503)942-5631 or write to Army Corps of Engineers Recreation Information, Cottage Grove, OR 97424.

Location: Take exit 174 off Interstate 5 in Cottage Grove, then go four miles east on Row Road to the campground entrance road.

Trip note: This large campground is set along the shore of Dorena Lake, a reservoir where fishing, swimming, boating and waterskiing are among the recreation options.

Site **5**
BAKER BAY COUNTY PARK
on Dorena Lake

Campsites, facilities: There are 34 sites for trailers or motor homes up to 20 feet long. Picnic tables and fire grills are provided. Piped water and sanitary services are available. A store is located within one mile. Pets and motorbikes are permitted. Boat docks and launching facilities are nearby.

Reservations, fee: No reservations necessary; $3 fee per night. Open late April to late October.

Who to contact: Phone (503)942-7669 or write to Lane County Recreation Department, Eugene, OR 97401.

Location: Take exit 174 of Interstate 5 in Cottage Grove, then travel eight miles east on Row Road to the campground.

Trip note: This campground is set along the shore of Dorena Lake, a reservoir where fishing, waterskiing, canoeing, swimming and boating are among the recreation options.

Site **6**
SHARPS CREEK
on Sharps Creek

Campsites, facilities: There are ten sites for tents, trailers or motor homes up to 20 feet long. Picnic tables and fire grills are provided. Piped water, pit toilets and firewood are available. Leashed pets are permitted.

Reservations, fee: No reservations necessary; no fee. Open all year.

Who to contact: Phone (503)683-6600 or write to Bureau of Land Management, P.O. Box 10266, Eugene, OR 97401.

Location: Take exit 174 off Interstate 5 at Cottage Grove, then travel 18 miles east on Row River Road and four miles south on Sharps Creek Road to the campground.

Trip note: This campground is set along the bank of Sharps Creek. Like nearby Site 7, this is just far enough off the beaten path to be missed by most campers.

Site **7**
RUJADA
on Layng Creek
UMPQUA NATIONAL FOREST

Campsites, facilities: There are ten sites for tents, trailers or motor homes up to 22 feet long. Picnic tables and fire grills are provided. Flush toilets and piped water are available. Leashed pets are permitted.

Reservations, fee: No reservations necessary; no fee. Open late May to late

September.

Who to contact: Phone the Cottage Grove Ranger District at (503)942-5591 or write to Umpqua National Forest, P.O. Box 38, Cottage Grove, OR 97424.

Location: From Cottage Grove, drive east past Dorena Drive to Culp Creek. Travel east on County Road 2400 out of the town of Culp Creek for four miles, then go two miles northeast on Forest Service Road 17 to the campground.

Trip note: This campground is set along the banks of Layng Creek. It's a good swimming spot about two miles upstream from its confluence with the Row River. This small, hidden spot is free and has piped water, a rare combination.

Site 8
PASS CREEK COUNTY PARK
near Roseburg

Campsites, facilities: There are ten tent sites and 30 sites for trailers or motor homes up to 30 feet long. Electricity, piped water, sewer hookups and picnic tables are provided. Flush toilets, showers and a playground are available. Bottled gas, a store, a cafe, a laundromat and ice are within one mile. Pets and motorbikes are permitted.

Reservations, fee: No reservations necessary; $7-9 fee per night. Open all year.

Who to contact: Phone (503)942-3281 or write to P.O. Box 87, Curtin, OR 97428.

Location: From Roseburg, travel 35 miles north on Interstate 5, then take exit 163 and drive to the park.

Trip note: This is a decent layover spot for travelers on Interstate 5. There are no other campgrounds within 25 miles in any direction.

Site 9
DOUGLAS COUNTY FAIRGROUNDS RV
near Umpqua River

Campsites, facilities: There are 50 sites for trailers or motor homes of any length. Electricity, piped water and picnic tables are provided. Flush toilets, sanitary services, showers and a playground are available. A store, a cafe, a laundromat and ice are located within one mile. Leashed pets are permitted.

Reservations, fee: No reservations necessary; $6 fee per night. Open all year.

Who to contact: Phone (503)440-4500 or write to P.O. Box 1550, Roseburg, OR 97470.

Location: Take exit 123 off Interstate 5 in Roseburg and follow the signs.

Trip note: This county park is near the Umpqua River, one of Oregon's prettiest rivers. There is often good fishing in season. Nearby recreation options include a golf course, bike paths and tennis courts.

Site 10
ALAMEDA AVENUE TRAILER PARK
near Umpqua River

Campsites, facilities: There are 35 sites for trailers or motor homes up to 30 feet long. Electricity, piped water and sewer hookups are provided. Flush toilets, sanitary services, showers and a laundromat are available. Bottled gas, a store, a cafe and ice are located within one mile. Pets and motorbikes are permitted.

Reservations, fee: Reservations accepted; $10 fee per night. Open all year.

Who to contact: Phone (503)672-2348 or write to 581 Northeast Alameda, Roseburg, OR 97470.

Location: In Roseburg, take the Garden Valley exit off Interstate 5 and travel east to Business Route 99. From there, go one-quarter mile north to Northeast Alameda Avenue.

Trip note: This is one of four parks in Roseburg. This park is near the Umpqua

River, which flows right through town. Nearby recreation options include a golf course, bike paths and tennis courts.

Site 11
NEBO TRAILER PARK
near Umpqua River

Campsites, facilities: There are 20 drive-through sites for trailers or motor homes of any length. Electricity, piped water and sewer hookups are provided. Flush toilets, sanitary services, showers, a laundromat and ice are available. Bottled gas, a store and a cafe are within one mile. Leashed pets are permitted.

Reservations, fee: Reservations accepted; $12 fee per night. Open all year.

Who to contact: Phone (503)673-4108 or write to 2071 Northeast Stephens, Roseburg, OR 97470.

Location: In Roseburg, take exit 125 and go northeast to Stephens Street.

Trip note: This is an option for motor home campers stopping in Roseburg. The park is near the Umpqua River. Nearby recreation options include a golf course, bike paths and tennis courts.

Site 12
TWIN RIVERS VACATION PARK
near Umpqua River

Campsites, facilities: There are 11 tent sites and 72 drive-through sites for trailers or motor homes of any length. Electricity, piped water, sewer hookups and picnic tables are provided. Flush toilets, bottled gas, showers, firewood, a store, a laundromat, ice and a playground are available. Pets and motorbikes are permitted. Boat launching facilities are nearby.

Reservations, fee: Reservations accepted; $8-13 fee per night. Open all year.

Who to contact: Phone (503)673-3811 or write to 433 River Forks Park, Roseburg, OR 97470.

Location: In Roseburg, take exit 125 off Interstate 5 and travel five miles west to Old Garden Valley Road. The park is 1.5 miles south.

Trip note: This is the only campground in Roseburg with tent sites as well as motor home sites. It's a wooded campground near the Umpqua River. Nearby recreation options include a golf course, a county park and bike paths.

Site 13
WHISTLER'S BEND
on North Umpqua River

Campsites, facilities: There are 24 sites for tents, trailers or motor homes up to 30 feet long. Picnic tables and fire grills are provided. Piped water, flush toilets, showers and a playground are available. Pets are permitted. Boat launching facilities are nearby.

Reservations, fee: No reservations necessary; $6 fee per night. Open all year.

Who to contact: Phone (503)673-4863 or write to P.O. Box 800, Winchester, OR 97495.

Location: From Roseburg, travel 15 miles east on Highway 138 to the park.

Trip note: This county park is set along the bank of the North Umpqua River. It can be an idyllic spot and is just a 20-minute drive from Interstate 5, yet it gets little pressure from outsiders.

Site 14
CAVITT CREEK FALLS
on Cavitt Creek

Campsites, facilities: There are eight sites for trailers or motor homes up to 20 feet long. Picnic tables and fire grills are provided. Pit toilets, piped water and firewood are available. Leashed pets are permitted.

Reservations, fee: No reservations necessary; $4 fee per night. Open May to late October.

Who to contact: Phone (503)672-4491 or write to Bureau of Land Management, 777 NW Garden Valley Boulevard, Roseburg, OR 97470.

Location: From Roseburg drive 18 miles east on Highway 138 to Glide. From Glide, travel seven miles southeast on Little River Road, then three miles south on Cavitt Creek Road to the campground.

Trip note: This campground is set along the bank of Cavitt Creek about three miles from its confluence with Little River. If you want to get deeper into the woods, Sites 18-21 provide options farther down the same road.

Site 15   ROCK CREEK
on Rock Creek

Campsites, facilities: There are 17 sites for tents, trailers or motor homes up to 18 feet long. Picnic tables and fire grills are provided. Vault toilets, piped water and firewood are available. Leashed pets are permitted.

Reservations, fee: No reservations necessary; $5 fee per night. Open May to late October.

Who to contact: Phone (503)672-4491 or write to Bureau of Land Management, 777 NW Garden Valley Boulevard, Roseburg, OR 97470.

Location: From Roseburg, drive 18 miles east on Highway 138 to Glide. From Glide, travel 12 miles northeast on Rock Creek Road to the campground.

Trip note: This campground is set along the bank of Rock Creek in a relatively obscure spot.

Site 16   MILL POND
on Rock Creek

Campsites, facilities: There are 12 sites for tents, trailers or motor homes up to 20 feet long. Picnic tables and fire grills are provided. Vault toilets, piped water, firewood and a group shelter are available. Some facilities are wheelchair accessible. Leashed pets are permitted.

Reservations, fee: No reservations necessary; $5-7 fee per night. Open May to late October.

Who to contact: Phone (503)672-4491 or write to Bureau of Land Management, 777 NW Garden Valley Boulevard, Roseburg, OR 97470.

Location: From Roseburg, drive 18 miles east on Highway 138 to Glide. From Glide, travel ten miles northeast on Rock Creek Road to the campground.

Trip note: This campground is set along the banks of Rock Creek. It is the first camp you will see along Rock Creek Road.

Site 17   SUSAN CREEK
on North Umpqua River

Campsites, facilities: There are 33 sites for trailers or motor homes up to 20 feet long. Picnic tables and fire grills are provided. Flush toilets, piped water and firewood are available. Some facilities are wheelchair accessible. Leashed pets are permitted.

Reservations, fee: No reservations necessary; $5-7 fee per night. Open May to late October.

Who to contact: Phone (503)672-4491 or write to Bureau of Land Management, 777 NW Garden Valley Boulevard, Roseburg, OR 97470.

Location: From Roseburg, travel 33 miles east on Highway 138 to the campground.

Trip note: This popular campground is set along the banks of the North Umpqua River. It's a good base camp for a fishing trip.

Site 18
WOLF CREEK
on Little River
UMPQUA NATIONAL FOREST

Campsites, facilities: There are nine sites for tents, trailers or motor homes up to 16 feet long. Picnic tables and fire grills are provided. Flush toilets and piped water are available. Some facilities are wheelchair accessible. Leashed pets are permitted.

Reservations, fee: Reservations required for groups, with a $35 fee per night. Open mid-May to late October.

Who to contact: Phone the North Umpqua Ranger District at (503)496-3532 or write to Umpqua National Forest, 18781 North Umpqua Highway, Glide, OR 97443.

Location: From Roseburg, drive 18 miles east on Highway 138 to Glide. From Glide, travel 12 miles southeast on County Road 17 to the campground.

Trip note: This campground is set along the banks of the Little River near the Wolf Creek Civilian Conservation Center. If you want to get deeper into the interior of the Cascades, Sites 22 and 23 are two choices that are about 15 miles east.

Site 19
EMILE CREEK
on Little River
UMPQUA NATIONAL FOREST

Campsites, facilities: There are four sites for trailers or motor homes up to 20 feet long. Picnic tables and fire grills are provided. Vault toilets, piped water and firewood are available. Leashed pets are permitted.

Reservations, fee: No reservations necessary; no fee. Open May to late October.

Who to contact: Phone the North Umpqua Ranger District at (503)496-3532 or write to Umpqua National Forest, 18781 North Umpqua Highway, Glide, OR 97443.

Location: From Roseburg, drive 18 miles east on Highway 138 to Glide. From Glide, travel 14 miles southeast on County Road 17 to the campground.

Trip note: This little-used campground is set along the banks of the Little River, not far from Sites 17, 18 and 20.

Site 20
COOLWATER
on Little River
UMPQUA NATIONAL FOREST

Campsites, facilities: There are seven sites for tents, trailers or motor homes up to 16 feet long. Picnic tables and fire grills are provided. Vault toilets and hand-pumped water are available. Leashed pets are permitted.

Reservations, fee: No reservations necessary; no fee. Open year-round.

Who to contact: Phone the North Umpqua Ranger District at (503)496-3532 or write to Umpqua National Forest, 18782 North Umpqua Highway, Glide, OR 97443.

Location: From Roseburg, drive 18 miles east on Highway 138. From Glide, travel 15.5 miles southeast on County Road 17 to the campground.

Trip note: This campground gets little use and is set along the banks of the Little River. Even though this is a fairly remote setting, it's not too long a drive from Roseburg.

Site **21**
WHITE CREEK
on Little River
UMPQUA NATIONAL FOREST

Campsites, facilities: There are four sites for tents, trailers or motor homes up to 31 feet long. Picnic tables and fire grills are provided. Vault toilets and hand-pumped well water are available. Leashed pets are permitted.

Reservations, fee: No reservations necessary; no fee. Open year-round.

Who to contact: Phone the North Umpqua Ranger District at (503)496-3532 or write to Umpqua National Forest, 18782 North Umpqua Highway, Glide, OR 97443.

Location: From Roseburg, drive 18 miles east on Highway 138 to Glide. From Glide, go 16.5 miles east on County Road 17. The campground is one-quarter mile east on Forest Service Road 2792.

Trip note: This campground is set at the confluence of White Creek and Little River. Hiking and fishing are two of the recreation options here.

Site **22**
HEMLOCK LAKE
on Hemlock Lake
UMPQUA NATIONAL FOREST

Campsites, facilities: There are 13 sites for tents, trailers or motor homes up to 22 feet long. **No piped water** is available. Picnic tables and fire grills are provided. Vault toilets are available. Leashed pets are permitted. Boat docks and launching facilities are nearby. No motors are permitted on the lake.

Reservations, fee: No reservations necessary; no fee. Open June to late October.

Who to contact: Phone the North Umpqua Ranger District at (503)496-3532 or write to Umpqua National Forest, 18782 North Umpqua Highway, Glide, OR 97443.

Location: From Roseburg, drive 18 miles east on Highway 138 to Glide. Travel on County Road 17 east from Glide for 16.5 miles, then go 15.5 miles east on Forest Service Road 27.

Trip note: This is a little-known jewel of a spot. For starters, it is set along the shore of Hemlock Lake. An eight-mile loop trail called the Yellow Jacket Loop is just south of the campground. For finishers, another trail leaves camp and heads north for about three miles to the Lake in the Woods campground. From there it is just a short hike to either Hemlock Falls or Yakso Falls.

Site **23**
LAKE IN THE WOODS
on Lake in the Woods
UMPQUA NATIONAL FOREST

Campsites, facilities: There are 11 sites for tents, trailers or motor homes up to 16 feet long. Picnic tables and fire grills are provided. Flush toilets and hand-pumped well water are available. Leashed pets are permitted.

Reservations, fee: No reservations necessary; no fee. Open June to late October.

Who to contact: Phone the North Umpqua Ranger District at (503)496-3532 or write to Umpqua National Forest, 18782 North Umpqua Highway, Glide, OR 97443.

Location: From Roseburg, drive 18 miles east on Highway 138 to Glide. Travel on County Road 17 east from Glide for 16.5 miles, then go 11 miles east on Forest Service Road 27.

Trip note: This campground is set along the shore of little Lake in the Woods. There are several good hikes available. One of them leaves the camp and heads south for about three miles to the Hemlock Lake campground. Two others nearby trails provide short, scenic hikes to either Hemlock Falls or Yakso Falls.

Site 24

SCAREDMAN CREEK
on Canton Creek

Campsites, facilities: There are ten sites for tents, trailers or motor homes up to 18 feet long. Picnic tables and fire grills are provided. Vault toilets and hand-pumped well water are available. Leashed pets are permitted.

Reservations, fee: No reservations necessary; no fee. Open May to late October.

Who to contact: Phone (503)672-4491 or write to Bureau of Land Management, 777 NW Garden Valley Boulevard, Roseburg, OR 97470.

Location: From Roseburg, drive 39 miles east on Highway 138 to Steamboat. From Steamboat, go three miles north on Canton Creek Road to the campground.

Trip note: This campground is set along the banks of Canton Creek. It's a small camp that is virtually unknown to out-of-towners.

Site 25

ISLAND
on Umpqua River
UMPQUA NATIONAL FOREST

Campsites, facilities: There are seven sites for tents, trailers or motor homes up to 22 feet long. Picnic tables and fire grills are provided. Piped water, vault toilets and firewood are available. Leashed pets are permitted.

Reservations, fee: No reservations necessary; no fee. Open year-round.

Who to contact: Phone the North Umpqua Ranger District at (503)496-3532 or write to Umpqua National Forest, HC 60, Box 101, Idleyld Park, OR 97447.

Location: From Roseburg, drive 40 miles east on Highway 138. The campground is set just off the highway to the right along the Umpqua River.

Trip note: This campground is set along the banks of the Umpqua River at a spot popular for both fishing and rafting. Nearby Sites 26 and 27 provide a more primitive setting.

Site 26

CANTON CREEK
near Umpqua River
UMPQUA NATIONAL FOREST

Campsites, facilities: There are five sites for tents, trailers or motor homes up to 16 feet long. Picnic tables and fire grills are provided. Piped water and vault toilets are available. Leashed pets are permitted.

Reservations, fee: No reservations necessary; $4 fee per night. Open mid-May to late October.

Who to contact: Phone the North Umpqua Ranger District at (503)496-3532 or write to Umpqua National Forest, HC 60, Box 101, Idleyld Park, OR 97447.

Location: From Roseburg, drive east on Highway 138 to Steamboat, then go 400 yards northeast on Forest Service Road 38 to the campground.

Trip note: This campground is set at the confluence of Canton and Steamboat Creeks, less than a mile from the Umpqua River. This site gets little use. No fishing is permitted on Steamboat or Canton Creeks because they are spawning areas for steelhead and salmon.

Site 27

STEAMBOAT FALLS
on Steamboat Creek
UMPQUA NATIONAL FOREST

Campsites, facilities: There are 11 sites for tents, trailers or motor homes up to 21 feet long. Picnic tables and fire grills are provided. Piped water and vault toilets are available. Leashed pets are permitted.

Reservations, fee: No reservations necessary; no fee. Open year-round.

Who to contact: Phone the North Umpqua Ranger District at (503)496-3532 or write to Umpqua National Forest, HC 60, Box 101, Idleyld Park, OR 97447.

Location: From Roseburg, drive east on Highway 138 to Steamboat, then go six miles northeast on Forest Service Road 38. The camp is one mile further on Forest Service Road 3810.

Trip note: This campground is set along the banks of Steamboat Creek, near Steamboat Falls and a fish ladder which provides passage for steelhead and salmon on their migratory, upstream journey. No fishing is permitted in Steamboat Creek.

Site **28**
APPLE CREEK GROUP CAMP
on Umpqua River
UMPQUA NATIONAL FOREST

Campsites, facilities: There are eight group sites for tents, trailers or motor homes up to 21 feet long. Picnic tables and fire grills are provided. Vault toilets are available. There is **no piped water.** Leashed pets are permitted.

Reservations, fee: No reservations necessary; no fee. Open year-round.

Who to contact: Phone the North Umpqua Ranger District at (503)496-3532 or write to Umpqua National Forest, 18782 North Umpqua Highway, Glide, OR 97443.

Location: From Roseburg, travel east on Highway 138, continuing 23 miles past Idleyld Park. The camp is next to the highway.

Trip note: This campground is set along the banks of the Umpqua River at a popular spot for rafting and fly fishing.

Site **29**
HORSESHOE BEND
on Umpqua River
UMPQUA NATIONAL FOREST

Campsites, facilities: There are 34 sites for tents, trailers or motor homes up to 22 feet long. Picnic tables and fire grills are provided. Piped water, flush toilets, a laundromat, and a store are available. Some facilities are wheelchair accessible; the camp is partially modified for the physically challenged. Leashed pets are permitted. Raft launching facilities are nearby.

Reservations, fee: No reservations necessary; $6 fee per night. Open mid-May to late September.

Who to contact: Phone the North Umpqua Ranger District at (503)496-3532 or write to Umpqua National Forest, HC 60, Box 101, Idleyld Park, OR 97447.

Location: From Roseburg, travel east from Glide on Highway 138 for 48 miles, then follow Forest Service Road 4730 a short distance to the campground.

Trip note: This campground is set in the middle of a big bend in the Umpqua River. Rafting and fly fishing are both popular here.

Site **30**
TWIN LAKES
on Big Twin Lake, hike-in only
UMPQUA NATIONAL FOREST

Campsites, facilities: There are six tent sites. Picnic tables and fire pits are provided. A pit toilet is available. There is **no piped water.** Leashed pets are permitted. Boat docks are nearby.

Reservations, fee: No reservations necessary; no fee. Open mid-June to late October.

Who to contact: Phone the North Umpqua Ranger District at (503)496-3532 or write to Umpqua National Forest, 18782 North Umpqua Highway, Glide, OR 97443.

Location: From the North Umpqua Ranger Station, take Highway 138 one-quarter mile west. Turn on Little River Road No. 17 and drive 20 miles. The road becomes Forest Service Road 27. Continue to Forest Service Road 2715 (about three miles east of the Lake of the Woods campground). Turn left on Forest Service Road 2715 and drive eight miles to its junction with Forest Service Road 2715-530. Turn left and drive to the end of the road, where the trailhead for Twin Lakes Trail No. 1500 is located. It is a 1.75-mile hike to the campground.

Trip note: This remote campground is set along the shore of Big Twin Lake at 4,800 feet elevation. The lake covers 14 acres with a depth of 48 feet. It's a place of quiet and great beauty.

Site **31**
BOULDER FLAT
on Umpqua River
UMPQUA NATIONAL FOREST

Campsites, facilities: There are ten sites for tents, trailers or motor homes up to 22 feet long. Picnic tables and fire grills are provided. Piped water and vault toilets are available. A store, a laundromat and ice are located within five miles. Leashed pets are permitted. A raft launch is nearby.

Reservations, fee: No reservations necessary; no fee. Open May to February.

Who to contact: Phone the North Umpqua Ranger District at (503)496-3532 or write to Umpqua National Forest, 18782 North Umpqua Highway, Glide, OR 97443.

Location: From Roseburg, drive 54 miles east on Highway 138 to the campground.

Trip note: This campground is set along the banks of the Umpqua River at the confluence of Boulder Creek. A trail follows Boulder Creek north from camp for 10.5 miles through the Boulder Creek Wilderness, a climb in elevation from 2,000 to 5,400 feet. It's a good thumper for backpackers.

Site **32**
TOKETEE LAKE
on Toketee Lake
UMPQUA NATIONAL FOREST

Campsites, facilities: There are 33 sites for tents, trailers or motor homes up to 22 feet long. **No piped water** is available. Picnic tables and fire grills are provided. Vault toilets are available. Leashed pets are permitted. Boat docks and launching facilities are nearby.

Reservations, fee: No reservations necessary; no fee. Open mid-April to late October.

Who to contact: Phone the Diamond Lake Ranger District at (503)498-2531 or write to Umpqua National Forest, HC 60, Box 101, Idleyld Park, OR 97447.

Location: From Roseburg, drive about 60 miles east on Highway 138, then one mile on Forest Service Road 34 to the campground.

Trip note: This campground is set along the shore of Toketee Lake. The North Umpqua Trail passes near camp and continues north along the river for many miles.

Site **33**
WHITEHORSE FALLS
on Clearwater River
UMPQUA NATIONAL FOREST

Campsites, facilities: There are five tent sites. **No piped water** is available. Picnic tables and fire grills are provided. Vault toilets are available. Leashed pets are permitted.

Reservations, fee: No reservations necessary; no fee. Open June to late October.

Who to contact: Phone the Diamond Lake Ranger District at (503)498-2531 or write to Umpqua National Forest, HC 60, Box 101, Idleyld Park, OR 97447.

Location: From Roseburg, travel 67 miles east on Highway 138 to the campground.

Trip note: This campground is set along the Clearwater River, one of the coldest streams in Umpqua National Forest. The small camp is in a primitive setting, yet it's adjacent to the highway.

Site **34**   **CLEARWATER FALLS**
                        on Clearwater River
                        UMPQUA NATIONAL FOREST

Campsites, facilities: There are eight tent sites and four sites for trailers or motor homes up to 16 feet long. **No piped water** is available. Picnic tables and fire grills are provided. Piped water and vault toilets are available. Leashed pets are permitted.

Reservations, fee: No reservations necessary; no fee. Open mid-May to late October.

Who to contact: Phone the Diamond Lake Ranger District at (503)498-2531 or write to Umpqua National Forest, HC 60, Box 101, Idleyld Park, OR 97447.

Location: From Roseburg, drive on Highway 138 for 70 miles. At Forest Service Road 4785 head south to the campground.

Trip note: This campground is set along the banks of the Clearwater River. The attraction here is the cascading section of stream called Clearwater Falls.

Site **35**   **BROKEN ARROW**
                        on Diamond Lake
                        UMPQUA NATIONAL FOREST

Campsites, facilities: There are 142 sites for tents, trailers or motor homes of any length. Picnic tables and fire grills are provided. Flush toilets and piped water are available. Leashed pets are permitted. Some facilities are wheelchair accessible. Boat docks, launching facilities and rentals are nearby.

Reservations, fee: No reservations necessary, except for groups. Call MISTIX at (800)283-CAMP ($6 MISTIX fee); $6 fee per night. Open late May to mid-September.

Who to contact: Phone the Diamond Lake Ranger District at (503)498-2531 or write to Umpqua National Forest at HC 60, Box 101, Idleyld Park, OR 97447.

Location: From Roseburg, drive 80 miles east on Highway 138. Turn on Forest Service Road 4795 and drive to the campground.

Trip note: This campground is set at 5,200 feet elevation near the south shore of Diamond Lake, the largest natural lake in Umpqua National Forest. Boating, fishing, swimming, hiking and bicycling are among the options here. Diamond Lake is adjacent to Mount Thielsen Wilderness, Crater Lake National Park and Mount Bailey, all of which offer a variety of recreation opportunities year-round. Diamond Lake is quite popular with anglers because of its good trout trolling, particularly in early summer.

Site **36**   **DIAMOND LAKE**
                        on Diamond Lake
                        UMPQUA NATIONAL FOREST

Campsites, facilities: There are 156 sites for tents, trailers or motor homes up to 40 feet long. Picnic tables and fire grills are provided. Flush toilets, piped water and firewood are available. Leashed pets are permitted. Boat docks, launching facilities and rentals are nearby.

Reservations, fee: Reservations provided through MISTIX by calling (800)283-CAMP ($6 MISTIX fee); $7 fee per night. Open mid-May to late October.

Who to contact: Phone the Diamond Lake Ranger District at (503)498-2531 or write to Umpqua National Forest, HC 60, Box 101, Idleyld Park, OR 97447.

Location: From Roseburg, drive 80 miles east on Highway 138. From there, go two miles south on Forest Service Road 4795 to the campground.

Trip note: This campground is set along the east shore of Diamond Lake. See the trip note for Site 35 for recreation information.

Site **37**
THIELSEN VIEW
on Diamond Lake
UMPQUA NATIONAL FOREST

Campsites, facilities: There are 60 sites for tents, trailers or motor homes up to 30 feet long. Picnic tables and fire grills are provided. Piped water and vault toilets are available. Leashed pets are permitted. Some facilities are wheelchair accessible. Boat docks, launching facilities and rentals are nearby.

Reservations, fee: No reservations necessary; $6 fee per night. Open late May to late September.

Who to contact: Phone the Diamond Lake Ranger District at (503)498-2531 or write to Umpqua National Forest, HC 60, Box 101, Idleyld Park, OR 97447.

Location: From Roseburg, drive on Highway 138 east for about 80 miles, then go south on Forest Service Road 4795 to the campground.

Trip note: This campground is set along the west shore of Diamond Lake. See the trip note for Site 35 for information on recreation opportunities.

Site **38**
EAST LEMOLO
on Lemolo Lake
UMPQUA NATIONAL FOREST

Campsites, facilities: There are six sites for tents, trailers or motor homes up to 22 feet long. **No piped water** is available. Picnic tables and fire grills are provided. Vault toilets are available. Leashed pets are permitted. Boat docks, launching facilities and rentals are nearby.

Reservations, fee: No reservations necessary; no fee. Open mid-May to late October.

Who to contact: Phone the Diamond Lake Ranger District at (503)498-2531 or write to Umpqua National Forest, HC 60, Box 101, Idleyld Park, OR 97447.

Location: From Roseburg, travel 74 miles east on Highway 138, then three miles north on Forest Service Road 2610. The park is located about two miles east on Forest Service Road 2666.

Trip note: This campground is on the eastern shore of Lemolo Lake, where boating and fishing are some of the recreation possibilities. Boats with motors are allowed. The North Umpqua River and adjacent trail are just beyond the north shore of the lake. If you hike for two miles northwest of the lake, you can reach spectacular Lemolo Falls.

Site **39**
INLET
on Lemolo Lake
UMPQUA NATIONAL FOREST

Campsites, facilities: There are 13 sites for tents, trailers or motor homes up to 22

feet long. **No piped water** is available. Picnic tables and fire grills are provided. Vault toilets are available. Leashed pets are permitted. Boat docks, launching facilities and rentals are nearby.

Reservations, fee: No reservations necessary; no fee. Open mid-May to late October.

Who to contact: Phone the Diamond Lake Ranger District at (503)498-2531 or write to Umpqua National Forest, HC 60, Box 101, Idleyld Park, OR 97447.

Location: From Roseburg, drive 74 miles east on Highway 138, then three miles north on Forest Service Road 2610. The camp is about three miles east on Forest Service Road 2666.

Trip note: This campground is set along the eastern inlet of Lemolo Lake. See the trip note for Site 38 for recreation details.

Site 40 POOLE CREEK
on Lemolo Lake
UMPQUA NATIONAL FOREST

Campsites, facilities: There are 60 sites for tents, trailers or motor homes up to 22 feet long. Picnic tables and fire grills are provided. Piped water and vault toilets are available. Leashed pets are permitted. Boat docks, launching facilities and rentals are nearby.

Reservations, fee: Reservations available through MISTIX by calling (800)283-CAMP ($6 MISTIX fee); $5 fee per night. Open mid-May to late October.

Who to contact: Phone the Diamond Lake Ranger District at (503)498-2531 or write to Umpqua National Forest, HC 60, Box 101, Idleyld Park, OR 97447.

Location: From Roseburg, drive 72 miles east on Highway 138, then four miles north on Forest Service Road 2610 to the campground.

Trip note: This campground is on the western shore of Lemolo Lake and not far from Lemolo Lake Resort which is open for recreation year-round. See the trip note for Site 38.

Site 41 LEMOLO LAKE RESORT
on Lemolo Lake

Campsites, facilities: There are five tent sites and 32 drive-through sites for trailers or motor homes of any length. Electricity, piped water, sewer hookups and picnic tables are provided. Flush toilets, bottled gas, sanitary disposal services, showers, a store, a cafe, a laundromat and ice are available. Pets and motorbikes are permitted. Boat docks, launching facilities and rentals are nearby.

Reservations, fee: Reservations accepted; $5-10 fee per night; MasterCard and Visa accepted. Open all year.

Who to contact: Phone (503)496-0900 or write to HC 60, Box 79B, Idleyld Park, OR 97447.

Location: From Diamond Lake, go west on Highway 138 for 10.5 miles, then go five miles north on Lemolo Lake Road to the resort.

Trip note: This resort is on the western shore of Lemolo Lake and offers recreation opportunities year-round.

Site 42 CONTORTA POINT
on Crescent Lake
DESCHUTES NATIONAL FOREST

Campsites, facilities: There are 12 sites for tents, trailers or motor homes up to 22 feet long. Picnic tables and fire grills are provided. Piped water, vault toilets and

firewood are available. Leashed pets are permitted. Boat docks and launching
facilities are located a mile away at the Spring campground (Site 43).

Reservations, fee: No reservations necessary; no fee. Open June to late September.

Who to contact: Phone the Crescent Ranger District at (503)433-2234 or write to
Deschutes National Forest, Box 208, Crescent, OR 97733.

Location: From Eugene, drive southeast on Highway 58 to Crescent Lake. The
turnoff is just past Odell Lake. Drive 11 miles southwest on Forest Service
Road 60, then one mile on Forest Service Road 280.

Trip note: This campground is on the southern shore of Crescent Lake, where
swimming, boating and waterskiing are among the summer pastimes. A number
of trails from the nearby Spring campground (Site 43) provide access to lakes
in the Diamond Peak Wilderness. A parking area for snowmobiles and
cross-country skiers is at the north end of the lake.

Site 43
SPRING
on Crescent Lake
DESCHUTES NATIONAL FOREST

Campsites, facilities: There are 68 sites for tents, trailers or motor homes up to 22
feet long. Picnic tables and fire grills are provided. Piped water, vault toilets
and firewood are available. Leashed pets are permitted. Boat docks are nearby.

Reservations, fee: No reservations necessary; $7 fee per night. Open June to late
October.

Who to contact: Phone the Crescent Ranger District at (503)433-2234 or write to
Deschutes National Forest, Box 208, Crescent, OR 97733.

Location: From Eugene, drive southeast on Highway 58 to the town of Crescent
Lake. Drive eight miles west on Forest Service Road 60 from Crescent Lake,
then turn northeast on the entrance road to the campground.

Trip note: This campground is on the southern shore of Crescent Lake. See the trip
note for Site 42.

Site 44
CRESCENT LAKE
on Crescent Lake
DESCHUTES NATIONAL FOREST

Campsites, facilities: There are 47 sites for tents, trailers or motor homes up to 21
feet long. Picnic tables and fire grills are provided. Piped water, vault toilets
and firewood are available. Leashed pets are permitted. Boat docks, launching
facilities and rentals are nearby.

Reservations, fee: No reservations necessary; $7 fee per night. Open mid-May to
late October.

Who to contact: Phone the Crescent Ranger District at (503)433-2234 or write to
Deschutes National Forest, Box 208, Crescent, OR 97733.

Location: From Eugene, drive southeast on Highway 58 to the town of Crescent
Lake. From Crescent Lake, go three miles southwest on Forest Service Road
60 to the campground.

Trip note: This campground is set along the north shore of Crescent Lake. A trail
from the campground heads into the Diamond Peak Wilderness and also
branches north to Odell Lake.

Site 45
ODELL TRAILER PARK
between Crescent and Odell Lakes

Campsites, facilities: There are 33 drive-through sites for trailers or motor homes

of any length. Electricity, piped water, sewer hookups and picnic tables are provided. Flush toilets, showers and a laundromat are available. Bottled gas, sanitary services, a store, a cafe and ice are located within one mile. Leashed pets are permitted.

Reservations, fee: Reservations accepted; $11 fee per night; MasterCard and Visa accepted. Open May to October.

Who to contact: Phone (503)354-1441 or write to Box 91, Crescent Lake, OR 97425.

Location: From Eugene, drive southeast on Highway 58 to Crescent Lake. In the town of Crescent Lake, take the Crescent Lake Road exit off Highway 58. The park is at the junction.

Trip note: This motor home park is centrally located between Crescent and Odell Lakes, both of which offer good boating and fishing. There are good hiking trails in the backcountry of nearby Diamond Peak Wilderness.

Site 46
ODELL CREEK
on Odell Lake
DESCHUTES NATIONAL FOREST

Campsites, facilities: There are 22 sites for tents, trailers or motor homes up to 22 feet long. Picnic tables and fire grills are provided. Piped water, vault toilets and firewood are available. Leashed pets are permitted. Boat docks, launching facilities and rentals are nearby.

Reservations, fee: No reservations necessary; $5 fee per night. Open mid-May to late September.

Who to contact: Phone the Crescent Ranger District at (503)433-2234 or write to Deschutes National Forest, Box 208, Crescent, OR 97733.

Location: From Eugene, drive southeast on Highway 58 to Odell Lake. At the east end of the lake, take Forest Service Road 680 and drive 400 yards to the campground.

Trip note: This campground is set along the south shore of Odell Lake, where you can fish, swim and hike. A trail from the camp heads southwest into the Diamond Peak Wilderness and provides access to several small lakes in the backcountry.

Site 47
SUNSET COVE
on Odell Lake
DESCHUTES NATIONAL FOREST

Campsites, facilities: There are 26 sites for tents, trailers or motor homes up to 22 feet long. Picnic tables and fire grills are provided. Piped water, vault toilets and firewood are available. Leashed pets are permitted. Boat docks, launching facilities and rentals are nearby.

Reservations, fee: No reservations necessary; $6 fee per night. Open mid-May to mid-October.

Who to contact: Phone the Crescent Ranger District at (503)433-2234 or write to Deschutes National Forest, Box 208, Crescent, OR 97733.

Location: From the junction of Highway 58 with Crescent Lake Road, go 2.5 miles northwest on Highway 58 to the campground.

Trip note: This campground is set along the southeast shore of Odell Lake. See the trip note for Site 46.

Site **48**

PRINCESS CREEK
on Odell Lake
DESCHUTES NATIONAL FOREST

Campsites, facilities: There are 46 sites for tents, trailers or motor homes up to 22 feet long. Picnic tables and fire grills are provided. Piped water, vault toilets and firewood are available. Showers, a store, a laundromat and ice are available within five miles. Leashed pets are permitted. Boat docks and rentals are nearby.

Reservations, fee: No reservations necessary; $7 fee per night. Open mid-May to late October.

Who to contact: Phone the Crescent Ranger District at (503)433-2234 or write to Deschutes National Forest, Box 208, Crescent, OR 97733.

Location: Go 5.5 miles northwest of the junction of Crescent Lake Road on Highway 58 to the campground.

Trip note: This campground is set along the east shore of Odell Lake. See the trip note for Site 46 for recreation details.

Site **49**

TRAPPER CREEK
on Odell Lake
DESCHUTES NATIONAL FOREST

Campsites, facilities: There are 32 sites for tents, trailers or motor homes up to 22 feet long. Picnic tables and fire grills are provided. Piped water, vault toilets and firewood are available. A store, a laundromat and ice are within five miles. Leashed pets are permitted. Boat docks and rentals are nearby.

Reservations, fee: No reservations necessary; $7 fee per night. Open mid-May to late October.

Who to contact: Phone the Crescent Ranger District at (503)433-2234 or write to Deschutes National Forest, Box 208, Crescent, OR 97733.

Location: Go 5.5 miles northwest of the junction of Crescent Lake Road on Highway 58 to the campground.

Trip note: This campground is set along the east shore of Odell Lake. See the trip note for Site 46 for recreation details.

Site **50**

SHELTER COVE RESORT
on Odell Lake

Campsites, facilities: There are ten tent sites and 70 drive-through sites for trailers or motor homes up to 30 feet long. Electricity and picnic tables are provided. Flush toilets, showers, a store, a cafe and ice are available. Leashed pets are permitted. Boat docks, launching facilities and rentals are nearby.

Reservations, fee: No reservations necessary; $6-9 fee per night; MasterCard and Visa accepted. Open late April to mid-October.

Who to contact: Phone (503)343-8995 or write to Cascade Summit, OR 97425.

Location: From Eugene, drive southeast on Highway 58 to Odell Lake. Take the West Odell Road turn off Highway 58 at the north end of Odell Lake, then drive 2.5 miles south on West Odell Road to the campground.

Trip note: This private resort is set along the north shore of Odell Lake.

Site **51**

GOLD LAKE
on Gold Lake
WILLAMETTE NATIONAL FOREST

Campsites, facilities: There are 25 sites for tents, trailers or motor homes up to 16

feet long. Picnic tables and fire grills are provided. Piped water, vault toilets and pets are permitted. Boat docks and launching facilities are nearby.

Reservations, fee: No reservations necessary; $5 fee per night. Open June to late September.

Who to contact: Phone the Oakridge Ranger District at (503)782-2291 or write to Willamette National Forest, 46375 Highway 58, West Fir, OR 97492.

Location: From Eugene, drive 61 miles southeast on Highway 58, then two miles northeast on Forest Service Road 500 to the campground.

Trip note: This campground is set along the shore of Gold Lake, where fishing, swimming and boating (for boats without motors) are permitted. The campground is set along a trail that provides access to numerous small lakes to the west and Waldo Lake to the north.

Site **52**   **SHADOW BAY**
on Waldo Lake
WILLAMETTE NATIONAL FOREST

Campsites, facilities: There are 92 sites for tents, trailers or motor homes up to 22 feet long. Picnic tables and fire grills are provided. Piped water, flush toilets and pets are permitted. Boat docks and launching facilities are nearby.

Reservations, fee: No reservations necessary; $6 fee per night, $12 per night for a double site. Open June to late September.

Who to contact: Phone the Oakridge Ranger District at (503)782-2291 or write to Willamette National Forest, 46375 Highway 58, Westfir, OR 97492.

Location: From Eugene, travel 59 miles southeast on Highway 58, then 5.5 miles north on Forest Service Road 5897, then two miles west on Forest Service Road 5896 to the campground.

Trip note: This camp is set at 5,400 feet elevation, tucked away along the southeast shore of Waldo Lake. For hikers, a trail circles the lake and intersects several other trails that provide access to many small backcountry lakes.

Site **53**   **NORTH WALDO**
on Waldo Lake
WILLAMETTE NATIONAL FOREST

Campsites, facilities: There are 58 sites for tents, trailers or motor homes up to 22 feet long. Picnic tables and fire grills are provided. Piped water and flush toilets are available. Pets are permitted. Boat docks and launching facilities are nearby.

Reservations, fee: No reservations necessary; $6 fee per night, $12 for a double. Open June to late September.

Who to contact: Phone the Oakridge Ranger District at (503)782-2291 or write to Willamette National Forest, 46375 Highway 58, Westfir, OR 97492.

Location: From Eugene, travel 59 miles southeast on Highway 58, then 10.5 miles north on Forest Service Road 5897, then two miles west on Forest Service Road 5898 to the entrance road to the campground.

Trip note: Mosquitos are bad news here in July. See the trip note for Site 52.

Site **54**   **TIMPANOGAS**
on Timpanogas Lake
WILLAMETTE NATIONAL FOREST

Campsites, facilities: There are ten sites for tents, trailers or motor homes up to 21 feet long. Picnic tables and fire grills are provided. Piped water, vault toilets and firewood are available. Leashed pets are permitted. Boat docks are nearby.

Only boats without motors are permitted.

Reservations, fee: No reservations necessary; $4 fee per night. Open mid-June to mid-October.

Who to contact: Phone the Rigdon Ranger District at (503)782-2283 or write to Willamette National Forest, 49098 Salmon Creek Road, Oakridge, OR 97463.

Location: From Eugene, travel 38 miles southeast on Highway 58 (two miles past Oakridge), then one-half mile on County Road 360. The camp is 38 miles southeast on Forest Service Road 21.

Trip note: This remote campground is set along the shore of little Timpanogas Lake in the Cascades National Recreation Area. A trailhead adjacent to camp provides access into the backcountry. There is a hike-in campground about two miles away at Indigo Lake which has five primitive sites and pit toilets. It is accessible by trail from this camp.

Site **55**
INDIGO SPRINGS
near Willamette River
WILLAMETTE NATIONAL FOREST

Campsites, facilities: There are three sites for tents, trailers or motor homes up to 16 feet long. Picnic tables and fire grills are provided. Vault toilets and firewood are available. There is **no piped water.** Leashed pets are permitted.

Reservations, fee: No reservations necessary; no fee. Open mid-April to mid-November.

Who to contact: Phone the Rigdon Ranger District at (503)782-2283 or write to Willamette National Forest, 49098 Salmon Creek Road, Oakridge, OR 97463.

Location: From Eugene, drive 38 miles southeast on Highway 58 (two miles past Oakridge), then one-half mile on County Road 360. From there, go 29 miles southeast on Forest Service Road 21. The camp is on the left.

Trip note: This campground sits along the bank of Indigo Creek, not far from its confluence with the Middle Fork of the Willamette River. It gets it name from the several large springs in the area.

Site **56**
SACANDAGA
on Willamette River
WILLAMETTE NATIONAL FOREST

Campsites, facilities: There are 20 sites for tents, trailers or motor homes up to 21 feet long. Picnic tables and fire grills are provided and vault toilets and firewood are available. There is **no piped water.** Leashed pets are permitted.

Reservations, fee: No reservations necessary; no fee. Open mid-April to mid-November.

Who to contact: Phone the Rigdon Ranger District at (503)782-2283 or write to Willamette National Forest, 49098 Salmon Creek Road, Oakridge, OR 97463.

Location: From Eugene, drive 38 miles southeast on Highway 58 (two miles past Oakridge), then one-half mile on County Road 360. From there, go 25 miles southeast on Forest Service Road 21. The camp is on the right.

Trip note: This primitive campground sits on a bluff overlooking the Willamette River. It's adjacent to historic Rigdon Meadows, the site of a stage coach station in pioneer days.

Site 57
CAMPERS FLAT
on Willamette River
WILLAMETTE NATIONAL FOREST

Campsites, facilities: There are five sites for tents, trailers or motor homes up to 21 feet long. Picnic tables and fire grills are provided. Piped water, vault toilets and firewood are available. Leashed pets are permitted.

Reservations, fee: No reservations necessary; $3 fee per night. Open mid-April to mid-November.

Who to contact: Phone the Rigdon Ranger District at (503)782-2283 or write to Willamette National Forest, 49098 Salmon Creek Road, Oakridge, OR 97463.

Location: From Eugene, drive 38 miles southeast on Highway 58 (two miles past Oakridge), then one-half mile on County Road 360. The camp is 20 miles south on Forest Service Road 21.

Trip note: This campground is set along the Middle Fork of the Willamette River.

Site 58
SECRET
on Willamette River
WILLAMETTE NATIONAL FOREST

Campsites, facilities: There are six sites for tents, trailers or motor homes up to 15 feet long. Picnic table and fire grills are provided. Vault toilets are available, but there is **no piped water.** Leashed pets are permitted.

Reservations, fee: No reservations necessary; no fee. Open mid-April to mid-November.

Who to contact: Phone the Rigdon Ranger District at (503)782-2283 or write to Willamette National Forest, 49098 Salmon Creek Road, Oakridge, OR 97463.

Location: From Eugene drive southeast on Highway 58 two miles past Oakridge, then one-half mile on County Road 360. From there, go 18 miles south on Forest Service Road 21.

Trip note: This campground is set along the Middle Fork of the Willamette River. It attracts few people. Despite its nice setting, nobody seems to know about it.

Site 59
SAND PRAIRIE
on Willamette River
WILLAMETTE NATIONAL FOREST

Campsites, facilities: There are 20 sites for tents, trailers or motor homes up to 22 feet long. Picnic tables and fire grills are provided. Flush toilets and piped water are available. Some of the facilities are wheelchair accessible. Leashed pets are permitted. A boat launch is nearby on Hills Creek Reservoir.

Reservations, fee: No reservations necessary; $7 fee per night, $14 per night for a double site. Open mid-April to mid-November.

Who to contact: Phone the Rigdon Ranger District at (503)782-2283 or write to Willamette National Forest, 49098 Salmon Creek Road, Oakridge, OR 97463.

Location: From Eugene, drive 38 miles southeast on Highway 58 two miles past Oakridge, then one-half mile on County Road 360. From there, go 11 miles south on Forest Service Road 21.

Trip note: This peaceful campground is set in a forest of old-growth trees along the Middle Fork of the Willamette River, just south of Hills Creek Lake. It is located at the Middle Fork Trail trailhead. This 40-mile trail was completed in the early 1990s.

Site 60
PACKARD CREEK
on Hills Creek Reservoir
WILLAMETTE NATIONAL FOREST

Campsites, facilities: There are 33 sites for tents, trailers or motor homes up to 30 feet long. Picnic tables and fire grills are provided. Piped water, vault toilets and firewood are available. Some facilities are wheelchair accessible. Leashed pets are permitted. Boat docks and launching facilities are nearby.

Reservations, fee: No reservations necessary; $7 fee per night, $14 per night for a double site. Open mid-April to mid-November.

Who to contact: Phone the Rigdon Ranger District at (503)782-2283 or write to Willamette National Forest, 49098 Salmon Creek Road, Oakridge, OR 97463.

Location: From Eugene, drive 38 miles southeast on Highway 58 two miles past Oakridge, then one-half mile southeast on County Road 360. The camp is five miles south on Forest Service Road 21.

Trip note: This is the lake I almost drowned in, a story detailed in Chapter Five under hypothermia. The campground is set at 1,600 feet elevation along the west shore of Hills Creek Reservoir, a 2,900-acre reservoir where fishing and boating are popular. No boats with motors are permitted on the Larison Cove arm of the lake.

Site 61
FERRIN
on Willamette River
WILLAMETTE NATIONAL FOREST

Campsites, facilities: There are seven sites for tents, trailers or motor homes. Picnic tables and fire grills are provided. Vault toilets are available. There is **no piped water**. Leashed pets are permitted.

Reservations, fee: No reservations necessary; no fee. Open late April to mid-October.

Who to contact: Phone the Oakridge Ranger District at (503)782-2291 or write to Willamette National Forest, 46375 Highway 58, Westfir, OR 97492.

Location: From Eugene, drive 35 miles southeast on Highway 58 and you'll see the campground. It is located two miles west of Oakridge.

Trip note: This campground is set along the banks of the Middle Fork of the Willamette River, not far from Oakridge. It's a free spot to lay out your sleeping bag for the night.

Site 62
DECEPTION CREEK MOBILE PARK
on Willamette River

Campsites, facilities: There are 15 sites for trailers or motor homes of any length. Electricity, piped water and sewer hookups are provided. Flush toilets, sanitary services, showers, a laundromat and ice are available.

Reservations, fee: Reservations accepted; $12 fee per night; MasterCard and Visa accepted. Open all year.

Who to contact: Phone (503)782-3555 or write to 46372 Highway 58, Westfir, OR 97492.

Location: From Eugene, drive 33 miles southeast on Highway 58. The camp is located three miles west of Oakridge.

Trip note: This motor home park is set along the Middle Fork of the Willamette River between the towns of Oakridge and Hemlock.

Site **63**	**SHADY DELL** on the Middle Fork of Willamette River WILLAMETTE NATIONAL FOREST

Campsites, facilities: There are nine sites for tents, trailers or motor homes up to 15 feet long. Picnic tables and fire grills are provided. Piped water, vault toilets and firewood are available. Sanitary services, a cafe and a laundromat are available within five miles. Some of the facilities are wheelchair accessible. Leashed pets are permitted. Boat docks and launching facilities are nearby at the south end of Lookout Point Lake.

Reservations, fee: No reservations necessary; $3 fee per night. Open May to late October.

Who to contact: Phone the Lowell Ranger District at (503)937-2129 or write to Willamette National Forest, Lowell, OR 97452.

Location: From Eugene, drive 33 miles southeast on Highway 58. The camp is located five miles west of Oakridge.

Trip note: This campground is set along the banks of the Middle Fork of the Willamette River, not far from Lookout Point Lake, a long narrow reservoir that sits adjacent to Highway 58.

Site **64**	**BLACK CANYON** on the Middle Fork of Willamette River WILLAMETTE NATIONAL FOREST

Campsites, facilities: There are 72 sites for tents, trailers or motor homes up to 22 feet long. Picnic tables and fire grills are provided. Piped water, vault toilets and firewood are available. Sanitary services, a cafe and a laundromat are within five miles. Some of the facilities are wheelchair accessible. Leashed pets are permitted. Boat docks and launching facilities are nearby at the south end of Lookout Point Lake.

Reservations, fee: No reservations necessary; $5 fee per night. Open May to late October.

Who to contact: Phone the Lowell Ranger District at (503)937-2129 or write to Willamette National Forest, Lowell, OR 97452.

Location: From Eugene, drive 30 miles southeast on Highway 58. The camp is located six miles west of Oakridge.

Trip note: This campground is set along the banks of the Middle Fork of the Willamette River, not far from Lookout Point Lake, where fishing and boating are popular.

Site **65**	**SALMON CREEK FALLS** on Salmon Creek WILLAMETTE NATIONAL FOREST

Campsites, facilities: There are 14 tent sites and six sites for trailers or motor homes up to 16 feet long. Picnic tables are provided. Piped water and vault toilets are available. A store, a cafe, a laundromat and ice are available within five miles. Leashed pets are permitted.

Reservations, fee: No reservations necessary; $5 fee per night. Open late April to mid-October.

Who to contact: Phone the Oakridge Ranger District at (503)782-2291, or write Willamette National Forest, 46375 Highway 58, Westfir, OR 97492.

Location: From Eugene, drive southeast on Highway 58 to Oakridge, then 3.5 miles

northeast on Forest Service Road 24 (Salmon Creek Road) to the campground.
Trip note: This campground is set along the bank of Salmon Creek. It is just far
enough from Highway 58 to get missed by most campers.

Site **66**   **KIAHANIE**
on the Middle Fork of Willamette River
WILLAMETTE NATIONAL FOREST

Campsites, facilities: There are 21 sites for tents, trailers or motor homes up to 16
feet long. Picnic tables and fire grills are provided. Piped water, vault toilets
and firewood are available. Leashed pets are permitted.
Reservations, fee: No reservations necessary; $5 fee per night. Open late April to
mid-October.
Who to contact: Phone the Oakridge Ranger District at (503)782-2291 or write to
Willamette National Forest, 46375 Highway 58, Westfir, OR 97492.
Location: From Eugene, drive southeast on Highway 58 to Oakridge, then go two
miles to Westfir. Head 19 miles northeast on Forest Service Road 19 to the
campground.
Trip note: I almost hate to reveal it, but this is one heck of a spot for fly fishing.
This remote campground is set along the North Fork of the Middle Fork of the
Willamette River. You want quiet, you came to the right place. An even more
remote campground is farther north on Forest Service Road 19 at Site 67.

Site **67**   **BOX CANYON HORSE CAMP**
near Chucksney Mountain
WILLAMETTE NATIONAL FOREST

Campsites, facilities: There are 13 sites that allow horse and rider to camp close
together. Picnic tables, fire grills and corrals are provided. Firewood, a manure
disposal site and vault toilets are available. There is **no piped water.** Leashed
pets are permitted.
Reservations, fee: No reservations necessary; no fee. Open mid-May to
mid-September.
Who to contact: Phone the Blue River Ranger District at (503)822-3317 or write to
Willamette National Forest, Blue River, OR 97413.
Location: Take Highway 126 east from the town of Blue River for 3.5 miles, then
go 30 miles south on Forest Service Road 19 (Aufderheide Forest Drive).
Trip note: Only 80 miles from Eugene, this unique and secluded campground offers
trails into several wilderness areas, including the Chucksney Mountain Trail,
Crossing-Way Trail and Grasshopper Trail. It's a good base camp for a
backpacking trip.

Site **68**   **SKOOKUM CREEK**
near Three Sisters Wilderness
WILLAMETTE NATIONAL FOREST

Campsites, facilities: There are eight tent sites. Picnic tables and fire grills are
provided. Firewood, piped water and vault toilets are available. Leashed pets
are permitted.
Reservations, fee: No reservations necessary; no fee. Open mid-May to
mid-September.
Who to contact: Phone the Blue River Ranger District at (503)822-3317 or write to
Willamette National Forest, Blue River, OR 97413.
Location: Take Highway east from the town of Blue River for 3.5 miles, then go

30 miles south on Forest Service Road 19 (Aufderheide Forest Drive) to Box Canyon. From there, drive south for three miles on Forest Service Road 1957 to the campground.

Trip note: This remote campground is set near the border of the Three Sisters Wilderness. A trailhead at camp provides access to numerous lakes and other trails in the backcountry. This is a primitive, little-known spot.

Site **69**
BLAIR LAKE
on Blair Lake
WILLAMETTE NATIONAL FOREST

Campsites, facilities: There are six tent sites. Picnic tables are provided. Piped water, firewood and a pit toilet is available. Leashed pets are permitted. Boat docks are nearby.

Reservations, fee: No reservations necessary; no fee. Open June to mid-October.

Who to contact: Phone the Oakridge Ranger District at (503)782-2291 or write to Willamette National Forest, 46375 Highway 58, Westfir, OR 97492.

Location: From the town Oakridge on Highway 58, travel one mile east on County Road 149 eight miles northeast on Forest Service Road 24. From there, go seven miles on Forest Service Road 1934 (a gravel road not recommended for motor homes or trailers).

Trip note: This campground is set at 4,800 feet elevation along the shore of little Blair Lake. Boats without motors are permitted and fishing can be good.

Site **70**
BLUE POOL
on the Middle Fork of Willamette River
WILLAMETTE NATIONAL FOREST

Campsites, facilities: There are 25 sites for tents, trailers or motor homes up to 16 feet long. Picnic tables and fire grills are provided. Piped water and vault toilets are available. Leashed pets are permitted.

Reservations, fee: No reservations necessary; $5 fee per night. Open late April to mid-October.

Who to contact: Phone the Oakridge Ranger District at (503)782-2291 or write to Willamette National Forest, 46375 Highway 58, Westfir, OR 97492.

Location: From Eugene, drive 45 miles southeast on Highway 58 to the campground.

Trip note: This campground is set along the Middle Fork of the Willamette River at 2,000 feet elevation. With easy access to the river, it's a decent layover spot.

Site **71**
WEST CULTUS
on Cultus Lake, hike-in or boat-in only
DESCHUTES NATIONAL FOREST

Campsites, facilities: There are 15 tent sites that are accessible by boat or on foot. Picnic tables and fire grills are provided. Vault toilets are available. There is no piped water. Leashed pets are permitted. Boat docks, launching facilities and rentals are nearby.

Reservations, fee: No reservations necessary; no fee. Open June to late September.

Who to contact: Phone the Bend Ranger District at (503)388-5664 or write to Deschutes National Forest, 1230 NE Third, Bend, OR 97701.

Location: From Bend take Highway 46 west for 45 miles. Turn west on Forest Service Road 4635 and travel 1.5 miles to the parking area. Then travel by boat about three miles to the west shore of the lake.

Trip note: This campground is set at 4,700 feet elevation along the west shore of

Cultus Lake. It is accessible by trail or boat only. It's about three miles from the parking area to the campground. This is a good spot for waterskiing, fishing and swimming. Trails branch out from the campground and provide access to numerous small backcountry lakes.

Site 72   CULTUS LAKE
on Cultus Lake
DESCHUTES NATIONAL FOREST

Campsites, facilities: There are 54 sites for tents, trailers or motor homes up to 22 feet long. Picnic tables and fire grills are provided. Piped water and vault toilets are available. Leashed pets are permitted. Boat docks, launching facilities and rentals are nearby.

Reservations, fee: No reservations necessary; $8 fee per night. Open June to October.

Who to contact: Phone the Bend Ranger District at (503)388-5664 or write to Deschutes National Forest, 1230 NE Third, Bend, OR 97701.

Location: From Bend take Highway 46 west for 45 miles. Turn west on Forest Service Road 4635 and travel 1.5 miles to a parking area. Travel by boat to the eastern shore of the lake.

Trip note: This campground is along the east shore of Cultus Lake, not far from a resort. It is a popular spot for windsurfing, waterskiing, swimming, fishing and hiking.

Site 73   LITTLE CULTUS LAKE
on Little Cultus Lake
DESCHUTES NATIONAL FOREST

Campsites, facilities: There are ten sites for tents, trailers or motor homes up to 22 feet long. Picnic tables and fire grills are provided. Piped water and vault toilets are available. Leashed pets are permitted. Boat docks, launching facilities and rentals are nearby.

Reservations, fee: No reservations necessary; no fee. Open late May to late September.

Who to contact: Phone the Bend Ranger District at (503)388-5664 or write to Deschutes National Forest, 1230 NE Third, Bend, OR 97701.

Location: From Bend drive 45 miles west on Highway 46. Turn west on Forest Service Road 4635 and drive one-half mile to Forest Service Road 4630 and turn left. Drive 1.5 miles to Forest Service Road 600, then turn left and drive one mile to the campground.

Trip note: This campground is set along the shore of Little Cultus Lake. The campsites are not clearly marked. It's a popular spot for swimming, fishing, boating (speed restricted) and hiking. Nearby trails access numerous backcountry lakes, and the Pacific Crest Trail passes about six miles west of camp.

Site 74   CULTUS CORRAL GROUP CAMP
near Cultus Lake
DESCHUTES NATIONAL FOREST

Campsites, facilities: There are 11 sites for tents, trailers or motor homes of any length. Picnic tables and fire grills are provided. Vault toilets and a corral are available. There is no piped water. Leashed pets are permitted. Boat docks, launching facilities and rentals are nearby.

Reservations, fee: Reservations accepted; no fee. Open June to October.

Who to contact: Phone the Bend Ranger District at (503)388-5664 or write to Deschutes National Forest, 1230 NE Third, Bend, OR 97701.

Location: From Bend, take Highway 46 for 43 miles. Turn right on Forest Service Road 4630, travel one-quarter mile to the campground entrance.

Trip note: This campground is about one mile from Cultus Lake, near many trails that provide access to backcountry lakes. The Pacific Crest Trail passes about ten miles from the camp, making this a good base camp for a backpacking trip.

Site **75**
IRISH AND TAYLOR
near Pacific Crest Trail
DESCHUTES NATIONAL FOREST

Campsites, facilities: There are five tent sites. Picnic tables and fire grills are provided. Pit toilets are available. There is **no piped water**. Leashed pets are permitted. Boat docks, launching facilities and rentals are nearby.

Reservations, fee: No reservations necessary; no fee. Open mid-June to mid-September.

Who to contact: Phone the Bend Ranger District at (503)388-5664 or write to Deschutes National Forest, 1230 NE Third, Bend, OR 97701.

Location: From Bend, go 43 miles southwest on Highway 46 (Cascade Lakes Highway), then 3.5 miles southwest on Forest Service Road 4630. The camp is 6.5 miles west on Forest Service Road 600. This is a rough road—high-clearance vehicles only—but it's worth the ride.

Trip note: This remote campground is set between two small lakes, about a mile from the Pacific Crest Trail. Other nearby trails provide access into the backcountry. It's little known, beautiful and free.

Site **76**
QUINN RIVER
on Crane Prairie Reservoir
DESCHUTES NATIONAL FOREST

Campsites, facilities: There are 41 sites for tents, trailers or motor homes up to 30 feet long. Picnic tables and fire grills are provided. Piped water and vault toilets are available. Leashed pets are permitted. Boat docks are nearby.

Reservations, fee: No reservations necessary; $7 fee per night. Open late April to mid-October.

Who to contact: Phone the Bend Ranger District at (503)388-5664 or write to Deschutes National Forest, 1230 NE Third, Bend, OR 97701.

Location: From LaPine, travel 2.5 miles north on US 97, then turn west on County Road 43 and drive 11 miles to County Road 42. Continue west for nine miles. Turn north on County Road 46 (Cascade Lakes Highway) and drive four miles to the campground.

Trip note: This campground is set along the western shore of Crane Prairie Reservoir, a popular spot for anglers. A large parking lot is available for boats and trailers.

Site **77**
ROCK CREEK
on Crane Prairie Reservoir
DESCHUTES NATIONAL FOREST

Campsites, facilities: There are 32 sites for tents, trailers or motor homes up to 22 feet long. Picnic tables and fire grills are provided. Piped water, a fish cleaning station and vault toilets are available. Leashed pets are permitted. Boat docks and launching facilities are nearby.

Reservations, fee: No reservations necessary; $7 fee per night. Open mid-May to mid-October.

Who to contact: Phone the Bend Ranger District at (503)388-5664 or write to Deschutes National Forest, 1230 NE Third, Bend, OR 97701.

Location: From LaPine, travel 2.5 miles north on US 97, then turn west on County Road 43 and drive 11 miles to County Road 42 and continue west for nine miles. Turn north on County Road 46 (Cascade Lakes Highway) and drive three miles to the campground.

Trip note: This campground is set along the west shore of Crane Prairie Reservoir and is an option to Site 76.

Site 78   COW MEADOW
on Deschutes River
DESCHUTES NATIONAL FOREST

Campsites, facilities: There are 20 sites for tents for tents, trailers or motor homes up to 16 feet long. Picnic tables and fire grills are provided. Vault toilets are available. There is **no piped water.** Leashed pets are permitted. Boat docks are nearby.

Reservations, fee: No reservations necessary; no fee. Open May to mid-October.

Who to contact: Phone the Bend Ranger District at (503)388-5664 or write to Deschutes National Forest, 1230 NE Third, Bend, OR 97701.

Location: From LaPine, travel 2.5 miles north on US 97, then turn west on County Road 43 and drive 11 miles to County Road 42 and continue west for nine miles. Turn north on County Road 46 (Cascade Lakes Highway) and drive seven miles to the campground entrance road on the right. Note: The entrance road is muddy at times.

Trip note: This campground is set along the Deschutes River, near the north end of Crane Prairie Reservoir. It's a pretty spot and the price is right.

Site 79   CRANE PRAIRIE
on Crane Prairie Reservoir
DESCHUTES NATIONAL FOREST

Campsites, facilities: There are 147 sites for tents, trailers or motor homes. Picnic tables and fire grills are provided. Piped water and vault toilets are available. Leashed pets are permitted. Boat docks, launching facilities and rentals are nearby.

Reservations, fee: No reservations necessary; $8 fee per night. Open May to October.

Who to contact: Phone the Bend Ranger District at (503)388-5664 or write to Deschutes National Forest, 1230 NE Third, Bend, OR 97701.

Location: From LaPine drive 2.5 miles north on US 97, turn west on County Road 43 and drive 11 miles to County Road 42. Continue west for 5.5 miles, then turn north on Forest Service Road 4270 and drive 4.5 miles to the campground entrance.

Trip note: This campground is set along the north shore of Crane Prairie Reservoir.

Site 80   CRANE PRAIRIE RESORT
on Crane Prairie Reservoir

Campsites, facilities: There are 20 sites for trailers or motor homes. Electricity, piped water, sewer hookups and picnic tables are provided. Bottled gas, firewood, a store and ice are available. Leashed pets are permitted. Boat docks, launching facilities and rentals are nearby.

Reservations, fee: Reservations accepted; $10 fee per night; MasterCard and Visa accepted. Open late April to mid-October.

Who to contact: Phone (503)385-2173 or write to P.O. Box 322, LaPine, OR 97739.

Location: From Bend, travel 48 miles southwest on Highway 46 (Cascade Lakes Highway). Turn on Forest Service Road 4270 and drive seven miles to the resort entrance.

Trip note: This resort is set along the north shore of popular Crane Prairie Reservoir, a good spot for canoeing and fishing. No waterskiing is permitted.

Site **81**

MILE
on Deschutes River
DESCHUTES NATIONAL FOREST

Campsites, facilities: There are eight sites for tents, trailers or motor homes up to 22 feet long. Picnic tables and fire grills are provided. Vault toilets are available. There is **no piped water.** Leashed pets are permitted.

Reservations, fee: No reservations necessary; no fee. Open late May to late September.

Who to contact: Phone the Bend Ranger District at (503)388-5664 or write to Deschutes National Forest, 1230 NE Third, Bend, OR 97701.

Location: From Bend, travel 40 miles southwest on Highway 46 (Cascade Lakes Highway) to the campground.

Trip note: This quiet campground is set along the banks of the headwaters of the Deschutes River. It's a quiet, primitive spot.

Site **82**

DESCHUTES BRIDGE
on Deschutes River
DESCHUTES NATIONAL FOREST

Campsites, facilities: There are 15 sites for tents, trailers or motor homes up to 22 feet long. Picnic tables and fire grills are provided. Piped water and vault toilets are available. Leashed pets are permitted.

Reservations, fee: No reservations necessary; $6 fee per night. Open June to October.

Who to contact: Phone the Bend Ranger District at (503)388-5664 or write to Deschutes National Forest, 1230 NE Third, Bend, OR 97701.

Location: From Bend, travel 41 miles southwest on Highway 46 (Cascade Lakes Highway) to the campground.

Trip note: This wooded campground is set along the banks of the Deschutes River.

Site **83**

WEST SOUTH TWIN
on South Twin Lake
DESCHUTES NATIONAL FOREST

Campsites, facilities: There are 24 sites for trailers or motor homes up to 22 feet long. Picnic tables and fire grills are provided. Piped water and flush toilets are available. Leashed pets are permitted. Boat docks, launching facilities and rentals are nearby.

Reservations, fee: No reservations necessary; $8 fee per night. Open mid-May to mid-October.

Who to contact: Phone the Bend Ranger District at (503)388-5664 or write to Deschutes National Forest, 1230 NE Third, Bend, OR 97701.

Location: From LaPine, travel 2.5 miles northeast on US 97, then 11 miles west on County Road 43. From there, go five miles west on County Road 42 and 1.5 miles south on Forest Service Road 4260.

Trip note: This campground is set along the western shore of South Twin Lake, a major access point to the Wickiup Reservoir. It's a popular fishing spot with very good kokanee salmon fishing.

Site **84**

GULL POINT
on Wickiup Reservoir
DESCHUTES NATIONAL FOREST

Campsites, facilities: There are 80 sites for tents, trailers or motor homes up to 30 feet long. Picnic tables and fire grills are provided. Piped water, sanitary dump station and vault toilets are available. Leashed pets are permitted. Boat docks, launching facilities and rentals are nearby.

Reservations, fee: No reservations necessary; $8 fee per night. Open May to October.

Who to contact: Phone the Bend Ranger District at (503)388-5664 or write to Deschutes National Forest, 1230 NE Third, Bend, OR 97701.

Location: From LaPine, travel 2.5 miles northeast on US 97, then 11 miles west on County Road 43. Continue another 2.5 miles west on County Road 42 to Forest Service Road 4260, turn south and drive to the campground.

Trip note: This campground is set along the north shore of Wickiup Reservoir. You'll find good fishing for kokanee salmon here.

Site **85**

NORTH TWIN LAKE
on North Twin Lake
DESCHUTES NATIONAL FOREST

Campsites, facilities: There are ten sites for tents, trailers or motor homes up to 22 feet long. Picnic tables and fire grills are provided. Vault toilets are available. There is **no piped water**. Leashed pets are permitted. Boat docks, launching facilities and rentals are nearby.

Reservations, fee: No reservations necessary; no fee. Open June to late September.

Who to contact: Phone the Bend Ranger District at (503)388-5664 or write to Deschutes National Forest, 1230 NE Third, Bend, OR 97701.

Location: From LaPine, travel 2.5 miles northeast on US 97, then 11 miles west on County Road 43. Continue another five miles west on County Road 42 to Forest Service Road 4260, then turn south and drive one-half mile to the campground.

Trip note: This campground is set along the shore of North Twin Lake and is a popular weekend spot for families.

Site **86**

SHEEP BRIDGE
near Wickiup Reservoir
DESCHUTES NATIONAL FOREST

Campsites, facilities: There are 17 sites for tents, trailers or motor homes up to 22 feet long. Picnic tables and fire grills are provided. Piped water and vault toilets are available. Leashed pets are permitted.

Reservations, fee: No reservations necessary; no fee. Open May to mid-October.

Who to contact: Phone the Bend Ranger District at (503)388-5664 or write to Deschutes National Forest, 1230 NE Third, Bend, OR 97701.

Location: From LaPine, travel 2.5 miles north on US 97, then go 11 miles west of LaPine on County Road 43, and five miles west on County Road 42. The camp is one-half mile west on County Road 4260.

Trip note: This campground is set along the channel north of Wickiup Reservoir. It is in an open, treeless area that has minimal privacy and is dusty in summer.

Site **87**
SOUTH TWIN LAKE
on South Twin Lake
DESCHUTES NATIONAL FOREST

Campsites, facilities: There are 21 sites for tents, trailers or motor homes up to 22 feet long. Picnic tables and fire grills are provided. Piped water and flush toilets are available. Leashed pets are permitted. Boat docks, launching facilities and rentals are nearby.

Reservations, fee: No reservations necessary; $8 fee per night. Open May to mid-October.

Who to contact: Phone the Bend Ranger District at (503)388-5664 or write to Deschutes National Forest, 1230 NE Third, Bend, OR 97701.

Location: From LaPine, travel 2.5 miles northeast on US 97, then 11 miles west on County Road 43. Continue west on County Road 42 to Forest Service Road 4260, turn south and drive 1.5 miles to the campground.

Trip note: This campground is set along the shore of South Twin Lake, a popular spot for swimming and fishing.

Site **88**
NORTH DAVIS CREEK
near Wickiup Reservoir
DESCHUTES NATIONAL FOREST

Campsites, facilities: There are 17 sites for tents, trailers or motor homes up to 22 feet long. Picnic tables and fire grills are provided. Piped water and vault toilets are available. Leashed pets are permitted. Boat docks and launching facilities are nearby.

Reservations, fee: No reservations necessary; $5 fee per night. Open May to late October.

Who to contact: Phone the Bend Ranger District at (503)388-5664 or write to Deschutes National Forest, 1230 NE Third, Bend, OR 97701.

Location: From LaPine, travel 2.5 miles north on US 97, then 11 miles west on County Road 43. The camp is nine miles west on County Road 42 and four miles south on County Road 46.

Trip note: This campground is set along a western channel of Wickiup Reservoir. The area was logged in 1987 because of pine beetle infestation. In late summer, the reservoir level tends to drop.

Site **89**
RESERVOIR
on Wickiup Reservoir
DESCHUTES NATIONAL FOREST

Campsites, facilities: There are 28 sites for tents, trailers or motor homes up to 22 feet long. Picnic tables and fire grills are provided. Piped water and vault toilets are available. Leashed pets are permitted. Boat docks are nearby.

Reservations, fee: No reservations necessary; no fee. Open May to late October.

Who to contact: Phone the Bend Ranger District at (503)388-5664 or write to Deschutes National Forest, 1230 NE Third, Bend, OR 97701.

Location: Travel 11 miles west of LaPine on County Road 43, then nine miles west on County Road 42. The camp is nine miles south on County Road 46.

Trip note: This campground is set along the south shore of Wickiup Reservoir, where the kokanee salmon fishing is good. This camp is best in early summer, before the lake level drops. Because of pine beetle infestation, the area was logged in 1987.

Site 90
LAVA FLOW
on Davis Lake
DESCHUTES NATIONAL FOREST

Campsites, facilities: There are 12 sites for tents, trailers or motor homes up to 22 feet long. Picnic tables and fire grills are provided. Vault toilets and firewood are available. There is **no piped water.** Leashed pets are permitted. Boat docks are nearby.

Reservations, fee: No reservations necessary; no fee. Open late May to late October.

Who to contact: Phone the Crescent Ranger District at (503)433-2234 or write to Deschutes National Forest, Box 208, Crescent, OR 97733.

Location: From Crescent (a small town on US 97), travel nine miles west on County Road 61, then nine miles north on Forest Service Road 46. The camp is located two miles north on Forest Service Road 850.

Trip note: This campground is set along the east shore of Davis Lake. It is a very shallow lake that provides good duck hunting during the fall. During early summer, there is some fishing.

Site 91
EAST DAVIS LAKE
on Davis Lake
DESCHUTES NATIONAL FOREST

Campsites, facilities: There are 33 sites for tents, trailers or motor homes up to 22 feet long. Picnic tables and fire grills are provided. Piped water, firewood and vault toilets are available. Leashed pets are permitted. Boat docks and launching facilities are nearby.

Reservations, fee: No reservations necessary; $5 fee per night. Open mid-May to late October.

Who to contact: Phone the Crescent Ranger District at (503)433-2234 or write to Deschutes National Forest, Box 208, Crescent, OR 97733.

Location: From Crescent (a small town on US 97), travel nine miles west on County Road 61, then 6.5 miles north on Forest Service Road 46. The camp is 1.5 mile west on Forest Service Road 46855.

Trip note: This campground is set along the south shore of Davis Lake.

Site 92
WEST DAVIS LAKE
on Davis Lake
DESCHUTES NATIONAL FOREST

Campsites, facilities: There are 25 sites for tents, trailers or motor homes up to 22 feet long. Picnic tables and fire grills are provided. Piped water, firewood and vault toilets are available. Leashed pets are permitted. Boat docks are nearby.

Reservations, fee: No reservations necessary; $5 fee per night. Open mid-May to late October.

Who to contact: Phone the Crescent Ranger District at (503)433-2234 or write to Deschutes National Forest, Box 208, Crescent Lake, OR 97425.

Location: From Crescent (a small town on US 97),, drive nine miles west on County Road 61, then three miles north on Forest Service Road 46. The camp is four miles on Forest Service Road 4660.

Trip note: This campground is set along the south shore of Davis Lake.

Site **93**
CRESCENT CREEK
on Crescent Creek
DESCHUTES NATIONAL FOREST

Campsites, facilities: There are ten sites for tents, trailers or motor homes up to 22
feet long. Picnic tables and fire grills are provided. Piped water, firewood and
vault toilets are available. Leashed pets are permitted.

Reservations, fee: No reservations necessary; $4 fee per night. Open May to late
October.

Who to contact: Phone the Crescent Ranger District at (503)433-2234 or write to
Deschutes National Forest, Box 208, Crescent, OR 97733.

Location: From Crescent (a small town on US 97), travel eight miles west on County
Road 61 to the campground.

Trip note: This is one of the Cascade's classic hidden campgrounds. It is set along
the banks of Crescent Creek at 4,500 feet elevation.

Site **94**
WICKIUP BUTTE
on Wickiup Reservoir
DESCHUTES NATIONAL FOREST

Campsites, facilities: There are five sites for tents, trailers or motor homes up to 22
feet long. Picnic tables and fire grills are provided. Piped water and vault toilets
are available. Leashed pets are permitted. Boat docks and launching facilities
are nearby.

Reservations, fee: No reservations necessary; no fee. Open May to late October.

Who to contact: Phone the Bend Ranger District at (503)388-5664 or write to
Deschutes National Forest, 1230 NE Third, LaPine 97701, OR 97739.

Location: From LaPine, go 2.5 miles northeast on US 97, then seven miles west on
County Road 43. The camp is located another seven miles west on Forest
Service Road 44.

Trip note: This campground is set along the southeast shore of Wickiup Reservoir.
It is one of the better camps on the lake because of the logging in other areas.
Kokanee salmon fishing is good during early summer.

Site **95**
BULL BEND
on Deschutes River
DESCHUTES NATIONAL FOREST

Campsites, facilities: There are four sites for tents, trailers or motor homes. Picnic
tables and fire grills are provided. Vault toilets are available. There is **no piped
water.** Pets are permitted.

Reservations, fee: No reservations necessary; no fee. Open April to October.

Who to contact: Phone the Bend Ranger District at (503)388-5664 or write to
Deschutes National Forest, 1230 NE Third Street, Bend, OR 97701.

Location: From LaPine, travel 2.5 miles northeast on US 97, then eight miles west
on County Road 43. The camp is 1.5 miles southwest on Forest Service Road
4370.

Trip note: This campground is set on the inside of a major bend in the Deschutes
River. A mini float trip can be made by starting at the upstream end of camp,
floating around the bend and then taking out at the downstream end of camp.

Site 96

FALL RIVER
on Fall River
DESCHUTES NATIONAL FOREST

Campsites, facilities: There are 12 sites for tents, trailers or motor homes up to 22 feet long. Picnic tables and fire grills are provided. Vault toilets are available. There is **no piped water.** Leashed pets are permitted.

Reservations, fee: No reservations necessary; no fee. Open June to mid-October.

Who to contact: Phone the Bend Ranger District at (503)388-5664 or write to Deschutes National Forest, 1230 NE Third, Bend, OR 97701.

Location: From Bend, travel 16.5 miles south on US 97, then 15 miles southwest on County Road 42 to the campground.

Trip note: This campground is set along Fall River. Fishing is restricted to artificials only. Check the regulations for other restrictions.

Site 97

PRINGLE FALLS
on Deschutes River
DESCHUTES NATIONAL FOREST

Campsites, facilities: There are seven sites for tents, trailers or motor homes up to 22 feet long. Picnic tables and fire grills are provided. Vault toilets are available. There is **no piped water.** Leashed pets are permitted.

Reservations, fee: No reservations necessary; no fee. Open April to October.

Who to contact: Phone the Bend Ranger District at (503)388-5664 or write to Deschutes National Forest, 1230 NE Third, Bend, OR 97701.

Location: From LaPine, travel 2.5 miles northeast on US 97, then seven miles west on County Road 43. The camp is about one-half mile northeast on Forest Service Road 4360.

Trip note: This campground is set along the Deschutes River fairly close to Pringle Falls. It is a popular canoe launching point.

Site 98

LAPINE STATE PARK
on Deschutes River

Campsites, facilities: There are 145 sites with full or partial hookups for trailers or motor homes of any length. Picnic tables are provided. Flush toilets, sanitary services, showers, firewood and a laundromat are available. Some facilities are wheelchair accessible. Leashed pets are permitted.

Reservations, fee: No reservations necessary; $9-11 in the summer, $6-8 off-season. Open mid-April to late October.

Who to contact: Phone (503)536-2428 or write to P.O. Box 5309, Bend, OR 97708.

Location: From LaPine, travel eight miles north on US 97, then go three miles west on the entrance road to the park.

Trip note: This state park is set along the banks of the Deschutes River. Trout fishing and canoeing are very good.

Site 99

SWAMP WELLS HORSE CAMP
near Arnold Ice Caves
DESCHUTES NATIONAL FOREST

Campsites, facilities: There are five primitive sites for tents, trailers or motor homes up to 22 feet long. Picnic tables and fire grills are provided. Firewood and vault toilets are available. There is **no piped water.** Leashed pets are permitted.

Reservations, fee: No reservations necessary; no fee. Open April to late November.

Who to contact: Phone the Fort Rock Ranger District at (503)388-5674 or write to Deschutes National Forest, 1230 NE Third Street, Bend, OR 97701.

Location: From Bend, travel 1.5 miles south on US 97, then six miles east on Forest Service Road 18. The camp is five miles south on Forest Service Road 1810, then three miles southeast on 1816. You'll be traveling on a dirt road, but a well-marked one.

Trip note: After looking at the zone map, this campground may appear to be quite remote, but it is actually in an area that has been heavily logged. It is a good place for horseback riding and the trails that go south re-enter the forested areas. Nearby are the Arnold Ice Caves, a system of lava tubes that are fun to explore. A Forest Service map details trail options.

Site 100   BIG RIVER
on Deschutes River
DESCHUTES NATIONAL FOREST

Campsites, facilities: There are five tent sites and eight sites for tents, trailers or motor homes up to 22 feet long. Picnic tables and fire grills are provided. Piped water and vault toilets are available. Leashed pets are permitted. Boat docks and launching facilities are nearby.

Reservations, fee: No reservations necessary; no fee. Open April to October.

Who to contact: Phone the Bend Ranger District at (503)388-5664 or write to Deschutes National Forest, 1230 NE Third, Bend, OR 97701.

Location: From Bend, go 16.5 miles south on US 97, then five miles southwest on County Road 42.

Trip note: This is a nice spot along the banks of the Deschutes River in a nice location. Rafting, fishing and boating using motors are permitted. Access is easy.

Site 101   ALLEN'S RIVERVIEW TRAILER PARK
on Little Deschutes River

Campsites, facilities: There are 20 sites for tents, trailers or motor homes of any length. Electricity, cable TV, piped water, sewer hookups and picnic tables are provided. Flush toilets, bottled gas, showers, firewood, a recreation hall and a laundromat are available. Leashed pets are permitted.

Reservations, fee: Reservations accepted; $7-12 fee per night. Open all year.

Who to contact: Phone (503)536-2382 or write to 52731 Huntington Road, LaPine, OR 97739.

Location: Travel 2.5 miles north of LaPine on US 97, then one mile west at Wickiup Junction. The camp is one mile north on Huntington Road.

Trip note: This campground is set along the bank of the Little Deschutes River. It's missed by a lot of highway travelers; they just plain don't know about it.

Site 102   HIGHLANDER MOTEL & TRAILER PARK
near Little Deschutes River

Campsites, facilities: There are 20 drive-through sites for trailers or motor homes up to 35 feet long. Electricity, piped water and sewer hookups are provided. Flush toilets, bottled gas, sanitary services, showers, a store, a cafe and ice are available. A laundromat is located within one mile. Pets and motorbikes are permitted.

Reservations, fee: Reservations accepted; $6 fee per night; MasterCard and Visa accepted. Open all year.

Who to contact: Phone (503)536-2131 or write to P.O. Box 322, LaPine, OR 97739.
Location: This campground is located in LaPine at the north edge of town.
Trip note: This campground is near the Little Deschutes River. A golf course and tennis courts are nearby.

Site **103**   **FAR-E-NUF RV PARK**
on Little Deschutes River

Campsites, facilities: There are two tent sites and 18 drive-through sites for trailers or motor homes of any length. Electricity, piped water, cable TV hookups, sewer hookups and picnic tables are provided. Flush toilets, sanitary services, showers, firewood, a laundromat and ice are available. Bottled gas, a store and a cafe are within one mile. Pets and motorbikes are permitted.
Reservations, fee: Reservations accepted; $8-10 fee per night. Open April to mid-October.
Who to contact: Phone (503)536-2265 or write to 52158 Elderberry Lane, LaPine, OR 97739.
Location: From LaPine, go 2.5 miles north on US 97, then 2.5 miles west at Wickiup Junction. The camp is one-half mile south on Pine Forest and 400 yards east on Wright Avenue.
Trip note: So you think you've come far enough, eh? If you want a spot in a privately-run motor home park near the bank of the Little Deschutes River, you've found it.

Site **104**   **McKAY CROSSING**
on Paulina Creek
DESCHUTES NATIONAL FOREST

Campsites, facilities: There are ten sites for tents, trailers or motor homes up to 22 feet long. Picnic tables and fire grills are provided. Vault toilets are available. There is **no piped water.** Leashed pets are permitted.
Reservations, fee: No reservations necessary; no fee. Open June to late October.
Who to contact: Phone the Fort Rock Ranger District at (503)388-5674 or write to Deschutes National Forest, 1230 NE Third Street, Bend, OR 97701.
Location: From LaPine, travel five miles north on US 97, then three miles southeast on County Road 21. The camp is two miles east on Forest Service Road 2120.
Trip note: This campground is set along the bank of Paulina Creek. A nearby trail travels east for six miles to Paulina Lake (also reachable by car, see Site 105).

Site **105**   **PAULINA LAKE**
on Paulina Lake
DESCHUTES NATIONAL FOREST

Campsites, facilities: There are 69 sites for trailers or motor homes up to 30 feet long. Picnic tables and fire grills are provided. Piped water, flush toilets, showers and a laundromat are located within five miles. **No piped water** is available. Leashed pets are permitted. Boat docks, launching facilities and rentals are nearby.
Reservations, fee: No reservations necessary; $8 fee per night. Open late May to late October.
Who to contact: Phone the Fort Rock Ranger District at (503)388-5674 or write to Deschutes National Forest, 1230 NE Third Street, Bend, OR 97701.
Location: Travel five miles north of LaPine on US 97, then go 13 miles east on County Road 21.

Trip note: This campground is set along the south shore of Paulina Lake at 6,300 feet elevation. The recreation options here include boating, sailing, fishing and hiking. Nearby trails provide access to the remains of volcanic activity, including craters and obsidian flows.

Site **106**   **CHIEF PAULINA HORSE CAMP**
on Paulina Lake
DESCHUTES NATIONAL FOREST

Campsites, facilities: There are 13 sites for tents, trailers or motor homes up to 30 feet long. Picnic tables and fire grills are provided. Piped water and vault toilets are available. Leashed pets are permitted. Boat docks and rentals are nearby.

Reservations, fee: Reservations required; fee depends on the size of the group. Open late May to late October.

Who to contact: Phone the Fort Rock Ranger District at (503)388-5674 or write to Deschutes National Forest, 1230 NE Third Street, Bend, OR 97701.

Location: From LaPine, travel five miles north on US 97, then go 15 miles east on County Road 21.

Trip note: This campground is set near the south shore of Paulina Lake. Horse trails and a vista point are nearby. See the trip note for Site 105 for additional recreation information.

Site **107**   **LITTLE CRATER**
on Paulina Lake
DESCHUTES NATIONAL FOREST

Campsites, facilities: There are 50 sites for tents, trailers or motor homes up to 30 feet long. Picnic tables and fire grills are provided. Piped water and vault toilets are available. Leashed pets are permitted. Boat docks, launching facilities and rentals are available nearby.

Reservations, fee: No reservations necessary; $8 fee per night. Open late May to late October.

Who to contact: Phone the Fort Rock Ranger District at (503)386-5674 or write to Deschutes National Forest, 1230 NE Third Street, Bend, OR 97701.

Location: From LaPine, travel five miles north on US 97, then 15 miles east on County Road 21.

Trip note: This campground is set along the east shore of Paulina Lake near Newberry Crater. See the trip note for Site 105.

Site **108**   **NORTH COVE**
on Paulina Lake, hike-in only
DESCHUTES NATIONAL FOREST

Campsites, facilities: There are six tent sites. **No piped water** is available. Picnic tables and fire grills are provided. Showers and a laundromat are located within five miles. Leashed pets are permitted. Boat docks, launching facilities and rentals are nearby.

Reservations, fee: No reservations necessary; no fee. Open mid-May to late October.

Who to contact: Phone the Fort Rock Ranger District at (503)388-5674 or write to Deschutes National Forest, 1230 NE Third Street, Bend, OR 97701.

Location: Go five miles north of LaPine on US 97, then go 13 miles east on County Road 21. Park and hike 1.5 miles to campground on north shore of Paulina Lake.

Trip note: See the trip note for Site 105 for additional recreation information.

Site **109**
WARM SPRINGS
on Paulina Lake, walk-in only
DESCHUTES NATIONAL FOREST

Campsites, facilities: There are five tent sites. Picnic tables are provided. Firewood is available. A laundromat is located within five miles. **No piped water** is available. Pets are permitted. Boat docks, launching facilities and rentals are nearby.

Reservations, fee: No reservations necessary; no fee. Open mid-May to late October.

Who to contact: Phone the Fort Rock Ranger District at (503)388-5674 or write to Deschutes National Forest, 1230 NE Third Street, Bend, OR 97701.

Location: From LaPine, travel five miles north on US 97, then 16 miles east on County Road 21. Park and hike one-half mile to the campground on the northeast shore of Paulina Lake.

Trip note: See the trip note for Site 105 for additional recreation information about Paulina Lake.

Site **110**
CINDER HILL
on East Lake
DESCHUTES NATIONAL FOREST

Campsites, facilities: There are 110 sites for tents, trailers or motor homes up to 30 feet long. Picnic tables and fire grills are provided. Piped water and vault toilets are available. Leashed pets are permitted. Boat docks, launching facilities and rentals are nearby.

Reservations, fee: No reservations necessary; $8 fee per night. Open late May to late October.

Who to contact: Phone the Fort Rock Ranger District at (503)388-5674 or write to Deschutes National Forest, 1230 NE Third Street, Bend, OR 97701.

Location: From LaPine, travel five miles north on US 97, then 18 miles east on County Road 21.

Trip note: This campground is set along the northeast shore of East Lake at an elevation of 6,400 feet. Boating, fishing and hiking are among the recreation options here.

Site **111**
EAST LAKE
on East Lake
DESCHUTES NATIONAL FOREST

Campsites, facilities: There are 29 sites for tents, trailers or motor homes up to 30 feet long. Picnic tables and fire grills are provided. Piped water and vault toilets are available. Leashed pets are permitted. Boat docks, launching facilities and rentals are nearby.

Reservations, fee: No reservations necessary; $8 fee per night. Open late May to late October.

Who to contact: Phone the Fort Rock Ranger District at (503)388-5674 or write to Deschutes National Forest, 1230 NE Third Street, Bend, OR 97701.

Location: From LaPine, travel five miles north on US 97, then 17 miles east on County Road 21.

Trip note: This campground is set along the south shore of East Lake. Boating and fishing are popular here, and hiking trails provide access to signs of former volcanic activity in the area.

Site **112**   **HOT SPRINGS**
                                   on East Lake
                       DESCHUTES NATIONAL FOREST

Campsites, facilities: There are 42 sites for tents, trailers or motor homes up to 30
   feet long. Picnic tables and fire grills are provided. Piped water, firewood and
   vault toilets are available. Leashed pets are permitted. Boat docks, launching
   facilities and rentals are nearby.
Reservations, fee: No reservations necessary; $8 fee per night. Open late May to
   late October.
Who to contact: Phone the Fort Rock Ranger District at (503)388-5674 or write to
   Deschutes National Forest, 1230 NE Third Street, Bend, OR 97701.
Location: Drive five miles north of LaPine on US 97, then 17 one-half miles east
   on County Road 21.
Trip note: This campground is set along the south shore of East Lake. See the trip
   note for Site 111 for additional recreation information.

Site **113**   **EAST LAKE RESORT & RV PARK**
                                   on East Lake

Campsites, facilities: There are ten tent sites and 38 drive-through sites for trailers
   or motor homes of any length. Electricity, piped water, sewer hookups and
   picnic tables are provided. Flush toilets, bottled gas, sanitary services, showers,
   firewood, a store, a cafe, a laundromat, ice and a playground are available. Pets
   and motorbikes are permitted. Boat launching facilities and rentals are nearby.
Reservations, fee: Reservations accepted; $10 fee per night. Open mid-May to
   mid-October.
Who to contact: Phone (503)536-2230 or write to P.O. Box 95, LaPine, OR 97739.
Location: From LaPine, travel six miles north on US 97, then 18 miles east on East
   Lake-Paulina Lake Road.
Trip note: This resort is set along the east shore of East Lake.

Site **114**   **CHINA HAT**
                       DESCHUTES NATIONAL FOREST

Campsites, facilities: There are 14 sites for tents, trailers or motor homes up to 30
   feet long. Picnic tables and fire grills are provided. Vault toilets are available.
   There is **no piped water.** Leashed pets are permitted.
Reservations, fee: No reservations necessary; no fee. Open May to late October.
Who to contact: Phone the Fort Rock Ranger District at (503)388-5674 or write to
   Deschutes National Forest, 1230 NE Third Street, Bend, OR 97701.
Location: From LaPine, drive east on Forest Service Road 22 for about 30 miles,
   then north for six miles on Forest Service Road 18.
Trip note: This remote campground is set at 5,100 feet elevation in a rugged,
   primitive setting. Hunters use it as a base camp in the fall.

Site **115**   **CABIN LAKE**
                       DESCHUTES NATIONAL FOREST

Campsites, facilities: There are 14 sites for tents, trailers or motor homes up to 30
   feet long. Picnic tables and fire grills are provided. Vault toilets are available.
   There is **no piped water.** Leashed pets are permitted.
Reservations, fee: No reservations necessary; no fee. Open mid-May to late October.
Who to contact: Phone the Fort Rock Ranger District at (503)388-5674 or write to

Deschutes National Forest, 1230 NE Third Street, Bend, OR 97701.

Location: From LaPine, drive about 30 miles east on Forest Service Road 22, then south on Forest Service Road 18 for six miles.

Trip note: This remote campground is set at 4,500 feet elevation. It's adjacent to the campground is an 80-year-old bird blind—a great place to watch birds.

Site 116
PRAIRIE
on Paulina Creek
DESCHUTES NATIONAL FOREST

Campsites, facilities: There are 14 sites for tents, trailers or motor homes up to 30 feet long. Picnic tables and fire grills are provided. Piped water, firewood and vault toilets are available. Leashed pets are permitted.

Reservations, fee: No reservations necessary; $5 fee per night. Open mid-May through October.

Who to contact: Phone the Fort Rock Ranger District at (503)388-5674 or write Deschutes National Forest, 1230 NE Third Street, Bend, OR 97701.

Location: From LaPine, travel five miles north on US 97, then three miles southeast on County Road 21 to the campground.

Trip note: This camp is set along the banks of Paulina Creek. Nearby is the trailhead for the Peter Skene Ogden National Recreation Trail.

Site 117
CORRAL SPRING
WINEMA NATIONAL FOREST

Campsites, facilities: There are seven sites for tents, trailers or motor homes up to 22 feet long. Picnic tables and fire grills are provided. Firewood and vault toilets are available. There is **no piped water.** A store, a cafe, a laundromat and ice are located within five miles. Leashed pets are permitted.

Reservations, fee: No reservations necessary; no fee. Open mid-May to late October.

Who to contact: Phone the Chemult Ranger Station at (503)365-2229 or write to Winema National Forest, P.O. Box 150, Chemult, OR 97731.

Location: From Chemult, travel 2.5 miles north on US 97, then go two miles west on Forest Service Road 9774.

Trip note: This campground is set next to Corral Spring. There's not much out here, but it's just what some of you people cruising US 97 will want.

Site 118
DIGIT POINT
on Miller Lake
WINEMA NATIONAL FOREST

Campsites, facilities: There are 64 sites for tents, trailers or motor homes up to 30 feet long. Picnic tables and fire grills are provided. Piped water, firewood, a sanitary disposal station and flush toilets are available. Leashed pets are permitted. Boat docks and launching facilities are nearby.

Reservations, fee: No reservations necessary; $5 fee per night. Open mid-June to October.

Who to contact: Phone the Chemult Ranger Station at (503)365-2229 or write to Winema National Forest, P.O. Box 150, Chemult, OR 97731.

Location: From Chemult, travel one mile north on US 97, then 12 miles west on Forest Service Road 9772.

Trip note: This campground is set along the shore of Miller Lake, a popular spot for boating, fishing, swimming and waterskiing. Nearby trails provide access to backcountry lakes and the Pacific Crest Trail passes two miles from camp.

CRATER LAKE

♦

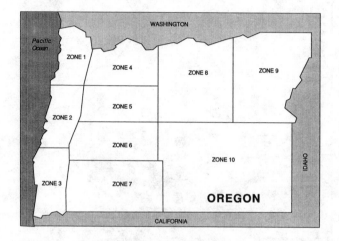

SOME HIGHLIGHTS

96 CAMPGROUNDS

Crater Lake National Park

Pacific Crest Trail

South Umpqua River

Umpqua National Forest

Rogue River

Rogue River National Forest

Williamson River

Upper Klamath Lake

Winema National Forest

Fremont National Forest

Sky Lakes Wilderness

Mountain Lakes Wilderness

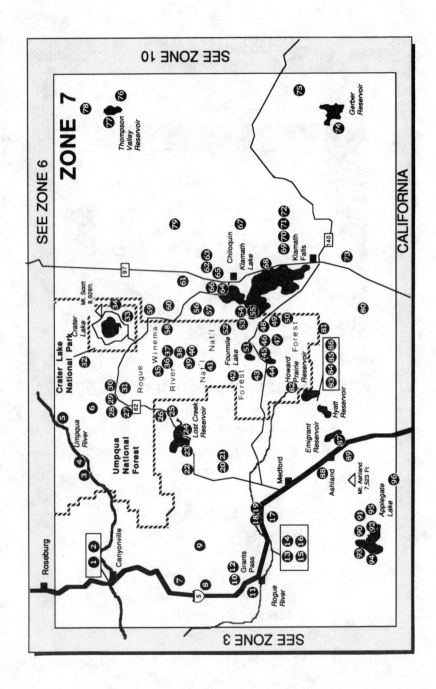

Site **1**

STANTON PARK
on South Umpqua River

Campsites, facilities: There are 20 tent sites and 20 sites for trailers or motor homes up to 30 feet long. Electricity, piped water, sewer hookups and picnic tables are provided. Flush toilets, showers and a playground are available. Bottled gas, sanitary disposal services, a store, a cafe, a laundromat and ice are located within one mile. Pets and motorbikes are permitted. A boat launch is nearby.

Reservations, fee: No reservations necessary; $7-9 fee per night. Open all year.

Who to contact: Phone (503)839-4483 or write to Canyonville, OR 97417.

Location: Take exit 99 off Interstate 5 in Canyonville (follow the sign), then drive one mile north on the frontage road to the campground.

Trip note: This campground is set along the banks of the South Umpqua River. It is an all-season spot with a good beach for swimming in the summer, good steelhead fishing in the winter and wild grape picking in the fall.

Site **2**

SURPRISE VALLEY MOBILE VILLAGE
on South Umpqua River

Campsites, facilities: There are 15 tent sites and 25 drive-through sites for trailers or motor homes of any length. Electricity, piped water, sewer hookups and picnic tables are provided. Flush toilets, showers and a laundromat are available. Leashed pets are permitted.

Reservations, fee: No reservations necessary; $10 fee per night. Open all year.

Who to contact: Phone (503)839-8181 or write to P.O. Box 909, Canyonville, OR 97417.

Location: From Canyonville, go three miles north on Interstate 5 to exit 102, then one mile east on Gazley Road.

Trip note: This motor home park is set near the South Umpqua River. Nearby recreation options include bike paths. For a more remote setting, Sites 3-5 are the answer.

Site **3**

DUMONT CREEK
on South Umpqua River
UMPQUA NATIONAL FOREST

Campsites, facilities: There are five sites for tents, trailers or motor homes up to 16 feet long. Picnic tables and fire grills are provided. Vault toilets are available. There is **no piped water.** Leashed pets are permitted.

Reservations, fee: No reservations necessary; no fee. Open late May to late October.

Who to contact: Phone the Tiller Ranger District at (503)825-3201 or write to Umpqua National Forest, 28712 Tiller Trail Highway, Tiller, OR 97484.

Location: Go 23 miles north of Shady Cove on Highway 227, then six miles northeast on County Road 46. The camp is 5.5 miles northeast on Forest Service Road 28.

Trip note: This campground is set along the banks of the South Umpqua River. It's quiet, primitive and remote.

Site **4**

BOULDER CREEK
on South Umpqua River
UMPQUA NATIONAL FOREST

Campsites, facilities: There are eight sites for tents, trailers or motor homes up to 15 feet long. Picnic tables and fire grills are provided. Vault toilets are available.

There is **no piped water.** Leashed pets are permitted.

Reservations, fee: No reservations necessary; no fee. Open late May to late October.

Who to contact: Phone the Tiller Ranger District at (503)825-3201 or write to Umpqua National Forest, 27812 Tiller Trail Highway, Tiller, OR 97484.

Location: From Shady Cove, go 23 miles north on Highway 227, turn east on County Road 46 for six miles. The camp is seven miles northeast on Forest Service Road 28.

Trip note: This campground is set along the banks of the South Umpqua River.

Site **5**
CAMP COMFORT
on the South Fork of Umpqua River
UMPQUA NATIONAL FOREST

Campsites, facilities: There are eight sites for tents, trailers or motor homes up to 15 feet long. Picnic tables and fire grills are provided. Vault toilets are available. There is **no piped water.** Leashed pets are permitted.

Reservations, fee: No reservations necessary; no fee. Open late May to late October.

Who to contact: Phone the Tiller Ranger District at (503)825-3201 or write to Umpqua National Forest, 27812 Tiller Trail Highway, Tiller, OR 97484.

Location: From Shady Cove, travel 23 miles north on Highway 227, turn east on County Road 46 for six miles. The camp is seven miles northeast on Forest Service Road 28.

Trip note: This campground is set along the banks of the South Umpqua River, deep in the Umpqua National Forest. Trailheads providing access to the Rogue-Umpqua Divide Wilderness can be found at the ends of Forest Service roads west of the camp.

Site **6**
COVER
on Jackson Creek
UMPQUA NATIONAL FOREST

Campsites, facilities: There are seven sites for tents, trailers or motor homes up to 16 feet long. Picnic tables and fire grills are provided. Vault toilets are available. There is **no piped water.** Leashed pets are permitted.

Reservations, fee: No reservations necessary; no fee. Open late May to late October.

Who to contact: Phone the Tiller Ranger District at (503)825-3201 or write to Umpqua National Forest, 27812 Tiller Trail Highway, Tiller, OR 97484.

Location: From Canyonville, drive east on Highway 227 to Tiller. From Tiller, go east on Highway 227 for 300 yards, then northeast on County Road 46 for six miles. The camp is 12 miles east on Forest Service Road 29.

Trip note: This campground is set along the banks of Jackson Creek. If you want quiet, this is the right place. Just about nobody knows about this one.

Site **7**
MEADOW WOOD RV RESORT & CAMPGROUND
in Glendale

Campsites, facilities: There are 20 tent sites and 63 drive-through sites for trailers or motor homes of any length. Electricity, piped water and picnic tables are provided. Flush toilets, bottled gas, sanitary disposal services, showers, firewood, a recreation hall, a store, a laundromat, ice, a playground and a swimming pool are available. Pets and motorbikes are permitted.

Reservations, fee: Reservations accepted; $10-12 fee per night; MasterCard and Visa accepted. Open March to late October.

Who to contact: Phone (503)832-2959 or write to 862 Autumn Lane, Glendale, OR

97442.

Location: Southbound, take exit 86 off Interstate 5 in Glendale. Drive three miles south on the frontage road and about 400 yards east on Barton Road. The camp is one mile south. Northbound, take exit 83 off Interstate 5 in Glendale and follow the same directions.

Trip note: This is a good option for motor home campers looking for a spot along Interstate 5. All the amenities are available.

Site **8**
JOE CREEK WATERFALL RV PARK
on Joe Creek

Campsites, facilities: There are 20 tent sites and 20 drive-through sites for trailers or motor homes of any length. Electricity, piped water, sewer hookups and picnic tables are provided. Flush toilets, bottled gas, sanitary disposal services, showers, firewood, a recreation hall, a store, a cafe, a laundromat and ice are available. Pets and motorbikes are permitted. Discounts are given to Good Sam members.

Reservations, fee: Reservations accepted; $7-15 fee per night; MasterCard and Visa accepted. Open all year.

Who to contact: Phone (503)474-0250 or write to 699 Jump Off Joe Creek Road, Grants Pass, OR 97526.

Location: Go ten miles north on Interstate 5 from Grants Pass. Take exit 66 and go 400 yards north on Jump Off Joe Creek Road. Follow the signs to the campground.

Trip note: This wooded campground is set along Joe Creek. Hiking trails and bike paths are nearby. You are just far enough out of Grants Pass to feel apart from civilization.

Site **9**
ELDERBERRY FLAT
on Evans Creek

Campsites, facilities: There are ten primitive tent sites. Picnic tables and fire grills are provided. Firewood and vault toilets are available. There is **no piped water.** Leashed pets are permitted. Toilets are wheelchair accessible.

Reservations, fee: No reservations necessary; no fee. Open late May to late October.

Who to contact: Phone (503)770-2200 or write to Bureau of Land Management, 3040 Biddle Road, Medford, OR 97501.

Location: From Gold Hill, take Highway 234 northeast. Turn on Meadows and go 12 miles northwest. From there, go eight miles north on Fork Evans Road to the campground.

Trip note: This campground is set along the banks of Evans Creek. Virtually unknown, it's only about a 30-minute drive from Interstate 5.

Site **10**
GRANTS PASS OVERNITERS
near Grants Pass

Campsites, facilities: There are 40 tent sites and 63 drive-through sites for trailers or motor homes of any length. Electricity, piped water, sewer hookups and picnic tables are provided. Flush toilets, bottled gas, showers, a laundromat, ice and a swimming pool are available. A store is located within one mile. Pets and motorbikes are permitted.

Reservations, fee: Reservations accepted; $12 fee per night. Open all year.

Who to contact: Phone (503)479-7289 or write to 5941 Highland, Grants Pass, OR 97526.

Location: From Grants Pass, go three miles north on Interstate 5 to exit 61E, then go north on the frontage road to the park.

Trip note: This wooded park is set in a rural area just outside Grants Pass. There are several other campgrounds in the area.

Site 11   BEND O' THE RIVER RV PARK
on Rogue River

Campsites, facilities: There are five tent sites and 20 drive-through sites for trailers or motor homes of any length. Electricity, piped water, sewer hookups and picnic tables are provided. Flush toilets, sanitary disposal services, showers, firewood, a store, a cafe, a laundromat and ice are available. Pets and motorbikes are permitted.

Reservations, fee: Reservations accepted; $6-9 fee per night. Open all year.

Who to contact: Phone (503)479-2547 or write to 7501 Lower River Road, Grants Pass, OR 97526.

Location: Take exit 58 off Interstate 5 in Grants Pass, then go south on 6th Street to G Street. The park is located seven miles west on Upper River Road.

Trip note: This campground is set along the banks of the Rogue River. It's a pretty spot far enough out of Grants Pass to have its own unique feel.

Site 12   ROGUE VALLEY OVERNITERS
near Rogue River

Campsites, facilities: There are two tent sites and 26 drive-through sites for trailers or motor homes of any length. Electricity, piped water and sewer hookups are provided. Flush toilets, sanitary disposal services, showers and a laundromat are available. Bottled gas, a store, a cafe and ice are available within one mile. Pets and motorbikes are permitted.

Reservations, fee: Reservations accepted; $11-16 fee per night. Open all year.

Who to contact: Phone (503)479-2208 or write to 1806 Northwest 6th Street, Grants Pass, OR 97526.

Location: Take exit 58 off Interstate 5 in Grants Pass, then follow 6th Street south for about 400 yards.

Trip note: This park is just off the freeway in Grants Pass, the jump-off point for trips down the Rogue River. The summer heat in this part of Oregon can surprise visitors in late June and early July.

Site 13   CIRCLE W CAMPGROUND
on Rogue River

Campsites, facilities: There are seven tent sites and 25 drive-through sites for trailers or motor homes of any length. Electricity, piped water, sewer hookups and picnic tables are provided. Flush toilets, sanitary disposal services, showers, a store, a laundromat, ice and a playground are available. Bottled gas and a cafe are located within one mile. Leashed pets are permitted. Boat docks are nearby.

Reservations, fee: Reservations accepted; $10-13.50 fee per night. Open mid-March to mid-November.

Who to contact: Phone (503)582-1686 or write to 8110 Rogue River Highway, Grants Pass, OR 97527.

Location: Take the Rogue River exit (exit 48) off Interstate 5, then go one mile west on Highway 99.

Trip note: This campground is set along the Rogue River. Nearby options include chartered boat trips down the Rogue River, a golf course and tennis courts.

Site 14   HAVE A NICE DAY CAMPGROUND
on Rogue River

Campsites, facilities: There are 16 tent sites and 30 drive-through sites for trailers or motor homes of any length. Electricity, piped water, sewer hookups and picnic tables are provided. Flush toilets, bottled gas, sanitary disposal services, showers, a laundromat, ice and a playground are available. A store and a cafe are located within one mile. Pets and motorbikes are permitted. Boat docks and launching facilities are nearby.

Reservations, fee: Reservations accepted; $12 fee per night. Open all year with limited winter facilities.

Who to contact: Phone (503)582-1421 or write to 7275 Rogue River Highway, Grants Pass, OR 97527.

Location: Take exit 48 off Interstate 5, cross the river and travel 1.5 miles west on Highway 99.

Trip note: This campground is set along the Rogue River.

Site 15   LESCLARE RV PARK & CAMPGROUND
on Rogue River

Campsites, facilities: There are ten tent sites and 38 sites for trailers or motor homes of any length. Electricity, piped water, sewer hookups and picnic tables are provided. Flush toilets, sanitary disposal services, showers, a store, a laundromat and ice are available. A cafe is located within one mile. Leashed pets are permitted.

Reservations, fee: Reservations accepted; $11 fee per night; MasterCard and Visa accepted. Open all year.

Who to contact: Phone (503)479-0046 or write to 2956 Rogue River Highway, Grants Pass, OR 97527.

Location: In Grants Pass, go south on 6th Street to Highway 99, then go two miles southeast on Highway 99.

Trip note: This wooded campground is set along the Rogue River. Jet boats offer chartered trips down the Rogue. A golf course is nearby.

Site 16   RIVERFRONT TRAILER PARK
on Rogue River

Campsites, facilities: There are two tent sites and 20 sites for trailers or motor homes of any length. Electricity, piped water, sewer hookups and picnic tables are provided. Flush toilets, sanitary disposal services, showers, a laundromat and ice are available. Bottled gas, a store and a cafe are located within one mile. Pets and motorbikes are permitted. Boat docks and launching facilities are nearby.

Reservations, fee: Reservations accepted; $10-13 fee per night. Open all year.

Who to contact: Phone (503)582-0985 or write to 7060 Rogue River, Grants Pass, OR 97527.

Location: From Rogue River, take Highway 99 two miles west to the park.

Trip note: This campground is set along the Rogue River, near the same recreation opportunities as Site 15.

Site 17   VALLEY OF THE ROGUE STATE PARK
on Rogue River

Campsites, facilities: There are 21 sites for tents or self-contained motor homes and

152 sites with full or partial hookups for trailers or motor homes of any length. Picnic tables and fire grills are provided. Flush toilets, sanitary disposal services, showers, firewood, a laundromat, a meeting hall and group campsites are available. A restaurant is nearby. Some facilities are wheelchair accessible. Leashed pets are permitted. Boat launching facilities are nearby.

Reservations, fee: No reservations necessary; $9-11 in summer, $6-8 off-season. Open all year with limited winter facilities.

Who to contact: Phone (503)582-1118 or write to 3792 North River Road, Gold Hill, OR 97525.

Location: From Grants Pass, travel 12 miles east on Interstate 5 to the turnoff for the park.

Trip note: This state park is set along the banks of the Rogue River. Recreation options include swimming and boating. It's a popular spot, often filled to near capacity during summer months.

Site 18   KOA GOLD'N ROGUE
on Rogue River

Campsites, facilities: There are 30 tent sites and 45 drive-through sites for trailers or motor homes of any length. Electricity, piped water, sewer hookups and picnic tables are provided. Flush toilets, bottled gas, sanitary disposal services, showers, firewood, a recreation hall, a store, a laundromat, ice, a playground and a swimming pool are available. A cafe is located within one mile. Pets and motorbikes are permitted. Boat launching facilities are nearby.

Reservations, fee: Reservations accepted; $14.50-17.50 fee per night; MasterCard and Visa accepted. Open early January to late October.

Who to contact: Phone (503)855-7710 or write to P.O. Box 320, Gold Hill, OR 97525.

Location: In Gold Hill on Interstate 5, take the South Gold Hill exit (exit 40) and go 400 yards to Blackwell Road. The camp is about another 400 yards south.

Trip note: This campground is set along the banks of the Rogue River and near a golf course, bike paths, tennis courts and the Oregon Vortex. It's one of the many camps located between Gold Hill and Grants Pass.

Site 19   LAZY ACRES RV
on Rogue River

Campsites, facilities: There are 50 sites for trailers or motor homes of any length. Electricity, piped water, sewer hookups and picnic tables are provided. Flush toilets, bottled gas, cable TV, a dump station, a playground, a cafe and a laundromat are available. Pets and motorbikes are permitted. Boat docks are nearby.

Reservations, fee: No reservations necessary; $10 fee per night; MasterCard and Visa accepted. Open all year.

Who to contact: Phone (503)855-7000 or write to 1550 2nd Ave, Gold Hill, OR 97525.

Location: In Gold Hill, take the South Gold Hill exit and go one-quarter mile north, then 1.2 miles west on 2nd Avenue.

Trip note: This newly remodeled, wooded campground is set along the Rogue River, and offers the same recreation options as Site 18.

Site 20   FLY-CASTERS CAMPGROUND & TRAILER PARK
on Rogue River

Campsites, facilities: There are 30 sites for trailers or motor homes of any length.

Electricity, piped water, sewer hookups and picnic tables are provided. Flush toilets, bottled gas, showers and a laundromat are available. A store, a cafe and ice are located within one mile. Leashed pets are permitted. Boat launching facilities are nearby.

Reservations, fee: Reservations accepted; $8 fee per night. Open all year.

Who to contact: Phone (503)878-2749 or write to P.O. Box 1170, Shady Cove, OR 97539.

Location: From Medford, drive north on Highway 62 for 23 miles and you will see the camp along the highway. It is set 2.7 miles south of the junction of Highways 62 and 227.

Trip note: This is a good base camp for motor home drivers who want to fish or hike. It is set along the banks of the Rogue River. The county park in Shady Cove offers picnic facilities and a boat ramp. Lost Creek Lake is about a 15-minute drive to the northeast.

Site 21 SHADY TRAILS RV PARK & CAMPGROUND
on Rogue River

Campsites, facilities: There are 27 tent sites and 48 drive-through sites for trailers or motor homes of any length. Electricity, piped water, sewer hookups and picnic tables are provided. Flush toilets, cable TV hookups, bottled gas, sanitary disposal services, showers, a store, ice and a playground are available. A cafe is located within one mile. Pets and motorbikes are permitted. Boat launching facilities are nearby.

Reservations, fee: Reservations accepted; $8-12 fee per night. Open all year.

Who to contact: Phone (503)878-2206 or write to Box 1299, Shady Cove, OR 97539.

Location: From Medford, drive 23 miles north on Highway 62 to the campground.

Trip note: This park is set along the banks of the Rogue River.

Site 22 BOB'S RV CAMPGROUND
on Rogue River

Campsites, facilities: There are ten tent sites and 37 drive-through sites for trailers or motor homes of any length. Electricity, piped water, sewer hookups and picnic tables are provided. Flush toilets, bottled gas, sanitary disposal services, showers, a laundromat, ice and a playground are available. A store and a cafe are located within one mile. Pets and motorbikes are permitted. Boat docks and launching facilities are nearby. Discounts are given to Good Sam members.

Reservations, fee: Reservations accepted; $8-12 fee per night. Open all year.

Who to contact: Phone (503)878-2400 or write to 27301 Highway 62, Trail, OR 97541.

Location: From Medford, drive north on Highway 62. From the junction of Highways 62 and 227, continue east on Highway 62 for three more miles.

Trip note: This campground is set along the Rogue River about six miles from Lost Creek Lake, where boat ramps and picnic areas are available for day-use.

Site 23 ROGUE ELK COUNTY PARK
on Rogue River

Campsites, facilities: There are 20 sites for trailers or motor homes up to 15 feet long. Picnic tables and fire grills are provided. Piped water and vault toilets are available. Leashed pets are permitted.

Reservations, fee: No reservations necessary; $8 fee per night. Open July to late October.

Who to contact: Phone (916)465-2241 or write to Jackson County Department of Parks and Recreation, 10 South Oakdale, Medford, OR 97501.
Location: Drive 27 miles northeast of Medford on Highway 62 to the campground.
Trip note: This campground is set along the Rogue River about five miles from Lost Creek Lake. Boat ramps and picnic areas are available at the lake.

Site 24   JOSEPH STEWART STATE PARK
on Lost Creek Lake

Campsites, facilities: There are 50 sites for tents or self-contained motor homes and 151 sites with water and electrical hookups for trailers or motor homes of any length. Picnic tables and fire grills are provided. Flush toilets, sanitary disposal services, showers, firewood and a playground are available. Some facilities are wheelchair accessible. Leashed pets are permitted. Boat launching facilities are nearby.
Reservations, fee: No reservations necessary; $9-10 in summer, $6-7 off-season. Open mid-April to late October.
Who to contact: Phone (503)560-3334 or write to 35251 Highway 62, Trail, OR 97541.
Location: From Medford, go 34 miles northeast on Highway 62.
Trip note: This state park is set along the shore of Lost Creek Lake, a reservoir with a marina, beach and boat rentals. There are eight miles of hiking trails and bike paths available throughout the park. This nice spot gets attention from Oregonians in the area but is missed by most other people.

Site 25   MILL CREEK
near Upper Rogue River
ROGUE RIVER NATIONAL FOREST

Campsites, facilities: There are eight sites for tents. Picnic tables and fire grills are provided. Vault toilets are available. There is **no piped water.** Leashed pets are permitted.
Reservations, fee: No reservations necessary; no fee. Open all year.
Who to contact: Phone the Prospect Ranger District at (503)560-3623 or write to Rogue River National Forest, Prospect, OR 97536.
Location: From Medford, travel 37 miles northeast on Highway 62, then one mile east on Forest Service Road 30.
Trip note: This campground is set along the bank of Mill Creek about two miles from the upper Rogue River. It is one in a series of remote, primitive camps near Highway 62 that is missed by out-of-towners.

Site 26   RIVER BRIDGE
on Upper Rogue River
ROGUE RIVER NATIONAL FOREST

Campsites, facilities: There are six sites for tents. Picnic tables and fire grills are provided. Vault toilets are available. There is **no piped water.** Leashed pets are permitted.
Reservations, fee: No reservations necessary; no fee. Open late May to early September.
Who to contact: Phone the Prospect Ranger District at (503)560-3623 or write to Rogue River National Forest, Prospect, OR 97536.
Location: From Medford, travel 39 miles northeast on Highway 62, then one mile north on Forest Service Road 6210.

Trip note: This campground is set along the bank of the upper Rogue River. The Upper Rogue River Trail passes the camp and follows the river for many miles to the Pacific Crest Trail in Crater Lake National Park. This is a good spot to start the hike.

Site **27**
NATURAL BRIDGE
on Upper Rogue River Trail
ROGUE RIVER NATIONAL FOREST

Campsites, facilities: There are 16 sites for tents, trailers or motor homes up to 22 feet long. Picnic tables and fire grills are provided. Vault toilets are available. There is **no piped water.** Leashed pets are permitted.

Reservations, fee: No reservations necessary; no fee. Open late May to early September.

Who to contact: Phone the Prospect Ranger District at (503)560-3623 or write to Rogue River National Forest, Prospect, OR 97536.

Location: From Medford, travel 45 miles north on Highway 62, then one mile west on Forest Service Road 300.

Trip note: The upper Rogue River runs underground at this spot. The Upper Rogue River Trail passes camp and follows the river for many miles to the Pacific Crest Trail in Crater Lake National Park.

Site **28**
ABBOTT CREEK
on Abbott and Woodruff Creeks
ROGUE RIVER NATIONAL FOREST

Campsites, facilities: There are nine tent sites and 12 sites for tents, trailers or motor homes up to 22 feet long. Picnic tables and fire grills are provided. Pump water and vault toilets are available. Leashed pets are permitted.

Reservations, fee: No reservations necessary; $3 fee per night. Open late May to late October.

Who to contact: Phone the Prospect Ranger District at (503)560-3623 or write to Rogue River National Forest, Prospect, OR 97536.

Location: From Medford, travel 42 miles northeast on Highway 62, then 3.5 miles northwest on Forest Service Road 68.

Trip note: This campground is set at the confluence of Abbott and Woodruff Creeks about two miles from the Upper Rogue River.

Site **29**
UNION CREEK
near Upper Rogue River
ROGUE RIVER NATIONAL FOREST

Campsites, facilities: There are 71 sites for tents, trailers or motor homes up to 16 feet long. Picnic tables and fire grills are provided. Piped water and pit toilets are available. Leashed pets are permitted.

Reservations, fee: No reservations necessary; $4 fee per night. Open late May to early September.

Who to contact: Phone the Prospect Ranger District at (503)560-3623 or write to Rogue River National Forest, Prospect, OR 97536.

Location: From Medford, travel 46 miles north on Highway 62.

Trip note: This campground is more developed than nearby Sites 25-27. It is set along the bank of Union Creek where it joins other creeks to form the Upper Rogue River. The Upper Rogue River Trail passes near camp.

Site **30**   FAREWELL BEND
on Upper Rogue River
ROGUE RIVER NATIONAL FOREST

Campsites, facilities: There are 61 sites for tents, trailers or motor homes up to 22 feet long. Picnic tables and fire grills are provided. Piped water and flush toilets are available. Some facilities are wheelchair accessible. Leashed pets are permitted.

Reservations, fee: No reservations necessary; $6 fee per night. Open late May to early September.

Who to contact: Phone the Prospect Ranger District at (503)560-3623 or write to Rogue River National Forest, Prospect, OR 97536.

Location: From Medford, travel 46.5 miles north on Highway 62.

Trip note: This campground is set along the bank of the Upper Rogue River near the Rogue River Gorge. The Upper Rogue River Trail passes near camp. It attracts a lot of the campers who also visit Crater Lake.

Site **31**   HUCKLEBERRY MOUNTAIN
near Crater Lake National Park
ROGUE RIVER NATIONAL FOREST

Campsites, facilities: There are 15 sites for tents, trailers or motor homes up to 21 feet long. Picnic tables and fire grills are provided. Pumped water and vault toilets are available. Leashed pets are permitted.

Reservations, fee: No reservations necessary; no fee. Open July to late October.

Who to contact: Phone the Prospect Ranger District at (503)560-3623 or write to Rogue River National Forest, Prospect, OR 97536.

Location: Travel 35 miles northeast of Medford to Prospect. From there continue 17.5 miles northeast of Prospect on Highway 62, then four miles south on Forest Service Road 60.

Trip note: This campground is set at 5,400 feet elevation, about 15 miles from the entrance to Crater Lake National Park. It is a prime hideaway for people who have visited Crater Lake and it's just far enough off the highway to get missed by most travelers.

Site **32**   HAMAKER
near Upper Rogue River
ROGUE RIVER NATIONAL FOREST

Campsites, facilities: There are 15 sites for tents, trailers or motor homes up to 15 feet long. Picnic tables and fire grills are provided. Pumped water and vault toilets are available. Leashed pets are permitted.

Reservations, fee: No reservations necessary; $4 fee per night. Open late June to early September.

Who to contact: Phone the Prospect Ranger District at (503)560-3623 or write to Rogue River National Forest, Prospect, OR 97536.

Location: From Medford, travel 47 miles northeast on Highway 62, then 11 miles north on Highway 230. Continue 600 yards east on Forest Service Road 6530.

Trip note: This campground is set at 4,000 feet elevation along Hamaker Creek. The Upper Rogue River passes near camp. This is a prime little spot for Crater Lake visitors.

Site **33**
MAZAMA
near Pacific Crest Trail
CRATER LAKE NATIONAL PARK

Campsites, facilities: There are 198 sites for tents, trailers or motor homes up to 32 feet long. Picnic tables and fire grills are provided. Piped water, flush toilets, sanitary disposal services, showers, a store, firewood and ice are available. Some facilities are wheelchair accessible. Pets and motorbikes are permitted.

Reservations, fee: No reservations necessary; $7 fee per night. Open early July to late September.

Who to contact: Phone (503)594-2511 or write to Crater Lake Lodge, P.O. Box 128, Crater Lake, OR 97604.

Location: From Klamath Falls, go 22 miles north on US 97, then 30 miles northwest on Highway 62.

Trip note: This campground is set adjacent to the ranger station at Annie Springs. The Pacific Crest Trail passes near camp. The only trail access down to Crater Lake is at Cleetwood Cove. Some of the park facilities are open in the winter for cross-country skiing along the unplowed roadways. Winter access to the park is available only from the west on Highway 62 to Rim Village. This is one of the two campgrounds at Crater Lake.

Site **34**
LOST CREEK
near the Crater Lake Pinnacles
CRATER LAKE NATIONAL PARK

Campsites, facilities: There are 12 sites for tents, trailers or small motor homes. There is also one group site, available by reservation. Picnic tables and fire grills are provided. Piped water and flush toilets are available. Pets and motorbikes are permitted.

Reservations, fee: No reservations necessary; no fee. Open early July to late September.

Who to contact: Phone Crater Lake National Park at (503)594-2211 or write to P.O. Box 7, Crater Lake, OR 97604.

Location: From Klamath Falls, go 22 miles north on US 97, then 30 miles northwest on Highway 62 to the Annie Springs junction. Take Rim Drive around the lake until the road to the Pinnacles, turn left and drive five miles to the campground.

Trip note: In good weather, this is a prime spot in Crater Lake National Park—you avoid most of the crowd that is driving the Rim Road. This primitive campground is set near little Lost Creek and The Pinnacles, a series of craggy spires. The only trail access down to Crater Lake is at Cleetwood Cove. Some of the park facilities are open in the winter for cross-country skiing along the unplowed roadways. Winter access to the park is available only from the west on Highway 62 to Rim Village.

Site **35**
IMNAHA
near Sky Lakes Wilderness
ROGUE RIVER NATIONAL FOREST

Campsites, facilities: There are four sites for tents. Picnic tables and fire grills are provided. Vault toilets are available. There is **no piped water.** Leashed pets are permitted.

Reservations, fee: No reservations necessary; no fee. Open all year.

Who to contact: Phone the Butte Falls Ranger District at (503)865-3581 or write to

Rogue River National Forest, P.O. Box 227, Butte Falls, OR 97522.

Location: From Medford, travel 35 miles northeast on Highway 62 to Prospect, then 12 miles east on Forest Service Road 37 to the campground.

Trip note: This campground is set along Imnaha Creek. Trailheads at the ends of the nearby Forest Service roads lead east into the Sky Lakes Wilderness. It's a good base camp for a wilderness trip.

Site **36**   **SOUTH FORK**
on the South Fork of Rogue River
ROGUE RIVER NATIONAL FOREST

Campsites, facilities: There are six sites for tents, trailers or motor homes up to 15 feet long. Picnic tables and fire grills are provided. Vault toilets are available. There is **no piped water**. Leashed pets are permitted.

Reservations, fee: No reservations necessary; no fee. Open all year.

Who to contact: Phone the Butte Falls Ranger District at (503)865-3581 or write to Rogue River National Forest, P.O. Box 227, Butte Falls, OR 97522.

Location: From Medford, travel 15 miles north on Highway 62, then 32 miles east on Forest Service Road 34.

Trip note: This campground is set along the South Fork of the Rogue River. To the east, trails at the end of the nearby Forest Service roads provide access to the Sky Lakes Wilderness. A map of Rogue River National Forest details all back roads, trails and waters.

Site **37**   **BIG BEN**
near the South Fork of Rogue River
ROGUE RIVER NATIONAL FOREST

Campsites, facilities: There are two sites for tents, trailers or motor homes up to 15 feet long. Picnic tables and fire grills are provided. Vault toilets are available. There is **no piped water**. Leashed pets are permitted.

Reservations, fee: No reservations necessary; no fee. Open all year.

Who to contact: Phone the Butte Falls Ranger District at (503)865-3581 or write to Rogue River National Forest, P.O. Box 227, Butte Falls, OR 97522.

Location: From Medford, travel 15 miles northeast on Highway 62, then 33 miles east on Forest Service Road 34. Drive south one mile on Forest Service Road 37 to the campground.

Trip note: This is one of the tiniest official campgrounds in the western U.S. and most folks don't have a clue that it exists. It is set along Big Ben Creek near its confluence with the South Fork of the Rogue River. Nearby trails at the ends of nearby Forest Service roads provide access to the Sky Lakes Wilderness to the east.

Site **38**   **PARKER MEADOWS**
on Parker River
ROGUE RIVER NATIONAL FOREST

Campsites, facilities: There are eight sites for tents, trailers or motor homes up to 15 feet long. Picnic tables and fire grills are provided and pumped water and vault toilets are available. Leashed pets are permitted.

Reservations, fee: No reservations necessary; $3 fee per night. Open mid-June to late September.

Who to contact: Phone the Butte Falls Ranger District at (503)865-3581 or write to Rogue River National Forest, P.O. Box 227, Butte Falls, OR 97522.

Location: From Medford, travel 14 miles northeast on Highway 62, then 18 miles east to Butte Falls. Go ten miles southeast of Butte Falls on County Road 30, then 11 miles northeast on Forest Service Road 37.

Trip note: This campground is set at 5,000 feet elevation along the bank of Parker Creek. Nearby, at the ends of the Forest Service roads, are trailheads that lead into to the Sky Lakes Wilderness. This is a nice spot, complete with water.

Site **39**
SNOWSHOE
near Snowshoe Butte
ROGUE RIVER NATIONAL FOREST

Campsites, facilities: There are five sites for tents, trailers or motor homes. Picnic tables and fire grills are provided. Pumped water and vault toilets are available. Leashed pets are permitted.

Reservations, fee: No reservations necessary; $3 fee per night. Open all year.

Who to contact: Phone the Butte Falls Ranger District at (503)865-3581 or write to Rogue River National Forest, P.O. Box 227, Butte Falls, OR 97522.

Location: From Medford, travel 14 miles northeast on Highway 62, then 18 miles east to Butte Falls. Travel nine miles southeast of Butte Falls on County Road 30, then five miles northeast on Forest Service Road 3065.

Trip note: This campground is set at 4,000 feet elevation near Snowshoe Butte and is a nice, secluded spot that is missed by many.

Site **40**
FOURBIT FORD
on Fourbit Creek
ROGUE RIVER NATIONAL FOREST

Campsites, facilities: There are seven sites for tents. Picnic tables and fire grills are provided. Pumped water and vault toilets are available. A store, a cafe and ice are located within five miles. Leashed pets are permitted. Boat docks, launching facilities and rentals are nearby.

Reservations, fee: No reservations necessary; $3 fee per night. Open late May to late September.

Who to contact: Phone the Butte Falls Ranger District at (503)865-3581 or write to Rogue River National Forest, P.O. Box 227, Butte Falls, OR 97522.

Location: From Medford, travel 15 miles northeast on Highway 62, then 18 miles east to Butte Falls. From Butte Falls, travel nine miles southeast on County Road 30, then one mile northeast on Forest Service Road 3065.

Trip note: This campground is set along Fourbit Creek. It's one in a series of hidden spots tucked away near County Road 30.

Site **41**
WHISKEY SPRINGS A AND B
near Fourbit Creek

Campsites, facilities: There are 36 sites for tents, trailers or motor homes up to 16 feet long. Picnic tables and fire grills are provided. Piped water and vault toilets are available. Leashed pets are permitted. Boat docks, launching facilities and rentals are nearby.

Reservations, fee: No reservations necessary; $4 fee per night. Open late May to early September.

Who to contact: Phone the Butte Falls Ranger District at (503)865-3581 or write to Rogue River National Forest, P.O. Box 227, Butte Falls, OR 97522.

Location: From Medford, travel 15 miles northeast on Highway 62, then 18 miles east to Butte Falls. From Butte Falls, travel nine miles southeast on County

Road 30, then 300 yards on Forest Service Road 3317.

Trip note: This campground is at Whiskey Springs, near Fourbit Creek. A nature trail is nearby. This is one of the larger, more developed backwoods Forest Service camps in the area.

Site 42   WILLOW LAKE RESORT
on Willow Lake

Campsites, facilities: There are 35 tent sites and 45 drive-through sites for trailers or motor homes up to 30 feet long. Electricity, piped water, sewer hookups and picnic tables are provided. Flush toilets, sanitary disposal services, showers, firewood, a store, a cafe, a laundromat, ice and a playground are available. Pets and motorbikes are permitted. Boat docks, launching facilities and rentals are nearby.

Reservations, fee: Reservations accepted; $8 fee per night; MasterCard and Visa accepted. Open all year.

Who to contact: Phone (503)865-3229 or write to 7800 Fish Lake, Butte Falls, OR 97533.

Location: Take Interstate 5 to Highway 62 in Medford, travel 14 miles on Highway 62, then 25 miles east on Butte Falls Highway. From there, go two miles southeast on Willow Lake Road.

Trip note: This campground is on the shore of Willow Lake. Nearby recreation options include hiking trails and a small marina.

Site 43   WILLOW PRAIRIE
near Fish Lake
ROGUE RIVER NATIONAL FOREST

Campsites, facilities: There are ten sites for tents, trailers or motor homes up to 15 feet long. Picnic tables and fire grills are provided. Pumped water and vault toilets are available. A store, a cafe and ice are located within five miles. Leashed pets are permitted. Boat docks, launching facilities and rentals are nearby.

Reservations, fee: No reservations necessary; $3 fee per night. Open late May to late September.

Who to contact: Phone the Butte Falls Ranger District at (503)865-3581 or write to Rogue River National Forest, P.O. Box 227, Butte Falls, OR 97522.

Location: From Medford, travel 31.5 miles east on Highway 140, then 1.5 miles north on Forest Service Road 37. The camp is one mile west on Forest Service Road 3738.

Trip note: This spot is primarily used as a horse camp. A map of Rogue River National Forest details the back roads and can help you get here. The campground is set near the origin of the west branch of Willow Creek. Fish Lake is four miles south.

Site 44   NORTH FORK
near Fish Lake
ROGUE RIVER NATIONAL FOREST

Campsites, facilities: There are seven tent sites. Picnic tables and fire grills are provided. Vault toilets are available. There is **no piped water.** Leashed pets are permitted. Boat docks, launching facilities and rentals are nearby.

Reservations, fee: No reservations necessary; no fee. Open late May to early September.

Who to contact: Phone the Ashland Ranger District at (503)482-3333 or write to Rogue River National Forest, 645 Washington Street, Ashland, OR 97520.

Location: From Medford, travel 31.5 miles east on County Road 140, then one-half mile south on Forest Service Road 37.

Trip note: Here is a small campground that is close to the highway, close to Fish Lake, yet missed by out-of-towners. Why? Because it is on a Forest Service road where motor homes fear to tread.

Site **45**
FISH LAKE
on Fish Lake
ROGUE RIVER NATIONAL FOREST

Campsites, facilities: There are ten tent sites and 17 sites for trailers or motor homes up to 22 feet long. Picnic tables and fire grills are provided. Piped water, flush toilets, a store, a cafe and ice are available. Leashed pets are permitted. Boat docks, launching facilities and rentals are nearby.

Reservations, fee: No reservations necessary; $6 fee per night. Open July to late October.

Who to contact: Phone the Ashland Ranger District at (503)482-3333 or write to Rogue River National Forest, 645 Washington Street, Ashland, OR 97520.

Location: From Medford, travel 33 miles east on Highway 140.

Trip note: This campground is on the north shore of Fish Lake. Recreation options include boating, fishing, hiking and bicycling. If this campground is full, Sites 46 and 47 provide options.

Site **46**
DOE POINT
on Fish Lake
ROGUE RIVER NATIONAL FOREST

Campsites, facilities: There are 25 sites for tents, trailers or motor homes up to 22 feet long. Picnic tables and fire grills are provided. Piped water, flush toilets, a store, a cafe and ice are available. Leashed pets are permitted. Boat docks, launching facilities and rentals are nearby.

Reservations, fee: No reservations necessary; $6 fee per night. Open July to late October.

Who to contact: Phone the Ashland Ranger District at (503)482-3333 or write to Rogue River National Forest, 645 Washington, Ashland, OR 97520.

Location: From Medford, travel 33 miles east on Highway 140.

Trip note: This campground is set along the north shore of Fish Lake. Recreation options include boating, fishing, hiking and bicycling.

Site **47**
FISH LAKE RESORT
on Fish Lake

Campsites, facilities: There are 25 tent sites and 50 sites for trailers or motor homes up to 30 feet long. Electricity, piped water, sewer hookups and picnic tables are provided. Flush toilets, bottled gas, sanitary disposal services, showers, a recreation hall, a store, a cafe, a laundromat and ice are available. Pets and motorbikes are permitted. Boat docks, launching facilities and rentals are nearby.

Reservations, fee: Reservations accepted; $9 fee per night; MasterCard and Visa accepted. Open May to mid-October.

Who to contact: Phone (503)949-8500 or write to P.O. Box 40, Medford, OR 97501.

Location: Drive five miles north of Medford on Highway 62, then 30 miles east on

Highway 140. The camp is one-half mile south on Fish Lake Road.

Trip note: This campground is set along Fish Lake, where hiking, bicycling, fishing and boating are some of the options. This is the largest of the three camps at Fish Lake.

Site 48   LAKE OF THE WOODS RESORT
on Lake of the Woods

Campsites, facilities: There are 30 sites for trailers or motor homes up to 32 feet long. Electricity, piped water, sewer hookups and picnic tables are provided. Flush toilets, showers, a store, a cafe, a laundromat and ice are available. Sanitary disposal services are located within one mile. Leashed pets are permitted. Boat docks, launching facilities and rentals are nearby.

Reservations, fee: Reservations accepted; $8 fee per night; MasterCard and Visa accepted. Open early May to November.

Who to contact: Phone (503)949-8300 or write to 950 Harriman, Klamath Falls, OR 97601.

Location: From Klamath Falls, travel northwest on Highway 140 for 35 miles, then one mile south on Lake of the Woods Road. The resort is west on Rainbow Bay Road.

Trip note: This campground is on the shore of Lake of the Woods, a popular spot for boating and fishing. A trail leads east from the resort and provides access to numerous lakes in the Mountain Lakes Wilderness.

Site 49   ASPEN POINT
on Lake of the Woods
WINEMA NATIONAL FOREST

Campsites, facilities: There are 61 sites for tents, trailers or motor homes up to 22 feet long. Picnic tables and fire grills are provided. Piped water, flush toilets and showers are available. Leashed pets are permitted. Boat docks, launching facilities and rentals are nearby.

Reservations, fee: No reservations necessary; $6 fee per night. Open late May to late September.

Who to contact: Phone the Klamath Ranger District at (503)883-6824 or write to Winema National Forest, 1936 California Avenue, Klamath Falls, OR 97601.

Location: Travel 32.5 miles northwest of Klamath Falls on Highway 140, then one-half mile south on Forest Service Road 3704. The camp is 100 yards west of Forest Service Road 3704.

Trip note: This campground is on the shore of Lake of the Woods.

Site 50   SUNSET
on Lake of the Woods
WINEMA NATIONAL FOREST

Campsites, facilities: There are 67 sites for tents, trailers or motor homes up to 22 feet long. Picnic tables and fire grills are provided. Piped water, firewood and flush toilets are available. Some facilities are wheelchair accessible. Leashed pets are permitted. Boat docks, launching facilities and rentals are nearby.

Reservations, fee: Reservations available through MISTIX at (800)283-CAMP beginning in 1991; $6 fee per night. Open June to mid-September.

Who to contact: Phone the Klamath Ranger District at (503)883-6824 or write to Winema National Forest, 1936 California Avenue, Klamath Falls, OR 97601.

Location: From Klamath Falls, travel 31 miles northwest on Highway 140, then 2.5

miles southwest on County Road 533. The camp is one-half mile west on Forest Service Road 3738.

Trip note: This campground is on the shore of Lake of the Woods.

Site 51
FOURMILE LAKE
at Fourmile Lake
WINEMA NATIONAL FOREST

Campsites, facilities: There are 25 sites for tents, trailers or motor homes up to 22 feet long. Picnic tables and fire grills are provided. Hand-pumped well water, firewood and vault toilets are available. Leashed pets are permitted. Boat docks, launching facilities and rentals are nearby.

Reservations, fee: No reservations necessary; $3 fee per night. Open June to late September.

Who to contact: Phone the Klamath Ranger District at (503)883-6824 or write to Winema National Forest, 1936 California Avenue, Klamath Falls, OR 97601.

Location: From Klamath Falls, travel 33 miles northwest on Highway 140, then three miles north on Forest Service Road 3661.

Trip note: This campground is the only camp on the shore of Fourmile Lake. There are several trails nearby that provide access to Sky Lakes Wilderness. The Pacific Crest Trail passes about two miles from camp.

Site 52
COLD SPRINGS
near Sky Lakes Wilderness
WINEMA NATIONAL FOREST

Campsites, facilities: There are two tent sites. Picnic tables and fire grills are provided. Pit toilets are available. There is **no piped water.** Leashed pets are permitted.

Reservations, fee: No reservations necessary; no fee. Open June to late September.

Who to contact: Phone the Klamath Ranger District at (503)883-6824 or write to Winema National Forest, 1936 California Avenue, Klamath Falls, OR 97601.

Location: From Klamath Falls, travel 28 miles northwest on Highway 140, then north on Forest Service Road 3651, a gravel road, for 11 miles to the end of the road.

Trip note: This campground is set near the source of one of the tributaries to Lost Creek and near a trailhead that provides access to numerous lakes in Sky Lakes Wilderness. The Pacific Crest Trail passes about two miles from camp. It's used primarily as a jump-off point for backpackers.

Site 53
ODESSA
near Klamath Lake
WINEMA NATIONAL FOREST

Campsites, facilities: There are five tent sites. Picnic tables and fire grills are provided. Firewood and vault toilets are available. There is **no piped water.** Leashed pets are permitted. Boat docks, launching facilities and rentals are nearby.

Reservations, fee: No reservations necessary; no fee. Open mid-May to late September.

Who to contact: Phone the Klamath Ranger District at (503)883-6824 or write to Winema National Forest, 1936 California Avenue, Klamath Falls, OR 97601.

Location: From Klamath Falls, travel 21.5 miles northwest on Highway 140, then one mile northeast on Forest Service Road 3639.

Trip note: This campground is set along Odessa Creek, near the shore of Upper Klamath Lake. Boating and fishing are allowed, but not waterskiing. This lake can provide excellent fishing for rainbow trout on both flies and Rapalas.

Site 54   HARRIMAN SPRINGS RESORT & MARINA
on Upper Klamath Lake

Campsites, facilities: There are six tent sites and 17 drive-through sites for trailers or motor homes. Electricity, piped water, sewer hookups and picnic tables are provided. Flush toilets, showers, firewood, a cafe, a laundromat and ice are available. Bottled gas, sanitary disposal services and a store are located within one mile. Pets and motorbikes are permitted. Boat docks, launching facilities and rentals are nearby.

Reservations, fee: Reservations accepted; $7 fee per night. Open April to late October.

Who to contact: Phone (503)356-2323 or write to Harriman Route, Box 79, Klamath Falls, OR 97601.

Location: Travel 27 miles northwest of Klamath Falls on Highway 140, then two miles north on Rocky Point Road.

Trip note: This resort is set along the shore of Pelican Bay at the north end of Upper Klamath Lake, adjacent to the Upper Klamath National Wildlife Refuge. Trout fishing is good, especially ideal from a canoe.

Site 55   ROCKY POINT RESORT
on Upper Klamath Lake

Campsites, facilities: There are five tent sites and 28 drive-through sites for trailers or motor homes of any length. Electricity, piped water, sewer hookups and picnic tables are provided. Flush toilets, bottled gas, sanitary disposal services, showers, firewood, a recreation hall, a store, a cafe, a laundromat, ice and a playground are available. Leashed pets are permitted. Boat docks, launching facilities and rentals are nearby.

Reservations, fee: Reservations accepted; $10 fee per night. Open April to mid-November.

Who to contact: Phone (503)356-2287 or write to Harriman Route, Box 92, Klamath Falls, OR 97601.

Location: From Klamath Falls, travel 27 miles northwest on Highway 140, then three miles north on Rocky Point Road.

Trip note: See the trip note for Site 54.

Site 56   FORT CREEK RESORT
on Wood River

Campsites, facilities: There are ten tent sites and 18 sites for trailers or motor homes of any length. Electricity, piped water, sewer hookups and picnic tables are provided. Flush toilets, showers, a recreation hall, a laundromat and a swimming pool are available. Bottled gas, a store, a cafe and ice are located within one mile. Pets and motorbikes are permitted.

Reservations, fee: Reservations accepted; $10 fee per night. Open mid-May to October.

Who to contact: Phone (503)381-2207 or write to P.O. Box 457, Fort Klamath, OR 97626.

Location: From Klamath Falls, travel 21 miles north on US 97, then 12.5 miles north on Highway 62. The campground is just before Fort Klamath on Highway

62.

Trip note: This campground is on the banks of the Wood River, just outside of Fort Klamath, the origin of numerous military campaigns in the late 1800s against the Modoc Indians.

Site **57**   FORT KLAMATH LODGE & RV PARK
on Wood River

Campsites, facilities: There are five tent sites and 11 sites for trailers or motor homes of any length. Electricity, piped water, sewer hookups and picnic tables are provided. Flush toilets, bottled gas, showers and a laundromat are available. A store and ice are located within one mile. Pets and motorbikes are permitted.

Reservations, fee: Reservations accepted; $10 fee per night; MasterCard and Visa accepted. Open all year.

Who to contact: Phone (503)381-2234 or write to P.O. Box 428, Fort Klamath, OR 97626.

Location: From Klamath Falls, travel 21 miles north on US 97, then 14.5 miles north on Highway 62. The campground is 1.5 miles northwest of Fort Klamath.

Trip note: See the trip note for Site 56.

Site **58**   SEVENMILE MARSH
near Sky Lakes Wilderness
WINEMA NATIONAL FOREST

Campsites, facilities: There are two tent sites. Picnic tables and fire grills are provided. Firewood and pit toilets are available. There is **no piped water.** Leashed pets are permitted.

Reservations, fee: No reservations necessary; no fee. Open mid-May to late September.

Who to contact: Phone the Klamath Ranger District at (503)883-6824 or write to Winema National Forest, 1936 California Avenue, Klamath Falls, OR 97601.

Location: From Klamath Falls, travel 21 miles north on US 97, then 13 miles north on Highway 62 to Fort Klamath. From there, drive west on County Road 1419 for three miles, then six miles northwest on Forest Service Road 3334.

Trip note: This campground is set near Sevenmile Marsh, at a trailhead that provides access to Sky Lakes Wilderness. The Pacific Crest Trail passes 1.5 miles from camp This tiny camp is used primarily as a jump-off point for backpackers.

Site **59**   CRATER LAKE CAMP & RV PARK
near Crater Lake National Park

Campsites, facilities: There are 50 tent sites and 36 drive-through sites for trailers or motor homes of any length. Electricity, piped water, sewer hookups and picnic tables are provided. Flush toilets, showers, firewood, a store, a laundromat, ice and a playground are available. Pets and motorbikes are permitted.

Reservations, fee: Reservations accepted; $8 fee per night; MasterCard and Visa accepted. Open mid-May to October.

Who to contact: Phone (503)381-2275 or write to P.O. Box 485, Fort Klamath, OR 97626.

Location: From Klamath Falls, travel 21 miles north on US 97, then 19 miles north on Highway 62 to the campground.

Trip note: This campground is located near the south entrance to Crater Lake National Park. It gets heavy traffic during the summer months.

Site **60** ### JACKSON F. KIMBALL STATE PARK
on Wood River

Campsites, facilities: There are six primitive sites for tents, trailers or motor homes of any length. Picnic tables and fire grills are provided. Firewood and vault toilets are available. There is **no piped water.** Leashed pets are permitted.

Reservations, fee: No reservations necessary; $8 fee per night. Open mid-April to late October.

Who to contact: Phone (503)783-2471 or write to Chiloquin, OR 97624.

Location: From Klamath Falls, travel 21 miles north on US 97, then 13 miles north on Highway 62 to Fort Klamath. From there, drive three miles north on Highway 232.

Trip note: This campground is set near the Wood River. It's another nice spot just far enough off the main drag that most tourists don't have a clue about it.

Site **61** ### WILLIAMSON RIVER
near Collier State Park
WINEMA NATIONAL FOREST

Campsites, facilities: There are three tent sites and seven sites for trailers or motor homes up to 30 feet long. Picnic tables and fire grills are provided. Hand-pumped well water and vault toilets are available. A restaurant is located within five miles. Leashed pets are permitted.

Reservations, fee: No reservations necessary; $4 fee per night. Open June to late October.

Who to contact: Phone the Chiloquin Ranger District at (503)783-2221 or write Winema National Forest, P.O. Box 357, Chiloquin, OR 97624.

Location: From Chiloquin, travel 5.5 miles north on US 97, then one mile northeast on Forest Service Road 3412.

Trip note: Another great little spot is discovered, this one with excellent trout fishing. This campground is set along the banks of the Williamson River. A map of Winema National Forest details the back roads and trails. Collier State Park provides a nearby side trip option.

Site **62** ### WALT'S COZY CAMP
on Williamson River

Campsites, facilities: There are 20 tent sites and 34 drive-through sites for trailers or motor homes of any length. Electricity, piped water, sewer hookups and picnic tables are provided. Flush toilets, bottled gas, showers and firewood are available. A store, a cafe, a laundromat and ice are available. Pets and motorbikes are permitted.

Reservations, fee: Reservations accepted; $8 fee per night. Open April to early November.

Who to contact: Phone (503)783-2537 or write to P.O. Box 243, Chiloquin, OR 97624.

Location: From Chiloquin, travel three miles north on US 97.

Trip note: This campground is set along the banks of the Williamson River, near Collier State Park. It is one of three camps in the immediate area. For a more remote setting, Sites 67 and 79 are available to the east.

Site **63**
COLLIER MEMORIAL STATE PARK
on Williamson River

Campsites, facilities: There are 18 sites for tents or self-contained motor homes and 50 sites with full hookups for trailers or motor homes of any length. Picnic tables and fire grills are provided. Flush toilets, sanitary disposal services, showers, firewood, a laundromat and a playground are available. Some facilities are wheelchair accessible. Leashed pets are permitted. A day-use hitching area is also available.

Reservations, fee: No reservations necessary; $9-11 in summer, $6-8 off-season. Open mid-April to late October.

Who to contact: Phone (503)783-2471 or write to Chiloquin, OR 97624.

Location: From Klamath Falls, travel 30 miles north on US 97.

Trip note: This campground is set at the confluence of Spring Creek and the Williamson River. A nature trail and a museum are available.

Site **64**
NEPTUNE PARK RESORT
on Williamson River

Campsites, facilities: There are 15 tent sites and 18 sites for trailers or motor homes of any length. Electricity, piped water, sewer hookups and picnic tables are provided. Flush toilets, bottled gas, showers, a store, and ice are available. Pets and motorbikes are permitted. Boat docks and launching facilities are nearby.

Reservations, fee: Reservations accepted; $10 fee per night; MasterCard and Visa accepted. Open all year.

Who to contact: Phone (503)782-2489 or write to HC 30, Box 115, Chiloquin, OR 97624.

Location: From Chiloquin, travel west at the Modoc Point sign and go four miles north. From there, follow the signs.

Trip note: This campground is set along Upper Klamath Lake.

Site **65**
WATERWHEEL CAMPGROUND & RV PARK
on Williamson River

Campsites, facilities: There are 20 tent sites and 24 drive-through sites for trailers or motor homes of any length. Electricity, piped water, sewer hookups and picnic tables are provided. Flush toilets, bottled gas, sanitary disposal services, showers, firewood, a store, a laundromat, ice and a playground are available. A cafe is available within one mile. Pets and motorbikes are permitted. Boat docks and launching facilities are nearby.

Reservations, fee: Reservations accepted; $11 fee per night; MasterCard and Visa accepted. Open all year.

Who to contact: Phone (503)783-2738 or write to HC 30, Box 91, Chiloquin, OR 97624.

Location: From Chiloquin, travel one-quarter mile south on US 97.

Trip note: This rural campground is set along the banks of the Williamson River. Hiking trails are nearby. This is an okay layover spot.

Site **66**
WILLIAMSON RIVER RESORT
on Williamson River

Campsites, facilities: There are eight sites for trailers or motor homes of any length. Electricity, piped water and picnic tables are provided. Bottled gas, sanitary disposal services, a store and ice are available. A cafe is located within one mile. Leashed pets are permitted. Boat docks, launching facilities and rentals are nearby.

Reservations, fee: Reservations accepted; $6 fee per night; MasterCard and Visa accepted. Open all year.

Who to contact: Phone (503)783-2071 or write to HC 30, Box 78, Chiloquin, OR 97624.

Location: From Chiloquin, travel 5.5 miles on Modoc Point Road.

Trip note: This resort is set along the banks of the Williamson River.

Site 67   POTTER'S TRAILER PARK
on Sprague River

Campsites, facilities: There are 17 tent sites and 23 drive-through sites for trailers or motor homes of any length. Electricity, piped water, sewer hookups and picnic tables are provided. Flush toilets, bottled gas, showers, firewood, a recreation hall, a store, a cafe, a laundromat and ice are available. Pets and motorbikes are permitted.

Reservations, fee: Reservations accepted; $8 fee per night. Open all year with limited winter facilities.

Who to contact: Phone (503)783-2253 or write to Star Route 2, Chiloquin, OR 97624.

Location: Go 12 miles east of Chiloquin on Sprague River Highway.

Trip note: This campground is set along the banks of the Sprague River. For the most part, the area east of Klamath Lake doesn't get much attention. But if you want to check out a relatively nearby spot that is out in booger country, check out Site 79.

Site 68   HAGELSTEIN PARK
on Upper Klamath Lake

Campsites, facilities: There are five tent sites and five sites for trailers or motor homes of any length. Picnic tables and fire grills are provided. Piped water and flush toilets are available. Leashed pets are permitted. Boat docks and launching facilities are nearby.

Reservations, fee: No reservations necessary; no fee. Open April to late November.

Who to contact: Phone (503)882-2501 or write to County Parks Department, Klamath Falls, OR 97601.

Location: From Klamath Falls, travel nine miles north on US 97.

Trip note: This county park is set along the shore of Upper Klamath Lake. This is the only campground along the eastern shore of the lake. The others are on the northwest end (Sites 53-55) or the southern end (Sites 69-72). Trout fishing can be superb here.

Site 69   KOA KLAMATH FALLS
on Upper Klamath Lake

Campsites, facilities: There are 18 tent sites and 73 drive-through sites for trailers or motor homes of any length. Electricity, piped water, sewer hookups and picnic tables are provided. Flush toilets, bottled gas, sanitary disposal services, showers, a recreation hall, a store, a laundromat, ice, a playground and a swimming pool are available. A cafe is located within one mile. Pets and motorbikes are permitted. Boat docks and launching facilities are nearby.

Reservations, fee: Reservations accepted; $10 fee per night; MasterCard and Visa accepted. Open all year with limited winter facilities.

Who to contact: Phone (503)884-4644 or write to 3435 Shasta Way, Klamath Falls, OR 97601.

Location: From Klamath Falls, travel 1.5 miles northwest on US 97, then one block west on Shasta Way.

Trip note: This campground is set along the shore of Upper Klamath Lake, near the marina. Hiking trails and tennis courts are nearby.

Site 70   MALLARD CAMPGROUND
on Upper Klamath Lake

Campsites, facilities: There are ten tent sites and 43 drive-through sites for trailers or motor homes of any length. Electricity, piped water, sewer hookups and picnic tables are provided. Flush toilets, showers, a recreation hall, a laundromat, ice and a swimming pool are available. Bottled gas, a store and a cafe are located within one mile. Pets and motorbikes are permitted.

Reservations, fee: Reservations accepted; $10 fee per night; MasterCard and Visa accepted. Open all year with limited winter facilities.

Who to contact: Phone (503)882-0482 or write to Route 5, Box 1348, Klamath Falls, OR 97601.

Location: From Klamath Falls, travel 3.5 miles north on US 97.

Trip note: This campground is near Hanks Marsh on the southeast shore of Upper Klamath Lake. Nearby recreation options include a golf course, bike paths and a marina.

Site 71   NORTH HILLS MOBILE PARK
near Upper Klamath Lake

Campsites, facilities: There are 15 sites for trailers or motor homes of any length. Electricity, piped water and sewer hookups are provided. A laundromat and a swimming pool are available. Bottled gas, a store, a cafe and ice are within one mile. Leashed pets are permitted.

Reservations, fee: Reservations accepted; $6 fee per night. Open all year with limited winter facilities.

Who to contact: Phone (503)884-9068 or write to 3611 Highway 97N, Klamath Falls, OR 97601.

Location: Travel two miles north of Klamath Falls on US 97.

Trip note: This park is near Upper Klamath Lake. A golf course, hiking trails, a marina and tennis courts are nearby.

Site 72   WISEMAN'S MOBILE COURT & RV
near Upper Klamath Lake

Campsites, facilities: There are eight tent sites and 12 sites for trailers or motor homes of any length. Electricity, piped water and sewer hookups are provided. Flush toilets, sanitary disposal services, showers and a laundromat are available. Bottled gas is located within one mile. Leashed pets are permitted.

Reservations, fee: Reservations accepted; $12 fee per night. Open all year.

Who to contact: Phone (503)882-4081 or write to 6800 South 6th, Klamath Falls, OR 97603.

Location: Take Highway 140 and drive 4.5 miles east from Klamath Falls.

Trip note: See the trip note for Site 71.

Site 73

TINGLEY LAKE ESTATES
near Klamath Falls

Campsites, facilities: There are six tent sites and ten drive-through sites for trailers or motor homes of any length. Electricity, piped water, sewer hookups and picnic tables are provided. Flush toilets, sanitary disposal services, showers, a laundromat and a playground are available. A store, a cafe and ice are located within one mile. Pets and motorbikes are permitted. Boat docks are nearby.

Reservations, fee: Reservations accepted; $8 fee per night. Open all year.

Who to contact: Phone (503)882-8386 or write to 11800 Tingley, Klamath Falls, OR 07603.

Location: From Klamath Falls, go seven miles southwest on US 97, then two miles east on Old Midland Road. The camp is one-half mile west on Tingley Road.

Trip note: This privately-operated park provides a layover spot for travelers crossing the Oregon border on US 97.

Site 74

GERBER RESERVOIR
on Gerber Reservoir

Campsites, facilities: There are 50 sites for tents, trailers or motor homes up to 30 feet long. Picnic tables and fire grills are provided. Piped water, firewood and vault toilets are available. Leashed pets are permitted. Boat launching facilities are nearby.

Reservations, fee: No reservations necessary; $2 fee per night. Open mid-May to mid-October.

Who to contact: Phone (503)947-2177 or write to Bureau of Land Management, P.O. Box 151, Lakeview, OR 97630.

Location: From Klamath Falls, travel 19 miles east on Highway 140, then drive southeast for about 17 miles to the turnoff for the reservoir and go 11 miles northeast on Gerber Road.

Trip note: This campground is set at 4,800 feet elevation along the west shore of Gerber Reservoir. Just about nobody has heard of Gerber Reservoir, since it's set out in the middle of nowhere. And that's just how we like it!

Site 75

LOFTON RESERVOIR
on Lofton Lake
FREMONT NATIONAL FOREST

Campsites, facilities: There are ten tent sites and seven sites for trailers or motor homes up to 22 feet long. Picnic tables and fire grills are provided. Well water and vault toilets are available. Leashed pets are permitted. Boat docks and launching facilities are nearby.

Reservations, fee: No reservations necessary; no fee. Open June to late October.

Who to contact: Phone the Bly Ranger District at (503)353-2427 or write to Fremont National Forest, Bly, OR 97622.

Location: Drive 54 miles east of Klamath Falls on Highway 140 to Bly. From Bly, continue 13 miles southeast on Highway 140, then seven miles south on Forest Service Road 3715. From there, go 1.5 miles northeast on Forest Service Road 3715A. From Lakeview, drive about 30 miles east on Highway 140, then continue as above.

Trip note: This remote campground is set along the shore of little Lofton Lake. Other lakes are nearby and are accessible by Forest Service roads. This area marks the beginning of the Southeast Basin, a sandy area that extends to Idaho.

Site **76**

EAST BAY
on Thompson Reservoir
FREMONT NATIONAL FOREST

Campsites, facilities: There are ten sites for tents, trailers or motor homes. Picnic tables and fire grills are provided. Firewood, well water and vault toilets are available. Leashed pets are permitted. Boat launching facilities are nearby.

Reservations, fee: No reservations necessary; no fee. Open mid-May to late October.

Who to contact: Phone the Silver Lake Ranger District at (503)576-2107 or write to Fremont National Forest, Silver Lake, OR 97638.

Location: From the town of Silver Lake, go one-half mile west on Highway 31, then 13 miles south on Forest Service Road 28. From there, go 1.5 miles west on Forest Service Road 2823-014.

Trip note: This campground is set along the east shore of Thompson Reservoir. It is a long way from home and you'd best bring all your supplies with you. Site 78 is an even more primitive setting along a stream.

Site **77**

THOMPSON RESERVOIR
on Thompson Reservoir
FREMONT NATIONAL FOREST

Campsites, facilities: There are 19 sites for tents, trailers or motor homes up to 22 feet long. Picnic tables and fire grills are provided. Piped water, firewood, and vault toilets are available. Leashed pets are permitted. Boat launching facilities are nearby.

Reservations, fee: No reservations necessary; no fee. Open mid-May to late October.

Who to contact: Phone the Silver Lake Ranger District at (503)576-2107 or write to Fremont National Forest, Silver Lake, OR 97638.

Location: From the town of Silver Lake, travel one mile west on Highway 31, then 14 miles south on Forest Service Road 27. The camp is one mile east on Forest Service Road 2700-287.

Trip note: This campground is set along the north shore of Thompson Reservoir. Fishing and boating are permitted. See the trip note for Site 76.

Site **78**

SILVER CREEK MARSH
near Silver Creek
FREMONT NATIONAL FOREST

Campsites, facilities: There are five tent sites. Picnic tables and fire grills are provided. Well water, firewood and vault toilets are available. Leashed pets are permitted.

Reservations, fee: No reservations necessary; no fee. Open mid-May to late October.

Who to contact: Phone the Silver Lake Ranger District at (503)576-2107 or write to Fremont National Forest, Silver Lake, OR 97638.

Location: From the town of Silver Lake, travel one mile west on Highway 31, then ten miles south on Forest Service Road 27. The camp is 200 yards southwest on Forest Service Road 2700-049.

Trip note: This campground is set adjacent to Silver Creek Marsh near Silver Creek. It's a small, quiet spot that gets little attention.

Site **79**
HEAD OF THE RIVER
on Williamson River
WINEMA NATIONAL FOREST

Campsites, facilities: There are six sites for tents, trailers or motor homes up to 30 feet long. Picnic tables and fire grills are provided. Firewood and vault toilets are available. There is **no piped water.** Leashed pets are permitted.

Reservations, fee: No reservations necessary; no fee. Open June to mid-October.

Who to contact: Phone the Chiloquin Ranger District at (503)783-2221 or write to Winema National Forest, P.O. Box 357, Chiloquin, OR 97624.

Location: From Chiloquin, go five miles north east on County Road 858, then 27 miles northeast on County Road 600. The camp is one mile north on Forest Service Road 3037.

Trip note: This campground is set along the headwaters of the Williamson River. Just about nobody knows about this small, lonely spot.

Site **80**
TOPSY
on Upper Klamath River

Campsites, facilities: There are 12 sites for trailers or motor homes. Picnic tables and fire grills are provided. Pit toilets and firewood are available. There is **no piped water.** Leashed pets are permitted. Boat launching facilities are nearby.

Reservations, fee: No reservations necessary; no fee. Open April to late October.

Who to contact: Phone (503)776-3774 or write to Bureau of Land Management, 3040 Biddle Road, Medford, OR 97504.

Location: From Klamath Falls, travel 17 miles west on Highway 66 then one mile south on Topsy County Road.

Trip note: This campground is set along the Upper Klamath River. This is a good spot for trout fishing and a top river for rafters (for experts only). There is Class IV and V whitewater at Caldera, Satan's Gate, Hell's Corner and Three Rocks.

Site **81**
SURVEYOR
on Spender Creek

Campsites, facilities: There are eight primitive sites for tents, trailers or motor homes up to 20 feet long. Picnic tables and fire grills are provided. Piped water, firewood and vault toilets are available. Leashed pets are permitted.

Reservations, fee: No reservations necessary; no fee. Open June to late October.

Who to contact: Phone (503)776-3744 or write to Bureau of Land Management, 3040 Biddle Road, Medford, OR 97504.

Location: From Ashland, travel 20 miles east on Dead Indian Road, then ten miles east to Keno.

Trip note: This campground is set at 5,200 feet elevation. It is an obscure, little spot near Spencer Creek.

Site **82**
DALEY CREEK
on Daley Creek
ROGUE RIVER NATIONAL FOREST

Campsites, facilities: There are five tent sites. **No piped water** is available. Picnic tables and fire grills are provided. Vault toilets are available. Leashed pets are permitted.

Reservations, fee: No reservations necessary; no fee. Open late May to early September.

Who to contact: Phone the Ashland Ranger District at (503)482-3333 or write to Rogue River National Forest, 645 Washington, Ashland, OR 97520.

Location: Go 25 miles northeast of Ashland on County Road 364, then 1.5 miles north on Forest Service Road 37.

Trip note: This campground is set along the banks of Daley Creek. It is a primitive and free alternative to camping at the nearby, more developed Fish Lake campsites (Sites 45-47) or Hyatt Lake and Howard Prairie Reservoir campsites (Sites 83-86).

Site **83**
CAMPER'S COVE
on Hyatt Lake

Campsites, facilities: There are 25 drive-through sites for trailers or motor homes up to 30 feet long. Electricity, piped water, sewer hookups and picnic tables are provided. Flush toilets, bottled gas, showers, firewood, a store, a cafe and ice are available. Leashed pets are permitted. Boat docks are nearby.

Reservations, fee: Reservations accepted; $8 fee per night; MasterCard and Visa accepted. Open April to late October.

Who to contact: Phone (503)482-1201 or write to P.O. Box 222, Ashland, OR 97520.

Location: Travel 18 miles east of Ashland on Highway 66, then three miles northeast on Hyatt Lake Road. The camp is 2.5 miles on Hyatt Prairie Road.

Trip note: This campground is set along the shore of Hyatt Lake. The Pacific Crest Trail passes about one mile away.

Site **84**
HOWARD PRAIRIE LAKE RESORT
on Howard Prairie Lake

Campsites, facilities: There are 155 tent sites and 285 sites for trailers or motor homes of any length. Electricity, piped water, sewer hookups and picnic tables are provided. Flush toilets, bottled gas, sanitary disposal services, showers, firewood, a store, a cafe, a laundromat and ice are available. Pets are permitted. Boat docks, launching facilities and rentals are nearby.

Reservations, fee: No reservations necessary; $5 fee per night; MasterCard and Visa accepted. Open mid-April to late October.

Who to contact: Phone (503)773-3619 or write to P.O. Box 4709, Medford, OR 97501.

Location: From Ashland, take Highway 66 east to Dead Indian Road, go 19 miles east to Howard Prairie Road and drive five miles south to the reservoir.

Trip note: This wooded campground is set along the shore of Howard Prairie Lake, where hiking, swimming, fishing and boating are among the recreation options. This is one of the largest campgrounds within more than a hundred miles.

Site **85**
HYATT LAKE RESORT
on Hyatt Lake

Campsites, facilities: There are 20 tent sites and 55 drive-through sites for trailers or motor homes of any length. Electricity, piped water, sewer hookups and picnic tables are provided. Flush toilets, bottled gas, sanitary disposal services, showers, a store, a cafe, a laundromat, ice and a playground are available. Pets and motorbikes are permitted. Boat docks, launching facilities and rentals are nearby.

Reservations, fee: Reservations accepted; $7 fee per night; MasterCard and Visa accepted. Open April to November.

Who to contact: Phone (503)482-0525 or write to P.O. Box 447, Ashland, OR 97520.

Location: Go 18 miles east of Ashland on Highway 66, then three miles northeast on Hyatt Lake Road. The camp is one mile on Hyatt Prairie Road.

Trip note: This campground is set along the shore of Hyatt Lake, where hiking, fishing and swimming are some of the recreation options. This is a downscaled option to the resort at adjacent Howard Prairie Reservoir (Site 84).

Site 86   HYATT LAKE
on Hyatt Lake

Campsites, facilities: There are 20 tent sites, and 27 sites for tents, trailers or motor homes of any length. Picnic tables and fire grills are provided. Piped water, showers, flush toilets, a sanitary disposal station are available. A boat ramp is nearby. Leashed pets are permitted.

Reservations, fee: No reservations necessary; $4-7 fee per night. Open mid-April to mid-October.

Who to contact: Phone (503)776-3744 or write to Bureau of Land Management, 3040 Biddle Road, Medford, OR 97504.

Location: From Ashland, go 20 miles east on Highway 66, then go five miles north on East Hyatt Lake Road. There are two campgrounds.

Trip note: This campground is on the east shore of Hyatt Lake. Nearby recreation options include a marina and a stable. A swimming beach is nearby and the lake has become good for fishing. It was treated and restocked in the spring of 1990.

Site 87   KOA GLENYAN
near Emigrant Lake

Campsites, facilities: There are 30 tent sites and 38 drive-through sites for trailers or motor homes of any length. Electricity, piped water, sewer hookups and picnic tables are provided. Flush toilets, bottled gas, sanitary disposal services, showers, firewood, a recreation hall, a store, a cafe, a laundromat, ice, a playground and a swimming pool are available. Pets and motorbikes are permitted.

Reservations, fee: Reservations accepted; $10 fee per night; MasterCard and Visa accepted. Open late February to late October.

Who to contact: Phone (503)482-4138 or write to 5310 Highway 66, Ashland, OR 97520.

Location: Travel 3.5 miles east on Highway 66 from Ashland.

Trip note: This campground offers shady sites near Emigrant Lake. Nearby recreation options include a golf course, hiking trails, bike paths and tennis courts. It's an easy jump from Interstate 5 at Ashland.

Site 88   JACKSON HOT SPRINGS
near Ashland

Campsites, facilities: There are 30 tent sites and 20 drive-through sites for trailers or motor homes of any length. Electricity, piped water, sewer hookups and picnic tables are provided. Flush toilets, showers, a cafe, a laundromat, ice and a swimming pool are available. Bottled gas is located within one mile. Leashed pets are permitted.

Reservations, fee: No reservations necessary; $9 fee per night. Open all year.

Who to contact: Phone (503)482-3776 or write to 2253 Highway 99N, Ashland, OR 97520.

Location: Near Ashland, take exit 19 off Interstate 5, and travel west for one mile to the stoplight, then turn right and drive 500 feet.

Trip note: This campground has mineral hot springs that empty into a swimming pool, not a hot pool (76 degrees). Hot mineral baths are available in private rooms. Nearby recreation options include a golf course, hiking trails, bike paths and tennis courts.

Site 89
MOUNT ASHLAND
on Pacific Crest Trail
ROGUE RIVER NATIONAL FOREST

Campsites, facilities: There are eight sites for tents, trailers or motor homes up to 15 feet long. Picnic tables and fire grills are provided. Vault toilets are available. There is **no piped water** is available. Leashed pets are permitted.

Reservations, fee: No reservations necessary; no fee. Open July to late October.

Who to contact: Phone the Oak Knoll Ranger District at (916)465-2241 or write to Klamath National Forest, 1312 Fairlane Road, Yreka, CA 96097. (Yes, the address and phone number are correct.)

Location: From Ashland, travel 12 miles south on Interstate 5. Turn west on County Road 993 and drive one mile. Turn on Forest Service Road 20 and drive for nine miles to the campground.

Trip note: This campground is set at 6,000 feet elevation along the Pacific Crest Trail. On clear days, there are great lookouts, particularly to the south where California's 14,000-foot Mount Shasta is an awesome sight.

Site 90
FLUMET FLAT
on Applegate Reservoir
ROGUE RIVER NATIONAL FOREST

Campsites, facilities: There are 23 sites for tents, trailers or motor homes up to 21 feet long. Picnic tables and fire grills are provided. Piped water, flush toilets, showers, a store, a cafe, a laundromat and ice are available. Some facilities are wheelchair accessible. Leashed pets are permitted.

Reservations, fee: Reservations required; $5 fee per night. Open late May to early September.

Who to contact: Phone the Star Ranger District at (503)899-1812 or write to Rogue River National Forest, 6941 Upper Applegate Road, Jacksonville, OR 97530.

Location: From Jacksonville, travel eight miles southwest on Highway 238, nine miles southwest on County Road 10 and one mile southwest on Forest Service Road 1095.

Trip note: This campground is set along the banks of the Applegate River about six miles north of Applegate Reservoir. A nature trail is nearby.

Site 91
BEAVER SULPHUR
on Applegate Reservoir
ROGUE RIVER NATIONAL FOREST

Campsites, facilities: There are ten sites for tents. Picnic tables and fire grills are provided. Vault toilets are available. There is **no piped water.** Leashed pets are permitted. Boat docks and launching facilities are nearby.

Reservations, fee: No reservations necessary; $2 fee per night. Open June to September.

Who to contact: Phone the Star Ranger District at (503)899-1812 or write to Rogue River National Forest, 6941 Upper Applegate Road, Jacksonville, OR 97530.

Location: From Jacksonville, travel eight miles southwest on Highway 238, nine

miles southwest on County Road 10 and three miles east on Forest Service
Road 20.

Trip note: This campground is set along the banks of Beaver Creek, about seven
miles from Applegate Lake. It's tiny and hidden.

Site **92**
FRENCH GULCH
on Applegate Reservoir, walk-in only
ROGUE RIVER NATIONAL FOREST

Campsites, facilities: There are nine walk-in sites for tents. Picnic tables and fire
grills are provided. Piped water and vault toilets are available. Leashed pets
are permitted. Boat docks and launching facilities are nearby.

Reservations, fee: No reservations necessary; $3 fee per night. Open late May to
early September.

Who to contact: Phone the Star Ranger District at (503)899-1812 or write to Rogue
River National Forest, 6941 Upper Applegate Road, Jacksonville, OR 97530.

Location: From Jacksonville, travel eight miles southwest on Highway 238, then
14 miles south on County Road 10. From there go 1.5 miles east on Forest
Service Road 1075. A short walk is required.

Trip note: This campground is set along the shore of Applegate Reservoir. It's a
popular summer fishing spot for Ashland anglers.

Site **93**
CARBERRY
on Applegate Reservoir, walk-in only
ROGUE RIVER NATIONAL FOREST

Campsites, facilities: There are ten walk-in sites for tents, trailers or motor homes.
Picnic tables and fire grills are provided. Vault toilets are available. There is
no piped water. Leashed pets are permitted. Boat docks and launching facilities
are nearby.

Reservations, fee: No reservations necessary; $2 fee per night. Open June to
September.

Who to contact: Phone the Star Ranger District at (503)899-1812 or write to Rogue
River National Forest, 6941 Upper Applegate Road, Jacksonville, OR 97530.

Location: Go eight miles southwest on Highway 238, then 18 miles south on County
Road 10. A short walk is required.

Trip note: This campground is set along the southwest shore of Applegate Reservoir.
It's a smaller and more primitive option to nearby Site 92.

Site **94**
WATKINS
on Applegate Reservoir, walk-in only
ROGUE RIVER NATIONAL FOREST

Campsites, facilities: There are 14 walk-in sites for tents. **No piped water** is
available. Picnic tables and fire grills are provided. Vault toilets are available.
Leashed pets are permitted. Boat docks and launching facilities are nearby.

Reservations, fee: No reservations necessary; $2 fee per night. Open June to
September.

Who to contact: Phone the Star Ranger District at (503)899-1812 or write to Rogue
River National Forest, 6941 Upper Applegate Road, Jacksonville, OR 97530.

Location: From Jacksonville, go eight miles southwest on Highway 238, then 17
miles south on County Road 10.

Trip note: This campground is set along the southwest shore of Applegate Reservoir.

Site **95**

SQUAW LAKE
on Squaw Lake, walk-in only
ROGUE RIVER NATIONAL FOREST

Campsites, facilities: There are 11 walk-in sites for tents, trailers or motor homes.
No piped water is available. Picnic tables and fire grills are provided. Vault
toilets are available. Leashed pets are permitted. Boat docks are nearby.

Reservations, fee: Reservations required; $2 fee per night. Open year-round.

Who to contact: Phone the Star Ranger District at (503)899-1812 or write to Rogue
River National Forest, 6941 Upper Applegate Road, Jacksonville, OR 97530.

Location: Travel eight miles southwest of Jacksonville on Highway 238, then 14
miles south on County Road 10. The camp is eight miles southeast on Forest
Service Road 1075.

Trip note: This campground is set along the shore of little Squaw Lake. Numerous
trails are in the area. It's a more intimate setting than the larger Applegate Lake
to the west.

Site **96**

WRANGLE
near Pacific Crest Trail
ROGUE RIVER NATIONAL FOREST

Campsites, facilities: There are five sites for tents. **No piped water** is available.
Picnic tables and fire grills are provided. Vault toilets are available. Leashed
pets are permitted.

Reservations, fee: No reservations necessary; no fee. Open early June to late
October.

Who to contact: Phone the Star Ranger District at (503)899-1812 or write to Rogue
River National Forest, 6941 Upper Applegate Road, Jacksonville, OR 97530.

Location: From Ashland, travel three miles north on Highway 99 to Talent, then
drive south on Forest Service Road 22 for 17 miles until it ends at Forest Service
Road 20. Head west on Road 20 for 4.5 miles. The entrance road to the
campground is on the right.

Trip note: This campground is set at the headwaters of Wrangle Creek in the
Siskiyou Mountains. The Pacific Crest Trail passes near camp. A map of Rogue
River National Forest details hiking trails and streams, as well as backcountry
roads.

COLUMBIA

◆

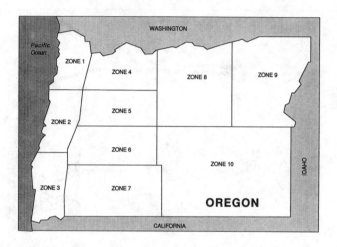

SOME HIGHLIGHTS

43 CAMPGROUNDS

Ochoco National Forest

Prineville Reservoir

Malheur National Forest

Strawberry Mountain Wilderness

Umatilla National Forest

Umatilla River

John Day River

Cold Springs National Wildlife Refuge

McKay Creek National Wildlife Refuge

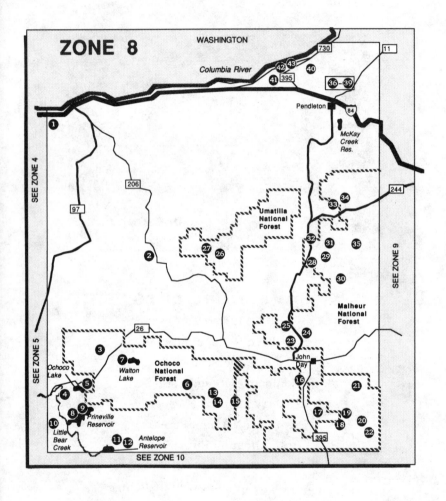

ZONE 8

WASHINGTON

Columbia River

730

11

42 43

40

41 395

36 — 39

Pendleton

84

McKay
Creek
Res.

SEE ZONE 4

206

97

1

Umatilla
National
Forest

244

33 34

SEE ZONE 9

27 26

2

32 31

35

28 29

30

Malheur
National
Forest

SEE ZONE 5

26

3

7

Walton
Lake

Ochoco
National
Forest

25

24

23

John
Day

5

Ochoco
Lake

6

13

15

16

21

4

14

17

19

20

8 9

Prineville
Reservoir

18

22

10

Little
Bear
Creek

11 12

Antelope
Reservoir

395

SEE ZONE 10

Site **1** **DESCHUTES RIVER STATE RECREATION AREA**
on Deschutes Rivers

Campsites, facilities: There are 34 primitive sites for tents, trailers or motor homes up to 30 feet long. Picnic tables and fire grills are provided. Piped water and flush toilets are available. Pets are permitted.

Reservations, fee: No reservations necessary; $8 fee per night. Open mid-April to late October.

Who to contact: Phone (503)739-2322 or write to Star Route Box 29, Wasco, OR 97065.

Location: Travel 12 miles east on Interstate 84 from The Dalles, then go five miles southeast on Highway 206.

Trip note: This park is set along the Deschutes River at the mouth of the Columbia River. There's a small day-use state park called Heritage Landing across the river, which has a boat ramp and rest room facilities. The Army Corps of Engineers offers a free train ride and tour of the dam at The Dalles during the summer. Good rafting and steelhead fishing possibilities are a bonus here, in season. For 25 miles upstream, the river is mostly inaccessible by car. A hiking trail from the camp goes up the west bank into that area.

Site **2** **SHELTON WAYSIDE**
near Fossil

Campsites, facilities: There are 36 primitive sites for tents, trailers or motor homes up to 30 feet long. Picnic tables and fire grills are provided. Piped water, firewood and vault toilets are available. Pets are permitted.

Reservations, fee: No reservations necessary; $6 fee per night. Open mid-April to late October.

Who to contact: Phone (503)575-2773 or write to Clyde Holiday State Park at P.O. Box 9, Canyon City, OR 97820.

Location: Go ten miles southeast of Fossil on Highway 19.

Trip note: This is a good layover if you are stuck in the area with no place to camp for the night; there are no campgrounds on major roadways for an hour's drive in any direction. The closest options are primitive sites (Sites 26 and 27), accessible by Forest Service roads.

Site **3** **WILDCAT**
on the East Fork of Mill Creek
OCHOCO NATIONAL FOREST

Campsites, facilities: There are 17 sites for tents, trailers or motor homes up to 30 feet long. Picnic tables and fire grills are provided. Piped water, firewood and vault toilets are available. Pets are permitted.

Reservations, fee: No reservations necessary; $4 fee per night. Open mid-April to late October.

Who to contact: Phone the Prineville Ranger District at (503)447-9641 or write to Ochoco National Forest, 221 East 3rd Street, Prineville, OR 97754.

Location: From Prineville, travel nine miles east on US 26, then nine miles northeast on County Route 122. The camp is two miles on Forest Service Road 33.

Trip note: This campground is set along the East Fork of Mill Creek at a trailhead that provides access into the Mill Creek Wilderness. This spot is little-known, except by backpackers with knowledge of the local area.

CRYSTAL CORRAL RV PARK
Site **4**
near Ochoco Lake State Park

Campsites, facilities: There are 20 tent sites and 22 drive-through sites for trailers or motor homes of any length. Electricity, piped water and sewer hookups are provided. Flush toilets, bottled gas, showers, a store, a cafe, a laundromat and ice are available. Pets and motorbikes are permitted. Boat docks, launching facilities and rentals are nearby.

Reservations, fee: Reservations accepted; $7 fee per night. Open all year.

Who to contact: Phone (503)447-5932 or write to HC 69, Box 91, Prineville, OR 97754.

Location: Travel eight miles east of Prineville on US 26.

Trip note: This motor home park is not far from Ochoco Lake State Park (Site 5), where recreation options include boating and fishing.

OCHOCO LAKE STATE PARK
Site **5**
on Ochoco Reservoir

Campsites, facilities: There are 22 primitive sites for tents, trailers or motor homes up to 30 feet long, and a special area for hikers and bicyclists. Picnic tables and fire grills are provided. Piped water, firewood and flush toilets are available. Pets are permitted. Boat launching facilities are nearby.

Reservations, fee: No reservations necessary; $2-8 fee per night. Open mid-April to late October.

Who to contact: Phone 503-575-2773 or write to Clyde Holiday State Park at P.O. Box 9, Canyon City, OR 97820.

Location: Travel seven miles east of Prineville on US 26.

Trip note: This is one of the nicer camps along Highway 26 in eastern Oregon. This state park is on the shore adjacent to Ochoco Lake, where boating and fishing are popular pastimes.

DEEP CREEK
Site **6**
on the North Fork of Crooked River
OCHOCO NATIONAL FOREST

Campsites, facilities: There are six sites for tents, trailers or motor homes up to 22 feet long. Picnic tables and fire grills are provided. Piped water, firewood and vault toilets are available. Pets are permitted.

Reservations, fee: No reservations necessary; no fee. Open June to mid-October.

Who to contact: Phone Big Summit Ranger District, Ochoco National Forest at (503)447-9645 or write to Ochoco National Forest, 2321 East Third, Prineville, OR 97754.

Location: From Prineville, travel 16.5 miles east on US 26, then 8.5 miles northeast on County Route 22. The camp is 23.5 miles southeast on Forest Service Road 42.

Trip note: This camp is small and gets little use, but it is set at a nice spot—the confluence of Deep Creek and the North Fork of the Crooked River.

WALTON LAKE
Site **7**
on Walton Lake
OCHOCO NATIONAL FOREST

Campsites, facilities: There are 23 sites for tents, trailers or motor homes up to 22 feet long. Picnic tables and fire grills are provided. Piped water, firewood and vault toilets are available. Pets are permitted. Boat docks and launching facilities are nearby.

Reservations, fee: No reservations necessary; $5 fee per night. Open June to late September.

Who to contact: Phone Big Summit Ranger District at (503)447-9645 or write to Ochoco National Forest, 2321 East Third, Prineville, OR 97754.

Location: Travel 16.5 miles east of Prineville on US 26, then 14 miles northeast on County Route 123. The camp is seven miles northeast of the Ochoco Ranger Station on Forest Service Road 22.

Trip note: This campground is set along the shore of Walton Lake. Fishing and swimming are popular and boats without motors are allowed. Hikers can explore a nearby trail that leads south to Round Mountain.

Site **8**

PRINEVILLE RESERVOIR RESORT
on Prineville Reservoir

Campsites, facilities: There are 75 drive-through sites for trailers or motor homes of any length. Electricity, piped water and picnic tables are provided. Flush toilets, bottled gas, sanitary disposal services, showers, firewood, a store, a cafe, a laundromat and ice are available. Pets are permitted. Boat docks, launching facilities and rentals are nearby.

Reservations, fee: Reservations accepted; $10 fee per night; MasterCard and Visa accepted. Open mid-March to mid-October.

Who to contact: Phone to (503)447-7468 or write to 1300 PLR, Prineville, OR 97754.

Location: Travel on US 26 for one mile east of Prineville, then go one mile south on Combs Flat Road. The camp is 18 miles south on Prineville Reservoir Road.

Trip note: This resort is set along the shore of the Prineville Reservoir, a good spot for watersports and fishing.

Site **9**

PRINEVILLE RESERVOIR
on Prineville Reservoir

Campsites, facilities: There are 48 tent sites and 22 sites for trailers or motor homes of any length. Electricity, piped water, sewer hookups and picnic tables are provided. Flush toilets, showers, firewood and a laundromat are available. A cafe is located within one mile. Pets are permitted. Boat docks and launching facilities are nearby.

Reservations, fee: Reservations accepted; $8 fee per night. Open mid-April to late October.

Who to contact: Phone to (503)447-4363 or write to Box 1050, Prineville, OR 97754.

Location: From Prineville, travel one mile east on US 26, then go one mile south on Combs Flat Road. Travel 16 miles southeast on Prineville Reservoir Road to the reservoir.

Trip note: This state park is set along the shore of the Prineville Reservoir. Swimming, boating, fishing and waterskiing are among the options available here. This is one of two campgrounds on the lake; the other is Site 8 (motor homes only). Site 10 provides another option, set on the Crooked River below the Prineville Dam.

Site **10**   **LOWER CROOKED RIVER**
                   on Crooked River near Prineville Dam

Campsites, facilities: There are 30 tent sites. Picnic tables and fire grills are
   provided. Piped water and vault toilets are available. Pets are permitted.
Reservations, fee: No reservations necessary; no fee. Open late April to December.
Who to contact: Phone (503)447-4115 or write to Bureau of Land Management,
   P.O. Box 550, Prineville, OR 97754.
Location: From Prineville, travel 16 miles south on Highway 27.
Trip note: This campground is set along the banks of the Crooked River, just below
   the Prineville Dam.

Site **11**   **ANTELOPE RESERVOIR**
                     on Antelope Reservoir
                   OCHOCO NATIONAL FOREST

Campsites, facilities: There are 24 sites for tents, trailers or motor homes up to 30
   feet long. Picnic tables and fire grills are provided. Piped water, firewood and
   vault toilets are available. Pets are permitted. Boat docks and launching
   facilities are nearby.
Reservations, fee: No reservations necessary; $3 fee per night. Open late April to
   late October.
Who to contact: Phone the Prineville Ranger District at (503)447-9641 or write to
   Ochoco National Forest, 2321 East Third, Prineville, OR 97754.
Location: From Prineville, travel 29 miles southeast on Highway 380, then 11 miles
   south on Forest Service Road 17. The camp is 300 yards east on Forest Service
   Road 17.
Trip note: This campground is set along the west shore of Antelope Reservoir.
   Fishing can be good and boating with motors is permitted. This is also a good
   lake for canoes.

Site **12**   **WILEY FLAT**
                      on Wiley Creek
                   OCHOCO NATIONAL FOREST

Campsites, facilities: There are five sites for tents, trailers or motor homes up to 30
   feet long. Picnic tables and fire grills are provided. Piped water, firewood and
   vault toilets are available. Pets are permitted.
Reservations, fee: No reservations necessary; $2 fee per night. Open mid-June to
   late October.
Who to contact: Phone the Prineville Ranger District at (503)447-9641 or write to
   2321 East Third, Prineville, OR 97754.
Location: Go 34 miles southeast of Prineville on Highway 380, then ten miles
   southeast on Forest Service Road 16. The camp is one mile west on Forest
   Service Road 16.
Trip note: This campground is set along Wiley Creek. It is a nice, hidden spot with
   minimal crowds and piped water. A map of Ochoco National Forest details
   nearby hiking trails and access roads. Site 14 provides a nearby, but more
   primitive, alternative.

Site **13**
WOLF CREEK
on Wolf Creek
OCHOCO NATIONAL FOREST

Campsites, facilities: There are 17 sites for tents, trailers or motor homes up to 22 feet long. Picnic tables and fire grills are provided. Piped water, firewood and vault toilets are available. Leashed pets are permitted.

Reservations, fee: No reservations necessary; $3 fee per night. Open mid-April to late October.

Who to contact: Phone the Paulina Ranger District at (503)477-3713 or write to Ochoco National Forest, HC 68, Box 6015, Paulina, OR 97751.

Location: Travel 3.5 miles east of Paulina on County Road 380, then 6.5 miles north on County Road 113. The camp is 1.5 miles north on Forest Service Road 142.

Trip note: This campground is set along the banks of Wolf Creek, a nice stream that runs through Ochoco National Forest. It's a quality spot.

Site **14**
SUGAR CREEK
on Sugar Creek
OCHOCO NATIONAL FOREST

Campsites, facilities: There are ten sites for tents, trailers or motor homes up to 21 feet long. Picnic tables and fire grills are provided. Firewood and vault toilets are available. There is **no piped water**. Pets are permitted.

Reservations, fee: No reservations necessary; $3 fee per night. Open mid-April to late October.

Who to contact: Phone the Paulina Ranger District at (503)477-3713 or write to Ochoco National Forest, HC 68, Box 6015, Paulina, OR 97751.

Location: From Paulina, go 3.5 miles east on County Road 380, then 6.5 miles north on County Road 113. The camp is two miles east on Forest Service Road 158.

Trip note: This campground is on the banks of Sugar Creek. It is one of three primitive camps in the outback of the Ochoco National Forest. The others are Sites 13 and 15. All are small and remote.

Site **15**
FRAZIER
on Frazier Creek
OCHOCO NATIONAL FOREST

Campsites, facilities: There are 12 sites for tents, trailers or motor homes up to 21 feet long. Picnic tables and fire grills are provided. Firewood and vault toilets are available. There is **no piped water**. Pets are permitted.

Reservations, fee: No reservations necessary; no fee. Open mid-May to late October.

Who to contact: Phone the Paulina Ranger District at (503)477-3713 or write to Ochoco National Forest, HC 68, Box 6015, Paulina, OR 97751.

Location: From Paulina, travel 3.5 miles east on County Road 380, then two miles north on County Road 113. The camp is ten miles east on County Road 135 and six miles on Forest Service Road 158.

Trip note: This campground is set along the banks of Frazier Creek. There are some dirt roads adjacent to camp that are good for mountain biking. It is advisable to obtain a map of Ochoco National Forest.

Site 16
STARR
near Starr Springs
MALHEUR NATIONAL FOREST

Campsites, facilities: There are five tent sites and nine sites for trailers or motor homes up to 25 feet long. Picnic tables and fire grills are provided. Firewood and vault toilets are available. There is **no piped water.** Pets are permitted.

Reservations, fee: No reservations necessary; no fee. Open early May to November.

Who to contact: Phone (503)575-2110 or write to Malheur National Forest, 139 NE Dayton Street, John Day, OR 97845.

Location: From John Day travel 15 miles south on US 395.

Trip note: This is a good layover for travelers on US 395. It is set adjacent to Starr Springs near an area that is popular in winter for skiing.

Site 17
WICKIUP
on Wickiup Creek
MALHEUR NATIONAL FOREST

Campsites, facilities: There are eight sites for tents, trailers or motor homes up to 16 feet long. Picnic tables and fire grills are provided. Piped water, firewood and vault toilets are available. Pets are permitted.

Reservations, fee: No reservations necessary; no fee. Open early May to November.

Who to contact: Phone (503)575-2110 or write to Malheur National Forest, 139 NE Dayton, John Day, OR 97845.

Location: Travel ten miles south of John Day on US 395 and eight miles southeast on Forest Service Road 15.

Trip note: This campground is set along the bank of Wickiup Creek.

Site 18
PARISH CABIN
on Bear Creek
MALHEUR NATIONAL FOREST

Campsites, facilities: There are three tent sites and 16 sites for tents, trailers or motor homes up to 32 feet long. Picnic tables and fire grills are provided. Piped water and vault toilets are available. Pets are permitted.

Reservations, fee: No reservations necessary; no fee. Open mid-May to late November.

Who to contact: Phone (503)575-2110 or write to Malheur National Forest, 139 NE Dayton, John Day, OR 97845.

Location: From John Day, travel ten miles south on US 395, then 16 miles southeast on Forest Service Road 15 to the campground.

Trip note: This campground is set along the bank of Bear Creek.

Site 19
CANYON MEADOWS
on Canyon Meadows Reservoir
MALHEUR NATIONAL FOREST

Campsites, facilities: There are 15 sites for tents, trailers or motor homes up to 16 feet long. Picnic tables and fire grills are provided. Piped water, firewood and vault toilets are available. Pets are permitted. Boat launching facilities are nearby.

Reservations, fee: No reservations necessary; no fee. Open mid-May to late October.

Who to contact: Phone (503)575-2110 or write to Malheur National Forest, 139 NE Dayton, John Day, OR 97845.

Location: From John Day, go south on US 395 for ten miles, then nine miles southeast on Forest Service Road 15. The camp is five miles northeast on Forest Service Road 1520.

Trip note: This campground is on the shore of Canyon Meadows Reservoir, where non-motorized boating, fishing and hiking are recreation options.

Site **20**
INDIAN SPRINGS
near Strawberry Mountain Wilderness
MALHEUR NATIONAL FOREST

Campsites, facilities: This is a primitive campground with no designated sites. **No piped water** or pit toilets are available. Pets are permitted.

Reservations, fee: No reservations necessary; no fee. Open June to mid-October.

Who to contact: Phone (503)575-2110 or write to Malheur National Forest, 139 NE Dayton Street, John Day, OR 97845.

Location: From John Day, travel ten miles south on US 395, then east on Forest Service Road 15 for about 15 miles to Forest Service Road 16. Turn left and go 2.5 miles, then turn left on Forest Service Road 1640 and go seven miles north (gravel then dirt road).

Trip note: This campground is set at Indian Springs, a pretty spot near Bear Creek. A side trip option is to drive the 77-mile loop around the Strawberry Mountain Wilderness. A map of Malheur National Forest details the back roads. Backpackers and hikers will find many trailheads along the Forest Service road.

Site **21**
STRAWBERRY
on Strawberry Creek
MALHEUR NATIONAL FOREST

Campsites, facilities: There are 11 sites for tents, trailers or motor homes up to 16 feet long. Picnic tables and fire grills are provided. Piped water and vault toilets are available. Pets are permitted.

Reservations, fee: No reservations necessary; no fee. Open June to mid-October.

Who to contact: Phone (503)820-3311 or write to Malheur National Forest, 139 NE Dayton, John Day, OR 97845.

Location: From John Day, travel 13 miles east, then go 8.5 miles south on County Road 60, then 2.5 miles south on Forest Service Road 6001.

Trip note: This campground is set along the bank of Strawberry Creek. Nearby trails provide access into the Strawberry Mountain Wilderness, to Strawberry Lake and Strawberry Falls. It is a pretty area. There are two other primitive campgrounds, Slide Creek and McNaughton Spring, that are along the entrance road to Strawberry. They have camping facilities, but no piped water. No fee is charged.

Site **22**
BIG CREEK
near Strawberry Mountain Wilderness
MALHEUR NATIONAL FOREST

Campsites, facilities: There are 14 sites for tents, trailers or motor homes up to 16 feet long. Picnic tables and fire grills are provided. Piped water and vault toilets are available. Pets are permitted.

Reservations, fee: No reservations necessary; no fee. Open mid-May to mid-November.

Who to contact: Phone (503)820-3311 or write to Malheur National Forest, 139 NE Dayton, John Day, OR 97845.

Location: From John Day, travel ten miles south on US 395, then southeast on Forest Service Road 15 for 16 miles, then eight miles east on Forest Service Road 16, and one half mile north on Forest Service Road 815.

Trip note: This campground is set along the bank of Big Creek. Nearby Forest Service roads provide access into Strawberry Mountain Wilderness.

Site 23

CLYDE HOLLIDAY WAYSIDE
near John Day River

Campsites, facilities: There are 30 sites for trailers or motor homes of any length. Electricity, picnic tables and fire grills are provided. Piped water, firewood, sanitary disposal services, showers and flush toilets are available. Some facilities are wheelchair accessible. Pets are permitted.

Reservations, fee: No reservations necessary; $7 fee per night. Open mid-April to late October.

Who to contact: Phone to (503)575-2773 or write to 511 Hillcrest Road, John Day, OR 97845.

Location: Travel seven miles west of John Day on US 26.

Trip note: This roadside campground is set near the John Day River. Of special interest in John Day is Kam Wah Chung, a Chinese herbalist's office from the 1880s that is now a museum administered by the State Parks Department.

Site 24

MAGONE LAKE
on Magone Lake
MALHEUR NATIONAL FOREST

Campsites, facilities: This camp was reconstructed in 1990 with 14 family campsites, with four of them designed for handicapped access. An additional group camping area is designed for six families, with a bonus three walk-in sites. There are 16 sites for tents, trailers or motor homes up to 16 feet long. Picnic tables and fire grills are provided. Piped water, firewood and vault toilets are available. Pets are permitted. Boat docks and launching facilities are nearby.

Reservations, fee: No reservations necessary; $4 fee per night. Open mid-May to November.

Who to contact: Phone (503)575-2110 or write to Malheur National Forest, 139 NE Dayton Street, John Day, OR 97845.

Location: From John Day, travel eight miles west, then go nine miles north on US 395, then eight miles northeast on Forest Service Road 36. The camp is two miles north on Forest Service Road 3618.

Trip note: This campground is set along the shore of little Magone Lake. A 1.5-mile trail rings the lake, and a half-mile trail is routed to Magone Slide, a unique geological formation.

Site 25

BEECH CREEK
on Beech Creek
MALHEUR NATIONAL FOREST

Campsites, facilities: There are five sites for tents, trailers or motor homes up to 16 feet long. Picnic tables and fire grills are provided. Piped water and vault toilets are available. Pets are permitted.

Reservations, fee: No reservations necessary; no fee. Open June to November.

Who to contact: Phone (503)575-2110 or write to Malheur National Forest, 139 NE Dayton Street, John Day, OR 97845.

Location: From John Day, travel eight miles west on US 26, then 16 miles north on

US 395 to the campground.

Trip note: This campground is set along Beech Creek.

Site 26
BULL PRAIRIE
on Bull Prairie Lake
UMATILLA NATIONAL FOREST

Campsites, facilities: There are 25 sites for tents, trailers or motor homes up to 31 feet long. Picnic tables and fire grills are provided. Piped water, sanitary disposal services, firewood and vault toilets are available. Pets are permitted. Boat docks and launching facilities are on site.

Reservations, fee: No reservations necessary; $5 fee per night. Open May to October.

Who to contact: Phone the Heppner Ranger District at (503)676-9187 or write to Umatilla National Forest, P.O. Box 7, Heppner, OR 97836.

Location: From the junction of Highway 26 and 19, drive north on Highway 19 just over two miles from Spray, then 12 miles north on Highway 207. The camp is three miles northeast on Forest Service Road 2039 (paved).

Trip note: This campground is set along the shore of Bull Prairie Lake. Boating (no motors permitted), swimming, fishing and hunting are some of the options here. This spot attracts little attention from out-of-towners.

Site 27
FAIRVIEW
near Bull Prairie Lake
UMATILLA NATIONAL FOREST

Campsites, facilities: There are five sites for trailers or motor homes up to 16 feet long. Picnic tables and fire grills are provided. Firewood and vault toilets are available. There is **no piped water**. Pets are permitted. Boat docks and launching facilities are nearby at Bull Prairie Lake.

Reservations, fee: No reservations necessary; no fee. Open May to late October.

Who to contact: Phone the Heppner Ranger District at (509)676-9187 or write to Umatilla National Forest, P.O. Box 7, Heppner, OR 97836.

Location: From the junction of US 26 and Highway 19, drive a little over two miles past Spray on Highway 19, then 11.5 miles north on Highway 207. The camp is 500 yards west on Forest Service Road 400.

Trip note: This campground is set adjacent to Fairview Springs near Mahogany Butte. It's a small, primitive site known by very few people.

Site 28
TOLLBRIDGE
on the North Fork of John Day River
UMATILLA NATIONAL FOREST

Campsites, facilities: There are six sites for tents, trailers or motor homes up to 31 feet long. Picnic tables and fire grills are provided. Piped water and vault toilets are available. Pets are permitted.

Reservations, fee: No reservations necessary; $4 fee per night. Open June to mid-October.

Who to contact: Phone the North Fork John Day Ranger District at (503)427-3231 or write to Umatilla National Forest, P.O. Box 158, Ukiah, OR 97880.

Location: From Dale, go one mile northeast on US 395, one half mile southeast on Forest Service Road 55 and 100 yards on Forest Service Road 10.

Trip note: This campground is set at the confluence of Desolation Creek and the North Fork of the John Day River, and is adjacent to the Bridge Creek Wildlife Area. It's small and secluded.

Site **29**
GOLD DREDGE
on North Fork of John Day River
UMATILLA NATIONAL FOREST

Campsites, facilities: There are five sites for trailers or motor homes. **No piped water,** picnic tables, or fire grills are provided, but pit toilets are available.
Reservations, fee: No reservations necessary; no fee. Open May to September.
Who to contact: Phone the North Fork John Day Ranger District at (503)427-3231 or write to Umatilla National Forest, P.O. Box 158, Ukiah, OR 97880.
Location: From Pendleton, travel 64 miles south on US 395 to Dale, then drive east on Forest Service Road 55 for six miles to the crossroads. Continue east on Forest Service Road 5506 for 2.5 miles to the campground.
Trip note: This campground is set along the banks of the North Fork of the John Day River, a federally certified wild and scenic river. Hunting, fishing and gold prospecting are some of the options here.

Site **30**
ORIENTAL CREEK
on North Fork of John Day River
UMATILLA NATIONAL FOREST

Campsites, facilities: There are five primitive tent sites. Picnic tables and fire grills are provided and pit toilets are available. There is **no piped water.**
Reservations, fee: No reservations necessary; no fee.
Who to contact: Phone the North Fork John Day Range District at (503)427-3231 or write to Umatilla National Forest, P.O. Box 158, Ukiah, OR 97880.
Location: From Pendleton, travel 64 miles south on US 395 to Dale, then drive east on Forest Service Road 55 for six miles to the crossroads. Continue east on Forest Service Road 5506 for 10.5 miles to the campground.
Trip note: This campground is set at 3,500 feet elevation along the banks of the North Fork of the John Day River. Nearby trails provide access to the North Fork John Day Wilderness. Hunting, fishing, gold prospecting are some of the options here, but no motorbikes are permitted in the Wilderness Area.

Site **31**
DRIFT FENCE
near Ross Springs
UMATILLA NATIONAL FOREST

Campsites, facilities: There are three sites for tents, trailers or motor homes up to 16 feet long. **No piped water,** picnic tables or fire grills are provided, but a vault toilet is available.
Reservations, fee: No reservations necessary; no fee. Open from June to November.
Who to contact: Phone the North Fork John Day Ranger District at (503)427-3231 or write to Umatilla National Forest, P.O. Box 158, Ukiah, OR 97880.
Location: From Ukiah, drive nine miles southeast on Forest Service Road 52 to the campground.
Trip note: This campground is set at 4,200 feet, adjacent to Ross Springs. This is a good area for elk and deer. The camp is adjacent to Blue Mountain National Forest Scenic Byway.

Site **32**
UKIAH-DALE FOREST STATE PARK
on Camus Creek

Campsites, facilities: There are 25 primitive sites for tents, trailers or motor homes up to 40 feet long. Picnic tables and fire grills are provided. Piped water, firewood and vault toilets are available. Pets are permitted.

Reservations, fee: No reservations necessary; $8 fee per night. Open mid-April to late October.

Who to contact: Phone (503)983-2277 or write to P.O. Box 85, Meacham, OR 97859.

Location: Go three miles south of Ukiah on US 395.

Trip note: This campground is set near the banks of Camus Creek. It's a good layover for visitors cruising US 395 looking for a spot for the night.

Site **33**
LANE CREEK
on Camus Creek
UMATILLA NATIONAL FOREST

Campsites, facilities: There are four sites for tents, trailers or motor homes up to 30 feet long. **No piped water** is available. Picnic tables and fire grills are provided. Vault toilets are available. Pets are permitted.

Reservations, fee: No reservations necessary; no fee. Open April to November.

Who to contact: Phone the North Fork John Day Ranger District at (503)427-3231 or write to Umatilla National Forest, P.O. Box 158, Ukiah, OR 97880.

Location: From Ukiah, travel 10.5 miles east on Highway 244.

Trip note: This campground is set along Camus Creek. There is good hunting and some fishing in Umatilla National Forest. A Forest Service map details the back roads.

Site **34**
BEAR WALLOW CREEK
on Bear Wallow Creek
UMATILLA NATIONAL FOREST

Campsites, facilities: There are nine sites for tents, trailers or motor homes up to 30 feet long. **No piped water** is available. Picnic tables and fire grills are provided. Vault toilets are available. Pets are permitted.

Reservations, fee: No reservations necessary; no fee. Open April to November.

Who to contact: Phone the North Fork John Day Ranger District at (503)427-3231 or write to Umatilla National Forest, P.O. Box 158, Ukiah, OR 97880.

Location: From Ukiah on US 395, travel ten miles east on Highway 244.

Trip note: This campground is set at the confluence of Bear Wallow Creek and Camus Creek. This is one of three camps off Highway 244. The others are Sites 33 and 35.

Site **35**
FRAZIER
on Frazier Creek
UMATILLA NATIONAL FOREST

Campsites, facilities: There are 25 sites for tents, trailers or motor homes up to 30 feet long. Picnic tables and fire grills are provided. Piped water and vault toilets are available. Pets are permitted.

Reservations, fee: No reservations necessary; no fee. Open June to November.

Who to contact: Phone the North Fork John Day Ranger District at (503)427-3231 or write to Umatilla National Forest, P.O. Box 158, Ukiah, OR 97880.

Location: From Ukiah, go 16 miles east on Highway 244, then one half mile south on Forest Service Road 5226. The camp is two miles east on Forest Service Road 20.

Trip note: This campground is set at 4,300 feet elevation along the banks of Frazier Creek. This is a popular hunting area that also has some fishing. It's advisable to obtain a map of Umatilla National Forest. It's a good staging area for motorcycles. Leyman Hot Springs provides a nearby trip option.

Site 36
BROOKE TRAILER PARK
near McKay Creek National Wildlife Refuge

Campsites, facilities: There are four tent sites and 20 drive-through sites for trailers or motor homes of any length. Electricity, piped water, sewer hookups and picnic tables are provided. Flush toilets, showers, a laundromat and ice are available. Bottled gas, sanitary disposal services, a store and a cafe are located within one mile. Pets are permitted.
Reservations, fee: Reservations accepted; $10 fee per night. Open all year.
Who to contact: Phone (503)276-5353 or write to 5 Northeast 8th Street, Pendleton, OR 97801.
Location: From Pendleton, travel three-quarters of a mile north on Highway 11, then one-quarter mile west on southeast Court Avenue.
Trip note: Waterfowl can be observed at the National Wildlife Refuge seven miles south of Pendleton. The Pendleton Mills and outlet are in town. Other nearby recreation options include a golf course, bike paths and tennis courts.

Site 37
RIVERVIEW TRAILER PARK
on Umatilla River

Campsites, facilities: There are 18 sites for trailers or motor homes of any length. Electricity and piped water are provided. Flush toilets, showers, a laundromat and a playground are available. A store, a cafe and ice are located within one mile. Pets are permitted.
Reservations, fee: Reservations accepted; $7 fee per night. Open all year.
Who to contact: Phone (503)276-7632 or write to 2712 Northeast Riverside, Pendleton, OR 97801.
Location: From Pendleton, travel one-quarter-mile northeast on Highway 11, then go one block east.
Trip note: This motor home park is set along the banks of the Umatilla River. Nearby recreation options include a golf course, bike paths and tennis courts.

Site 38
RV PARK
near Umatilla River

Campsites, facilities: There are 30 tent sites and 31 drive-through sites for trailers or motor homes of any length. Electricity, piped water, sewer hookups and picnic tables are provided. Flush toilets, sanitary services, showers, a laundromat and a playground are available. Bottled gas, a store, a cafe and ice are located within one mile. Motorbikes are permitted.
Reservations, fee: No reservations necessary; $12 fee per night. Open all year.
Who to contact: Phone to (503)276-5408 or write to 1500 Southeast Byers, Pendleton, OR 97801.
Location: From Pendleton, go one mile north on Highway 11, then one block west on 10th Street. The camp is located one-quarter mile east on 12th Street and one-quarter mile north on Byers.
Trip note: This campground is one block from the levee along the Umatilla River, where people fish and walk. The Pendleton Woolen Mills are around the corner.

Site 39
SHADEVIEW MOBILE HOME PARK
near Umatilla River

Campsites, facilities: There are eight drive-through sites for trailers or motor homes of any length. Electricity, piped water and sewer hookups are provided. Flush toilets and showers are available. Bottled gas, sanitary disposal services, a store, a cafe, a laundromat and ice are located within one mile. Pets are permitted.

Reservations, fee: Reservations accepted; $8.50 fee per night. Open all year.

Who to contact: Phone (503)276-0688 or write to 1417 Southwest 37th, Pendleton, OR 97801.

Location: Go one mile south of Pendleton on US 395, then one-quarter mile West on Southgate Place. The park is one block north on 37th Street.

Trip note: This park is set near the Umatilla River. A levee along the river offers walking and fishing opportunities. Nearby recreation options include marked bike trails and tennis courts. The Cold Springs National Wildlife Refuge is eight miles east of Hermiston and offers a large variety of waterfowl.

Site 40
HAT ROCK CAMPGROUND
near Columbia River

Campsites, facilities: There are 40 tent sites and 30 drive-through sites for trailers or motor homes of any length. Electricity, piped water, sewer hookups and picnic tables are provided. Flush toilets, sanitary disposal services, showers, a store, a cafe, a laundromat and ice are available. Pets are permitted. Boat docks and launching facilities are nearby.

Reservations, fee: Reservations accepted; $6 fee per night. Open all year.

Who to contact: Phone (503)567-4188 or write to Route 3, Box 3780, Hermiston, OR 97838.

Location: From Hermiston, go one mile southeast on Highway 207, then one half mile on State Park Road.

Trip note: This campground is not far from Hat Rock State Park, a day-use area with a boat launch along the banks of the Columbia River.

Site 41
BUTTER CREEK RECREATION COMPLEX
on Butter Creek

Campsites, facilities: There are 20 tent sites and 24 drive-through sites for trailers or motor homes of any length. Electricity, piped water, sewer hookups and picnic tables are provided. Flush toilets, bottled gas, sanitary disposal services, showers, a store, a cafe, a laundromat and ice are available. Pets are permitted.

Reservations, fee: Reservations accepted; $8-11 fee per night; MasterCard and Visa accepted. Open all year.

Who to contact: Phone (503)567-5469 or write to Route 1, Box 1929A, Hermiston, OR 97838.

Location: Take exit 182 off Highway 207 in Hermiston.

Trip note: This campground is set along the banks of Butter Creek.

Site 42
SHADY REST MOBILE HOME PARK
on Columbia River

Campsites, facilities: There are six tent sites and 24 drive-through sites for trailers or motor homes of any length. Electricity, piped water and sewer hookups are provided. Flush toilets, showers, a laundromat and a swimming pool are available. A store, a cafe and ice are located within one mile. Pets are permitted.

Boat docks and launching facilities are nearby.

Reservations, fee: Reservations accepted; $12 fee per night. Open March to late October.

Who to contact: Phone (503)922-5041 or write to Route 1, Box 240, Umatilla, OR 97882.

Location: Travel one half mile west of Umatilla on US 730.

Trip note: This campground is set along the Columbia River. Nearby recreation options include a golf course, a marina and tennis courts.

Site **43**
DUN-ROLLIN TRAILER PARK
near the Columbia River

Campsites, facilities: There are 15 sites for trailers or motor homes of any length. Electricity, piped water and sewer hookups are provided. Flush toilets, sanitary disposal services, showers, a laundromat and a playground are available. Bottled gas, a store, a cafe and ice are located within one mile. Pets and motorbikes are permitted.

Reservations, fee: Reservations accepted; $10 fee per night. Open all year.

Who to contact: Phone (503)567-6918 or write to 445 East Jennie, Hermiston, OR 97838.

Location: From Hermiston, travel one-quarter mile north on US 395 to Jennie, then go one-half mile east.

Trip note: This motor home park is not far from the Columbia River and Cold Springs National Wildlife Refuge. Nearby recreation options include a golf course, bike paths, a marina and tennis courts.

WALLOWA

◆

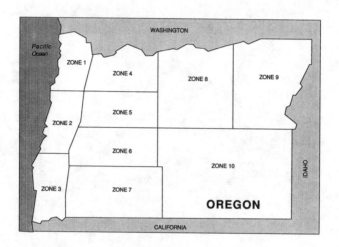

SOME HIGHLIGHTS

66 CAMPGROUNDS

Wallowa-Whitman National Forest

Grande Ronde River

Umatilla National Forest

Burnt River

Snake River

Eagle Cap Wilderness

Phillips Lake

Hells Canyon Wilderness

Lostine River

Imnaha River

Blue Mountain

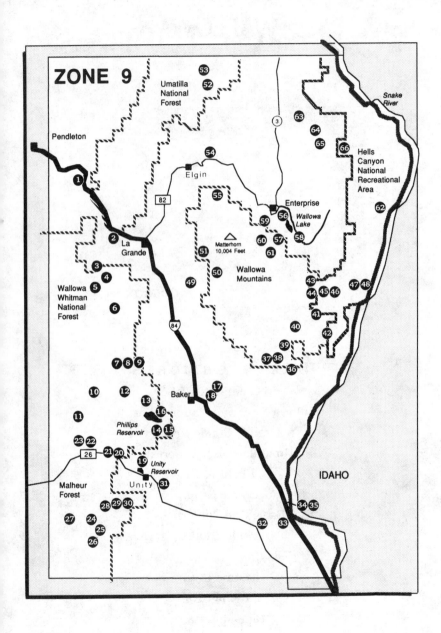

ZONE 9

Umatilla
National
Forest

Pendleton

Elgin

Snake
River

Hells
Canyon
National
Recreational
Area

Enterprise

Wallowa
Lake

Matterhorn
10,004 Feet

Wallowa
Mountains

La
Grande

Wallowa
Whitman
National
Forest

Baker

Phillips
Reservoir

IDAHO

Unity
Reservoir

Unity

Malheur
Forest

EMIGRANT SPRINGS STATE PARK
Site **1**
near Umatilla Indian Reservation

Campsites, facilities: There are 33 tent sites and 18 sites with full hookups for trailers or motor homes of any length. Picnic tables and fire grills are provided. Flush toilets, showers, firewood, a laundromat and a playground are available. Leashed pets are permitted.

Reservations, fee: No reservations necessary; $9-11 in summer, $6-8 off-season. Open mid-April to late October.

Who to contact: Phone (503)983-2277 or write to Meacham, OR 97859.

Location: From Pendleton, travel 26 miles southeast on Interstate 84 to the park.

Trip note: This wooded state park offers group camping and a display about the Oregon Trail. This is a good layover for people driving Interstate 84. It's set just south of the Umatilla Indian Reservation.

HILGARD JUNCTION STATE PARK
Site **2**
on Grande Ronde River

Campsites, facilities: There are 18 primitive sites for tents, trailers or motor homes up to 20 feet long. Picnic tables and fire grills are provided. Piped water, a sanitary disposal service, firewood and vault toilets are available. Some facilities are wheelchair accessible. Leashed pets are permitted.

Reservations, fee: No reservations necessary; $8 fee per night. Open all year with limited winter facilities.

Who to contact: Phone (503)983-2277 or write to LaGrande, OR 97850.

Location: Travel eight miles west of LaGrande on Interstate 84 to Starkey Road.

Trip note: This roadside campground is set along the banks of the Grande Ronde River at the foot of the Blue Mountains. It is surrounded by Umatilla National Forest.

TIME AND A HALF
Site **3**
on Grande Ronde River
WALLOWA-WHITMAN NATIONAL FOREST

Campsites, facilities: There are five tent sites. Picnic tables and fire grills are provided. Piped water, firewood and vault toilets are available. Leashed pets are permitted.

Reservations, fee: No reservations necessary; no fee. Open late May to late November.

Who to contact: Phone the LaGrande Ranger District at (503)963-7186 or write to Wallowa-Whitman National Forest, Box 907, Baker, OR 97814.

Location: Go nine miles northwest of LaGrande on Interstate 84 to the Hilgard junction, then 13 miles southwest on Highway 244. From there, go 4.5 miles south on Forest Service Road 51.

Trip note: This campground is set along the banks of the Grande Ronde River. If this small camp is full, try the next three camps listed. They are also small, primitive Forest Service campgrounds located just south on the same Forest Service road system.

SPOOL CART
Site **4**
on Grande Ronde River
WALLOWA-WHITMAN NATIONAL FOREST

Campsites, facilities: There are five sites for tents, trailers or motor homes up to 22 feet long. Picnic tables and fire grills are provided. Firewood and vault toilets are available. There is **no piped water.** Leashed pets are permitted.

Reservations, fee: No reservations necessary; no fee. Open late May to late November.

Who to contact: Phone the LaGrande Ranger District at (503)963-7186 or write to Wallowa-Whitman National Forest, Box 907, Baker, OR 97814.

Location: Go nine miles northwest of LaGrande on Interstate 84, then 13 miles southwest on Highway 244. From there, go seven miles south on Forest Service Road 51.

Trip note: This small, rustic camp is set at 3,800 feet elevation on the banks of Grande Ronde River. It is advisable to obtain a map of Wallowa-Whitman National Forest that details the back roads and side trips available.

Site 5
RIVER
on Grande Ronde River
WALLOWA-WHITMAN NATIONAL FOREST

Campsites, facilities: There are six sites for tents, trailers or motor homes up to 22 feet long. Picnic tables and fire grills are provided. Firewood and vault toilets are available. There is **no piped water.** Leashed pets are permitted.

Reservations, fee: No reservations necessary; no fee. Open late May to late November.

Who to contact: Phone the LaGrande Ranger District at (503)963-7186 or write to Wallowa-Whitman National Forest, Box 907, Baker, OR 97814.

Location: From LaGrande, travel nine miles northwest on Interstate 84, then 13 miles southwest on Highway 244. The camp is 11 miles south on Forest Service Road 51.

Trip note: This campground is set along the banks of the Grande Ronde River. This is one of four small, primitive camps along Forest Service Road 51 and adjoining Road 5125.

Site 6
WOODLEY CAMPGROUND
on Grande Ronde River
WALLOWA-WHITMAN NATIONAL FOREST

Campsites, facilities: There are seven sites for tents, trailers or motor homes up to 22 feet long. Picnic tables and fire grills are provided. Firewood and vault toilets are available. There is **no piped water.** Leashed pets are permitted.

Reservations, fee: No reservations necessary; no fee. Open late May to late November.

Who to contact: Phone the LaGrande Ranger District at (503)963-7186 or write to Wallowa-Whitman National Forest, Box 907, Baker, OR 97814.

Location: From LaGrande, go nine miles northwest on Interstate 84, then 13 miles southwest on Highway 244. The camp is 12 miles south on Forest Service Road 51, then six miles southeast on Forest Road 5125.

Trip note: This campground is set along the banks of the Grande Ronde River. Hiking trails are available, detailed on Forest Service maps.

Site 7
ANTHONY LAKE
on Anthony Lake
WALLOWA-WHITMAN NATIONAL FOREST

Campsites, facilities: There are 47 sites for tents, trailers or motor homes up to 22 feet long. Piped water and picnic tables are provided. Firewood, a cafe and ice are available. Some facilities are wheelchair accessible. Leashed pets are permitted. Boat docks, launching facilities and rentals are nearby.

Reservations, fee: No reservations necessary; $5 fee per night. Open July to late September.

Who to contact: Phone the Baker Ranger District at (503)523-4476 or write to Wallowa-Whitman National Forest, Box 907, Baker, OR 97814.

Location: From Haines, go 17 miles northwest on County Road 1146, then nine miles west on Forest Service Road 73.

Trip note: This campground is set along the banks of Anthony Lake, where boating without motors is permitted. Several smaller lakes are within two miles by car or trail. These are ideal for trout fishing from a raft, float tube or canoe. The trailhead for the Elkhorn Crest Trail is near here.

Site **8**
GRANDE RONDE LAKE
on Grande Ronde Lake
WALLOWA-WHITMAN NATIONAL FOREST

Campsites, facilities: There are eight tent sites and four sites for trailers or motor homes up to 16 feet long. Picnic tables and fire grills are provided. Piped water, firewood and vault toilets are available. Leashed pets are permitted. Boat docks and launching facilities are nearby.

Reservations, fee: No reservations necessary; $3 fee per night. Open July to mid-September.

Who to contact: Phone the Baker Ranger District at (503)523-4476 or write to Wallowa-Whitman National Forest, Box 907, Baker, OR 97814.

Location: Travel 17 miles northwest of Haines on County Road 1146, then 9.5 miles west on Forest Service Road 73. The camp is one half mile northwest on Forest Service Road 43.

Trip note: This campground is set at 7,200 feet elevation, along the shore of Grande Ronde Lake, a small lake where the trout fishing can be good. A nearby trail leads north to the Aurelia Mine site. Several other trails are south near Anthony Lake. A map of Wallowa-Whitman National Forest details the possibilities.

Site **9**
MUD LAKE
on Mud Lake
WALLOWA-WHITMAN NATIONAL FOREST

Campsites, facilities: There are 14 tent sites and seven sites for trailers or motor homes up to 16 feet long. Picnic tables and fire grills are provided. Piped water, firewood and vault toilets are available. Leashed pets are permitted. Boat docks, launching facilities and rentals are nearby.

Reservations, fee: No reservations necessary; $3 fee per night. Open July to mid-September.

Who to contact: Phone the Baker Ranger District at (503)523-4476 or write to Wallowa-Whitman National Forest, Box 907, Baker, OR 97814.

Location: From Haines, travel 17 miles northwest on County Road 1146, then nine miles west on Forest Service Road 73.

Trip note: This campground is set along the shore of Mud Lake. It's a small lake and the trout fishing can be fairly good here.

| Site **10** | **NORTH FORK JOHN DAY**
on the North Fork of John Day River
UMATILLA NATIONAL FOREST |

Campsites, facilities: There are seven sites for tents, trailers or motor homes up to 22 feet long. Picnic tables and fire grills are provided. Vault toilets are available. There is no piped water. Leashed pets are permitted.

Reservations, fee: No reservations necessary; no fee. Open June to late September.

Who to contact: Phone the John Day Ranger District at (503)427-3231 or write to Umatilla National Forest, P.O. Box 158, Ukiah, OR 97880.

Location: From Ukiah, travel 38.5 miles southeast on Forest Service Road 52.

Trip note: This campground is set along the banks of the North Fork of the John Day River. This is an ideal base camp for a wilderness backpacking trip. Trails from camp lead into the North Fork John Day Wilderness. The camp is located at the intersection of Elkhorn and Blue Mountain National Forest Scenic Byways.

| Site **11** | **OLIVE LAKE**
on Olive Lake
UMATILLA NATIONAL FOREST |

Campsites, facilities: There are six sites for tents, trailers or motor homes up to 31 feet long. **No piped water** is available. Picnic tables and fire grills are provided. Firewood and vault toilets are available. Leashed pets are permitted. Boat docks and launching facilities are available.

Reservations, fee: No reservations necessary; no fee. Open June to late September.

Who to contact: Phone the John Day Ranger District at (503)427-3231 or write to Umatilla National Forest, P.O. Box 158, Ukiah, OR 97880.

Location: From Dale, travel one mile northeast on US 395, then one half mile southeast on Forest Service Road 55. The camp is 26 miles southeast on Forest Service Road 10.

Trip note: This campground is set at 6,000 feet elevation along the shore of Olive Lake, located between two sections of the North Fork John Day Wilderness. Nearby trails provide access to the wilderness. Motorbikes and mountain bikes are not permitted in the wilderness.

| Site **12** | **McCULLY FORKS**
on McCully Creek
WALLOWA-WHITMAN NATIONAL FOREST |

Campsites, facilities: There are three tent sites and four sites for trailers or motor homes up to 16 feet long. Picnic tables and fire grills are provided. Firewood and vault toilets are available. There is **no piped water.** Leashed pets are permitted.

Reservations, fee: No reservations necessary; no fee. Open late May to late October.

Who to contact: Phone the Baker Ranger District at (503)523-4476 or write to Wallowa-Whitman National Forest, Box 907, Baker, OR 97814.

Location: From Baker, travel southwest on Highway 7 to the 410 junction. Turn right and travel six miles northwest on Highway 410. The campground is located three miles past Sumpter.

Trip note: This campground is set along the banks of McCully Creek. It is an easy access campground that is free and primitive.

Site 13
DEER CREEK CAMPGROUND
on Deer Creek
WALLOWA-WHITMAN NATIONAL FOREST

Campsites, facilities: There are eight sites for trailers or motor homes up to 16 feet long. Picnic tables and fire grills are provided. Firewood and vault toilets are available. Leashed pets are permitted.

Reservations, fee: No reservations necessary; no fee. Open early May to late October.

Who to contact: Phone the Baker Ranger District at (503)523-4476 or write to Wallowa-Whitman National Forest, Box 907, Baker, OR 97814.

Location: From Baker, travel 26 miles southwest on Highway 7, then three miles north on Forest Service Road 6550.

Trip note: This campground is set along the banks of Deer Creek, about nine miles from Phillips Lake. The camp is nestled below Elkhorn Ridge.

Site 14
MILLERS LANE
on Phillips Lake
WALLOWA-WHITMAN NATIONAL FOREST

Campsites, facilities: There are seven sites for tents, trailers or motor homes up to 15 feet long. Picnic tables and fire grills are provided. Firewood and vault toilets are available. There is **no piped water.** Leashed pets are permitted. Boat docks are nearby.

Reservations, fee: No reservations necessary; no fee. Open May to mid-November.

Who to contact: Phone the Baker Ranger District at (503)523-4476 or write to Wallowa-Whitman National Forest, Box 907, Baker, OR 97814.

Location: From Baker, travel 24 miles southwest on Highway 7 just past Phillips Lake, then 3.5 miles southeast on Forest Service Road 2226.

Trip note: This campground is set along the south shore of Phillips Lake. It is a long, narrow lake, the largest lake in the region. This is one of three camps on the lake. Only Site 16 has piped water.

Site 15
SOUTHWEST SHORE
on Phillips Lake
WALLOWA-WHITMAN NATIONAL FOREST

Campsites, facilities: There are 18 sites for tents, trailers or motor homes up to 15 feet long. Fire grills, firewood and vault toilets are available. There is **no piped water.** Pets are permitted. Boat docks and launching facilities are nearby.

Reservations, fee: No reservations necessary; no fee. Open May to mid-November.

Who to contact: Phone the Baker Ranger District at (503)523-4476 or write to Wallowa-Whitman National Forest, Box 907, Baker, OR 97814.

Location: From Baker, travel 24 miles southwest on Highway 7, then 2.5 miles southeast on Forest Service Road 2226.

Trip note: This campground is set along the south shore of Phillips Lake, a four-mile long reservoir created by the Mason Dam on the Powder River. It's one of three primitive camps on the lake. Nearby Site 16 has piped water.

Site 16
UNION CREEK
on Phillips Lake
WALLOWA-WHITMAN NATIONAL FOREST

Campsites, facilities: There are 58 sites for tents, trailers or motor homes up to 22

feet long. Electricity, piped water, sewer hookups and picnic tables are provided. Flush toilets, firewood and ice are available. Some facilities are wheelchair accessible. Leashed pets are permitted. Boat docks and launching facilities are nearby.

Reservations, fee: No reservations necessary; $8 fee per night. Open mid-April to mid-November.

Who to contact: Phone the Baker Ranger District at (503)523-4476, or Forest Service specialist Frank Bennett at (503)894-2210 or write to Wallowa-Whitman National Forest, P.O. Box 907, Baker, OR 97814.

Location: Travel 17 miles southwest of Baker on Highway 7.

Trip note: This campground is set along the north shore of Phillips Lake. It is easy to reach, yet missed by travelers on Interstate 84. It's one of three camps on the lake; this is the only one with piped water.

Site 17   MOUNTAIN VIEW TRAV-L PARK
near Beaver Creek

Campsites, facilities: There are 11 tent sites and 49 drive-through sites for trailers or motor homes of any length. Electricity, piped water, sewer hookups, cable TV hookups, and picnic tables are provided. Flush toilets, sanitary disposal services, showers, a laundromat, ice, a playground and a swimming pool are available. Bottled gas, a store and a cafe are located within one mile. Pets and motorbikes are permitted.

Reservations, fee: Reservations accepted; $10-13 fee per night. Open all year with limited winter facilities.

Who to contact: Phone (503)523-4824 or write to 845 Hughes Lane, Baker, OR 97814.

Location: From Baker, go one-half mile west on Campbell, then one mile north on Cedar. The camp is one mile west on Hughes Lane.

Trip note: This grassy campground is set near Beaver Creek.

Site 18   LARIAT MOTEL RV PARK
in Baker

Campsites, facilities: There are 20 sites for trailers or motor homes of any length. Electricity, piped water, sewer hookups and picnic tables are provided. Flush toilets, sanitary disposal services, showers, a laundromat and ice are available. Bottled gas, a store and a cafe are located within one mile. Leashed pets are permitted.

Reservations, fee: Reservations accepted; $10 fee per night; MasterCard and Visa accepted. Open all year, but with limited winter facilities.

Who to contact: Phone (503)523-6381 or write to 880 Elm Street, Baker, OR 97814.

Location: Take exit 306 off Interstate 84 in Baker.

Trip note: The Oregon Trail Museum is located in the heart of town.

Site 19   UNITY LAKE STATE PARK
on Unity Reservoir

Campsites, facilities: There are 11 sites for tents or self-contained motor homes, and ten with partial hookups for trailers or motor homes of any length. Picnic tables and fire grills are provided. Piped water, flush toilets, showers, sanitary disposal station and firewood are available. Some facilities are wheelchair accessible. Leashed pets are permitted. Boat docks and launching facilities are nearby.

Reservations, fee: No reservations necessary; $9-11 in summer, $6-8 off-season.

Open mid-April to late October.

Who to contact: Phone (503)575-2773 or write to Huntington, OR 97907.

Location: Travel 47 miles east of John Day on US 26. Turn north (left) on Highway 245 and drive three miles to the park.

Trip note: This campground is set along the east shore of Unity Reservoir. It's easy to reach and a popular spot when the weather is good.

Site **20**

WETMORE
on the Middle Fork of Burnt River
WALLOWA-WHITMAN NATIONAL FOREST

Campsites, facilities: There are ten sites for tents, trailers or motor homes up to 16 feet long. Picnic tables and fire grills are provided. Piped water, firewood and vault toilets are available. Some facilities are wheelchair accessible. Leashed pets are permitted.

Reservations, fee: No reservations necessary; no fee. Open late May to mid-September.

Who to contact: Phone the Unity Ranger District at (503)446-3351 or write to Wallowa-Whitman National Forest, P.O. Box 907, Baker, OR 97814.

Location: Travel ten miles northwest of Unity on US 26 to the campground.

Trip note: This campground is set near the Middle Fork of Burnt River. It's a good base camp for a fishing or hiking trip. The stream can provide good trout fishing. Trails are detailed on a map of Wallowa-Whitman National Forest.

Site **21**

OREGON
on Road Creek
WALLOWA-WHITMAN NATIONAL FOREST

Campsites, facilities: There are eight sites for tents, trailers or motor homes up to 16 feet long. Picnic tables and fire grills are provided. Piped water and vault toilets are available. Leashed pets are permitted.

Reservations, fee: No reservations necessary; no fee. Open late May to mid-September.

Who to contact: Phone the Unity Ranger District at (503)446-3351 or write to Wallowa-Whitman National Forest, P.O. Box 907, Baker, OR 97814.

Location: Drive eight miles northwest of Unity on US 26 to the campground.

Trip note: This campground is set along the banks of Road Creek. There are hiking trails in the area. There is easy access with good recreation potential.

Site **22**

DIXIE
near Bridge Creek

Campsites, facilities: There are ten sites for tents, trailers or motor homes up to 20 feet long. Picnic tables and fire grills are provided. Vault toilets, a store, a cafe and ice are available. Hand-pumped well water is available. Leashed pets are permitted.

Reservations, fee: No reservations necessary; no fee. Open June to November.

Who to contact: Phone Long Creek Ranger District at (503)575-2110 or write to Malheur National Forest, 139 NE Dayton Street, John Day, OR 97845.

Location: Travel 11 miles northeast of Prairie City on US 26, then one-half mile north on Forest Service Road 365.

Trip note: This campground is set at Dixie Summit at 5,300 feet elevation, near Bridge Creek. It is just far enough off US 26 to get missed by almost everybody, yet close enough to provide easy access.

Site 23   MIDDLE FORK
on the Middle Fork of John Day River

Campsites, facilities: There are 11 sites for tents, trailers or motor homes up to 20 feet long. Picnic tables and fire grills are provided. Vault toilets are available. There is **no piped water.** Leashed pets are permitted.

Reservations, fee: No reservations necessary; no fee. Open mid-June to November.

Who to contact: Phone Long Creek Ranger District at (503)575-2110 or write to Malheur National Forest, 139 NE Dayton Street, John Day, OR 97845.

Location: From Prairie City, travel 15 miles northeast on US 26, then one mile north on Highway 7. The camp is five miles northwest on County Road 20.

Trip note: This campground is set along the banks of the Middle Fork of the John Day River. It is a rustic spot that is easy to reach.

Site 24   ELK CREEK
on Elk Creek

Campsites, facilities: There are five tent sites. Picnic tables and fire grills are provided. Vault toilets are available. There is **no piped water.** Leashed pets are permitted.

Reservations, fee: No reservations necessary; no fee. Open mid-May to mid-November.

Who to contact: Phone Prairie City Ranger District at (503)820-3311 or write to Malheur National Forest, 139 NE Dayton Street, John Day, OR 97845.

Location: Go 8.5 miles southeast of Prairie City on County Road 62, then 16 miles southeast on Forest Service Road 13. The camp is 1.5 miles south on Forest Service Road 16.

Trip note: This campground is set at the confluence of the North and South Forks of Elk Creek. It is advisable to obtain a map of Malheur National Forest that details the back country roads.

Site 25   NORTH FORK MALHEUR
on Malheur River

Campsites, facilities: There are five tent sites. Picnic tables and fire grills are provided. Vault toilets are available. There is **no piped water.** Leashed pets are permitted.

Reservations, fee: No reservations necessary; no fee. Open mid-May to mid-November.

Who to contact: Phone Prairie City Ranger District at (503)820-3311 or write to Malheur National Forest, 139 NE Dayton Street, John Day, OR 97845.

Location: From Prairie City, travel 8.5 miles southeast on County Road 62, then 16 miles southeast on Forest Service Road 13. Travel two miles south on Forest Service Road 16, then take the left fork (Forest Road 1675) and drive two miles to the campground.

Trip note: This secluded campground is set along the banks of the North Fork of Malheur River, a designated wild and scenic river.

Site 26   LITTLE CRANE
on Little Wet Creek

Campsites, facilities: There are five tent sites. Picnic tables and fire grills are provided. Vault toilets are available. There is **no piped water.** Leashed pets are permitted.

Reservations, fee: No reservations necessary; no fee. Open June to mid-November.

Who to contact: Phone Prairie City Ranger District at (503)820-3311 or write to Malheur National Forest, 139 NE Dayton Street, John Day, OR 97845.

Location: From Prairie City, travel 8.5 miles southeast on County Road 62, then 16 miles south on Forest Service Road 13. The camp is 5.5 miles south on Forest Service Road 16.

Trip note: This campground is set along the banks of Little Wet Creek, good stream for sneak-fishing for trout. There are also some good hiking trails in the area, detailed on the Forest Service map.

Site **27**
TROUT FARM
near Prairie City

Campsites, facilities: There are eight sites for tents, trailers or motor homes up to 21 feet long. Picnic tables and fire grills are provided. Piped water, showers and vault toilets are available. Leashed pets are permitted.

Reservations, fee: No reservations necessary; no fee. Open May to mid-November.

Who to contact: Phone Prairie City Ranger District at (503)820-3311 or write to Malheur National Forest, 139 NE Dayton Street, John Day, OR 97845.

Location: From Prairie City, go 8.5 miles southeast on County Road 62, then seven miles south on Forest Service Road 14.

Trip note: This is a good spot for a trout fishing trip or a family picnic. There is a small pond at the campground with a trail that is wheelchair accessible. No other camps are in the immediate area.

Site **28**
ELK CREEK #2
on the South Fork of Burnt River
WALLOWA-WHITMAN NATIONAL FOREST

Campsites, facilities: There are six dispersed sites for tents, trailers or motor homes up to 15 feet long. Picnic tables and fire grills are provided. Piped water, firewood and vault toilets are available. Leashed pets are permitted.

Reservations, fee: No reservations necessary; no fee. Open late May to mid-September.

Who to contact: Phone the Unity Ranger District at (503)446-3351 or write to Wallowa-Whitman National Forest, P.O. Box 907, Baker, OR 97814.

Location: Travel 49 miles east of John Day on US 26 to Unity. In Unity, turn southwest on Forest Road 6005 (South Fork Road) and drive ten miles to the campground.

Trip note: This campground is set along the bank of the South Fork of Burnt River. It is a small, obscure camp, yet has piped water and an adjacent stream.

Site **29**
SOUTH FORK
on the South Fork of Burnt River
WALLOWA-WHITMAN NATIONAL FOREST

Campsites, facilities: There are 29 sites for tents, trailers or motor homes up to 16 feet long. Picnic tables and fire grills are provided. Piped water, firewood and vault toilets are available. Leashed pets are permitted.

Reservations, fee: No reservations necessary; no fee. Open late May to mid-September.

Who to contact: Phone the Unity Ranger District at (503)446-3351 or write to Wallowa-Whitman National Forest, P.O. Box 907, Baker, OR 97814.

Location: From Unity, drive six miles southwest on Forest Service Road 6005

(South Fork Road) to the campground.

Trip note: This campground is set along the banks of the South Fork of Burnt River. It's a nice trout creek with good evening bites for anglers who know how to sneak-fish.

Site 30
STEVENS CREEK
on the South Fork of Burnt River
WALLOWA-WHITMAN NATIONAL FOREST

Campsites, facilities: There are six dispersed sites for tents, trailers or motor homes of any length. Picnic tables and fire grills are provided. Piped water, firewood and vault toilets are available. Leashed pets are permitted.

Reservations, fee: No reservations necessary; no fee. Open late May to mid-September.

Who to contact: Phone the Unity Ranger District at (503)446-3351 or write to Wallowa-Whitman National Forest, P.O. Box 907, Baker, OR 97814.

Location: From Unity, turn south on South Fork Road (Forest Service Road 6005) and drive seven miles to the campground.

Trip note: This campground is set along the banks of the South Fork of Burnt River and is an option to the other small camps along Burnt River.

Site 31
UNITY MOTEL & TRAILER COURT
near Unity Reservoir

Campsites, facilities: There are three tent sites and 11 sites for trailers or motor homes. Electricity, piped water, sewer hookups and picnic tables are provided. Flush toilets, showers and a laundromat are available. Bottled gas, a store, a cafe and ice are located within one mile. Pets and motorbikes are permitted.

Reservations, fee: Reservations accepted; $7 fee per night; MasterCard and Visa accepted. Open all year with limited winter facilities.

Who to contact: Phone (503)446-3431 or write to P.O. Box 87, Unity, OR 97884.

Location: Travel 49 miles east of John Day on US 26 to Unity. This campground is located in town off US 26.

Trip note: This campground is in town. Possible side trips include visiting Unity Reservoir, Unity Lake State Park and exploring the nearby Burnt River.

Site 32
BROGAN TRAILER PARK & CAMPGROUND
near Willow Creek

Campsites, facilities: There are 15 tent sites and 30 drive-through sites for trailers or motor homes of any length. Electricity, piped water, sewer hookups and picnic tables are provided. Flush toilets, showers, a laundromat and ice are available. Bottled gas, a store and a cafe are located within one mile. Leashed pets are permitted.

Reservations, fee: Reservations accepted; $8 fee per night. Open April to late December.

Who to contact: Phone (503)473-3737 or write to P.O. Box 23, Brogan, OR 97903.

Location: Drive 24 miles north of Vale on US 26 to Brogan. The campground is in town.

Trip note: This rural campground is set on the inner edge of the west's Great Basin. Nearby side trips include Willow Creek, which runs along US 26, or Malheur Reservoir, set northwest of Brogan.

Site 33
FAREWELL BEND STATE PARK
on Snake River

Campsites, facilities: There are 43 tent sites and 53 sites with partial hookups for trailers or motor homes of any length. Piped water and picnic tables are provided. Flush toilets, sanitary disposal services, showers and firewood are available. Leashed pets are permitted. Boat launching facilities are nearby.

Reservations, fee: No reservations necessary; $8-10 in summer, $6-8 off-season. Open all year with limited winter facilities.

Who to contact: Phone (503)869-2365 or write to Huntington, OR 97907.

Location: From Ontario, travel 25 miles northwest on Interstate 84 to the park entrance.

Trip note: This campground is set along the banks of the majestic Snake River. It's one of three camps in the immediate area. See the zone map.

Site 34
SPRING RECREATION SITE
on Snake River

Campsites, facilities: There are and 14 sites for tents, trailers or motor homes up to 30 feet long. Picnic tables and fire grills are provided. Piped water, sanitary disposal services and vault toilets are available. Leashed pets are permitted. Boat launching facilities are nearby.

Reservations, fee: No reservations necessary; $3 fee per night. Open May to October including limited and some off-season weekends.

Who to contact: Phone (503)473-3144 or write to 100 Oregon Street, Vale, OR 97918.

Location: From Ontario, drive 25 miles north on Interstate 84 to Huntington. At Farewell Bend turn east onto Highway 30 and drive 3.5 miles to the campground.

Trip note: This campground is set along the banks of the Snake River. It is one of three camps in the immediate area.

Site 35
SPRING RECREATION LAKE
on Snake River

Campsites, facilities: This campground closed for renovation in 1990, is designed with 14 sites for tents, trailers or motor homes. Call for availability. Picnic tables and fire grills are provided. Piped water, sanitary disposal services and vault toilets are available. Leashed pets are permitted. Boat launching facilities are nearby.

Reservations, fee: No reservations necessary; no fee. Open May to October including limited and some off-season weekends.

Who to contact: Phone (503)523-6391 or write to Bureau of Land Management, P.O. Box 987, Baker City, OR 97814.

Location: From Huntington, travel 3.5 miles northeast on Snake River Road.

Trip note: This campground is set along the banks of the majestic Snake River. It's one of three camps in or near Huntington.

Site 36
EAGLE FORKS
on Eagle Creek
WALLOWA-WHITMAN NATIONAL FOREST

Campsites, facilities: There are seven sites for tents, trailers or motor homes up to 21 feet long. Picnic tables and fire grills are provided. Firewood and vault

toilets are available, but there is **no piped water.** Leashed pets are permitted.
Reservations, fee: No reservations necessary; no fee. Open June to late October.
Who to contact: Phone the Pine Ranger District at (503)742-7511 or write to Wallowa-Whitman National Forest, P.O. Box 907, Baker, OR 97814.
Location: Drive 41 miles east of Baker on Highway 86 to Richland. From Richland, travel 11 miles via a county road and Forest Service Road 7735.
Trip note: This campground is set at the confluence of Little Eagle Creek and Eagle Creek. A trail leaves camp and follows the creek northwest for five miles. It's a prime day-hike, yet the spot attracts few people.

Site 37   TAMARACK
on Eagle Creek
WALLOWA-WHITMAN NATIONAL FOREST

Campsites, facilities: There are ten sites for tents, trailers or motor homes up to 22 feet long. Picnic tables and fire grills are provided. Piped water, firewood and vault toilets are available. Leashed pets are permitted.
Reservations, fee: No reservations necessary; no fee. Open June to late October.
Who to contact: Phone the Pine Ranger District at (503)742-7511 or write to Wallowa-Whitman National Forest, P.O. Box 907, Baker, OR 97814.
Location: From Baker, drive 23 miles northeast on Highway 203 to the town of Medical Springs. From Medical Springs, travel 15.5 miles southeast on Forest Service Road 67 to the bridge across Eagle Creek. The camp is 300 yards east on Forest Service Road 77.
Trip note: This campground is set along the banks of Eagle Creek. This is a good spot for a fishing and hiking trip in a remote setting.

Site 38   TWO COLOR
on Eagle Creek
WALLOWA-WHITMAN NATIONAL FOREST

Campsites, facilities: There are 14 sites for tents, trailers or motor homes up to 22 feet long. Picnic tables and fire grills are provided. Piped water, firewood and vault toilets are available. Leashed pets are permitted.
Reservations, fee: No reservations necessary; no fee. Open mid-June to late October.
Who to contact: Phone the LaGrande Ranger District at (503)963-7186 or write to Wallowa-Whitman National Forest, P.O. Box 907, Baker, OR 97814.
Location: From Baker, drive 23 miles northeast via Interstate 84 and Highway 203 to the town of Medical Springs. From Medical Springs, go 15.5 miles southeast on Forest Service Road 6700, then 1.5 miles northeast on Forest Service Road 7755.
Trip note: This campground is set along the banks of Eagle Creek, about a mile north of Site 37, which has piped water.

Site 39   McBRIDE
on Brooks Ditch
WALLOWA-WHITMAN NATIONAL FOREST

Campsites, facilities: There are five sites for tents, trailers or motor homes up to 16 feet long. Picnic tables and fire grills are provided. Vault toilets are available, but there is **no piped water.** Leashed pets are permitted.
Reservations, fee: No reservations necessary; no fee. Open mid-May to late October.
Who to contact: Phone the Pine Ranger District at (503)742-7511 or write to Wallowa-Whitman National Forest, P.O. Box 907, Baker, OR 97814.

Location: Drive 52 miles east of Baker on Highway 86 to Halfway. Go six miles northwest of Halfway on Highway 442, then go 2.5 miles west on Forest Service Road 7101.

Trip note: This campground is set along the banks of Brooks Ditch. It's a little-used, primitive and obscure camp.

Site **40**
FISH LAKE
on Fish Lake
WALLOWA-WHITMAN NATIONAL FOREST

Campsites, facilities: There are 20 sites for tents, trailers or motor homes up to 22 feet long. Picnic tables and fire grills are provided. Piped water, firewood and vault toilets are is available. Leashed pets are permitted. Boat launching facilities are nearby.

Reservations, fee: No reservations necessary; no fee. Open late May to early-September.

Who to contact: Phone the Pine Ranger District at (503)742-7511 or write to Wallowa-Whitman National Forest, P.O. Box 907, Baker, OR 97814.

Location: From Baker, travel 52 miles east on Highway 86 to Halfway. From Halfway, go five miles north on County Route 733, then 18.5 miles north on Forest Service Road 66.

Trip note: This campground is set along the shore of Fish Lake, a good base camp for a fishing trip. Side trip options include hiking out on nearby trails that lead to mountain streams.

Site **41**
TWIN LAKES
near Twin Lakes
WALLOWA-WHITMAN NATIONAL FOREST

Campsites, facilities: There are nine sites for tents, trailers or motor homes up to 22 feet long. Picnic tables and fire grills are provided. Firewood and vault toilets are available, but there is **no piped water.** Leashed pets are permitted.

Reservations, fee: No reservations necessary; no fee. Open July to mid-September.

Who to contact: Phone the Hells Canyon National Recreation Area at (503)426-3151 or write to Wallowa-Whitman National Forest, P.O. Box 907, Baker, OR 97814.

Location: From Baker, travel 52 miles east on Highway 86 to Halfway. From Halfway, go five miles north on County Road 733, then 24 miles north Forest Service Road 66.

Trip note: This campground is set between the little Twin Lakes. Nearby trails provide access to backcountry lakes and streams. See a Forest Service map for details.

Site **42**
LAKE FORK
on Lake Fork Creek
WALLOWA-WHITMAN NATIONAL FOREST

Campsites, facilities: There are 11 sites for tents, trailers or motor homes up to 22 feet long. Picnic tables and fire grills are provided. Piped water and vault toilets are available. Leashed pets are permitted.

Reservations, fee: No reservations necessary; $3 fee per night. Open June to late November.

Who to contact: Phone the Hells Canyon National Recreation Area at (503)426-3151 or write to Wallowa-Whitman National Forest, P.O. Box 907, Baker, OR

97814.

Location: From Baker, travel 62 miles east on Highway 86, then eight miles north on Forest Service Road 39.

Trip note: This campground is set along the banks of Lake Fork Creek, an ideal jump-off point for a backpacking trip. A trail from camp follows the creek west for about ten miles to Fish Lake. It continues beyond Fish Lake to several smaller lakes.

Site 43
LICK CREEK
on Lick Creek
WALLOWA-WHITMAN NATIONAL FOREST

Campsites, facilities: There are 12 sites for tents, trailers or motor homes up to 30 feet long. Picnic tables and fire grills are provided. Piped water, firewood and vault toilets are available. Leashed pets are permitted.

Reservations, fee: No reservations necessary; $3 fee per night. Open mid-June to late November.

Who to contact: Phone the Hells Canyon National Recreation Area at (503)426-3151 or write to Wallowa-Whitman National Forest, P.O. Box 907, Baker, OR 97814.

Location: Travel south of Enterprise on Interstate 82 to Joseph. From Joseph, go 7.5 miles east on Highway 305, then 15 miles south on Forest Service Road 39.

Trip note: This campground is set along the banks of Lick Creek, in Hells Canyon National Recreation Area. Piped water is provided and it is secluded and pretty.

Site 44
EVERGREEN
on Imnaha River
WALLOWA-WHITMAN NATIONAL FOREST

Campsites, facilities: This is a group campsites for tents, trailers or motor homes up to 31 feet long. **No piped water** is available. Picnic tables and fire grills are provided. Vault toilets are available. Leashed pets are permitted.

Reservations, fee: No reservations necessary; no fee. Open June to late November.

Who to contact: Phone the Hells Canyon National Recreation Area at (503)426-3151 or write to Wallowa-Whitman National Forest, P.O. Box 907, Baker, OR 97814.

Location: Travel south of Enterprise on Interstate 82 to Joseph. Take Highway 305 east from Joseph for 7.5 miles, then go 29 miles south on Forest Service Road 39. The camp is eight miles southwest on Forest Service Road 3960.

Trip note: This campground is set along the banks of the Imnaha River in Hells Canyon National Recreation Area. It's one of seven camps in the vicinity; see zone map for others.

Site 45
HIDDEN
on Imnaha River
WALLOWA-WHITMAN NATIONAL FOREST

Campsites, facilities: There are ten sites for tents, trailers or motor homes up to 30 feet long. Picnic tables and fire grills are provided. Piped water, firewood and vault toilets are available. Leashed pets are permitted.

Reservations, fee: No reservations necessary; $3 fee per night. Open June to late November.

Who to contact: Phone the Hells Canyon National Recreation Area at (503)426-3151 or write to Wallowa-Whitman National Forest, P.O. Box 907, Baker, OR 97814.

Location: Travel south of Enterprise on Interstate 82 to Joseph. From Joseph, take Highway 305 east 7.5 miles, then go 29 miles southeast on Forest Service Road 39. The campground is seven miles southwest on Forest Service Road 3960.

Trip note: This campground is set along the banks of the Imnaha River, in the Hells Canyon National Recreation Area. It is essential to obtain a map of Wallowa-Whitman National Forest that details back roads and hiking trails.

Site 46   INDIAN CROSSING
on Imnaha River
WALLOWA-WHITMAN NATIONAL FOREST

Campsites, facilities: There are 15 sites for tents, trailers or motor homes up to 30 feet long. Piped water, picnic tables and fire grills are provided. Firewood and vault toilets are available. Leashed pets are permitted. Horse facilities are available.

Reservations, fee: No reservations necessary; $3 fee per night. Open June to late November.

Who to contact: Phone the Hells Canyon National Recreation Area at (503)426-3151, or to write to Wallowa-Whitman National Forest, P.O. Box 907, Baker, OR 97814.

Location: Travel south of Enterprise on Interstate 82 to Joseph. From Joseph, go 7.5 miles east on Highway 305, then 29 miles south on Forest Service Road 39. The campground is nine miles southwest on Forest Service Road 3960.

Trip note: This campground is set at the end of the road along the banks of the Imnaha River, in Hells Canyon National Recreation Area. The trailhead for the Eagle Cap Wilderness is nearby. Obtain a Forest Service map for side trip possibilities.

Site 47   BLACKHORSE
on Imnaha River
WALLOWA-WHITMAN NATIONAL FOREST

Campsites, facilities: There are 17 sites for tents, trailers or motor homes up to 30 feet long. Picnic tables and fire grills are provided. Piped water, firewood and vault toilets are available. Leashed pets are permitted.

Reservations, fee: No reservations necessary; $3 fee per night. Open June to late November.

Who to contact: Phone the Hells Canyon National Recreation Area at (503)426-3151 or write to Wallowa-Whitman National Forest, P.O. Box 907, Baker, OR 97814.

Location: Travel south of Enterprise on Interstate 82 to Joseph. Travel 7.5 miles east of Joseph on Highway 305, then go 29 miles southeast on Forest Service Road 39.

Trip note: This campground is set along the banks of the Imnaha River in Hells Canyon National Recreation Area. It's a secluded spot in Wallowa-Whitman National Forest.

Site 48   OLLOKOT
on Imnaha River
WALLOWA-WHITMAN NATIONAL FOREST

Campsites, facilities: There are 12 sites for tents, trailers or motor homes up to 30

feet long. Picnic tables and fire grills are provided. Piped water and vault toilets are available. Leashed pets are permitted.

Reservations, fee: No reservations necessary; $3 fee per night. Open June to late November.

Who to contact: Phone the Hells Canyon National Recreation Area at (503)426-3151 or write to Wallowa-Whitman National Forest, P.O. Box 907, Baker, OR 97814.

Location: Travel south of Enterprise on Interstate 82 to Joseph. From Joseph, go 7.5 miles east on Highway 305, then 30 miles southeast on Forest Service Road 39.

Trip note: This campground is set along the banks of the Imnaha River in Hells Canyon National Recreation Area. It's a primitive option.

Site **49**   **CATHERINE CREEK STATE PARK**
on Catherine Creek

Campsites, facilities: There are ten sites for tents, trailers or motor homes up to 30 feet long. Picnic tables and fire grills are provided. Piped water, firewood and flush toilets are available. Some facilities are wheelchair accessible. Leashed pets are permitted.

Reservations, fee: No reservations necessary; $8 fee per night. Open mid-April to late October.

Who to contact: Phone (503)963-6444 or write to LaGrande, OR 97850.

Location: From LaGrande, drive southeast on Highway 203 about eight miles past Union.

Trip note: This campground is set along the banks of Catherine Creek. It's a pleasant, easy-to-reach park that is little known to out-of-towners.

Site **50**   **NORTH FORK CATHERINE TRAILHEAD**
near Eagle Cap Wilderness
WALLOWA-WHITMAN NATIONAL FOREST

Campsites, facilities: There are five tent sites and five sites for trailers or motor homes up to 22 feet long. Picnic tables and fire grills are provided. Vault toilets are available. There is **no piped water.** Leashed pets are permitted.

Reservations, fee: No reservations necessary; no fee. Open mid-June to late October.

Who to contact: Phone the LaGrande Ranger District at (503)963-7186 or write to Wallowa-Whitman National Forest, P.O. Box 907, Baker, OR 97813.

Location: From the LaGrande, travel 14 miles southeast on Highway 203 to Union. Drive ten miles southeast of Union on Highway 203, then four miles east on Forest Service Road 7785. The camp is 3.5 miles northeast on Forest Service Road 7785.

Trip note: This campground is set along the North Fork of Catherine Creek at a trailhead that provides access to various lakes and streams in the Eagle Cap Wilderness. It's a good jump-off point for a hiking trip. A National Forest map details the possibilities.

Site **51**   **MOSS SPRINGS**
near Eagle Cap Wilderness
WALLOWA-WHITMAN NATIONAL FOREST

Campsites, facilities: There are seven sites for tents, trailers or motor homes up to 22 feet long. Picnic tables and fire grills are provided. Firewood, horse facilities and vault toilets are available. Leashed pets are permitted.

Reservations, fee: No reservations necessary; no fee. Open July to mid-September.

Who to contact: Phone the LaGrande Ranger District at (503)963-7186 or write to Wallowa-Whitman National Forest, P.O. Box 907, Baker, OR 97814.

Location: Travel 15 miles west of LaGrande to Cove. Drive 1.5 miles southeast of Cove on County Road 602, then eight miles east on Forest Service Road 6220.

Trip note: This campground is set at a trailhead that provides access to the Eagle Cap Wilderness, a good jump-off point for a multi-day backpacking trip. It is advisable to obtain a map of Wallowa-Whitman National Forest.

Site 52   JUBILEE LAKE
on Jubilee Lake
UMATILLA NATIONAL FOREST

Campsites, facilities: There are 51 sites for tents, trailers or motor homes up to 22 feet long. Picnic tables and fire grills are provided. Piped water, firewood and flush toilets are available. Leashed pets are permitted. Boat docks and launching facilities are nearby.

Reservations, fee: No reservations necessary; $5-7 fee per night. Open July to mid-October.

Who to contact: Phone the Walla Walla Ranger District at (509)522-6290 or write to Umatilla National Forest, 1415 West Rose Avenue, Walla Walla, WA 99362.

Location: From Elgin, travel 23.5 miles northwest on Highway 204, then 12 miles northeast on Forest Service Road 64. The camp is 700 yards south on Forest Service Road 250.

Trip note: This campground is set along the shore of Jubilee Lake at 4,800 feet elevation. It's a good area for fishing, hiking and hunting. Boats are permitted, but electric motors only. A 2.5-mile trail loops around the lake and provides a side trip and fishing access for shore anglers.

Site 53   MOTTET
near the South Fork of Touchet River
UMATILLA NATIONAL FOREST

Campsites, facilities: There are seven sites for tents. Picnic tables and fire grills are provided. Spring water, firewood and vault toilets are available. Leashed pets are permitted. Rangers urge everyone to pack out their garbage.

Reservations, fee: No reservations necessary; no fee. Open July to mid-October.

Who to contact: Phone the Walla Walla Ranger District at (509)525-6290 or write to Umatilla National Forest, 1415 West Rose Avenue, Walla Walla, WA 99362.

Location: Travel 17 miles east of Pendleton via Highway 11 to Weston. From Weston, travel 17.5 miles east on Highway 204, then two miles east on Forest Service Road 64. Continue 800 yards on Forest Service Road 20. High clearance vehicles recommended.

Trip note: This campground is set at 5,200 feet elevation, adjacent to a trailhead which leads down to the South Fork of the Touchet River. It's a nice spot, located far from the beaten path.

Site 54   MINAM STATE RECREATION AREA
near Grande Ronde River

Campsites, facilities: There are 12 primitive sites for tents, trailers or motor homes of any length. Picnic tables and fire grills are provided. Piped water, firewood and vault toilets are available. Leashed pets are permitted.

Reservations, fee: No reservations necessary; $8 fee per night. Open mid-April to late October.

Who to contact: Phone (503)432-8855 or write to Elgin, OR 97827.

Location: From LaGrande, drive 20 miles northeast on Interstate 82 to Elgin. From Elgin, continue 15 miles northeast on Interstate 82, then go one-half mile north.

Trip note: This campground is set along the banks of the Minam River. Morning and evening trout fishing can be decent. This is a good launch point to float the Wild and Scenic Grande Ronde River.

Site 55   BOUNDARY
near Eagle Cap Wilderness
WALLOWA-WHITMAN NATIONAL FOREST

Campsites, facilities: There are eight tent sites. Picnic tables and fire grills are provided. Firewood and vault toilets are available, but there is **no piped water.** Leashed pets are permitted.

Reservations, fee: No reservations necessary; no fee. Open mid-June to November.

Who to contact: Phone the Eagle Cap Ranger District at (503)426-3104 or write to Wallowa-Whitman National Forest, P.O. Box 907, Baker, OR 97814.

Location: From Wallowa, travel five miles south on County Route 515, then two miles south on Forest Service Road 8250-040.

Trip note: This campground is set along the banks of Bear Creek at a trailhead that provides access to the Eagle Cap Wilderness. It's a good jump-off point for a multi-day backpack trip.

Site 56   MOUNTAIN VIEW MOTEL & TRAILER PARK
near Wallowa Lake

Campsites, facilities: There are 20 tent sites and 25 drive-through sites for trailers or motor homes of any length. Electricity, piped water, sewer hookups and picnic tables are provided. Flush toilets, sanitary disposal services and showers are available. Bottled gas, a store, a cafe and a laundromat are located within one mile. Leashed pets are permitted.

Reservations, fee: Reservations accepted; $7 fee per night; MasterCard and Visa accepted. Open all year.

Who to contact: Phone (503)432-2982 or write to Route 1, Box 87, Joseph, OR 97846.

Location: Travel south Enterprise on Interstate 82 to Joseph. This campground is located one mile west of Joseph on Interstate 82.

Trip note: This park is not far from Wallowa Lake. Nearby recreation options include a golf course, hiking trails, bike paths and a riding stable.

Site 57   HURRICANE CREEK
near Eagle Cap Wilderness
WALLOWA-WHITMAN NATIONAL FOREST

Campsites, facilities: There are ten sites for tents, trailers or motor homes up to 15 feet long. Picnic tables and fire grills are provided. Firewood and vault toilets are available, but there is **no piped water.** Leashed pets are permitted.

Reservations, fee: No reservations necessary; no fee. Open mid-June to late October.

Who to contact: Phone the Eagle Cap Ranger District at (503)426-3104 or write to Wallowa-Whitman National Forest, P.O. Box 907, Baker, OR 97814.

Location: Travel south of Enterprise on Interstate 82 to Joseph. This campground is located 3.5 miles southwest of Joseph on Forest Service Road 8205.

Trip note: This campground is set at the edge of the Eagle Cap Wilderness. It's a good jump-off point for a wilderness backpacking trip. It's essential to obtain maps of the area from the ranger district.

Site **58**
WALLOWA LAKE STATE PARK
on Wallowa Lake

Campsites, facilities: There are 89 tent sites and 121 drive-through sites for trailers or motor homes of any length. Group campsites are available. Electricity, piped water, sewer hookups and picnic tables are provided. Flush toilets, sanitary disposal services, showers, firewood and a laundromat are available. A store, a cafe and ice are located within one mile. Some facilities are wheelchair accessible. Leashed pets are permitted. Boat docks, launching facilities and rentals are nearby.

Reservations, fee: Reservations accepted; $8 fee per night. Open mid-April to late October.

Who to contact: Phone (503)432-8855 or write to Route 1, Box 323, Joseph, OR 97846.

Location: Travel south of Enterprise on Interstate 82 to Joseph. From Joseph, go six miles south on Interstate 82 to the south shore of the lake.

Trip note: This campground is set along the shore of scenic Wallowa Lake. Trailheads that provide access into Eagle Cap Wilderness are nearby.

Site **59**
WILLIAMSON
on Lostine River
WALLOWA-WHITMAN NATIONAL FOREST

Campsites, facilities: There are ten sites for tents, trailers or motor homes up to 16 feet long. **No piped water** is available. Picnic tables and fire grills are provided. Vault toilets are available. Leashed pets are permitted.

Reservations, fee: No reservations necessary; no fee. Open mid-June to November.

Who to contact: Phone the Eagle Cap Ranger District at (503)426-3104 or write to Wallowa-Whitman National Forest, P.O. Box 907, Baker, OR 97814.

Location: From Wallowa, travel eight miles southeast on Interstate 82 to Lostine. From Lostine, go seven miles south on County Road 551, then four miles south on Forest Service Road 8210.

Trip note: This campground is set along the banks of the Lostine River. Nearby trails provide access to the Eagle Cap Wilderness. This is another in a series of little-known primitive sites in the area.

Site **60**
SHADY
on Lostine River
WALLOWA-WHITMAN NATIONAL FOREST

Campsites, facilities: There are 16 sites for tents, trailers or motor homes up to 16 feet long. **No piped water** is available. Picnic tables and fire grills are provided, vault toilets are available. Leashed pets are permitted.

Reservations, fee: No reservations necessary; no fee. Open mid-June to November.

Who to contact: Phone the Eagle Cap Ranger District at (503)426-3104 or write to Wallowa-Whitman National Forest, P.O. Box 907, Baker, OR 97814.

Location: From Wallowa, travel eight miles southeast on Interstate 82 to Lostine. Drive seven miles south of Lostine on County Road 551, then ten miles south on Forest Service Road 8210.

Trip note: This campground is set along the banks of the Lostine River. Nearby trails provide access to the Eagle Cap Wilderness.

TWO PAN
Site **61**
on Lostine River
WALLOWA-WHITMAN NATIONAL FOREST

Campsites, facilities: There are nine tent sites. **No piped water** is available. Picnic tables and fire grills are provided. Vault toilets are available. Leashed pets are permitted.

Reservations, fee: No reservations necessary; no fee. Open mid-June to November.

Who to contact: Phone the Eagle Cap Ranger District at (503)426-3104 or write to Wallowa-Whitman National Forest, P.O. Box 907, Baker, OR 97814.

Location: From Wallowa, travel eight miles southeast on Interstate 82 to Lostine. Drive seven miles south of Lostine on County Road 551, then 11 miles south on Forest Service Road 8210.

Trip note: This campground is set at the end of the Forest Service road on the banks of the Lostine River. Adjacent trails provide access to numerous lakes and streams in the Eagle Cap Wilderness. At 5,600 feet elevation, this is a prime jump-off spot for a multi-day wilderness adventure.

SADDLE CREEK
Site **62**
near Hells Canyon Wilderness
WALLOWA-WHITMAN NATIONAL FOREST

Campsites, facilities: There are six sites for tents, trailers or motor homes up to 15 feet long. Picnic tables and fire grills are provided. Firewood and vault toilets are available, but there is **no piped water.** Leashed pets are permitted.

Reservations, fee: No reservations necessary; no fee. Open July to late November.

Who to contact: Phone the Hells Canyon National Recreation Area at (503)426-3151 or write to Wallowa-Whitman National Forest, P.O. Box 907, Baker, OR 97814.

Location: From Enterprise, drive to the small town of Imnaha on Highway 350. Head 24 miles southeast of Imnaha on Forest Service Road 4240.

Trip note: This campground is set at 6,900 feet elevation. Trails are nearby that provide access to Saddle Creek and the Hells Canyon Wilderness. A map of Wallowa National Forest details the trails in area.

COYOTE
Site **63**
near Coyote Springs
WALLOWA-WHITMAN NATIONAL FOREST

Campsites, facilities: There are 21 sites for tents, trailers or motor homes up to 22 feet long. Picnic tables and fire grills are provided. Firewood and vault toilets are available, but there is **no piped water.** Leashed pets are permitted.

Reservations, fee: No reservations necessary; no fee. Open mid-May to December.

Who to contact: Phone the Wallowa Valley Ranger District at (503)432-2171 or write to Wallowa-Whitman National Forest, P.O. Box 907, Baker, OR 97814.

Location: From Enterprise, travel 15 miles north on Highway 3, then 25 miles northeast on Forest Service Road 46 to the campground.

Trip note: This campground is set at 4,800 feet elevation, adjacent to Coyote Springs. It is one of three primitive camps in the vicinity.

Site 64

DOUGHERTY
near Dougherty Springs
WALLOWA-WHITMAN NATIONAL FOREST

Campsites, facilities: There are ten sites for tents, trailers or motor homes up to 22 feet long. Picnic tables and fire grills are provided. Vault toilets are available, but there is **no piped water.** Leashed pets are permitted.

Reservations, fee: No reservations necessary; no fee. Open June to late November.

Who to contact: Phone the Hells Canyon National Recreation Area at (503)426-3151 or write to Wallowa-Whitman National Forest, P.O. Box 907, Baker, OR 97814.

Location: Travel 15 miles north of Enterprise on Highway 3, then 30 miles northeast on Forest Service Road 46.

Trip note: This campground is set at 5,000 feet elevation adjacent to Dougherty Springs. It is one in a series of remote camps set near natural springs.

Site 65

VIGNE
on Chesnimnus Creek
WALLOWA-WHITMAN NATIONAL FOREST

Campsites, facilities: There are 12 sites for tents, trailers or motor homes up to 22 feet long. Picnic tables and fire grills are provided. Piped water, firewood and vault toilets are available. Leashed pets are permitted.

Reservations, fee: No reservations necessary; no fee. Open mid-April to late November.

Who to contact: Phone the Wallowa Valley Ranger District at (503)432-2171 or write to Wallowa-Whitman National Forest, P.O. Box 907, Baker, OR 97814.

Location: Go 15 miles north of Enterprise on Highway 3, then ten miles northeast on Forest Road 46, then ten miles east on Forest Road 4625.

Trip note: This campground is set along the banks of Chesnimnus Creek. It is the only Forest Service camp in the area that has piped water available.

Site 66

BUCKHORN
near Buckhorn Lake
WALLOWA-WHITMAN NATIONAL FOREST

Campsites, facilities: There are six sites for tents, trailers or motor homes up to 16 feet long. Picnic tables and fire grills are provided. Firewood and vault toilets are available, but there is **no piped water.** Leashed pets are permitted.

Reservations, fee: No reservations necessary; no fee. Open June to late November.

Who to contact: Phone the Hells Canyon Ranger District at (503)426-3151 or write to Wallowa-Whitman National Forest, P.O. Box 907, Baker, OR 97814.

Location: Travel three miles south on Interstate 82 from Enterprise, then go 22 miles northeast on County Road 772. Continue ten miles northeast on Forest Road 46.

Trip note: This campground is set at 5,200 feet elevation adjacent to Buckhorn Springs. It's a small, primitive and obscure camp that gets little use.

SOUTHEAST BASIN

◆

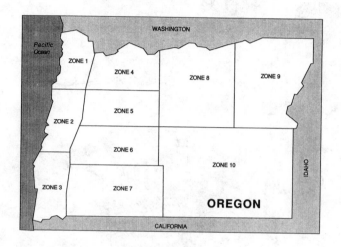

SOME HIGHLIGHTS

---

31 CAMPGROUNDS

Fremont National Forest

Malheur National Wildlife Refuge

Ochoco National Forest

Malheur National Forest

Owyhee Lake

Emigrant Creek

Hart Mountain

National Antelope Refuge

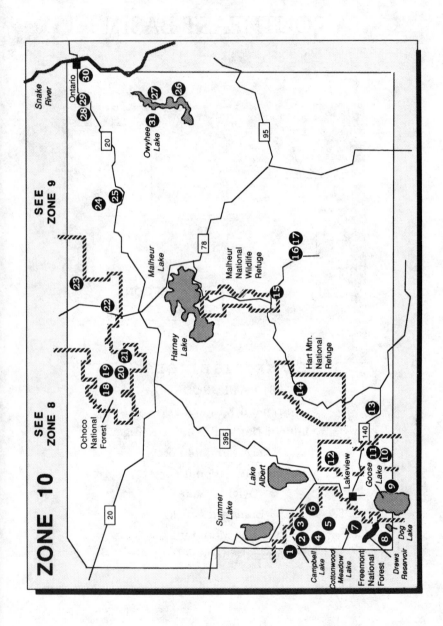

Site **1**
LEE THOMAS
on the North Fork of Sprague River
FREMONT NATIONAL FOREST

Campsites, facilities: There are seven sites for tents, trailers or motor homes up to 16 feet long. Picnic tables and fire grills are provided. Piped water and vault toilets are available. Leashed pets are permitted.

Reservations, fee: No reservations necessary; no fee. Open April to late October.

Who to contact: Phone the Paisley Ranger District at (503)943-3114 or write to Fremont National Forest, Paisley, OR 97636.

Location: From Paisley on Highway 31, travel one mile west of Paisley on County Road 2-8, then 22.5 miles west on Forest Service Road 3315. Drive one mile south on Forest Service Road 28, then continue for five miles on Forest Service Road 3411 to the campground.

Trip note: This campground is set along the North Fork of the Sprague River. This is located in the interior of Fremont National Forest, a genuine hideaway.

Site **2**
CAMPBELL LAKE
on Campbell Lake
FREMONT NATIONAL FOREST

Campsites, facilities: There are 15 sites for tents, trailers or motor homes up to 16 feet long. Picnic tables and fire grills are provided. Well water and vault toilets are available. Leashed pets are permitted. A boat launch is nearby. No gas motors are permitted on the lake, electric motors only.

Reservations, fee: No reservations necessary; no fee. Open mid-June to late September.

Who to contact: Phone the Paisley Ranger District at (503)943-3114 or write to Fremont National Forest, Paisley, OR 97636.

Location: From Paisley on Highway 31, travel one mile west on County Route 2-8, then 22.5 miles west on Forest Service Road 3315. Drive three miles south on Forest Service Road 28 to the campground.

Trip note: This campground is set along the shore of Campbell Lake. No boats with gas motors are permitted. Good side trips are available in Fremont National Forest. A Forest Service map details the back roads.

Site **3**
DEADHORSE LAKE
on Deadhorse Lake
FREMONT NATIONAL FOREST

Campsites, facilities: There are 13 sites for tents, trailers or motor homes up to 16 feet long. Picnic tables and fire grills are provided. Well water and vault toilets are available. Leashed pets are permitted. A boat launch is nearby.

Reservations, fee: No reservations necessary; no fee. Open mid-June to September.

Who to contact: Phone the Paisley Ranger District at (503)943-3114 or write to Fremont National Forest, Paisley, OR 97636.

Location: From Paisley on Highway 31, travel one mile west on County Road 2-8, then 23 miles west on Forest Service Road 3315. From there, go three miles south on Forest Service Road 28, then three miles west on Forest Service Road 2800-033.

Trip note: This campground is set along the shore of Deadhorse Lake about a mile from Campbell Lake. Boats with electric motors are permitted, but gas motors are prohibited. Good side trips are available in Fremont National Forest.

Site **4**
CORRAL CREEK
near Gearhart Mountain Wilderness
FREMONT NATIONAL FOREST

Campsites, facilities: There are five sites for tents, trailers or motor homes up to 16 feet long. Picnic tables and fire grills are provided. Vault toilets are available. There is **no piped water.** Leashed pets are permitted.

Reservations, fee: No reservations necessary; no fee. Open June to late October.

Who to contact: Phone the Bly Ranger District at (503)353-2427 or write to Fremont National Forest, Bly, OR 97622.

Location: Drive 67 miles east of Klamath Falls on Highway 140 to the town of Quartz Mountain, then head northeast on Forest Service Road 3660 for about 16 miles to the junction of Forest Service Road 34. Turn right and drive 200 yards to the campground.

Trip note: This campground is set along Corral Creek adjacent to a trailhead that provides access to the Gearhart Mountain Wilderness.

Site **5**
HAPPY CAMP
on Dairy Creek
FREMONT NATIONAL FOREST

Campsites, facilities: There are nine sites for tents, trailers or motor homes up to 16 feet long. Picnic tables and fire grills are provided. Piped water and vault toilets are available. Leashed pets are permitted.

Reservations, fee: No reservations necessary; no fee. Open June to late October.

Who to contact: Phone the Paisley Ranger District at (503)943-3114 or write to Fremont National Forest, Paisley, OR 97636.

Location: From Paisley on Highway 31, travel one mile south on County Road 2-8, then 18 miles south on Forest Service Road 33. From there, go three miles south on Forest Service Road 28, then three miles west on Forest Service Road 2800-047.

Trip note: This campground is set along Dairy Creek, about eight miles east of the Corral Creek campground, which has a trailhead that provides access to the Gearhart Mountain Wilderness.

Site **6**
MARSTERS SPRING
on Chewaucan River
FREMONT NATIONAL FOREST

Campsites, facilities: There are ten sites for tents, trailers or motor homes up to 22 feet long. Picnic tables and fire grills are provided. Well water and vault toilets are available. Leashed pets are permitted.

Reservations, fee: No reservations necessary; no fee. Open mid-May to mid-November.

Who to contact: Phone the Paisley Ranger District at (503)943-3114 or write to Fremont National Forest, Paisley, OR 97636.

Location: Travel one mile west of Paisley on County Road 2-8, then seven miles south on Forest Service Road 33.

Trip note: This pretty campground is set along the banks of the Chewaucan River. It is the first of five camps in this nice area. See the zone map for further details.

Site 7   COTTONWOOD MEADOWS
on Cottonwood Meadow Lake
FREMONT NATIONAL FOREST

Campsites, facilities: There are 19 sites for tents, small trailers or motor homes. Picnic tables and fire grills are provided. Piped water and vault toilets are available. Leashed pets are permitted. Boat docks are nearby.

Reservations, fee: No reservations necessary; no fee. Open mid-June to late October.

Who to contact: Phone the Lakeview Ranger District at (503)947-3334 or write to Fremont National Forest, Lakeview, OR 97630.

Location: From Lakeview, travel 24 miles west on Highway 140, then eight miles northeast on Forest Service Road 3870.

Trip note: This campground is set along the shore of Cottonwood Meadow Lake. It is one of the better spots in the vicinity for fishing and hiking. Boats with electric motors are allowed on the lake, but gas motors are prohibited.

Site 8   DOG LAKE
on Dog Lake
FREMONT NATIONAL FOREST

Campsites, facilities: There are eight sites for tents, trailers or motor homes up to 16 feet long. **No piped water** is available. Picnic tables and fire grills are provided. Vault toilets are available. Leashed pets are permitted. A boat launch is nearby.

Reservations, fee: No reservations necessary; no fee. Open mid-May to late October.

Who to contact: Phone the Lakeview Ranger District at (503)947-3334 or write to Fremont National Forest, Lakeview, OR 97630.

Location: Travel ten miles west of Lakeview on Highway 140, then five miles south on County Road 112. The camp is another 13 miles west on Forest Service Road 4017.

Trip note: This campground is set along the west shore of Dog Lake. Fishing and boats with motors are permitted. Forest service roads on the east side of the lake provide access to some small lakes and Horseshoe Creek.

Site 9   GOOSE LAKE STATE PARK
on Goose Lake

Campsites, facilities: There are 48 sites with water and electrical hookups for trailers or motor homes up to 30 feet long. Picnic tables and fire grills are provided. Flush toilets, showers and firewood are available. Leashed pets are permitted. Boat launching facilities are nearby.

Reservations, fee: No reservations necessary; $10 in summer months, $7 off-season. Open mid-April to late October.

Who to contact: Phone (503)947-3111 or write to New Pine Creek, OR 97635.

Location: Go 14 miles south of Lakeview on US 395, then one mile west.

Trip note: This park is set along the east shore of Goose Lake. This out-of-the way area attracts waterfowl from the Pacific Flyway.

Site 10   DEEP CREEK
on Deep Creek
FREMONT NATIONAL FOREST

Campsites, facilities: There are three tent sites and five sites for trailers or motor homes. Picnic tables and fire grills are provided. Vault toilets are available.

There is **no piped water.** Leashed pets are permitted.

Reservations, fee: No reservations necessary; no fee. Open mid-June to late October.

Who to contact: Phone the Lakeview Ranger District at (503)947-3334 or write to Fremont National Forest, Lakeview, OR 97630.

Location: From Lakeview, travel six miles north on US 395, then eight miles east on Highway 140. The campground is 16 miles south on Forest Service Road 3915.

Trip note: This campground is set along the banks of Deep Creek. Site 7 provides a relatively close camping option.

Site 11
WILLOW CREEK
on Willow Creek
FREMONT NATIONAL FOREST

Campsites, facilities: There are 11 sites for tents, trailers or motor homes up to 22 feet long. Picnic tables and fire grills are provided. Well water and vault toilets are available. Leashed pets are permitted.

Reservations, fee: No reservations necessary; no fee. Open mid-June to late October.

Who to contact: Phone the Lakeview Ranger District at (503)947-3334 or write to Fremont National Forest, Lakeview, OR 97630.

Location: Travel six miles north of Lakeview on US 395, then eight miles east on Highway 140. The campground is another ten miles south on Forest Service Road 3915.

Trip note: This campground is set along the banks of Willow Creek, not far from a dirt road that heads north to Burnt Creek. A Forest Service map details the back roads.

Site 12
MUD CREEK
on Mud Creek
FREMONT NATIONAL FOREST

Campsites, facilities: There are six sites for tents, trailers or motor homes up to 16 feet long. Picnic tables and fire grills are provided. Piped water and vault toilets are available. Leashed pets are permitted.

Reservations, fee: No reservations necessary; no fee. Open mid-June to late October.

Who to contact: Phone the Lakeview Ranger District at (503)947-3334 or write to Fremont National Forest, Lakeview, OR 97630.

Location: Travel six miles north of Lakeview on US 395, then eight miles east on Highway 140. The camp is seven miles north on Forest Service Road 3615.

Trip note: This campground is set along the banks of Mud Creek. Drake Peak at 8,405 feet is nearby. No other camps are in the immediate vicinity.

Site 13
ADEL STORE & PARK
in Adel

Campsites, facilities: There are eight sites for trailers or motor homes of any length. Electricity, piped water and sewer hookups are provided. Flush toilets, showers, a store, a cafe and ice are available. Pets and motorbikes are permitted.

Reservations, fee: No reservations necessary; $7 fee per night.

Who to contact: Phone (503)947-3850 or write to P.O. Box 19, Adel, OR 97620.

Location: From Lakeview, travel 30 miles east on Highway 140 to Adel. The motor home park is in town.

Trip note: Recreation options in the area include rockhounding, or visiting the Hart Mountain National Antelope Refuge, 40 miles north of town.

Site **14**
HART ANTELOPE REFUGE
near Adel

Campsites, facilities: There are 12 primitive sites for tents, trailers or motor homes up to 20 feet long. Leashed pets are permitted.

Reservations, fee: No reservations necessary; no fee. Open May to November with limited facilities in the winter and on some off-season weekends. The road is often impassable in the winter.

Who to contact: Phone (503)947-3315 or write to Plush, OR 97637.

Location: Travel 43 miles northeast of Adel on a paved, then gravel road to Refuge headquarters.

Trip note: This unique refuge offers canyons and hot springs. Some of Oregon's largest antelope herds roam this large area. The closest camping option is in Adel at Site 13.

Site **15**
PAGE SPRINGS
near Malheur National Wildlife Refuge

Campsites, facilities: There are 15 sites for tents, trailers or motor homes up to 24 feet long. Picnic tables and fire grills are provided. Piped water, firewood and vault toilets are available. Leashed pets are permitted.

Reservations, fee: No reservations necessary; $3. Open year-round.

Who to contact: Phone (503)573-5241 or write to Bureau of Land Management, HC 74-12533, Highway 20 West, Burns, OR 97738.

Location: Travel 61 miles south of Burns on Highway 205 to Frenchglen, then three miles east of Frenchglen on Steens Mountain Road to the campground.

Trip note: This campground is set adjacent to Page Springs and the Malheur National Wildlife Refuge. The Frenchglen Hotel is administered by the state parks department and offers overnight accommodations and food.

Site **16**
JACKMAN PARK
near Malheur National Wildlife Refuge

Campsites, facilities: There are five primitive tent sites and five sites for trailers or motor homes up to 24 feet long. Picnic tables are provided. Firewood and pit toilets are available. There is **no piped water.** Leashed pets are permitted.

Reservations, fee: No reservations necessary; $3 fee. Open July to late October.

Who to contact: Phone (503)573-5241 or write to Bureau of Land Management, HC 74-12533, Highway 20 West, Burns, OR 97738.

Location: Travel 20 miles east of Frenchglen on Steens Mountain Road.

Trip note: Set at 8,100 feet elevation in the eastern Oregon desert, this is one of three camps in the area. Site 15 is nearby and Site 13 is about 15 miles northeast at the southeast end of the Malheur National Wildlife Refuge. No other camps are within an hour's drive.

Site **17**
FISH LAKE
on Fish Lake

Campsites, facilities: There are 20 sites for tents, trailers or motor homes up to 24 feet long. Picnic tables and fire grills are provided. Piped water, firewood and vault toilets are available. Leashed pets are permitted. Boat launching facilities are nearby.

Reservations, fee: No reservations necessary; $3 fee. Open July to late October.

Who to contact: Phone (503)573-5241 or write to Bureau of Land Management,

HC 74-12533, Highway 20 West, Burns, OR 97738.

Location: Travel 16 miles east of Frenchglen on Steens Mountain Road.

Trip note: Located at 7,900 feet elevation, this campground is set along the shore of little Fish Lake.

Site 18
DELINTMENT LAKE
on Delintment Lake
OCHOCO NATIONAL FOREST

Campsites, facilities: There are 24 sites for tents, trailers or motor homes up to 30 feet long. Picnic tables and fire grills are provided. Piped water, and vault toilets are available. Some facilities are wheelchair accessible. Leashed pets are permitted. Boat docks and launching facilities are nearby.

Reservations, fee: No reservations necessary; $4 fee per night. Open June to mid-October.

Who to contact: Phone the Snow Mountain Ranger District at (503)573-7292 or write to Ochoco National Forest, HC 74, Box 12870, Burns, OR 97738.

Location: From Hines, drive a half mile south on US 20, then turn north on Forest Service Road 47 and drive about ten miles. Turn left on Forest Service Road 41 and travel about 30 miles to the campground.

Trip note: This campground is set along the shore of Delintment Lake, originally a beaver pond which was gradually developed into a lake covering 57 acres. Here's a secret: rainbow trout here average 12 to 18 inches.

Site 19
EMIGRANT
near Emigrant Creek
OCHOCO NATIONAL FOREST

Campsites, facilities: There are five sites for tents, trailers or motor homes up to 30 feet long. Picnic tables and fire grills are provided. Piped water and vault toilets are available. Leashed pets are permitted.

Reservations, fee: No reservations necessary; $3 fee per night. Open mid-June to mid-October.

Who to contact: Phone the Snow Mountain Ranger District at (503)573-7292 or write to Ochoco National Forest, HC 74, Box 12870, Burns, OR 97738.

Location: Travel one mile south of Hines on US 20, then 25 miles northwest on Forest Service Road 47. The camp is another ten miles west on Forest Service Road 43.

Trip note: This campground is set in a meadow of Emigrant Creek. This is one of three camps in the immediate area.

Site 20
FALLS
on Emigrant Creek
OCHOCO NATIONAL FOREST

Campsites, facilities: There are five sites for tents, trailers or motor homes up to 30 feet long. Picnic tables and fire grills are provided. Piped water, firewood and vault toilets are available. Leashed pets are permitted.

Reservations, fee: No reservations necessary; $3 fee per night. Open mid-June to mid-October.

Who to contact: Phone the Snow Mountain Ranger District at (503)573-7292 or write to Ochoco National Forest, Star Route 4, Box 12870 Highway 20, Burns, OR 97720.

Location: From the Hines, travel one mile south on US 20, then 25 miles northwest on Forest Service Road 47. The camp is another 8.5 miles west on Forest Service Road 43.

Trip note: This campground is set along the banks of Emigrant Creek. It's a small, quiet layover for out-of-town visitors.

Site **21**   **YELLOWJACKET**
on Yellowjacket Lake
MALHEUR NATIONAL FOREST

Campsites, facilities: There are 20 sites for tents, trailers or motor homes up to 22 feet long. Picnic tables, hand-pumped well water and vault toilets are available. Leashed pets are permitted. A boat launch is nearby.
Reservations, fee: No reservations necessary; no fee. Open late May to mid-October.
Who to contact: Phone the Burns Ranger District at (503)573-7292 or write to Malheur National Forest, Burns, OR 97720.
Location: Travel one mile south of Burns on US 20, then 32 miles northwest on Forest Service Road 47. The camp is another four miles east on Forest Service Road 37.
Trip note: This campground is set along the shore of Yellowjacket Lake. Fishing can be fair, depending upon the time of the year. Boats without motors are encouraged.

Site **22**   **IDLEWILD**
in Divine Canyon
MALHEUR NATIONAL FOREST

Campsites, facilities: There are 24 sites for tents, trailers or motor homes up to 30 feet long. Picnic tables and fire grills are provided. Piped water and vault toilets are available. Leashed pets are permitted.
Reservations, fee: No reservations necessary; no fee. Open late May to mid-October.
Who to contact: Phone the Burns Ranger District at (503)573-7292 or write to Malheur National Forest, Burns, OR 97720.
Location: From Burns, travel 17 miles north on US 395.
Trip note: This campground is set in Divine Canyon. It's a popular spot for visitors traveling up US 395 and in need of a stopover. It provides easy access.

Site **23**   **ROCK SPRINGS**
near Rock Springs
MALHEUR NATIONAL FOREST

Campsites, facilities: There are eight primitive sites for tents, trailers or motor homes up to 21 feet long. Picnic tables and fire grills are provided. Piped water and vault toilets are available. Leashed pets are permitted.
Reservations, fee: No reservations necessary; no fee. Open late May to mid-October.
Who to contact: Phone the Burns Ranger District at (503)573-7292 or write to Malheur National Forest, Burns, OR 97720.
Location: Travel 34 miles north from Burns on US 395, then 4.5 miles east on Forest Service Road 17. The camp is one mile southeast on Forest Service Road 1836.
Trip note: This campground is set adjacent to Rock Springs. It is far enough off US 395 to get completely missed by most long-range travelers, yet close enough to provide a good overnight rest stop if you know of it. Now you do.

Site **24**
CHUCKAR PARK
near North Fork of Malheur River

Campsites, facilities: There are 18 sites for tents, trailers or motor homes up to 30 feet long. Picnic tables and fire grills are provided. Piped water and vault toilets are available. Leashed pets are permitted.

Reservations, fee: No reservations necessary; $3 fee per night. Open April to late November.

Who to contact: Phone (503)473-3144 or write to 100 Oregon Street, Vale, OR 97918.

Location: From Vale, drive 56 miles west on US 20 to Juntura. Travel six miles northwest of Juntura on a Beulah Reservoir Road.

Trip note: This campground is set along the banks of the North Fork of the Malheur River. The area in general provides habitat for chuckar, an upland game species. Hunting can be good in season during the fall, but requires much hiking in rugged terrain.

Site **25**
OASIS RV PARK
in Juntura

Campsites, facilities: There are ten tent sites and 22 drive-through sites for trailers or motor homes of any length. Electricity, piped water and sewer hookups are provided. Flush toilets, showers, a cafe and ice are available. Bottled gas and a store are located within one mile.

Reservations, fee: Reservations accepted; $8.50 fee per night; MasterCard and Visa accepted. Open all year.

Who to contact: Phone (503)277-3605 or write to P.O. Box 277, Juntura, OR 97911.

Location: From Vale, travel 56 miles west on US 20. This park is located in Juntura.

Trip note: This is one of two camp possibilities in this area; the other is Site 22, which is in a more primitive setting. Other than these two camps, the closest options are almost an hour's drive away.

Site **26**
LESLIE GULCH
on Owyhee Lake

Campsites, facilities: There are ten sites for tents, trailers or motor homes up to 20 feet long. Picnic tables and fire grills are provided. Vault toilets are available. There is **no piped water.** Leashed pets are permitted. Boat launching facilities are available on site.

Reservations, fee: No reservations necessary; no fee. Open April to November.

Who to contact: Phone (503)473-3144 or write to 100 Oregon Street, Vale, OR 97918.

Location: From Homedale, drive south on US 95 to Leslie Gulch Recreation Area turnoff (McBridge Creek Road) and travel west for 25 miles to the campground.

Trip note: This campground is set along the east shore of Owyhee Lake. Warm water fishing, waterskiing and hiking are among the recreation options in this high desert area. Site 27 provides the other option at this lake. No other campgrounds are located within an hour's drive.

Site **27**
LAKE OWYHEE STATE PARK
on Owyhee Lake

Campsites, facilities: There are 30 sites for tents or self-contained motor homes, and ten sites with water and electrical hookups for trailers or motor homes of any length. Picnic tables and fire grills are provided. Flush toilets, sanitary disposal station, showers and firewood are available. Leashed pets are permitted. Boat docks and launching facilities are available nearby.

Reservations, fee: No reservations necessary; $9-10 in summer, $6-7 off-season. Open mid-April to late October.

Who to contact: Phone (503)372-2331 or write to Nyssa, OR, 97913.

Location: Go eight miles south of Nyssa on Highway 201, then 28 miles southwest on Owyhee Lake Road.

Trip note: This state park is set along the shore of Owyhee Lake. This is a good lake for waterskiing in the day and for fishing for warm water species in the morning and evening. Site 26 provides the only other camping option at the lake.

Site 28   PROSPECTOR TRAVEL TRAILER PARK
in Vale

Campsites, facilities: There are 28 drive-through sites for trailers or motor homes of any length. Picnic tables are provided. Flush toilets, bottled gas, sanitary disposal services, showers, a laundromat and ice are available. A store and a cafe are located within one mile. Pets and motorbikes are permitted.

Reservations, fee: Reservations accepted; $10 fee per night. Open April to December.

Who to contact: Phone (503)473-3879 or write to Route 3, Box 4634, Vale, OR 97918.

Location: Drive one-half mile north of Vale on US 26, then one block east on Hope.

Trip note: This is one of two camps (Site 29) for motor home travelers in Vale.

Site 29   WESTERNER TRAILER PARK
on Willow Creek

Campsites, facilities: There are ten drive-through sites for tents, trailers or motor homes of any length. Electricity, cable TV hookups, piped water, sewer hookups and picnic tables are provided. Flush toilets, showers, a laundromat and ice are available. Bottled gas, a store, a cafe and a swimming pool are located within one mile. Pets and motorbikes are permitted.

Reservations, fee: Reservations accepted; $8.50 fee per night; MasterCard and Visa accepted. Open all year.

Who to contact: Phone (503)473-3947 or write to 317 A Street East, Vale, OR 97918.

Location: This campground is in Vale at the junction of US 20 and US 26.

Trip note: This campground is set along the banks of Willow Creek.

Site 30   WEST GATE MOTORHOME PARK
near Snake River

Campsites, facilities: There are ten drive-through sites for trailers or motor homes of any length. Electricity, piped water and sewer hookups are provided. Flush toilets, showers, a recreation hall and a laundromat are available. Bottled gas, a store, a cafe and ice are located within one mile. Pets are permitted.

Reservations, fee: Reservations accepted; $7 fee per night. Open all year.

Who to contact: Phone (503)889-4068 or write to 2511 Southwest 4th, Ontario, OR 97914.

Location: Go one-half mile west of Ontario on US 30, then two miles west on Highway 201.

Trip note: This park is set near the banks of the Snake River. Nearby recreation options include an 18-hole golf course and tennis courts.

Site **31**   **TWIN SPRINGS**
                              near Twin Springs

Campsites, facilities: There are six campsites for tents, trailers or motor homes. Picnic tables and fire grills are provided, piped water and vault toilets are available. Leashed pets are permitted.

Reservations, fee: No reservations necessary; no fee. Open April to late November.

Who to contact: Phone (503)473-3144 or write to 100 Oregon Street, Vale, OR 97918.

Location: From Vale, drive four miles west on US 20. Turn south on Dry Creek Road (mostly gravel) and drive 30 miles to the campground.

Trip note: This small, little-known camp is set at Twin Springs and an old homestead. It's popular rockhound country.

- INDEX KEY -

Campgrounds are indexed in bold capitals and followed by these codes

B	Boating
BF	Bass fishing
C	Bicycling
CP	County Park
D	Pets allowed
F	Fishing
G	Golf course nearby
H	Hiking
K	Hunting
M	Motor home sites
N	Nature activities
NC	No fee
NF	National Forest
NP	National Park
P	No water
Q	Rafting
R	Horse corrals/riding
S	Swimming
SA	Salmon fishing
SF	State Forest
SP	State Park
T	Tent sites
TF	Trout fishing
W	Wheelchair access
X	Winter sports

WASHINGTON

Zone 1 ... Olympic
pages 57-88

Zone 2 ... Southwest
pages 89-108

Zone 3 ... Puget Sound
pages 109-128

Zone 4 ... North Cascades
pages 129-144

Zone 5 ... Mount Baker
pages 145-162

Zone 6 ... Mount Rainier
pages 163-198

Zone 7 ... Mt. St. Helens
pages 199-222

Zone 8 ... Wenatchee
pages 223-246

Zone 9 ... Colville
pages 247-278

Zone 10 ... Spokane
pages 279-306

Zone 11 ... Yakima
pages 307-318

Zone 12 ... SE Plains
pages 319-338

OREGON

Zone 1 ... Tillamook
pages 341-356

Zone 2 ... Umpqua
pages 357-380

Zone 3 ... Siskiyou
pages 381-400

Zone 4 ... Mount Hood
pages 401-438

Zone 5 ... Willamette
pages 439-476

Zone 6 ... Cascade
pages 477-516

Zone 7 ... Crater Lake
pages 517-550

Zone 8 ... Columbia
pages 551-566

Zone 9 ... Wallowa
pages 567-590

Zone 10 ... SE Basin
pages 591-602

•FIND YOUR IDEAL CAMPGROUND•

Finding a campsite shouldn't be frustrating. Neither should be using an index. That's been our motivation in designing this one. You'll find every campground indexed here (set apart with bold capital letters). We've used codes showing the type of park setting, available facilities and activities at each campground and placed a key on every page for easy reference.

Because campers decide on a location for a camping trip first, we've included cities, parks, lakes, mountains, rivers, and other landmarks to orient you (and give you plenty of options). Zone references (**Z**) are given within the index where they are most useful. And, so you can find your way around the book easily, zone page numbers are included in the key as well. Learn your way around this index and you'll always find the ideal site for every trip!

5-Y RESORT ON PEARRYGIN LAKE (WA Z9) B, D, G, H, M, N, Q, R, T: 259

- A -

Abbott Creek: 527
ABBOTT CREEK (OR Z7) D, M, NF, T: 527
Aberdeen: 98
Acme: 140
Adams Creek: 203
ADAMS FORK (WA Z7) B, D, H, M, NF, T: 203
Adel: 596-597
ADEL STORE & PARK (OR Z10) D, M, N: 596
Agate Beach: 77
AGATE BEACH TRAILER AND RV PARK (OR Z2) D, M: 359
Agate Beach Wayside: 359
Agness: 389-390
AGNESS RV PARK (OR Z3) B, D, F, M, NF, T: 394
AHTANUM CAMP (WA Z11) D, NC, T, X: 313
Ahtanum Creek: 313
Ahtanum Creek, Middle Fork: 313
Ahtanum Creek, North Fork: 314
AINSWORTH STATE PARK (OR Z4) D, F, M, SP: 407
AL'S RV TRAILER PARK (WA Z1) B, G, M: 73
ALAMEDA AVENUE TRAILER PARK (OR Z6) C, D, G, M: 481
Albany: 441, 454
ALBANY TRAILER PARK (OR Z5) D, M, T: 454
ALDER DUNE (OR Z2) B, D, M, NF, T: 366
ALDER FLAT (OR Z4) HIKE-IN,

D, H, NC, NF, P, T: 429
Alder Lake: 177-178, 366
ALDER LAKE (WA Z6) B, D, NC, T: 177
ALDER LAKE PARK (WA Z6) B, M, T: 178
ALDER SPRINGS (OR Z5) D, H, NF, P, T: 450
ALDER THICKET (WA Z12) D, H, K, M, NC, NF, P, T: 330
Aldrich Lake: 126
ALDRICH LAKE MULTIPLE USE AREA (WA Z3) B, D, H, NC, SF, T: 126
ALLEN SPRINGS (OR Z5) D, F, H, M, NF, T: 464
ALLEN'S RIVERVIEW TRAILER PARK (OR Z6) D, M, T: 511
ALLINGHAM (OR Z5) D, F, M, NF, T: 462
ALPINE (OR Z4) D, H, NF, T, X: 413
Alpine Lakes Wilderness: 158, 161, 233, 239-243
ALPINE RV PARK AND CAMPGROUND (WA Z4) D, H, M, T: 141
Alsea: 363
Alsea Bay: 361, 364
ALSEA BAY TRAILER PARK (OR Z2) B, C, D, F, M: 361
Alsea River: 362-364
Alta Lake: 265
ALTA LAKE STATE PARK (WA Z9) B, D, G, M, R, S, T: 265
ALTAIRE (WA Z1) D, M, NP, T: 70
Amanda Park, town of: 61
American Forks: 188
AMERICAN FORKS (WA Z6) D, H, M, NF, T: 186
AMERICAN HERITAGE CAMPGROUND (WA Z6) D, G,

ABOUT THE AUTHOR

Author **Tom Stienstra** is recognized as one of the West's premier outdoors writers. His outdoors column is syndicated in papers throughout the country and he is the camping editor for Western Outdoor News.

Tom is an avid adventurer. As a full-time outdoors writer, he has traveled throughout the West in search of prime fishing, hiking, and camping areas. Among his many adventures are fishing expeditions for Great White sharks, a month-long hunt for Bigfoot and several 200-mile hikes. He frequently leads seminars on the outdoors, Great White sharks, bears and world-class adventures.

He has won a number of writing awards. In 1988, he was awarded first place for the nation's best feature outdoors column. In 1989, he won first and second place awards for "Pride in America" from the Outdoor Writers Association of America.

His books include PACIFIC NORTHWEST CAMPING, CALIFORNIA CAMPING, ROCKY MOUNTAIN CAMPING, GREAT OUTDOOR ADVENTURES OF THE BAY AREA AND NORTHERN CALIFORNIA and SALMON MAGIC.

In PACIFIC NORTHWEST CAMPING, Tom brings his entertaining style to the practical aspects of camping in the Pacific Northwest. He reveals more than 1,400 campgrounds, including primitive wilderness area sites and urban RV parks. The detailed maps and Tom's insightful trip notes make PACIFIC NORTHWEST CAMPING the most complete, useful and entertaining camping guide ever written about the Pacific Northwest.

Outdoor titles available from Foghorn Press include

- **CALIFORNIA CAMPING** (3rd Edition) by Tom Stienstra
  describing 1500 campgrounds throughout the state
- **PACIFIC NORTHWEST CAMPING** (2nd Edition) by Tom Stienstra
  describing 1400 campgrounds in Washington and Oregon
- **ROCKY MOUNTAIN CAMPING** by Tom Stienstra
  describing 1200 campgrounds in Colorado, Wyoming and Montana
- **GREAT OUTDOOR ADVENTURES or Tom Stienstra's Almanac**
  describing 132 adventures in the Bay Area and Northern California
- **CALIFORNIA GOLF** (2nd Edition) by Mark Soltau
  describing over 600 golf courses throughout the golf vacation state

ORDER INFORMATION

All Foghorn Press outdoor books are $15.95.
We accept visa or mastercard.

Phone Orders
Our toll free number in California is (800)842-7477.
To order from outside the state, please phone (415)641-5777.

Mail Orders
Enclose your name and street address along with a check or money order
or visa/mastercard number (please include expiration date and phone
number) for the total book amount plus $3 shipping. Mail to:

Foghorn Press/Order Dept.
P.O. Box 77845
San Francisco, CA 94110

Books are shipped via UPS within 48 hours of receipt of your order.

Courtesy discount
If you currently own an old edition of any Foghorn Press title, you may
mail in the title page from that edition with an order for an new edition
of the same book and take a $3 courtesy discount off the $15.95 price.
Edition information is located on the title page of each book—please
verify yours before taking advantage of this discount. This can only be
redeemed through Foghorn Press at P.O. Box 77845, San Francisco, CA
94110.

Book or Outdoor Trade Outlets
Please call to receive the new Foghorn Press catalog and quantity
discount information.